The Short Oxford History of the Modern World

General Editor: J. M. Roberts

The Short Oxford History of the Modern World
General Editor: J. M. Roberts

Rebellions and Revolutions

China from the 1800s to 2000

Second edition

Jack Gray

OXFORD

UNIVERSITY PRESS

OXFORD

UNIVERSITY PRESS

Great Clarendon Street, Oxford OX2 6DP

Oxford University Press is a department of the University of Oxford.
It furthers the University's objective of excellence in research, scholarship,
and education by publishing worldwide in

Oxford New York

Auckland Bangkok Buenos Aires Cape Town Chennai
Dar es Salaam Delhi Hong Kong Istanbul Karachi Kolkata
Kuala Lumpur Madrid Melbourne Mexico City Mumbai Nairobi
São Paulo Shanghai Singapore Taipei Tokyo Toronto

Oxford is a registered trade mark of Oxford University Press
in the UK and in certain other countries

Published in the United States
by Oxford University Press Inc., New York

© Jack Gray 2002

The moral rights of the author have been asserted

Database right Oxford University Press (maker)

First edition 1990

British Library Cataloguing in Publication Data

Data available

Library of Congress Cataloging in Publication Data

Data available

ISBN 0–19–870069–5

1 3 5 7 9 10 8 6 4 2

Typeset in Minion and Congress Sans
by RefineCatch Limited, Bungay, Suffolk
Printed in Great Britain by
T.J. International Ltd., Padstow, Cornwall.

TO MAISIE

Preface to the First Edition

The historian of modern China is not given much room for manœuvre in his choice of themes. They impose themselves. The first is the causes of the collapse of the Chinese Empire which, founded two centuries before Christ, had survived into the modern age; the failure of what had hitherto been the most promising quarter of mankind—probably the most productive, possibly the best governed and certainly the most innovative—sets a fascinating problem.

The second question raised is the prolonged failure of China to respond to the challenge posed by the coming of the West, and the question is sharpened by the unavoidable contrast with the success of Japan which, when subjected by the Western powers to precisely the same regime as they had imposed on China, moved with extraordinary rapidity to modernize and join the ranks of the industrialized powers. Related to this is the question whether the privileges of the foreign powers in China proved to be on balance a hindrance or help to her transformation; and here the fact that Japan succeeded so well, in spite of the imposition of the same privileges, throws doubt on the idea that foreign privilege was the decisive factor in preventing China's modernization. More important, the records of the Chinese economy in the early twentieth century, gradually made available by modern scholarship, suggest that the assertion that China's efforts failed miserably is not altogether true, and has persisted only as one of the nationalist and communist myths which must be eliminated before any valid assessment of modern China's history can be attempted.

When we move on to the rise and victory of the Chinese Communist Party we face the question whether this was really the result of a broad-based 'peasant revolution', or whether its cause was essentially military, and it was perhaps possible only because the Japanese invasion of China, being directed against the ports and urban centres defended by the Nationalists, left comparatively unscathed the remoter rural areas in which the Communists operated, leaving them free to build up formidable military strength through guerrilla campaigns.

The major theme presented by post-revolutionary China starts from Mao Zedong's rejection of Stalinism in the late 1950s and the gradual hammering out, through much strife and agony, of a Chinese alternative to the Soviet-style command economy, an alternative which has implications far beyond the borders of China in so far as it presents new possibilities not only for Marxist socialism but for the rest of the Third World in its struggle against poverty. Not the least interesting aspect of this alternative is that it represents the incorporation into socialism of certain traditional Chinese economic values and expectations; the 'socialism with Chinese characteristics' advocated by Deng Xiaoping is perhaps Chinese in a sense of which Deng and his fellow reformers are not fully conscious.

The revival of these traditional values raises the further question of how far China in the course of revolution has remained Chinese. The dilemma of her first modern nationalists was that the drastic changes necessary to preserve China as a nation might destroy her as a culture and eliminate everything that gave the Chinese their identity. Yet perhaps tradition has proved to be tougher than they expected. The traditional political culture has survived the revolution very well. As with the Poles, the Hungarians and the Czechs, the nation's world of historical images and references has not altogether been replaced by Marxism. The great historical figures of Confucian virtue and vice may still be more real to most Chinese than Marx and Lenin. When in 1959 Marshal Peng Dehuai was advised by his friends to cease his criticism of Mao Zedong's Great Leap Forward, he identified himself not with some figure from socialist history but with the Ming official Hai Rui, who had reprimanded the Emperor at the risk of his life. When in 1962 a group of Chinese intellectuals started a campaign against the Marxist assertion that there is no morality above class, they began at the grave of Confucius. Perhaps the most striking evidence of all comes from a recent Chinese urban opinion poll (1987) which showed that 'filial disobedience' was still the moral defect most strongly condemned.

The final theme which presents itself to our attention is the evolution of China's new place in the family of nations. When, after 1949, the new regime had ruthlessly squeezed out all foreign economic interests, China found it necessary to enter into a fraternal treaty with the Soviet Union which, ironically, reasserted many of the features of the 'unequal treaties' imposed on China in the nineteenth century. Khrushchev rescinded these arrangements, but by this time the divergence of interests and ideology between China and the Soviet Union had reached such a point that he earned no gratitude for his liberality. Thus China, having incurred the enmity of the United States of America since the Korean War, now chose to brave the hostility of the other superpower. To find a way out of this dangerous isolation, Mao Zedong chose to reach a *rapprochement* with the United States. Yet perhaps more significant in the long run than this diplomatic revolution will be China's part, now steadily increasing, in the rapid economic growth of the Far East. The value of trade accross the Pacific is now greater than the value of trade across the Atlantic, as a result of the development of Japan, Taiwan, South Korea, Hong Kong, and Singapore—all of them communities within or derived from the old Chinese Confucian world. In this astonishing shift in the balance of economic power from West to East, China has not yet fully brought to bear the massive weight of her vast resources or the energies of a thousand million people who are as industrious, as enterprising, and as receptive to training as Japan's ninety million. When she does the world will be changed.

In view of the importance of these broad themes, it may surprise readers to find that in the author's analysis political narrative here and there plays a larger part than is altogether fashionable today. There are several reasons for this. For most of the period the 'great forces of history' in China were often conspicuous by their absence. Chinese society, 'big in the middle and small at both ends' as Mao Zedong himself once admitted, had not been articulated to the point where organized interest-groups systematically competed with each other and gave shape to politics. In these conditions decisions were made largely by the small élites in and around governments. At the same time, China's problems were of a kind which could not be readily solved without the sustained and single-minded leadership of the State, but until the Communists came to power in 1949 this leadership was fitful and feeble; it is important to understand why this was so. More generally, it is the author's opinion, formed in the course of some years of concern with development studies, that in matters of modernization 'whate'er is best adminstered' is usually best; there is little point in arguing, for example, as to whether such-and-such a country should choose a strategy of export promotion or of import substitution if its government is too incompetent, corrupt, or apathetic to pursue either course effectively, and it is a melancholy fact that many Third World governments fall into this category. On the other hand, the most successful countries in the Third World, often actually countries with few resources, are those which have vigorous, intelligent, and committed government. Finally, as historians well know, the construction of a close and detailed political narrative is more often than not the only effective way to pierce the mists of nationalist and ideological mythology and of quasi-sociological generalization, and to avoid simply replacing one stereotype with another.

Those engaged in research on modern Chinese history are not numerous; they are on the whole personally known to each other and regularly exchange ideas. In these circumstances to pick out a few individuals for acknowledgment of their help would be invidious. The list of selected reading at the end of the book can provide, and is intended to provide, a full acknowledgment of the author's indebtedness to his many friends and colleagues. At the same time, in spite of considerable recent research on the modern history of China, there are places in the story at which one is still dependent on the research of a single author. The account here of the state of China's inner frontiers and the role of Russia there in the nineteenth century leans heavily on the research of Joseph Fletcher, see *Cambridge History of China*, vol. 10, chapter 7 and 8. The narrative of the peasant movement in China before 1927 makes much use of the work of Roy Hofheinz, *The Broken Wave*. The systematic research of Lee Hong-Yung, published in his *The Politics of the Chinese Cultural Revolution*, amply confirmed my own tentative conclusions concerning the split in the Red movement during the early stages of the Cultural Revolution.

I should like to thank Dr John Roberts, the General Editor of this series, and Dr Ivon Asquith of OUP for the great patience they have shown during the prolonged preparation of this volume.

J.G.

Institute of Development Studies
at the University of Sussex
November 1988

Preface to the Second Edition

The final chapter of the first edition, which runs from 1976 to 1989, has been rewritten as well as extended to the present day. Recent research has added considerably to our understanding of the whole post-1976 process of economic reform in China.

The one specific criticism made of the first edition was that I had been 'remarkably easy on Mao'. I have therefore rewritten the last pages of the penultimate chapter in which an attempt was made to judge his career. Many scholars both in China and the West now concur in my opinion that Mao's heritage to China was by no means entirely negative. He was, at any rate, a much more complex and interesting character than the conventional stereotype suggests.

Discussions with readers have suggested that they would be helped by a few words on the methodological principles applied in the book. The first is that objectivity requires not indifference but empathy. The second is that those involved in a situation under analysis must be assumed to be rational and of good intent unless and until they are proved otherwise. The third is that ideology seldom explains anything; it is a word that has become so ambiguous that it is better forgotten. The fourth is that all potential causal factors in the situation under scrutiny must be recognized, understood, and incorporated. The fifth and final principle is that in judging great men who are struggling with vast and intractable problems, a little humility will do the historian no harm.

Finally, my thanks are due to Fiona Kinnear of Oxford University Press for her guidance and help in the preparation of this second edition, and to Matthew Cotton for his help in the final editing. I owe special thanks to Peter Nolan for his help with economic figures for the late 1990s.

J.G.
Centre for the Study of Democratisation,
University of Warwick
May 2002

Contents

List of maps and tables

Maps

Table

Chronology

Based on Colin McKerras, with the assistance of Robert Chan, *Modern China: A Chronology from 1842 to the Present* and Colin McKerras: *The New Cambridge Handbook of Modern China*. Readers who want to pursue the study of modern Chinese history further would be well advised to keep these books at hand.

1833	Dec. 10	Lord Napier appointed to lead a mission to China.
1834		The British Government decides that the East India Company's monopoly of trade with China will not be renewed.
	Oct. 11	Lord Napier dies of illness in China.
1836	May 17	Xu Naiqi memorializes the Emperor, arguing that the best solution to the opium problem is to legalize the opium trade.
	June	Charles Elliot appointed British Superintendent of Trade.
	Sept. 19	The Emperor orders abolition of the opium trade.
1838–9		Opium imports to China reach 40,000 chests.
1839	Mar. 10	Lin Zexu arrives at Canton as Imperial commissioner to put down the opium trade.
	24	Lin Zexu confines the British traders in their warehouses at Canton. They are held for six weeks.
	27	Superintendent of Trade Charles Elliot orders the British opium traders to surrender their stocks of opium.
	May 24	The British community leaves Canton.
	July 12	The killing of a Chinese peasant, Lin Weihi, in a brawl near Hong Kong precipitates a further crisis.
1840	Aug. 30	As the British Expedition reaches the Beihe and threatens the forts guarding Tianjin, the Emperor appoints Qishan, Governor-General of Zhili, to negotiate with them.
	Sept. 17	Qishan persuades the British to return to Canton to continue negotiations there.
1841	Jan. 7	Elliot captures the Bogue forts guarding the approaches to Canton.
	20	Qishan and Elliot sign the Qunbi Convention, which their respective governments refuse to ratify.
	30	The Emperor appoints Yishan to command a force to annihilate the British.
	Apr. 30	Elliot dismissed and replaced by Sir Henry Pottinger.
	Aug.	Pottinger arrives in Hong Kong.
1842	Mar. 18	Lin Zexu exiled to Kuldya (Yili).
	June 19	The British take Shanghai.
	July 31	The British take Jinjiang, leaving Nanjing open to attack.

	Aug. 4	British warships reach Nanjing.
	Aug. 20	Qiying and Yilibu board the *Cornwallis* for negotiations.
	29	The Treaty of Nanjing.
1843	June	Hong Xiuquan studies *Good Words to Exhort the Age*.
	Oct. 18	Supplementary Treaty of the Bogue.
1844	Mar. 19	Qiying made Governor-General of Guangdong and Guangxi.
	Apr. 2	Hong Xiuquan and Feng Yunshan leave Huaxian to preach in Guangdong and Guangxi.
	July 3	Sino-American Treaty of Wangxia.
1845	June 13	Nian rebels defeat an imperial force in Shandong.
1846	July 25	The British troops withdraw from Zhoushan Island.
1847	Apr. 3	The British attack Canton in protest at exclusion from the city.
	9	Qiying promises entry to Canton after two years.
1848	July 4	Xu Guangqin appointed Governor-General of Guangdong and Guangxi, Ye Mingshen Governor of Guangdong.
	Dec. 30	Palmerston forbids the use of force to secure entry into Canton.
1849	Apr. 1	Xu Guangqin informs Bonham that the Emperor has refused entry into Canton because of unanimous popular opposition.
	May 7	Xu Guangqin and Ye Mingshen rewarded for their resistance to British entry into Canton.
1850	Mar. 9	Yi Zhu ascends the throne, with reign title Xian Feng.
	Aug.	Russia establishes a base at the mouth of the Amur.
	Sept.	Imperial troops defeated by Taipings at Jintian.
	Dec. 1	Degradation of Muchanga and Qiying.
1851	Jan. 1	Taipings win a major victory at Guiping (Guangxi).
	11	Hong declares himself Tian Wang.
	Aug. 26	The Treaty of Kuldya: Russian trade allowed at Kuldya (Yili) and Tarbagatai, but not at Kashgar.
	Sept. 11	Taipings take Yong'an (Guangxi).
1852		Ye Mingshen becomes acting Governor-General of Guangdong and Guangxi.
	June 3	Taipings checked at Battle of Soyi Ford. Fung Yunshan is wounded and subsequently dies during 1852.
1853	Jan. 12	Taipings complete occupation of Wuhan cities, which they soon relinquish.
	Feb. 24	Taipings take Anqing (Anhui).
	Mar. 4	Taipings take Wuhu (Anhui).
	15	Jiangsu request for British help against the Taipings refused.
	29	Taipings take Nanjing.
	31	Imperial troops form the Great South Camp.
	May 5	Bonham visits Taiping court at Nanjing.

	June 10	Taiping northern expedition crosses the Yellow River.
	Sept. 8	The Small Swords society takes the walled city of Shanghai.
1854	Mar. 9	Taiping northern expedition begins its retreat.
	May 5	Taiping reinforcements for the northern expedition defeated in Shandong.
	June 17	The Red Turbans (Triads) begin revolt in Guangdong.
	23	Three foreign inspectors appointed to collect Shanghai customs.
	Nov. 3	Talks begin at Dagu (in Tianjin) on treaty revision.
	5	Foreign proposals for treaty revision rejected.
	Dec. 2	Taiping western expedition severely defeated at Tianjiazhen.
	7	Ye Mingshen's request for British assistance against the Red Turbans refused.
1855	Jan. 31	Zeng Guofan's naval forces defeated at Jiujiang (in Jiangxi).
	Feb. 17	The walled city of Shanghai retaken from the Small Swords society with French help.
	May 21	The Red Turbans (Triads) defeated in Guangdong.
	31	Final destruction of Taiping northern expedition.
1856	Jun. 20	Taipings, in alliance with Nian, crush the Great South Camp.
	July 1	France demands redress for the murder of the missionary Chapdelaine.
	Aug. 2	Yellow River completes its change of course.
	Sept. 2	In Nanjing, Wei Changhui massacres Xang Yiuqing, his family and followers.
	Oct.	Wei Changhui forces Shi Dakai to flee, and massacres his family. Customs duty on opium set at 20 yuan per chest.
	8	The lorcha *Arrow* boarded by Chinese troops.
	25	British attack Canton, following Ye Mingshen's refusal to apologize over the *Arrow* incident.
1857	July 2	Elgin arrives in Hong Kong.
	12	Muslim rebels under Ma Rulong rise in Yunnan.
	Dec. 11	Ye Mingshen rejects British and French demands.
	29	Canton taken by British and French forces.
1858	Jan. 5	Ye Mingshen captured.
	Feb. 22	Ye Mingshen shipped to India.
	May 17	Court rejects British, French, American and Russian demands.
	20	Dagu falls to British and French forces.
	28	The Treaty of Aigun (signed by Muraviev and Yishan): China cedes the North bank of the Amur.
	June 13	Russian Treaty of Tianjin signed.
	18	United States Treaty of Tianjin signed.
	25	British Treaty of Tianjin signed.
	27	French Treaty of Tianjin signed.
	29	Qiying commits suicide on the orders of the Court.
	Sept. 27	Taipings crush the Great North Camp.

1859	Apr. 22	Arrival of Hong Rengan in Nanjing.
	June 20	Bruce, Bourboulon, and Ward arrive at Dagu to go to Beijing and are prevented from landing.
	25	British and French attack on the Dagu fort fails.
1860	Mar. 19	Taiping Li Xiucheng takes Hangzhou to draw Qing forces off Nanjing.
	May 6	Li Xiucheng breaks up the Great South Camp.
	July	Muraviev founds Vladivostok.
	Aug. 1	British and French forces land near Tianjin.
	19	Li Xiucheng defeated by British and French forces at Shanghai.
	Sept. 18	Parkes and others imprisoned (13 killed) by Sengelincin, who is defeated. Yixin (Prince Gong) ordered to negotiate with Great Britain and France.
	22	The Emperor flees.
	Oct. 18–20	The old Summer Palace burnt down by the British and French.
	24–8	Yixin signs Convention of Beijing with Great Britain and France.
	Nov. 14	By a convention signed with Russia, China cedes all territory east of the Ussuri River.
	Dec. 3	Li Xiucheng's western expedition defeated in Anhui.
1861	Mar. 11	Establishment of the Zongli Yamen.
	19	The Nian army threatens Kaifeng.
	July 7	Yixin memorializes proposing purchase of foreign ships and guns.
	Aug. 22	Death of the Xian Feng Emperor, succeeded by Zai Qun with the reign title Tong Zhi.
	Sept. 5	Taipings lose Anqing, a decisive turning-point.
	Nov. 8	Su Shun executed.
	Dec.	Zeng Guofan sets up an arsenal in Anhui. Chinese edition of *North China Daily News (Shanghai Xinbao)* starts publication.
1862	Feb. 10	Li Xiucheng defeated outside Shanghai by Ward's 'Ever Victorious Army'.
	19	Zeng Guofan buys a foreign steamship. The Court orders 800,000 taels to be spent on foreign ships and arms.
	Mar. 1	Ma Rulong, Yunnan Muslim rebel, surrenders.
	9	Shi Dakai forced into Guizhou.
	June 3	Li Hongzhang's Huai army defeats Li Xiucheng, with foreign help, outside Shanghai.
	29	Muslims attack Xi'an, beginning the north-west Muslim revolt.
	July 11	Tong Wen Guan (Foreign Languages School) opens.
	Nov. 3	Li Xiucheng's attempt to raise the siege of Nanjing repulsed.
1863	Jan. 9	Order in council allows British officers to serve in the Qing forces.
	Mar.	Renewed Muslim revolt in Yunnan, led by Du Wenxiu.
	June 13	Shi Dakai surrenders.

	July 13	Li Hongzhang refuses permission for a railway between Suzhou and Shanghai.
	Aug. 6	Shi Dakai executed.
	Dec. 4	Taipings at Suzhou surrender, and their leaders are treacherously executed by Li Hongzhang.
1864	June 2	Li Hongzhang memorial calls for investigation of all kinds of foreign machinery.
	3	Xinjiang Muslim rebellion begins, led by Burhannudin.
	July 19	Fall of Nanjing; end of the Taiping Rebellion.
1865	Jan.	Buzurg Khan and Yakub Beg enter Xinjiang from Khokand and occupy Kashgar.
	24	Sengelincin defeated by Nian at Lushan (in Hunan).
	27	W. A. P. Martin's translation of Wheaton's *Elements of International Law* presented to the throne.
	Apr.	Establishment of Hong Kong and Shanghai Banking Corporation.
	2	Yixin degraded.
	23	Yixin restored.
	Sept.	Establishment of the Jiangnan Arsenal.
1866	Apr. 11	Xinjiang Muslims take Tarbagatai.
	Sept. 24	The Nian break out of Zeng Guofan's barrier dikes at Kaifeng.
	25	Zuo Zongtang sent to Shaanxi-Gansu to put down Hui rebellion.
	Nov. 26	Li Hongzhang appointed Imperial Commissioner in charge of Hunan and Huai armies.
	Dec. 7	Li Hongzhang appointed to subdue the Nian.
	11	The Tong Wen Guan opens new departments of mathematics and astronomy.
1867	Jan. 11, 23	Qing forces heavily defeated by East and West Nian armies.
	May	Li Hongzhang founds Jinling Arsenal at Nanjing.
	Nov. 21	Burlinghame Mission leaves.
1868	Jan. 5	East Nian annihilated near Yangzhou (in Jiangsu).
	18	Fuzhou dockyard begins work. The Jiangnan Arsenal produces its first steamship.
	Aug. 16	West Nian annihilated in Shandong.
1869	Jan. 14	Clarendon reprimands Sir Rutherford Alcock, British ambassador to China, for seizing the Jiangnan Arsenal's new ship over the 'Yangzhou Incident', when the China Inland Mission in Yangzhou was attacked.
	Mar. 24	British Government expresses dissatisfaction over the behaviour of British naval forces at Chaozhou after a clash with villagers. Increasing attacks on missions and converts throughout the year.

1870	June 21	The Tianjin massacre.
	Nov. 8	Yakub Beg takes Turfan.
1871	May 12	17-year-old Guizhou Miao rebellion finally defeated. First Chinese students leave for abroad (United States).
	June 3	Undersea cable from Shanghai to London completed.
	8	Death of Wo Ren, the conservative idealogue. Yakub Beg signs a treaty with the Russians, opening Xinjiang to Russian trade.
	July 4	Russian troops occupy Kuldya (Yili).
	Dec. 10–14	Rebel city of Dali in Yunnan, attacked and the Muslim leader Du Wenxiu forced to surrender on 26 Dec.
1873	Feb. 23	Tong Zhi Emperor assumes power from the Regents.
	24	Powers demand audience with the Emperor.
	June 14	China Merchant Steamship Navigation Company set up by Li Hongzhang.
	29	Powers received in audience by the Emperor.
	Nov. 4	Gansu Hui rebellion defeated by Zuo Zongtang.
1874	Mar. 15	Franco-Vietnamese Treaty of Saigon establishes French sovereignty over Cochin China.
	May 7	Japanese land in Taiwan.
	Oct. 31	Japan withdraws from Taiwan on payment of an indemnity of half a million taels.
1875	Feb. 21	Margary killed.
	Mar. 19	Great Britain demands redress for the death of Margary.
	June 12	Death of Tong Zhi Emperor, aged 18.
	14	Two empresses dowager become regents again.
	Aug. 28	China's first ambassador, Guo Songtao, appointed to Great Britain.
1876	Feb. 27	Japan asserts independence of Korea and signs treaty with her.
	May 29	Death of Yakub Beg.
	Sept. 13	The Zhefu (Chefoo) Convention.
1879	Apr. 4	Japan annexes the Liuqiu (Ryukyu) Islands.
	Oct. 2	Chong Hou signs the Treaty of Livadia with Russia, ceding considerable territory round Kuldya and conceding substantial trade privileges.
	Dec. 4	Zuo Zongtang denounces the Treaty of Livadia.
1880	Feb. 19	The Treaty of Livadia renounced by China.
	Sept. 5	Zuo Zongtang's Lanzhou woollen mill starts work.
1881		The Treaty of St Petersburg replaces the Treaty of Livadia.
	Feb. 14	Establishment of Kaiping coal-mine.
1882	Mar. 22	Kuldya handed back to China.
	Apr. 25	French force occupies Hanoi.
	May 3	China protests at French action in Indo-China.

	July 23	Pro-Chinese *coup d'état* in Korea when the regent, the Taewongun, seizes power.
	24	The Chinese remove the Taewongun to China to avoid complications.
	Aug. 30	Japan makes a treaty with Korea, obtaining the right to post troops at her Seoul consulate; the treaty is made without reference to China.
	Dec. 20	France and China agree joint guarantee of the independence of Annam.
1883	May 19	The Black Flags defeat the French near Hanoi, but are soon forced to retreat.
	Oct. 26	Li Hongzhang advises that China is too weak to fight France.
	Nov. 30	Zhang Zhidong demands stand against France.
1884	Apr. 8	Yixin dismissed from all offices because of defeat over Annam, along with the whole Grand Council.
	May 11	Li Hongzhang signs treaty with France conceding French claims.
	June 23	Further fighting takes place in Indo-China between French and Chinese troops.
	July 12	France demands an indemnity.
	Aug. 5	France bombards gun emplacements on Taiwan.
	23	France destroys Fuzhou shipyard and Fujian fleet.
	Dec. 6	In Korea, Yuan Shikai defeats Japanese guards to reverse a pro-Japanese coup.
1885	Apr. 18	China and Japan agree to withdraw troops from Korea.
	June 9	After further defeats, China and France sign treaty confirming French protectorate over Annam.
	Oct.	Founding of Shanghai Polytechnic Institute by British missionary John Fryer.
1886	Jan. 1	Burma declared part of British India, but Great Britain allows Burma to continue to send tribute.
	Sept. 2	Yehenala (Cixi) announces prolongation of her regency.
1887	June 11	Zhang Zhidong founds the Guangya Academy, with a partly Western curriculum.
	Dec. 1	Beijing orders Tibetan troops to withdraw from Lingtu in Sikkim to prevent a clash with Great Britain.
1888	Mar.	The British destroy Tibetan positions at Lingtu, and complete their occupation of Sikkim in September.
	Nov. 19	Weng Tonghe refuses to transmit Kang Youwei's first 10,000-word memorial to the Emperor.
	Dec. 17	Li Hongzhang creates the Beiyang fleet.
1889	Mar. 4	The Guang Xu Emperor assumes power.
	Apr. 2	Zhang Zhidong proposes a railway from Beijing to Hankou.

1890	Mar. 17	British control of Sikkim confirmed by treaty with China.
	Dec. 4	Zhang Zhidong sets up Hanyang iron and steel works.
1891		Kang Youwei's *The Forged Classics of Xin* is printed.
1894	Mar. 17	Tonghak rebellion breaks out in Korea.
	May 31	Korean king asks for Chinese assistance.
	June 5	Japanese army sent to Seoul.
	8	Chinese troops arrive in Korea.
	25	Legations of America, Russia, France, and Great Britain request simultaneous withdrawal of Chinese and Japanese troops from Korea.
	Aug. 1	Outbreak of Sino-Japanese War.
	Sept. 17	Beiyang fleet destroyed in action with the Japanese navy.
	Nov. 24	Sun Yatsen founds the Revive China Society in Honolulu.
1895	Apr. 17	The Treaty of Shimonoseki signed.
	23	Triple intervention (Russia, Germany, France) urges return of Liao-dong to Japan.
	May 2	Kang Youwei and 603 graduates protest against the Treaty of Shimonoseki.
	3	Kang Youwei obtains the *jinshi* degree.
	5	Kang Youwei has audience with the Emperor.
	29	Kang Youwei sends letter of protest at the Treaty of Shimonoseki, calls for reforms, and the Emperor approves.
	June 2	Japan having invaded Taiwan, China surrenders the island.
	Oct. 26	Sun's first rising takes place at Canton and is defeated.
	Nov. 7	Japan returns Liaodong to China in return for an increased war indemnity.
1896	Mar. 23	China borrows £16 million at 5% interest from the Hong Kong and Shanghai Banking Corporation and the Deutsche–Asiatische Bank to pay the Japanese indemnity.
	27	Li Hongzhang leaves on goodwill mission to the United States and Europe.
	May 13	Yuan Shikai sets up a military academy at Tianjin.
	June 2	In St Petersburg Li Hongzhang signs the secret Sino-Russian treaty of alliance which includes Russia's right to extend the Trans-Siberian Railway through Manchuria.
	5	France signs contract with China to build a railway from Annam to Guangxi.
	15	The Big Swords society attacks Christian converts and missionaries in Shandong.
	Oct. 11	Sun Yatsen is kidnapped in London and detained at the Chinese legation, but is released on 23 Oct. on the intervention of the Foreign Office.
	20	The Court sets up a general railway company.
	Nov. 12	The Court decides to set up a Western-style bank.
1897	Mar. 1	France secures non-alienation of Hainan.

	June 21	Liu Kunyi, Zhang Zhidong, and other provincial officials appeal to the Court to suppress the Boxers.
	July 3	A second Open Door note proposes respect for the integrity of China.
	9, 28	Five officials, including two members of the Zongli Yamen, executed for being pro-foreign.
	16	After an incident on the Amur River, Russia invades Manchuria.
	Aug. 14	The Allies enter Beijing.
	15	Yehenala (Cixi) flees.
	Oct. 1	Li Hongzhang appointed Governor-General of Zhili.
	22	Sun's second rising (in Huizhou, Guangdong) fails.
1901	Apr. 21	Yikuang (Prince Qing) appointed head of the new Bureau of Government Affairs; this marks the beginning of new reforms.
	Aug. 29	The Court reforms examinations; 8-legged essay again abolished.
	Sept. 7	Signing of Boxer protocol which includes an indemnity of 450 million taels, the razing of the Dagu forts, and the stationing of foreign troops at Tianjin, Tangshan, Shanhaiguan, and other places in Zhili. Yan Fu completes his translation of Adam Smith's *Wealth of Nations*.
1902		In the course of the year, foot-binding condemned, intermarriage between Chinese and Manchus legalized, Christian converts to be equal to others before the law, an educational system and a national syllabus created, all provinces ordered to send students abroad, certain Hanlin compilers and graduates to study at Imperial University.
	Jan. 30	Anglo-Japanese alliance concluded.
1903	Apr. 8	The Russians refuse to evacuate Manchuria without a non-alienation agreement *re* Manchuria; Japan protests on 30 Apr.
	July 1	The British Younghusband Expedition reaches Lhasa.
1904	Jan. 13	Zhang Zhidong and others propose the phasing out of traditional examinations.
	Feb. 8	The Russo-Japanese War begins when Japan attacks Lushun.
	May 15	Tibet declares war on Great Britain.
	Aug. 3	British troops reach Lhasa.
	Sept. 7	Tibet agrees to have no dealings with any foreign power without British consent.
	Oct. 23	Rising in Hunan led by Huang Xing of the China Revival Society is defeated.
1905	Mar. 10	Japan wins decisive victory over Russia at Mukden (Shenyang).
	July 2	Yuan Shikai, Zhang Zhidong, and others call for constitutional government within twelve years.
	16	The Court orders a mission abroad to study constitutions.

	30	Sun and others meet in Tokyo to form the Tong Meng Hui (Chinese United League), formally set up on 20 Aug.
	Sept. 5	The Treaty of Portsmouth ends the Sino-Russian War. China's sovereignty restored in Manchuria, but Japan gets lease of the Liaodong Peninsula and the Chinese Eastern Railway north to Changchun. Yan Fu's translation of J. S. Mill's *System of Logic* is published.
1906	Apr. 8	Great Britain agrees with China not to interfere in Tibetan affairs.
	Sept. 1	The Court announces that a constitution is to be drafted.
	Nov. 6	The Six Boards abolished and replaced by eleven ministries.
	20	Command of four out of six divisions of the Beiyang Army is put in Manchu hands.
	Dec. 4	Two more Nationalist revolts, in Jiangxi and Hunan, quickly suppressed.
1907	Feb. 19	Further Nationalist revolt (in Guangdong) defeated.
	Apr. 20	Manchuria divided into three provinces: Fengtian, Jilin, Heilongjiang.
	May 22	The third Nationalist revolt (in Guangdong) defeated.
	June 2	The fourth Nationalist revolt (in Guangdong) defeated.
	July 6	Nationalist rising in Anhui kills the governor, but is defeated.
	Sept. 1	Further Nationalist revolt in Guangdong defeated after an initial victory; this is regarded as the fifth rising associated with Sun Yatsen.
	20	An imperial edict orders establishment of a national assembly.
	Oct. 19	An imperial edict is issued setting up elected provincial assemblies.
	Nov. 30	Nationalist revolt in Guangxi defeated.
1908	Jan. 13	Contract with Deutsche Asiatische Bank for a loan to build the Tianjin–Pukou Railway.
	Mar.	From March onwards, mass boycott of Japanese goods over Japanese reaction to the seizure of a Japanese ship (the *Tatsu Maru*) smuggling arms.
	6	Contract with Great Britain for a loan to build the Shanghai–Hangzhou–Ningbo Railway.
	13	Hanyang Arsenal, Daye iron-mines and Pingxiang coal-mines merged to form the Hanyeping Coal and Iron Company.
	Nov. 14	Death of the Guangxu Emperor.
	15	Death of Yehenala (Cixi).
	Dec. 2	Pu Yi ascends the throne as Emperor, with reign title Xuan Tong.
1909	Jan. 1	China regains control of the Beijing–Hankou Railway from Belgium.
	2	Yuan Shikai ordered to retire.
	Dec. 7	The Dalai Lama protests at the dispatch of Chinese troops to Tibet.

1910	Jan. 26	Petition from provincial assemblies for the immediate opening of Parliament.
	Feb. 12	Further Nationalist rising in Guangzhou is put down.
	Apr.	Yunnan–Annam Railway completed.
	May 23	Formation of an international consortium to handle loans to China.
	June 27	The Court turns down request for an immediate parliament, having decreed a national assembly, half elected, half appointed.
	July 4	Japan and Russia sign a secret treaty recognizing each other's rights in Manchuria.
	Nov. 4	An imperial edict that Parliament be convened in 1913 instead of 1916 is issued.
	Dec. 18	The National Assembly's demand for responsible cabinet government is rejected by the Court.
1911	Jan. 30	Nationalist rising in Canton put down, 86 revolutionaries killed.
	May 8	Great Britain agrees to end opium imports by 1917.
	9	An edict nationalizes all China's railways.
	20	Loan from consortium to build Sichuan–Hankou and Hankou–Canton railways, £10 million at 5% interest.
	June 17	The Railway Protection League set up in Sichuan.
	Sept. 7	Thirty Railway Protection League demonstrators killed by imperial troops.
	Oct. 10	Wuhan rising takes place.
	18	Consuls at Hankou proclaim their neutrality.
	22	The New Army rebels in Changsha; Hunan declares independence.
	29	Shanxi proclaims independence.
	31	The New Army rebels in Jiangxi.
	Nov.	At various dates, Guizhou, Jiangsu, Guangxi, Anhui, Shandong and Sichuan join the revolution.
	Dec. 2	Conference of representatives of all provinces sets up a provincial government.
	25	Sun Yatsen arrives from overseas.
1912	Jan. 1	Official proclamation of the Republic.
	5	Acting President Sun recognizes all treaties made by the imperial government and agrees to protect foreign interests.
	Feb. 12	The Qing Emperor abdicates.
	13	Yuan Shikai declares support for the Republic. Sun declares his willingness to resign in favour of Yuan Shikai.
	14–15	Yuan Shikai elected provisional President.
	15	Nanjing is named as the capital of the new republic.
	29	Cao Kun's 3rd Division mutinies in Beijing in protest at the removal of the capital to Nanjing.
	Mar. 13	Tang Shaoyi becomes Prime Minister.

	15	Yuan Shikai begins to borrow heavily from the four-power international consortium and other groups.
	Apr. 2	The Senate decides to establish the capital at Beijing.
	May 5	British troops move into Tibet.
	12	Yuan Shikai prohibits private organizations from taking part in politics.
	June 1	Russia invades Kuldya (Yili).
	June 15	Tang Shaoyi resigns as Prime Minister and is succeeded by Lu Zhengxiang.
	July 14	Five members of the Cabinet (of whom four are Tong Meng Hui members) resign.
	Aug. 10	A general election takes place.
	Sept. 24	Contract with a Belgian syndicate to build a railway from Luoyang (Henan) to Xi'an (Shanxi).
	Sept. 25	Zhao Binglin succeeds as Prime Minister.
	Nov. 3	Russia recognizes the independence of Mongolia. China protests. Mongolia and Tibet form an alliance under which each recognizes the other's independence.
1913	Mar. 20	Song Jiaoren assassinated.
	Apr. 8	First meeting of the elected National Assembly.
	26	Zhao Binglin obtains a loan of £25 million from a group of five foreign banks without parliamentary approval.
	29	The Senate declares the loan of 26 Apr. null and void.
	May 1	Zhao Binglin resigns because of the assassination of Song Jiaoren and is succeeded by Duan Qirui as acting Prime Minister.
	July 12	Li Liejun declares the independence of Jiangxi; followed by Jiangsu, Anhui, Guangdong and Hunan.
	Sept. 1	This 'second revolution' ends when Yuan Shikai's troops take Nanjing.
	11	Xiong Xiling's cabinet formed.
	Nov. 4	Yuan Shikai orders the dissolution of the Nationalist Party and ousts its MPs.
	26	Yuan Shikai orders that a Political Council should replace the National Assembly.
1914	Feb. 12	Prime Minister Xiong Xiling resigns and is replaced by Sun Baoqi.
	May 1	Yuan Shikai annuls the provisional Constitution and promulgates the Constitutional Compact.
	July 3	At a conference at Simla Great Britain recognizes the autonomy of Tibet; China does not ratify the agreement.
	28	Austria–Hungary declares war on Serbia: outbreak of World War I.
	Aug. 15	Japan sends an ultimatum to Germany demanding the handing over of Qingdao, Shandong.
	Nov. 7	Japan occupies Qingdao.

	Dec. 3	The Twenty-one Demands; formally presented 20 Jan. 1915.
	29	Yuan Shikai's presidential election law; the President to be elected for ten years and to be eligible for re-election.
1915	Mar. 10	Geming Dang denounces the Twenty-one Demands and calls for the overthrow of Yuan Shikai.
	May 8	Yuan Shikai accepts modified Twenty-one Demands.
	Sept. 1	The Council of State calls for the restoration of the monarchy.
	Dec. 5	Chen Qimei and others unsuccessfully attack the Jiangnan Arsenal.
	25	Cai E, Tang Jiyao, and others organize the National Protection Army.
	31	Yuan Shikai assumes the throne.
1916	Jan. 6	Chen Jiongming rebels against the pro-Yuan Governor of Guangdong, Long Jiguang.
	May 8	The National Protection Army sets up a separate national government in Canton, the Military Affairs Council.
	June 6	Death of Yuan Shikai.
	7	Vice-President Li Yuanhong succeeds as President, with Feng Guozhang as Vice-President.
	29	Duan Qirui appointed Prime Minister.
	July 14	Canton Military Affairs Council disbanded.
	Aug. 1	The National Assembly (dissolved by Yuan in 1914) reconvenes.
	Oct. 31	Death of Huang Xing, leader of the Wuhan rising.
	Dec. 26	Li Yuanhong appoints Cai Yuanpei as Vice-Chancellor of Beijing University.
1917	Jan. 1	Hu Shi advocates literary reform (the use of the colloquial written form, *bai hua*) in *New Youth* magazine.
	Feb. 16	Great Britain assures Japan of support for her assumption of German rights in Shandong.
	May 23	Li Yuanhong dismisses Duan Qirui as Prime Minister as a result of his unconstitutional proceedings *re* entry to World War I. A quick succession of prime ministers follows: Wu Tingfang (23 May), Jiang Zhaozong (12 June), Li Jingxi (24 June).
	June 14	Zhang Xun arrives in Beijing with 5,000 men to 'mediate'.
	July 1	Zhang Xun restores Pu Yi to the throne, and Duan Qirui as Prime Minister.
	2	Li Yuanhong appoints Feng Guozhang as Acting President.
	12	Zhang Xun driven from Beijing.
	Aug. 14	Declaration of war on Germany.
	26	Feng Guozhang seeks a truce with the South.
	Sept. 10	An alternative (military) government is set up at Canton, with Sun as Generalissimo.
	Oct. 10	War between North and South begins in Hunan.

	Nov. 2	By the Lansing–Ishi Agreement, the United States recognizes that Japan has special rights in China because of their propinquity.
	15	Duan Qirui resigns and is replaced by Wang Shizhen.
1918	Feb. 26	Sun Yatsen's supporter Cheng Biguang assassinated at Canton.
	Mar. 23	Feng Guozhang forced by northern warlords to restore Duan Qirui as Prime Minister. War with the South continues.
	May 4	The Canton military government replaced by a seven-man committee dominated by southern military leaders.
	15	New Canton government requests a peace conference.
	21	Sun Yatsen leaves Canton in disgust.
	June 14	Assassination of Lu Jianzhang by Xu Shuzheng, follower of Duan Qirui.
	Aug. 3	Allied intervention in Siberia begins; the intervention is joined by Chinese troops, 18 Aug.
	Oct. 10	The newly elected National Assembly elects Xu Shichang as President. Duan Qirui resigns and is replaced by Qian Nengxun. Peace negotiations with Canton follow.
	15	Li Dazhao's *Victory of Bolshevism* is published in *New Youth* magazine.
	Nov. 16	Beijing orders a truce with the South.
	Dec. 2	Powers (USA, Great Britain, France, Italy, and Japan) call for an end to the civil war.
1919	Apr. 6	Publication of translation of the Communist Manifesto in the *Weekly Critic*.
	May	Li Dazhao publishes *My Marxist Views* in *New Youth*.
	May 1	John Dewey lectures in China (until 11 June).
	4	The May Fourth Movement; it spreads and persists until 10 Jun. The Government dismisses pro-Japanese ministers and on 13 May accepts the resignation of Prime Minister Qian Nengxun.
	13	North–South talks end in failure.
	June 28	Chinese delegates refuse to sign the Treaty of Versailles.
	July 25	The Karakhan Declaration issued by the Soviet Union.
	Sept. 24	Jin Yunpeng appointed Prime Minister.
	Oct. 10	Sun Yatsen's Geming Dang (the Revolutionary Party) becomes the Guomindang (the Nationalist Party).
	Dec.	The Society for the Study of Socialism founded in Beijing University.
	28	Death of Feng Guozhang.
1920	Mar.	Ministry of Education adopts *bai hua* as the language of textbooks.
	Apr. 1	End of Siberian intervention, except for Chinese and Japanese troops.
	30	Chinese troops withdraw from Siberia.

	May	Under the influence of Voitinsky of the Comintern, Chen Duxiu and others secretly form the Chinese Communist Party.
	26	North–South war breaks out again when the South attacks Baoqing (Hunan) as Wu Peifu withdraws.
	July 12	Cao Kun and Zhang Zuolin condemn Duan Qirui.
	14	War between the Anhui and Zhili cliques. Fengtian assists Zhili. Duan Qirui defeated.
	19	Duan Qirui resigns from all posts.
	Aug. 9	Jin Yunpeng appointed acting Prime Minister.
	16	Chen Jiongming, on Sun's orders, marches to oust the Guangxi troops from Canton.
	Sept. 27	Second Karakhan Declaration is issued by the Soviet Union.
	29	Chen Jiongming takes Canton.
	Oct. 12	Bertrand Russell arrives in China to lecture and stays for a year.

1921

	May 5	Sun Yatsen made Extraordinary President of the Canton government.
	20	President Xu Shichang orders war on the South, in alliance with Lu Rongting of Guangxi.
	July	The Chinese Communist Party sets up China Labour Union Secretariat in Shanghai, headed by Zhang Guotao.
	6	Soviet troops take Ulan Bator (Urga) and defeat the White Guards.
	15	The Guomindang army takes Nanning (in Guangxi).
	23–31	The First Congress of the Chinese Communist Party.
	31	The First Congress elects a Central Committee, including Chen Duxiu and Zhang Guotao.
	Sept. 1	Wu Peifu makes truce with the South.
	19	The Peking Union Medical College opens.
	Oct.	Liang Shuming publishes *The Cultures of East and West and their Philosophies.*
	Nov. 5	Russia makes a treaty with Mongolia without reference to China.
	12	The Washington Conference opens.
	Dec. 4	Sun Yatsen goes to Guangxi to organize a northern expedition.
	7	Sun Yatsen lectures on *The Three Principles of the People.*
	24	Liang Shiyi becomes Prime Minister with the support of Zhang Zuolin.

1922

	Jan. 13	The Hong Kong seamen's strike begins.
	25	Liang Shiyi forced from office and replaced by Yan Huiqing.
	Feb. 3	Sun Yatsen orders the Northern Expedition to begin.
	26	General strike in Hong Kong.
	Mar. 3	British open fire on strikers in Shatin, killing four.
	5	Hong Kong strike ends with the strikers winning wage increases.
	21	Assassination of Sun's chief of military supplies, Deng Keng, probably at the instigation of Chen Jiongming.

Apr. 28		The First Zhili–Fengtian war begins.
May		Peng Pai begins to organize the peasants in Haifeng, Guangdong.
	4	Zhang Zuolin defeated.
June	1	Cao Kun and Wu Peifu invite Li Yuanhong to resume the Presidency.
	11	Li Yuanhong resumes the Presidency when Xu Shichang resigns.
	16	Chen Jiongming attacks Canton; Sun Yatsen takes refuge on a gunboat.
July		The Second Congress of the Chinese Communist Party votes for a united front with the Guomindang.
	2	The Northern Expedition troops return to Guangdong to assist Sun Yatsen.
Aug.	5	Tang Shaoyi becomes Prime Minister.
	9	Sun Yatsen flees to Hong Kong.
	22	Sun Yatsen holds a meeting on the reorganization of the Guomindang; Chen Duxiu, Secretary-General of the Communist Party, participates.
Sept.	13	Anyuan miners, led by Liu Shaoqi, strike for higher wages and recognition of their union; successful.
	19	Wang Chonghui becomes Prime Minister.
Oct.	1	Japanese troops withdraw from Siberia.
	23	Strike at Kailan mines lasts until 16 Nov., but fails.
Nov.	11	Third Karakhan Declaration; the Soviet Union re-asserts her claim to the Chinese Eastern Railway.
	29	Wang Daxie becomes Prime Minister.
Dec.	10	Japan returns Qingdao to China.
	11	Wang Zhengting becomes Prime Minister.

1923	Jan.	4	Wang Zhengting resigns as Prime Minister, and is succeeded by Zhang Shaoceng, who resigns on 13 June.
		16	Sun Yatsen recaptures Canton.
		26	The Sun Joffe Declaration.
	May	6	Bandits seize and wreck a train in Shandong and kidnap almost 300, including 35 foreigners; this event throws untimely doubt on China's ability to keep order.
	June		Mao Zedong elected to the Central Committee of the Chinese Communist Party.
		3	The Third Congress of the Chinese Communist Party reasserts hope of a united front.
		4	Troops loyal to Wu Peifu attack the organized workers of the Beijing–Hankou Railway; 30 killed.
		13	Cao Kun forces President Li Yuanhong to retire.
	Sept.	2	Chiang Kaishek arrives in Moscow, returning on 15 Dec.
	Oct.	5	Cao Kun elected President.
		6	Borodin of the Comintern arrives to advise Sun Yatsen.

1924	Jan.	10	Cao Kun appoints Sun Baoqi as Prime Minister.

	Jan. 20–30	First Congress of the Guomindang.
	May 3	Sun Yatsen appoints Chiang Kaishek as Commandant of the Whampoa Military Academy and Commander-in-Chief of the Nationalist forces.
	Aug. 2	Song Ziwen appointed by Sun Yatsen to manage the central bank of the Canton regime.
	9	Sun Yatsen orders Chiang Kaishek to deal with the Canton Merchants' Corps.
	Sept. 1	War between Jiangsu and Zhejiang precipitates the second Zhili–Fengtian war.
	14	Yan Huiqing becomes Prime Minister.
	Oct. 15	The Canton Merchants' Corps defeated by Whampoa cadets.
	23	Feng Yuxiang breaks with Wu Peifu and occupies Beijing.
	24	Yan Huiqing's cabinet resigns.
	Nov. 2	Cao Kun resigns as President; Huang Fu is Acting President.
	3	Feng Yuxiang forces Wu Peifu out of Tianjin. The war ends.
	21	Duan Qirui announces 'Aftermath Conference'.
	24	Duan Qirui appointed Chief Executive.
	Dec. 31	Sun Yatsen (already mortally ill) arrives in Beijing for the Aftermath Conference.
1925	Jan. 22	The Fourth Congress of the Chinese Communist Party.
	Mar. 12	Death of Sun Yatsen.
	May 30	The May the 30th Incident: British police inspector orders fire on student–worker demonstration; nine Chinese killed.
	June 1	At a further demonstration, the British kill four more Chinese.
	3	30,000 students demonstrate in Beijing over the May the 30th Incident.
	4	Diplomatic corps rejects a Chinese accusation against Great Britain and puts the responsibility for the May the 30th Incident on the demonstrators; a wave of demonstrations follows throughout China, with many further deaths.
	19	General strike in Hong Kong in protest at the May the 30th Incident.
	23	British and French troops kill 52 demonstrators at Canton.
	July 1	A new national government formally set up at Canton.
	Aug. 20	Assassination of Liao Zhongkai, leader of the left-wing Guomindang.
	Nov. 4	Final destruction of Chen Jiongming's power in Guangdong.
	22	Revolt of Guo Songling against Zhang Zuolin.
	23	The Western Hills Group founded to oppose the United Front.
	Dec. 23	Guo Songling defeated in Fengtian.
	24	Feng Yuxiang takes Tianjin.
1926	Jan.	The Hunan Peasant Movement begins.
	1–9	Second Congress of the Guomindang.
	5	Zhang Zuolin forms an alliance with Wu Peifu against Feng Yuxiang.

	19	War breaks out between Zhang Zuolin and Feng Yuxiang.
	20	In the *Zhongshan* incident, Chiang Kaishek curbs the power of the Communists within the Guomindang.
	Apr. 9	Troops of Feng Yuxiang force Duan Qirui to flee.
	18	Feng Yuxiang's army retreats from Beijing.
	July 1	Chiang orders the northern expedition to begin.
	Oct. 10	Wuchang falls to the northern expedition.
	Nov. 8	Nanchang falls.
1927	Jan. 1	The Guomindang moves the capital to Wuhan.
	Feb. 19	After clashes in Hankou, Great Britain relinquishes the Concession there and at Jiujiang.
	Mar.	Publication of Mao Zedong's *Report on the Peasant Movement in Hunan.*
	22	Shanghai falls to the Guomindang.
	Apr. 12	Chiang Kaishek attacks and eliminates the Communist-led workers' pickets in Shanghai.
	27	The Fifth Congress of the Chinese Communist Party (to 5 May) decides to try to preserve the United Front with the Wuhan government.
	June 6	Yan Xishan gives his allegiance to Chiang Kaishek.
	21	Feng Yuchang appeals to Wuhan to unite with Nanjing.
	July 15	Wuhan Guomindang orders all Communists within the Guomindang to renounce allegiance; this marks the end of the United Front.
	Aug. 1	The Communist Party launches an unsuccessful rising in Nanchang.
	7	An emergency Communist Party conference at Jinjiang adopts a policy of radical land reform; Chen Duxiu dismissed as Secretary General of the Chinese Communist Party and replaced by Qu Qiubai.
	Sept. 8	The Autumn Harvest Uprising, led by Mao Zedong, fails.
	Oct.	Mao Zedong retreats to Jinggang Shan.
	Nov. 13	Foundation of The Lufeng Soviet, followed by Haifeng on 18 Nov., in eastern Guangdong.
	Dec. 1	Chiang Kaishek marries Song Meiling.
	11	The Canton Commune, suppressed by 13 Dec.
1928	Feb. 28	Lufeng and Haifeng Soviets suppressed.
	Apr. 20	Japanese forces land at Qingdao, fearing that approaching Guomindang forces may attack their interests.
	28	Li Dazhao executed in Beijing.
	May 3	Armed clash at Jinan between Nationalist and Japanese forces; Chiang Kaishek orders the Nationalist forces to withdraw.
	June 4	Assassination of Zhang Zhuolin by Japanese extremists.
	12	Nationalist army takes Tianjin.
	18	The Sixth Congress of the Chinese Communist Party in Moscow (to 11 July). Qu Qiubai replaced by Xiang Zhongfa, with Li Lisan as the real holder of power.

	July	A series of treaties (between now and Dec.) between China and the Powers sets new tariffs.
	Oct. 10	Chiang Kaishek elected Chairman of the Nationalist government. The presidents of the Five Yuan are Tan Yankai, Hu Hanmin, Wang Chonghui, Dai Jitao, and Cai Yuanpei, under the new Organic Law.
1929	Jan. 1–25	Conference on demobilization held in Nanjing; it is unsuccessful.
	14	Mao Zedong and Zhu De leave Jinggang Shan.
	19	Death of Liang Qichao.
	Feb. 10	After a battle with local Nationalist government forces, Mao Zedong establishes a new base at Ruijin, Jiangxi.
	Mar. 15–18	Third National Congress of the Guomindang.
	26	Chiang Kaishek launches a campaign against the Guangxi warlords, who are defeated by the end of April.
	May 23	Han Fuju defects from Feng Yuxiang.
	July 10	China seizes the Chinese Eastern Railway from the Soviet Union; military clashes follow.
	Aug. 30	Peng Pai executed.
	Oct. 27	Feng Yuxiang attacks in Henan; defeated by 22 Nov.
	Dec. 22	China, after a series of defeats, accepts restoration of the status quo *re* the Chinese Eastern Railway.
1930	Feb. 17	China secures the agreement of the Powers to set up Chinese courts in the International Settlement, replacing the mixed courts.
	26	A Communist Party circular sets the Li Lisan line.
	Mar. 8	A soviet set up at Pingjiang in Hunan.
	Apr. 18	Great Britain agrees to restore Weihaiwei to China.
	May 1	Chiang Kaishek declares war on Feng Yuxiang and Yan Xishan.
	July 13	The 'Enlarged Conference' meets in Beijing.
	27	Peng Dehuai seizes Changsha for the Communist Party but is driven out.
	Aug. 1–2	Mao Zedong and Zhu De fail to take Nanchang.
	15	Yan Xishan defeated at Jinan, Shandong.
	Sept. 22	Great Britain agrees to hand back the Boxer indemnity payments to China, to be used for railways and educational purposes.
	23	Zhang Xueliang, son of and successor to Zhang Zuolin, occupies Beijing.
	Oct. 3	Chiang Kaishek takes Kaifeng from Feng Yuxiang.
	9	And takes Loyang; end of the war.
	Nov. 5	First encirclement campaign begins against the Ruijin Soviet.
	16	The Comintern condemns the Li Lisan line.
	18	Mao Zedong's wife, Yang Kaihui, executed at Changsha.
	Dec. 8	The Futian Incident, in which Mao Zedong puts down a pro-Li Lisan mutiny in his own ranks.

	27	First encirclement campaign defeated.
1931	Jan. 8	Fourth plenum of the Sixth Central Committee of the Communist Party dismisses Li Lisan, Qu Qiubai and others from the Central Committee; they are replaced by 'returned students' Chen Shaoyu, Qin Bangxian, and others.
	Feb. 7	He Mingxiong, Shanghai Communist leader, executed.
	May 16–30	Second encirclement campaign defeated.
	28	A rebel government formed in Canton headed by Wang Jingwei, Li Zongren, and Tang Shaoyi, in protest at the arrest of Hu Hanmin by Chiang Kaishek.
	June 24	Xiang Zhongfa, Communist Party Secretary-General, executed in Shanghai.
	July 1	Third encirclement campaign ordered, but called off on 18 Sept., after Japan occupies a Chinese camp outside Mukden (Shenyang).
	Sept. 26	A vast demonstration in Shanghai demands resistance to Japanese aggression in Manchuria.
	Nov. 19	Japan seizes Tsitsihar, capital of Heilongjiang.
	Dec. 16	Deng Yanda, third-party leader, executed for treason by the Nationalist government. Chiang Kaishek resigns all his posts.
	28	At the first plenum of the Guomindang a standing committee is set up under Lin Sen as Party Chairman and including Chiang Kaishek, Wang Jingwei, and Hu Hanmin.
	29	Japan completes the occupation of Manchuria.
1932	Jan. 28	Japan attacks Shanghai; the 19th Route Army resists. Wang Jingwei becomes President of the Executive Yuan.
	Feb. 18	Puppet administrative council in Manchuria proclaims independence.
	21	The Nationalist government states it will never recognize the independence of Manchuria.
	Mar. 9	Formal establishment of Manzhouguo (in Japanese, Manchukuo).
	Apr. 15	The Ruijin Soviet declares war on Japan.
	May 5	Cease-fire agreement signed at Shanghai.
	June 18	Start of the fourth encirclement campaign.
	Sept. 3	Assassination of war-lord Zhang Zongchang.
	Oct. 2	The Lytton Commission Report on the Manchurian situation published.
	11	Zhang Guotao driven out of Hebei–Hunan–Anhui soviet area, moves to Sichuan and sets up a new soviet.
1933	Jan.	The Chinese Communist Party Central Committee moves from Shanghai to the Ruijin Soviet.
	Feb. 27	Japan attacks Jehol.
	Mar.	Decisive Communist Party victories bring fourth encirclement campaign to an end.
	1	Currency reform, based on a new 88% silver dollar.

	Apr. 29	Japan invades Chahar.
	May 31	Tanggu Truce signed, by which China relinquishes Manchuria and Jehol to Japan in return for cessation of fighting.
	June 2	Land reform verification campaign begins in Ruijin.
	Oct. 6	Fifth encirclement campaign begins.
	24	Inner Mongolia declares autonomy.
	Nov. 20	Chen Mingshu of the 19th Army, and third-party forces, proclaim a new national government in Fujian.
1934	Jan. 21	Guomindang troops bring Fujian separatist government to an end.
	Feb. 19	Chiang Kaishek launches his New Life Movement.
	Mar. 1	Pu Yi proclaimed Emperor of Manchukuo by the Japanese.
	Apr. 17	Japan states her opposition to all foreign technical, financial or military assistance to China except her own.
	Aug. 27	Birthday of Confucius officially celebrated.
	Oct. 16	Red Army abandons Ruijin; the Long March begins.
1935	Jan. 6–8	Communist Party politburo meets at Zunyi, Guizhou.
	8	Mao Zedong elected Chairman of the politburo at Zunyi.
	Feb. 9	Zhang Guotao, defeated at Tongjiang, Sichuan, retreats west.
	20	Censorship of all films imposed by the Nationalist government.
	Mar. 4	Russia sells the Chinese Eastern Railway to Manchukuo; China protests on 18 Mar.
	May 16	Sheng Shicai, militarist in control of Xinjiang, reaches agreement with the Soviet Union for aid.
	30	First Route Red Army crosses the Dadu River after the capture of the chain bridge at Luding, Sichuan.
	June 10	The He-Umezi Agreement by which China withdraws troops and officials from Hebei.
	16	Junction of the forces of Mao Zedong and Zhang Guotai in Sichuan (Mougong).
	18	Qu Qiubai executed.
	Oct. 26	Mao Zedong's forces reach the Shaan-Gan-Ning Soviet at the end of the Long March.
	Nov. 1	Wang Jingwei wounded in an assassination attempt.
	5	Beijing students protest at persecution of students, claiming that 300,000 have been killed and demanding civil rights.
	19	He Long and Ren Bishi abandon the Hubei–Hunan–Sichuan–Guizhou Soviet.
	25	A puppet government declares 22 *xian* in east Hebei independent, at Japanese instigation; China protests on 29 Nov.
	Dec. 9	Noted student demonstration in Beijing against Japanese imperialism; it is suppressed but agitation spreads to other cities.
1936	Feb. 20	The Nationalist government publishes an emergency decree empowering military police to fire on demonstrating students.

	Mar. 12	The Soviet Union and the People's Republic of Mongolia sign a military alliance; China protests, 7 Apr.
	May 12	Death of Hu Hanmin.
	June 23	Chiang Kaishek's troops force the Communist Party out of its Wayaobao base to Baoan (both in Shaanxi).
	Aug. 19	Guangxi militarists set up a separate government in Guangxi, but dissolve it on 6 Sept. after agreement with Chiang Kaishek.
	Oct. 22	Troops of Zhang Guotao and He Long make junction with Mao Zedong's forces in Gansu.
	Nov. 21–2	Communist Party defeats Guomindang forces at Shanchengkao, Gansu.
	24	Fu Zuoyi defeats Prince De, leader of the Mongol nationalists and protégé of Japan.
	25	Germany and Japan sign anti-Comintern protocol.
	Dec.	Communist Party moves to Yan'an, Shaanxi.
	12	The Xi'an Incident: Chiang Kaishek arrested by Zhang Xueliang.
	25	Zhang Xueliang releases Chiang Kaishek.
1937	July 7	The Lugou Qiao (Marco Polo Bridge) Incident sparks off the second Sino-Japanese War.
	28	Japan takes Beijing and Tianjin on 30 July.
	Aug. 21	Russia and China sign a non-aggression pact.
	Sept. 13	Japan takes Datong, Shanxi.
	25	Lin Biao defeats Japanese forces at Pingxiangguan, Shanxi.
	Nov. 9	Chiang Kaishek orders the evacuation of Shanghai.
	20	The Nationalist capital is moved to Chongqing, Sichuan.
	Dec. 13	Japan takes Nanjing, which is then sacked with extreme brutality.
	24	Fall of Hangzhou.
	27	Fall of Ji'nan, Shandong.
1938	Apr. 1	Zhang Guotao formally expelled from the Communist Party, having earlier defected.
	7	Chinese under Li Zongren defeat Japanese forces at Taierzhuang, Shandong.
	May 12	Amoy falls.
	June 6	Kaifeng, capital of Henan, falls.
	7	Nationalist troops breach the Yellow River dikes to impede the Japanese advance; great loss of civilian life follows.
	July	A brief war between the Soviet Union and Japan on the border with Manchuria, ending (12 Aug.) with the restoration of the status quo.
	Oct. 21	Canton falls.
	26	Wuhan falls.
1938	Dec. 18	Wang Jingwei defects to the Japanese.
1939	Mar. 28	Nanchang, capital of Jiangxi, falls.

	May	The Communist New Fourth Army forms a liberated area on the south bank of the Yangzi Estuary.
	11	Renewed hostilities between Japan and the Soviet Union in Outer Mongolia.
	June 28	Chiang Kaishek appointed Chairman of the Supreme National Defence Council.
	30	After serious battles between the Guomindang and Communist Party troops, Chongqing issues 'Measures for Restricting the Activities of Alien Parties', signalling the virtual end of the United Front.
	Aug. 20	Japan defeated by the Soviet Union at the Battle of Nomonhan.
	Sept. 3	Outbreak of World War II.
	8	Chiang Kaishek appointed Chairman of the Joint Board of Directors of the four national banks.
	Oct. 6	Japan defeated in the First Battle of Changsha.
	Nov. 20	Chiang Kaishek appointed President of the Executive Yuan.
	Dec. 11	New wartime press censorship regulations introduce very sweeping censorship.
1940	Jan. 15	Mao Zedong's *On New Democracy* published.
	Apr. 1	Fu Zuoyi retakes Wuyuan, Suiyuan, from the Japanese.
	June 12	Yichang, Hubei, falls, bringing the Japanese forces to the foot of the Yangzi gorges.
	24	Japan demands the closing of the Burma Road.
	July 16	Chiang Kaishek, after agreement with the Communist Party, orders the New Fourth Army to move north of the Yangzi.
	18	Great Britain agrees to close the Burma Road through which China receives military supplies.
	Aug. 20	The Red Army launches its 'Hundred Regiments' offensive against the Japanese.
	Nov. 1	The Soviet Union negotiates with Sheng Shicai exclusive rights to tin mining in Xinjiang.
	Dec. 5	Conclusion of the Hundred Regiments offensive.
1941	Jan. 4	The New Fourth Army virtually destroyed by Nationalist forces in south Anhui.
	May	The Rectification Movement opens with Mao Zedong's speech 'Reform Our Study'.
	June 22	Germany invades the Soviet Union.
	July 1	The central government of the Nationalist Republic resumes the land tax.
	Aug.	Japanese counter-attack as a result of the Hundred Regiments offensive; the Border Region areas are greatly reduced.
	20	New base of re-formed New Fourth Army in north Jiangsu is successfully defended against Japanese attacks.
	Sept. 3	China retakes Fuzhou, Fujian.
	5	Regulations for Farmers' Bank are issued, to arrange for loans to assist the government in its policy of equalizing land ownership.

	29–30	China wins the Second Battle of Changsha.
	Dec. 7	The Japanese attack the American Pacific fleet at Pearl Harbour.
	25	Hong Kong occupied by the Japanese.
1942	Jan. 15	China wins the Third Battle of Changsha.
	Feb.	Japan begins a mopping-up campaign against the Communist Party bases in the north.
	1	Mao Zedong's *Rectify the Party's Style of Work* is published.
	15	Singapore falls.
	Mar. 7	Rangoon falls.
	June	Japan defeated in an attempt to destroy the Communist Party base in south-east Shanxi.
	2	Lend-lease signed.
	Oct. 2–7	Wendell Wilkie arrives in China as special envoy of the President of the United States.
	5	Sheng Shicai repudiates the agreement with the Soviet Union and orders all Russians out.
	Nov.	Japan fails to destroy Communist Party bases in Shandong and north Jiangsu. Stillwell assumes command as Chief-of-Staff of the China theatre.
1943	Jan. 11	Treaties signed with the United States and Great Britain abolishing extraterritoriality, the Concessions, and the Boxer Protocol.
	Feb.	Another Japanese campaign against the Communist Party in north-west Shanxi is defeated.
	Mar. 10	Publication of Chiang Kaishek's *China's Destiny*.
	June 2–14	China defeats Japanese attacks in Hubei.
	Dec. 1	Cairo (Conference) Declaration; Manchuria, Taiwan and the Pescadores declared to be Chinese, and Korea to be independent.
1944	Feb.–Apr.	The Communist 8th Route Army makes gains in Jehol and Hebei against the Japanese.
	Apr. 18	Japan begins new transcontinental offensive.
	22	Fall of Zhengzhou, Henan.
	May 25	Fall of Luoyang, Henan.
	June 6	D-Day; the Allies land on the beaches of Normandy.
	15	First United States air raid on Japan, from a base in Chengdu.
	18	Fall of Changsha.
	20	Vice-President Henry Wallace arrives in Chongqing.
	July 1–23	China participates in the Bretton Woods Conference.
	Sept.	Establishment of the China Democratic League.
	25	Chiang Kaishek demands the recall of Stillwell.
	Oct. 5	Japan retakes Fuzhou
	29	Stillwell recalled by Roosevelt.
	Nov. 7	Patrick Hurley flies to Yan'an.
	11	Fall of Guilin.

	Dec. 15	China Expeditionary Force retakes Bhamo in Burma.
1945	Jan. 28	Japan completes her control of the Beijing–Hankou–Canton railway. Road link from India to China reopened after Japanese defeats in Burma.
	Feb. 4–11	Yalta Conference secretly agrees that Russia will invade Manchuria and lease Port Arthur (Lushun).
	Apr. 23	The Seventh Congress of the Chinese Communist Party opens, with Mao Zedong's speech 'On Coalition Government' the following day.
	May 7	Surrender of Germany.
	Aug. 6	Hiroshima atom-bombed.
	8	The Soviet Union declares war on Japan.
	9	Nagasaki atom-bombed.
	14	Japan surrenders unconditionally. The Soviet Union and China agree to joint control of railways in Manchuria.
	20	The Soviet Union occupies Harbin, Changchun, and Mukden (Shenyang).
	25	Treaty of Friendship and Alliance between the Soviet Union and China.
	28	Mao Zedong flies to Chongqing for discussions with Chiang Kaishek.
	Sept. 20	The United States dispatches marines to China to assist in the disarming of the Japanese.
	Oct. 1	The Communist Party and the Guomindang in Chongqing agree to avoid civil war, but the agreement is not subsequently honoured.
	31	Guomindang troops sent against Shaanxi–Hebei–Shanxi–Henan; the Communist Party areas are defeated.
	Nov. 27	Hurley (United States Ambassador since 8 Jan.) resigns, criticizing United States policy; succeeded by General George C. Marshall.
	Dec. 7	The Soviet Union declares that Manchuria's industrial equipment is war booty.
	28	Mao Zedong orders the creation of rural bases in Manchuria.
1946	Mar. 23	The Soviet Union informs China that she will withdraw from Manchuria by the end of April. (Withdrawal had already started, and Chinese Communist Party troops had entered Changchun on 23 Jan. and Mukden on 26 Jan.; Chiang Kaishek had begun to airlift troops to Manchuria on 3 Jan.).
	May 1	Communist Party forces renamed the People's Liberation Army.
	4	Communist Party directive on the land question.
	July 12	Civil war begins, with Guomindang attacks in Jiangsu and Anhui.
	15	Assassination of the poet Wen Yido.

	Dec. 25	Massive student anti-USA protests over the alleged gang-rape of the Beijing student Shen Chong by American soldiers.
1947	Jan. 28	United States withdraws from mediation between the Guomindang and the Communist Party.
	Feb. 28	Demonstration in Taiwan against Guomindang mal-administration; it spreads, but is brutally suppressed.
	Mar. 19	The Guomindang captures Yan'an—symbolic, but of little military consequence.
	Apr. 4	The People's Liberation Army launches a major offensive in Shanxi.
	May 6	The PLA launches a major offensive in Shandong.
	13	The PLA launches a major offensive in Manchuria.
	20	Major student demonstrations in Nanjing and Tianjin fired on by military police.
	June 30	Lin Biao forces the Yellow River.
	Aug. 24	A. L. Wedermeyer, sent by Truman on a fact-finding mission to China, publicly condemns the Nationalist government and calls for drastic reforms.
	Oct. 10	The Communist Party issues the Outline Land Law.
	Nov. 9–15	The PLA takes Longhai Railway from Xuzhou to Zhongzhou.
	12	The PLA takes Shijiazhuang.
	Dec. 30	Galloping inflation shows in new exchange rate of 290,000 yuan to the £.
1948	Jan. 5	The China Democratic League (in Hong Kong) calls for unity with the Communist Party and others to overthrow Chiang Kaishek.
	Feb. 11	Mao Zedong criticizes the Outline Land Law.
	Sept. 12	The PLA launches final campaign in Manchuria.
	20	Wholesale price index in Nanjing reaches 8,740,600 after new gold yuan note collapses.
	Nov. 2	The PLA completes conquest of Manchuria.
	Dec. (early)	The PLA launches final campaign to take Beijing and Tianjin.
1949	Jan. 15	Tianjin falls.
	19	The Nationalist government offers peace talks.
	21	Chiang Kaishek retires and hands over to Li Zongren.
	31	Beijing occupied.
	Apr. 21	Mao Zedong orders a countrywide PLA advance.
	23	Nanjing falls.
	May 16–17	Wuhan falls.
	27	Shanghai falls.
	July 1	Publication of Mao Zedong's *On the People's Democratic Dictatorship*.
	Sept. 21	Chinese People's Political Consultative Conference opens.
	27	The CPPCC adopts the Organic Law.
	29	The CPPCC adopts the Common Programme.

	Sept. 30	The Central Committee elects Mao Zedong Chairman of the Chinese People's Republic.
	Oct. 1	Zhou Enlai appointed Prime Minister and Minister of Foreign Affairs. The People's Republic of China proclaimed.
	Nov. 30	The PLA takes Chongqing.
	Dec. 10	Chiang Kaishek departs for Taiwan.
	16	Mao Zedong arrives in Moscow.
1950	Jan. 13	The Soviet Union boycotts the Security Council because of its vote against the expulsion of the Republic of China.
	14	The People's Republic of China orders all official United States personnel to leave China.
	Feb. 14	Treaty of Friendship, Alliance and Mutual Assistance between the Soviet Union and China.
	May 1	New marriage law promulgated.
	June 25	Outbreak of the Korean War.
	27	Zhou Enlai denounces Truman's order to the United States 7th Fleet to prevent any attack on Formosa.
	29	Trade Union law promulgated.
	30	Agrarian reform law promulgated.
	Nov. 2	Chinese and United States troops clash in Korea for the first time.
	Dec. 29	All United States-sponsored educational, cultural, charitable, and religious organs in China put under Chinese control.
1951	Jan. 4	Seoul falls to Chinese and North Korean troops.
	Feb. 1	The United Nations condemns China as an aggressor in Korea.
	21	Campaign against counter-revolutionaries begins.
	Apr. 30	Confiscation of foreign business begins with the requisition of property of the Asiatic Petroleum Company (Shell Oil Ltd.).
	May 14–15	Chinese and North Korean troops are driven out of Seoul.
	18	The United Nations imposes an embargo on trade with China.
	20	The *People's Daily* condemns the film *The Story of Wu Xun*.
	23	Agreement with Tibet states that Tibet is part of China, but autonomous.
	July 1	Armistice negotiations begin in Korea.
	Aug.	The Three Antis movement begins in Manchuria.
	Sept. 3	Provisional regulations for law courts and the procuratorate promulgated.
	9	Chinese troops reach Lhasa.
	Dec. 7	The Three Antis movement is adopted on a national scale.
1952	Feb. 1	The Five Antis movement is launched; announced completed 15 July.
	June 1	Sino-Japanese trade agreement signed.
	July 4	End of the Three Antis movement.
	5	Basic completion of land reform announced.
	Sept. 15	China agrees to the prolongation of Soviet Union occupation of Lushun.

	Oct. 10	Gao Gang appointed chairman of the new State Planning Commission.
	Dec. 31	The Changchun Railway returned to China.
1953	Jan. 1	First Five Year Plan begins.
	5	Mao Zedong issues an inner-Party directive to 'combat bureaucracy, commandism and violations of law and discipline'.
	Mar. 1	Promulgation of Electoral Law of the People's Republic of China.
	5	Death of Stalin.
	July 16	The *People's Daily* announces a campaign against Catholic 'imperialist elements'; 20 arrested in Shanghai, others about this time elsewhere.
	27	Armistice signed in Korea.
	Aug.	'General line for transition to socialism' supersedes 'new democracy'.
	Dec. 8	Elections take place for the National Party Congress.
	16	Central Committee adopts Resolution to Develop Agricultural Producers' Co-operatives.
1954	Feb. 6–10	At fourth plenum of the Seventh Party Congress, Liu Shaoqi condemns 'independent kingdoms', and begins the attack on Gao Gang and Rao Shushi (appointed one year before as chairmen of North-east and East China administrative committees respectively).
	Mar. 31	Gao Gang and Rao Shushi expelled from the Party.
	Apr. 26	Geneva Conference on Indo-China situation opens; China participates.
	June 21	Final declaration of the Geneva Conference divides Vietnam at the 17th parallel.
	July 19	Regional administrative committees abolished.
	Sept. 20	Adoption of the Draft Constitution of the People's Republic of China.
	27	First meeting of the National People's Congress.
	29	Khrushehev arrives in Beijing.
	Oct. 12	Agreement signed for the withdrawal of the Soviet Union from Lushan, end of Soviet Union participation in joint-stock companies, and a new long-term credit of 520 million roubles.
	16	Mao Zedong gives support to criticism of the Hu Shi school, and in particular against Yu Pingbo's book on *A Dream of Red Mansions*.
	Nov. 1	Census results announced; mainland population 582 million.
	Dec. 2	Taiwan and the United States sign mutual defence treaty.
1955	Feb. 5	Campaign against writer Hu Feng begins.
	Apr. 18–24	First Bandung Conference of Asian and African nations.
	July 18	Hu Feng arrested as a counter-revolutionary.

	July 30	Mao Zedong's report 'On the Co-operative Transformation of Agriculture' calls for speeding up collectivization.
	Oct. 4–11	Sixth plenum of the Seventh Central Committee adopts Mao Zedong's policy on collectivization and issues the Resolution on the Question of Agricultural Co-operation.
1956	Jan. 14	Zhou Enlai calls for more liberal treatment of intellectuals.
	15	The imposition of joint State private ownership of industrial and commercial enterprises is begun with a celebratory rally in Beijing; followed by the same in other cities this month.
	25	Supreme State Conference adopts Mao Zedong's radical Twelve Year Draft National Programme for Agricultural Development.
	Feb. 25	Khrushchev condemns Stalin and the personality cult.
	Apr. 7	The Soviet Union agrees to provide 55 more factories and a railway from Lanzhou to Aktogai.
	25	Mao Zedong's speech on 'The Ten Great Relationships'.
	May 2	Mao Zedong gives his speech on the Hundred Flowers policy to the Supreme State Congress.
	Aug. 18	The Soviet Union and China reach agreement over joint exploitation of the Amur Basin.
	Sept. 15–27	The Eighth National Congress of the Communist Party (the first since liberation) adopts a revised Party constitution which contains no reference to the Thought of Mao Zedong.
	27	Second Five Year Plan adopted, to run from 1957.
1957	Jan. 7	The Soviet Union and China issue a joint communiqué on expanding the ties among socialist countries.
	Feb. 17	Meeting of Supreme State Conference (to 1 Mar.); Mao Zedong gives his speech 'On the Correct Handling of Contradictions among the People'.
	Apr. 27	Rectification campaign announced against bureaucratism, sectarianism, and subjectivism.
	May 1	The period of the Hundred Flowers begins (to 7 June).
	June 8	The *People's Daily* attacks abuse of the rectification campaign, signal for the anti-rightist campaign.
	Oct. 4	Sputnik, the first artificial satellite, successfully launched by the Soviet Union.
	15	Agreement on new technology for national defence between the Soviet Union and China; according to a later Chinese statement (15 Aug. 1963), the Soviet Union promised China a sample atom bomb.
	15	Yangzi bridge opened at Wuhan.
	Nov. 17	Mao Zedong, in Moscow, in a speech to Chinese students, says 'the east wind prevails over the west wind'.
	Dec. 12	National Economic Planning Conference adopts a draft plan for 1958: proposes catching up with Great Britain in 15 years, and includes the Twelve Year Plan for Agriculture.

1958	Apr. 29	The first People's Commune, 'the Sputnik Commune', is founded in Henan.
	May 5–23	Second Session of the Eighth Party Congress launches the Great Leap Forward.
	25	Fifth plenum of the Eighth Central Committee elects Lin Biao Deputy Chairman of the Central Committee.
	June 13	Ma Yinchu, Vice-Chairman of Beijing University, is criticized for his 'Malthusian' population theory.
	July 31	Khrushehev arrives in Beijing.
	Aug. 3	Final communiqué on international problems issued at the conclusion of Khrushchev's visit fails to mention the problem of the recovery of Taiwan.
	17–30	Enlarged Politburo meeting at Beidahe, Hebei, approves the People's Communes.
	Dec. 10	At Wuchang, the sixth plenum of the Eighth Central Committee issues the Resolution on Some Questions Concerning People's Communes, the first check to Great Leap Forward extremes, and announces that Mao Zedong will not stand for re-election as Chairman of the People's Republic of China.
1959	Mar. 10	Tibetan rebellion begins; the Dalai Lama flees from Lhasa.
	Apr. 27	Liu Shaoqi appointed Chairman of the People's Republic of China.
	June	Serious flooding is reported in Guangdong.
	July–Aug.	Severe drought affects 30% of arable in 17 provinces and autonomous regions.
	Aug. 12–16	Lushan plenum (eighth plenum of the Eighth Central Committee); 1959 targets reduced, but asserts that the principal danger to the Great Leap Forward is 'right opportunism'. Peng Dehuai criticizes the Great Leap Forward.
	14	Locusts in Henan, Hebei, Anhui, and Jiangsu.
	16	Peng Dehuai and his supporters dismissed as an 'Anti-Party clique' by the Central Committee.
	25	Armed clash on the Sino-Indian border.
	Sept. 17	Lin Biao appointed Minister of Defence and Luo Ruiqing Chief of Staff.
	26	Nehru asserts the legality of the McMahon Line.
	30	Khrushchev arrives in Beijing, fresh from Camp David talks (25–7 Sept.) with Eisenhower.
1960	Mar. 17	Catholic Bishop of Shanghai (Gong Pinmei) sentenced to life for 'setting up counter-revolutionary organizations and training special agents'.
	18	American Bishop James Walsh sentenced to 20 years for spying.
	Apr. 16	Sino-Soviet split begins with *People's Daily* reasserting Lenin's theory of the nature of imperialism.
	17	Lu Ping replaces Ma Yinchu as Vice-Chairman of Beijing University.

	June 21	The Chinese interpretation of imperialism is attacked by Khrushchev at the Third Congress of the Rumanian Workers' Party.

June 21   The Chinese interpretation of imperialism is attacked by Khrushchev at the Third Congress of the Rumanian Workers' Party.

July 16   The Soviet Union announces the withdrawal of her technicians from China.

Nov. 5   Liu Shaoqi and Deng Xiaoping arrive in Moscow for the 43rd anniversary of the October Revolution; three weeks of bitter argument follow.

Dec. 29   China reveals the extent of the 1960 natural disasters, the worst in a century.

1961   Feb.–May   Agreements with Australia and Canada to import grain.

Mar. 1   *Red Flag* calls for the Hundred Flowers to bloom again.

Apr.   Widespread reports of serious drought in the north and floods in the south: nine provinces affected, much starvation.

Oct. 19   Zhou Enlai addresses CPSU Congress in Moscow, and condemns 'one-sided censure of any fraternal party'.

Nov.   Wu Han's play *The Dismissal of Hai Rui* is published in Beijing as a book.

1962   May 11   China protests at Indian intrusion into western Tibet.

June 26   Via Warsaw talks, the United States states that she will not support any Guomindang attack on the mainland from Taiwan.

Sept. 24–7   Tenth plenum of the Eighth Central Committee: Mao Zedong's speech of the 24th exhorts 'Never forget class struggle'.

Oct. 20   Sino-Indian Border War begins.

Nov. 6–12   National forum on Confucius' ideas held in Jinan.

20   Indian defence collapses.

Dec. 1   Chinese troops in India begin voluntary withdrawal to 20 km. behind their former line of control.

15   Khrushehev attacked in *People's Daily* for 'adventurism followed by capitulationism' over the installation of missiles in Cuba.

1963   Feb. 2–27   Political work conference of the People's Liberation Army; Draft Regulations Governing Political Work in the PLA promulgated by the Central Committee on 27 Feb. to ensure Party control of the PLA.

May 2   *Chinese Youth* carries Mao's instruction, 'Learn from Comrade Lei Feng'.

20   Central Work Conference in Hangzhou issues 'Draft Resolution of the Central Committee on Some Problems in Current Rural Work' (First Ten Points): opening of the Socialist Education Campaign in the countryside.

July 5   Bilateral Sino-Soviet talks open in Moscow but fail.

31   China denounces the Partial Nuclear Test Ban Treaty of 5 Aug. (United States, the Soviet Union, and Great Britain)

Sept.   At Central Work Conference, Mao Zedong calls for drama on modern themes; 'Later Ten Points' is issued.

	6	China accuses the Soviet Union of 'large-scale subversive activities in the Yili region'.
1964	Feb. 1	'Learn from the PLA' campaign begins with a *People's Daily* editorial.
	Apr. 10–15	At the preparatory meeting for the second Afro-Asian Conference, Foreign Minister Chen Yi frustrates an invitation extended to the Soviet Union by India.
	June 5–13	Festival of Beijing Operas on Contemporary Themes.
	16	Mao Zedong makes a speech at a Central Committee Work Conference on the need to train revolutionary successors.
	July	Wang Guangmei, wife of Liu Shaoqi, reports to a conference in Shanghai on her 'Taiyuan Experience'.
	Aug. 18	At a conference in Beijing, Mao Zedong attacks Yang Xianzhen, the philosopher who argued that the main movement of dialectics is 'from two into one'.
	Sept. 10	Central Committee adopts 'Revised Later Ten Points' ('Some Concrete Policy Formulations of the CCPCC on the Rural Socialist Education Movement').
	Oct. 15	Khrushchev resigns; is succeeded by Kosygin as Prime Minister and Brezhnev as First Secretary of the CPSU.
	16	China's first nuclear test takes place.
	Nov. 5–13	Zhou Enlai leads delegation to Moscow for the 47th anniversary of the October Revolution.
	Dec. 21–2	At the National People's Congress, Zhou Enlai states that China has repaid almost all her foreign debt.
1965	Jan. 14	'Some Problems Currently Arising in the Course of the Rural Socialist Education Movement' (23 Articles), drafted by Mao Zedong, issued by the Politburo.
	Mar. 7	The *People's Daily* praises part-work part-study schools. A campaign in favour of them follows, in which Liu Shaoqi is the main spokesman.
	23	The *People's Daily* denounces Moscow meeting of 19 communist parties (1–5 Mar.) and asserts that the new Soviet leaders are continuing Khrushchev's revisionism.
	May 10	*Red Flag* publishes Luo Ruiqing's article 'Commemorate the Victory over German Fascism'.
	23	System of PLA ranks abolished.
	June 26	Mao Zedong calls for the health service to give priority to the rural areas.
	Sept. 3	*Red Flag* publishes Lin Biao's *Long Live the Victory of People's War*.
	Nov. 10	Yao Wenyuan's article attacking *The Dismissal of Hai Rui* is published in Shanghai *Wen Hui Bao*.
	30	The *People's Daily* belatedly reprints Yao's article.
	Dec. 8	Central Committee conference in Shanghai condemns the errors of Luo Ruiqing.

1966   Feb. 1   The *People's Daily* attacks Tian Han's play *Xie Yaohuan*.
            Mar. 22   Communist Party declines invitation to attend CPSU 23rd Congress.
            Apr. 16   The *People's Daily* attacks *The 3-Family Village* and *Evening Talks at Yanshan*.
            May 7   Mao Zedong writes to Lin Biao: PLA should learn politics, military affairs and culture, and become 'a great school'.
            16   The Politburo sets up Cultural Revolution group under its Standing Committee; Luo Ruiqing formally dismissed.
            25   Editor and entire board of the *Beijing Daily* are dismissed.
            June(early) Liu Shaoqi put in charge of the Cultural Revolution and sends work-teams into the colleges.
            2   The *People's Daily* reproduces Nie Yuanzi's poster attacking Lu Ping, Vice-Chairman of Beijing University.
            4   Lu Ping dismissed.
            Aug. 5   Mao Zedong's poster 'Bombard the Headquarters' is published.
            8   Central Committee issues sixteen-point directive to guide the Cultural Revolution.
            10   The *People's Daily* attacks the economic theories of Sun Yefang and condemns the use of profit targets as indicators of efficiency.
            18   Mass Cultural Revolution rally at Tiananmen, at which the Red Guards appear for the first time.
            20   Red Guards begin attacks on the 'four old things'.
            Sept.   Publication of the 'Little Red Book' (*Mao Zhuxi Yulu*, the Thoughts of Chairman Mao).
            Oct. 23   Liu Shaoqi and Deng Xiaoping produce self-criticisms.
            27   Guided-missile nuclear weapon test successful.
            Dec. 26   The *People's Daily* calls for extension of the Cultural Revolution to industrial enterprises.

1967   Jan.   In the 'January Revolution', radicals organize seizures of power in Shanghai.
            1   It is announced that the 1966 harvest was a record, and all main industrial targets were exceeded.
            11   Central Committee condemns 'economism'.
            13   Central Committee forbids armed struggle.
            23   PLA instructed to intervene on the side of the revolutionary masses.
            31   First Revolutionary Committee set up (in Heilongjiang). Radical education reforms announced, including the abolition of all examination systems.
            Feb. 5   Shanghai People's Commune created briefly.
            11   Condemnation of 'false takeovers'—the 'February Adverse Current'.
            Mar. 30   'Top person in the Party taking the capitalist road', i.e. Liu Shaoqi, is attacked on the radio and (1 Apr.) in *Red Flag*.

Apr. 6   Central Committee Military Affairs Commission forbids opening fire on mass organizations even if controlled by counter-revolutionary elements. But serious violence nevertheless mounts.

June 17   China explodes her first hydrogen bomb.

July 14   Wang Li and others arrive in Wuhan to deal with the situation involving Chen Zaidao, commander of Wuhan military region.

20   Wang Li and Xie Fuzhi are kidnapped in Wuhan; Zhou Enlai flies to Wuhan and secures their release.

Aug. 22   Office of the British chargé d'affaires in Beijing burned down by Red Guards.

Sept. 1   Zhou Enlai orders all Red Guards to return home, abjure violence, and cease attacks on foreign embassies.

24   Mao Zedong returns from six-province tour of inspection.

Oct. 14   Central Committee orders resumption of classes at all levels of education.

17   Posters in Beijing denounce Wang Li as ultra-leftist.

Nov. 25   Zhou Enlai reveals the breakdown of rail transport as a result of the Cultural Revolution.

1968   Feb. 6   *Wen Hui Bao* denounces anarchism; a campaign begins to restore order.

Mar. 21   Zhou Enlai asserts that there is a new 'February Adverse Current', i.e. another attempt to restore criticized leaders and officials.

Apr. 18   Violence reaches a peak at Wuzhou (in Guangxi), where a group called Allied Command attack the April the 22nd Revolutionary Rebel Grand Army, which is wiped out with the death of several thousand Red Guards. Faction fighting in Guangdong is constant at this time.

May 7   First May the 7th school opens in Heilongjiang.

July 27   Worker–Peasant Mao Zedong Thought Teams sent into Qinghua University.

28   Mao Zedong severely reprimands Red Guard leaders Nie Yuanzi and Kuai Dafu.

Aug. 23   China condemns the invasion of Czechoslovakia.

Oct. 13–31 Enlarged twelfth plenum of the Eighth Central Committee adopts a new Party constitution.

14   *Red Flag* calls for rebuilding the Party.

31   Liu Shaoqi expelled from the Party and dismissed from all posts.

1969   Feb. 21   The *People's Daily* publishes a new Mao Zedong directive which calls for reasonable targets: 'in drawing up plans, it is necessary to mobilize the masses and see to it that there is enough leeway'.

Mar. 2   Sino-Soviet clash at Damansky Island (Zhenbao) on the Ussuri River.

	Apr. 1–24	Ninth National Congress of the Communist Party produces a new Party constitution with Mao Zedong Thought as the theoretical basis.
	July 8	Another Sino-Soviet clash, on the Amur near Khabarovsk.
	21	United States Government eases restrictions on travel to China.
	Aug. 13	Another clash, at Yumin in Xinjiang.
	Oct. 20	Talks open in Beijing on the Sino-Soviet border problem.
	Dec. 19	The United States eases the trade embargo.
1970	Mar. 22	The *Liaoning Daily* promotes the Anshan Constitution, which sought to create workers' control of the Anshan iron and steel complex, on its anniversary.
	Apr. 24	China puts her first satellite into orbit.
	July 10	The American Catholic Bishop Walsh is released.
	Aug. 23	Second plenum of the Ninth Central Committee at Lushan. Jiangxi (to 25 Sept.); Lin Biao attempts through surrogates to ensure that the office of Chairman of the People's Republic of China is included in the draft State constitution. Mao Zedong regards this as the 'surprise attack'.
	15	Mao Zedong writes to the whole Party calling for criticism of Chen Boda.
1971		Throughout the year, provincial and city Party committees elect new first secretaries (26 of them, making 28 to date).
	Jan. 1	Successful end of the Third Five Year Plan announced, and the beginning of the Fourth.
	Mar. 22–4	Lin Biao's son, Lin Liguo, accused of plot to overthrow Mao Zedong.
	Apr. 10–17	United States table tennis team visits China, and is received by Zhou Enlai.
	July 9–11	Kissinger visits Beijing secretly.
	Sept. 12	Lin Biao tries and fails to assassinate Mao Zedong, according to later statements.
	13	Lin Biao killed in a plane crash in Mongolia.
	Oct. 25	The United Nations admits the People's Republic of China.
1972	Jan. 1	The *People's Daily* releases the first official production statistics for ten years.
	Feb. 21	Nixon arrives in Beijing.
	28	Joint China–US statement agrees that there is only one China, and that the United States will progressively reduce her forces in Taiwan.
	Mar. 30	Vietcong begin Tet offensive; China gives moral support.
	Aug. 1	Movement to criticize Lin Biao launched.
	Sept. 25–30	Japanese Prime Minister Tanaka Kakuei visits China; it is agreed that full diplomatic relations will be resumed; Japan repudiates the treaty of 1952 with Taiwan.
	Dec. 29	Chinese imports of technology resume, with a contract with Tokyo Engineering Company for ethylene plant.

1973	Jan. 1	Joint New Year editorial, new Mao Zedong directive: 'Dig tunnels deep, store grain everywhere, and never seek hegemony'.
	Apr. 11–16	Vienna Philharmonic Orchestra visits China.
	12	It is revealed indirectly that Deng Xiaoping is a Vice-Premier again.
	Aug. 7	Yang Rongguo's article 'Confucius—a Thinker who Stubbornly Upheld the Slave System' published in the *People's Daily*, beginning of the 'Criticize Lin Biao and Confucius' campaign.
	24–8	Tenth National Congress of the Communist Party. New State constitution; Wang Hongwen, introducing it, says that the Cultural Revolution will be a recurring phenomenon.
	Sept. 24	Brezhnev states that China 'did not even take the trouble to reply' to the Soviet Union proposal for a treaty of non-aggression.
	Oct. 1	Joint editorial publishes Mao Zedong's directive on work-study classes for cadres.

When China's economic reform begins, decision-making becomes less formal. Reform is carried through by decentralized trial-and-error experiments, in which precise dates are less relevant than periodization.

1974		In his last public speech, Zhou Enlai revives the Four Modernizations proposals of 1964.
	Jan. 1	Launch of the 'campaign to criticize Lin Biao and Confucius'. Widespread changes of regional military command take place, probably in order to break up Lin Biao's network of support.
	11	China claims the Spratly Islands.
	19–20	China expels Vietnam from Xisha (Paracel) in the Spratly Islands.
	Apr. 12	Deng Xiaoping is mentioned as Vice-Premier.
	May 20	China establishes diplomatic relations with Malaysia (to 2 June).
	Nov. 29	Death of Peng Dehuai.

1975	Jan. 8–10	Second plenum of the Tenth CCPCC. Deng Xiaoping elected Vice-Chairman.
	Apr. 5	Death of Chiang Kaishek.
	May 3	At a Political Bureau meeting, Mao tells Jiang Qing, Wang Hongwen, Zhang Chunqiao, and Yao Wenyuan not to act as a 'gang of four'.
	Autumn	Three proposals on the question of the Four Modernizations, submitted by Deng Xiaoping, Hu Yaobang, and Hu Qiaomu, are condemned by the Gang of Four as 'three poisonous weeds'.
	Dec. 19	Zhao Ziyang mentioned as first secretary of Sichuan Provincial Party Committee.

1976	Jan. 8	Death of Zhou Enlai.

	Feb. 3	Hua Guofeng appointed acting premier in succession to Zhou Enlai.
	Apr. 4	Demonstrations in Beijing in memory of Zhou Enlai are suppressed by force.
	7	Hua Guofeng appointed first Vice-Chairman of the CCPCC and premier of the State Council. Deng Xiaoping dismissed from all posts.
	July 28	Devastating earthquake in Tangshan, Hebei.
	Sept. 9	Death of Mao Zedong.
	Oct. 6	Fall and imprisonment of the Gang of Four.
	Dec. 25	Mao's speech of 25 Apr. 1956 'On the Ten Great Relationships' is formally published.

1977–8   Commune and brigade enterprises allowed to engage in all trades and to buy and sell throughout the country. They are also encouraged to process agricultural products.

1977	June 2	Deng Xiaoping publicly supports the slogan 'practice is the sole criterion of truth'.
	July 21	Third plenum of the Tenth CCPCC confirms Hua Guofeng as Chairman. Deng Xiaoping named as Vice-Chairman.

1978–81   Inflation: retail price of non-staple food trebles.

1978		Attempts to recentralize the economy under Hua Guofeng's Ten Year Plan cease by the end of the year.
		USA begins to share intelligence and to hold regular consultations with China, and to sell China arms.
		Creation of the Chinese Academy of Social Sciences marks the acceptance of social science research.
	Feb.	First session of the Fifth NPC ratifies Hua Guofeng's Ten Year Plan.
	16	Sino-Japanese trade agreement.
	July 3	China ends economic and technical aid to Vietnam.
	Aug. 12	Peace treaty signed with Japan.
	Nov.	*People's Daily* calls for specific legal protection for the civil rights stipulated in the Constitution.
	19	Beginning of Democracy Wall democratization protest.
	Dec. 5	Wei Jingsheng's poster 'The fifth Modernization'.
	18–22	Third plenum of the Eleventh Central Committee. Economic reform begins.

1979–81   Output of heavy industry falls marginally while light industry increases by 30%. This illustrates the transformation of sectoral priorities taking place.

Planned targets reduced annually. State-owned enterprises (SOEs) allowed to sell surplus on the market.

In spite of inconsistencies of policy, the profits retained by SOEs increase year by year.

Retail prices of non-staple foods treble.

1979ff		Attempts begin to make state-owned enterprises pay fees for fixed capital and borrow working capital from the banks. Depreciation allowance increased. Retention of profits established, but the level too low to have incentive effect. Annual growth of commune and brigade enterprises, planned at 4% per annum, exceeds 20%.
1979		Soviet Union increases naval patrols in Far Eastern waters, partly from Camran Bay in Vietnam.
	Jan.	Theory Conference called by Hu Yaobang sets the parameters of the subsequent debates on democratization. Many of the principal speakers at the Conference thereafter act as leaders of the democratization movement, with Hu's support.
	Jan. 1	PRC and USA establish diplomatic relations.
	7	China denounces Vietnamese aggression against Kampuchea.
	28	Deng Xiaoping visits the USA (to 5 Feb.).
	Feb.	Wu Han's play *The Dismissal of Hai Rui* restaged.
	17	China invades Vietnam and takes Langson city (to 5 Mar.).
	Mar. 16	Foreign Minister Huang Hua announces that Chinese troops have withdrawn from Vietnam.
	30	At a forum on the Party's theoretical work, Deng proposes the 'four cardinal principles': the socialist road, the dictatorship of the proletariat, the leadership of the CCP, and upholding Marxism-Leninism-Mao Zedong Thought.
	July 1	Second session of the Fifth NPC: new code of Criminal Law and Criminal Procedure. Organic Law of the Local People's Congresses and Local People's Governments.
	3	China withdraws economic aid from Vietnam.
	13	Following experiments by Zhao Ziyang in Sichuan, five documents are issued offering autonomy to state-owned enterprises.
	Oct. 16	Wei Jingsheng sentenced to 15 years.
1980–1		Retrenchment, in an attempt to control inflation. Workers' management, inherited from the Cultural Revolution, is drastically reduced.
1980	onwards	The number of products allocated by the state begins to fall, reduced to about 20 by the 1990s, but the reduction is not steady.
1980		Wan Li, who favoured decollectivization of agriculture, becomes Vice-President in charge of rural work. Decollectivization spreads.
		On the instruction of Chen Yun, economy to include both planned production and production for the market, but the relations between them not defined.
		First local elections.
		Chen Yun is replaced by Zhao Ziyang in day-to-day management of the economy.

	Life tenure of state posts abolished.
	Wang Ruoshui publishes articles on alienation in socialist society.
Jan.	Attempt begins to change from profit remittance to tax; but the most profitable firms gain least.
Feb. 23–9	Fifth plenum of the Eleventh Party Congress. Hu Yaobang and Zhao Ziyang elected to the Standing Committee of the Political Bureau. Wang Dongxing, Wu De, and other Cultural Revolution supporters resign from the CC. Liu Shaoqi posthumously rehabilitated.
Apr. 17	China joins the International Monetary Fund.
May. 15	China joins the World Bank.
Aug. 18	Professional organizations permitted, within limits, to elect their own leaders.
Sept.	The second session of the Fifth NPC abolishes Mao's 'four great freedoms' asserted in the Cultural Revolution Constitution of 1975, namely, putting up wall posters, conducting debates, launching demonstrations, and mounting strikes.
10	Third session of the Fifth NPC. Hua Guofeng replaced as Prime Minister by Zhao Ziyang. Resignation of Deng Xiaoping and other vice-premiers on grounds of old age. Deng, however, informally retains supreme power.
Oct. 20	Trial of the Gang of Four and associates begins.
Nov. 3	While standing as a candidate in local elections in Beijing, Wang Juntao calls for comprehensive democratization.

1981–5	Sixth Five Year Plan; cautious growth targets rapidly exceeded by 1984.
	Rural incomes double.
	Savings explosion. By 1983, bank loans account for 13% of SOE investment. Retained profits rise to 45%.

1981	Jan. 25	Gang of Four sentenced.
	June 29	Sixth plenum of the Eleventh Party Congress accepted resignation of Hua Guofeng as Chairman of the CCP. Hu Yaobang becomes Party Chairman and Deng Xiaoping chairman of the Military Commission. The plenum adopts 'Resolution on Certain Questions in the History of our Party Since the Founding of the PRC', condemning the Cultural Revolution and the role of Mao Zedong in it. 'The chief responsibility . . . does indeed lie with Comrade Mao Zedong.'
	Aug.	Elections at county level and below completed. For the first time, there is a choice of candidates, but democrats elected are not permitted to take their seats.
	Dec. 16	$US 1.37 billion Japanese financial aid to Chinese industry is agreed.

| 1982–3 | Increasing macroeconomic problems as a result of reforms lead to retrenchment and retreat from reforms. |

1982		Energy crisis alleviated, mainly by growth of small collective coal mines.
		USA relaxes export licensing on goods to China.
		Deng Liqun appointed Director of Propaganda, a victory for the conservative veterans.
	Jan.	Abolition of the communes. Commune and brigade enterprise renamed township and village enterprise.
	11	Deng Xiaoping's 'one country, two systems' for Taiwan is proposed
	Aug. 17	Agreement reached on programme of investment priorities, supported by the World Bank and Japan.
		Sino-US agreement to limit US sales of weapons to Taiwan.
	Sept. 6	Twelfth Party Congress adopts a new CCP Constitution, replacing the position of Party Chairman with that of Secretary-General: Hu Yaobang thus becomes Secretary-General. Ye Jianying, Deng Xiaoping, Zhao Ziyang, Li Xiannian, and Chen Yun elected to the Political Bureau Standing Committee. Deng elected chairman of the Military Commission.
	24	China and Britain agree to begin discussions on the future of Hong Kong.
	Oct. 7, 16	China tests first submarine launch missiles.
	Dec. 4	Fifth session of the Fifth National People's Congress announces that China's population expansion has reached one thousand million with an annual rate of increase of 1.4%.
1983	Jan.	Wang Ruoshui's first article on Marxist Humanism.
	Mar. 6	*People's Daily* publishes Zhou Yang's speech at the celebration of the anniversary of the death of Marx, asserting that 'alienation is an objective fact'.
	June 18	Fourth session of the Sixth NPC elects Li Xiannian as President of PRC.
	Oct. 11	Second plenum of the Twelfth Central Committee. Deng Xiaoping personally launches a campaign against 'spiritual pollution', in criticism of members of Hu Yaobang's intellectual entourage.
		China's application to join the International Atomic Energy Agency approved.
	Nov. 23–30	Hu Yaobang visits Japan, the first visit of a CCP leader to a non-socialist country.
1984ff.		As price reform narrows the gap between planned and market prices, tax-for-profit becomes more effective, though still not wholly equitable.
		State-owned enterprises permitted to sell over-plan products at market prices.
1984		By this date, although reform of state-owned enterprises largely ineffective, rapid growth of collective enterprise has more than compensated.

1984		Tax-for-profit again tried and again failed.
		Reagan states that China is a 'friendly non-aligned nation'.
		China takes steps to mend relations with India, Burma, and Mongolia.
		Relaxation of restrictions on private enterprise.
	Jan.	China begins to join international organizations, including non-government organizations.
	1	Exchange rates unified at market rate.
	10	Zhao Ziyang begins an official visit to the USA and Canada.
	Feb.	'Spiritual pollution' campaign brought to end by Hu Yaobang.
	Apr. 26	Reagan visits China (to 1 May).
	May 30	Zhao Ziyang visits Western Europe (to 16 June).
	June	First public opinion polls permitted.
	July 28	China participates in the Los Angeles Olympic Games.
	Sept. 1	China's first nuclear reactor declared operational.
	Oct.	Following a letter from Zhao Ziyang to the Political Bureau a firm plan is set out for further economic reform. All goods to be voluntarily traded, further economic growth to be market-led. This plan however is a statement of intent not immediately implemented. Dual pricing begins.
		Fourth Congress of the All-China Federation of Literary and Art Circles demands increased freedoms. This marks a brief political thaw.
	Dec.	Gorbachev elected General Secretary of the CPSU.
	19	Joint Declaration on Hong Kong, enshrining 'one country, two systems' principle, to be maintained for 50 years.
1985–9		Rural incomes cease to rise.
1985		A year of deflationary policies.
		Grain procurement abolished (but later restored).
		China begins friendly overtures to Vietnam.
		Deng Liqun retires as Director of Propaganda.
		Li Peng elected to the Secretariat of the Political Bureau.
	Mar.	Lu Binyan publishes 'A Second Kind of Loyalty'.
	summer	Hu Yaobang organizes seminars for high-ranking officials on the rule of law.
	July	Wan Li, at a conference on Research in the Soft Sciences, calls for policy to be based on scientific and democratic procedures, and for the protection of the rights of researchers.
	Sept.	Chen Yun attacks Hu Yaobang for tolerating 'spiritual pollution'.
	16	Fourth plenum of the Twelfth CCPCC. Sixty-four members retire on grounds of old age. Among them are Political Bureau members including Ye Jianying.
	Oct. 28	Zhao Ziyang visits Latin America (to 12 Nov.).
	Nov. 2	Ma Deng rejects Marxist economics in an article in *Workers' Daily*, 'Ten Major Changes in China's Study of Economics'.
	20	Students protest in Beijing against growing Japanese influence in China.

1986–90	Seventh Five Year Plan reasserts the new sectoral priorities agreed on in 1979: agriculture, consumer goods, and then heavy industry. Planning now to be based on anticipated growth paths rather than central allocation of materials.
1986–9	Party groups gradually eliminated from enterprise management. Agricultural input prices increase by 15% per annum. Use of organic fertilizers decreases.
1986	Contract system applied to all workers in state enterprises. Measures taken, with some success, to bring import and export prices into line with world prices. Public enthusiasm for reform diminishes because of rising inflation. Under Gorbachev, the Soviet Union reduces troops on the border with China.
Feb.	People's Revolution in the Philippines.
Mar. 10	China becomes a member of the Asian Development Bank.
Spring	Hu Qili invites scientists and social scientists to pursue their own policy-related research.
Apr. 2	Yu Guangyuan asserts that Lenin had no experience of socialist construction.
12	New Civil Law Code promulgated.
Mid-April	Fei Xiaotong recommends that the Chinese People's Consultative Conference should be made a second chamber.
June	Hu Yaobang, speaking abroad, quotes Montesquieu's 'liberty means doing anything permitted by law'.
July 11	China applies to rejoin GATT, of which she had been a member until 1950.
Aug.	A group of newspaper editors in Harbin proposes the creation of non-official newspapers. The proposal is rejected.
3	NCNA reports China's first bankruptcy of a state-owned enterprise (the Shenyang Explosion-Prevention Equipment Factory).
Sept. 10	Yan Jiaqi writes that 'democracy needs a web of rules, regulations, institutions, laws, morals, public opinion and conventions'. He quotes the 17th-century Chinese philosopher Huang Zongxi.
26	Shanghai Stock Market reopens for the first time since Liberation.
28	Deng Xiaoping, in a speech at the sixth plenum of the Twelfth Central Committee, insists on retaining the condemnation of 'bourgeois liberalism' in the resolution. Hu Yaobang prevents distribution of the speech.
Oct. 12–18	Queen Elizabeth II visits China.
Nov. 22	*Guangming Ribao* (Enlightenment Daily) points out that South Korea, Taiwan, and Japan have assimilated Western values without losing their national cultures.

Late November	Wang Ruowang calls for a multi-party system.
Dec.	State-owned enterprises given long-term contracts.
5	Several thousand students march in Hefei, Anhui province, demanding greater democracy. Similar student demonstrations in many cities, including Beijing.
15	*People's Daily* argues that Western 'concepts, ideas and theories are not only the spiritual wealth of the bourgeoisie, but are also part and parcel of the civilization of mankind'.

1987	Organic Law of Villagers' Committees attempts to introduce competitive village elections; this first attempt proves ineffective.
	Democratization of South Korea.
Jan. 16	Demotion of Hu Yaobang. Censorship office set up soon after.
17	Fang Lizhi expelled from the CCP.
Mar. 26	Joint declaration that sovereignty of Macau will be transferred to the PRC on 20 Dec. 1999, on basis of 'one country, two systems'.
May 11	Yang Baikui, colleague of Yan Jiaqi, advises intellectuals to join other social groups in political action.
June 4–21	Zhao Ziyang tours Eastern Europe.
Sept.–Oct.	Riots in Tibet.
Oct. 6	US Senate condemns China's actions in Tibet.
8	NPC Foreign Affairs Committee condemns US interference in China's internal affairs.
25	Thirteenth Party Congress (to 1 Nov.). Chen Yun and Li Xiannian step down. Zhao Ziyang becomes Secretary-General, Li Peng acting Prime Minister. Deng Xiaoping leaves the Central Military Commission, to be succeeded by Zhao Ziyang. Yang Shangkun replaces Li Xiannian as President of the PRC. China said to be in the 'Primary Stage of Socialism'. After public consultation, the Congress promises substantial and specific measures of democratization.
Nov. 2	First plenum of the Thirteenth CCPCC confirms Zhao Ziyang as CCP Secretary-General.

1988	Protection for private enterprise strengthened in a new state Constitution.
	Managerial authority in SOEs defined by law.
	China agrees to limit arms sales to the Middle East.
	River Elegy television film asserts that China is still 'feudal'.
	In this year inflation running at 19%. Strong deflationary policies enforced.
	Systematic (but still cautious) shedding of state-owned enterprise workers begins.
Feb. 25	New democratic constitution established in South Korea.
Mar.	Riots in Qinghai.
14	Naval clash between China and Vietnam in the Spratly Islands which China claims.

25	Seventh NPC (to 13 Apr.). Li Peng confirmed as Prime Minister. Proceedings of the Congress televised and widely discussed in the media.
Apr. 8	NPC elects Yang Shangkun as PRC President (replacing Li Xiannian) and Wang Zhen as Vice-President (replacing Ulanfu). Wan Li replaces Peng Zhen as chairman of the NPC Standing Committee.
May	Soviet Union begins withdrawing troops from Afghanistan.
Aug. 15–17	Political Bureau meeting allows prices for most commodities to be regulated by the market. This causes accelerated inflation.
Nov. 10–24	Li Peng makes his first overseas trip as premier, visiting Thailand, Australia, and New Zealand.
Dec. 1–3	Qian Qichen visits the Soviet Union, first visit by a Chinese foreign minister since Zhou Enlai in 1956.
1989 Feb. 1	*Qiushi*, reform journal, gives a coded warning of the increase in the power of Li Peng.
25–6	US President George Bush visits China.
Apr. 15	Death of Hu Yaobang.
17	Students occupy Tiananmen Square.
25	Deng Xiaoping and the Political Bureau Secretariat decide on RMRB editorial describing the student demonstration as 'turmoil'.
30	Zhao Ziyang returns from Korea and opposes the RMRB editorial.
May 1	Deng Xiaoping refuses to condemn a strong pro-democracy speech made by Su Shaozhi at the Second Theory Conference, held on the tenth anniversary of the First.
4	Zhao angers Deng Xiaoping by a speech to the Asian Development Bank meeting, making light of the student demonstrations.
13	Around 1,000 students begin a hunger strike.
15–18	Gorbachev makes the first visit of a Soviet leader to China since 1959.
16	Secretariat of the Political Bureau decides on declaration of martial law.
19	Zhao Ziyang visits Tiananmen Square, says, 'We have come too late!', and weeps.
20	Declaration of martial law. Demonstrators respond by calling for the resignation of Li Peng. Meanwhile the army refuses to act against people who erect barricades.
21	Zhao Ziyang and Hu Qili dismissed for opposing martial law.
29	'Goddess of Democracy' erected in Tiananmen Square.
June 2	Over 1,000,000 Beijing citizens rise to resist the approach of the troops.
4	Troops clear Tiananmen Square; several hundred citizens are killed.

June 5	Bush announces suspension of all government-to-government sales to China and commercial export of weapons, in protest against the Beijing massacre.
24	Fourth plenum of the Thirteenth CCPCC dismisses Zhao Ziyang from all posts, replaced by Jiang Zemin as General Secretary.
26	World Bank announces deferment of consideration of seven new development loans to China because of the Tiananmen incident and the repression which followed.
July 15	Leaders of the seven major industrial capitalist countries condemn China for suppression of the pro-democracy movement, but only limited economic sanctions are imposed.
Aug.	Communism collapses in Poland after the communists are defeated in the June elections.
Oct.	Honecker sacked as Party head in East Germany, followed by the collapse of communism. The fall of the Berlin Wall symbolizes this collapse.
Nov.	The 'Thirty-Nine Points' embody post-Tiananmen attempts by the new government to reverse economic reform.
9	Fifth plenum accepts Deng's request to resign as chairman of the Military Commission. Replaced by Jiang Zemin, with Yang Shangkun as first vice-chairman of the Commission and Yang Baibing as secretary.
Dec.	Havel elected in Czechoslovakia.
26	Ceauşescu executed.
1990 ff.	After the Tiananmen Incident, under international sanctions, growth rates in China fall rapidly. Real urban incomes shrink. Profits of SOEs are drastically reduced, and some managers refuse to renew their contracts.
	Increasing opposition to growing inequalities, expressed in a literature of protest.
	Attempts to revert to pre-1972 foreign policy as part of post-Tiananmen reaction prove unsustainable, and foreign policy reverts to that of the 1980s.
1990	It is reported that China, in breach of her 1988 undertaking, has sold a nuclear reactor to Iran, nuclear technology and nuclear missile launchers to Pakistan, and missiles to Iran. Iraq, and Saudi Arabia. She subsequently refuses to join the Non-proliferation Treaty and the Missile Technology Control regime, or to put the export of nuclear materials under the International Atomic Energy Agreement
Feb. 2	US Export–Import Bank grants a loan of $US10 million to China's National Offshore Oil Corporation.
Apr. 4	Seventh NPC adopts Basic Law of the Hong Kong Special Administrative Region of the PRC.

	Oct. 22	The European Community lifts sanctions. Post-Tiananmen sanctions then end completely when China abstains from Security Council vote sanctioning the Gulf War, but does not vote against the war.
	Dec. 19	Shanghai Securities Exchange opens.
1991–3		Foreign investment is renewed, after the withdrawal of international sanctions, and reaches 20% of China's total fixed investment.
1991		Township and village enterprises now producing almost 50% of industrial output value, and 45% of manufactured exports. Foreign investment (mainly from Hong Kong and Taiwan) in these enterprises soars.
	Jan. 26	Wang Dan sentenced to 4 years' imprisonment for his part in leading the Tiananmen demonstrations.
	Feb.	Zou Jiahua, head of the State Planning Commission, calls for reduction of state mandatory plans; this marks the failure of conservative attempts to reverse economic reform.
	12	Chen Ziming and Wang Juntao sentenced to 13 years' imprisonment for their part in the Tiananmen demonstrations. Many other convictions follow.
	Mar. 23	Ministry of Agriculture issues urgent circular calling for greater development of township and village enterprises to prevent further redundant labourers pouring into the coastal regions.
	25	Seventh NPC (to 9 Apr.). Tenth Five Year Plan. It is reported that absolute poverty has been virtually eliminated throughout China.
	Apr. 8	Mayor of Shanghai Zhu Rongji and Minister of the State Planning Commission Zou Jiahua appointed Vice-Premiers.
	9	NPC adopts the Income Tax Law for Enterprises with Foreign Investment (joint ventures) and the Income Tax Law for Foreign Enterprises, and the Civil Procedure Law of the PRC.
	May 14	Suicide of Jiang Qing.
	15–19	Jiang Zemin visits the Soviet Union.
	16	China and the Soviet Union settle the eastern section of their common frontier.
	Sept.	New autonomy charter drawn up for SOEs by Zhu Rongji, providing better protection of the rights of the enterprises.
	Nov. 10	Relations with Vietnam normalized.
	Dec. 11–16	Li Peng visits India, the first Chinese premier to do so since 1960. He reaches agreement on economic relations and technological co-operation.
1992		Urban annual inflation rate reaches 22%.
		Stock exchanges resume trade in Shanghai and Shenzhen, but only 7% of shares bought by individuals, most of the rest by government institutions.

Feb. 21	USA lifts ban on high-technology exports to China.
Mar.	China accedes to the Treaty on Non-proliferation of Nuclear Weapons.
Oct.	Deng Xiaoping's southern speeches call for accelerated economic reform and restored (though limited) freedom of political debate.
4	Foreign Ministry confirms recent underground nuclear test.
19	First plenum of the Fourteenth CC chooses a new Standing Committee of the Political Bureau, including Zhu Rongji, Liu Huaqing, and Hu Jintao, who replace Yao Yilin and Song Ping. Yang Shangkun, Wan Li, and others resign their Political Bureau membership.

1993   Grain and oil prices freed.

Private enterprises permitted to trade abroad and to enter into joint ventures.

Bulk of state revenue no longer derived from state-owned enterprise profits but from value-added tax.

Many state-owned enterprises become joint-stock companies with limited liability, but bulk of shares remain in public hands Inflation remains serious.

State personnel to be selected by open competitive examination.

Ninety-five per cent of state-owned enterprise workers now covered by unemployment provision, but no provision made for non-establishment workers.

Gross value of output of township and village enterprises rose 35% in 1993.

Mar. 27	NPC appoints Jiang Zemin as state president (replacing Yang Shangkun). Jiang Zemin also becomes chairman of the Central Military Commission. Qiao Shi is appointed chairman of the NPC Standing Committee.
June 20	State Council announces abolition of many fees and taxes imposed on peasants.
Sept. 15	Wei Jingsheng, imprisoned since 1979, is released one year early on probation.
Nov. 14	Third plenum of the Fourteenth Central Committee: 'Establishment of a Socialist Market System'. It is once more asserted that the market should be allowed to play a basic role in allocating resources; that the government should manage the national economy by mainly economic means, and should not intervene directly in the management of enterprises.
Dec. 24	People's Bank given a role in macroeconomic policies.

1994   Exchange rate unified at market rate at the second attempt; the first attempt was in 1984.

Enterprises in all forms of ownership (state, collective, and private) to be taxed at the same rate. State Compensation Law allows citizens to sue the state.

Apr. 25	Grain rationing reimposed in some areas. Exports of rice and maize suspended.
May 26	President Clinton announces extension of MFN trading status; the announcement includes expectations concerning human rights but no preconditions.
July 4	Death of North Korean President Kim Il Sung.
Sept. 3	Agreement on the western section of the boundary between the PRC and the Russian Federation signed.
25–8	Fourth plenum of the Fourteenth Party Congress: 'Socialism with Chinese Characteristics' is reasserted.
Oct. 5	International conference to honour Confucius. This illustrates the revival of interest in Confucianism.
31	Li Peng visits South Korea.
Nov. 8–22	Jiang Zemin visits Singapore, Malaysia, Indonesia, and Vietnam.

1995	Mar. 11	USA and China sign Agreement on Intellectual Property Rights.
	17	When NPC appoints two new Vice-Premiers, Wu Bangguo and Jiang Chunyun, both have numerous votes recorded against their appointment.
	Apr. 10	Death of Chen Yun.
	June 27	NCNA publishes new regulations on foreign investment which encourage shifting investment to central and western regions, and encourage investment in agriculture, energy, and communications.
	Dec. 13	Wei Jingshen imprisoned for the second time, sentenced to 14 years.

1996		Draft law protecting township and village enterprises arouses great opposition in the NPC, but the law is passed.
		Bumper grain harvest: grain imports fall by 42% and exports increase by 42.3%
		By this date, employment in township and village enterprises (formerly commune and brigade enterprises) accounts for one-third of the labour force (excluding the agricultural labour force).
		Revisions to Criminal Procedure Law to regulate administrative detention and the power of procuracy to prosecute, and to strengthen access by the defence to prosecution evidence.
	Mar. 8–20	China sends surface-to-surface missiles towards Taiwan and holds naval and air force exercises in the Taiwan Straits, on the eve of the Taiwan elections.
	13	In response to China's military exercises in the Taiwan Straits, US planes demonstrate in support of Taiwan.
	20	USA agrees to sell Stinger missiles to Taiwan, but refuses Taiwan's request for submarines.
	May 15	USA retaliates against Chinese infringements of the 1993 China–USA agreement on intellectual property rights.

June 8   China carries out a nuclear test, provoking strong international protest.

July 18   Foreign Ministry spokesman criticizes Japan for encroaching on the Diaoyu Islands.

29   China announces a further nuclear test, but states that a Chinese moratorium on all nuclear tests will go into effect the next day.

Sept. 24   China signs the Comprehensive Nuclear Test Ban Treaty.

Dec. 16   State Council ratifies the appointment of Tung Chee Hwa as first chief executive of the Hong Kong Special Administrative Region.

1997   Urban unemployment, official figures 8 million, but many analysts believe the figure is nearer 20 million.

Chinese Academy of Social Sciences states that township and village enterprises are 'likely to be the primary and strategic focus of national growth'.

Growth of state-owned enterprise profits exceeds the growth of losses. Eighty per cent of loss-making firms are small, traditional, or specialized. Overall profits of the sector, 11%.

Far Eastern economic crisis begins.

As a consequence of the Far Eastern economic crisis, state-owned enterprise profits halved.

Feb. 19   Death of Deng Xiaoping.

Apr. 26   Death of Peng Zhen.

July 1   Ceremonial return of Hong Kong to Chinese sovereignty.

Sept. 18   At Fifteenth CCP Congress, the CCP Constitution is amended to take 'Marxism-Leninism, Mao Zedong Thought and Deng Xiaoping Theory as its guide to action'.

NCNA publishes the full list of the new CCPCC Standing Committee. Prominent absences include Qiao Shi, Yang Baibing, and Zou Jiahua.

Oct. 26   Jiang Zemin visits USA (to 3 Nov.). Joint communiqué on 29 Oct. announces 'China–USA Strategic Partnership'.

27   China signs the International Covenant on Economic, Social, and Cultural Rights.

Nov. 11–16   Li Peng visits Japan.

16   Release of Wei Jingsheng, who immediately goes to the USA for medical treatment.

1998   Jiang Zemin reasserts Deng's Four Cardinal Principles. Procurement of grain restored.

New thaw in summer 1998 renews call for political reform, but the thaw proves to be brief.

Record grain harvest.

Survey shows a massive loss of arable land through transfer to non-agricultural uses. However, US satellite surveys have suggested that there is 47% more arable land in China than the official figures show.

		Heilongjiang suffers its worst floods in recorded history.
	Mar.	Decision that henceforth the state will pay the pensions of SOE workers, in place of the enterprises.
	17	Zhu Rongji succeeds Li Peng as premier.
	21	Zhu Rongji visits Britain and France (to 4 Apr.).
	Apr. 15	Supreme People's Court President Xiao Yang calls for the introduction of live TV and radio broadcasts of trials as a step towards an open legal system.
	May 14	Foreign Ministry condemns India's nuclear tests of May 11 and 13.
	June 3	Jiang Zemin declares that China opposes all nuclear tests and asserts she will hold no further tests.
	27	President Clinton visits China. He is permitted, in a television broadcast, to argue that free markets and democracy are inseparable.
	July 16	Former Beijing Mayor Chen Xitong is sentenced to 16 years for corruption.
	Sept. 14	Death of Yang Shangkun.
	Oct. 5	China signs the International Covenant on Civil and Political Rights.
	14	CCPCC adopts the 'Resolution of the CCPCC on Several Major Issues concerning Agriculture and Rural Work', calling for the raising of farmers' incomes and for boosting the vitality of the rural economy.
	27	PRC Villagers' Committees Organization Law attempts again to make village government more representative and accountable (first attempt was in 1987).
	Dec. 21–2	The three founders of the new China Democracy Party Xu Wenli, Wang Youcai, and Qin Yongmin are imprisoned for subversion.
1999	Mar. 6	For the first time in PRC history, an elected village head is voted out in an election (in Jili, near Harbin).
	25	Foreign Ministry condemns NATO, and especially the USA, for bombing Yugoslavia.
	Apr. 24	State Environmental Protection Administration announces that China will invest RMBY66. 7 billion in 836 key projects to clean up the Haibe and Liaohe rivers.
	25	The Falungong religious sect holds a meeting in Beijing: the meeting is broken up and the sect harassed and repressed thereafter.
	May 7	USA bombs Belgrade Chinese Embassy.
	8	China protests against this. Clinton apologizes.
	8 and 9	Many thousands of students and others demonstrate in Beijing, Shanghai, Guangzhou, and Chengdu, in protest against the incident.
	25	The USA accuses China of having stolen nuclear secrets from the USA since the 1970s. A Chinese Foreign Ministry statement denies this.

June 24		World Bank approves $US160 million towards the Chinese Western Poverty Reduction Project.
	25	Technological Innovation Fund for Technology-Based Small and Medium Enterprises is founded, with initial funds of 1 billion yuan.
July 22		Falungong declared an illegal organization.
Sept. 9		Guangdong provincial People's Congress holds a legislative hearing open to the public, who are able to speak on and oppose proposed legislation.
Nov. 19		China expresses 'strong resentment' towards a US House of Representatives resolution condemning China for imprisoning Fajungong practitioners.
Dec. 26		Beijing court sentences four Falungong organizers to 7 to 18 years for using the sect to cause deaths, obtain state secrets, and other illegal activities.
2000	Feb. 5	In Beijing, police break up a Falungong demonstration marking Chinese New Year, beating and detaining some demonstrators.
	21	Falungong practitioner Chen Zixiu dies in prison in Weifang, Shandong, following serious police brutality.
	27	China condemns the US State Department's human rights report for 1999 for its attacks on China's human rights.
	29	Rioting following the bankruptcy of a molybdenum mine in Liaoning is suppressed by the army. Many similar incidents continue to take place. Among the causes are the effects of the Far Eastern economic crisis, and China's attempts at adjustment preceding accession to the World Trade Organization.
Mar.		Democratization is completed in Taiwan.
	9	China protests against an American Defence Department decision to sell defence missiles and an anti-aircraft radar system to Taiwan.
	10, 11	Execution of eleven Uygur nationalists.
Apr. 13		Police arrest about 200 members of the Falungong after a demonstratation in Tiananmen Square.
	25	Falungong hold demonstration in Tiananmen Square on the anniversary of their first rally in the Square (1999). It is suppressed.
May 20		In his speech at the ceremony inaugurating him as President of Taiwan, Chen Shui-bian pledges not to declare the independence of Taiwan during his term of office 'as long as the CCP regime has no intention to use military force against Taiwan'.
	24	From 1 June, Beijing's 5,000 neighbourhood committees to be chosen by direct popular election.
July 5		China, Russia, Kazakhstan, Kyrgyzstan, and Tajikistan agree to co-operate in opposing Muslim terrorism.

10 China rejects the conditions laid down by the World Bank for China's Western Poverty Reduction Project (see 24 June 1999).

18 Vladimir Putin and Jiang Zemin jointly oppose the US proposal for a national missile defence system.

Emperors of the late Qing dynasty

Reign Title	Personal Name	Dates of Reign
Jia Qing	Yong Yan, b. 1760, 5th son of the Qian Long Emperor	1796–1821
Dao Guang	Min Ning, b. 1782, 2nd son of the Jia Qing Emperor	1821–51
Xian Feng	Yi Zhu, b. 1831, 4th son of the Dao Guang Emperor	1851–62
Tong Zhi	Zai Qun, b. 1856, only son of the Xian Feng Emperor	1862–75
Guang Xu	Zai Tian, b. 1871, nephew of the Xian Feng Emperor	1875–1908
Xuan Tong	Pu Yi, b. 1906, nephew of the Guang Xu Emperor	1908–12

The Imperial examination system

The course of the examining process began with an examination at the *xian* (county) level, passing of which qualified the candidate to sit a prefectural test for acceptance on a short list of candidates who were then examined at the prefectural capital under the province's director of education. There was a quota for each *xian* for the number who could succeed in this test.

Graduates were called *shengyuan* (government students), but were more popularly known as *xiucai* (cultivated talents), and became officially members of the 'gentry', with the right to a stipend and to various privileges under the law.

Every three years examinations were held at provincial level under an examiner appointed by the Emperor. Graduates were called *juren* (recommended men); again, each *xian* (county) was given a quota.

Every three years two levels of examinations were held in the capital; the first produced a short list of candidates who, at the second level, were examined again under the personal supervision of the Emperor. Graduates were called *jinshi* (presented scholars). There were in this case quotas by province.

The most distinguished metropolitan graduates were usually appointed to be members of the Hanlin Academy, the supreme institution of Chinese scholarship.

Notes on Chinese names

The new Pinyin system of romanization of Chinese words is used throughout this book, with the exception of certain personal names and place-names familiar in the West only in dialect form or in a non-Chinese form; in these cases, on the first occurrence of the name, the familiar form will be given first and will be followed by the Pinyin form in parentheses: e.g., Chiang Kaishek (Jiang Jieshi). Both forms are listed in the index.

The Pinyin system of spelling corresponds more closely than the old system to the phonetic expectations of English-speaking readers: for example, in the previous Wade-Giles system *pan* indicated the sound *ban* and the sound *pan* had to be represented by *p'an*. In Pinyin, *pan* is *pan* and *ban* is *ban*.

There are, however, three initial consonants which are not pronounced as they would be in English. (i) *q* is pronounced *ch*, as in *ch*air; (ii) *c* is pronounced *ts*, as in ou*ts*ide; and (iii) *x* is pronounced *sh*, as in *sh*e, but is more sibilant (between *sh*e and *see*).

There are very few different surnames in China, and the fact that the Chinese language depends so much on tones (not indicated in Pinyin) increases the number of apparent homophones and near homophones. The reader is advised to think of each Chinese name as a single word: for example, to think of Wu Peifu as Wupeifu; this reduces the potential confusion.

The strict Pinyin orthography has been altered in two ways: first, by omitting the umlaut which occurs in some syllables but which makes little difference to pronunciation; second, by inserting an apostrophe between the syllables of a word whose composition is ambiguous in Pinyin (for example, the town of Xian—pronounced She-ann—could equally well be pronounced misleadingly as a single syllable, and it is therefore written as Xi'an).

Two Chinese provinces have names which, in the absence of tonal differentiation, are the same: *shanxi*. In Pinyin, therefore, an exception is made in order to distinguish them as Shanxi and Shaanxi (formerly distinguished in the old international post-office romanization as Shansi and Shensi).

There are three further possible sources of confusion over place-names; they are not the result of problems of translation but it is convenient to note them here: (1) During the republican period the old banner lands of Inner Mongolia were divided into three new provinces, Suiyuan, Chahar, and Jehol (Reher). These were abolished when the Chinese People's Republic was founded, and Inner Mongolia was redivided into autonomous Mongol administrations. (2) Under the Empire the province surrounding Beijing was called Zhili, which means 'directly subordinate', the area being ruled from the capital. When the Nationalist Republic moved the capital to Nanjing in 1927, Zhili was renamed Hebei. (3) The name Wuhan is an abbreviation of the names of the three cities of the conurbation which straddles the middle Yangzi: Wuchang, Hankou, and Hanyang. Wuhan is used here except in contexts in which it is necessary to be specific as to which city is in question.

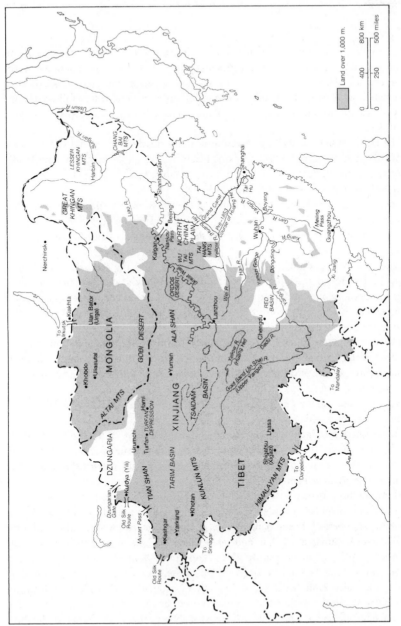

Map 1. China: physical

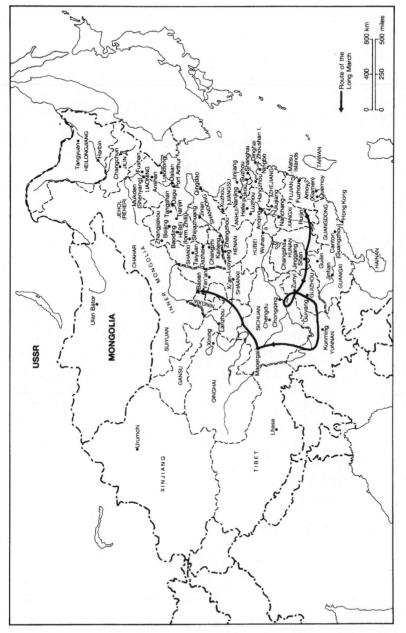

Map 2. China: political

1

The traditional society

European views on China

To Europeans of the eighteenth-century Enlightenment the Chinese Empire seemed to show the possibility of a polity based on reason without hereditary privilege or religious authority, ruled by a philosopher-king counselled by philosophers. Yet by the start of the next century, China had come to symbolize almost the opposite: a polity stifled by the power of a self-perpetuating élite who were both the guardians of a quasi-religious tradition and the servants of an arbitrary despot.

The remoteness of China has always made it easy for Europeans to project their own problems on to their accounts of Chinese life, and it was Europe which had changed rather than China. After the French Revolution traditional privilege was no longer the main enemy in Europe, while from the Industrial Revolution onwards a new concept of society had arisen, in which the creative force was not the great legislator but the free citizen. It might be possible to argue that China provided an image of the first; but she could provide no image of the second.

Yet such a sudden change of mind did not take place only as the result of a shift of subjective viewpoint. Objective factors assisted.

Longer experience of China had made it difficult to maintain the idealized view propagated by the Jesuits who had been represented in Beijing (Peking) since 1582. Anxious as they were to use the high morality of the pagan Chinese as a stick with which to beat back-sliding Christians, a sour note began to be heard in their letters home as the eighteenth century wore on.

The British meanwhile were gaining acquaintance with China through trade at Canton (Guangzhou). This had begun, inauspiciously, in 1637 when five British ships, having been refused permission to trade, shot their way in and forced the authorities to accept them. Trade developed rapidly and peacefully thereafter. The British were not inclined by tradition to set much store by philosophical despots. Nor were they, like the Jesuits, offered the flattering opportunity of a place at the Celestial Court, but had to put up with seasonal occupation of a row of warehouses in Canton, the walls of which were increasingly plastered with hostile Chinese placards. They came to China from experience in India, and thought they understood oriental government; they expected to find in China an arbitrary authority exercised over a cowed population, and naturally they found what they expected. Then experience showed that China, for all her pretensions to superiority, was hopelessly vulnerable to naval artillery; and the British were soon returning Chinese contempt with contempt.

China too was changing. The Manchu dynasty established by conquest in 1644 had reached its apogee and begun its descent, by a process so familiar that the Chinese ascribed to it the force of natural law. The long internal peace which the Manchus imposed had made possible rapid economic growth and unprecedented prosperity. The price was now to be paid, on the one hand in the consequences of a rapid growth of population, and on the other in growing laxity and corruption. By the time the British Government began its attempts to enter into political relations with the Chinese, the barbarities of the Chinese system were becoming more obvious than its virtues.

The demographic problem was fundamental. The population of China more than doubled during the eighteenth century alone, to about 300,000,000 (and has since trebled that figure). China's past population statistics are the result of registration for corvée and, later, for poll-tax, and can give evidence only of broad trends. The population had strong reasons to avoid registration, while disorder, though it might actually reduce the population, also tended to wreck the system of registration; thus when we find that the population of China at the beginning of the Ming dynasty (1368) is recorded as little more than half of the 100,000,000 recorded in the twelfth century, we are at liberty to suspect that registration had simply broken down. Then in 1713 poll-tax was abolished, while at the same time the Manchu rulers made it clear that they regarded evidence of increasing population as a tribute to their good government. The numbers recorded leapt to over 200,000,000 by the mid eighteenth century. Thereafter the figures are probably more dependable, relative to each other, and they show a rapid and sustained increase comparable with that of the population of the West since a similar date.

We can be confident that the population increased by 50 per cent in the fifty years between 1750 and 1800, rose again by 25 per cent in the next half-century, took another century to increase by a further 25 per cent, and in the thirty-five years following the 1949 revolution increased by almost 100 per cent. These figures seem to fit the known facts of economic and social conditions: 1750–1800, rapid growth owing to the good order maintained by the Manchu conquerors; 1800–50, some slowing down of growth as disorder spread, dependence on marginal land grew, the possibilities of easy internal migration decreased, and the rapid increase in the value of silver relative to copper injured peasant incomes; in the late nineteenth and early twentieth centuries, even slower growth as the adverse factors intensified to crisis point; and, finally, a very rapid rate of growth as post-revolution public health measures (the most unambiguous success of Communist government in China) began to bring the death-rate and the rate of infant mortality tumbling down almost to modern Western levels after 1949.

The effects were not at first entirely adverse. Production increased substantially, through migration to less developed regions of the country, through more intensive cultivation, and through the cultivation of more productive crops such as potatoes, sweet potatoes and peanuts introduced from abroad. The number and frequency of rural markets increased with remarkable rapidity. Commerce experienced an almost explosive growth.

In the long run, however, increased numbers, as they pressed on limited resources, inevitably produced sharper competition. The position of tenant cultivators *vis-à-vis* those with land to offer was weakened. The educated, whose numbers grew more rapidly than those of the population in general, faced intensified competition for public office. This competition had two results which in the long run seriously damaged Chinese public life: first, China's all-pervading patron client relationships were corrupted; and second, the number of minor functionaries attached to the offices of government, especially of local government, grew out of all proportion, creating a parasitic class of local power-brokers who used their positions to mulct the population, and who created a formidable barrier to any attempts at the reform of government.

The Jia Qing Emperor who succeeded the Qian Long (1736–96) Emperor in 1796 was keenly aware of the need for reform. The long dominance of Qian Long's favourite, He Shen, who had for over twenty years disposed of the patronage of the Empire and had succeeded in corrupting almost the whole governing apparatus, was ended promptly by the new ruler: He Shen was executed, his vast fortune confiscated, and his appointees dismissed. But the damage was almost irreversible. His clique was too deeply rooted. His minions were soon back in lucrative office. The Jia Qing Emperor resorted to extremes of frugality in order to maintain the imperial treasury, emptied by the White Lotus Rebellion (1796–1804), the first great peasant uprising in China in modern times, and the appalling embezzlement of public funds by those in charge of its suppression. Frugality alone, however, could solve nothing, and China entered the nineteenth century with her government at the lowest ebb of efficiency, honesty, and solvency.

Yet the decisive factor in Western views of China was not change in China, but change in Europe. These views reflected the consequences of the revolutions in Western Europe in productive capacity, in administrative efficiency, in the association of citizens with the state both in politics and in military service, in the new perspectives of economic development, and not least in the fire-power of European armies. In these new conditions the very virtues which had served so admirably in traditional China to maintain harmony in a vast agrarian society suddenly became vices. Most of what the Chinese prided themselves on—most of what they believed gave them their identity as Chinese—was to seem irrelevant or worse in the new world.

The first step to an explanation of China's modern predicament is to be sure of what we have to explain. The study of China's past is still influenced by two extremes of European past opinion. One extreme sees the disappearance of the Empire as the overthrow of a great civilization which could still have been viable and valuable in the modern world; the other as the inevitable collapse of an ancient ramshackle tyranny before the irresistible drive of the new way of life created in the West. The Chinese themselves still feel this dilemma painfully. While they feel compelled to value their past, which gives them their identity, many feel equally compelled, especially under Marxist influence, to condemn most of their history as a two-thousand-year dark age of 'feudalism'. The Communist revolution has by no means blunted the horns of this dilemma; on the contrary, it has given the problem a new and passionate political dimension, as many Chinese contrast the humanistic values of the Confucian past with the Marxist assertion that there can be no morality above class.

If we turn to the economic state of China we find similar contradictory views. It is argued that the traditional economy had such serious weaknesses that without revolution no progress could be expected. It is argued with equal force that until recent times the Chinese economy was as efficient as any, that progress continued, and that there were many signs to show that China could have created a modern economy for herself. One particular line of this latter argument goes on to find the cause of her failure to do so in the effects of imperialism.

Turning to the present, some have seen in contemporary China the image of a revolution of universal applicability; others have seen it as an enforced distortion of the natural development which should have taken place in China, had indeed already begun, and has since been carried through with astonishing success in other Chinese communities: in Taiwan, Hong Kong and Singapore.

The first problem is that of China's sheer size and variety. To compare the whole of China with any other country is in itself liable to invalidate comparisons. For example, to give an overall national figure for Chinese economic growth in the 1920s and 1930s is simply to bury the brisk development of China's coastal cities in the stagnation of her vast, poor, war-torn hinterland.

If questions of space complicate the problems of comparison, so do questions of time. To judge that China was slow to respond to new economic opportunities implies comparison; but while it is obvious that the pace of China as a whole was slow beside the exceptional pace of Japan, this does not prove that it was slow in comparison with, say, India, or with many other countries which even now have difficulty in modernizing their economies. It is reasonable to expect that there must be a fairly long gestation period in a pre-modern country which seeks to develop the skills of modern production, management and marketing. The question is whether China, or any part of China, took longer to learn than other comparable countries; and the answer is by no means certain.

The traditional economy

The most obvious geographical characteristic of China is her vast size and population. In land area China is exceeded only by the Soviet Union and Canada. In population she is unrivalled; one human being in five is Chinese, and her total population is greater than that of Western Europe and North America combined.

With size goes variety of conditions and resources. Topography and climate run from extreme to extreme; from the world's highest mountains to its lowest depression; from the tundra to the tropic; from desert and steppe to the rain forests and rubber plantations of Hainan Island.

China is a sloping shelf; its western end tilts up to the peak of Everest, its eastern end dips through plains of rich silt and alluvium and through marshes and salt-pans into the Pacific Ocean. One-fifth of China is over 15,000 feet in average altitude. Four-fifths is mountain. An area as large as Western Europe is high plateau, too arid for more than oasis cultivation, where the population density scarcely rises above 1 per square mile. At the other extreme are the lower valleys of the Yangzi and Pearl (Zhu Jiang) rivers, where the density is among the highest in the world (1,250 per square mile) and there is only one-third of an acre of land per capita.

The climate is dominated by two great seasonal movements of air: the moisture-laden summer monsoon from the South Pacific and the cold dry winter airstream from Siberia. The monsoon air sheds its rain as it moves north-west. South-east China has a rainfall close to that of Devon and Corn-wall (about 40 inches a year). By the time the monsoon reaches the North China Plain that rainfall is halved. It is halved again at the western end of the Great Wall, and halved again to create the desert conditions of the Tarim Basin. Even where rainfall is on average adequate it varies greatly from year to year, especially in the spring season of germination; every spring is a crisis. When the summer rains come, they can come as typhoon downpours which replace the threat of drought with the threat of flood; even in the north-western deserts oasis agriculture is as threatened by flash floods as by drought.

China's soil is as varied as her topography and climate. Mostly, however, it is not naturally of the highest fertility; the richness of the paddy fields of the populous provinces of central and southern China is man-made, the result of centuries of dung and tillage. In a sense, China is a vast Holland, a land of little polder farms worked at the intensity of gardening and dependent on human effort to maintain dams, dikes and fertility. Psychologically these conditions

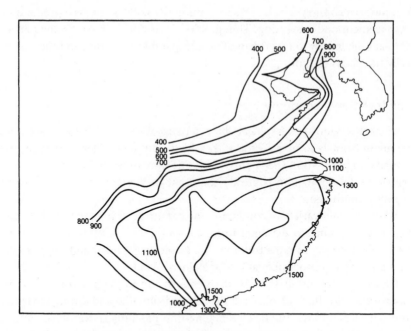

Map 3. Annual precipitation (millimetres)

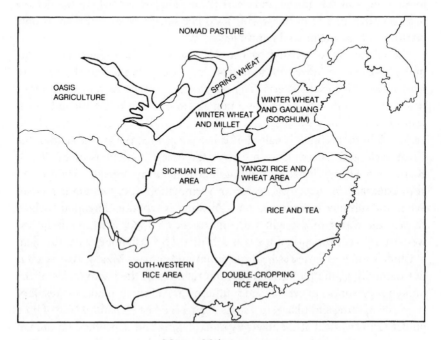

Map 4. Main crop areas

produce a contradiction: the sense of a high degree of mutual dependence in the maintenance of the infrastructure, combined with a passionate sense of independence in the maintenance of the soil. This contradiction still lies at the root of Chinese rural politics.

The vast majority of China's rural population live in compact, usually walled, villages of one-storeyed houses. Villages usually lie within sight of each other, as in rural France; clusters of low, tiled roofs on every horizon are part of the landscape. Villages were linked in the past in groups of about twenty around a periodic fair at which trade, local public affairs and marriage negotiations were carried on; since the abolition of the commune system in 1982 these natural groupings are reasserting themselves.

China's mineral resources are as vast and as varied as the rest of her characteristics. Judged even by the present inadequate surveying, they put her among the three countries richest in that respect. Her coal stocks are the greatest in the world. She has great reserves of iron ore, although mostly not of first-rate quality. She has at least 2 per cent of the world's known oil resources. She is rich in bauxite, tin, phosphates, fluorspar, gypsum, asbestos, cement, antimony, tungsten, and manganese. Her gold resources are of significant size and copper resources adequate for the foreseeable future. She is believed to have several large deposits of uranium. She is short only of lead, zinc, and certain ferro-alloys. If and when her rulers overcome their distaste for the export of non-renewable resources, the result of an irrational but widespread misinterpretation of the effects of the age of imperialism, she will be one of the world's greatest exporters of minerals; her economic future depends largely on this.

In contrast to the infinite variety of China in all other respects, stands the near-uniformity of her racial composition. Ninety-four per cent of her population are of Chinese (Han) race, or (to be more accurate) share the language and culture of Han and accept a common national identity, although racially the Chinese are in fact a mixture of acculturated aborigines. There are nevertheless over five hundred 'national minorities' in China, and although they form only a small part of the population they occupy half of China's territory, an area larger than Western Europe. Moreover, many are strung along vulnerable frontiers which divide them from fellow-nationals across the border. Their strategic importance in such cases is out of all proportion to their numbers. Some are aborigines in remote areas which Han acculturation has failed to penetrate; some are the remnants of former foreign conquerors, such as Manchus and Mongols; others (especially in the north-west) were subjected to China by conquest, and many of these are not even Mongoloid in race, such as the Turkic peoples of Xinjiang. The degree of acceptance of Chinese dominance varies. At one extreme the Manchus have been almost wholly integrated; at the other the Muslim Turks of the far west still cannot easily identify with infidel rulers.

The Han themselves are divided, and while all acknowledge a common national allegiance they also entertain local loyalties which have in the past compromised national unity many times, leading in fact to predictable lines of fission which can split open again in times of tension. The Chinese are (most passionately) a nation *vis-à-vis* the world outside; but they have internal rivalries not entirely beyond comparison with the rivalries of Europe. Every province has myths about the temperamental characteristics—usually deplorable—of the people of other provinces, and the people of one province often show a hostility of a quasi-racist kind to immigrants from elsewhere. In this sense, the oldest nation in the world is still engaged in nation-building.

China's economy on the eve of the Opium War was still agrarian. Agriculture was by far the greatest source of wealth. The value of its product vastly exceeded that of handicrafts, in spite of the existence of a dozen great cities with populations exceeding half a million. Possibly as much as 90 per cent of the population lived on the land outside the towns.

By the fifteenth and sixteenth centuries the old, mainly feudal, forms of tenure had given way to a free market in land. The last insignificant vestiges of serfdom were abolished in the eighteenth century. Some land was owned by landlords who rented to cultivators, some was in the hands of owner-operators. The proportion owned by each category then is not known, but as the distribution of landlordism was determined largely by local conditions of soil and climate and by the scale of local investment in irrigation, the pattern was probably much the same as that of the twentieth century as revealed by modern surveys: that is, most peasant families owned some land but many also rented in extra land, and a large minority depended wholly on rented land. Landlordism was not wholly the result of landless poverty; renting gave the system flexibility. By the early nineteenth century there were very few large estates; 250 acres would make one a gentleman of substance and influence and the patron of scores of peasant families. Yet landlordism was never regarded as morally acceptable; the ideal was that every family should own enough land for its support and for the employment of family members, and no one should own more. In spirit, if not altogether in fact, China was a land of independent peasants who owed nothing to anyone except the taxes they owed to the state.

Chinese history is therefore punctuated by peasant revolts which could sometimes bring down dynasties. There was a sort of entropy in China's agricultural system. The peasants' margin over subsistence was small, and the climate precarious; hard times meant debt, and at the rates of interest prevailing in an imperfectly monetized economy, debt was all but impossible to shake off. The lender foreclosed and the peasant became merely a tenant on his ancestral land. In this way peasant proprietorship was steadily eroded until the deprived rebelled. The resulting loss of life would often make men scarce rather than land, and peasant proprietorship would be restored.

An agrarian economy is not necessarily a subsistence economy. Most of the world's past civilizations have been sustained by the surplus production of their agricultural workers, and what could sustain the luxuries of Indian princely courts and Chinese vice-regal palaces could also, as far as quantity goes, have initiated modernizing investment.

The Chinese farmer sold about one-third of what he produced, and bought about one-third of what he consumed. Generally speaking, what he sold was truly a surplus; it consisted of as much of his subsistence-mixture of crops as he did not retain for his family's use. Even in the twentieth century there was only a handful of crops of which the typical farmer would sell as much as half; he consumed half even of the tobacco that he grew. Only a small fraction of the one-third of the crops which reached local markets would ever move beyond them. Yet so great was China's agricultural production that this small fraction created, in aggregate, an enormous commerce. Her great climatic range, while it made possible a degree of national self-sufficiency denied even to the whole of Western Europe, at the same time stimulated long-distance trade within China on a scale which made necessary, as in Europe's overseas trade, the creation of new forms of business organization. Part of this trade was in craft work of a high standard from particular places, such as the porcelain of Jingdezhen in Jiangxi, but not all long-distance trade was in goods exceptionally high in value relative to weight. Yunnan copper travelled to all those provinces which had no local supplies and which could not readily import copper from Japan; that is, to about twelve provinces out of eighteen. Sugar from the south was sold throughout China, as well as being exported to Japan and South-east Asia. Much of this sugar was exchanged for raw cotton from the Yangzi Delta, while the Yangzi area itself bought raw cotton from further north. Silk from the Yangzi also had a nationwide market, and large quantities were exported. The tea of the eastern provinces went everywhere at home and also went abroad. The iron of Foshan in Guangdong moved long distances within and beyond China. Soya products from the north-east were shipped to the Yangzi ports and distributed to the surrounding countryside. Timber moved long distances from the north and the west, across the more developed parts of China whose forest cover had long gone to feed the stoves of a fuel-starved population. Finally, although by far the greater part of the food supply was consumed on or near the farm, the total quantity of food which moved beyond this narrow range in order to feed a city population larger than the whole contemporary population of France, plus a comparable population in the smaller towns, plus another population of the same order of magnitude who planted cotton or cultivated mulberry trees instead of food crops, was certainly far greater than the total of the long-distance trade in grain in eighteenth-century Europe.

Such commerce on the national scale was made possible by China's system of navigable waterways, partly natural and partly man-made. The River Yangzi is navigable, even for ocean steamships, right through the heart of China to the city of Yichang, where further navigation is made more difficult by the Yangzi Gorges. The Yellow River (Huang He) is open to small-scale shipping almost as far west as Xi'an, though only as a result of constant dredging of its silt-laden bed. Tributaries navigable for hundreds of miles join these two great rivers to most of China's provincial capitals, while the Yangzi and Yellow rivers themselves are linked by the Grand Canal. Other canals of scarcely less grandeur fill out the system of rivers, while the delta regions are criss-crossed by an extraordinarily dense network of minor channels by which virtually every delta village has been brought into direct contact by water with the great cities of its area. Four-fifths of China, however, is too hilly or too arid to provide easily navigable waterways; though Chinese inventiveness in locks and ramps and special craft pressed the possibilities to extraordinary lengths, most of the area of China still remained beyond the reach of transport by water. Yet the total mileage of the littoral of China's navigable waterways in pre-modern times is of the same order of magnitude as the total navigable littoral of Europe and the British Isles, from the Baltic to the Mediterranean.

Between the shoulder-pole and sampan trade of the local market town and the junk-borne inter-regional trade just described was the trade carried on within each Chinese province. This has not hitherto been the subject of much research, although a glance at the map will show that many Chinese provinces form distinct natural marketing regions. The boundaries of most provinces are formed by mountainous watersheds. Almost every one is a natural geo-graphical region within which communication is relatively easy and beyond which, except down the main waterway, communication is relatively difficult. Consequently, each has a distinct economic life and a distinct local culture. As far as trade is concerned, the province was usually the main area in which locally produced goods were sold. In times of scarcity consciousness of this was expressed in resentment against the export of goods, especially of food-stuffs, to other parts of China. What proportion of China's marketed com-modities circulated at this provincial level of trade is not known, but it must have been large.

China's foreign trade, although very small in proportion to population because of the self-sufficiency which her size and variety bestowed on her, was also large in absolute terms. Oceanic navigation was with some exceptions forbidden, out of a not unreasonable conviction that all blue-water sailors in these days were potential pirates. In spite of this ban a huge trade was carried on in Chinese vessels to South-east Asia, including the Spanish Philippines, and this led to the gradual growth of large Chinese communities in the coun-tries of the area. A controlled but significant trade was carried on with Japan, permitted mainly because of the dependence of the provinces of East China on Japanese copper for minting. A considerable import of rice from Bangkok to Canton took place, while via the Liuqiu Islands trade was carried on with Satsuma in western Japan.

The first European traders to appear in Eastern waters bought spices with profits from the local trade of South-east Asia, and through this were drawn to the shores of China, from which there began a growing export of Chinese goods to Europe. Silk and tea were the main staples. This foreign trade in silk and tea was an extension of trade at home. The foreign market was marginal: China, as far as her foreign trade was concerned, sold her surplus; in fact both of the great export staples, silk and tea, being essentially peasant products, were largely the peasants' surplus. There was also a long-established over-land trade westwards, most of all with Russia in the form of an exchange of Chinese tea (in brick form) for Russian furs.

The caravan trails of Inner Asia also carried a growing trade in spite of the difficulties of terrain, with routes from Xinjiang west through Ferghana and south to Darjeeling and Srinagar. The growth of this commerce contributed to the gradual extension of Chinese power in the area during the eighteenth century.

Most non-agricultural production in China took place in peasant house-holds, primarily to supply the household itself. Yet perhaps we exaggerate this, even in the case of the most important product, cotton cloth.

Weaving was still done in many peasant homes, but as in other countries there was a tendency towards greater specialization in the hands of full-time weavers, and the concentration of weavers in particular villages or counties. As long as spinning was unmechanized, spinning work had to be very widely distributed because of the number of spinners necessary to keep one weaver at work. It was mainly carried on by peasant women during the slack season of agriculture. Even then, it was calculated that half the cost of a piece of finished cotton cloth was accounted for by the labour of spinning.

We are, however, too ready to assume from the near-universal distribution of spinning, and the wide distribution of weaving, that the cotton textile industry was overwhelmingly a peasant spare-time handicraft. While the common hard-wearing blue cloth which is the traditional working costume of the Chinese labourer was produced mainly on peasant looms, the many fine and elaborate cottons were not all the products of spare-time weavers. This is not to suggest that peasants cannot practise high-quality crafts, but simply that any product which catches the attention of a wider market because of its quality or distinction is almost bound to be subjected to a marketing organ-ization which in turn will tend to create a specialist labour force. One of the problems in research here is that in an agrarian society, these specialists are likely to continue to own land or to acquire it, and so the distinction between peasant and handicraft worker is obscured.

The production of cotton cloth was China's greatest industry, and the ques-tions involved are important for the wider question of how far premodern

China was already showing tendencies to develop towards modern, capitalist economic forms. This in turn is related to the broadest question of all: why was the subsequent process of economic modernization in China apparently so halting and imperfect?

In the early 1950s a controversy arose among the historians of the Chinese People's Republic on this question. Mao Zedong had expressed the opinion that China had already been developing towards a native capitalism, when the process was frustrated by imperialist aggression. No one involved in the debate dared to gainsay this ruling, but one result of the controversy was a considerable increase in our knowledge of China's pre-modern economy. What Chinese historians looked for as signs of capitalist development included the production of goods for a market, large-scale production, the existence of a free labour market, the division of labour and specialization, and increased cash-cropping of agricultural products used as industrial raw materials. All these signs of development were certainly present in eighteenth-century China.

First, a substantial part of cotton cloth production was for sale, with regular lines of goods produced for regular markets. There was a great concentration of production round Songjiang which, along with other areas of relatively concentrated production, sent its cloth to all parts of the Empire, while 'nankeens'—cotton cloth from the general area of Nanjing (Nanking) provided the first great export of China to the West.

The scale of operations varied from process to process. Dyeing and calendering (the process of finishing the cloth by the use of moisture, heat and pressure) showed the greatest tendency towards large-scale unified operations; in Suzhou there were ten or twenty thousand workers engaged in calendering, renting their equipment from big merchants. At the other end of the process of manufacture, there were merchants who organized the ginning and bowing of the raw cotton and sold the rovings to the spinners. And although spinning and weaving remained very largely domestic (though not necessarily peasant), the merchants—the great men of the inter-regional trade, and the smaller men who sold to them—often exercised considerable control.

There are many cases also of factory-scale production; in Hebei some cotton-ginning shops employed a hundred men, and in the city of Canton alone there were fifteen hundred spinning and weaving shops of similar size. The existence of separate groups of 'merchants' concerned with the organization of ginning, spinning, weaving, calendering, and dyeing shows the development of a significant degree of division of labour. Surviving records of the cotton industry do not refer specifically to a free labour market, but references to its existence in silk-manufacturing, given that the organization of the production of silk was not dissimilar to that of cotton, show its existence. There is also evidence of specialization in the growing of cotton, notwithstanding the fact that peasants, wherever soil and climate allowed, grew their own. In the three countries around the greatest centre of manufacture it is recorded that in the eighteenth century only 20 per cent or 30 per cent of the farmers grew rice; the rest grew cotton. The Kang Shen area in the dry coastal heights of Jiangsu province grew only cotton; and already in the seventeenth century it had been observed that almost the whole population of Jia Tong county in southern Jiangsu made their living in this way.

Silk fabrics were not, like cotton cloth, the normal wear of the labouring classes. The main centres of mulberry growing were in the Yangzi valley; the main use of the silk-oak was in Shandong and in Guangdong. The industry was therefore more concentrated than the cotton industry, and much more market-oriented, especially from the late eighteenth century when a huge export trade grew up. Silk weaving gave rise to an even greater range of products and styles than the weaving of cotton—brocades, damasks, gauzes, satins, etc., in endless variety. As in the cotton industry, all levels of organization existed side by side: independent weavers, others working in a putting-out system, and wage earners. Many examples of proto-factory organization are recorded. The scale of production along the southern shore of the Yangzi Estuary is shown by legislation of the Kang Xi reign period (1662–1723) forbidding ownership of more than one hundred satin looms; but by the Dao Guang period (1821–51) there were shops with over six hundred looms and over one thousand workmen, and the total of privately owned looms was about thirty thousand. Development in Hangzhou was of the same order, some shops having a thousand looms and three to four thousand workers. Similar conditions existed in Nanjing, Suzhou, Canton, and Chengdu. Much of this development occurred in the late eighteenth century, and was associated with the huge increase in exports due to the reduction of duties on Chinese silk by the British Government in 1750.

There is evidence to show the existence of a large-scale putting-out system: even as early as late Ming, in Wu county (Suzhou), according to a contemporary local gazetteer, 'the families spin and the weaving shops provide capital . . . if the dyeing vats close, several thousand dyers are dispersed; if the weaving shops close, again several thousand weavers are dispersed, all men who "eat their labour"'. The existence of a free labour market here is well attested: weavers 'assembled according to their special skills at certain bridges in the city to wait for work'. In fact, because the traditional effort to prevent migration from county to city was breaking down, the growth of such capitalist enterprise had to be tolerated in order to provide increased opportunities of employment.

Large-scale cash-cropping of mulberries was common. The Huzhou local gazetteer records that the landowners there 'planted hemp and mulberries by the 1,000 acres'. In Guangdong a hundred thousand peasant households specialized in growing mulberries. In 1852 the botanist Robert Fortune, travelling by boat in the Yangzi area, wrote that for 'two days . . . upwards of 100 miles I saw little else than mulberry trees'. Brokers bought mulberry leaves in bulk for the feeding of cocoons, which in turn were sold in bulk for reeling.

In the manufacture of porcelain at Jingdezhen, although the imperial potteries were the largest enterprises, there were two or three thousand private potteries employing a total of over a hundred thousand workers, while many of the successive processes of manufacture for the imperial kilns themselves were carried out in private proto-factories.

Other industries yield similar examples. In Yunnan, twenty or thirty copper-mining firms employed up to eighty thousand men, on capital ranging up to 200,000 ounces of silver. In Sichuan there were three thousand saltwells, some employing as many as three or four thousand men. There is evidence also of an increasing scale of operations in the processing of crops. Six families in Qiming, Shandong, employed over four thousand people in the processing of tobacco. We have examples from Hubei and Guangdong of tea-processing workshops each employing several hundreds. In Taiwan, the scale of sugar refining was such as to require a division of labour into seventeen jobs. Although specialist cultivators of cash crops undoubtedly remained a small minority of the rural population they were sufficiently numerous to provide the basis of a vast and growing trade in manufactures.

In all these trades penetration by merchant capital is apparent. Cash crops were often grown on credit. Large sectors of the textile industries operated on credit extended to domestic operatives. Even the fishermen of Zhejiang worked on credit from the Ningbo banks.

It is significant of the changes that were taking place from the seventeenth century that the old paternalistic controls and government monopolies were breaking down. In the salt-gabelle administration direct government production and sale had given way to private handling under licence. In the imperial silk mills and porcelain factories there was a tendency for government to procure rather than produce. The attempts to prevent the development of a free labour market were relinquished. The attempt to hold down silk prices by limiting exports failed, and the legislation against participation in ocean-going trade became a dead letter.

Since the fifteenth century there had been increasing monetization of the economy. In the more productive parts of China taxes had been commuted from grain to silver, and money rents began to replace rents in kind. A steady increase in the availability of silver produced a prolonged mild inflation. which tended to stimulate economic growth. One of the main factors was the steady inflow of silver earned by foreign trade. In the two and a half centuries up to 1830, silver to the value of perhaps three hundred and fifty million Mexican dollars was imported as a result of trade with Manila, Japan, the European East India companies and South-east Asia.

With increasing money new forms of banking arose. They appeared in two widely separated centres: in Shanxi, on the basis of substituting bank-clearance operations for the shipment of bullion by armed convoys; and in Ningbo, on the basis of the exchange of currencies and the assaying of silver, made necessary by China's chaotic currency. Although their origins were so different, the Shanxi banks and the Ningbo money-shops (*qian zhuang*) were both soon carrying on the normal functions of banking—deposit, credit and clearance. The Shanxi houses operated throughout the nation, acting as bankers to the Beijing government, and in foreign trade providing funds for the purchase of tea and silk for export and opium for import. The Ningbo firms, although most closely connected with the trade with South-east Asia in Chinese hands, played a considerable part in the inter-regional trade whose main focus was the lower Yangzi area, and especially in trade with Manchuria as that region filled up with Chinese immigrants.

It has been argued that the appearance here and there in China of relatively large-scale, proto-capitalist forms of enterprise means little; that such things being exceptional were therefore not significant. It is a poor argument. The evaluation of economic development in China is, rightly or wrongly, measured against the history of Western industrial revolution, and in these terms China's eighteenth-century proto-capitalist enterprises were no thinner on the ground than those of Europe at the same date.

In any case, the exact number of enterprises and of industries affected is not very important. The capacity for large-scale production, and for distribution over long distances, with adequate credit and with large-scale mobilization of capital through stable institutions, is proved. While there is no way of proving that in other circumstances China would have gone on to create independently a fully capitalist system—and no way of proving that she would not—it can at least be concluded that if China's later steps to economic modernization were faltering, the cause did not lie in an inability to rise above subsistence farming, individual craft production and the small family business.

The political system

The Confucian ideal of government was that of rule by an enlightened élite who, through study of the classics, had become committed to the moral norms which the classics expressed. The Emperor's role was to be the supreme patron of the Confucian scholars; the role of the scholars was to advise the Emperor and to govern by his authority. By the late imperial period China was apparently closer to the realization of the Confucian ideal of government than ever before. The great aristocratic families had been replaced by a widespread class of small gentry. Government and society were dominated by the Confucian élite. The apogee of their influence was probably reached in the early Qing dynasty, from the late seventeenth to the late eighteenth century.

Yet this victory was hollow. The scholars had come to unrivalled power, but as servants of the emperors. Organized in a bureaucracy, every member of which was subject to instant dismissal and arbitrary punishment by the autocrat, their role as his councillors was limited. Lacking an adequate base of independence in large hereditary properties, they depended primarily on their public careers. Mobility, down as well as up, was rapid; only a small minority of graduates were succeeded as graduates by their sons or grandsons.

The Emperors ensured that organized opposition by the Confucian officials was made as difficult as possible. No official could serve in his home area, and the tenure of his post was too short to permit him to put down roots where he found himself. No one man was given sole charge of any one branch of public affairs. Responsibilities were shared and overlapping, so that one official checked another. In these circumstances only the most vigorous official could succeed in positive action. All important matters had to be referred to Beijing, where the overworked Emperor himself provided the worst of all the bottlenecks of Chinese administration.

All bureaucracies tend to evade actions which may entail dangerous responsibilities, and to avoid novelty. The Chinese system exaggerated these characteristic faults to the point at which the official had a strong disincentive to do more than collect taxes, prevent disorders too serious to be covered up, and woo his superiors with bribes to ensure his own promotion. Even the Emperors themselves were frustrated, finding in the checks and balances they had created an insuperable obstacle to getting their own will carried out.

At the same time the official, so burdened from above with fear of responsibility, was in a position of complete irresponsibility towards those below. Chinese rulers moralized about public opinion—'heaven hears as my people hear; heaven sees as my people see'—but this public opinion was not permitted institutional or protected expression. All communications with officialdom were, by definition, petitions. Appeal against the actions of an official could only be to his superior in office, who had often as much reason as his underling to cover up evidence of maladministration or injustice.

There has long been controversy on the question of whether or not the Chinese village was self-governing. If it was so, it was by default, and because the central government lacked the resources to extend government to the grass-roots. Many important duties were performed by members of the local community on its behalf: the collection of the land tax, the registration of births and deaths and of property, and the duties of watch and ward. These unofficial functionaries were usually nominated by their fellow-citizens. The appearance of democracy of a sort is, however, specious. Such men were not representatives: they were hostages.

A striking illustration of the ambiguity of the late Confucian empire towards local institutions is shown in the history of the various forms of organization which were created in the villages. There was first the *baojia*, a hundred-and-tithing system the function of which was to assist in keeping the peace by registering all householders and reporting the presence of strangers;

although other tasks were put upon it, its responsibilities lay essentially in the field of public security. There was also the *lijia*, which duplicated registration but for land-tax purposes; this also became involved in police work. Then when the Sacred Edict was produced by the Kang Xi Emperor (1662–1723), and village scholars were appointed to expound it twice a month, to the duty of reading the Edict was added the duty of awarding appropriate praise or blame to local citizens, and this was soon extended to the reporting of malefactors.

Even the clans were brought into the business of spying. Confucians valued the clan as the proper flowering of the ethic of filial piety. The government encouraged the keeping of genealogies, the maintenance of ancestral shrines, and the acquisition of clan property. It also encouraged the clans to write their own rules of conduct. The next predictable step was to appoint from among the clan a functionary whose duty was to report on clan members who committed offences against national law.

Thus local institutions were all drawn into police work. The consequence was that no citizen of reputation would serve in these capacities; and institutions which might have represented the community, channelled its energies, and protected its interests, became further means of atomizing it.

Authoritarian government sooner or later usually becomes corrupt government. By the nineteenth century the evidence of almost universal corruption among the mandarinate is overwhelming. Yet we should not too quickly assume that this state of things was new. After the defeats which China suffered in the nineteenth century the Chinese were in a mood to blame their rulers. Experience of Western administration in Hong Kong and the Treaty Ports, and growing acquaintance with the countries of the West, had set new standards. Then to the Chorus of Chinese complaints were added the observations of foreign travellers who—forgetting how recent a thing, even in Europe, was public honesty—were able to indulge themselves in condemning the dishonesty of Chinese officials, which they contrasted with the scrupulous honesty of Chinese merchants. There is little doubt that dishonesty had increased, but there are few nineteenth-century complaints that had not been the subject of repeatedly expressed concern by the Chinese emperors of earlier periods. The deterioration represented a more unscrupulous abuse of opportunities which had always been available and always abused. Chinese officials were underpaid and were tacitly expected to increase their incomes by charging fees for their services. The result was to obscure the distinction between the official's private property and the public purse.

During the later Qing dynasty the average tenure of a district magistrate was less than one year. He knew little of his bailiwick, perhaps not even its dialect. Though he brought with him a private staff according to his means, its members too were strangers. His office was run largely by a permanent staff of local men, paid for out of fees and supplements added to taxation. They were not imperial appointees and were responsible only to the magistrate, who was seldom there long enough to catch up with their malpractices. These men were the real rulers of China; with the authority of the magistrate behind them, and a network of local contacts from gentry protectors to local hooligans, they enjoyed enormous and vicious power.

The limits of local misgovernment in China were simply the limits of what a patient population, devoted to the Confucian ideal of government but entertaining very low expectations of its practical operation, was willing to tolerate. The one legal avenue of redress was petition. The next step, if petition failed, was to riot. If that failed, one took to the hills and joined the bandits.

Apart from this crude—but often effective—means of securing the redress of grievances, there was little that could be done. On the whole, however, the saving grace of the system was that the bureaucracy could not penetrate very deeply into the countryside. Each district magistrate had under him on average, in the late eighteenth century, about a quarter of a million people. To govern them directly was impossible. In these circumstances the local magistrate was more like a District Officer of the British Empire than a French Prefect. Local affairs were decided by villagers prominent for their wealth, education, experience, or probity. Few legal disputes ever went to the magistrate: his justice was too slow and too expensive. Disputes were usually settled by the arbitration of neighbours; the magistrate's court was in practice one of appeal. Clans, guilds and villages kept the peace for themselves as best they could. Disorder was endemic. Clans carried on bloody feuds, sometimes with hired mercenaries. Villages fought each other annually over water rights. Banditry was widespread, and the bandits were often allied with members of the gentry, local government employees, or particular clans. Secret societies and village bullies ran protection rackets. If the depredations of bandits and hoodlums became intolerable, the village would arm itself and, with luck, inflict sufficient injury on the malefactors to secure a respite.

Nevertheless China was not unusually lawless. On the contrary, considering the remoteness of the magistrate and the paucity of the available armed forces; the scope which Chinese rural life offered for conflicts over land and water rights, rights in local fairs, tax assessments, and the assessment of forced labour; the increasing destitution, vagrancy, and migration produced by population increase; and that the law and its representatives did very little indeed—in spite of the theory of government—to protect the weak against the strong; the fact that most of the Chinese countryside was peaceful most of the time is more remarkable than the fact that disturbance was never far away.

The explanation of this relative stability does not lie in institutions, for there was little or nothing at that level of society except the ineffective *baojia* system. The explanation lies in social structures and in habits of mind which were maintained independent of police power or legal control. It was China's political culture rather than her political institutions which kept life going. The object of that culture was the maintenance of peace and stability in an agrarian society, in which change was neither sought nor anticipated. The highest value recognized in China was social harmony. The method by which the Chinese sought to realize this value was the control of conflict by the imposition of hierachically organized authority.

The socialization process

The process of socialization was perhaps more consciously and systematically applied in traditional China than in any other great civilization. Chinese Confucian philosophy is largely, indeed, a philosophy of socialization. It is concerned much less with defining the true, the good, and the beautiful than with discovering the means by which mankind can be brought, if not actually to accept these values, at any rate to behave as if they did. The process began in the home. The authority of the father was absolute, as the head of a hierarchy arranged by generation, age and sex, in which every member of the extended family was related in rank to every other. By the time the Chinese toddler had even mastered the vocabulary of this complex pecking order, he was hooked on hierarchy. Aggression was suppressed, dependence encouraged. What was owed to parents had no limits; therefore a sense of guilt for one's filial inadequacy is part of the Chinese personality. From the point of view of its political implications, the most significant characteristic induced by such an upbringing was a conviction that conflict is usually both futile and destructive.

When the young adult left home he found a similarly organized hierarchy in society. His duty was to obey his superiors and control his inferiors. His relations with others were not only defined but ritualized, in order to make their consequences even more difficult to evade. Subject to the arbitrary authority of his father and his elders at home, he accepted with the same guilt-ridden sense of filial obligation the authority of the teacher, the mandarin, and the Emperor. The vigorous conduct of change by democratic means is, obviously, unlikely to be advanced by the prevalence of expectations which lead to fear of conflict, inability to act within a peer group, and submission to authority. The story of Chinese politics in modern times is partly the story of a struggle, still unresolved, to shake off these burdens inherited from the past.

It is in such terms that modern Chinese radicals saw Confucianism and condemned it as a systematic emasculation of the individual spirit. In this, however, they were being less than just to their own heritage. There are other sides to Confucianism, which was not, in fact, essentially authoritarian. Confucius himself certainly preached a marked degree of deference towards rulers, but at the same time he insisted through his theory of the 'rectification of names' that a ruler who was such only in name—who played the tyrant and not the king—was owed no allegiance. And, after all, the life of Confucius himself—as a man who laid down the law on the right conduct of rulers, measured the rulers of his time by the standard of the ancient sage-kings and found them wanting, insisted that those in authority must listen to self-appointed sages like himself, and spread these subversive ideas among a band of students— was not such as to encourage unqualified acceptance of authority. His most influential interpreter, Mencius, carried his ideas further, even to the justification of regicide.

The Confucian concept of human nature was inappropriate as a justification of despotism. China's ancient Legalist thinkers argued for the necessity of despotism on the Hobbesian grounds that human beings were essentially selfish, and only an untrammelled authority exercising salutary punishments could prevent the life of man from reverting to the nasty, the brutish, and the short. The Confucians, on the other hand, argued that human beings were essentially sociable, though imperfectly so; that every man had within him— however deeply buried under wilful ignorance and self-indulgence—a conscience which could guide his conduct; and thus, as Mencius said, the meanest man had it in him to become a sage. On this view of human nature, no ruthless ruling hand was needed; every man was capable of making his own moral judgements. The capacity for moral judgement, however, had to be developed. It had to be directed towards the ideal of universal objectivity, in the sense of the extension of equal sympathy towards all. The main question that thereafter divided Chinese philosophers was the nature of objectivity, and it was there that theories which could be used to support authoritarianism found an opportunity to creep in.

We may contrast two main schools of thought at the risk of over-simplification. Zhu Xi, the great synthesizer of Song Dynasty neo-Confucianism, adopted a metaphysical view of the question: each and every thing in the world (and 'thing' included both physical objects and what we may call moral events) had its 'principle'. Knowledge of these principles made objectivity possible. Principles were eternal and unchanging; they existed 'above' the phenomena whose nature they determined, and they pre-existed them: before there was archery, the principle of the bow was already in existence. Principle, however, did not determine what a thing was in imperfect reality, but what it could be and ought to be. This theory opened the way for the imposition by authority of fixed and indisputable principles of conduct. The Emperors found it convenient to patronize the Zhu Xi school, which became from that time until the fall of the Empire the orthodox interpretation of Confucianism, Zhu Xi had intended no such authoritarian implication: on the contrary, his concept of unalterable principle was directed precisely against arbitrary conduct; but the concept was captured by the despots.

Many Chinese philosophers were uneasy about Zhu Xi's metaphysics. In the Ming dynasty Wang Yangming (1472–1529) condemned Zhu Xi's idea of seeking truth from the laborious investigation of the myriad of principles enshrined in the myriad of things, and argued that truth (he meant moral truth) was to be discovered by the response of a lively individual conscience to practical experience: principles were imposed on the world by the human mind. The revolutionary implications of such a theory in imperial China are obvious, but Wang's ideas were condemned by the orthodox who could not separate his idea of communion with one's own conscience from the very different Buddhist idea of meditation as a withdrawal from the world. Nevertheless, his ideas still retain a potent though unacknowledged influence in Chinese minds.

Perhaps Confucius and Mencius had already sold the pass. Both believed that morality was learned in the home. Pity, sympathy, consideration for others, the sense of justice, and the sense of loyalty are learned in the family or not at all. However, in their own troubled times they sought above all for the origins of loyalty. They found them in the respect and affection of the child for the father. They therefore stressed filial piety as the greatest of all virtues, and so opened the door to despotic abuses of the idea.

As for the Confucian belief that rulers must accept the counsel of those who had proved their virtue and wisdom, the Emperors found means here too of hoisting the Confucians with their own petard. Having first in the Han dynasty identified themselves as the supreme patrons of the sages, the Emperors went on to act as if they themselves were the supreme sages, popes as well as emperors.

The Confucian ideal of objectivity, of impartiality as between subjects, was also distorted to serve the autocracy. The Emperor, looking on all men with equal regard, was justified thereby in destroying all expressions of sectional interest; and in the name of Confucius he sought to atomize Chinese society.

If we were to halt our description of Confucianism at this point, it would be to agree with the most severe of its twentieth-century critics, and to judge it to be merely one of history's monumental failures. Yet it was not. It continued to exist not only in what it was, but in what it might be; Zhu Xi's metaphysics had a point: the principles of good government, he said, were not created by the great emperors Yao and Shun, and did not go out of existence with the bad emperors Zhou and Xie. They are the eternal aspirations of man. In this respect Zhu Xi can stand for Confucianism generally: ambiguous and consequently subject to manipulation, but fundamentally anti-authoritarian. It is a condemnation of arbitrary government on the grounds of the moral responsibility of every man, and of his intuitive understanding of a moral law above *raison d'état*. This condemnation, on these same grounds, is still a powerful factor in Chinese politics today.

2

The opening of China

The European trade with East Asia

The modern history of the Far East begins with the forcible opening of China in 1843 by Britain, the leader in the new technologies of which the Chinese (and the Japanese) knew nothing, having deliberately closed their doors to foreigners and foreign influence. This situation, however, was not preordained.

It could have been different; one might even argue that it should have been different. The great powers of Asia were not at first threatened by the Europeans. The Moguls were in full control of India. In China the Qing dynasty had built up the most extensive Chinese empire in history. In Japan the Tokugawa had restored order in 1600 and ruled Japan's feudal *daimyōs* with a rod of iron for more than two centuries thereafter.

The main enemies of the European newcomers were not the states of South and East Asia but the Arab traders, against whom the Portuguese fought a long and vicious war in the first decades of the sixteenth century, in the course of which they created a network of naval strongholds; but as far as the rulers of Asia were concerned it was not of much importance whether Arabs or Portuguese—or Dutch or British—paid the taxes in return for which they permitted trade.

Even when the Arabs had been forced to share their monopoly of the spice trade, the Europeans were by no means the only numerous and powerful group of armed traders in the East. The Chinese, with ships as large as the Portuguese carracks and much more efficient to windward, traded in growing strength throughout South-east Asia, and settled in the area in far greater numbers than Europeans. The Arabs themselves, far from totally defeated, were still extending their influence in the wake of the conversion of the Malay world to Islam. Japanese trader-pirates were aggressively active. The Europeans were drawn immediately into this intra-regional trade in order to earn funds locally with which to buy Asian commodities, and so to placate their home governments, which had strong mercantilist objections to the perpetual eastward drain of silver. And in the East there was silver to be earned, thanks to the Manila galleon which brought an annual cargo of bullion from the mines of South America. This Spanish silver lubricated the trade of the area, and in particular flowed into the pockets of Chinese traders at Manila in exchange for silk. Thence it fructified the economy of China's centres of silk and tea production in the lower Yangzi provinces.

The staples of the trade between East and West were tropical goods impossible to produce in temperate Europe—pepper and spices, tea from China, coffee from Java, cotton from India. Others were manufactures, such as cotton and silk goods, porcelain and lacquer-ware, which represented the 'high technology' commodities of the time. As trade widened it did not change its essential nature, which was the purchase of Asian goods by Europe; but the profits of Western participation in regional Asian trade were gradually substituted for the export of bullion from Europe, until in the end it was China's new adverse balance of trade with India that brought about the crisis in which China was forced open to the world.

This mingling of peoples, centred in South-east Asia and spreading to China and Japan, offered the possibility of mutual influence, to the extent that East and West might well have developed together.

For a long time the main carriers of Western knowledge to the East, and of Eastern ideas to the West, were the Jesuit missionaries who accompanied the Portuguese. In Beijing they sought to present Christianity as a faith complementary to Confucianism rather than in conflict with it. The time was ripe. As the Ming dynasty decayed, the official neo-Confucian interpretation of the classics, now closely associated in the minds of some Chinese scholars with increasingly despotic rule, began again to be questioned. The Jesuits had an opportunity to participate in the reinterpretation. Their teaching also revived China's flagging interest in technology. Jesuit scientists introduced European astronomical observation, the latest mathematics, records of European mechanical devices as well as theoretical mechanics, mining technology, the latest European medical knowledge, cartography, and last but not least, Western cannon and the methods of its manufacture and use. For China the potentialities of this new knowledge were great. The importance attached by the Chinese Court to the maintenance of an accurate calendar and the proof of the superiority of Western methods of astronomical calculation gave the Western missionaries a commanding place in astronomy in China. The introduction of the new mathematics brought to an end China's neglect of her own distinguished mathematical tradition, and proved fruitful. European cannon, imported or made in China to Western specifications, played a part in Ming resistance to the Manchu invaders. Some of the concepts of European mechanics passed into the Chinese language. The greatest long-term potential, however, lay less in particular subjects than in the new scientific methodology implied in them. Chinese science, unsurpassed in meticulous observation, was weak in the capacity to rationalize the knowledge gained. Western science could have complemented China's own tradition.

The cultural flow was by no means all from West to East. Indeed, Chinese influence on European taste was sufficiently pervasive for Europeans today to forget—so thoroughly was much of this influence assimilated—how much of Europe's cultural environment is Chinese in origin. However, the full extent of Chinese cultural influence is difficult to trace: while Western influence in China was channelled through a handful of individual missionaries who kept a record of what they did, Chinese influence came into Europe mainly in the baggage of anonymous merchants. Images of China also played a considerable part in the phase of European self-criticism which was induced by the widening of European horizons. Along with magnanimous Turks and philosophical Persians, the Chinese as exemplars of the world's greatest enlightened despotism played an important role in transforming Europe's self-image.

Similar cultural exchanges were taking place between the West and Japan, where the response was characteristically much more enthusiastic. Had these exchanges between East and West continued it is possible that the processes of industrialization and modernization, which in the event took place in Europe alone, might have been more general, and the world's subsequent history very different. But contacts were broken off when both China and Japan chose isolation as the best means of combating what was believed to be the subversive influence of Christianity. Both China and Japan brought Christian missionary activity to an end, and each confined maritime foreign trade to a single port, Canton in the case of China, Nagasaki in the case of Japan. Fruitful mutual contact between East and West was rendered all but impossible.

Until almost the end of the eighteenth century, trade, restricted though it was, went relatively smoothly. On the British side, the East India Company enjoyed in China as in India a monopoly of commerce, granted by parliamentary charter renewed at intervals. On the Chinese side, the Canton authorities limited trade with the foreign merchants to a group of Chinese merchant houses, the Hongs, nominally thirteen in number. The system was one which, although it had its irritations, also had its comforts and amenities for both sides. Personal relations between the East India Company's super-cargoes and the Hong merchants were warm and friendly.

At the end of the century circumstances changed. The Canton system of trade came under pressures which were eventually to break it up. The Company still laboured under the difficulty of providing silver in Canton to buy Chinese tea and silk. The Chinese market for British products was very restricted. Some woollen and cotton cloth was sold, but little else. The balance of trade between Britain and China was massively in China's favour. This was eventually redressed by imports of Indian goods, and it was from this form of the 'country' (intra-Asian) trade that the new, destructive pressures were to arise.

The decisive event, however, took place in Westminster. Defeat in the American War of Independence had badly prejudiced British overseas trade. Pitt passed in 1784 the Commutation Act which reduced British import duties on Chinese tea from an average of 110 per cent to an average of 10 per cent. He hoped that with tea thus reduced in price, consumption would so rise as to bring even from this far lower rate of taxation a greater revenue, and also that with duties so low the smuggling of tea into the British Isles would no longer be profitable, and the main incentive which took continental ships to China— the profits of tea destined to be smuggled into Britain—would be destroyed. He was right. Non-British European trade with China all but ceased, while tea, which hitherto had been a luxury of upper-class boudoirs, rapidly became Britain's national drink.

The problem was how to find silver for such massively increased purchases. Efforts to promote the sale of British manufactures in China were unsuccessful. It was in India that the solution was found, in rapidly increasing sales of Indian products to China. For a time, Indian raw cotton was sold in China in growing quantities, but for unknown reasons these imports dwindled quite abruptly. Indigo was also a significant earner of Chinese silver, but its replacement by synthetic Prussian blue brought the indigo business to a disastrous end. Cotton and indigo were then replaced by imports of opium.

British participation in this traffic in a dangerous narcotic, and the fact that the war subsequently fought with China appeared to have been undertaken in defence of it, produced highly emotional reactions at the time and has continued to produce them ever since. The conclusion of Chinese nationalists, and of many others, is that the British must have been a singularly unscrupulous lot. However, a closer look at the facts shows how the British, though inspired by no exceptional greed or ruthlessness, found themselves in the position of making war on China, apparently for a cause which disgusted even those most ready to support hostilities.

Opium had been used in China since the ninth century at the latest. It was accepted there, as elsewhere, as the only effective pain-killer known before the age of modern synthetic drugs. As elsewhere, it was also used to alleviate the symptoms of various diseases, including dysentery. In Europe as in China the medical science of the time could not have been practised without opium. Its import into Britain was legal; about five or six tons a year were imported in the early nineteenth century. Occasional cases of addiction occurred among those who took heavy doses over a long period to relieve chronic pain (as was believed to have been the case with Coleridge), but there was no general awareness of its dangers.

The British in India knew a little more but not much. There, opium in a very diluted form was commonly drunk as a stimulant, with no visible harm to the consumers; the toughest Indian troops in British service drank opium habitually without impairing their efficiency. At the same time enough damage was done in India by opium (if only among those richer and more at leisure than Bengali sepoys) to alert the Company to some extent to the dangers. Warren Hastings regarded it as 'a pernicious article of luxury', the consumption of which, in India, should be limited. In general, however, in India as in Britain, policy equated opium with alcoholic spirits, whose consumption should be regulated but not prohibited.

In China, when addiction to opium had become sufficiently serious to attract the attention of the imperial government in the early eighteenth century, its consumption and sale were made illegal in 1729, and its import in 1796. The Company's direct association with the drug began when in 1773 it inherited the Bengal Opium Monopoly, and found that China offered a market. The amount sold in China was small, and compatible with the use of the drug solely for medical purposes. The rapid growth of Chinese consumption, as measured by the growth of imports—the quantity of opium grown in China itself is not known, but probably it was always greater than that imported—began only in the last quarter of the eighteenth century. In 1767 China was importing about 1,000 chests, each containing about 140 lb. of opium. This was in total about 60 tons, and far less per capita than contemporary British imports of the drug for medical purposes. By 1799 China's imports had risen to 4,000 chests, a level at which it remained until 1830, when it doubled. By 1836 it was 30,000.

At the time it was not clear why widespread addiction occurred, although the answer was simple: in China opium was smoked, a form of consumption almost unknown elsewhere. The opium was mixed with tobacco. The morphia content of the mixture was low; but it was fatally easy to move on to smoking unadulterated opium with a morphia content of almost 10 per cent. It was a habit entirely outside the experience of the British, either at home or in India.

Until the early years of the nineteenth century the Company's policy was one of limited production with a high profit margin. Had it been possible to maintain this policy Chinese hostility might have been avoided. The threat to its maintenance came from western India, outside Company territory. There, private growers began to compete in shipping opium to China. The attempts of the Company in India to stamp this out led to corruption and tyranny so vicious as to threaten British influence among the Rajput princes, and in the end the growing of opium in the Malwa area had to be accepted. The Company was consequently forced into a price war, in the course of which opium ceased to be an expensive commodity. Mass consumption in China became possible.

It was only when the Chinese Government in 1821 had begun to react by attempting to put its anti-opium legislation into force for the first time that the degree of Britain's dependence on the drug trade became clear. This was one year before De Quincey published his *Confessions of an English Opium Eater*, which for the first time brought the use of opium as a narcotic to the attention of the British public. One-seventh of the East India Company's revenues in India came from opium, and it was the only elastic revenue available. About one-twelfth of British revenues at home came from import taxes on tea, which could be bought at a profit only if silver could be earned by the sale of opium. These were difficult problems enough, but much more important was the fact that Indian remittances to Britain, amounting to some £4 million a year, were (in exchange terms) paid out of silver earned in China from the sale of opium; therefore India's ability to absorb British exports depended on the flow of funds from China. The East India Company's exchequer at Canton, receiving 18 million Mexican dollars a year from opium sales, was the hub of British commerce in the East.

The whole appalling situation was revealed quite suddenly. Until 1821 no attempt whatsoever had been made by the Chinese authorities to implement or even to advertise the law. The Company had never been approached on the question by the Chinese Government. Another attempt was made in 1829. Soon after, the British Government and the public were first made fully aware of the extraordinary commercial and financial ramifications of the opium traffic in the course of the debates which preceded the abolition of the Company's monopoly of trade with China. Alarm was lulled, however, by the confident expectation in the mid thirties that China would legalize the import of opium in order to control it. The crisis in Canton then followed immediately, when the Emperor rejected legalization. It caught the British and Indian governments unprepared.

The devious process by which opium got to the Chinese consumer was such as to confuse the question of moral responsiblity for the trade. The Company in India encouraged the cultivation of the poppy and sold the refined opium at auction; thereafter it took no part in the trade. The opium was bought by private merchants, some British and some Parsee, and shipped to China on their account. It was consigned to commission agents in Canton; thus most of the opium did not belong to those who carried through the transaction in China. It was transferred at sea, where British jurisdiction did not apply and Chinese jurisdiction could not be enforced. It was taken ashore by Chinese boats crewed not by Cantonese but by Tanka, 'boat people', outcasts who lived by fishing, smuggling and piracy. Inland, the opium was distributed under the protection of members of anti-Manchu secret societies, such as the Triads. The Chinese opium merchants were usually financed by the great Shanxi banks, whose ability to act as the bankers of the Chinese Government came largely from the profits of the opium trade. On its way to shore, the drug paid 'squeeze' to the revenue authorities with the regularity of a tax. Much of this went into the coffers of the 'Hoppo', the controller of the Canton customs, and assisted him in fulfilling his extra-legal responsibility to supply the best part of a million dollars annually to the Emperor's private purse; thus even the Emperor himself participated in the profits of the trade.

After the Bengal–Malwa price war of the 1820s, when the price of opium plummeted in China, the moral consequences which ensued need no comment; but it was the apparent economic rather than the moral consequences which impelled the Chinese to urgent action. Chinese currency consisted of silver and copper. Silver was the unit of account; coinage was of copper. The relative value therefore of silver and copper was extremely important: instability in this relationship could have disastrous consequences, especially for the ordinary people who made payments in copper coins of obligations fixed in silver. In the first decades of the nineteenth century, the value of silver began to rise rapidly in China. A censor, drawing attention to this, attributed it wholly to the drain of silver to pay for opium.

In fact there were better reasons for the scarcity of silver. The issue of copper coinage in China had increased out of all proportion to the increase in silver. In the late seventeenth century, the average number of copper coins minted annually was of the order of two to three hundred million; by the early nineteenth century this had increased eightfold. Such a profligate increase in the copper currency was enough in itself to account for the soaring value of silver in relation to copper; but in addition the new coins were increasingly debased until their average weight was reduced by half; again this alone could account for the whole rise. As silver rose in value it was hoarded, both by private individuals and by government offices. It is in fact surprising that the relative value of silver rose between 1750 and 1838 by only about 50 per cent.

The opium trade did not create this situation, but it exacerbated it. Hitherto the foreign trade had resulted in a steady increase in China's stocks of silver. Now this flow ceased, and it appeared as if China was exporting silver, in payment mainly for opium, at a rate of $18 million a year. In fact this was not so; the Chinese were unaware that of that sum about 75 per cent did not leave the country at all. Paid into the East India Company's exchequer at Canton by the opium traders in return for bills of exchange on Calcutta or London, it was used to buy tea and silk.

The British were only dimly aware of this mounting alarm in Chinese governing circles. Their attention was on quite other problems at Canton. As long as all trade was conducted by the East India Company itself, either on the Company's account or by its servants and licensees as a privilege strictly limited, the situation was controllable. Now this began to change. The growth in the 'country' trade brought to Canton an increasing number of traders who resented the limitations which the Company imposed on their activities. By far the most important of these was their exclusion from the trade in tea, silk and other staple commodities. The private traders showed considerable ingenuity in evading control; they turned up at Canton as Prussian consul, or in possession of a privateer's licence from the Swedish government, and by such pretexts were able to join fully in trade and to erode the East India Company's monopoly. This monopoly was by now becoming unpopular in Britain as free-trade sentiment grew. In 1810 the Company's monopoly of trade in India had come to an end; it was impossible then to maintain the monopoly strictly at Canton.

The situation was novel in three distinct ways. First, the British Government had, inevitably, to take the place of the Company in protecting British citizens, and in doing so the Government would inevitably be guided not by commercial expediency, as the Company had been, but by the normal conventions of international law. Second, the Company had been able, though with increasing difficulty as the 'country' trade grew, to discipline the members of the British community; with the Company gone, law-breakers would have to be judged and punished by some form of British court, unless they were to be left to the tender mercies of China's antiquated and thoroughly corrupt judicial system, an alternative which was morally intolerable. The problems of jurisdiction, which had caused many alarms in the Company's time but had never in fact led to any worse event than a temporary stoppage of trade, now demanded urgent solution. Third, the new class of British manufacturers created by the Industrial revolution, entertaining hopes of increased overseas markets for their products, were not likely to be content merely with the abolition of the Company's monopoly, and were bound to use the utmost pressure to release trade from the severe restrictions put upon it by the Chinese Government. The exchange problem lent force to this demand. If the opium trade were to be abolished, British purchase of Chinese goods would be profitable only if substitute imports could be found; the obvious substitute was British manufactures, but the prospect of securing a sufficient sale of these—enough to earn Mexican $15,000,000 as against the Mexican $1,250,000 or so then earned—by means of trade at a single port seemed remote. The possiblility of at least reopening ports at which trade had formerly been permitted to Europeans thus became involved with the question of the opium trade.

Although the replacement of the Company by private traders exacerbated the problems of Sino-British relations, none of these problems was new. Yet the Canton system of trade, as it was when the Company's monopoly lapsed in 1833, had grown up largely in the preceding half century, and the worst irritants were the most recent. The British felt that they were gradually being deprived of rights which they had formerly enjoyed. During the first half of the eighteenth century the charges on trade were steadily increased, the limitation of trade in staple products to a small number of Chinese 'security' merchants was imposed, the last trade at ports other than Canton was squeezed out by prohibitive charges and government controls, and direct access by foreigners to imperial officials was forbidden. The systematic confirmation of these restrictions by decree, and their tightening up, was in fact a consequence of the attempts of the East India Company to appeal against them. In 1753 the Company petitioned the Chinese authorities, asking that the system of security merchants should be abolished, that there should be free access to Chinese officials, that the 'linguists' (interpreters) and 'compradors' (brokers) who were the essential intermediaries in carrying on business at Canton should not have to bribe the officials, and that the posting of anti-foreign placards should be banned. The Company struck trade in support of their demands, and as a result were received by the Canton Governor-General. Their triumph was short-lived, however; in 1755 a series of decrees spelled out, in a stricter form than ever, the details of the Canton system. The security merchant system was reaffirmed, and it was further stipulated that only Hong merchants could act in this capacity; other Chinese merchants, if they wanted to trade with foreigners, could do so only under the aegis of a Hong merchant, and only in mutual surety groups of five. The Hong merchants were made responsible for any crimes committed by foreign supercargoes and captains, while the captains were to be held responsible for crimes committed by any of their crew. No ship could be unloaded without the permission of a Hong merchant, who was then held responsible for the payment of all tariffs and harbour dues. Trade at ports other than Canton was now formally forbidden.

To these rules of trade were added severe restrictions on the residence and movement of foreigners. They were allowed to come to Canton only during the trading season. While there they were confined to an island on the outskirts of the city, in their 'factories', and could exercise only on the island itself, a place so small that one could walk its circumference in ten minutes. No wives or families were permitted.

Such restrictions suggest that the British traders in China led a grim, confined, and frustrated life. This was not entirely true. The factories were comfortable. Living was luxurious. Profits on trade for the Company, for individual Company servants, and for private traders were high enough to ensure the prospect of a comfortable early retirement at home—dysentery was a far greater threat to this prospect than any Chinese decrees. The system, well oiled by corruption, worked so smoothly that all the witnesses before the House of Commons Select Committee on Commerce with China (1830) agreed that 'business could be dispatched with greater case and facility at Canton than anywhere else in the world'. Hunter, an American merchant, wrote of the Hongs: 'As a body of merchants we found them able and reliable in their dealings, faithful to their contracts, and large-minded. The monopoly they enjoyed could not have been in the hands of a more able, liberal or genial class of men'. Their monopoly was in any case increasingly evaded. The Hongs (especially those who were financially weak) sold their name to private traders. Smuggling was widespread; not only was opium illegally imported in large quantities, but also saltpetre and salt. Silver was smuggled out, the restriction on the export of silk was a dead letter, and tutenag was also exported illegally. The limitation of trade to Canton was evaded by trading voyages up the coast. Just as the law forbidding Chinese participation in maritime trade had broken down, and just as paternalistic controls of manufacturing had been waived, so the attempts of the Chinese Government to maintain severe restrictions on commercial relations between Chinese subjects and foreigners were now equally threatened.

It was not in the interests of the new private foreign traders at Canton, however, to point to the advantages of the system. Their ambition was to secure complete freedom of trade, and the nature of the Canton system provided them with just those arguments which would work most powerfully on the trading classes at home. As long as the East India Company was active and itself an object of attack by the private traders, its members provided a truer picture of conditions in China, but after 1833 its counter-arguments were heard no more. When the British Government felt compelled to attempt to open up official relations with China after the end of the monopoly, it did so under public pressure to secure an end to all the restrictions of the Canton system.

There were three matters with which the British Government had to concern itself immediately. One sprang from the recent decay of the Hong system itself; most of the Hong merchants found themselves unable to finance expanding foreign trade. Another sprang from the disappearance of the Company with its power to discipline its servants and licensees. And a third sprang from the very fact of official British involvement with the Chinese authorities and the difficulty of accepting Chinese conventions of communication which denied equal status to representatives of the British Crown.

The problem of debts owed to foreigners by the Hong merchants was one which went back well into the eighteenth century. By 1770 only four out of the thirteen Hong houses could be considered solvent. The foreign trading community insisted that these debts were due to the 'vanity and extravagance' of the Chinese merchants, and also to official squeeze. The first explanation is contradicted by ample evidence that most Hong merchants were careful, competent and honest, and the second by the fact that official exactions, though large in absolute amount, were quite marginal to the value of commerce. The true explanation lies simply in the fact that China's economy, being only partly monetized, was unable to finance the trade. It had to be largely financed by the foreigners; but this process proved ruinous to the weaker Chinese firms. Interest rates in China were very high as compared with those in Europe; once in debt at such rates, it was difficult to get out. And once in debt to a British firm, the Hong merchant found himself in a poor bargaining position, forced not only to sell his goods at a low price but—a worse fate—forced to buy British cotton piece-goods for which there was only a very poor market.

In 1760 the Chinese Government had made it illegal for Chinese to borrow from foreigners. The law remained a dead letter as far as the incurring of debt was concerned but sprang instantly to life when British creditors appealed to the Chinese Government for redress, claiming that when a merchant went bankrupt his Chinese creditors were paid first and the foreign creditors never. The British were successful in bringing the matter before the Beijing government itself. The response was reasonable. Beijing, while refusing to take action on any debts incurred since the decree of 1760, and refusing to recognize interest amounting to more than the principal (this was Chinese law), at the same time instituted an insurance scheme by which the Hongs, who paid a small percentage of the value of their turnover into a common fund (the Consoo fund), could settle bad debts out of this fund. Beijing also provided a generous arrangement for repayment of principal plus 100 per cent interest over a number of years.

The problem of jurisdiction

The debt question was only a part of the wider problem of jurisdiction on the China coast. It was in questions of criminal jurisdiction, however, that the real problem lay. Chinese governments traditionally left foreign communities on Chinese soil to deal with crimes which occurred among themselves, and to keep the peace in their own way; but at the same time the authorities maintained the right to intervene in serious cases. To the mandarins, this measure of extraterritorial jurisdiction given to foreign communities was merely informal and expedient and in no sense represented a surrender of China's sovereign rights. To the foreigners, however, Chinese behaviour in this respect seemed inconsistent and dangerously unpredictable.

The reluctance of foreigners to be subjected to Chinese law and procedure was partly due to the appalling state of Chinese justice at that time, but a deeper reason to resist was the Chinese use of institutions of mutual surety, which made the group to which an individual belonged responsible for his crime if he himself were not delivered to justice. This was applied in the normal way to the foreign community, whose chiefs—supercargoes and ships' captains—could thus be held responsible for crimes committed by those under their authority. This was in fact the condition upon which the Chinese were willing to extend a degree of extraterritorial jurisdiction to the foreigners. Such an attitude ran completely counter to Western concepts of justice. Half a dozen scandalous cases after 1780 illustrated the difficulties and stiffened foreign resistance to Chinese jurisdiction.

The other side of the problem was that, with the East India Company's ability to control the behaviour of British subjects gone, offenders would either have to be left to China's disreputable police force (as disreputable among Chinese as among foreigners) or submitted to some sort of British jurisdiction. This was no merely theoretical problem. The Europeans who found their way to Canton were not always the best representatives of Christian civilization. Many were adventurers out to make a quick fortune before the health hazards of South China should deliver them untimely into the

British cemetery at Macao. Unscrupulous, violent, and openly contemptuous of the Chinese population, their behaviour led to increasing Chinese hostility. The British Government was well aware of this behaviour. In 1830 a Bill to provide for a British magistracy in Chinese waters passed the Commons, but it was thrown out of the Lords on the grounds that the extension of jurisdiction to the high seas was unconstitutional. The consequence of this judgement was obvious: if there was to be a British magistrate to control the unruly British in China, then there would have to be some British territory there on which he could operate. The subsequent annexation of Hong Kong stemmed partly from this.

The assumption behind such reasoning, of course, was that the problem would probably in the end have to be solved by some unilateral British action; the prospect of any normal form of communication between the two governments, through which a negotiated solution to this and other problems might be found, was remote.

On the question of communications, there have been two extreme opinions regarding the Chinese attitude. One is that China's refusal to permit direct communication represented an intolerable degree of Chinese arrogance and conceit, and a determination to keep foreigners in China from any means of protecting their interests. The other opinion is that it was not the Chinese who showed conceit and arrogance in the matter but the British, who sought to force the Chinese to accept a system of international relations in which they had neither interest nor concern. The truth is as usual more complex.

China's concept of international relations was derived from her geographical position. Until the age of oceanic trade China's long coastline was almost a closed frontier. On her inner frontiers the borders of China proper were almost as sharply marked as the sea from the shore, by the line between the wilderness and the sown. Within, the Chinese peasant had pushed his intensive cultivation to the margin of possibility; beyond that margin were the forest hunters of the north, the steppe nomads of the north-west, the peoples of the high Himalayas, and the aborigines of the tropical mountain valleys between China and the Indo-Chinese lands. To the north, the Great Wall symbolized this division between settled Chinese farming on the one hand and a shifting life of hunting, herding, or slash-and-burn cultivation on the other. Chinese territorial government with its bureaucratic administration was applied to the one; with the rest, relations were personal and quasifeudal. They were also precarious and unstable: today's client tribe was tomorrow's invading horde. The steppe nomads were the greatest threat. China had one great advantage, however: being by most standards incomparably more civilized than her neighbours, she could usually keep them in awe.

This moral authority was maintained by persuading Chinese and non-Chinese alike that China was the sole centre of civilization, that the Emperor was in principle the universal monarch, and that rebellion against him was against morality itself. The ritual expression of this idea (a useful idea which has occurred to rulers elsewhere from time to time) was the tribute system. At stipulated intervals of years, each of her neighbours acknowledged China's supreme authority by sending to Beijing a mission bearing tribute. It usually went home loaded with more gifts than it had brought; for generous imperial patronage, demonstrating China's inexhaustible riches, was an essential part of the system. So too was Chinese help in times of disaster, and Chinese mediation in such matters as disputed succession.

It was a logical inference from such an ideology that no country except the Chinese Empire could rightly be said to have 'officials', who were by definition the appointees and delegates of the Chinese Emperor, the only source of civilized power. Other peoples had military leaders, tribal chiefs, or headmen, but not officials.

The ideology, though derived from the problem of the subjugation and control of non-Chinese peoples (both within and without the frontiers of China proper), was equally important as a means of maintaining authority over the Chinese themselves. This claim to moral supremacy was the legitim-ation of Chinese government. When, therefore, the British demanded that Chinese officials should acknowledge the representatives of the British Crown as equals, and as representing an equal sovereign state, they were not dealing with mere protocol but were launching a dangerous attack on the whole fabric of political loyalty in China.

In the Company's time the issue had not arisen. As the representative of a private trading firm the chief supercargo could not aspire to be treated differ-ently from China's own private citizens; any communication with officialdom must be in the form of a petition, and any approach made to the authorities must be through the spokesman for one's mutual surety group, in this case the Hongs. The Company did not set its sights high; it sought the right of direct communication with the Hoppo (the representative of the Board of Revenue who farmed the customs, and who was not in fact even a gazetted official) and a right of appeal from the Hoppo to the Governor-General. It did not raise objections to the petition form of address. The situation was in any case eased by the characteristically pragmatic attitude taken by the Canton authorities. Although normally neither the Hoppo nor the Governor-General would communicate directly with the foreigners, in a crisis they did so: between 1731 and 1816 the supercargoes visited the Governor-General on seven occasions. In 1760 the Company even won an undertaking from the Governor-General that its representatives would have direct access to the Hoppo and an appeal to him; but this was not consistently honoured.

It was the introduction of official British representatives which created a crisis. The Chinese were less prepared to show inconsistency where the issue concerned persons making a firm claim to official status, while the British

Government was not inclined to let its point go, as the Company had so often done, simply in order to prevent a breakdown of trade.

The British Government did not, however, react to the situation with uncompromising jingoism. It is true that the British were familiar enough with other Asian monarchies whose arbitrary government was rationalized in extravagant pretensions and supported by demeaning rituals very like the Chinese kowtow; they had therefore scant sympathy with Beijing. At the same time, successive British governments gave full consideration to the policy alternatives: either to force the Chinese to accept international practice so that the British Government could play its normal role of protecting British subjects and British interests, or to ignore questions of protocol, communicate with the Chinese on Chinese terms, and hope that expanding trade and its increasing mutual benefits would eventually induce the Canton authorities and Beijing to accept some workable *modus vivendi*. Although the Duke of Wellington might incline to the latter, and Palmerston to the former, neither was wholly committed to his view. It was events rather than opinions which determined the eventual choice; and, as we shall see, even when China was prostrate before British arms in 1843, it was a *modus vivendi* which the British sought in the Treaty of Nanjing, rather than full Chinese submission to international practice.

Behind the formulation of British policy in China lay the belief that the situation in Canton had much in common with the circumstances in Bengal two generations before, in which Britain had been drawn into governing India. There was indeed one fixed point of agreement among all concerned with British relations in the Far East: China must not become another India. One eastern empire was enough. British trade in Bengal had been based on privileges given to the East India Company by decrees of the Mogul emperors; when Mogul power waned, local Indian rulers had proved reluctant to continue honouring these decrees. Eventually the Company, after innumerable futile protests, had taken into its own hands the administration of the Bengal treasury to ensure that British rights were honoured. Some elements at least of the Chinese situation seemed similar. Privileges formerly enjoyed had been withdrawn. Others were extended or withheld in an unpredictable way. It could be argued that these grievances originated with the provincial authorities in Canton and did not represent the will of the Emperor. It was also clear that the Chinese Empire was becoming feeble. In these circumstances, a repetition of the history of Bengal seemed alarmingly possible. If necessary, steps must be taken to ensure that British grievances were redressed by the Chinese Government before the situation became such that they could only be redressed by the imposition of British control. The analogy was, however, superficial. The late eighteenth-century Delhi emperors had no control over their satraps in Bengal and elsewhere, whereas the Beijing government was in full control of the local administration at Canton and in full agreement with its policy; most of the restrictions of which the British complained had in fact been confirmed by imperial decree. Yet the war with China which British governments were beginning to think possible would be in the nature of an armed demonstration that would bring the attention of Beijing to British grievances, secure their redress, and, by opening up normal communication, ensure that in future there would be no similar accumulation of combustibles.

The British records make it clear that whatever wider hopes the British business classes might entertain, the attention of the Government was fixed essentially on existing grievances. British governments were not concerned to force China to change her system of controlling commerce (though they were ready to try to persuade her), but simply to ensure that the existing system was made predictable and tolerable.

The first step taken to institute formal relations between British and Chinese governments was, ironically, taken at the suggestion of the Chinese. The Canton Governor-General, Lu Kun, aware that the East India Company's monopoly was coming to an end in 1833, expressed the hope that the British would appoint someone to replace the Company's chief supercargo in representing the British merchants. This request, coming after the entire failure of two British embassies sent to Beijing, seemed to be the breakthrough for which the British had waited. A mission under Lord Napier was sent. It set out with great hopes, and ended in frustration, anger, and the threat of war.

The mission was misconceived from the beginning. Lu Kun had certainly expressed the hope that the chief supercargo of the East India Company would be replaced by some sort of general manager of British commerce. What he got instead was an ambassador. Worse, although Napier's instructions were those appropriate to an embassy, he was not given a title which indicated this to the Chinese. He was, in fact, merely called 'Superintendent of Trade'. The Chinese were left in doubt as to whether the actions which he took against the precedents followed by the former chief supercargo of the Company represented the will of his government or his own pretensions. Nor was Napier's own conduct such as to mollify the suspicious Canton authorities. His instructions had been so framed as to occasion to these authorities the least possible offence. He was to exercise control over British subjects in the Canton River, assist them in their lawful pursuits, and enjoin them to conform to the laws of the Chinese Empire 'so long as these were fairly and equally administered'. He was to investigate the state of trade and the possibility of its extension to other parts of China and Japan, but was not to prejudice existing trade by the attempt. Although it was affirmed that 'the establishment of direct communication with the Imperial court at Peking would be desirable', Napier was not expected to pursue this; on the contrary, he was enjoined not to enter negotiations except when some extraordinary matter arose, and then only after reference home. He was to use no menacing language, to avoid appeals to the Navy, and to allow no British warship to pass the narrows of the

Canton River at the Bogue (the Bocca Tigris or Tiger's Mouth). He was, in fact, to arrive with as little fuss as possible and to confine himself to duties which were less than those of a consul, until in the fullness of time he might approach the Chinese on the wider issues to which his instructions referred. Perhaps the British Government should have anticipated that a proud, irascible Scottish peer, a veteran of Trafalgar, with naval ships at his command, would find this situation frustrating.

The Governor-General's response to Napier's arrival was reasonable. He had asked for, and expected, a senior merchant who could represent his fellow merchants. For the British to send a representative of the government was completely new; the Governor-General therefore very properly advised the Court that the admission of such a representative should have been negotiated, and that the purpose of his presence and the duties of his office should have been made known beforehand. He wanted credentials to forward to Beijing but Napier had none; he had asked for these, but Palmerston thought them unnecessary.

The Governor-General resolved that Napier would be treated as if he were simply the successor to the Company's chief supercargo until he could show that he was something more. In practice this meant that on his arrival in Chinese waters he would go to Macao, from there petition the Canton authorities for permission to come up river, and wait for his passport. Napier, however, having eluded the Chinese officials sent to intercept him, came straight to Canton and 'announced his arrival' in a letter which did not employ the petition form of address. The letter was returned to him. Characteristically, once Napier had arrived in Canton the Chinese authorities did not altogether adhere to their own rules. He was permitted to stay. Although he should have communicated through the Hongs, in fact an interview was arranged for him at which officials of Canton city were present. The next act in the drama, however, was farce. A second interview was arranged with the officials, but it broke down in a tussle over the arrangement of the chairs, an arrangement which would have put Napier in a position inferior to that of the Chinese officials.

By this time Napier was no longer able to maintain the pacific attitude that his instructions ordered. He referred to the Governor-General as a 'presumptuous savage'; he informed the British Government that trade could be extended in China by force 'with a facility unknown even in the capture of a paltry West Indian island'; and he wrote that the first objective of the Government 'should be to get a settlement on the same terms that every Chinaman, Pagan, Turk or Christian sits down in England'. It was the first time, but not the last, that a move to improve relations with China, begun in a spirit of forbearance and tolerance, ended in furious threats. Napier ordered up the frigates. The Chinese blockaded the factories. Only Napier's sudden illness and death prevented hostilities.

The rest of the mission remained in Chinese waters, but its influence was negligible. Wellington had succeeded Palmerston, and blamed Napier for having refused to follow Chinese custom. The new Superintendent, Sir John Francis Davis, a former Company supercargo and a pioneer sinologist, reinforced Wellington's view by arguing that the use of force could not be justified unless and until an approach had been made to Beijing and had failed. The Canton authorities avoided dealing with the mission. Even the Portuguese in Macao refused to recognize it.

In April 1835 Palmerston returned to the Foreign office. One of the members of Napier's mission, Charles Elliot, was a relative of Palmerston's friend Lord Minto. He had undertaken a correspondence with the Foreign Office on China and his ideas had impressed the new Foreign Secretary. Davis, as his senior, warmly recommended him as a future Superintendent. With these three advantages Elliot secured the appointment. His proposals for policy were also conciliatory, but he ended by making war.

Elliot saw no urgency. He believed that trading conditions were acceptable; indeed he argued that 'practically speaking, the aggregate of our trade with China is less burdened than it is in any other country with which we have commerce to an analogous extent'.

He took the view that Chinese protocol should be accepted until day-to-day relations had created a *modus vivendi*. He was of the opinion that the Chinese had not been averse to the idea of the mission, but that Napier had thrown the opportunity away by coming without permission to Canton. Elliot in fact announced his appointment to the Governor-General through the Hongs in a letter using the petition inscription, and in return received a courteous reply and an imperial edict granting him permission to come to Canton. This was too much for Palmerston. He insisted that Elliot should not use the petition form, and should refuse to correspond via the Hong merchants.

Yet the situation was not completely deadlocked. It was in the interests of the Canton authorities to have, in the city, someone to whom the British merchants would be responsible. When Elliot as instructed by Palmerston wrote directly to the Governor-General and without the petition inscription, the first Chinese reaction was certainly to tighten the rules: the Hongs were now instructed to open and read letters from foreigners, and not merely to pass them on still sealed. On Elliot's threatening to leave Canton, however, the Governor-General relented and agreed to accept letters directly.

Persistent firmness and courtesy from the British might well have succeeded in securing adequate means of communication. Unfortunately, these first concessions came too late. The opium crisis had arrived.

The opium crisis and war, 1836–1842

The first action against the opium trade had been taken in 1821 by Governor-General Ruan Yuan. He ordered the opium ships out of the river; they moved, but only further down the estuary to Lintin Island, which then became the centre of distribution of the drug, stored on board ships permanently anchored there. In 1829 there was another flurry of activity, but this again soon died down. In the mid-thirties Beijing began to consider the possibility of bringing the trade under control by legalizing it. The debate was initiated by a memorial from an official, Xu Naiqi, who had been in office at Canton and knew what the problems were. Former Canton Governor-General Ruan Yuan, one of China's greatest contemporary scholars, was now a grand councillor at the capital. He too favoured legalization and he was a man whom no one could suspect of being influenced towards this view either by venality or by indifference to the moral issue. Xu's memorial was probably inspired by Ruan, and it was supported by the influential members of the Xue-hai Tang, the great academy devoted to practical statesmanship which Ruan had founded in 1820 in Canton. Ruan Yuan's successors as Governor-General, Lu Kun and Deng Tingzhen, both favoured legalization. The essential argument of the pro-legalization party was that if imports were legalized and controlled the lawlessness and corruption associated with the drug trade could be eliminated and the Government would only have to deal with the addicts. Consumption could then be gradually eliminated.

Many British in Canton who heartily hated the opium trade had reached the same conclusions. It was only the big opium-runners who were against legislation, because their dominance of the trade depended on their financial ability to meet the costs involved in its illegality.

For some months in 1836 legalization seemed certain, and this was known to the foreigners in Canton; but the opposition rallied. It was led by officials remote from the scene who had no experience of the difficulties and were thus in a position to flourish the moral arguments without inhibition. Their arguments were difficult to gainsay. They pointed to the rapid spread of moral degradation, to the increasing grip of opium on the official classes. They pointed to the experience of the 1832 campaign against the Yao aborigines, when the soldiers sent against them were so weakened by addiction to opium that they were unable to fight. They pointed to the supposed drain of silver. They demanded immediate and drastic action, to save the army and the economy. The Emperor accepted their arguments, and a systematic movement to suppress opium began in late 1836.

Vigorous action was begun to put down the internal trade, the opium dens (which flourished openly) and the smoking habit. The new Governor-General, Deng Tingzhen, also ordered the foreign opium ships out of the river, but the merchants evaded this. Superintendent of Trade Elliot was wholly in sympathy with the Chinese actions, but when he wrote home that he might be obliged to intervene to stop the trade, Palmerston reminded him that he had no legal powers, and must 'neither encourage or protect' the traders. The Governor-General's measures, however, brought the trade to a standstill. Opium was unsaleable; even Matheson of the firm of Jardine & Matheson, the senior opium trader, began to think it possible that this time the Chinese would bring it to an end.

When news of the campaign reached India and London there was no disposition to oppose China's belated enforcement of her old prohibition. The Government had already stated in Parliament in 1833 that it 'was as anxious as anybody' to get rid of the opium trade, but would need time to work out some alternative source of revenue. The Governor-General of India, Auckland, responded to the news from China by assuming that the trade would end. Palmerston without hesitation acknowledged China's right to stop imports and asserted that 'any losses would have to be suffered by the parties' engaged in the trade.

The attempts of the opium merchants to evade the Governor-General's measures in 1837 were precisely of the kind to increase the British disposition to accept the abolition of the traffic. British boats manned by armed lascars were braving the Chinese anti-opium fleet to run the drug to the very Canton wharves. Heavily armed clippers, any one of which could have dealt with a whole fleet of Chinese war junks, were spreading opium up the entire Chinese coast. Armed clashes took place. Even David Jardine, Matheson's partner, was disgusted, and the American opium firm Russell & Co. announced their withdrawal from the trade in February 1839.

In Canton the three successive British superintendents Davis, Robinson, and Elliot all detested the trade and would have been delighted to see it abolished. Elliot left the Governor-General in no doubt that he would send on to his government any representations made with respect to the opium trade. Had there been normal communication between the two governments it is probable that the problem would have been solved; and the Governor-General was clearly disposed, in order to further the suppression of opium, to relax the barriers to communication.

This was the situation into which Imperial Commissioner Lin Zexu stepped on 10 March 1839. Lin Zexu was 54 when he arrived at Canton. He was the son of a family of small means which had nevertheless maintained a tradition of scholoarship. He took the highest (*jinshi*) degree at the early age of 26 and joined the Hanlin Academy, the highest distinction in Chinese scholarship. He was a leading member of the new reform party. An official of varied, practical and nation-wide experience, in 1837 he was serving as Governor-General of Hunan and Hubei. There he had carried out measures against opium with apparent success. His method was to invoke the help of the people via the local gentry in identifying both the dealers and the consumers, to execute all convicted of participation in the trade, to give addicts eighteen months to cure themselves under threat of execution if they failed, and to employ such medical methods as were known to assist them in overcoming the addiction (in Canton he sought the advice of Western medical missionaries). Hunan and Hubei, however, offered little parallel with Canton, the centre of the trade and the point of import; it is likely that in these provinces homegrown rather than imported opium was the problem. Lin Zexu was ill-prepared by his experience to take action at Canton.

He probably did not intend to invite a direct confrontation with the foreigners. In his correspondence with his fellow-reformer Gong Zizhen he expressed agreement with recommendations which Gong had made. One of these was that it would not be possible to attempt to stop the evil at its foreign source lest the barbarians and 'native rebels' (the anti-Manchu Triads, involved already in the internal distribution of the drug) should unite. Once at Canton, however, Lin was drawn into an attack on the foreign importers.

He was convinced that the foreign opium traders had no countenance from their governments at home. He assumed, as the letter which he wrote to Queen Victoria showed, that the import of opium into Britain must be illegal, as in China. He believed that British shipping was licensed and that the opium ships were vessels which had evaded licensing. He was unaware of the use of silver to buy tea, of the exchange problem, or of its political implications. He assumed that Elliot represented the opium merchants, and would not trust him as a channel of communication with Britain. In fact, Lin memorialized the throne only two days after his arrival at Canton that 'it is common knowledge that Elliot is not an English official, but a renegade merchant'.

Lin was thus totally unaware that he had an ally in Elliot, who condemned the opium trade as 'a traffic which every friend to humanity must deplore', who fully appreciated the difficulty the Chinese faced in trying to distinguish between the legal and the illegal trade and therefore agreed that 'the Chinese government had just grounds for harsh measures towards the lawful trade'. No reply was sent by Lin to Elliot's assurance, conveyed via the Governor-General, of 'his best efforts for fulfilling the reasonable purposes of this government, whenever they are authentically made known'.

Lin ordered the surrender of the opium stored down-river at Lintin. To him this was perfectly reasonable: he had already ordered the surrender of opium in the hands of the Chinese dealers, offering to spare them the death penalty if they conformed within a time limit. The two cases, however, were not the same. In the first place most of the opium at Lintin did not belong to the foreign merchants in India, and they had no legal right to surrender it. In the second place Lin did not have the force to seize the opium directly. Hence he resorted to the confinement of the British community in the factories.

It is not known at what stage he took this drastic decision. He demanded that Dent, the senior opium dealer since Jardine had left for home and retirement, be handed over to him. This he had a perfect legal right to expect, but there was no possibility that Elliot would allow Dent to be handed over to a Chinese court. He was prepared only to accompany Dent to an interview with Lin. This was not enough. So Lin moved troops into position round the factories. It was perhaps at this point that the decision was taken to hold their occupants as hostages for the surrender of the opium.

The British community were besieged in the factories for six weeks. Elliot was forced to order the surrender of the drug. The British traders complied, although the Superintendent had no legal power to give such an order. The surrendered drug was then burned and the ashes thrown into the Pearl River. By this act Lin Zexu had changed the whole issue as far as the British were concerned, from the suppression of the opium traffic, a cause with which the British authorities fully sympathized in spite of the great and ramified interests which the traffic supported, to the holding of British citizens, including innocent citizens, as hostages.

The news of Lin Zexu's confinement of the British community reached London on 21 September 1839, to be followed shortly by the information that Elliot had induced the merchants to surrender their opium by promising that the British Government would compensate them. It was at this point and in this way that the British public for the first time had the opium trade brought to their attention. *The Times* quickly serialized a book on its evils, put together by a young clergyman, Thilwell, mainly from material in the *Chinese Repository*, a journal published in Canton by an American missionary. An anti-opium society was promptly formed, led by Ashley (later Lord Shaftesbury). The Tory opposition prepared to launch an attack on Melbourne's administration. On the other side of the question the opium trader Jardine, arriving home opportunely from Canton, organized a campaign of pressure on the Government of a kind hitherto quite unknown in British politics. On his advice the question of the immorality of the opium trade was avoided in this campaign. The argument was confined to the responsibility of the Government, which had permitted if not encouraged the Company to grow opium in India specifically for the Chinese market. The Government must therefore compensate the merchants. The shame of the imprisonment of the community in Canton was fully exploited, and the impression given that the British had been forced to hand over their property out of fear for their lives. There was no one in Britain who could gainsay this interpretation, though it was, to say the least of it, exaggerated. The attention of the public was easily diverted from the confusing question of the immorality of opium to the manifest immorality of the holding of mostly innocent British citizens as hostages. As a Canton merchant not connected with the drug trade wrote, the crisis might have started from opium, but the problem now was how to restore the legal trade without 'the most cringing and humiliating concessions'.

Britain's decision to launch the war was made at a Cabinet meeting in which the question of compensation was the only point at issue. Was the Government to accept or repudiate Elliot's undertaking? It would have to accept it. Could the Government itself pay the compensation? No: Melbourne's administration had already a deficit, and there was no possibility that Parliament would accept the imposition of extra taxation for such a purpose. The Chinese therefore would have to pay for the opium, and for the expenses of the campaign fought to persuade them of the necessity.

Palmerston's letter to the Emperor of China put the case simply: he did not dispute China's right to forbid the import of opium, nor her right to seize contraband. The injustice was that the law had been allowed to become a dead letter, until suddenly without warning it was put into force 'with the utmost vigour and severity'.

His case was perhaps a little overstated. Governor-General Ruan Yuan had tried to put the law into force in 1821. It had been applied more vigorously in 1829. It was disingenuous to argue that the British had received no warning. On the other hand, British awareness of the strength of opinion in favour of legalization in both Canton and Beijing led the traders and the British Government to discount the warnings. The attack on opium in 1836, continued by Lin Zexu, was the first campaign they were forced to recognize as being in earnest. Rightly or wrongly they were indeed taken by surprise.

Meanwhile in the Pearl River the death of a Chinese peasant, Lin Weihi, in an obscure drunken brawl had brought a further crisis. Lin Zexu demanded that the culprit be handed over by the British, but no one knew which of a gang of drunken sailors was guilty. To enforce his demand Lin stopped the trade and withdrew the Chinese servants from the factories. A repetition of his imprisonment of the community seemed likely, so the British withdrew. The Macao authorities, in spite of orders from the Portuguese Government, would not risk their own safety by offering sanctuary there, so Elliot and the merchants landed on Hong Kong, where the opium ships which Elliot had been happy to order out of Lintin became the chief means of defence of the beleaguered community. These events confirmed the view that some place of refuge under British control was necessary, while in such a place, on British territory, a court could be set up which, among its other powers, might have power to take any necessary steps against opium smuggling.

The expedition which followed was not intended to perpetuate the opium trade, an aim which could have been secured quite simply by seizing an island off the Chinese coast and permitting Chinese traders to buy there. Although in the end an island base was acquired, it was not sought by the British Government. Hong Kong as a British colony grew by itself and was accepted by the Government only with great reluctance, and in fact the opium trade was at first forbidden at Hong Kong when it became a British possession and a British court was established.

The question of the drug traffic did not form any part of British demands. Nor were the British plenipotentiaries instructed to avoid the subject. On the contrary they were instructed to assure the Chinese negotiators that the British were not attempting to force the trade on them by war, and to suggest that legalization was the sensible first step to a solution.

The basic premise of the operation was that no more force should be used than was necessary to bring the Chinese Government to accept that British grievances were justified. It was hoped that a blockade of the Chinese coast would be enough. Palmerston was confident that if the blockade were extended north to include the Beihe (the coast off Tianjin) only a hundred miles from the capital, the Chinese Government would be brought to terms.

Elliot did not agree. He knew that a blockade would be ineffective. It would be impossible to enforce it on Chinese shipping to South-east Asia without a degree of ruthlessness which would be counter-productive. It would worry the government in Beijing very little. His alternative was a short sharp action in the Pearl River where the original provocation had been given. He had in mind the destruction of the forts of the Bocca Tigris (the Bogue) an action which could be carried out within a few hours with a minimum of casualties and minimal damage to civilian interests.

Palmerston's orders came. They were for a blockade; so most of the fleet sailed north, leaving Canton and its fortifications untouched.

Zhoushan (Chusan) Island off Hangzhou Bay was taken as a temporary base, and for the security of this base Ningbo on the mainland opposite was also occupied. At Zhoushan the naval commander, in his barrage covering the landing, used round shot instead of grape or canister, in order to minimize Chinese casualties. The army commander refused to billet his troops in Dinghai town in order to avoid creating hostility among the Chinese civilian population; instead he put them under canvas on a malarial swamp where fever and dysentery produced a death-rate which would scarcely have been acceptable in battle.

Meanwhile the fleet had moved up to the Beihe. The Chinese Court was forced to consider a change of policy. Lin Zexu's root-and-branch attack on the opium trade and his challenge to the foreigners had never commanded unanimous support. In particular, many Manchus, whose first consideration was the survival of their control of China rather than the welfare of the Chinese, had taken a more cautious view. The most powerful statesman at court, the Manchu Muchanga, was cautious and conciliatory, and the appearance of the barbarian ships at the Beihe after their triumphs off Hangzhou Bay restored his influence.

Qishan, the Governor-General of Zhili (now Hebei), off whose territory at Tianjin the ships lay, was one of those who had been critical of Lin Zexu although, like Lin, he was of the reform party. He now accepted for transmission to the Court the letter from Palmerston carried by the expedition. In this, most misleadingly, Lin's name had been so closely associated with the statement of British grievances that the Court gained the impression that the dismissal of Lin would serve to redress them. Muchanga and his party were already disposed to blame Lin, and the Emperor was brought round to their view. Lin had written in triumph, after his confiscation of the opium, that he had destroyed so much of the capital of the opium traders that they were unlikely to be able to revive the trade, and that—*a fortiori*—they would not have the resources to seek revenge. Yet the opium trade was growing faster than ever as the clippers followed the men-of-war up the coast, and the ability of the foreigners to take revenge had been made disastrously plain. Lin was degraded and exiled. The foreigners were so informed by Qishan. He persuaded them to remove themselves to a safer distance, by making half-promises of redress to be negotiated at the source of the trouble in Canton. He would follow them south, post-haste, to deal with the details.

Elliot was quick to accept his offer. His presence in the north was, he knew, a bluff which the northern monsoon would call within a few weeks. The ships could not hang about off the treacherous sandbanks of the river mouth in winds from that quarter. Nor, if they landed a force, could they follow it up over the shoals to give it the protection of naval guns. In any case only a fraction of the troops were fit for combat, thanks to their commander's folly. The fleet went south. Governor-General Qishan followed.

Qishan's success allowed the war party in Beijing to gain the upper hand once more. The Emperor decided on a war of annihilation. His strategy was to protract negotiations until the enemy were exhausted, while assembling the forces necessary to crush them. This was Qishan's task at Canton.

Elliot played into the hands of the war party. In his concern to minimize conflict he struck briefly and then withdrew to renew negotiations. He did this repeatedly, on each occasion enabling Qishan to report a devastating defeat as a victory. Qishan himself knew better. He was the first high official (and the first Manchu aristocrat) to see for himself the power of Western arms; but Elliot's 'ill-timed mercies', as the American missionary S. Wells Williams called them, enabled Qishan's rivals to condemn him to Beijing as pusillanimous if not treacherous.

For five weeks after Qishan's arrival in the south, Elliot negotiated in vain. An attack was then made on the outer Bogue forts. The British navy's first iron steamer, the *Nemesis*, drawing only six feet of water, went in beneath the angle of depression of the Chinese battery's guns and poured grape and canister straight through the embrasures. Fifteen hundred troops were landed to outflank the forts. The Manchu garrison fought gallantly, almost to the last man. The British did not suffer a single fatality. Elliot withdrew to let the lesson sink in; but the Emperor was informed of a victory. Qishan, though he hastened to make an agreement, dared not put his seal on it. So the British struck again, this time at the inner Bogue forts, and with the same devastating results. And again Elliot withdrew and waited, and again the report of a victory went to Beijing. When this second round of destruction had no effect, Elliot with reluctance ordered the fleet up-river to Canton. The *Nemesis* poked her way ahead through the mud-banks and found a route for the warships, which debouched into the main channel only five miles from the city. There again the British held their hand, and only when the Chinese launched a fire-raft attack (uselessly, on the last of the ebb) did the fleet move up and hoist the British flag once more over the Canton factories.

When even this had no result, General Gough took the heights round the city itself; and it was at this point that Elliot's policy showed its worst dangers. Gough's troops were ready to occupy the last obstacle in the way of an attack on Canton, the Hill of the Five-Storeyed Pagoda, from which there already fluttered the white flag of surrender, when he received Elliot's orders to proceed no further. Gough's inaction was promptly taken as a sign of weakness by the gentry of the Canton area, who had organized a popular militia. In consequence 700 British and Indian troops, caught in a typhoon downpour, were attacked by about 8,000 Chinese irregulars while their soaked muskets were useless. Under this harassment they retreated, though with negligible losses. The next day Gough's peremptory order to the Canton authorities to send the irregulars home was obeyed with alacrity, and this should have been the end of the matter; but then came the news from Elliot that a peace had been concluded. Gough's forces moved out down river, and the spectacle of his going created a myth by which it was believed—eventually even in Beijing— that the militia could defeat the foreigners. Thereafter, no official in Canton could attempt to conciliate the British without being accused of cowardice.

The peace which Elliot had signed at Qunbi (Chunpi) was repudiated by both governments; Qishan was put in chains for having, at last, told the Emperor the unpalatable truth and having advised him to accept the consequences. Hong Kong was the Emperor's sticking-point: he could not stomach the surrender of Chinese subjects to barbarian jurisdiction, not even the handful of fishermen and farmers on Hong Kong island. Palmerston for his part also completely repudiated the agreement, in one of the most savage despatches ever directed to a British representative. The indemnity, he asserted, was ridiculously small, and its payment so spread out that it could be recouped from taxes on British trade. None of the problems of Sino-British relations, except for the question of equality in communication, had been solved. The cession of Hong Kong, which Palmerston had never wanted, was no substitute for the opening of more ports to trade. Elliot was recalled.

Sir Henry Pottinger replaced Elliot as plenipotentiary, arriving in China in August 1841. He was a man of a different stamp. He had spent his life in India, for the most part as a political agent at the courts of Indian princes. He was prepared to treat the Celestial Court with the same brisk ruthlessness with which he had handled the emirs of Sind. He expressed no moral qualms about opium; he did not readily express moral qualms about anything. He was a man with no doubts, and he had the power behind him to impose his certainties.

A new military expedition was launched with the object of proceeding to the second stage of the original plan, now that the first had failed: the Grand Canal was to be cut at Nanjing. From the mouth of the Yangzi almost to Nanjing the British force—the army on the bank, the ships on the river— experienced virtually no opposition, although for thirty-six days the entire fleet, strung out along the river and sounding its way from one mud-hole to the next, was an easy target. At Jinjiang, however, as at all other places where they had been met, the Manchu bannermen fought with great courage, disputing every inch of the city streets. To the dismay of the British, when defeated they killed their wives and children, and then themselves. The Chinese would never have understood how shocked the British were at such behaviour, which was quite outside the European code of warfare. The British did not want to feel responsible, and they did not think they should be held responsible, for such desperation. They knew too little of the culture into which they had blundered to realize that the war, which to them was merely an armed protest with strictly limited objectives, was to their opponents the defence of civilization.

As the enemy approached Nanjing the Governor-General there frankly reported to Beijing that the city could not be defended. The Emperor was at last forced to accept defeat. The imperial clansman Yilibu, exiled after an accusation that he had shown himself too conciliatory to the foreigners at Ningbo during the first expedition, now found his ability to please them an asset. He was ordered to Nanjing.

At Nanjing he joined Qiying, also an imperial clansman. The seriousness with which the Beijing government now looked at the situation is shown by the appointment of these two princes of the blood to rescue Nanjing. Qiying circumspectly delayed making contact with the foreign ships until Jinjiang had fallen. After that disaster even the Emperor would be unlikely to go back on his order to make peace. Still with characteristic circumspection, Qiying sent one of Yilibu's domestic slaves, Zhang Xi, disguised as a mandarin of the fifth rank, to sound out the foreigners. Zhang Xi left a diary which, read along with British reports of his mission, shows that he gradually became convinced that the foreigners sought only trade not conquest. He reported this to Qiying, who in turn informed the Court, and in so doing accepted personal responsibility for the conclusion of a peace treaty based on the assumption that foreign demands, being essentially commercial, could be safely conceded. The main initial difficulty was to secure from the Emperor the acceptance of Pottinger's demands that the imperial commissioners must have plenipotentiary powers, and that they must negotiate in person. This done, Qiying, Yilibu, and the Nanjing Governor-General boarded the *Cornwallis*, where they bowed to the Queen's picture as an indication of their willingness to negotiate as equals.

The Treaty of Nanjing

The treaty was concluded with remarkable speed. The response of the Chinese negotiators to the various demands of the British shows the relative importance which they attached to the points involved. On the question of the cession of Hong Kong, they showed (as one would expect) much less alarm over the prospect of a British presence on an island in the Pearl River, which might be little different in practice from the presence of the Portuguese in Macao, than over the idea that Chinese citizens would be put under foreign rule. In the end the Chinese text of the Treaty of Nanjing left the status of Hong Kong ambiguous. It was the English version, stipulated to be the authoritative one, which stated that Hong Kong was to be ceded outright.

The two clauses of the treaty which future Chinese nationalists would come to regard with the greatest abhorrence, that which gave the British rights of extraterritoriality and that which made China's tariffs a matter of treaty right, were not strongly contested. Some degree of extraterritoriality was, as we have seen, a part of China's traditional method of dealing with foreign communities. As for the tariffs, Pottinger found that the merchants, who had complained loud and long at the severity of the duties charged, did not know in fact how much they had paid; the Hong merchants had always settled the duties for them. The draft tariff proposal put before the Chinese laid down as bargaining terms a duty of 5 per cent *ad valorem*. The Chinese accepted without demur: this figure was actually higher than the average of the existing official rates. On the other hand, illegal exactions now ceased.

Opium was not mentioned in the treaty, except for the stipulation of an indemnity, but the Chinese completely compromised their moral stand by offering to legalize the trade provided the British Government would guarantee the payment of a fixed tax. The British Government, not inclined to turn tax-farmer for Beijing, naturally refused. The question of the future of the trade was left unanswered. However, the new Hong Kong administration was instructed to outlaw the opium trade in Hong Kong, in the expectation that the officials of the mainland ports would take similar steps; but within a year it was obvious that the Chinese authorities were taking no action, and when pressed they declared themselves unable to deal with the problem. It therefore became pointless to exclude opium from Hong Kong. Had the Chinese authorities taken the action which their own law demanded and which the British fully expected, then in co-operation with British consuls charged under the treaty to assist in the suppression of smuggling, and with a government in Hong Kong which was not prepared to offer the trade any sanctuary there, the problem might have been solved. As it was, within a decade the

Chinese officials on the coast were welcoming the trade, allowing it to be carried on openly, and raising revenue from it. The British could thereafter feel that they had been absolved from responsibility—a poor moral argument but sufficient for the purpose.

The Treaty of Nanjing—the first of the 'unequal treaties'—is widely believed to have been an instrument of imperialism. Its details, however, make such a view difficult to sustain. Its clauses can be divided into three categories. The first includes the charges made as compensation for British property seized and destroyed and to cover the cost of the war; these charges were designed to be a deterrent to any future repetition of Lin's seizure of the British community as hostages. They did not bring about any permanent change in China's relations with Britain. The second category is concerned with the redress of the grievances occasioned by the tightening up of the Canton system in the later eighteenth century, and by the inconsistencies and uncertainties of its operation; into this category fall those clauses which specify the abolition of the bankrupt Hong system, the granting of defined extra-territorial rights, the stipulation in the treaty of the amount of taxes due on trade, and the rules of communication between British and Chinese authorities. The third category consists of the only British demands which went beyond the definition of existing rights—the opening up of other Chinese ports for trade and the cession of Hong Kong. It could be argued that as foreigners had formerly traded at these ports, they were to be reopened rather than newly opened, but whether this interpretation is acceptable or not, the demand was a very limited one. It applied only to four new southern ports; it involved no access to any part of China beyond these coastal towns themselves, except over short distances for recreational purposes; it involved no right to acquire land and property on Chinese soil, to exploit Chinese mineral resources, or to manufacture in China. It involved, in fact, the absolute minimum of tolerable conditions for commerce, on terms which did not even give the foreign trader direct access to his original suppliers or his final customers.

As for the cession of Hong Kong, the record of British discussions before the War shows that the original motive which led to the idea of taking over an island was to have a territory on which a British magistrate could operate in order to control British subjects. To this was added, after the threat that Lin Zexu might lock the British community up for a second time after the murder of the peasant Lin Weihi, the need for a place of refuge. Outright cession was not decided upon until late in the course of events, the British being prepared to consider arrangements by which Chinese residents in Hong Kong would remain under Chinese jurisdiction, and only in the end concluding that no such arrangement seemed practical. If territorial acquisition had been the point, or the establishment of a base from which to put pressure on China, the British had only to remain on Zhoushan, rather than evacuate that excellent position within striking distance of the major Yangzi cities and settle for a barren rock at the extremity of the country, a tiny island so unproductive and so unhealthy that even the most optimistic of men did not foresee its extraordinary future development, which was due more to the continued and increasing breakdown of public order in China than to the merits of Hong Kong itself.

The British were in fact uncertain as to the wisdom of annexing Hong Kong almost until the end. Lord Aberdeen actually ordered Pottinger to forbid further construction of permanent buildings on the island, on the grounds that it was not, and would not be, a British possession; but as Chinese merchants poured in, no orders could prevent the spontaneous creation of a new Sino-British settlement. The British Government was presented with a *fait accompli*.

The notion of the Treaty of Nanjing as the expression of ruthless imperialism arose later when circumstances had changed. By the end of the century Chinese nationalists saw in extraterritoriality an insult to and a derogation from Chinese sovereignty. The Treaty tariff, the original purpose of which had simply been to get the taxes on trade stipulated in order to prevent corruption, had become an obstacle (or so it was believed) to the protection of China's new infant industries. The competitive acquisition by the powers of armed bases on Chinese soil after 1894, a movement in which the British participated in order to be able (in British interests of course) the better to defend China's integrity and independence against the rapacity of Russia, led to the assumption that the cession of Hong Kong had been, and had been intended to be, the first such acquisition.

The Treaty of Nanjing was, in fact, a very mild one. China had suffered a devastating defeat. The victor could well have forced China to accept in her relations with the British everything regarded as normal under Western international law, and could in addition have annexed rich and populous territories. Instead, the British took the utmost pains to limit their demands to the bare minimum necessary to secure reasonable conditions for trade, and to introduce as little novelty as they could. British governments continued to see the future of relations with China in terms of alternatives: either to leave things as they were in the hope that continued and increasing contacts through trade would induce the Chinese to accept the necessary novelties, or to use force. Events led to the use of force; but in a sense it was used only to provide the basic conditions for a return to the first alternative, the patient and peaceful development of a *modus vivendi*. It is surprising to observe how little the system was actually changed. In the five ports now open, British merchants could stay all year and no longer had to come and go with the trade winds; they could bring their families with them; they had a consul to represent their interests, and laws to prevent the evasion of duties, which made the licensing of security merchants unnecessary even from the Chinese point of view. Otherwise things were much as they had been; the restrictions which remained were of far greater significance than those which had been abolished.

In 1845 France and the United States negotiated similar treaties with China. The Sino-American Treaty of Wangxia (Wanghia) included a 'most-favoured-nation' clause, and this was extended by the Chinese Emperor to all treaty powers as a mark of his undiscriminating benevolence.

Of the powers other than Great Britain which entered into treaty relations with China none had, at that date, interests of any importance, except perhaps the United States, but American traders mainly sold furs in China for cash, a simple form of commerce which did not involve them so deeply in the problems which the British faced, and only one American firm, Russell & Co., had been involved in the opium trade. The treaties were made with China more in the hope of future advantage and because, the British having done the fighting, they cost nothing. The Chinese, for their part, were ready to oblige in the hope that one foreign nation would check another, and they would not be at the mercy of the British.

3

The Taiping Rebellion

1850–1864

Disorder and rebellion

Throughout the last decades of the eighteenth century and the first decades of the nineteenth in China, scarcely a year passed without violent protest or armed rebellion. Some of this protest was scarcely distinguishable from banditry. Much was of the spontaneous rice-riot kind. On several occasions, however, small groups raised the banner of the Ming dynasty and marched against the foreign rulers. The Taiping Rebellion of 1850 was only the greatest of many outbreaks. A major rebellion broke out in 1796. Led by the White Lotus secret society, it began in the foothills of the middle Yangzi among migrant peasants whose maize monoculture on the hill slopes had disastrously accelerated the process of erosion. The rebellion, however, quickly spread far beyond the area in which such circumstances could account for it, lighting a train of explosive discontent which flashed across the whole of northern China, engulfing half of the provinces of the Empire in a decade of destructive war.

The White Lotus Rebellion was extinguished by 1806, but its embers continued to smoulder. Secret societies under other names, some of which were related to the White Lotus society itself, kept up sporadic resistance. In 1812 members of one such sect scaled the walls of the Forbidden City and were beaten off only through the courage of Prince Min-ning, the future Dao Guang Emperor. There were further attacks led by successors of the White Lotus in the 1820s and 1830s. In northern China, where the four provinces of Hebei, Henan, Shandong and Jiangsu meet, a group of mounted 'social bandits', the Nian, controlled most of the countryside; throughout the first half of the century it was a 'no-go' area for the officials of the Beijing government. In the early 1850s the Nian had gathered sufficient strength to launch a full rebellion, just when the Taiping rebels of the south were pouring down the Yangzi towards Nanjing.

The White Lotus society had spread its influence among the aborigines of central and south-west China, and in the 1830s the Miao rebelled. In 1836 the

Yao of Hunan, under White Lotus preachers, started a fitful war of resistance which flared up once more in 1855 during the chaos of the Taiping Rebellion.

In 1853 the Triads (the southern anti-Manchu secret society) of the West River in Guangdong rose in a movement which flashed down the river from lodge to lodge, and put Canton under siege.

At one point in 1854 the imperial government had lost control not only of the Pearl River to the Triads, but also a large area around Nanjing to the Taipings, Shanghai to a Triad offshoot called the Short Swords, and the lower Yellow River to the Nian. A broad band of territory from Canton to within one hundred miles of Beijing was in the hands of rebel groups. Before this surge of rebellion among the Han Chinese had been halted, risings were launched in north-west and south-west China by China's Muslim minorities. Into this sea of troubles the British, in alliance with the French, were to launch a second war on China in 1857. If these rebellions show the weakness of the imperial government the fact that the dynasty survived is, at the same time, evidence of the extraordinary resilience of traditional society. Sluggish, ill-co-ordinated and corrupt as the machinery was, it worked. When the dynasty finally fell in 1912 it was in circumstances far less perilous, on the surface at least, than those of the mid-nineteenth century.

The causes of this wave of rebellion are still unknown. Attempts have been made to explain events in terms of economic distress. Of this there was no lack, but there is little evidence that the rebellions were directly related to any particular cause of hardship. The argument most easily disposed of is that rebellion was the result of the destruction of traditional forms of handicraft employment in China by the competition of foreign manufactures: the great rebellions all began in areas far beyond the reach of foreign trade.

The occurrence of famine is often adduced as a cause. The incidence of dearth in China is given in the 'Veritable Records' (in which the major decisions made by the Emperor were recorded daily). They show that while distress sufficient to attract a reduction of taxes was widespread, the geo-graphical pattern of dearth in the twenty-five years (1825–49) before the main rebellions began bears no consistent relationship to the occurrence of major outbreaks.

There is one partial exception to this. The Nian Rebellion was immensely strengthened when between 1853 and 1855 the unpredictable Yellow River, flowing between artificial banks often higher than the surrounding fields, broke through these treacherous and decayed defences to switch its course from south to north of the Shandong peninsula, devastating thousands of square miles of plain around the mountain strongholds of the Nian rebels. The Nian ranks were swollen by recruits from among the millions made destitute, but the disaster did not cause the rebellion, which had already been in existence for most of a generation.

Resistance to landlordism is the explanation of rebellion which leaps most readily to Chinese minds, being at once the traditional and the Marxist expectation. Yet on this view also the records give no help: none of the rebellions began in an area known to suffer from land tenure conditions worse than average.

The hypothesis that increase in population, leading to an ever more adverse man–land ratio, was a major cause of rebellion is more plausible, if less fashionable. In its simple form, however—that is, that rebellion occurred where population pressure was most severe—this hypothesis would be difficult to prove. No rebellion of importance except the Triad 'Red Turban' rising of 1854 in Guangdong took place in a densely populated area; on the contrary, the major risings occurred in areas of relatively sparse population. The connections, if any, between population pressure and disorder were indirect. One obvious case is the role played by conflicts between migrating Han farmers and the aboriginal minorities of areas into which they moved in search of land. In Manchuria and Inner Mongolia, Han settlers were rapidly becoming a substantial majority of the population and were bitterly resented. In central China the pressure of increasing Chinese settlement was one cause of Miao and Yao rebellions, while the growing number of Chinese settlers and merchants in Xinjiang (Chinese Turkestan) played a major part in the perpetual disturbances of that Muslim area, disturbances which soon fed back into the adjacent area of China proper which was inhabited by Muslims of Han race. The Taiping Rebellion itself began, as we shall see, in a similar situation of strife between natives and migrants; but here it was the immigrant minority, the Hakka, who were under pressure and resorted to resistance.

Less directly, population pressure resulting in increasing competition among the gentry-graduate élite led both to the increased burden of maintaining the ever-growing swarm of petty office-holders and to inefficiency arising from the diversion of public funds into corrupt patron–client relationships. These consequences of unprecedented growth in population undoubtedly played a part in the general malaise out of which disaffection grew.

However the increased disorder of the 1830s and 1840s which provided the rich recruiting ground for the great rebellions of the fifties seems to have had a more easily identifiable cause. Until about 1825 a long slight inflation had kept peasant incomes abreast of the increasing exactions of the official and sub-official classes. Then prices plunged—the consequence of the frantic efforts of the government, almost bankrupted by corruption, to maintain its revenues by the minting of vast quantities of debased copper coinage. To this was added the cessation of the inflow of silver as opium imports grew. To meet tax demands assessed in silver the peasant landowner was forced to pay more in copper, while with the scarcity of silver the price he received for his crops was sharply reduced. The riots of the 1830s and 1840s were primarily tax riots; and it was where these protests were most numerous—the middle and lower Yangzi provinces—that the Taipings recruited the vast majority of their adherents.

China's alien rulers then lost a war to a handful of barbarians. The legitimacy of the alien government was put in question. So far as the statements of those who participated in rebellion are known, the immediate target of attack was the bureaucrat; the grievance was bad government, but as the protests surpassed the local scale the final target became the alien dynasty. Whatever else the rebellions may have been, they were nationalist.

Any explanation of rebellions in China in the nineteenth century solely in terms of material conditions is inadequate. Many rebellious groups had religious affiliations, to a degree which may surprise the reader who thinks of Chinese culture only in terms of the secular tradition of upper-class Confucianism. Pietistic Buddhism combined with vestiges of Manichaeism was the inspiration of the White Lotus rebels. Sufi sainthood was the flag of the Muslim rebels of the west. The Taiping Rebellion itself was led by a group who had embraced a form of Christianity. Although as usual the interconnections of social dislocation and religious revival are difficult to trace, China's mid-century situation shows a close association between them.

The origins of the rebellion

In 1814 the leader of the Taiping movement, Hong Xiuquan, was born in Huaxian, Guangdong, of a family of peasant proprietors. Recognizing his unusual ability, his family made sacrifices to ensure his schooling, but when he reached the age of 15 or 16 they could support him no further. He took employment as the village schoolteacher. He continued to study, however, and having come first in the local preliminary examinations, four times sat the provincial examinations at Canton. Like many young men of ability and originality, he failed to pass the conventionalized test into which the examination system had deteriorated, and which in any case would be passed, even at provincial level, by only one candidate in a hundred.

On his journey to Canton to take the examination for the second time in 1837 Hong had casually bought a pamphlet written by a Christian convert, Liang Afa, entitled 'Good Words to Exhort the Age'. He paid no attention to it at the time. Then on his return from his third failure in 1844 he suffered an acute mental breakdown. The story we have from Hong's associates claims that his own description of this experience was given immediately, but that its full significance was only understood later in the light of the 'Good Words'. It is equally possible that his description came only after reading the pamphlet. Hong claimed that during his illness he was caught up into a heaven of angels and beautiful maidens, a splendid paradise presided over by an old man who, while he wore the dress and sat in the pose of a traditional Chinese 'ancestor portrait', had a long golden beard. Hong's abdomen was cut open and his organs replaced. He was adopted as the younger brother of Jesus Christ. He was given a commission to cast out devils, and a magic sword and a seal. On his return to earth, the account goes, he took up his divine mission, identifying the devils partly with the idols of China's rural temples, but partly also with the Manchu rulers of China. His friends noted that he had become grave and authoritative.

An alternative explanation is that Hong under the frustration of his failures in the examinations developed illusions of grandeur and of persecution. And the brief and selective introduction to Christianity which he now had to hand was such as to meet Hong's mental needs. The author put Christianity in the context of his times, in a scene of decay, violence and corruption; his God was an Old Testament God of wrath as much as a God of love. This form of Christian message, with its pervading sense of China's accelerating moral decay, already had political overtones of alienation and potential rebellion.

Hong added his own personal revelation to the Christian story, and began to preach and to destroy idols. Among his first converts were two distant cousins, Feng Yunshan and Hong Rengan, both of whom were to play great parts in the movement and eventually to die for it. Both of them, like Xiuquan himself, were failed examinees. All three worked as village schoolteachers, but when they began to destroy idols they were dismissed. Hong Xiuquan and Feng Yunshan decided to leave the district. They walked three hundred miles from their village near Canton to the hills of Guangxi and there continued to preach. They belonged to the Hakka minority, and their message was readily received in the Hakka communities, increasingly hard-pressed by Cantonese hostility.

Hong then returned east to go to Hong Kong for religious instruction from the American Baptist missionary Isaachar Roberts. His time there was brief. Being penniless, he took the advice of fellow converts and asked Roberts for help towards his subsistence, and Roberts—vigilant against 'rice Christians'—declined to baptise him. Nevertheless he had now at least participated in Christian worship, and had read the Bible. He returned to Guangxi to find that Feng Yunshan had built up a congregation of 2,000. At this point we have no evidence that the movement was political: Hong's hymns, which are our main source for his personal ideas, were revised in later years so that the political applications of his religious beliefs may have been added only after the movement turned to rebellion. What we have for certain at this time is an evangelical movement of a kind familiar enough in Christian history—lower-class, intensely puritanical, ecstatic, and offering mutual support and personal dignity to the rejected.

Hong soon became locally known and respected. The authorities were tolerant. Yet however pacific the intentions of the Hakka God-worshippers may have been the circumstances in which they found themselves did not encourage peace. The whole area watered by the West River had by the 1840s become violently unstable. Whatever general factors may have operated, there were specific and immediate causes for disorder. The militia organized to oppose the British at Canton had been demobilized and many of its members had turned bandit; thirty bandit gangs operated in the area. The British navy had suppressed piracy on the South China coast, forcing the pirates upstream. Local communities then formed their own self-defence forces and had them recognized officially, but these forces were almost as dangerous as those of the bandits, being recruited from much the same sources. Finally, in such conditions the secret societies soon predictably transformed themselves from societies for mutual protection into protection rackets.

The society of Guangxi had its own particular tensions on which the forces of disorder fed. Non-Chinese aboriginal minority peoples were still numerous there. Partly assimilated and often prosperous, they nevertheless still suffered discrimination. In the mountains were many mines, some recently opened and employing 'incomers', a word which usually indicates the Hakkas, though some may have been aborigines. In the extensive forests were charcoal-burners, strongly organized for their own protection. The main problem, however, was that of the Hakkas—the 'Guest Clans'. They were migrants from the north. Although Chinese in race and speech, they differed markedly from the native (*bendi*) Cantonese. They were tough, pioneering hill farmers. They farmed the poorest areas, but with such industry that they were gradually edging their more fortunate Cantonese neighbours out. Their women, who did not bind their feet, worked beside them in the fields and often tended the farms while their husbands migrated to the mines or to man ships, burn charcoal, or emigrate. Even in the most prosperous Hakka houses the women still spun and sewed. In spite of all their disadvantages the Hakkas had reached what was probably the highest rate of literacy of any labouring group in China: 80 per cent of males could read, and they took a disproportionate number of places in the provincial examination, though few had sufficient means to advance beyond this level. They had the sort of proud and aggressive sense of identity which their position, combined with their characteristics, would lead one to expect. And, finally, they practised the local religions and accepted the local shamanistic beliefs, and did so with their characteristic intensity.

Their communities were scattered, while many individuals worked away from home in an isolation relieved only by membership of a secret society, the only refuge of the itinerant Chinese worker. They were thus especially vulnerable. They were soon victims of the growing disorder which put arms in the hands of the hostile Cantonese majority. For those who accepted Hong Xiuquan's new foreign faith the isolation was even greater. It led to an intensified sense of identity; the stark contrast between the saved few and the damned multitude, which nineteenth-century Calvinist Christianity preached so vividly, could rationalize the Hakkas' own position.

The pressure on the God-worshipping Hakkas was such that they found themselves drawn into conflict which could hardly fail to escalate to the point at which they were forced to defend themselves against imperial troops, and so become outlawed. At what point in this escalation Hong and his associates decided on rebellion is uncertain. We have accounts of a few incidents which were typical of the increasing tension, incidents recorded because they served to explain the first concentration of uprooted God-Worshippers at the foot of the Thistle Mountains. A militia unit passing through a Hakka village molested the inhabitants, and this led to a conflict after which the 130 villagers, dispossessed, left to join Feng Yunshan. In another village a Hakka concubine was kidnapped; after the ensuing fracas the whole village of 200 souls moved to join the original 130. A rich landlord and pawnbroker, head of the Wei clan, bought himself a military rank, and his son Wei Changhui—government lictor and one-time militiaman in Canton—erected a tablet to celebrate the occasion. The Weis being of Zhuang aboriginal blood, local Cantonese insulted the tablet. The Weis in revenge raided the Cantonese village and then joined the God-Worshippers; their wealth helped to sustain the growing number of the displaced. Two other rich clan chiefs, Hu Yiguang and Zeng Yuzhen, also put their means at the disposal of Hong's sect. Similar clashes forced other groups and clans to join the God-Worshippers. The leader of the local charcoal-burners, Yang Xiuqing, had already brought in his followers. Xiao Chaogui, a relation by marriage of the charcoal-burner (who was also the uncle of clan chief Zeng Yuzhen), had brought in his fellow farm labourers. Some of the Triad river pirates sought to join; most were put off by the strict discipline of the sect, but one group, led by Luo Dagang, became part of the movement.

By the end of 1850 there were at least 10,000 God-Worshippers in and around Jintian, perhaps even 30,000. As their numbers grew the authorities became alarmed. They ordered the God-Worshippers to disperse, and when they refused attacked them. The government forces were driven off and a deputy magistrate was killed. A full-scale attack on them was launched, but again the imperial forces were defeated. The Manchu commander was captured and beheaded; the God-Worshippers had crossed the Rubicon.

Whether or not rebellion had been planned it is certain that a serious conflict had been anticipated. For several years weapons had been secretly manufactured, wrapped in greased cloth and hidden in a lake. Many God-Worshippers who trekked to Jintian in 1849 and 1850 had sold or burned down their houses, and had turned all their assets into cash, which they paid into a common treasury. They had submitted to a rule which segregated the men from their wives and families, a measure clearly intended both to increase military mobility and to ensure loyalty. Finally, the speed with which the basic institutions of Hong's new kingdom were announced strongly suggests long-laid plans.

The name of his new kingdom was Taiping Tianguo—literally the Heavenly Kingdom of Transcendent Peace. The Chinese words are steeped in millenial meanings, but the concept was immediately derived from Christianity. Hong's Christian associates during his month in Hong Kong had observed the eagerness with which he had seized on the text, 'The Kingdom of God is at hand', and it was the Kingdom of God on Earth which Hong claimed to have founded on 11 January 1851.

His associates were a group interesting both for the range of their origins and for the limits of this range. Those whose names are important in the history of the rebellion include: a failed examinee and village schoolteacher (Feng Yunshan); an orphan charcoal-burner and former government clerk (Yang Xiuqing); a poor peasant and seller of faggots (Xiao Chaogui); a member of a rich Zhuang clan, lictor and former member of the Cantonese militia (Wei Changhui); a failed examinee from prosperous farming stock (Shi Dakai); a female bandit chief, outlawed after revenging the murder of her husband (Su San); a Triad leader and river pirate (Luo Dagang); a military cadet from a rich landlord family (Hu Yiguang); two wealthy money-lenders and pawnbrokers (Wu Keyi and Zhou Shengkun); a Guangdong merchant (Yu Tingzhang); a carpenter (Bin Fashou); a rural advocate (Huang Yukun); two thought to be from landlord families (Meng De-an and Chen Chengzhong); a scholar of considerable local repute (He Zhenquan); a former accountant with a Hong merchant (Wu Ruxiao); the head of a rich clan (Zeng Yuzhen); and a poor peasant (Li Xiucheng).

The most obvious characteristic of this group is its variety. It is by no means composed of peasants. Almost all would have been literate. About half might be supposed to have some administrative experience as clan heads or businessmen. Yet it is mainly rural. It includes not a single holder of a degree higher than that of *xiucai*. And all the evidence direct or indirect shows that the group was predominantly Hakka. All, with the exception of Hong Xiuquan himself and Feng Yunshan, were from the West River counties of Guangxi.

So far as we can guess at the motives of the revolt from the characteristics of its leading participants, it was not motivated by peasant discontent, nor by destitution: Shi Dakai's clan brought with them to Jintian 100,000 taels (ounces of silver). The only common bond is adherence to the God-Worshippers' faith. The main characteristic of recruitment was that whole Hakka clans joined. It represented ethnic, reinforced by religious, identity.

The Taiping kingdom

Hong's new system was proclaimed in broad outline soon after the Jintian rising, elaborated in 1851 after the capture of the city of Yongan, and fully promulgated after the capture of Nanjing in 1853, in the document now usually referred to as the Land Law of the Taiping Tianguo.

Hong's kingdom was a theocracy; every rule and every act was justified by religion, and the authority of the State was legitimized by Hong's revelations. But though a Christian kingdom, its institutions were Chinese. They were based on the 'Rites of Zhou' (Zhou Li), representing the supposed institutions of a part of ancient China. They expressed an ideal frequently resurrected by Chinese reformers; both Wang Mang (45 BC–AD 23) and Wang Anshi (1021–86) had tried to put this ideal into operation. The Rites have been regarded throughout Chinese history as embodying the perfectly equitable and ordered society, the institutional expression of Tai Ping, transcendent peace. The word *ping* has connotations of equality as well as of peace, and so the Rites have also been regarded as representing a Chinese tradition of egalitarian socialism. In fact, the institutions described are neither egalitarian nor socialist, but a rationalization of feudalism. In this ideal scheme of things all land is owned by the State. Society is hierarchical, from its basic groups of twenty-five families cultivating in peace and fighting in war and providing the surplus to maintain the State, up through successive ranks of territorial officials who are both civil and military leaders, to the Emperor at the top.

The Taipings in theory followed the Zhou Li system. All property belonged to God, that is, to the State; all money, valuables and products were paid into the Sacred Treasury. In return, rations and pay, graded according to rank, were issued. In theory the peasants were brought into the system, grouped as in the Zhou Li in communities of twenty-five families whose head—ostensibly elected—was called a 'sergeant' (*liang si-ma*), and who was commander, administrator, and preacher in one person. All surplus agricultural produce was to be requisitioned for the Sacred Treasury, and the cultivators left only with rations. Commerce and handicraft production were to be similarly organized.

Some features of this ideal Zhou Li system were appropriate to the circumstances of the rebellion. The 'Sacred Treasury' had been established even before the Jintian rising, when God-Worshippers, dispossessed of their land, had to depend on a common source of funds. It remained an important form of discipline thereafter in an insurgent army, dependent on plunder, which might well have disintegrated had the plunder not been appropriated and distributed by the central command. To set up basic communities of twenty-five farmer-soldiers did not prove possible, however; as one Taiping commander wrote, in a densely settled country there was no possibility of 'establishing military colonies'—a revealing phrase which suggests that the motive in adopting this Zhou Li ideal was rather remote from the 'proto-Communist' motivation with which the Taipings have since been credited.

The rules for election of local government were not applied. Some Taiping commanders encouraged local people to recommend candidates for local office, but as this happened only in the later stages of the rebellion, when the rebels had come to be feared and hated, the quasi-electoral system was worth little; by then no one of integrity or ability would serve them if he could avoid it. As for the common ownership of land, the idea appears in the 1853 land system document itself only to disappear; only one other surviving document alludes to it. No attempt was made to apply it. Perhaps it was simply taken up with the rest of the Zhou Li institutions and included pro forma.

One cannot build on this slender foundation the conclusion that the Taiping regime was socialist. A hierarchically organized theocratic tyranny which proposes to maintain itself by confiscating the entire surplus of the working population is scarcely to be called socialist. The facts of Taiping power in any case differed substantially from its theories. Six men, among whom Hong Xiuquan was only *primus inter pares*, divided power among them. Hong's title was Sovereign; the rest were wangs (kings). Each wang had his own administration. Among them Yang Xiuqing, the charcoal-burner, quickly achieved precedence, and his administration came to enjoy authority over the others; but this authority depended on Yang's personal pre-eminence, partly the result of the early death in battle of Feng Yunshan and Xiao Chaogui the faggot-seller, and partly of his successful claim to independent divine revelation.

It was a system far from egalitarian. An elaborate hierarchy developed in which officials at every level enjoyed the power of life and death over those below. Ritual, extravagant traditional symbolism of rank and office, and elaborate sumptuary legislation soon appeared. The leaders built themselves elaborate palaces. Even while the segregation of the sexes was still strictly applied to the rank and file, the Taiping leaders allowed themselves harems of a size determined by rank. In spite of Taiping profession of belief in equality of the sexes, women were bestowed as rewards for victory. Yet for the rank and file adultery was punished by death.

The claim of the Taipings to be Christian was hotly disputed by missionaries and others. Yet their adoption of an ancient Chinese theory of social and political organization does not of itself show that the Taipings were not Christian; the association of Christianity with Zhou Li institutions is no more strange than its association with the Roman and Byzantine empires, medieval feudalism and modern industrial society.

Hong Xiuquan believed in the Christian God. He acclaimed Christ as the Saviour. He based his teaching on the Bible. He practised baptism. He sought to impose on his followers a strict code of moral conduct drawn from Protestantism at its most austere. On these grounds he must be accepted as a Christian of a kind, but what damned Hong Xiuquan in the eyes of Western missionaries was the position which he allotted to himself in the Christian scheme of things. He claimed to be an independent source of Christian revelation, and to have been adopted as the second son of God. He acknowledged Yang Xiuqing's claim to be a third, and accepted that Yang was—or was possessed by—the Holy Spirit. To most nineteenth-century Christians such claims were both blasphemous and ludicrous. Yet as T. T. Meadows, the first historian of the Taipings, pointed out, many Christian mystics had expressed their religious experiences in similarly concrete terms, while young Chinese introduced to the Bible as literal truth would find no lack of precedents there for such adventures.

The religious ideas which Hong took from Christianity were quite alien to those dominant in China. He preached a strict monotheism, opposed both to the secular morality of educated Chinese and to the pantheism of popular religion. He insisted on the right of all men, not just the Emperor, to worship Heaven, and he preached the brotherhood of man on the grounds that all men (and women) were God's children. He extended this idea of brotherhood to people of all nations. His God was a God of equality, freedom, and universal love.

Yet it would be an equally reasonable view of Hong's religious development to say that Christian theory simply acted as the spark to bring to life buried aspects of Chinese belief. The classics included certain early beliefs in which Tian, 'Heaven', had some of the characteristics of the Judaeo-Christian God. This personification of Heaven could feel compassion and anger, was father and protector, and was the source of moral retribution. The influence of the secular morality of Confucius had relegated these ideas to the background of Chinese thought, but they were never repudiated, and the emperors of China continued, once a year, to sacrifice to Tian on the Altar of Heaven.

A second strand of thought from ancient times which chimed in with Christianity was Mozi's concept of universal brotherhood in which there were no degrees of love. Confucians condemned this as unrealistic, arguing that altruism could only be a much weakened reflection of the natural affections of the family. Mozi's work nevertheless continued to be read; indeed the ideal of a universal sympathy, if not love, which would be objective because undiscriminating, actually became central to Confucian thought. There are unmistakable verbal parallels with Mozi in one of the major Taiping documents (the 'Proclamation on the Origin of Principles for the Enlightenment of the Age'). One could thus argue that the Christian ideas which Hong found in the 'Good Words' pamphlet simply served to form a new pattern of existing Chinese ideas in Hong's mind.

There is, however, another twist in the relations of Christian to Taiping ideas. Between Christianity and the classics there lay the popular Chinese tradition of resistance expressed in the vernacular novels and organized in the secret societies. That the Taipings were influenced by this tradition is beyond doubt. References to the novels are frequent in their documents. Much of the symbolism of Hong's vision—magic sword and magic mirror, esoteric books, the Heavenly Net and the Earthly Trap—comes straight from the popular novels. And these novels were also the source of secret-society beliefs and rituals. The Peach-Garden Oath of mutual loyalty, taken by the three heroes of *The Romance of the Three Kingdoms*, was the model for all secret-society oaths.

The idea of brotherhood gained much of its emotional force from the novels. And the idea that Heaven bestows the mandate of the Empire loomed much larger in the 'little tradition' of the novels and the secret societies than in the 'great tradition' of Confucian scholarship. It is in the ritual documents of the Triads and other societies that one finds associated the ideas of Heaven as a father, of Heaven as the legitimator of government, of the Tian Guo or Heavenly Kingdom and the Tai Ping millennium, of equality between high and low, and of the brotherhood of men.

Many secret societies were also passionately nationalist. The main groups then in existence—the White Lotus society, the Heaven and Earth society (the Triads), and the Elder Brother society—had all been founded or revitalized as part of an anti-Manchu underground. So close is the parallel between some of the ideas of Hong and those of the nationalist secret societies that some authors have seen Hong as the greatest of the Triad leaders, and his rebellion as the climax of the Triad movement. This is certainly not literally true; Hong condemned the Triads for their futile adherence to the centuries-dead Ming cause, and he spurned them because they had lost their ideals and sunk into crime. Later, when they had nevertheless flocked to the Taiping standard in vast numbers, the old Guangxi God-Worshippers affirmed that it was Triad greed and cruelty which had ruined the cause. Yet the profound influence of the secret societies on Hong's thought is unmistakable. It is certain that he had passed through the ritual initiation of the Triads.

The last dimension of Chinese experience which may have been related to the Hakka's interpretation of Christianity is represented by south Chinese popular religious practices. The religion of the remote mountain areas was shamanistic. This may have reflected the continued influence of the aboriginal peoples of the area. Trance and possession by spirits were features of this religion, but while Christian theologians had quickly come to identify possession with evil spirits, according to Chinese beliefs possession was usually good. From this came the ecstatic dimension of Taiping Christianity.

The course of the rebellion

Even before the proclamation of Taiping Tianguo at Jintian, the Beijing government had learned of the alarming concentration of God-Worshippers and of their successful resistance to local imperial forces. Lin Zexu was recalled from disgrace and ordered south to deal with them, but died *en route* in November 1850. A former governor-general of Canton replaced him, but he died in May 1851. A Grand Secretary (Saishanga) was then appointed. The delay gave the Taiping forces a breathing space, for although the local Green Standard army (indigenous Chinese, as distinct from Manchu) out-numbered them ten to one, and river pirates who had joined the imperial service had blockaded the West River, the fierce valour of Hong's followers discouraged their enemies from attempting to do more than contain them. It was a classical insurgency situation, in which 'decayed tapsters and serving men' faced men who 'knew what they fought for and loved what they knew'.

After a month hemmed in at Jintian the Taipings broke through and fought their way to the town of Yongan, which they captured on 25 September 1851 and where they remained for three months, sustained by rich land-owners hostile to the Manchus. The imperialists invested the town. The insurgents' gunpowder was exhausted, but they cut their way out with the sword and annihilated the pursuit. They then marched to the city of Guilin and attacked it, the Hakka women racing their menfolk with the scaling ladders to be first into the city. Guilin, however, held out. The Taipings did not yet have the capacity to take well-fortified cities; that had to wait for the adherence to their cause of the miners of Hunan. They turned away from the city and marched north over the mountains to the head-waters of the Xiang River, the great tributary of the Yangzi which drains Hunan province.

Here on the upper Xiang River they met their first serious check, at the hands of forces which were in the end—though only after thirteen years of further fighting—to destroy them. Jiang Zhongyuan, one of the gentry of Hunan, had organized a force of 'braves' to deal with the rebellions which had persisted in the province since risings of the 1830s led by Miao aborigines. His braves were in the vicinity. On 10 June 1852 they met the Taipings at Soyi Ford. One-fifth of the insurgent force was destroyed. Here it was that Feng Yunshan was killed.

The rebels then faced a strategic decision: whether to retreat into Guangxi or to press on towards the Yangzi. Yang Xiuqing counselled advance. Local supporters helped the Taiping army to evade Jiang Zhongyuan's braves, guiding the rebels through the mountain passes. With this decision made, the rebels issued a proclamation appealing for the support of the Chinese people. The appeal, though couched in religious terms, was to nationalism against the corruption and rapacity of the Manchu regime. It contained no mention of land or of landlordism.

The rebels reached the Yangzi at Changsha, but the check at Soyi Ford had allowed the city to organize its defence under another leader of the Hunan braves, Lo Pingchang. Although Taiping miners breached the walls, Changsha's small force of defenders—6,000 to the Taipings' 40,000—held out until imperial reinforcements arrived.

Thwarted at Changsha, the insurgents faced their second strategic decision: whether to press on northwards and attack Beijing, or to swing east and establish themselves on the Yangzi. Yang Xiuqing at first favoured the bolder course, but doubts were raised as to whether the route north could sustain a force which, with women and children, now numbered about a quarter of a million. The question was perhaps decided by the adherence to the cause of a local shipowner, Tang Zhengcai, who put his vessels at the disposal of the

Taipings, and so enabled them to seize the shipping of the river and raise a fleet of 26,000 vessels large and small. Possession of this formidable water force was an irresistible attraction; yet the consequent decision to head east instead of north may in the end have been fatal.

The cities of the river below Changsha proved ill-defended. Wuhan was taken easily. When large imperial reinforcements were hurried to the spot the Taipings abandoned it and attacked downstream. The strategic cities of Jinjiang and Anqing were taken, and China's second capital, Nanjing, lay exposed. Some 17,000 defenders faced twenty times that number of insurgents whose ranks had been multiplied by the adherence of the Triads of the area, as well as by conscription. Taipings disguised as Buddhist monks infiltrated the city, while adherents from among the miners of Hunan breached the wall, and a tide of loose-haired, red-turbaned rebels, 'several (Chinese) miles wide and deep', poured into Nanjing.

The Taipings then launched two great expeditions designed to conquer China. One went north to attack Beijing. The other went west to consolidate the rebels' hold on the Yangzi and to penetrate Sichuan. The wisdom of this strategy was doubtful. Had they launched their whole force north they would probably have overturned the dynasty. On the other hand, had they concentrated all their troops in the Yangzi area, destroyed the two great imperial military camps already established north and south of Nanjing, taken advantage of the seizure of Shanghai by a secret society, the Short Swords, to occupy it while the powers were still hostile to Beijing, and then recaptured the cities of the middle Yangzi area (Wuhan, Nanchang and Changsha), they could have created a powerful southern empire which would have attracted all those in the north who preferred a native Chinese government. Instead they compromised. They left the imperial camps untouched, they ignored invitations to co-operate from the Shanghai Short Swords, and they split their forces in three in order at once to hold Nanjing, attack Beijing, and retake the middle Yangzi.

The western expedition was only partly successful. It failed to hold Wuhan, but it re-established Taiping control of Jinjiang and Anqing, the two towns which controlled the water route from the south-west to Nanjing. The northern expedition at first went well. Town after town fell as anti-Manchu groups within rose in support. Vast numbers of recruits joined the march. One hundred thousand men reached the Yellow River at Kaifeng. Here, however, the attack faltered. By one of these intrusive accidents of history, a freak rain storm soaked the rebels' gunpowder. During the delay that followed large forces of imperial troops and of local braves under gentry command were able to concentrate. Although in June 1853 the Taiping vanguard crossed the river, threatened Tianjin and threw the capital into panic, their force was spent. Autumn had arrived and the southerners were not equipped for a north Chinese winter. Reinforcements from Nanjing failed to win through. A long and bitterly contested withdrawal began. The retreating Taipings fought with extraordinary courage and tenacity, but cold, hunger, and incessant battle wore them down. The northern expedition army was entirely destroyed, and its captured leaders died by the thousand cuts. The Taipings had lost the initiative. There was now little hope that they could dislodge the Manchus. The best they could expect was to consolidate the south.

Between 1854 and 1856 the struggle for the Yangzi provinces swung back and forth; Wuhan was several times taken and recovered; Hunan and Hubei were penetrated but lost. The rebels took most of Jiangxi, although the provincial capital at Nanchang held out. By 1855 they also held much of Anhui and Jiangsu. Then in spring 1856 they destroyed the two great imperial camps, north and south of Nanjing. They were able to consolidate a strong quadrilateral of territory based on Luzhou, Jinjiang, Suzhou and Anqing. This area gave them annual revenues three times as great as the depleted resources of the Beijing government. They controlled the lower Yangzi. Had they created a convincing administration at Nanjing they could have tapped the resources of foreign trade; and the favour of the Western governments, then again at loggerheads with the Canton authorities, would certainly have followed.

Unfortunately the rebel government at Nanjing became less rather than more convincing as time passed. Hong Xiuquan took no part in affairs. His sanity came into doubt. He left decisions to Yang Xiuqing, and Yang's success in crushing the two imperial camps had swollen his ambition. Using his claim to independent religious revelation, he even ordered (in the voice of God the Father speaking through him) that Hong Xiuquan should be beaten for mistreating his wives, and Hong submitted. Fortunately the voice of God the Father then counselled mercy, and the Heavenly Emperor was spared the rod. Yang, however, pursued his moral advantages by demanding that he should be addressed in the term 'may you live ten thousand years', an honour hitherto reserved for the Sovereign.

Hong Xiuquan, at last made aware of Yang's ambitions, recalled the princes whom Yang had sent away on military expeditions. When Wei Changhui, the first to return, reached Nanjing he murdered Yang and his two brothers and massacred 20,000 of his followers. He then attacked his rival prince, Shi Dakai. Shi escaped over the wall in a basket, leaving his family in the city. Wei murdered them. He attacked the palace; but the Heavenly Emperor's Hakka wives fought him off until his own troops turned on him. Wei and his whole family and following were killed, and Shi Dakai was summoned back to assume the leadership.

Shi was an able man, both as commander and as administrator. He was the only one of the Taiping princes who made any serious attempt to rehabilitate the regions which his armies occupied. It is possible that he might have stopped the rot and revived the movement. Two of Hong Xiuquan's five original princes had died in battle, and two by assassination. Shi was the last.

Hong, however, no longer dared to trust any one man. While promoting Shi to supreme civil authority, at the same time he began to listen to the counsels of his own two opium-addicted elder brothers, who were corrupt, vicious and jealous of their exclusion from high office. Shi remained only a few months and then took the major part of the Taiping forces and marched west. This was not an act of desertion; Hong continued until the end to recognize Shi as a prince, while Shi himself continued to acknowledge his allegiance. His aim was to renew the rebellion, not to repudiate it. He raised vast new forces among the Triads of the south, and sought to conquer Hunan and Hubei; but he was forced ever further south-west, hemmed in, and finally betrayed by aborigines.

With the removal of any firm hand from control in Nanjing, the imperial government could now scarcely lose, provided it could replace with resolute officers and well-trained forces the pusillanimous and imbecile commanders who had first faced the rebellion.

New resistance to the Taipings had begun in Hunan. The rebels had been worsted by Jiang Zhongyuan's Hunan braves at Soyi Ford. They had been three times beaten back from the breached walls of Changsha by similar gentry-led local levies. The organizers of these levies were not career bureaucrats and members of the national establishment, but men of merely local reputation or none. Jiang Zhongyuan, the victor of Soyi Ford, had failed the metropolitan examination three times, and had been merely an 'expectant' director of local schools until the success of his militia against a local rebellion in 1847 won him a district magistracy. His defence of Changsha brought him the governorship of Anhui. In his origins, and in his rapid rise to high office in spite of failure in the examinations, he was typical of the new generation of leaders who were to arise out of the Taiping turmoil. He himself, however, did not live to join them. He committed suicide after defeat in the battle in which the Taipings took Luzhou, the key to south Anhui.

The emergence of such men from obscurity to mount a stubborn, even fanatical, struggle against the heretical Taipings was not accidental. They represented a movement. Its members had reacted against the arid and pedantic scholarship which had been the only safe intellectual pursuit during the Qian Long reign-period, and revived the essential concern of Confucianism with public affairs and public morals. In their generation disorder was the greatest problem; therefore their revived Confucianism was concentrated on the question of the restoration of harmony. The future anti-Taiping leaders were already associated in this movement of thought. The master–pupil relationships of this Confucian revival dominated the command structure of the new militia. The textbook of the movement, as far as the suppression of disorder is concerned, was the work (1582–7) of a Ming writer, Qi Jiguang, who had evolved means of dealing with the Japanese pirate raids of his time. There is evidence that the Taiping's military administration owed something to the same author. His main innovation was a military structure in which subordinates were in close personal relations with their superiors in a sort of quasi-feudal system of hierarchical loyalties. Such a form of organization was the antithesis of Chinese military tradition, which sought to impose an impersonal bureaucratic structure of military command, precisely in order to avoid the creation of dangerous personal loyalties. It was, however, to this model that the Hunan gentry leader Zeng Guofan turned, not without occasioning alarm in Beijing. His group of scholar-reformers was known as the Jingshi School (the School of Statesmanship) and had its centre at Changsha, the provincial capital of Hunan. Changsha from this time on was a centre first of reform and later of revolution. In Canton, Ruan Yuan's new academy (the Xue-hai Tang) was engaged in similar pursuits, although unlike the Changsha group its staff was entirely local (and from a Beijing point of view perhaps rather alarmingly so).

Another group consisted of scholars identified with the New Text interpretation of Confucianism—intense, quasi-religious, uncompromisingly puritanical. Lin Zexu was an adherent; so was Wei Yuan, the foremost writer on practical policy of his generation, who was exceptional in his realization that the critical condition of China was due largely to new problems which demanded new responses. Some have argued that the activities of these reforming scholars indicate a renaissance of Chinese public morality. At the level of scholarship their writings certainly show that Chinese thought was then by no means as bound by tradition as is generally thought. At the level of substantive reform, however, they were too few to arrest the continued decline of the dynasty.

Out of the Taiping crisis arose two men who were to become China's greatest statesmen in the following years. The first was Li Hongzhang. A graduate of the metropolitan examinations (a *jinshi*), and a protégé of Zeng Guofan, like his mentor he organized irregualr forces to oppose the rebels, in his home province of Anhui. By 1862 he was Acting Governor of the province, and by 1870 he was to hold the double appointment of Governor-General of Zhili and Superintendent of Trade for the Northern Ports; in this position he dominated China's foreign relations, combining a realistic acceptance of China's weakness with an attempt to increase national strength through a programme of limited industrialization. The second, Zuo Zongtang, rose to prominence in a similar way in Zhejiang. He was to go on to put down Muslim risings in the north-west by a policy which included the creation of an arsenal and a woollen mill and the establishment of military colonies. By these efforts he was able to ensure continued Chinese control of the passes on the frontier with Russia.

Before the war with Great Britain and then the Taiping Rebellion superseded all other policy concerns, meanwhile, the most urgent problem was the state of national revenue. There were three problems, assuming no possibility of fundamental changes in the system of taxation: the decay of the Grand Canal which bore the 'grain tribute', a special levy on the rich rice lands of the lower Yangzi; the breakdown of the official salt monopoly; and the state of the land tax which had become quite arbitrary as a result of the increasing imposition of supplementary local taxes on top of the regular land tax, fixed at its existing level in perpetuity as an act of imperial benevolence by the Kang Xi Emperor (1662–1723). The reform of these three institutions was the touchstone of the efforts of the Jingshi scholars. They succeeded in reforming the salt gabelle. On the other hand they failed in their attempt to have the transport of the grain tribute diverted to the sea route from the Canal, which was not only physically decayed but was also hopelessly tangled up in the corrupt vested interests of the officials and of the secret societies which controlled the labour force. Reform of the land tax also failed, as it was to fail again and again, up to and including the efforts to reform it of the Nationalist government of the 1930s. The only substantial achievement of the reformers was to contain rebellion, but the anti-insurgency institutions which they created did not produce—as they had hoped—a new level of public morality and efficiency.

In 1852 the Qing court sent Zeng Guofan back to his home province with the title 'Commissioner for Local Defence'. Zeng was from a poor Hunan rural family. His father had been the first member of the family to graduate, and worked as a local teacher. Guofan became a *jinshi* in 1838, and two years later had the distinction of joining the Hanlin Academy. He soon became a leading member of the new circle of reform scholars. Muchanga, the most powerful minister of the Dao Guang Emperor (1821–51), shared this interest, and adopted Zeng Guofan as a protégé.

On reaching Hunan, Zeng was not content merely to accept separate militia groups operating in their own localities. His policy was to build them into a mobile professional force. He sought officers of Confucian convictions and plain manners, and with the ability to handle civilians as well as soldiers. They were given the same ranks as the Green Standard forces (the army composed of Chinese, as opposed to the Manchu banners), but were much better paid and were pensioned. Zeng chose the top commanders; they chose their subordinate officers, who in turn recruited the rank and file largely from their own villages. The recruits were hardy peasants of good character; they signed on formally, and their families were responsible for their loyalty. Military regulations forbade opium smoking, rape, gambling, brawling and membership of secret societies.

Zeng's greatest quality was patience. He had formed a long-term plan on his arrival in Hunan and he steadily made his preparations, refusing to be distracted by appeals for help from beleaguered colleagues. His troops were blooded in putting down a series of Triad risings in Hunan in 1853. Then in 1854 came his first serious action with the Taipings, who were once more threatening Changsha. The first brush was almost a disaster for Zeng. He lost half of his new fleet; but his troops rallied and in turn defeated the rebels. Changsha was saved and Zeng had proved the worth of his ideas to the provincial governor, who henceforth gave his full co-operation. But as Zeng's victories accumulated, the Court became alarmed that 'a mere commoner . . . by shouting a slogan . . . could rally over 10,000 followers'. Zeng did not get his expected promotion.

His policy involved four principles: a small, disciplined, high-quality force of high morale; a fleet to deprive the rebels of free movement on the Yangzi; steady pressure downstream—'all through history,' he wrote, 'the suppression of rebellion in Jiangnan has demanded that one should first control the upper river'; and, finally, he believed that time was on his side. In the early years, however, Zeng did not command more than a fraction of the available forces, and could not secure unity. Until the fratricide among the Taipings in Nanjing in 1856 it was the rebel forces which enjoyed unity of command. Yet, although in some areas Taiping control was extended in these years, thanks to Zeng's persistence in organizing an effective naval arm they gradually but surely lost control of the river above Qiujiang and so could no longer operate easily in Hunan and Hubei. Zeng also held the Boyang Lake and thus the water route into Jiangxi. Down-river, moreover, the imperial forces had succeeded in reoccupying the two great northern and southern camps. The Taipings could still achieve victories, but they did so now largely by weight of numbers, and these greatly increased numbers created an insoluble problem in their relations with the population; the necessity of supplying such hosts brought them more and more into conflict with the people.

The government forces were not only inferior in numbers. They were also short of revenue. The first units of braves were maintained by subscriptions from the gentry, but the sort of army Zeng sought to build required vastly more money than such voluntary assistance could provide. The sale of rank and office provided most of the funds in the earlier years. Later the *likin*, a new tax on the transit of goods, became the main source of revenue, while through his good relations with the governors of the Yangzi provinces (eventually some of these were his own men, appointed on his recommendation) Zeng was able to divert revenue normally due to Beijing.

In Nanjing, after the fratricide, an attempt was made to create a new rebel leadership. The forces were reorganized into four armies. New commanders were found, among them Li Xiucheng, probably the most able of all the Taiping generals. In 1858 he destroyed the great northern camp once more and defeated a Qing relief force from the great southern camp. He made an alliance with the Nian rebels in Anhui and with their assistance was able to re-establish control over the southern part of the province, the main source of supplies for Nanjing. At the same time, the attempts of the other Taiping armies to re-conquer the middle Yangzi ended in defeat when Zeng Guofan's fleet broke out of the Boyang Lake to take Jinjiang. This marked the end of Taiping naval power.

In 1859 the rebellion entered a new phase, with the arrival at Nanjing of Hong Rengan. A cousin of Hong Xiuquan, he had been among the original converts. When Hong and Feng had moved to Guangxi, Rengan being younger than the others had remained behind to look after family affairs. In 1852 he went to Hong Kong and became a Christian catechist. His relations with Protestant missionaries were close and from them he learned much about Western ways of life. He added to his classical Chinese education some knowledge of western mathematics and the sciences. In 1854 he made an attempt to reach Nanjing via Shanghai, but he could not convince the Short Sword rebels (who then held the city) of his identity. In 1859 he tried again and succeeded. Hong Xiuquan warmly welcomed him: the two had been brought up as brothers. Rengan was immediately given supreme power.

He had three aims: to purify Taiping Christianity, to launch a Westernized reform programme, and to extend rebel power to the coast and ally with the foreign powers. His Christianity was orthodox and well informed. He began patiently to correct the grosser errors of Hong Xiuquan, though never attempting to dispute the validity of the Heavenly Emperor's religious experience. His general policies were outlined in a long memorial which Hong Xiuquan accepted. His first aim was to restore Nanjing's power by the centralization of political and military authority, and by setting up an independent accounting system of the Western kind in order to eradicate corruption. He believed that central authority would be strengthened by the establishment of local elections, by the encouragement of newspapers and by the use of 'secret boxes' in which citizens could deposit their suggestions. He proposed that families should no longer be regarded as sharing the guilt of an individual member, and that individual rights should in general be upheld. He wanted the protection of children against infanticide and against being sold into service, and the abolition of foot-binding, extravagant ceremonial, and long nails. He advocated a government health programme, social relief for the disabled and distressed, and the creation of new charitable and educational institutions.

His economic programme looked forward to the building of highways, railways, and steamships; the promotion of mining; the establishment of banks, insurance companies, and a postal system; and the encouragement of scientific progress and of innovation protected by patents. In fact, he replaced Hong Xiuquan's Zhou Li utopia with a vision of practical development under democratic forms.

The realization of this vision required contact with the Western powers. In his military planning Rengan therefore looked east to Shanghai rather than west to Wuhan and Changsha. He was nevertheless well aware of the importance of holding the quadrilateral round Nanjing. Luzhou had by then been exposed by the treachery of Li Xiucheng's Nian allies, Anqing was under pressure from the Hunan braves, and the two great camps had again been restored by the imperialists.

Rengan could not easily enforce a united strategy on the Taiping commanders, whose first priority was the defence of their own supply areas. Li Xiucheng's troops lived off the area east of Nanjing, Chen Yucheng's army off the area round Anqing. Rengan's strategy had to take account of this position. The plan of campaign in which he reconciled these discordant interests was ingenious. Li Xiucheng would move further east into the coastal provinces; this would enlarge his own territorial base, but would also draw off imperial troops from the great southern camp. He would then swing back to crush the camp. With the pressure on Nanjing relieved, with increased supplies from Jiangsu and Zhejiang, and perhaps with steamships bought on the coast, an attack would then be launched to the south-west by Li Xiucheng moving up the right bank of the river, and Chen Yucheng moving parallel on the left bank, to meet at Wuhan, draw the imperial forces off Anqing, and re-establish control of the middle Yangzi. With the Taiping rear thus restored, the coastal areas would be attacked and the coastal cities occupied.

The first stage of the plan went well. Li Xiucheng took Hangzhou, and when a relieving force had left the southern camp he doubled back by forced marches and took the weakened camp by surprise. The expedition to the south-west was then launched, but failed. Li Xiucheng did not unite with Chen Yucheng; according to his own later account he found the river in spate, and could not even get messengers over, far less take his troops across. He turned aside into Jiangxi. Chen, left alone, was forced to withdraw. Anqing fell to the imperial forces and Li's subsequent conquests in the coastal areas were inadequate compensation. Both Zeng Guofan and Hong Rengan were in agreement that Li's decision to pull out of the Wuhan campaign was the most serious military error the Taipings had ever made.

The foreign powers and the Taipings

When Li, with a new army of Triads, recruited in Jiangxi, overran most of southern Jiangsu, again marched east and approached Shanghai the attitude of the foreign powers became for the first time a factor in the situation. Hitherto the question of neutrality or intervention had been largely theoretical. Foreign interests had not been directly threatened. The first foreign reactions to the rebellion had been generally favourable. It appeared to have begun from the resistance of Chinese Christians to religious persecution, and then broadened into a nationalist revolution. On both counts the rebels could expect Western sympathy. Governments, however, took a narrower view: only if the Taipings could set up a viable government, and if that government provided acceptable conditions for trade, would it enjoy favour. The religious issue cut no ice with the British Board of Trade.

When the Taipings took Nanjing in 1853 the British were wrestling with the stubborn resistance of the Canton authorities to the full implementation of the 1843 Treaty of Nanjing. Any prospect of an alternative to the existing dynasty seemed inviting. Sir George Bonham, Governor of Hong Kong and Chief Superintendent of Trade, went in person to Nanjing within weeks of the Taiping occupation.

He was not impressed. He saw nothing to suggest that the rebels were capable of founding an effective government. He saw little sign of trade. As far as future relations between Nanjing and foreign governments were concerned. Taiping messages were conflicting. While on the one hand the foreigners were greeted as brothers in Christ, on the other the formal proclamations of the new government were expressed in the traditional and unacceptable language of universal empire (the only diplomatic language they possessed), and so cast doubt on their fraternal professions. If the tolerant Bonham could take a sour view of the rebels in 1853, when they were more favourably regarded than they would ever be again, it is not surprising that by 1860 foreign governments were hostile, or that opinion in the Treaty Ports offered little opposition to this hostility.

The first breach of neutrality did not express a change of policy. When in July 1860 Li Xiucheng's army took Songjiang, 25 miles from Shanghai, British troops were actually at that moment marching on Beijing in a third war which had proved necessary in order to enforce the treaty wrested from the unwilling Emperor in the second (see chapter 4). The decision to defend Shanghai against Li was not an expression of hostility to the Taipings, but simply of a determination to keep the rebels out of the city and prevent a repetition of the chaotic situation after 1853 when the Triad Short Swords had held it. Indeed the initiative in persuading the foreign governments to use their troops against the Taipings came not from foreign Treaty Port interests, but from Chinese refugee gentry and the Chinese trading community in Shanghai. Li Xiucheng was driven off with heavy casualties in a battle before the walls of Shanghai against British marines with artillery.

By then the situation was changing. The Treaty of Tianjin, just confirmed by the third war, in 1857 gave the British access to the Yangzi and to Wuhan and the rebellion was preventing the peaceful enjoyment of this access. A few months later Yixin (Prince Gong) came to power in Beijing. He was prepared to listen to the advice of the British envoy, Frederick Bruce. Bruce in turn fully supported Yixin, and was determined to see the Taipings destroyed. His dispatches show an unrelenting hostility towards them. It was entirely due to Bruce that Hong Rengan's plans for the development of China, on lines which should have been of great interest to any British government of the time, received no serious attention. Bruce dismissed Rengan's reform memorial. *A*

New Work for Aid in Government, a copy of which had been sent to each of the foreign consuls-general, as 'a crafty device to conciliate the support and sympathy of the missionary body at the time when the insurgents meditated the seizure of Shanghai'.

There was by then much less reason than before to suspect Taiping intentions. Their tariff policy was reasonable. Under Li Xiucheng the Suzhou silk trade actually expanded. The British were permitted to buoy the Yangzi channel, and were freely given a coaling station on the Yangzi in Taiping territory. Foreigners were less molested, on the whole, by rebel soldiers than by the Hunan braves, against whose hostility even Bruce himself was forced to protest to Zeng Guofan. Hong Rengan voluntarily granted foreigners a sort of extraterritorial jurisdiction, putting his missionary mentor Isaachar Roberts (whom he had invited to Nanjing) in charge of a special court. He asked for missionaries to come to Suzhou and offered them freedom to preach in the interior. Around Shanghai and in Ningbo the Taiping authorities behaved with extraordinary forbearance in the face of provocations, inspired by Bruce, which disgusted even the Treaty Port communities themselves.

Bruce's implacable hostility had the further serious consequence of weakening Rengan's position at the Nanjing court. There he was dependent on the favour of an Emperor whose mind had virtually failed, and he was at the mercy of the Emperor's vicious brothers. He had scant control over the Taiping generals. A very little foreign recognition and foreign assistance would have gone a long way to strengthen the hand of the only man in China whose vision of the country's future coincided with that of the Westerners. But thanks almost entirely to Bruce, Britain was now committed, against the better judgement of many of its servants in China, to support of the conservative Manchus.

In June 1861 Bruce wrote to Russell the Foreign Secretary arguing that the rebellion was destructive and futile as well as blasphemous and immoral, and recommending that neutrality be ended. T. T. Meadows, the most persistent defender of the Taipings in the British service and undoubtedly better informed than any of his colleagues, protested to Russell against this view. He was forbidden to have any further contact with Nanjing.

The first consequence was that a force of Filipinos, Chinese, and British deserters raised by the American mercenary Ward, already employed by the imperial authorities in Jiangsu against the Taipings (a force hitherto regarded with suspicion and irritation by the British, who had twice arrested Ward), was now countenanced and encouraged. The French formed a similar force.

The rebels had agreed not to attack Shanghai for a year in the hope that they could meanwhile persuade the foreign powers to revert to neutrality. When the year was up Li Xiucheng again approached the city and, after a request to the foreigners to remain neutral, attacked. Ward's 'Ever-Victorious Army' (his force had been given this flattering title by the grateful Chinese authorities), assisted by British and French troops, repulsed the attack. Li successfully counter-attacked and cleared the way to Shanghai, which he assaulted twice more in June and August 1862. But foreign artillery proved decisive. The British and the French were now fully committed to intervention. Captain (later General) Charles Gordon was seconded from the British army to command the force created by Ward, with full supplies of British arms, including heavy artillery.

Yet foreign intervention was of a limited nature and short duration. This, however, was not due to reluctance on the part of the foreign governments. It was the Chinese officials who set the limits, using both their own authority in the area and constant appeals to Beijing to prevent any dangerous escalation of foreign involvement. Li Hongzhang, who had risen to power in Anhui and Jiangsu (in much the same way as Zeng Guofan in Hunan), along with Zuo Zongtang in Zhejiang, were forced by their desperate circumstances to accept foreign help; but Zeng Guofan, who had been given extraordinary powers after the second fall of the great southern camp and was now in supreme command of the whole war against the rebels, was determined that while foreign forces might be allowed to assist in the coastal areas they would not be permitted to take part in the main campaign against Nanjing.

Given the consequently limited nature of foreign intervention, it would be difficult to argue that this intervention was the decisive factor in the defeat of the rebellion. In fact no intervention took place as long as there seemed to be any hope that the rebels could win. It was Taiping weakness and the perpetuation of the disorder which this weakness entailed rather than Taiping strength which the British feared.

The Taiping forces were stretched too far. While they were operating in Jiangsu and Zhejiang, Zeng Guofan's brother, Zeng Guoquan, met little resistance as he moved in on Nanjing. Luzhou had already fallen in 1862, leaving Nanjing exposed to attack from the west. Zeng Guoquan's troops established themselves boldly under the walls of Nanjing, where the Hunan braves dug themselves in and resisted forty days of Taiping bombardment with rockets and explosive shells. Li Xiucheng returned, bringing his entire family with him as a pledge of loyalty. But by the winter the walls had been mined and breached. Although the imperial forces had failed to enter against the fierce resistance of the defenders, who were now reduced to the original hard core of Guangxi converts, prolonged resistance was impossible. Li Xiucheng urged the Heavenly Emperor to leave the city. He refused. In July 1864 he died, whether poisoned by his own hand or as a result of disease brought on by the privations of the siege is not known.

In that same month Nanjing fell. So ended the longest, fiercest and most destructive war of the nineteenth-century world. A million insurgents were under arms. An area as great as that of France and Germany combined was devastated and much of it depopulated. No quarter was given, and none asked for; a hundred thousand Taipings died in Nanjing rather than surrender. Almost none survived.

Their religion died with them and left no trace. Their projected political and social revolution, if that was what they had truly intended, was not seriously attempted, although sheer devastation and loss of life did actually reduce the power of the landlords somewhat in the main areas of fighting. The Taipings, however, left behind them the myth of a mass uprising inspired (apparently) by millennial egalitarian dreams, to provide China's later socialist leaders with the substance of a heroic tradition; but by the same token the struggle created an alternative opposing myth, of the ability and the duty of Confucians to resist such insurrection. If Hong Xiuquan inspired Mao Zedong, Zeng Guofan equally inspired Chiang Kaishek.

4

Conflict with the Western powers

1843–1861

Anglo-Chinese relations, 1843–1857

In our concern with the events of the Taiping Rebellion, we have passed over the events of China's relations with the foreign powers from 1843 to 1860. We now return to these.

Before 1843 the community of foreign merchants at Canton had argued that expansion of trade with China was prevented only by certain political obstacles. These had now been removed. Traders had access, although only indirectly, to the most populous parts of China, and so to a market which, in the number of potential consumers, was as large as British India. It was not unnaturally assumed that in China the products of the power-looms of Lancashire would compete successfully with the products of China's handlooms.

British traders plunged into this new market with high hopes and a total lack of market research. Before the new ports were even officially opened they were swamped with Indian cotton yarn and British cotton piece-goods. The merchants combined to try to maintain prices, but as more ships hove up over the horizon they were forced to sell at heavy loss. After an initial expansion in 1843, trade contracted. It was not until 1856 that the legal trade once more achieved the level of 1843. The Select Committee of the House of Commons on Commercial Relations with China, 1847, accepted that trade had languished and that losses of 30–40 per cent were normal. The Lancashire branch of Jardine & Matheson, Matheson & Scott—who should have made a profit if anyone could—wrote to their parent firm in Hong Kong in 1847 that 'all our transactions in your quarter have so far been attended by heavy loss'.

The general opinion was that China's balance of trade severely limited her capacity to buy British goods. The markets for her tea and silk were not unlimited. Attempts to introduce Chinese sugar and grass-cloth fibre to the international market failed.

In 1852 Rutherford Alcock, the conscientious consul at Shanghai, wrote a report which explained with despairing candour the nature of British trade with China. He explained how Britain's commerce with China and India, then worth a total of £23 million, depended entirely on the illegal opium trade as the source of funds with which Chinese produce was bought and with which India settled her trading account with Britain:

What cordial relations of amity or commerce are possible under such conditions? Our whole trade is one of sufferance and compulsion, and by force alone can be maintained . . .

The same merchant who builds a large and splendid house of business at one of the five ports under the provisions of the Treaty, for the ostensible sale of our manufactured goods, and for the purchase in return of tea and silk . . . keeps a large and well-armed opium ship some short distance below the anchorage to supply him by the proceeds with funds at an advantageous rate wherewith to purchase these same teas. He makes an order for drug, which circulates with the same facility as a bank-note, and with that (added to the smaller quantity of longcloths sold) he concludes his bargain for a chop of tea or a hundred bales of silk; and not seldom at a rate which leaves no margin of fair profit. The only profit is made either on opium, the tea, or the silk, and only in prosperous seasons upon all. Rarely indeed to any amount upon our million and a half of manufactures.

Alcock's conclusion was that the opium trade should be legalized, at a tax sufficiently low to make smuggling unprofitable, but sufficiently high to discourage consumption. This at least would have removed the anomaly that in every transaction, one part was legal and the other illegal, with all the corruption and violence which were bound to follow.

The implicit assumption in his letter was that the legal import trade was limited simply by the loss of silver spent on the import of opium. Most contemporary comment was in agreement; the Select Committee on Commercial Relations with China reached this conclusion, British governments accepted it, and the new and influential *Economist* publicized the view. There was one dissenting voice. Mitchell, in the service of the new Hong Kong government, had in 1854 submitted to Sir George Bonham, as Governor of Hong Kong, a report on his own investigation of the British textile trade with China. Bonham, for unknown reasons, did not forward it to Westminster; it remained unread in the Hong Kong archives until the Earl of Elgin as envoy to China found it in the course of the Second Anglo-Chinese War—a war which conceivably might never have occurred had Mitchell's conclusions been known to the British Government and accepted then, as they were to be thereafter, as proof that the prospect of a vast Chinese market for British cottons was an illusion which British policy should not encourage.

Mitchell began by pointing out that of some £15 million representing the legal trade with China in 1854, and the revenue accruing from it, only a mere £1.5 million was represented by exports to China of British manufactures, a sum little larger than British exports to Naples. And the exports to China had actually decreased by £250,000 since 1843. He then gave his analysis. It contradicted the assumption that the Chinese hand-loom weaver was bound to fall victim to the superior cost-efficiency of the steam-driven loom:

The first thing that should have been borne in mind at the opening of our new trade in 1843 was this: that we were about to start in competion with the greatest manufacturing people in the world . . .

I would first of all observe that during nearly ten years of uninterrupted residence in this country . . . I have never yet seen a Chinaman wearing a garment of our longcloth, who had to get his daily bread by his daily labour . . . and the bare fact proves that there is something radically ill-adapted in the nature of our goods to the great bulk of this population . . .

Our longcloth is partially worn by the wealthier classes throughout the maritime cities, as indoor dishabille . . . but . . . they wear it because it happens to fall in their way and is cheaper, for such subordinate purposes, than their own materials . . .

Nothing could more clearly evince the light estimation in which our shirtings are held by this people . . . than the fact that the silk of those years went home to London packed in wrappers of Manchester longcloth!

The Chinese only take our goods at all because we take their teas . . . we bring the Chinese nothing that is really popular among them, except our opium . . . Opium is the only 'open sesame' to their stony hearts, and woe betide our trade the day we meddle with it.

The best mode of illustrating the question will be by a single example taken from the province with which I am best acquainted, that of Fukien, and I would beg to direct the particular attention of the Board of Trade to the beautiful and simple economy of it . . .

The Fukien farmer, among his other crops, raises a certain proportion of sugar . . . This sugar he disposes of in the spring to a trader at the nearest seaport, who ships it to Tientsin or some other northern port during the summer monsoon, undertaking to pay the farmer for it, part in money, and part in northern cotton when his junk returns . . .

When the harvest is gathered, all hands in the farmhouse . . . turn to carding, spinning and weaving this [northern] cotton, and out of this homespun stuff, a heavy and durable material, . . . they clothe themselves; and the surplus they carry to the market town . . . the manufacture varying from the coarsest dungaree to the finest nanking, all . . . costing the producer nothing beyond the raw material, or rather the sugar he exchanged for it.

So far back as 1844 I sent musters of this native cloth, of every quality, home to England, with the prices specified, and my correspondents assured me that they could not produce it in Manchester at the rates quoted, much less lay it down here . . .

The further history of British exports of cottons to China bears out Mitchell's analysis; the trade was never more than a small fraction of the magnitude of British trade in the same goods with India, and never more than a trivial percentage of total British exports of cotton goods. The Chinese peasant-weaver defeated Lancashire's machines.

If the high British expectations of an expanding and profitable trade were disappointed, so too were the equally buoyant hopes that a friendly *modus vivendi* could be developed on the basis of the Nanjing treaty. Events were, in fact, to repeat the pattern of before the Opium War by which amicable intentions were transformed into frustration, threats, and military action.

At first the auguries seemed favourable. At Beijing Muchanga supported Qiying throughout the Nanjing negotiations and continued to support him when he was commanded to remain at Canton in charge of foreign relations. Qiying persisted in the policy of attempting to soften British demands by professions of warm personal friendship for the British representative. These professions, as he was careful to inform Beijing, were quite insincere: he was merely playing the Confucian *gan-qing* (warm sentiments) card, the only promising card in China's very weak hand. Yet Qiying was undoubtedly sincere in his belief that good personal relations could allay the barbarian threat. In committing himself to this policy he risked accusations of treasonable relations with the enemy, and so risked his life. One cannot in these circumstances doubt the strength of his convictions. And one must note that they were matched on the British side by similar opinions. Both sides—for the moment—regarded the development of day-to-day amicable relations as the solution.

It was the population of Canton who ruined this prospect by their implacable opposition to British entry into the city. There is an irony here: free entry into and residence within the ports of trade was one of the conditions upon which the British insisted strongly, and yet at all the other ports the new foreign communities soon showed a preference for the suburbs, where they could maintain more easily their own standards of public hygiene and where they would be beyond the incessant noise of the Chinese city.

Such were the simple motives which led to the founding of the Foreign Concessions. It was circumstances at Shanghai, and not imperialist plans, which led to these small areas of foreign residence being withdrawn from Chinese administration. Before 1853 the foreign settlement there consisted of about 150 establishments. There were no Chinese residents other than servants and service traders. Then in 1853 the Taipings took Nanjing. Refugees of all classes poured into Shanghai. Soon after, the Chinese city was seized by the Short Sword rebels, and much of its resident population sought protection in the foreign area. Within a year there were 8,000 Chinese residences, and no means of providing for either sanitation or public order. The consuls therefore came to an arrangement with the local Chinese authorities by which the foreign lessees of land in the foreign area would meet once a year to consider such matters, and that this assembly would take the power to levy rates to cover the costs of providing roads, bridges, sanitation, and police. In this way the International Concession was created (the French, preferring to act independently, set up their own concession). When the precedent was followed at other Treaty Ports the negotiations were at government level, and this gave rise to the false assumption that they represented a deliberate and sinister invasion of Chinese sovereignty. Combined with extraterritoriality, which was also applied to subjects of the Western powers who were Chinese in race (and who outnumbered non-Chinese among the foreign community which was withdrawn from Chinese jurisdiction), in the long run the Concessions did result in an impairment of Chinese sovereignty within the small areas concerned (the largest of these areas was only about nine square miles), but no sinister imperialist motive was involved.

More important from this point of view was the permitted presence of foreign warships in the Treaty Ports. These could be, and were, used against Chinese citizens and on occasion against officials representing the Chinese Government. Yet one must not overestimate the political consequences; the gunboats were used to protect foreign nationals locally, and sometimes to exact reparation for injury done to them. They were not at this time used by the Western powers to put pressure on Chinese governments over policy matters, other than those concerned with the safety of foreign lives and property.

The foreigners had chosen to live outside the Chinese Treaty Ports. At Canton, however, the foreigners had no choice; the Cantonese would not let them inside, and so they had no opportunity to discover that perhaps here as elsewhere they would rather be outside.

The sources of Canton's furious hostility to the foreigners are not at all easy to determine. Such hostility had not proved to be general throughout the five ports. Indeed, in each port the experience of the British was different. At Shanghai the foreign traders were welcomed before the war had even ended. Relations were amicable enough at Amoy (Xiamen), until popular hostility was aroused by the evils of fraud and force attendant on the emigration of Chinese contract workers to the Guano Islands, and when these evils were allayed by co-operation between the British and Chinese governments, good relations were restored. At Ningbo there was no trouble but not much trade either. Of Fuzhou in the early years one cannot say that there were any relations at all. There was no trade. Only when the Triad rebellion at Canton in 1854 diverted tea supplies to the Fujian coast did some trade at Fuzhou begin.

At Canton the hostility generated during the war continued unabated. Part of the explanation may lie in the nature of the Cantonese themselves. They are not noted in China for their patience. They have always worn the cloak of Confucian deference rather lightly. Part of the explanation may lie in the ease with which in Canton a mob could be brought together. Sir John Davis, former East India Company super-cargo, pioneer sinologist, pre-war Superintendent of Trade, and post-war Governor of Hong Kong, exaggerated when he claimed that the Cantonese mob was 'the most vicious in the world'; but the mob existed and could be manipulated. Qiying himself reported as much to the throne.

The most probable explanation is that which the Cantonese themselves gave. They believed that China could have been successfully defended had the people been given arms. Further, they believed that proof of the effectiveness of popular military action had been demonstrated by Gough's apparent retreat from Canton. The movement to create a popular militia force, begun during the war, was continued. Qiying was faced with a city in arms, and was forced to appeal to the British to delay their entrance on the grounds, which were undoubtedly true, that he could not guarantee their safety. His government in Canton became steadily more unpopular nevertheless; he could justify in confidential memorials to the Court his apparently amicable personal relations with the foreigners, but he could not give such an explanation publicly. In 1847 an incident occurred which seriously weakened his position. Six British citizens, young clerks from merchant houses, went on a day's expedition up-river. On landing near a village they were attacked and murdered by the inhabitants. The British authorities demanded justice, and Qiying executed four of the villagers. To the British the murder of these young civilians was an act of barbarism; to the Cantonese, however, in their state of exalted patriotism, it was a justified act of war. Qiying's position was becoming intolerable; repeatedly he requested the permission of the Emperor to resign on the grounds of exhaustion and ill health, but was repeatedly refused. Then in February 1848 permission was at last given.

The date is significant. In 1847, the last instalment of the war indemnity having been paid, the British duly evacuated Zhoushan, which they had held as security. The threat of a British force stationed within striking distance of Nanjing was ended. From that date the relations between Britain and China deteriorated. Qiying was replaced by Xu Guangqin, who made public his sympathy with Cantonese hostility and who brought to an end all attempts at conciliation. He was not only permitted to do so by the Court but was loaded with honours for his resistance to foreign demands.

In 1850 the Dao Guang Emperor died. He was succeeded by his son under the reign title Xian Feng. He was only 19. As heir apparent—no doubt chafing at the power of Muchanga and encouraged in this by political rivals—he had already expressed his determination to resist the foreigners. Within a year both Muchanga and Qiying had been degraded. The British, in ignorance of Chinese conventions, had given the young Emperor an opportunity to get rid of both by addressing letters to them personally and so laying them open to a charge of seditious correspondence. In reality, however, the turning-point in policy had already arrived in 1847.

The British were not unduly perturbed. Relations elsewhere were acceptable, though the profits of trade had been disappointing. That they had not relinquished their hope of peaceful development was shown by an unusual appointment made to the consular service in China in 1847, an appointment which can only be explained by continued British faith in conciliation. That it was made by Palmerston, so much associated with the ready use of force to maintain British interests, makes it all the more significant. Dr John Bowring was appointed consul at Canton, in circumstances which indicate that this post—a humble one for so distinguished a man—was meant to be an apprenticeship for the Chief Superintendency. Bowring was not a career dip-lomat, but a West Country ironmaster. He was a man of wide culture and many languages who had been since 1830 Britain's principal international apostle of free trade. He was an evangelical in religion, the author of the still well-known hymn, 'In the Cross of Christ I Glory'. He had linked religion with commerce in an aphorism which will seem wholly blasphemous only to those who have forgotten Europe's mercantilist wars and the nineteenth-century hope that the end of mercantilism would mean the establishment of perpetual peace: 'Jesus Christ,' proclaimed Bowring, 'is Free Trade, and Free Trade is Jesus Christ.' In this spirit, he helped to found the Peace Society. He was well known in British intellectual life: he was one of Bentham's literary executors and had edited the first numbers of the *Westminster Review*; he was a friend of Mary Wollstonecraft Shelley.

Bowring accepted enthusiastically the current idea that the problems of relations with China could be solved by friendly day-to-day relationships over practical concerns. He believed that his talents and experience qualified him to achieve this, and his record supported the possibility. Yet he proceeded, within ten years, to bring about a second war with China almost single-handed, a war which disgusted his government by the triviality of its cause and the merchants by its ill timing, for trade had at last begun to be profitable.

Had Bowring served his consular probation in Shanghai instead of in the south, the subsequent history of British relations might have been different. In Shanghai, something like a *modus vivendi* was indeed being developed around a new institution, the Imperial Maritime Customs, which had not been antici-pated in the Treaty of Nanjing, was entirely the product of an emergency, and was at first regarded with deep suspicion by both the Chinese and British governments.

In its attempts at Nanjing to create a system acceptable to the Chinese, the British Government had imposed on British consuls in China the unprecedented responsibility of ensuring that British merchants met their tax obligations. This arrangement was explicitly stated to be a replacement for the abolished system of security merchants. In this way, the British conceded something to Chinese concepts of group responsibility. The consuls were also at first empowered to report to the Chinese authorities any case of smuggling by British subjects which came to their notice, and to seize and impound smuggled goods (which were meant to include opium); but as the other treaty powers imposed no such responsibility on their consuls Palmerston—invoking the most-favoured-nation clause—eventually relieved the British representatives of this charge.

When in 1853 the Taipings took Nanjing trade was paralysed and, silver being unobtainable, the foreign merchants were unable to pay their taxes on trade. In the same year, 1853, when Shanghai itself was seized by the Short Sword secret society the Chinese customs house ceased to operate. Consul Alcock ordered British merchants to pay their tariff dues into the consulate in cash or bills. The Chinese local authorities resisted this, but their attempt to solve the problem by setting up transit-duty stations inland was contrary to the treaty because this could have been used to circumvent the treaty tariff. On the British side the question was whether or not, under international law, customs duties were owed to a government which had ceased to govern the area concerned and could not offer protection. The Privy Council ruled that the duties were still owed; and it was with the promise of payment to Chinese authorities on the British IOUs held by the consul that Alcock was able to persuade the Chinese to accept the idea that the collection of duties should be supervised by a foreign appointee. It was in order to relieve honest traders from the disadvantage of having to compete with those who were willing to smuggle and able to do so through the absence (or the venality) of the Chinese customs officials—a possibility which threatened the basis of the treaty system. Three inspectors representing Britain, France and the United States were appointed, but the predominance of British trade put the real authority in the hands of the British inspector. Analogy with India, where the assumption of supervision of the Bengal revenues by the East India Company had proved to be the first step towards British political control, is tempting but misleading. Lord Clarendon, Palmerston's successor as Foreign Secretary, ruled firmly that the appointment of the inspectors, as employees of the Chinese Government, was entirely a matter for that government. They were thereafter so appointed, and proved faithful servants; some proved indeed to be more Chinese than the Chinese themselves in upholding the rights of the Empire.

This was the origin of the Imperial Maritime Customs, which were thereafter administered with a degree of honesty of which the Chinese magistracy at that time was regrettably incapable. The taxes on foreign trade which had hitherto gone for the most part into the pockets of local officials now reached the Government, to provide a new and ever-growing source of revenue. The inspectorate also provided advice based on a knowledge of Western interests and of international law. The customs service has been condemned by modern Chinese nationalists as yet another serious loss of Chinese sovereignty. It could perhaps be better seen as an example of means by which the benefits of modern administrative efficiency could be extended to pre-modern governments without a signficant loss of sovereignty.

The origins of the second war

It was not, however, until China had suffered further defeats that Beijing became reconciled to the creation of systematic co-operation of the kind foreshadowed by the new customs service. In fact China's policy after 1847 deliberately created a sort of 'Catch-22' for the foreign powers. The Emperor supported the policy of the Canton authorities of giving no interviews to foreigners except under duress; at the same time he ordered the authorities at the other ports to refer all matters of foreign policy to Canton.

An attempt was made to find a way out of this impasse by using the pretext of a forthcoming revision of the Treaty of Nanjing and of the parallel treaties made between China and powers other than Britain. The American Treaty of Wangxia provided for revision after twelve years, and Great Britain claimed the same right under the most-favoured-nation clause. In 1854 an attempt was made to open negotiations. Some of the provisions of Nanjing had not worked altogether well, and some of them had been evaded by the Chinese authorities.

The travels of Bowring (now accompanid by the US representative McLane) in his attempts to open negotiations for revision wearily repeated those of Elliot in the opening stages of the Opium War. The Governor-General at Canton, Ye Mingshen, obstructed all attempts to discuss the subject. Bowring and McLane therefore went to Shanghai in the hope that they could communicate with Beijing through the authorities there. After delays, they were persuaded by the Governor, Qierhanga, that an edict had been sent to Ye Mingshen at Canton ordering him to treat. Bowring and McLane, with this assurance, returned south. There, after the usual evasions and frustrations, they learned that Ye had no powers to negotiate more than trivial changes. Bowring and McLane boarded ship again, and sailed for Shanghai once more. There they informed the Governor that they were going north to the Beihe and would expect to be met by an official having full powers to negotiate. Arriving in the north, they were met by a salt commissioner who 'just happened' to be in the neighbourhood, and who agreed to inform the Court—unofficially—of their proposals. They were then invited to occupy a palatial encampment already prepared; it was, however, miles from any habitation, and such Chinese citizens as curiosity attracted to the scene were driven off with whips.

The proposals put by the British and American governments were similar, except that the American document did not, as did the British, include a request for legalization of the opium trade; McLane personally agreed with the now general opinion that legalization was the only possible solution, but his government would not support him. Some clauses were directly concerned with Chinese failure to maintain certain sections of the treaties. An additional export tax had been put on tea, in contravention of the treaty tariff. Inland transit dues were also (it was strongly suspected) being used to increase taxes on foreign trade. The foreigners had still not achieved access to Canton. Their chief representatives in China still did not have regular access to the chief provincial authorities, especially at Canton. Other clauses dealt with problems which had been revealed since the treaties were put into operation; they proposed changes, but on the basis of the existing treaties. These proposals covered regulation of China's chaotic currencies; arrangements for co-operation to suppress piracy; regulations for emigration by Chinese labourers; and better co-operation from the Chinese authorities in legal disputes over the foreign renting of property, which was made almost impossible around Canton by gentry opposition.

The rest of the proposals represented hopes of further improvement of relations and extension of trade, but to be brought about by negotiation and not under the threat of force. First, a request for a resident minister in Beijing; the foreign plenipotentiaries were convinced that the lack of direct communication with the capital could in the end result only in renewed possibility of war. Second, a proposal for the opening of Tianjin as a treaty port, if necessary by surrendering the right to trade at Ningbo. Third, a proposal—put in more for form's sake than out of any real hope or expectation—for the free opening of the interior of China to foreign travel and residence. Finally the British draft, but not the American, invited discussion of the possible legalization of the opium trade.

The envoys waited for five days in their tented village at the Beihe before receiving the imperial reply. It was a refusal to discuss any point of substance. 'In all these matters, existing arrangements must be adhered to . . . impossible to permit . . . change would be inconvenient . . . already covered by existing treaty stipulations. . . .' Even those demands which concerned breaches of the existing treaties were waved away; in particular, entry to Canton was refused. That this reply was an act of conscious defiance is strongly suggested by the fact that after Bowring's first visit to Shanghai the Intendant of Circuit, Wu Jianzhang, who was in charge of day-to-day management of foreign trade at Shanghai, was impeached on a charge of having embezzled the duties which the British consul had collected when the Chinese customs post was closed by the rebels.

The British and American governments accepted the rejection of treaty revision without too much perturbation. There was no crisis. More dangerous for the future, perhaps, was its effect on Bowring himself, who ever since his arrival in China had suffered one frustration heaped on another. His very virtues were against him. His predecessor, Sir George Bonham, who after a lifetime of service in the East entertained no high expectations of the despotic governments with which he dealt, could take a tolerant attitude: 'If the Chinese do not love us,' he wrote home, 'it must be confessed that they have hardly reason to; and if they often oppose us by duplicity and bad faith, is not that the natural defence of the weak?' Bowring, on the other hand, with his passionate Christian-radical belief in the perfectibility of man, his unusually wide cultural sympathies, and his pride in his own proven powers of persuasion, had come to China with the highest expectations, which had all the further to fall when he found himself faced with the obstruction offered by Governor-General Ye Mingshen.

Bowring's career in Canton had begun with a muddle over protocol of the sort already familiar. When he had informed the Chinese authorities of his arrival he had expected to be received at least by the Superintendent of Finances, who was by the treaty his corresponding equal. Instead the Governor of Canton appointed a military officer to meet him in a Hong warehouse—a double put-down: barbarian tribesmen are dealt with by the military, and merchants belong in warehouses. In both respects, the Governor was deliberately repudiating the precedents established by the treaty. Bonham wrote requesting that the precedents be followed. The Governor refused.

Within days of his arrival Bowring was immersed in the atmosphere of rumour, misinformation, uncertainty, and anxiety engendered in Canton by the refusal of the high authorities to communicate, and the consequent fear and silence on the part of even those Chinese whose business brought them into close contact with the foreigners. Bowring's dispatches as Governor of Hong Kong do not reveal this atmosphere, but one finds it thick and heavy in the records of the consulate itself. Bowring had almost no opportunity to communicate with the Chinese authorities. At one stage his hopes were raised when, in answer to a letter requesting safe conduct for the captain of a British ship wrecked and plundered on Hainan, at the expense of the British Government, the Canton Governor replied with great politeness that it was the duty of his officials to look after the comfort of the victims and that the Chinese authorities would meet the trifling expense. Bowring failed to see in this exceptional emphasis on benevolence the distinction which the Governor was taking the opportunity to make between what was due from imperial grace and favour and what would be withheld because it had been gained by force.

Chinese policy was consistent. Its aim was as far as possible to nullify the treaties. On the one hand, the implementation of treaty privileges was obstructed by a sort of sullen work-to-rule which was relaxed only when force was threatened. On the other hand, any foreign request which was regarded as being compatible with the pre-war exercise of imperial benevolence was politely entertained. The response over the captain of the wrecked lugger is one example. Another was Ye Mingshen's willingness to discuss the problems of currency reform. And the Court itself, in its reply to the proposals for treaty revision, indicated that it would be possible to discuss the question of the new tax on tea, the request for remission of duties owed at Shanghai owing to the rebellion, and the possibility that wrong judgements had been made in legal cases between foreigners and Chinese—all reasonable subjects for traditional imperial benevolence.

The well-informed British official Meadows was of the opinion that the Chinese were still quite unable to believe that the claims of the foreign leaders to represent their distant governments were genuine. The attitude of Chinese officials he illustrated by a statement which he composed from many conversations he had overheard:

How should they be government officers? Even allowing that they have a subordinate sovereign [*wang*] in their country, is it likely that he would be sending out great numbers of his officials several months' voyage from his own places? Does our emperor send his officers and troops to Cochin-China, Siam and other places to the south? No, but great numbers of our people go to these places, where they keep together, submit to their own headmen, and often create disturbances and fight with the natives just as the English barbarians do here. Their being sent from their own country is mere pretence.

Chinese official correspondence tends to confirm Meadows's view. The issues were not described, except when it was unavoidable, in terms of relations between two states, but only in terms of relations between China on the one hand and on the other the individuals who acted as spokesmen for the foreign communities. The Chinese Government dealt with them as it would have dealt with powerful pirate chiefs. Only one Chinese statesman had ever attempted to open correspondence with the British Government at home, when Lin Zexu wrote his appeal to Queen Victoria to stop the opium trade. A reply might have convinced the Chinese that they were dealing with a government, but no reply was sent. In the case of relations with Russia the Chinese had shown that, in spite of the theory of universal Chinese sovereignty, they would if necessary acknowledge the existence of another government and treat with it as an equal. The Western governments, however, failed fully to convince the Chinese that they were involved. From beginning to end, the problem of the foreigners is treated in the Chinese correspondence largely as a problem of public order.

In this sense, victory in the Opium War had failed to achieve the aim for which the war had been fought: to reach a position in which relations between Britain and China could be developed by peaceful diplomatic interchange between two equal states, each acknowledging the interests, rights and responsibilities of the other. No doubt this failure was due to China's wilful ignorance of the outside world. But this ignorance, in spite of the defeat already suffered, was sustainable only through lack of an urgent motive for learning. Only Lin Zexu and a handful of his friends had felt any such urgency, and they had been discredited.

There was thus a strong case from the point of view of the treaty powers for fighting the war over again. Yet no such intention is evident. The interests in China of the treaty powers other than Britain were marginal. As for Britain, the legal trade at last began to achieve profits in 1856 and there was no desire to risk what had been gained. Finally the Crimean War caused the withdrawal from China of such attention as Britain and France had hitherto given. In 1856 there seemed little chance of renewed hostilities with China. The war which came was generated locally, at Canton.

When the 1854 Triad risings around Canton were put down at the end of that year, many of the defeated rebels turned pirate. The Canton river passage became hazardous. Disorder had driven many Chinese merchants to seek refuge on Hong Kong, which now began to grow rapidly. At the same time the Canton authorities chose, rather inconsistently, to treat Hong Kong as foreign territory for purposes of commerce, with the result that Chinese merchants could trade with Hong Kong only under licence. For both these reasons the Hong Kong government decided to grant the right to fly the British flag to small vessels plying between Canton and the colony. In October 1856 one such small vessel, the *Arrow*, while lying at Canton and flying the British flag, was boarded by Chinese troops and its Chinese crew arrested on suspicion of connections with pirates. Parkes, the aggressive Canton consul, promptly demanded not only the return of the crew, but a public apology from Governor Ye Mingshen. Bowring supported him. Although he had several times in the past upheld China's rights against the opinions of his subordinates he did not do so in this instance. Perhaps he was tempted to seek a *casus belli*. Ye Mingshen's policy of obstruction had worn out Bowring's patience. He had already put on record his belief that 'something harder than brain bullets' would be necessary at Canton. The founding member of the Peace Society was now looking forward to war. He called the Royal Navy up-river.

When the news arrived in Britain, both government and opposition, the one in private and the other in public, deplored these events and put the personal responsibility upon Bowring, who was relieved of his post at the first decent opportunity. The ministry fell to a motion of censure on the handling of the *Arrow* incident.

Returned to power in the subsequent election, however, the Government decided to pursue the war and to take the opportunity to secure the full and proper implementation of the existing treaties. It was hoped that the capture of Canton and the removal of Governor Ye Mingshen from power would be enough to force the Court to negotiate. If this was not enough a swift landing would be made at Dagu near Tianjin supported by nine or ten gunboats, in order to paralyse Chinese opposition without further bloodshed. It was the first war over again. A careful distinction was made between the redress of grievances for which the use of force was justified, and new extensions of treaty rights which should be sought only by negotiation. The French Government, which had decided to join with Britain after the murder in China of two French missionaries, concurred. The American representative Reed at first deplored war on so trivial a cause as the *Arrow* incident; but when he was able to see the documents taken from Ye Mingshen's office, which showed conclusively that the Beijing government knew and approved of his behaviour, Reed felt fully justified in having supported the two allies. Britain and France, along with the USA and Russia, sent identical notes to Beijing.

British actions, however, soon put a strain on this *ad hoc* alliance. After Canton fell the plan for a bloodless coup failed when Elgin's gunboats were delayed, allowing the Dagu forts to be strengthened. Seymour, the naval commander, refused to land without first silencing the forts. Serious hostilities were made inevitable. Elgin himself, after serious study of the records of British relations with China, had become convinced that the only way to prevent continuing strife and perhaps repeated war was promptly to inflict upon the Chinese the most unambiguous defeat, then to demand all that Britain eventually sought, and to do so under the menace of renewed hostilities; and—so far as the style of his negotiations was concerned—to behave with systematic and peremptory harshness. He had decided, in fact, to exceed his instructions.

In the north, contact was made with the Governor-General of Zhili, Tan Tingxiang, and others before hostilities began. The Russian and American representatives attempted to use their good offices as neutrals to bring the two sides together. This proved impossible because of the insuperable objection of the Chinese to two ideas. First was the demand for a resident ambassador in Beijing, the issue which when forced on the Chinese by Elgin was to lead to a third war. Second was the notion that a representative of the Emperor could be given 'full powers' to negotiate. When the precedent of Qiying's powers was raised, the mandarins declared that he had forged them. It was when the Governor-General of Zhili finally declared that there was no way in which he could obtain full powers that the allies, on 20 May 1858, attacked the Dagu forts and opened the way to Tianjin.

In Reed's discussions with the Zhili Governor-General it appeared that the Chinese were now prepared, while rejecting the presence of embassies at the capital, to consider the possibility of a right of direct correspondence under seal and on equal terms with the Council of State. While rejecting the opening of inland and river markets, they were willing to open formally the six Chinese ports at which illegal trade (mainly in opium) was already carried on; none of these was of any potential importance. As soon as the forts were taken and the Grand Canal exposed, word came promptly from Beijing that two envoys had been ordered to Tianjin with full powers. They were Manchus of high rank, Gueiliang and Huashana. On the British side, Elgin, having formally met them once, kept his distance and left negotiations principally to two young members of his mission, Wade and Lay. They pressed British demands with great harshness, and under repeated threats of renewed force.

Then Qiying suddenly reappeared and announced that he had been sent by the Emperor to do what he could. He resumed his former blandishments. Lay drew from his boot a copy, taken from the Canton archives, of one of Qiying's earlier memorials which proved the insincerity of his professions of friendship. Qiying was reduced to tears. He left in despair, was tried for having deserted his post, and condemned to take his own life. In these circumstances, the Chinese acceptance of British terms was almost the equivalent of unconditional surrender. To the end they protested, especially against the admission of foreign ambassadors to Beijing.

Besides stipulating the right of a British representative to reside in the capital, the new treaty, the Treaty of Tianjin (Tientsin), exacted a war indemnity of 4 million taels for Great Britain; opened ten further treaty ports in addition to the existing five; permitted foreigners to travel anywhere in China under passport; fixed inland transit duties on foreign imports at a maximum of 2.5 per cent *ad valorem*; gave freedom of movement throughout China for missionaries; and legalized the trade in opium. Four of the new treaty ports were on the Yangzi River, extending upstream to China's second capital, Nanjing. The prospect of foreign shipping on China's most vital river was regarded with great alarm by the Manchu government; but their greatest horror was reserved for the prospect of foreign ambassadors at the capital. To the Emperor himself this meant the end of the tribute system, the denial of his claim to universal sovereignty, and the undermining of the legitimation of imperial government. Beijing had no intention of submitting to such dangerous humiliation. The Chinese negotiators at Tianjin assured the Emperor that while the treaties must be accepted for the moment, 'Your Majesty only needs to charge your servants with mismanagement' to reduce the treaties to 'waste paper'. The legalization of the opium trade was accepted by the Chinese Government without objection, however. The authorities of central China already admitted opium freely, imposing taxes on the trade in order to increase revenues to be used to suppress the Taiping Rebellion.

The terms of the French treaty were similar, France obtaining an indemnity of 2 million taels. The United States also made a new treaty. The three treaties were assimilated to each other through the 'most-favoured-nation' clause.

Elgin's performance at Tianjin, so completely at variance with his personal character, which was as urbane as it was humane, was deliberate and calculated; but his perturbed French colleague, Baron Gros, wrote home: 'I have come to the view that the concessions demanded are exorbitant, and perhaps even dangerous for England . . . I have not left my English colleague ignorant of my belief that his government will be obliged to use force to secure the execution of concessions obtained by force alone.' He was to be proved right.

Elgin's cousin Frederick Bruce, who had acted as the secretary of his mission at Tianjin, was appointed envoy to Beijing. To save the Chinese Court the embarrassment of having to receive him publicly he was not given the title of ambassador. He was not expected to reside permanently at Beijing; the duration of his stay was negotiable. The British Government insisted, however, that Bruce must be admitted to Beijing, and if the Chinese resisted they were to be informed that such resistance would result only in the permanence of the mission at the capital. He was to take with him 'a sufficient naval force'. It was known that the Mongol general Sengelincin (better known in the British Army as 'Sam Collinson') had been given command of 50,000 troops, and had strengthened the Dagu forts and staked the river. When on 25 June 1859 the British sought to force their way ashore, the forts opened fire. The British boats found themselves on the shoals under heavy bombardment. More than half of the landing party were casualties, including Admiral Hope. It was at this point that, in a famous incident, the American Commodore Tatnall used his steamer to tow several launches of British marines into the battle, exclaiming that blood was thicker than water. In spite of this fraternal help, the British retreated.

The third war, 1860

The reaction at home to Bruce's action was mixed. It could be argued that having been refused peaceful passage Bruce should, according to international law, have retired and remonstrated with the Chinese Government before using force. Moreover, the Chinese had offered a peaceful welcome at a point ten miles up the coast, though only after the forts had already been attacked. From this place the American envoy was in fact conducted to Beijing and received there, but in humiliating conditions which would not have been accepted had they been anticipated. Against this argument, however, were the circumstances surrounding the incident: China's open preparations to resist, the uncertainty over what Bruce's reception might be even if he reached the shore in peace, and his dependence on presumptive evidence of Chinese intentions. Such arguments on either side, however, did not alter the fact that Britain, in the person of her envoy, had suffered a humiliation, any acceptance of which was likely to put the British position in China back to the period before the first war. A third war was inevitable, and this was agreed by British statesmen without demur.

An ultimatum was sent to Beijing in March 1860, demanding the admission in due form of the British envoy. This and all other demands were refused. and the refusal was accompanied by a warning that the people of the Treaty Ports would be incited against the foreigners. The threat showed that the victory at Dagu had vastly encouraged the hawks at Court; but it was not a threat to be taken seriously. The Canton militia had already proved unable to defeat regular troops. Meanwhile central China had become dependent on foreign assistance against the Taipings, and the authorities there preferred to let the north do the fighting, as they were to do again in the Boxer Rising.

The Anglo-French forces landed off Tianjin on 1 August 1860, meeting no resistance. The Chinese immediately offered to accept the ultimatum. Elgin replied that March had been the time to consider the ultimatum of March. Tianjin fell. The Chinese submitted completely. Nevertheless when negotiations commenced it was found that Sengelincin's forces were drawn up for an ambush. The members of the French and British missions sent to open negotiations as requested were seized and imprisoned, and thirteen members of the escort were murdered. War was renewed and Beijing taken. The allies looked around for some single act of vengeance for the murder of their representatives which would not involve loss of life. The French wanted to burn down the Imperial Palace itself but the British thought this might only drive the Chinese Government to follow the Emperor who had already departed 'on a hunting trip' to Jehol (Reher). The Summer Palace, however, had already been looted both by allied soldiers and by local Chinese and was already severely damaged. So it was decided to burn the rest of it to the ground.

In return for Chinese action in opposing the landing of the British envoy the Convention of Beijing added new terms to the Treaty of Tianjin: a larger indemnity and the opening of Tianjin as a sixteenth treaty port. After the conclusion of the Tianjin treaty, Elgin, having ruthlessly made his point, had entered into the negotiations of the details of the agreement with an amiability equal to his previous truculence. The concessions thus made by Elgin at Tianjin to Chinese sentiment, that the British representative would not be a full ambassador, and that he need not reside actually in Beijing and would be expected to visit the capital only as business required, were now withdrawn; there was to be an ambassador permanently resident at the Chinese court.

China's inner frontiers and the advance of Russia

While the Western nations were extending their power to areas outside Europe the Chinese were themselves engaged in territorial expansion into non-Chinese areas. This expansion doubled the area of China in the course of the eighteenth century. By the end of that century more than half of the territory of the Manchu empire consisted of lands whose native populations were not Chinese. Conquest, the expansion of Chinese trade, and the settlement of land by Chinese emigrants paralleled Western—and more closely Russian—imperialism. This contemporary process of Chinese imperialist expansion was as oppressive and as brutal as anything elsewhere.

There were four main areas outside China proper under Manchu-Chinese rule: Manchuria, homeland of the conquerors of China, underdeveloped, and largely depopulated by the migration of the Manchu forces to China; Mongolia, inhabited by nomadic herdsmen who practised a form of Buddhism derived from Tibet; Xinjiang (Sinkiang), also known as Chinese Turkestan, whose inhabitants were mostly Turkic Muslims strongly influenced by Sufi traditions; and Tibet.

Manchu policy did not in principle favour an expansion of Chinese settlement or of Chinese influence into these areas, foreseeing the inevitability of expensive and dangerous conflicts. Yet it could not prevent it. With the population of China growing rapidly, the pressure to expand by migration was irresistible. At the same time the development of commerce in Chinese hands in these areas, theoretically subject to strict limitations, went on apace; and the Beijing government (or more truly its representatives in the frontier areas) became increasingly dependent on this trade as a source of taxes.

Mongolia was the area most strongly affected by Han expansion, but this worked in combination with indigenous changes. The population of Mongolia had decreased. Nomadism declined, and Han settlers began to cultivate the more fertile land. Monasticism was still growing rapidly, until by the early nineteenth century some 30 per cent of the male population had taken vows. Monasteries increased in size and towns grew round them. Increasing urbanization promoted increased trade, largely in the hands of Han merchants. As Mongolian incomes tended to be seasonal there was ample opportunity for usury. The Han traders were the main usurers, and through this came into possession of much land.

The traditional leaders of Mongolian nomad society were appointed by the Manchus as bannermen, but were given only a limited military role. They paid tribute to the Qing court and their vassals in turn paid tribute or taxes in kind to them. They had the power to allocate pasture. Slaves were common, and freemen a privileged class, as were monks. Native oppression was increased by Chinese penetration. Yet although Mongolia suffered more than any other frontier area it was at this time the least rebellious. The Qing had successfully co-opted its leaders.

Turkestan was more intractable. Like Mongolia it was divided by geography. The area north of the Tian Shan range, Dzungaria, was geographically part of Mongolia; it was mainly steppe, but there was much potential arable which Chinese settlers were now being encouraged to cultivate with grants of land by the Qing court. There were also military colonies of Chinese troops, who were encouraged to remain after demobilization. Most of the immigrants were Hui—Muslims of Han race. The native Turkic inhabitants were also Muslims. Hostility to Chinese penetration in Dzungaria was therefore not religious (in contrast to hostility elsewhere in Xinjiang); it was Chinese economic domination that was resented. In the other main part of Turkestan, the Tarim Basin, the population at the end of the eighteenth century numbered only about 300,000, mostly Muslims of Turkic stock. Theirs was an area of oasis agriculture, uncertainly irrigated by melting snows, where ancient trade routes ran from oasis to oasis, westwards through Kokhand and south to Tibet and Darjeeling. Qing rule in Turkestan was indirect, and its peoples were allowed to live in their own way. The *begs* (princes), however, had been sinicized and turned into an official class holding power at the will of the Emperor. In return they enjoyed exemption from taxation and were given grants of land and of slaves whose numbers rapidly grew.

At the western frontier of Turkestan the Qing faced a situation not unlike that created by the presence of foreign traders at Canton. Much of the cross-frontier trade of the area was handled by merchants from the independent state of Kokhand, whose prosperity and revenues were largely dependent upon trade with and via Turkestan. It was an aggressive little mercantile state, and its merchants and rulers were constantly chafing against the restrictions imposed upon commerce by the Qing government. As at Canton, trade was permitted only with security merchants and under passports. The trade was ruthlessly milked for taxes by a system which discriminated heavily in favour of Chinese merchants.

Tibet, although subject to Chinese suzerainty, did not at this time (or indeed until after 1951) suffer from Chinese penetration either by peasants or by merchants. Under Chinese suzerainty, it enjoyed almost complete autonomy. The Chinese chose to regard the members of its lay bureaucracy as members of the imperial mandarinate, but they were in fact chosen by Lhasa. Tibet was a theocracy, ruled by incarnate Buddhas, and in imitation of China it had adopted a policy of almost complete exclusion. This served to protect the arbitrary authority of the lamas and also to protect the maintenance of the government trade monopolies from which this clerical ruling class profited. The vast majority of the population were simple farmers. The Chinese Emperor was the highest patron of Lamaist Buddhism—a concept which allowed the Emperor to think of the Dalai Lama as his client, and the Dalai Lama to think of the Emperor as his disciple. Both sides could enjoy the advantage of the relationship without disturbance of their illusions because the remoteness of Tibet ensured that there were few conflicts.

Manchuria as a frontier area presented a special problem. As the homeland of China's conquerors, it was for a century and a half strictly protected from Chinese immigration; by 1800, however, this protection could not be maintained. There was land and to spare: in the nineteenth century southern Manchuria rapidly filled up with Chinese peasant immigrants.

The interest of the Chinese imperial government in the frontier areas was strategic rather than economic. Trade with them and beyond them was of marginal importance—of far less significance even than the trade at Canton, or the unacknowledged maritime trade between southern China and Southeast Asia. The real interest of Beijing in these remote and relatively unproductive regions was to prevent the coalescing of nomad or other groups into a power which could again, as so often in the past, threaten China's security. The means used was to patronize local rulers, draw them into relations of personal loyalty to the Emperor, and encourage their sinicization. The danger was, however, that these native rulers would then become alienated from their own people, as China's individualistic property relations, exploited by them, replaced older bonds.

The disadvantage of this traditional policy as it survived into the modern world was that political allegiance was personal, not territorial. China had no clear frontiers; indeed even when a frontier was defined, as in the Treaty of Nerchinsk in 1689 with Russia, the Chinese seem to have attached little importance to it, setting up their boundary markers on the line which they found most convenient, even though it was in fact many miles inside Chinese territory. Another disadvantage was that the very success of the Qing in exploiting the many tribal, racial, and religious divisions of the area had weakened the capacity of its peoples to resist not only Chinese but Russian penetration.

In 1689 the Treaty of Nerchinsk had defined a part of the border, and the further Treaty of Kiakhta in 1727 had extended this demarcation westwards. Significantly the Manchu government, faced with a strong power on its inner frontiers, quickly dropped its pretence of universal sovereignty and negotiated with Russia as an equal; nevertheless the forms of the tributary system were saved by offering the Russians, in addition to trade at two points on the border, the opportunity to send a trading caravan every three years, provided its leader would perform the usual ceremonies. The Russians also obtained the privilege of a resident ecclesiastical mission in Beijing. In 1792 the two powers sought in a further agreement to solve some of the problems which had arisen, but without much success. On the inner frontiers, as on the coast, the rapid development of Chinese commerce soon burst the paternalistic bonds applied to it by the Beijing court. Russian and Chinese traders illegally exchanged goods at various points on the border, and the local authorities, always short of funds, were happy to accept new taxable assets.

By 1824 the value of the trade at Kiakhta had risen to almost 16 million roubles a year. In addition there was unrecorded trade at other frontier crossings. The staples of the trade were Russian furs, and Chinese tea, silk, and cotton. European manufactures also found their way into China through Russian hands.

After 1824, however, the trade began to wane. Russia found herself with an adverse trade balance in the East. The causes are not clear, but the growth of the sea-borne trade certainly played a part. Another factor was that central Asian fur supplies were becoming exhausted, while American furs could reach China more cheaply; the Russians were forced further east in search of new supplies.

In 1803 St Petersburg had decided to request from Beijing an extension of commercial privileges on the frontier, and in addition the right to participate in the maritime trade. An embassy was sent, headed by Count Iu. A. Golovkin. Russia's requests were not marked by modesty. Golovkin sought the opening of the entire frontier to Russian trade, unrestricted caravan trade in the interior of China, exclusive right to trade at Nanjing, trade with India via Tibet, navigation of the Amur River and a trading post at its mouth, and the opening of Canton to Russian shipping.

Meanwhile in 1821 St Petersburg also attempted to open relations with

Ranjit Singh, the ruler of the Punjab. The mission did not reach the Punjab, but the attempt renewed British fears of the possibility of the penetration of India by Russian influence. The Russians at the same time were expressing alarm that their trade with China might be virtually eliminated by British competition via Canton. In 1845 a Russian investigator disguised as a Kazakh visited Tarbagatai in Xinjiang and confirmed that British goods preponderated there among imported manufactures. In 1841 the Russians sought to gain an advantage over Great Britain by informing the Chinese that the export of opium to China via Russia had been forbidden; in fact no such prohibition was enforced or enforceable, and opium continued to flow into China via Xinjiang, to the alleviation of Russia's adverse trade balance. Pressure was applied through the Russian ecclesiastical mission in Beijing to induce the Chinese to legalize trade at Kuldya (Yili) and Tarbagatai. Local Manchu officials favoured this, and Beijing could not enforce the existing restrictions at such a distance. The Treaty of Kuldya was therefore agreed in 1851, opening these places to trade. The Chinese, however, rejected the opening of Kashgar, much desired by Russia in order to facilitate trade with Tibet and India.

Further east, around the Amur, the Chinese were in a weak position. The right bank of the river was only thinly settled, the left bank scarcely at all. Into this area Russian subjects continued to press in search of furs and, as their numbers grew, in search of arable land for their support. In 1849 G. I. Nevelskoi sailed down the Amur and proved it navigable. He found British, American, and French ships at its mouth, and so to Russia's worries over commerce was added the strategic worry of the possibility of the dominance of Siberia from the mouth of the Amur by the Western powers. N. N. Muraviev, the Russian Governor of Siberia, promptly raised the Russian flag at the mouth of the river; the government in St Petersburg condemned his action, but the Tsar supported him: 'Where the Russian flag has once been hoisted it must not be lowered.' The new Russian post was settled and fortified.

Muraviev then dissuaded the Tsar from seeking a new border agreement, which might have limited eventual further Russian expansion. During the Crimean War he sent a strong force to hold the mouth of the Amur, informing Beijing that he was doing so to protect the area from the British and French. The area had been denuded of its normal force of bannermen by the Taiping Rebellion, and China could not resist. Muraviev then demanded the cession of the left bank and the confirmation of existing Russian settlements. China protested that in 1853 Qing possession of both banks of the Amur had been confirmed by Russia, but the Russians continued to increase their settlements and their military forces.

Soon after came the second war with the Western powers and the negotiations at Tianjin. Here, the Russians acted with a degree of cynical duplicity for which modern history offers few parallels. Having first refused to associate themselves with the British and French on the grounds that they 'would use neither force nor threats against the Chinese Empire', the Russians then began two sets of negotiations. In Manchuria, Yishan (who had faced the British in the first stages of the Opium War) found himself helpless in the face of Russia's military occupation of the Amur, and accepted a treaty by which this vast area was ceded to Russia. Meanwhile the Russian emissary at Tianjin, Putiatine, was falsely assuring the naïve officials in Beijing that Great Britain and France supported Russia's demands; he did not, however, press for the cession of the Amur, leaving that to his compatriots in the north. The treaty which he concluded at Tianjin made no mention of the Amur.

Meanwhile, in order to strengthen their position before a British ambassador arrived in Beijing (an event which Putiatine secretly urged the Chinese Government to resist), the Russians extended their settlements in the north and moved further up the Ussuri and Sungari rivers. Then came the third war. The new Russian negotiator, Ignatiev, was asked by the Chinese to mediate—a measure of their desperation, for they had at last awakened to the threat of Russian expansion. Again, like Putiatine, Ignatiev falsely assured the Court that the British and French supported Russia's demands; but he crowned even Putiatine's duplicity: when the demands were resisted he threatened that he would recall the recently departed British and French forces. By the Treaty of Beijing, Ignatiev secured the opening of the entire Chinese border to Russian trade and influence, with in addition the proviso that the most-favoured-nation clause would not apply. Soon after, Russia secured a further agreement by which duties on overland imports from Russia would be taxed at one-third less than imports by sea. Russian gains were so great that they were alarmed themselves, lest the Western European powers would feel forced to respond by establishing their influence in Korea. The Russian advance was prudently halted for the time being; but Russian territorial ambitions remained undiminished.

Meanwhile China's own form of imperialism—the transformation of Manchu suzerainty over the non-Chinese peoples of the western regions by Han settlement and into Han commercial dominance—went on apace. Han expansion was not simply a spontaneous movement of population. Some of the most influential scholars of the age, most notably the New Text reformers such as Wei Yuan and Kong Zizhen, were urging the Qing government to develop Xinjiang and Mongolia systematically by means of Han penetration.

The most massive Chinese settlement was in Inner Mongolia. The best of the old pastures were broken up by the ploughs of Chinese peasants and the nomads made desperate. The Mongol princes and the heads of monasteries added to the distress by their increasing exploitation, a result of their increasing indebtedness to Chinese merchant-users. Mongol society fell into deep distress. Two very different efforts were made to alleviate conditions. The Mongol Prince Toghtaktu ('To the Terrible') launched a policy of development within his own banner lands after 1821. He opened mines and textile workshops, encouraged agricultural diversification, set out to provide universal and compulsory education, and attempted to reduce the power of the monasteries. He found few allies, however, and when those threatened by his reforms took to arms his Qing overlords gave him no support. The second effort was a popular revolt of poor peasants, both Mongol and Chinese, in 1861. It was quickly stamped out. The decline of Mongol society, hastened by syphilis and tuberculosis, continued unchecked. Han immigration also continued, encouraged after 1860 by growing Chinese fear of Russia.

In Mongolia, the Qing Emperor as the supreme patron of Buddhist monasticism could control the country through the support of the monasteries. In Muslim Xinjiang he had no such advantage. There, infidel rule was a perpetual affront. The population looked west to the Muslim world and they did not have to look very far for a patron. The khans of Kokhand gave support to the Sufi sects of the western Tarim Basin who were the most ready among Xinjiang's population to offer resistance to the Qing.

In 1817 Kokhand allowed the exiled Sufi leader Jahangir to invade Xinjiang and gave him military support. The first invasion was not successful, but when a Qing commander massacred the unprotected women and children of a group of rebels, the people of the area flocked to Jahangir's standard. He harassed the Qing banner troops, though they were vastly superior in numbers. They were besieged in their cantonments, leaving the countryside to the rebels. The revolt lasted for seven years, until Jahangir was betrayed for the reward which the Qing had offered. Peace had scarcely been restored, however, when the khan of Kokhand launched another invasion. He was defeated, not so much by the imperial authorities as by the growing hostility of the population to the savagery of his soldiers. Although forced to withdraw, he remained nevertheless a menace; but his demands were merely commercial, and therefore, it seemed to Beijing, he could be bought off. Between 1832 and 1835 an agreement was reached relaxing the restrictions on trade and accepting the appointment of a Kokhandi as supervisor of trade in Altishahr. The Qing court congratulated themselves on this successful damage limitation. When the British launched their war on China in 1839, Beijing promptly sent its Xinjiang experts to Canton. The Treaty of Nanjing was accepted with less alarm than one might have expected, because of the Kokhand precedent.

The Qing-Kokhand accord permitted Kokhand to station a political resident at Kashgar and commercial subordinates elsewhere, who enjoyed the extraterritorial jurisdiction applicable to all foreigners in Altishahr. Much of this represented the conditions normally sought by Muslim merchants trading abroad; and on the European side the Turkish Capitulations, by which Turkey had conceded to European traders the equivalent of these normal rights of Muslim merchants, formed a parallel precedent in European minds. The accord with Kokhand and the treaty with the British thus confirmed—though more explicitly than the Chinese would have conceded without force—

expectations on both sides. Similar arrangements were made with traders from Kashmir and Badakhshan.

In one respect, however, the arrangements in Xinjiang went further. The foreign residents taxed the trade. The Qing therefore had no financial incentive to govern the trading towns of the far west. They withdrew to their line of guard posts. In this way their authority in western Xinjiang was undermined.

Although Beijing was forced to make concessions in the far west of Xinjiang, in Dzungaria systematically subsidized Han colonization continued. In 1844 the exiled Lin Zexu was in charge of the process. In 1847 and in 1852 Kokhand again stirred up religious-based opposition in Xinjiang. The Qing were successful in restoring order, but their victories were followed by savage reprisals which merely intensified religious fervour, and by 1860 Xinjiang was on the verge of a jihad.

Tibet was soon to be as threatened by Great Britain as the lands further north and north-west were by Russia. At first the British in India were prepared to exercise restraint. Their motive was actually a reluctance to enter into conflict with China. It was the Russian advance into central Asia which changed British policy; they were determined to forestall the possible establishment of Russian influence in Lhasa. This was the motive for their absorption of Kumaon and Garwhal, which brought them into direct contact with Tibet, at the conclusion of a war with Nepal (1814–16), thus risking the Chinese hostility they had hitherto chosen to avoid; but in the event Beijing refused to acknowledge responsibility towards China's Nepalese tributary. As a result of the war Tibet lost her own tributary of Sikkim to Britain. The policy of the Indian government, however, was still to avoid contact with Tibet unless contact proved necessary; but the perpetual turbulence, dislocation of trade, and threats to the balance of power among the many small independent and tributary states on the Tibetan border drew the British in step by step.

The Tibetans, who in practice conducted their foreign policy independently of China, responded to the possibility of British pressure by insisting that Tibet was under Qing protection. This was a myth, but the British accepted it. It was only towards the end of the eighteenth century, when it became clear that China was in no real sense involved in Tibet, that the British began to explore the possibility of a new relationship with Lhasa.

By the mid-nineteenth century, therefore, contradictory developments were taking place on the inner frontiers of China. While Chinese economic dominance grew, Manchu political authority weakened. Han penetration aroused hostility and resistance with which the Qing were less and less able to deal. Russia stood ready to exploit any weakness, and was very willing and able to join in the Manchus' game of divide and rule among the Mongols and Muslims of the north and west. China was distracted, facing both a threat from the sea and a threat from the steppe, and was able to respond adequately to neither.

5

The self-strengthening movement

Opportunities, political and economic, 1861–1894

The years 1861 to 1894, between the end of the Third War with the West and the outbreak of the First Sino-Japanese War, were make-or-break years for the reform of the old system. The period had begun with defeat, and rebellion still raged. The Taipings were to hold Nanjing for three more years. In the north the Nian rebels, strengthened by remnants of the Taipings, still maintained their power. In the south-west, in the north-west, and in Chinese Turkestan, Muslim rebels controlled large areas. Yet during this span of over thirty years China enjoyed many advantages. Defeat by modern weapons had forced some degree of realism upon Beijing. The need for the acquisition of these modern weapons was accepted, and with their aid the Chinese Government was able to destroy the rebellions one by one.

China's main international advantage was that the Western powers were in agreement that they must co-operate with each other in order to preserve the unity and integrity of China, to assist China to increase her strength, and to induce the government in Beijing to accept the responsibilities and assume the powers of a unified and centralized state and to accept international law as the basis of China's relations with the world.

It may be argued that this view is difficult to reconcile with the steady encroachment on China's frontiers which proceeded throughout the period. China proper, however, was not much touched by these encroachments. It was the remote, non-Chinese borderlands and the tributary states which were detached from Chinese influence. The theory of universal sovereignty, upon which Chinese claims to rule beyond the area populated by the Han were based, proved in the nineteenth century to be a source of weakness. China had no frontiers; imperial government shaded off through feudal suzerainty into tribute relations long drained of political significance. These areas had become a power vacuum. The advance of Russia across the Asian heartland, scarcely controllable from St Petersburg, found little to check it. The extension of British power in and beyond India, motivated mainly by concern for the security of possessions surrounded by areas which were constant sources of conflict, brought British authority into Nepal and Burma, historically tributaries of China but tributaries in which the imperial government no longer exercised any discernible influence. As the distance shortened between the areas of British and Russian rule, the existence of the remaining power vacuum between them became a source of constant apprehension to both. In Indo-China the French were advancing piecemeal, drawn in more by a series of *faits accomplis* created by French adventurers than by any consistent French policy of expansion.

The Chinese Government further weakened an already weak position by the ambiguous attitude which it took to its dependencies and tributaries. As far as their north-eastern homeland was concerned, the Manchus certainly did not relinquish territory and control willingly, but as far as the tributaries now troubled by foreign incursion were concerned, the Qing court was more inclined to deny than to assert its theoretical responsibilities; to assert them might bring only war and indemnities. Even in the case of Korea, whose relationship with China was much closer than that of any other tributary and whose geographical position dictated that Beijing should in no circumstances have tolerated the replacement there of Chinese influence by any other, China at first disclaimed all responsibility.

The loss of China's fringe areas might be regarded, in China's circumstances at that time, as a source of increased strength rather than weakness; to cling to remote territories which then contributed little or nothing to Chinese life, and which China did not have the capacity to develop or to defend, was merely to give hostages to fortune.

Chinese patriots often condemn the co-operative policy of the powers as representing in reality a common front against China, which deprived her of the normal possibility of gaining her ends and protecting her interests by allying with one power against another. It is an argument, however, which ignores the regrettable realities of China's situation. China could have offered favours; but nothing would have led more swiftly to her dismemberment than a policy of discrimination in the granting of privileges between one power and another.

Such a policy was prevented by the most-favoured-nation clause, although this too has been attacked as a serious invasion of China's sovereignty. It tended, certainly, to increase the effect of a new concession given to any one power by automatically bestowing it upon all, tightening the grip of Treaty Port privilege on China by a sort of ratchet motion. On the other hand, by removing the possibility that any one power could gain the advantage of an exclusive privilege, it removed the main motive for the competitive pursuit of such privileges.

That a policy of co-operation would be carried out with complete consistency is too much to expect. The interests of the various powers, and their position *vis-à-vis* China, differed too much. The ability of the powers as a group to check the actions of any one power varied with circumstances.

Nevertheless the deep differences of interest, attitude, and opportunity which were later, at the end of the century, to destroy the policy of co-operation—and which were first to put China in imminent danger of partition and then paradoxically to save her from such a fate—did not decisively influence policy in the years between 1860 and 1894. It was the defeat of China by Japan in 1895 which precipitated a hectic scramble for a position of advantage in China; but there was a deeper reason for this change. The co-operative policy was based on agreement among the Western powers that the creation of a strong and wealthy China was in the best interests of all, on the fact that China was now making some attempt to increase her wealth and strength, and on the hope that she was succeeding. The relinquishment of the co-operative policy signalled the relinquishment of that hope.

In the 1860s China undoubtedly enjoyed an opportunity to modernize such as she was not to have again. The powers urged modernization on her, and offered advice, encouragement, and assistance, while at the same time counselling their citizens and each other not to entertain unrealistic expectations of the likely pace of change. The Imperial Maritime Customs provided a large and buoyant new revenue, while its foreign supervisors, as servants of the Chinese Government, worked faithfully and conscientiously to contribute to the development of a modern infrastructure. Many of China's provinces were now in the hands of competent governors who had reached power not through the moribund examination system but through the rough apprenticeship of the Taiping Rebellion. Their experience of civil war had also familiarized them, via modern arms, with modern industry, and so disposed them to favour at least a limited degree of modernization. Finally Japan (Confucian like China, but traditionally held in low regard by the Chinese) had embarked on a dramatically effective drive for modernization which set the Chinese an example, stimulating at once as an encouragement, a reproach, and a threat.

The results of the limited modernization movement in China were not entirely insignificant. The reason why this partial success came to look like a total failure was the extraordinary rise of Japan. Conditions had changed, however. The situation in which international trade was growing rapidly as a proportion of total world economic activity, and was thus offering the possibility of relatively easy accumulation of capital, ended with the century. China missed the last bus, which Japan had caught.

Court politics after 1860

During the late 1850s the most powerful man at court was Su Shun, an imperial clansman then in his forties. He held the rank of Adjutant-General, one of three men of this rank to whom had fallen the task of ruling China amid the difficulties of the Taiping Rebellion and foreign invasion when the

Xian Feng Emperor, in despair, gave himself up to dissipation. Su Shun, a man of severe and forceful personality, soon emerged as the most effective of the three. He was the author of the policy of entrusting to the Chinese gentry the suppression of the rebellion. He was, in his conservative way, a reformer, but his severity made him bitter enemies. In 1859 he ordered the execution of a Grand Secretary and three of the Grand Secretary's colleagues for their involvement in a case of corrupt practice in the provincial examinations of the Beijing area. (It was also Su Shun who ordered the death by suicide of Qiying when he left the Tianjin negotiations in despair.) As President of the Board of Revenue he had the ungrateful task of attempting to clear up the corruption—which involved officials, bankers and even princes of the blood—caused by the efforts of the Government to raise funds by the issue of debased coinage and paper money, which depreciated as soon as issued.

As a former President of the Board of Ceremonies, which handled China's tribute relations, he was of all the conservatives at court the most bitterly opposed to the reception of foreign ambassadors in Beijing. Forced to accept, he continued to insist that the ambassadors must perform the kowtow. It was on his advice that the Emperor ordered that the landing of the British envoy should be resisted by force. The occupation of the capital left him unreconciled to defeat. He retreated to Jehol with the dying Emperor.

During his absence Yixin (Prince Gong), left to negotiate with the British and French, became convinced that the Western powers were less of a threat than had been supposed. It became obvious that both powers entertained much goodwill towards China. It was a matter of astonishment too that although they held the capital and the fate of the dynasty in their hands, they went peaceably home once they had secured the limited concessions they sought. Yixin was convinced that the foreigners took their undertakings seriously and that, this being so, the acceptance of Western international law by China might prove to be to her advantage.

Su Shun, however, had been appointed by the dying Emperor to the council of eight regents who, in association with the two Empresses dowager, were to rule in the name of the infant sovereign. Su Shun was about to return to the capital, accompanying the body of the late Emperor, and plainly he would present a formidable obstacle to the new conciliatory policies advocated by Yixin. He and his fellow regents were therefore surprised in their beds, while *en route* home, and were arrested. He and two others were executed.

In 1860 Yixin, sixth son of the Dao Guang Emperor and younger brother of the late Xian Feng Emperor, was 27 years old. Left in Beijing when the Emperor fled to Jehol, Yixin was forced to exchange (with Elgin) the text of the Tianjin Treaty, sign the new Convention of Beijing, and at the same time sign (with Ignatiev) the treaty which ceded to Russia all the land east of the Ussuri River. Although young, he had the support of Grand Councillor Wen Xiang, a Manchu in his forties and a man of considerable experience. There was nothing in Wen Xiang's previous career to lead one to expect that he would be predisposed to the conciliation of foreigners or to the adoption of measures of modernization; however, he was highly respected in China for honest and straightforward dealing, and his possession of these characteristics may have helped him recognize that the Westerners with whom he found himself in contact were not as devious and full of dark schemes as barbarians were traditionally held to be, but that on the contrary they said no more than they meant and meant no more than they said. Within a year he and Yixin had secured the establishment of a virtual foreign office, the Zongli Yamen, which dealt with other countries as equal sovereign states. A language school for diplomats, the Tong Wen Guan, followed soon after. And in 1861 he won acceptance for the creation of a small modernized force of bannermen which five years later showed its mettle when a detachment of 4,000 men saved Mukden (Shenyang) from an attack by 30,000 bandits. In various such ways Wen Xiang showed himself ready to accept change: he told W. A. P. Martin, the foreign director of the new language school, that China would 'learn all the good things possible from you people of the West'.

With China's policies in the hands of Yixin and Wen Xiang at court, supported in the provinces by those loyal governors who had risen through resistance to the Taipings and their protégés (several of whom were now governors themselves), China might have been expected to make a good beginning in modernizing at least some aspects of life. Had the power of Yixin and Wen Xiang been untrammelled this might have been so, but it was by no means unchallenged. Yixin's rise, although made possible by the support of Yehenala (Cixi), the senior Empress Dowager, incurred her jealousy. The fact that her own position was barely legitimate rendered her insecure. She had no strong convictions in favour of, or against, the limited degree of modernization which had been put in train. Her concern was to maintain a political balance in Beijing, in which both sides would have to appeal to her as arbiter. The death of Su Shun had checked the power of the conservatives, but that power she soon partly restored. Yixin's half-brother Yihuan, who was married to Yehenala's younger sister, put himself at the head of a faction bitterly hostile to change; yet he had no principles beyond a hatred of all things foreign, and for the rest was willing to encourage Yehenala in her inclinations towards political indecision, corrupt patronage, and personal extravagance.

In consequence, although Yixin had been given the rank of 'Prince Councillor' (a title hitherto bestowed only on the sons of the founder of Manchu power and unused for more than two centuries), his position was far from secure. He could not give full support to the schemes of development proposed to him by Li Hongzhang and other officials, who in the end found it necessary, if they were to win any concessions at all, to gain the favour of the conservatives. The Zongli Yamen, although apparently very powerful, being in composition virtually a sub-committee of the inner cabinet, was under constant fire from the conservatives. Its members were accused of exceeding their powers, of truckling to the foreigners, and even of treachery. Yehenala was persuaded to insist that no decisions on foreign relations could be taken by the Yamen without submitting them to a palace conference, which the conservatives could dominate.

In 1865 Yixin was abruptly deprived of all his offices, soon after he had been loaded with further honours for his part in defeating the Taipings. The rebellion being over, there was that much less reason for Yehenala to accept his supremacy. Whether or not she intended his dismissal to be permanent we cannot know, but in response to appeals from many court officials he was reinstated in a few days, though deprived of his rank of Prince Councillor. In 1873 he was again dismissed, but reinstated the following day. Thereafter he remained in power, but with diminishing influence. The more successful he was in maintaining peace with the foreigners the less tolerable his power appeared.

The conservative faction had the support of several men who, as imperial tutors, were guardians of Confucian orthodoxy. One, Wang Tonghe, was later to favour reform and become a patron of the 1898 Reform Movement, converted like many more by the humiliating defeat of China by Japan in 1895. In the 1860s and 1870s, however, he was one of the conservative ideologues. Of these, the most notorious was the Mongol, Wo Ren. While still in a junior position he had submitted a memorial which reasserted the orthodox principle that officials should be chosen for their moral worth rather than their expertise. It was believed at the time that his memorial convinced the Emperor that Qiying, then still at Canton and an advocate of the creation of a body of experts in foreign affairs, should be removed from office. Since 1855 Wo Ren had tutored Yixin's elder brother, who in turn was to become tutor in Manchu to the Emperor and to pass the extreme conservatism of Wo Ren to his own sons. It was they who distinguished themselves at the end of the century by persuading the Court to support the Boxers.

The conservatives, with Wo Ren as their spokesman, soon won a victory which slowed the faltering pace of experimental modernization to a crawl. In 1866–7 Wen Xiang, in a move to break down the barriers to the acceptance of Western learning, proposed that scholars who had already obtained the *juren* degree should be encouraged to enter the new diplomatic language school as students, and at the end of their course should be given a 'special recommendation' for promotion in the public service. The Dowager approved, but the scheme was immediately attacked by a censor. Wo Ren joined the debate, producing a memorial which was as eloquent as it was obscurantist, identifying foreign technology with Daoist magic, pouring scorn on the idea of employing barbarians as teachers, and asserting the old principle that China's safety lay not in weapons but in the virtue and loyalty of her people. Wo Ren was backed by the scholar class in general. Although Wen Xiang's programme was not abolished, no scholar of reputation would join it. Although training in Western ideas continued to develop, Wo Ren's successful opposition undoubtedly slowed the pace by discouraging the participation of able men.

The lack of human resources therefore, was a major constraint on modernization. It was probably more important than the lack of money. The Imperial Maritime Customs provided the Government with large revenues which, being new, were not already appropriated to fixed purposes. A considerable part of this large and increasing sum was devoted to schemes of development. The funds thus provided were mostly transferred to provincial authorities for the financing of particular schemes; these funds acted as a kind of inducement investment, which encouraged the provincial authorities to find further means of development from their own local resources.

China's total investment in state-patronized industries, especially from 1866 (when the war indemnity was finally paid off, out of Maritime Customs revenue) to 1894, was by no means inconsiderable, and the scope of the developments undertaken was very wide. If these enterprises had been as successful as their founders hoped, and had in consequence been followed up by private Chinese investors, China might well by 1914 or so have laid the foundations of self-reliant industrialization in the Japanese manner.

In spite of the purblind reaction of Wo Ren and his supporters, there was a wide measure of agreement on the need for limited reforms. At the minimum there was no disagreement on the necessity of reforms aimed at the rehabilitation of the areas of China which had been the most devastated and disrupted by rebellion. The reformers assumed that the restoration of the prosperity of gentry society was the proper aim, for such had been the damage done in the Yangzi provinces that many gentry families were unable, even with government support, to recover their former property; there was undoubtedly a shift in the distribution of land ownership from the gentry to the peasant cultivators, although wherever possible the reforming provincial authorities restored the old property relations. Reform, at least in the sense of post-rebellion rehabilitation, was intended to be comprehensive; the movement was referred to as 'the Tong Zhi Restoration' (the restoration of the Tong Zhi reign period), a term from traditional historiography which indicates the recovery of a dynasty in decline.

Reform was focused on the land tax. The protégés of Li Hongzhang and Zeng Guofan, in power in the Yangzi area, sought to check the regressiveness of the land-tax assessments by abolishing the privileges legally enjoyed by the greater gentry families. They sought to limit the power of the yamen underlings to impose extra levies, although recognizing that local government could not function without local taxes. They attempted to exclude government employees from tax farming. They hoped to bring to an end the bribing of officials in order to secure reduced tax assessments, a practice indulged in as much by the poorer as by the richer proprietors. There was also an attempt to reduce the savage extra assessment which had been put on the counties of the south bank of the Yangzi Estuary at the beginning of the dynasty as a punishment for the stubborn resistance which their people had put up against the Manchu conquest, a burden which was still unchanged. Yet although the post-Taiping governors were honest, competent and thorough, their efforts at this most basic reform of all, the reform of the land tax, had only a temporary effect.

In the military field foreign arms were accepted, and with more reluctance foreign drill; but the reorganization of the national armed forces proceeded only slowly. The most necessary reform was to cut down the Green Standard forces to a fraction of their swollen numbers and modernize the remainder. This was done in two provinces under the influence of Li Hongzhang, but failed to spread. The new armed forces built up in opposition to the Taipings suffered a mixed fate. Zeng Guofan's Hunan army was by 1864 in hands other than those of the young reformers of the Practical Statesmanship (Jingshi) movement who had been his early lieutenants. Under cruder men who had risen from the ranks they had reverted to the corruption and brutality of traditional Chinese armies—so much so that the Hunan army had to be disbanded as a threat to public order. Li Hongzhang's Huai army, however, survived, went on to defeat the Nian rebels, and to become the nucleus of future military modernization. It was significant for the future that because the Government left the initiative in modernizing the army to the provinces, and most of the financing also, the centrifugal forces released in the struggle against the rebellions were perpetuated.

In the field of administrative reform little was done, and what was done was entirely within the traditional framework. Such new institutions as were created were called 'bureaux', a term intended to indicate their *ad hoc* and temporary nature. The Taiping period indeed saw two serious inroads into the traditional system whereby, ideally at least, degrees were bestowed only on the results of examinations, and appointments made only by the Emperor. The purchase of degrees had rapidly increased, in the attempt to raise the means to fight the rebels. Offices as well as degrees could now be purchased. At the same time, appointments were more and more being made by the provincial authorities themselves, partly to posts in the civil establishment and partly as advisers employed by provincial officials, personal advisers in theory but now paid out of public funds. Thus the attempts of the reforming governors to secure assistants of integrity and ability actually further undermined the traditional system.

At the same time, in the circumstances of the rebellion in which the affected provincial authorities were forced to use their own initiative, the group of officials who headed each provincial government had drawn together in an unprecedented way. Hitherto the possibility of effective resistance to imperial orders had been minimized by the fact that the governor-general, the governor, the superintendent of revenue, and the chief judicial officer each had the authority to memorialize the throne individually; and mutual jealousy ensured that it was difficult for them to maintain a common front. This had now broken down and the officials of a province tended to present to the throne an agreed view.

For the time being the deterioration of central authority did not weaken China. The new provincial rulers were as loyal as they were vigorous. In the most populous parts of China government probably improved in the second half of the nineteenth century. Only in the next century did this deterioration begin to show its inevitable consequences.

There was a consensus that the modern weapons coming into use should be manufactured in China. Arsenals were established. It was agreed that China should build her own naval steamships. The textile mills opened by Li Hongzhang and Zuo Zongtang were accepted on the grounds that they would manufacture uniforms. Beyond that, there was no widespread support for industrialization.

In 1865–6 Robert Hart, as head of the Imperial Maritime Customs, produced a memorandum which was accepted by the Zongli Yamen and submitted to the Throne. It argued the case for the building of railways, the opening of modern mines, the introduction of the telegraph, and the need to send diplomatic representatives abroad. Hart, however, assumed that foreign investment and foreign participation would be necessary, and this was enough to ensure that the proposal was dismissed immediately; even Li Hongzhang was adamantly against the introduction of foreign capital.

In 1867, in view of the imminence of revision of the treaties, the Government invited the opinions of the high officials of the capital and the provinces, in a letter outlining the demands which the foreigners were likely to make. The demands anticipated involved the creation of railways, the opening of mines and other industrial developments. All but a small and predictable handful of the respondents were against any such developments.

Opposition to foreign capital set one of the limits to modernizing development. Another was the belief of officials that private merchants and manufacturers, being by definition self-seeking and irresponsible, could not be trusted in the control of basic industries closely related to national security. As for consumer industries, although Li Hongzhang appreciated the wealth-creating possibilities of machine production in agriculture and manufacturing industry, the strength of Chinese prejudice against labour-saving innovations which would 'break rice bowls' was too strong.

A further restriction was put on the possibilities of development by Chinese hostility to the opening of factories on Chinese soil by foreigners. For this reason the most natural and effective means of the transmission of modern technology—the experience gained by Chinese staff and workers in modern factories introduced by foreigners—was for the most part unavailable. Only in ship-repairing yards. Treaty Port public utilities, and a very few small clandestine manufacturing enterprises was such experience obtainable, and the numbers so employed were very limited.

The second obvious avenue for the transmission of technology was the dispatch of students abroad. This began, but against every sort of obstacle the conservatives could impose. The largest group sent abroad at this time consisted of 120 adolescent boys sent in groups of 30 a year from 1872 to Connecticut to study in American schools; they became so rapidly Westernized, however, that the scheme was brought to an abrupt halt in 1881. A handful of students (numbered in tens rather than in hundreds) were also sent abroad for technical training in connection with the new arsenals and shipyards which were established at this time, but it was not until the first years of the twentieth century that significant numbers were trained abroad, and returned students began to exert an intellectual influence.

China's first modernization efforts therefore took place within severe self-imposed restraints: no foreign-owned industry; no foreign investment; no general industrialization; no legal changes which might protect and encourage enterprise, including that of returned emigrant Chinese businessmen who could have provided a very valuable channel of technology transmission; no encouragement of private enterprise in basic and defence-oriented industries; little or no incentive offered to train, either in China or abroad, in industrial disciplines; and, finally, no systematic attempt to maximize exports in order to accumulate capital.

Gradually the mood changed. The first naïve supposition, that all that was necessary to strengthen China was to acquire modern arms and all that was necessary for this was to import the necessary technology, began to give way. It was realized that unless the contribution of individuals to successful production was rewarded with official promotion, it would be impossible to recruit the necessary personnel. Li Hongzhang and his associates fully realized that one of the significant differences between China and the West was that in the West success in production and innovation was highly rewarded.

Then, with the Japanese example rapidly yielding its humiliating lessons, it began to be appreciated that a strong economy was the necessary basis of a strong defence. Yet the insistence on rejecting all foreign investment made it very difficult to develop mining and the necessary means of transporting coal and iron ore. The new arsenals, shipyards, mines, and steelworks operated in a vacuum, with neither infrastructure nor complementarities.

Gradually it came to be realized that dependence on officially sponsored industries and such private capital as could be attracted into the Government's ill-managed, ill-costed, and precarious industries would never be enough. Private enterprise must be encouraged, and if this was so then there must be changes in law and in official practice towards merchants before investors would have the necessary confidence.

Then came what was perhaps the most significant, and difficult, change: an appreciation of the impossibility of altering the technological basis of production in China without changes in social values. But this development had to wait for the new century and for a new generation.

Meanwhile, modernization went on with halting steps. The first initiatives were taken by the three greatest of the anti-Taiping leaders. Zeng Guofan and Li Hongzhang had been astonished at the effectiveness of British artillery, and by 1863 had created three small arsenals. Zuo Zongtang was impressed more by foreign warships than by the inferior French field-guns available in his area, and pushed for the creation of a naval dockyard at Fuzhou. The Court approved in 1866. Meanwhile Li Hongzhang had in 1865 established the large Jiangnan Arsenal, while a second comparable enterprise had been set up at Tianjin.

From these beginnings in the manufacture of arms and of warships, officially sponsored industrialization began to spread into the civil sector. The form of organization chosen was called 'government supervision and merchant management' (*guandu-shangban*). Official sponsorship and control thus dominated industrial development until the field was opened up to private enterprise by two later changes: the granting of permission to foreigners to open factories in the Treaty Ports, by the Treaty of Shimonoseki, 1895, and the passing of legislation from 1904 onwards giving legal protection to merchants, provisions for incorporation, and limited liability.

Li Hongzhang was the pioneer of *guandu-shangban* enterprise. He created the China Merchants' Steamship Navigation Company, which competed successfully with the foreign steamship lines in China's coastal trade. He opened at Kaiping in Henan China's first modern coal-mines, later developed into a coal, iron ore, and steel-making complex. He opened mills for the manufacture of cotton yarn and cotton cloth. His leading role was taken over by a fellow reformer, Zhang Zhidong, first as Canton, and then as Wuhan Governor-General. Zhang created a steelworks at Wuhan, textile mills, and factories producing cement, glass, paper, cotton yarn and cloth, and leather goods. Some other provincial leaders made similar attempts.

Although the scope of these first Chinese industrial enterprises was impressive and the total capital invested in them considerable, they were not on the whole successful. Historians formerly tended to dismiss them as examples of the inefficiency of any business conducted by any government, no further analysis of their history being necessary. It is an argument which, when the dramatic success of similar government-controlled pioneer industries in Japan is taken into account, can hardly be sustained. What was wrong with *guandu-shangban* enterprise was not government participation but *bad* government participation; and it did not improve over the years. On the contrary, it deteriorated as the more successful enterprises came to be seen as new sources of official perquisites and sinecures.

There were other causes of failure. Most fundamental, perhaps, was that while the assertion that merchants must be trusted, protected, and recognized as indispensable to China's wealth and strength came to be accepted, the change of heart was not accompanied by a corresponding change of behaviour. Officials continued to exercise arbitrary power; indeed in this respect the situation grew worse. Li Hongzhang, the first of the sponsors of *guandu-shangban* enterprise, was also the most liberal. He accepted the normal conventions of Chinese business in which shareholders were usually content to leave the operation of the business to a manager who was allowed full authority. In Li's scheme the Government replaced the shareholders, and the enterprises were run by experienced merchants, with a minimum of official interference. In contrast, Zhang Zhidong, although forced in theory to concede greater power to private businessmen because of the reluctance they had shown to invest in government concerns, took a much more bureaucratic attitude and attempted to keep a tight grip on management.

To some extent the conflict between private entrepreneurs and gazetted officials was mediated by the growth of new groups whose position was part-official, part-merchant. On the one hand the possibility of the purchase of rank and office allowed the merchant to play an official role, while on the other it was coming to be accepted that officials might with approval act as entrepreneurs. Even this, however, did not prevent official interference from prejudicing management. As a consequence, private investment in *guandu-shangban* enterprise, at first popular because it provided a means which the Chinese polity otherwise lacked of protecting business, became steadily less attractive. The official industrial pioneers, as time passed, became more rather than less dependent on government funds. There was then of course a corresponding increase in government power over the enterprises.

The faults of such government supervision were predictable. Commercial decisions were taken by unqualified officials. The Government, anxious to recover its investment, discouraged plough-back while the merchants, because they never had full confidence in the relationship, were even less disposed to accept long-term risks. The Government, usually creditor rather than shareholder, expected to be repaid in full if a firm went into liquidation; it was the private shareholders who lost. Successful firms, such as the China Merchants' Steamship Navigation Company, were raided for funds to help ailing ventures. Most fundamental of all, the officials were not primarily concerned with the promotion of commercially viable development; thus, for example, Zhang Zhidong sited his Wuhan steelworks where it could be under his own eye, ignoring the distance of his site from the sources of his raw materials, so adding costs which doubled the price of his finished steel.

It is sometimes argued that foreign competition was the main cause of the failure of *guandu-shangban* enterprise. This is improbable. Foreigners were not allowed to establish enterprises in the heavy industry sector, while imports of high-bulk commodities such as coal, iron and steel, cement, and glass would not have been able to compete with any competent Chinese enterprise. Advocates of this explanation also choose to forget that the economic privileges which foreigners enjoyed were insignificant in comparison with the privileges which the Chinese Government could and did bestow on these infant industries. The Steamship Navigation Company was given a monopoly of the transport of tribute grain from the Yangzi to Tianjin. The Wuhan iron and steel complex was given a monopoly of the supply of rails for the building of railways then in prospect. The new textile mills were given similar monopoly markets.

Foreign relations, 1861–1894

While it is true that in the years succeeding the Second War there was a revolution in China's attitude to the world, this revolution was not complete. Nor was it to prove irreversible. The most obvious deficiency in China's new policy was the lack of representation abroad. The strength of conservative hostility to the establishment of Chinese embassies was such that the individuals who at this time went abroad to represent the Chinese Government for particular purposes were shunned and reviled on their return. In 1865 Robert Hart argued strongly to the Zongli Yamen that for as long as China had no ambassadors, and so lacked direct contact with foreign governments, she would be at the mercy of the foreign representatives in Beijing, whose attitudes were often more belligerent than those of their governments at home. The Zongli Yamen was open to such an argument but not the Court.

In 1866 the Yamen made a tentative move in the direction of representation abroad by promoting Hart's Secretary for Chinese Correspondence, Bin Qun, to a suitable rank and sending him in the company of Hart (who was going on home leave) to Europe. He made the round of Europe's capitals and was well received.

In the following year Burlingame, the retiring American minister in Beijing, was invited to become an informal Chinese ambassador. He set off with two Chinese companions to America and Europe. He and his Chinese colleagues received unambiguous assurances from the governments of both the United States and the United Kingdom that neither government had any intention of exerting pressure on China to gain further advantages. Yet on their return Burlinghame's Chinese companions, the bearers of this good news, were treated more in the proverbial manner of the bearers of bad news; they were banished to the frontier. Burlingame was not there to protect them, having died of pneumonia in St Petersburg.

The paradox of the situation at court was that the more successful the policies of Yixin and Wen Xiang proved in securing friendly relations with foreign countries, the more the conservatives felt that they could relapse into complacent arrogance.

Throughout these years the conciliatory party was increasingly embarrassed by local attacks on Chinese converts to Christianity and on missionaries. Anti-Christian activities in China sprang from a variety of fears and prejudices, were differently motivated among different classes, and while partly spontaneous were sometimes encouraged by the gentry. It was widely believed that they were supported by powerful members of the Court, in an alliance which foreshadowed Manchu support for the last and greatest paroxysm of anti-Christian feeling in China, the Boxer Rising of 1900. It was even believed that Yixin's brother himself instigated the Tianjin massacre of 1870, and while the immediate circumstances of this incident seem sufficient to account for the events without resort to such an explanation, the fact that the story was accepted as perfectly credible is evidence enough of the atmosphere of the time.

Much of the hostility to the missionaries was based on superstitious fears, such as concern that the building of churches and mission stations was interfering with the geomantic influences of the landscape. Much of the trouble sprang from the dissemination of an anti-Christian literature of quite incredible viciousness and obscenity, in which every sort of vice or perversion of sex and cruelty were represented as the normal religious practice of Christians, a literature so abominable that beside it the worst of traditional European anti-Semitic outpourings seem uninventive. Hostility also often expressed a belief that the economic misfortunes of the poor were the result of foreign influence.

Some of the hostility was justified. Chinese religious sects traditionally provided protection for their members. In the case of Christian converts this protection was based, in the last analysis, on the foreign gunboat. The Zongli Yamen reported that in all the years during which it had dealt with foreigners no single case was known in which a missionary had reprimanded any of his converts.

Anti-Christian incidents occurred in hundreds each year. They were fed especially by French support to the Catholic Church, whose celibate representatives were in any case usually prepared to penetrate much further beyond the security of the Treaty Ports than their married Protestant colleagues. Catholic bishops claimed to correspond with provincial governors on equal terms. In the Chinese cities the Church Visible set out to be very visible indeed, its cathedrals often dominating the skyline as they had in medieval Europe. The Catholic clergy, in assuming Chinese dress, chose to adopt the costume of the Confucian gentry, to the fury of the élite of a country where sumptuary conventions were an expression of the whole hierarchical conception of good order and harmony. The enforcement of the claims of the Catholic Church for the return of the property it had acquired in China two centuries before was a constant source of anger. It may be added that as the Catholics gained far more converts than the Protestants, they contributed more to, and suffered more from, hostility.

The cause of the Tianjin massacre was as follows. The nuns of the convent in Tianjin paid premiums for orphans brought to them for care. The population believed that the children were cruelly maltreated and put to death for necromantic purposes. The belief was sufficiently widespread for the Zhili Governor-General (Chong Hou) to investigate the convent in person. He proclaimed himself satisfied that the activities of the nuns were simply charitable. But the belief and the hostility it engendered were unaffected. In 1870 the French consul in a burst of anger appeared with a pistol, demanded justice for the nuns, and shot at the *xian* magistrate. The shot killed the magistrate's servant. An uproar followed in which ten nuns, two priests, two French officials and three unconcerned Russian merchants were killed.

The gunboats restored order. The French government demanded redress. Zeng Guofan was called in by Beijing to negotiate. He shared none of the hostility towards Christianity felt by the gentry and the lower classes, and he was no lover of disorder. He recommended severe punishments, including the execution of fifteen offenders. The anti-foreign elements at Court condemned him as a traitor, and he was replaced as negotiator by Li Hongzhang; but Li's prescription proved to be even more severe. France was amply satisfied, and, when a Chinese mission of apology arrived in Paris, Thiers assured its leader that France had no wish that anyone should be executed, merely that good order should be maintained. Anti-Christian activity died down considerably thereafter.

Five years later, in 1875, another but rather different incident led to tension with Britain. It had been arranged with the Chinese Government that a British exploratory expedition should cross into China from Upper Burma. A young British consular official, Margary, travelled across China to Yunnan to meet the explorers. Against the advice of the local authorities there, that they could not be responsible for his safety, he chose to press on into aboriginal territory. *En route* he was murdered along with his Chinese train. Britain demanded compensation, and to this Sir Thomas Wade, the British ambassador in China, added other demands, which he forced Beijing to accept in the Zhefu (Chefoo) Convention. The Convention not only stipulated compensation for the family of the murdered man and a mission of apology but also exacted concessions quite unrelated to the event, including the opening of four more ports. On the other hand, concessions were made to China on the exemption of foreign goods from the *likin*, internal transit tax, and an increase in the import tax on opium. The British Government, however, refused to support its ambassador. The Convention was not ratified for ten years, that is until 1885.

Again, as after the Tianjin massacre, China sent a mission of apology.

Unlike preceding missions, this proved to be the beginning of permanent representation abroad; its members were not brought home, but were left in the capitals of the West. In this way the Zongli Yamen circumvented opposition to the dispatch of ambassadors.

Meanwhile the Chinese had been forced to dismantle another barrier to normal relations with the world. The young Tong Zhi Emperor having reached his majority in 1873 and assumed the reins of government, it became impossible for the Court to continue to deny to the foreign diplomats in the capital the right of audience. The kowtow was the stumbling block; the foreigners were willing to do only such obeisance to the Chinese emperor as they would do to their own sovereigns. The Court was forced to accept, but such face as could be saved was saved; the ambassadors were made to wait for many hours before being given a perfunctory interview in a pavilion reserved for the reception of tribute missions.

The chief guarantee of China's security lay in the determination of the British Government to refrain from pressing on China changes which might weaken the imperial government. Britain, moreover, used her influence to discourage other powers from using such pressure. France and the United States agreed.

In adopting such a self-denying policy Whitehall was strongly influenced by the Mitchell Report, which has already been quoted, suggesting that the first euphoric hopes of a vast trade in China had been illusory. The Report having been transmitted to London, British governments from then on acted on the assumption that little would be gained by any further opening up of China; the potential profits were not worth the risk of injury to the stability of the imperial regime and therefore to existing British trade. In vain the Old China Hands demanded a forward policy. With the approach of the revision of the Tianjin Treaty they launched a campaign to secure the complete opening of China, but Clarendon would have none of it. He instructed the British ambassador in Beijing, Sir Rutherford Alcock, to accept any arrangement satisfactory to the Chinese. The result was the Alcock Convention of 1869, the first international treaty which China negotiated from a position of equality: minor concessions made by the Chinese to ease restrictions on trade and travel were balanced by British concessions on tariff rates, including increased import duties on opium and increased export duties on silk. The Old China Hands responded with a clamorous protest. The British Government felt unable to support Alcock, and the convention was not signed. China's first equal treaty was thus aborted by the force of Treaty Port opinion. At least, however, the process of treaty revision had not further damaged Chinese interests. In fact, paradoxically, the episode of the Alcock Convention was a sort of victory for China, for the British Government had shown that it preferred to have no changes at all rather than impose changes in response to aggressive pressure from Treaty Port interests.

Meanwhile the decay of the old tribute system was made further apparent when in 1873 Japan intervened on behalf of fifty-four sailors from the Liuqiu Islands who had been killed by aborigines in Taiwan. Japan's claim to jurisdiction in the Liuqius was based on the fact that since 1609 half of the islands had been subject, and the other half tributary, to the western Japanese fief of Satsuma. As tribute missions were profitable, the king of the Liuqius had preferred to continue quietly to pay tribute to China as well; and so the Chinese were left in ignorance of the Japanese connection.

Japan invaded Taiwan. The Chinese guns manufactured in the Nanjing Arsenal proved useless. China was forced to accept that Japan had the right to represent the Liuqius, and five years later the Japanese annexed the islands completely.

Meanwhile on China's inner frontiers another rising of Sufi Muslims in Xinjiang had broken out, and the Russians took advantage of the situation to occupy the Kuldya region, north of the Muzart Pass. Yakub Beg from Kokhand also invaded Xinjiang. He was encouraged by the British who hoped that he would create a strong power which could check Russia's advance. China could do nothing, cut off from the Xinjiang rebels by another Muslim rebellion in the north-west. Both Britain and Russia courted Yakub Beg and recognized his new state.

With a threat in Taiwan and a threat in Xinjiang, the Chinese faced the fact that they were now vulnerable from both the sea and the steppe. There was a debate. One side argued that Xinjiang was barren and also indefensible; the greater threat came from the sea. The other side argued, on the contrary, that there was no great threat from the sea, whereas the loss of Xinjiang, by leaving Mongolia exposed, would seriously weaken the security of Beijing. Zuo Zongtang took a more sophisticated view. He argued that while the West wanted only trade, if Russia was permitted to absorb Chinese territory the West might then be tempted to redress the balance by seeking Chinese territory also. Zuo won the argument and was commissioned to restore Chinese power in the north-west. His campaign lasted from 1875 to 1877. Yakub Beg was forced to suicide. The main point in the expedition, however, had been to remove the excuse for Russian intervention and to recover Kuldya. A representative, Chong Hou, was sent to St Petersburg to negotiate. There in his inexperience he signed away three-quarters of Kuldya including the Muzart Pass, and agreed to an 'indemnity' of five million roubles and to Russian navigation of the upper Sungari River giving access to Manchuria. However, after a year of further negotiation Russia withdrew her claim to the Kuldya territory in exchange for an increased indemnity, by the Treaty of St Petersburg, 1881.

Thus unexpectedly reprieved on her north-western frontier, China within two years faced another threat, this time in the south. France had established her influence in Vietnam by restoring the Nguyen dynasty in 1802. Indo-China was then brought under French control by a series of treaties. The Annamese, who normally were by no means disposed to interpret their position of tributary to China in any but a cultural sense, now requested assistance from Beijing. Chinese irregulars, the 'Black Flags', were already operating against the French, and in 1883 China sent regular troops. Yixin and Li Hongzhang believed that China was not yet sufficiently strong to oppose the French, but the recent defeat of France by Prussia had encouraged a group of young hawks who had formed the 'Purist' party. The hawks also had a more serious argument, that France would not be content simply to conquer a non-Chinese tributary state but would use that conquest as a springboard to penetrate China via Yunnan and Guangdong. When a further French expedition was sent to Vietnam it was met by a Chinese army. The Chinese were defeated and forced to negotiate. On 11 May 1884 the French secured Chinese recognition of all French treaties with Annam. The Purists protested at this, and when they were offered command against the French they enthusiastically accepted the challenge. Their enthusiasm was shortlived. The French sank China's southern squadron, destroyed the Fuzhou naval yard, blockaded Taiwan and intercepted the grain tribute. A Chinese victory on land restored China's self-respect but did nothing to check the devastating operations of the French navy; so in spite of victory in battle China was forced once again to a humiliating peace, and to the loss of her influence in Indo-China.

The first Sino-Japanese war, 1894

The problem of the southern frontier was less urgent and less dangerous than the threat which was developing in Korea. In 1875 an armed Japanese surveying team clashed with Korean troops. Although Korea was China's closest and most strategically placed tributary, the Zongli Yamen, apprehensive of trouble, asserted that China had no responsibility for Korean policy, internal or external. Japan then proceeded to make a treaty with the Koreans which recognized Korea as an independent state. The treaty was on the familiar lines provided by the Western treaties with China and Japan.

Chinese abdication of responsibility for Korean policy left Japan free to establish control of Korea. Robert Hart of the Imperial Maritime Customs pointed out to the Zongli Yamen the probable consequences. He convinced Li Hongzhang, and China reasserted her claims of suzerainty by establishing a Chinese Resident in Seoul, encouraging Korea to open relations with the West, and supervising as the suzerain power the negotiation of the subsequent treaties. This reassertion of influence was supported by the Western powers, although all recognized that China's new interpretation of her ancient link with Korea as constituting a virtual protectorate had little foundation.

The abrupt opening up of Korea under Chinese pressure split Korean opinion. A reforming party led by the Korean Queen favoured Japanese assistance.

The former regent, the Taewongun, led the opposition. After an attempted coup against the Queen in which seven Japanese officers were killed, the Chinese, to pre-empt any punitive action by the Japanese, arrested the Taewongun and detained him in China, but were still obliged to concede to Japan the right to station troops in Seoul to protect the Japanese legation there. Soon after, as Korea's internal struggles continued, more Chinese troops were also sent to the peninsula and a young military official, Yuan Shikai (who was eventually to be the first President of the Chinese Republic), was despatched to supervise Korean government. Then Japan, taking advantage of the Sino-French war in Annam, forced Li Hongzhang to an agreement which virtually established a Sino-Japanese condominium at Seoul. The conflict took on a new international dimension at this point. Russia seized Port Lazarev in north-east Korea. Britain responded by seizing an island base, Port Hamilton. Japan in these circumstances backed away, and actually began to encourage China to reassert her authority in Korea. The Japanese retreat, however, was only *pour mieux sauter*. By 1894 she was ready. In that year a rebellion led by a Korean religious group, the Tonghak, an anti-Christian sect, broke out. The Korean Government appealed to China for help. The Japanese encouraged Yuan Shikai to attack the rebels, and then promptly sent in an expedition to support them.

Li Hongzhang was confident of Western support, but none came. This was the first of many occasions in which Britain and the United States, although recognizing clearly where their interests lay and although fully aware of the international consequences of the weakening of China's security, willed the end but grudged the means, and left China to fight her own battle—a battle which in the long run was not only against Japan but also against Russia, which was now an active claimant to influence in Korea.

War between China and Japan was declared on 1 August 1894. China was routed on both land and sea. The Japanese public, jubilant over their easy victory, expected that Japan would take control not only of Korea but also of Manchuria, Taiwan, Shandong, Jiangsu, Fujian, and Guangdong. Their hopes, however, were premature by half a century; it was not until the Second World War that Japan was able to assert control of these areas of China for a time. On this occasion her territorial demands were moderated to include only the Liaodong peninsula, on the south coast of Manchuria, and Taiwan. Even this, however, was too much for the other powers. Russia, France, and Germany intervened to force the Japanese to disgorge Liaodong under threat of war, though Britain and the United States did not join the intervention. The Treaty of Shimonoseki, 1895, thus amended, stipulated the recognition of the independence of Korea; a huge indemnity of 230 million taels; the opening of Chongqing, Suzhou, Hangzhou and Shaxi to trade; the right of Japanese nationals to engage in manufacturing in China; and the cession of Taiwan and the Liuqiu Islands.

The war had put China's policy of limited modernization to the test and proved it worthless. Defeat showed that modern arms were useless in pre-modern hands. In a sense it vindicated the old arch-reactionary Wo Ren, who believed that China's true strength lay in the capacity to mobilize her people; but the conditions of such successful mobilization in the modern world were not those which Wo Ren had envisaged; they were those which the Japanese had embraced. The climate of opinion in China changed overnight. Contempt and derision were now poured not upon the heretical supporters of change, but upon their orthodox opponents.

The Western powers were as disillusioned as the Chinese public. From differing motives they had supported the unity and integrity of China, and to this policy they had been true in their fashion. It now seemed possible that China's unity and integrity were past salvation. The powers hastened to complete their contingency plans for the partition of China by staking out their spheres of influence. The first step was the competitive acquisition of naval bases on the coast of China.

In this competition Russia began with an advantage. The pusillanimous policy of Great Britain and the United States, the two powers most strongly interested in the preservation of China's intergrity, had left China isolated in the struggle with Japan. Russia had then stepped in as the leader of the triple intervention and saved Liaodong for China (or, more properly, for future absorption by Russia). She now offered loans to China to assist in the repayment of the monstrous indemnity imposed by the Japanese, an indemnity the annual instalments of which exceeded Beijing's total revenue. China, disappointed by the failure of Britain to come to her aid, had no choice but to accept, in full knowledge of the dangers, reliance on one rapacious neighbour against the other. In a secret Sino-Russian agreement the Russians exacted their price. Arguing that if Russia were to be in a position to give China military help against Japan she needed the shortest possible railway route to Vladivostok, and that this meant the building of a line across Chinese territory, its protection by Russian 'railway guards', and the cession of a strip of territory along the line, de Witte, the Russian Minister of Finance, secured a dominating position for Russia in Manchuria. To guard against the further assertion of Russian power Germany then seized the opportunity of the murder of two missionaries in Shandong to exact from China a 99-year lease of the port of Jiaozhou. The Russian response was, having first considered whether to take over Dairen or Port Arthur, to take over both. This was followed by the further exaction from China of the right to build a railway through the Liaodong peninsula to the border of Korea; Liaodong, so recently saved from Japan, now passed into Russian control. The British secured a lease of Weihaiwei and the Hong Kong New Territories (1898). France followed with a lease of Guangzhou Bay. By non-alienation agreements and other arrangements Japan gained a sphere of influence in Fujian; France in Guangdong,

Guangxi, and Yunnan; and Germany in Shandong. It was accepted that the Yangzi region was of special interest to Britain.

China's situation was made even more dangerous by the alliance of Russia and France and by the self-imposed isolation of her most natural ally, Great Britain. The British, conscious at last of the danger of further inactivity, sought a way out of isolation. Approaches to Germany failed. Britain therefore turned to Japan, whose navy in combination with the Royal Navy could out-match any Franco-Russian naval combination. Just as China had been forced to accept the protection of one aggressor, so the British in their belated attempt to protect China's integrity were forced into a perverse alliance with the other.

Fear of imminent partition precipitated the 1898 Reform Movement in China. Yet it can now be seen that the danger was much less acute than the Chinese supposed. While all the powers had their contingency plans for parti-tion drawn up, they were not equally ready to accept partition as a solution. Their economic interests differed sharply. Britain traded with all of China; exclusive control of the Yangzi region would have been poor compensation for the possible loss of trade in other regions. The United States had nothing to hope for from partition, there being no part of China in which she could claim to have special interests. On the other hand, French trade in China was rela-tively undeveloped; her hopes of profit lay more in lending and investment. Exclusive control of a part of China might facilitate such operations and could also be used to avoid commercial competition on equal terms. The traders of undeveloped Russia suffered severely in conditions of free competition, and consequently a major motive of Russian territorial expansion was the hope of using political domination to eliminate commercial competition. Such a motive might point to acceptance of a partition of China, but Russia had wider ambitions. She hoped in time to absorb all of China, and a partition, especially one in which Japan was able to halt the Russian advance into Liaodong and Korea, would have closed off this possibility.

The German attitude was ambiguous. On the one hand, Germany's belated search for colonial empire prompted the acquisition of power in Shandong. On the other hand, her growing ability to compete commercially led her mercantile interests to incline to the British view and stress the importance of free access to the whole of China.

Germany therefore entered into an agreement with Britain in 1901 that neither would seek to acquire Chinese territory. This agreement was perhaps in itself enough to prevent the partition of China. It was certainly of more importance than the subsequent Open Door declarations proposed by the United States and supported by Britain. The first of these (1899) asked only for the preservation of equal commercial opportunities in China, implicitly in the event of partition. The second (1900), which asked more positively for the preservation of China's integrity, had little effect. The response of those

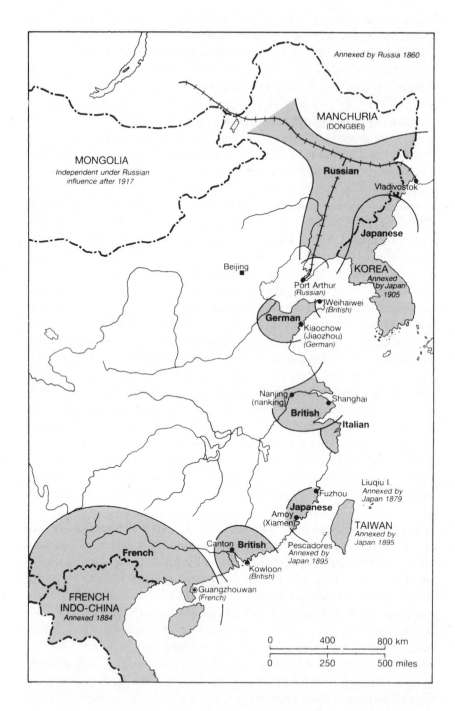

Map 5. Concessions and spheres of influence, *c.*1900 (After *Cambridge History of China*, xi, 114)

powers most likely to do damage to China's integrity was at best non-committal. The Anglo-German agreement, although confined to only two powers, was explicit and binding.

The question of imperialism

The battle for concessions is usually regarded as a high point of imperialism in China. The meaning of the word imperialism is ambiguous. It is an '-ism' word, intended to apply to ideas and not to facts. It describes an attitude of mind, or a set of principles and policies, concerning the desirability of exercising political domination beyond one's own national borders. From this original meaning it has been extended to the facts of political domination abroad, whether they are inspired by imperialist ideas or not. One consequence has been that the actual, and varied, motives for the exertion of such dominance become obscured, and the differing degrees of commitment to territorial expansion on the part of different countries are also obscured. The meaning of the word, having shifted from imperialism as an idea to imperialism as a set of objective facts, has then made a further move to imperialism as a historical process, in which conscious ideas play only a minor role and in which certain facts inevitably come into existence. This is the so-called Marxist concept of imperialism. In fact it owes much more to Lenin than to Marx. It has at least the virtue of being relatively precise. In the advanced stage of capitalism the capitalists, who cannot but accumulate more funds than they can profitably invest at home, seek outlets for investment abroad. Organized in competing nation states, they seek to limit international capitalist competition by monopolizing investment opportunities in particular areas of the world through political domination. They seek in particular for areas which provide protected markets and protected sources of raw materials. The results for the countries dominated are always the same, and on balance always bad. Their existing social and economic structure is broken down and replaced by a set of dependent relationships with the metropolitan power.

The general applicability of this theory of 'economic imperialism' does not concern us here, although many of the criticisms which must be made of it with respect to its application to Chinese history would probably apply more widely. The most obvious fact of course is that China did not lose her sovereignty, though she suffered some marginal limitation of it. This limitation arose through the exaction from China by the other powers of certain 'privileges'; but most of these privileges were in fact merely incomplete substitutes for rights mutually enjoyed by the citizens of those countries which subscribed to existing international practices, rights which were generally open to Chinese citizens in all the countries concerned. The two most obvious limitations on Chinese sovereignty, extraterritorial jurisdiction and the treaty tariff, certainly bound China in ways in which other nations were not bound; but in origin they had been enforced simply in order to secure clarifications of, and consistency in, existing Chinese practices.

It is equally clear that the pursuit of political domination of Chinese territory bore no relation to advanced capitalism. The two powers committed to systematic expansion, Russia and Japan, were the least advanced economically, and they were certainly the last countries involved which could be considered to be suffering from a surfeit of investment capital. The most advanced capitalist power, Great Britain, showed no interest whatever in the acquisition of Chinese territory; with the power to dominate the entire coast of China unchallenged for half a century she had merely acquired, and then only with reluctance, one tiny island at the southern extremity of the Chinese Empire, in order to provide security for her traders who had been held hostage at Canton. Although Britain had at this time the largest private investments in China, these were mostly trade-related. As for loans to the Chinese Government, they were inspired largely by the British Government as part of its policy of preserving Chinese independence, and were entered into by British lenders without enthusiasm; the pressure which the Foreign Office imposed on British banks can be documented. The theory of economic imperialism also clearly implies a search for territory from which, by the use of tariffs, the rigging of freight rates, and other means, competition can be excluded. Again, the power, least disposed to such policies was Britain, the most advanced capitalist power, which from the Treaty of Nanjing onwards sought no exclusive privileges from China and bent all its efforts to the maintenance of free trade. And again it was backward Russia which sought for special advantages.

Thus in the crisis following the defeat of China by Japan in 1894–5 it was the most advanced capitalist powers—Britain, the United States and laterally Germany—which opposed the partition of China and so saved her from dismemberment at the hands of the predatory feudal powers, Russia and Japan. In sum, the Leninist theory of imperialism, if it is to fit China, has to be stood on its head: imperialism was not connected with the last stage of capitalism but with the first.

6

Reform and revolution

The reform movement of 1898

Defeat by Japan in 1894–5 was the greatest shock that the Chinese had suffered since the Opium War. The victor was not a great Western power, but a small Asian country. The defeated Chinese forces were as modern as those of the enemy. The old excuses would not work this time. The conservatives were at last put on the defensive. These were the circumstances in which the Hundred Days of Reform commenced, led by young graduates. They had gained the ear of the young Emperor Zai Tian, who had succeeded to the throne as a minor in 1875 with the reign title Guang Xu. One should not see them, a group of a dozen young men, as a tiny clique, isolated and helpless before universal opposition. They looked forward to considerable support, and their hopes of success were not entirely unfounded.

A generation had passed since the language school, the Tong Wen Guan, had begun after 1861 to publish the first translations of Western books. The work of translation had been taken up by others. From technology, mathematics, and international law the translators had passed on to the classical works of European culture and politics, until by the 1890s most of the main ideas of the West were available in Chinese or in Japanese. The relevance of these ideas was argued daily in new, Western-style newspapers in Chinese.

Protestant missionaries played an indispensable role in the introduction of Western ideas. The publications of the Society for the Diffusion of Christian and General Knowledge were influential, while at the same time they fostered a readership for the new Chinese press. The first of these newspapers were founded by missionaries and their associates, and those that followed by independent and non-Christian Chinese. There was also a very rapid development in the publication of new journals, most of which supported reform. Far too numerous to be dealt with by the official censorship, they were not confined to the Treaty Ports, but were also produced in most of the provincial capitals. Many were closely related to new 'study societies'—disguised political associations—which were also a remarkable feature of this time. Of the influential Western books, one of the most important was Mackenzie's *The Nineteenth Century: a History*, an uncompromising glorification of the

European idea of progress. This was a notion that challenged traditional Chinese concepts of a static society in which the maintenance of stability was the criterion of success. In so questioning the whole 'golden age' basis of Chinese social and political morality, the intellectual foundation for reform was thus laid.

The Reform Movement did not wholly depend upon the translation of Western works. Many Chinese writings on reform were already current and influential. What most obviously distinguished the thought of their authors from that of the previous generation was their acceptance of the painful idea that it was not enough to adopt certain Western techniques and use them to preserve Chinese values. Values must also change.

The most powerful expression of the views of the more conservative reformers who clung to Chinese values, Governor-General Zhang Zhidong's *Exhortation to Learning*, was published in the actual year of the Reform itself. Written by one who had been the most vigorous of China's reforming states-men, it was designed to make the case in favour of reform but at the same time to warn against changes which would threaten Confucian culture. The new generation, however, were aware of the ambiguity of Zhang's resounding slogan, 'Chinese values, Western means': Yan Fu, the influential translator of Adam Smith and Herbert Spencer, was quick to point out that Western means and Western values were inextricably related.

There were three possible attitudes to the traditional culture: to continue to insist, like Zhang Zhidong, on the superiority of Chinese values; to repudiate them and accept the values of the West, an attitude which no Chinese of this generation could wholly take; or to mediate the necessary changes by finding in the Chinese heritage itself some means of rationalization of the acceptance of Western values. This last theme was already common ground among many of the reform writers, and it was such writers who prepared the ground for a reinterpretation of Confucianism from a conservative creed looking back to the golden age to a millenial vision of the future. Much of this writing was very special pleading, well deserving the familiar Chinese condemnation of historians who 'distort the past to manipulate the present'. Much of it, how-ever, drew genuinely on buried alternatives within the Confucian tradition.

One such alternative had been growing in popularity since the eighteenth century. Its advocates were especially radical because they did not confine themselves to proposing different interpretations of the classical texts, but denied the authority of some of the texts themselves. There were in existence two versions of the classics. Until the usurpation (AD 9–23) of Wang Mang only one had been known. Having been orally preserved by scholars after the first Qin Emperor destroyed the Confucian books, the texts had been written down in the new Han script current at the time of their recovery. Then, during Wang Mang's usurpation, a new version was discovered (in suspiciously supernatural circumstances), written in the ancient 'tadpole' characters. The two versions came to be distinguished as the 'modern script' (*jin-wen*) and the 'ancient script' (*gu-wen*), and it was the latter which became accepted thereafter. Yet two books in particular in the ancient script canon continued to have a doubtful reputation. They were of special importance because they comprised so large a part of the historical records of ancient times, which Confucius had claimed to preserve and interpret. One was the *Classic of History* itself, in the ancient script version. The other was the *Zuo Commentary* on the *Spring and Autumn Annals* which told the story of Confucius' own state of Lu, presided over by his ideal ruler, the Duke of Zhou. In the eighteenth century the adherents of the modern script version of the classics were given new encouragement when the ancient script of the *Classic of History* was proved a forgery. It was also shown that the *Zuo Commentary* was actually a separate chronicle which had been manipulated to form, quite inappropriately, a commentary on the *Spring and Autumn Annals*. The modern-text school had always argued thus, and had been especially devoted to an alternative surviving commentary on the Annals, the *Gong Yang*.

Of course, the choice of the texts to which one gave credence was not determined by textual criticism alone. Behind all the philology were differing views of the meaning of Confucianism. Modern-text scholars were passionate reformers; their adherents included Lin Zexu and his close friend Gong Zizhen. They took a quasi-religious attitude to Confucius, worshipping him as 'the uncrowned king' rather than respecting him simply as the greatest of teachers. They combined a sort of religious determinism with pragmatic reforming vigour, in a manner familiar enough in the West but much less common among the schools of Confucianism. Their values were essentially the social values of Confucius, but to them the means of achieving these values was the active response of the committed individual to the actual circumstances of his own time. Within this view, and derived from the modern-text scholar's belief in the significance of the prescriptions of the *Book of Changes*, was also the idea that the most effective action is that which recognizes and exploits the tendencies of the times. One can perceive in this system of belief the elements that brought such scholars, at this juncture in Chinese history, to the leadership of the Reform Movement in association with the Protestant missionaries. They were much more disposed than any other group within Confucianism to embrace the Western notion of progress sustained by the initiative of individuals, and of a morality whose rules of application evolve in relation to changes in circumstances. It was almost predictable that some modern-script scholar would soon find, in the texts which they favoured, an appropriate Confucian rationale for comparable Western attitudes. Kang Youwei provided it.

Kang (1858–1925) was born in Guangdong to a family of scholars. He studied under a teacher, Zhu Ciqi, who took a keen interest in the history of Chinese institutional changes over the centuries, and whose teaching therefore disposed his pupils to take a relativist view of institutions. Kang, however, like many young thoughtful Chinese in every generation, was not content with orthodox studies, even the most liberal, and like so many other distinguished thinkers of the past he left home and the classroom for a period of solitary reading and meditation in the mountains. There he underwent a mystical experience in which in a sudden vision he saw that 'I and all things are one'. His experience was not without precedent: several of the great figures of Confucian thought had undergone this flash of intuitive enlightenment. The idea came from Buddhism rather than Confucianism, but for Confucians it implied no other-worldly quietism. It was a prelude to action, a springboard to vigorous participation in affairs.

The greatest thinker whose career had begun in this way was the Ming dynasty philosopher Wang Yangming. Wang's philosophy stressed that the moral order was to be understood not as something in the external world, but as something inherent in man himself, in the individual conscience. Introspection, in which a man measured his own unruly desires against an infallible inner knowledge of moral truth, was the only source of wisdom. Wang equally emphasized that moral self-knowledge existed to be applied; it was useful only as the compelling force of practical action in the world of society and politics.

Wang was not the first Chinese to undergo this mystical experience and to interpret it as a categorical imperative to act without fear or favour. And Kang Youwei was not the last; young Mao Zedong recorded in one of his youthful notebooks a similar though less dramatic enlightenment from which he drew similar implications.

Kang Youwei's mystical enlightenment was succeeded by another, less mystical but equally mind-opening experience; on his way to Shanghai he passed through Hong Kong. There he saw for the first time what modern Western government and enterprise could do. He found it impossible any longer to maintain the notion that the foreigners were China's inferiors in all but material force. He found a new world, some of whose values were visible in the very streets. He sought to learn all he could of it. He made contact with missionaries, and he later acknowledged that he owed his conversion to the cause of reform chiefly to the writings of two of them. Timothy Richard and Young J. Allen.

In 1888 Kang went to Beijing and submitted his first memorial. The Imperial College refused to transmit it to the Court because Kang was not a graduate. He returned south, resolved on four things: to pass the metropolitan examination and so, as a graduate, to win the right to be heard; to provide an intellectual justification of reform in terms which Confucianists could acknowledge; to organize public pressure for reform; and to gain the ear of the Emperor. In 1895 he took the degree of *jinshi* with the highest honours. Already he had opened his own academy in Guangdong where he expounded his revolutionary interpretation of Confucianism and his plans for reform to a growing group of young disciples. These ideas were published in two books. The first, *The Forged Classics of Xin*, took up the attack which the modern-text school had maintained against the ancient-text tradition, and sought to prove that the ancient-text versions of the classics were entirely spurious, having been faked to provide a legitimation of Wang Mang's usurpation. By this means Kang sought to undermine orthodox resistance to reform. His second book, like his first, took up modern-text ideas but developed them far beyond their original implications. Modern-text scholars had long argued that the manifest differences in laws, customs, and institutions between the three dynasties of the golden age (Xia, Yin, and Zhou) showed that change was inherent in history. This much was by now almost common ground in China, but Kang in his second work went on to argue from certain elements in the modern-text canon that change would inevitably go through three phases: the era of chaos, the era of rising peace, and the final era of universal peace. He then identified the Western idea of progress with the era of rising peace. The most shocking argument he used was implicit in the very title: known in the West as *Confucius the Reformer*. The Chinese title includes one half of the phrase, 'to distort the past in order to manipulate the present'; the rest of the phrase is implicit. Confucius insisted that he had done no more than transmit the historical records of the great ancient rulers. Kang denied this. The golden age which Confucius described had never existed; it was a vision of the future.

Kang meanwhile was engaged in political organization. He played a leading part in the creation of the new 'study societies'. This name was a euphemism for associations which were in fact created for a political purpose: to force the Court at Beijing to undertake reform through the pressure of public opinion. This purpose made their existence illegal, and after the first flurry of reform activity following the Treaty of Shimonoseki of 1895 they were suppressed. They survived nevertheless by various subterfuges. Kang's own Self-Strengthening Society became a newspaper publishing house. Censorship made this role also precarious, but at least the organization won a respite; and by one of the many paradoxes of imperialism, Chinese newspapers could evade censorship by putting themselves nominally under foreign ownership.

China's failure to regenerate herself in the modern world is often explained in terms of broad historical tendencies and social forces. Perhaps the final explanation will be of this kind; but in the particular case of the failure of reform in 1898 it seems to be more readily explicable by the situation at court and by the actions of individuals in positions of power. Indeed it could be argued that the great social forces were conspicuous here only by their absence. In the claustrophobic struggles within the Court, the constituencies to which both reformers and conservatives could appeal scarcely extended beyond the vermilion walls of the Forbidden City itself. While the study societies mobilized such support for reform as existed in the country as a whole, their membership was very small, and their influence depended on the support of a few great individual officials such as the reforming Governor-General of Hubei and Hunan, Zhang Zhidong, and the military commander Yuan Shikai. Only through such patrons could they participate in the struggle at Court, and in the event their patrons took no action.

The most significant fact of 1898 is the simplest and most obvious fact: that for thirty years the Dowager Empress Yehenala, the former imperial concubine, by the exploitation of Chinese family obligations, by systematic and single-minded intrigue, and very probably by murder, had contrived to maintain her power by securing the succession of one child emperor after another, so that imperial authority was in abeyance virtually from 1861 until the end of the dynasty. During that time Yehenala had removed from the scene everyone with sufficient courage to oppose her, leaving in the great offices of state only such men as would bow to the orders of her eunuch favourites. By 1898, although the Emperor officially ruled, the 63-year-old Dowager still pulled the strings from her retirement.

In spite of these unfavourable circumstances the young Emperor Zai Tian, thanks to two liberal-minded tutors, Weng Tonghe and Sun Jianai, grew up with a strong sense of his imperial duties, a knowledge of English, an interest in Western ideas, and a determination to save China from the extinction that seemed to threaten her. After the beginning of the Scramble for Concessions, he sent word to the Dowager that he would not rule a doomed country, and that unless he was given power to reform China he would abdicate. Yehenala, in the face of this direct challenge, had no alternative but to agree. At the same time, she took the necessary steps to secure her position. Her faithful follower Rong Lu was made governor-general of the metropolitan province and commander of the new modern armed forces around Beijing, and an edict was issued ordering all officials civil and military who owed their position to her benevolence to put their gratitude on record.

Yehenala was not against all change. She had supported the efforts of Li Hongzhang and Zeng Guofan, and she retained her confidence in Zhang Zhidong even though his reforms in Hunan and Hubei went far further than any previous attempts and had already brought to his area many of the innovations that Zai Tian and his young advisers were now to attempt to apply to the whole country.

After the Emperor's message demanding the right to exercise his proper authority had been sent to the Dowager, a memorial, inspired as the first formal step to reform, was submitted to the Emperor by a sympathetic censor, Yang Shenxiu, and a Hanlin Academy reader, Xu Zhijing, requesting that 'the policy of the country should be settled'. An edict in response to this was immediately issued by the young Emperor, stating that policy henceforth would be based upon the abolition of outworn customs and the study of Western ideas. On 12 July 1898 and on the initiative of Weng Tonghe, Kang Youwei was summoned for an audience.

The policies of Kang Youwei, which Emperor Zai Tian adopted with little change, can be divided (true to his modern-text beliefs) into a minimum and a maximum programme. His minimum programme was concerned with what he regarded as the three essential preconditions of further reform: the modernization of the traditional examination system, the elimination of sinecures, and the creation of a system of modern education. His maximum programme, towards which no steps were taken during these Hundred Days, was a constitutional monarchy.

The reformers have frequently been accused by historians of bringing down opposition upon their own heads by attempting to push through radical reforms in too short a time. This is too simple a judgement. Much of what they sought to do had already been done in Hunan by Zhang Zhidong. A good many of their apparent novelties had precedents in Chinese history and could hardly be said to represent drastic new departures. And they were at great pains to avoid arousing unnecessary opposition. The establishment of schools and colleges to teach Western subjects went no further than the reformers of Hunan had already gone, and the study of the classics remained the basis of education. The setting up of bureaux to superintend the building of railways and the development of mines, to undertake research into tea production, to supervise the silk industry, and in general to encourage both agricultural and industrial production, were scarcely radical acts in an age when several trusted viceroys had already opened mines, encouraged railways, built textile factories and patronized chambers of commerce. As for the development of agriculture and sericulture by the establishment of state institutions to promote the diffusion of the best available techniques, such policies had a longer history in China than in the West.

The issue in education which was most likely to arouse widespread and bitter opposition was the abolition of the traditional examinations. They were the centre of the system, the point at which those educated in Confucian moral norms were introduced into the government of the Empire. There were probably a million young men in China who had already prepared themselves for the orthodox examinations and whose hopes would be dashed were the examinations to be abolished. The reformers, themselves almost all distinguished graduates, knew this well enough, and made no attempt to destroy the system abruptly. Their only drastic measure was to abolish the notorious eight-legged essay; but this had been the target of many reformers in the past; many great Confucian thinkers had condemned it or severely criticized it. One Qing emperor, Kang Xi, had actually abolished it, though it had soon been revived. And although this particular part of the examination was abolished by Zai Tian and his young consellors, the principle that the examinations would consist in the first place of essays on the Four Books and the Five Classics was maintained. There were important qualifications, however. Questions on the classical texts were to be concerned with application to contemporary problems. They were to be supplemented by questions on 'Western' subjects, in the first instance those relevant to economics. As the student moved upwards through the various levels of examination, this Western content was to be increased.

There is no evidence that a million student voices were immediately raised in protest. The country scarcely knew what the changes were. The opposition at court, in fact, used false rumours to attempt to create opposition beyond; but of that opposition—spontaneous or contrived—we know nothing. On the evidence, it was not youth but age which opposed reform—the gerontocracy in power in the central ministries, the Six Boards, and at Court.

In the abolition of sinecures and redundant posts the reformers appreciated that a comprehensive policy of rationalization of the bureaucracy would take time. The posts actually abolished were all notorious examples of waste. At the same time, the Emperor ordered that those who had been made redundant should be maintained in Beijing on the grounds that the development of China would require more rather than fewer officials. It may be that the abolition of sinecures was still a major factor in opposition to reform, but it could not have been because large numbers of officials were suddenly deprived of their livelihood. No such thing happened. It must also be remembered that there was nothing sacrosanct about the list of civil posts in China. Departments were frequently chopped and changed in numbers. They were seldom wholly abolished—the bureaucratic mind does not work like that—but cuts were perfectly familiar. The real problem was that sinecure posts were now more often occupied by Manchus than by Chinese.

In the actual struggles which took place at court over the Reform Movement two issues dominated. The first was the question of communication. The second was the question of patronage.

Kang Youwei's aims were democratic, at least to the extent that he wanted the people of China to be taken into the confidence of the Emperor, and the Emperor to be in touch with the aspirations of the people. Perhaps his ideas of democracy were limited to its usefulness as transmission belt and sounding board. Perhaps he saw in democracy primarily a method of mobilizing mass national feeling. Whatever the limits of his hopes, however, Kang's plans demanded the immediate creation of some means of direct communication between government and people, without the mediation of officialdom. Two problems were here involved. The first was that only officials of high rank could memorialize the Throne directly, and none of the young Emperor's youthful reforming counsellors had such rank; as a result, reform could not have been initiated at all had it not been for the sympathy of courageous officials of higher rank, who were prepared to put their names to proposals written by the reformers. Of these, the censor Yang Shenxiu subsequently suffered death for the part which he played, and Li Duanfen, an official who had proposed the foundation of a modern university, suffered exile. The second problem was that memorials to the Emperor had to pass through conventional official channels, and this process gave ample opportunity for the use of every device of protocol or pedantry in order to reject a document unwelcome to the bureaucrats. Zai Tian now decreed that any Chinese citizen, official or not, could address the Throne. He ordered the great offices of state to transmit to him all memorials from their own members, however junior, and to pass them on unopened. The bureaucrats resisted. A crisis came when a junior official of the Board of Ceremonies, Wang Chao, wrote a memorial urging the Emperor to pay a state visit to Japan to study Meiji reforms at first hand. This suggestion was more than the Board of Ceremonies could stomach. They refused to transmit the memorial. Zai Tian responded by degrading the entire membership of the Board. Such an act made conservative resistance certain.

The question of patronage was equally explosive. Yehenala's power had been built up by her assumption of imperial patronage. If Zai Tian succeeded in resuming the right to promote and demote, the Dowager's power would melt away like the snows of yesteryear. Her immediate supporters such as Rong Lu also enjoyed, by delegation from her, enormous patronage; they too had much to lose. Zai Tian was well aware of the limits of his authority in this respect. A Chinese emperor with normal power would probably have initiated reform by a purge of opposing ministers, who would have been degraded, exiled, imprisoned, or executed as the case demanded. Zai Tian could not take this normal autocratic course, but was compelled to use more devious ways. In general, he sought to find minor posts for his reforming counsellors, and to promote them to a rank which would permit their being employed in secretarial capacities within the Grand Council, the Council of Strategy, the Zongli Yamen, and the Six Boards of Government, and then to insist on their right to memorialize him directly over their own unbroken seals. In this position they might try to influence their conservative seniors, first by reason and then, if that failed, by the threat implied in their right to memorialize independently. Until the crisis over the state-visit memorial, however, Zai Tian made no attempt to appoint to or demote from a senior central office. At this point the Dowager's follower Rong Lu, possibly as a deliberate challenge, recommended to the Emperor forty of his own clients to assist in the reform. Zai Tian ignored him.

The wrangle over the memorial and the rejection of Rong Lu's recommendations were the real crises of the Hundred Days, and show the issues which were vital to Yehenala and the Court. They had little to do with the actual reforms which the young Emperor had decreed. They represented only the alarm of a usurper at the threat to her power, and the fury of her clients at the danger to their perquisites.

By then Zai Tian was aware that the reaction was near. He issued a decree appealing to his ministers in the capital and in the provinces to publicize his reform edicts, in the hope that Chinese public opinion would rally to his support. His appeal was in vain; and there was no other way in which he could reach his people.

When this failed he was forced to a final gamble. Of the three armies within reach of the capital and under the supreme authority of Rong Lu, one, stationed at Tianjin, was commanded by Yuan Shikai who was a patron of Kang Youwei's Self-Strengthening Society. Now the reformers were forced to put Yuan's support to the test. A secret emissary was sent to Tianjin, with the Emperor's order to Yuan to march on Beijing and arrest Yehenala. What happened is not known. It was widely believed then that Yuan revealed his orders to Rong Lu. The evidence is not conclusive; but certainly Yuan made no move and Rong Lu's guards suddenly moved in to arrest the Emperor and his counsellors.

The young Emperor remained under house arrest until his death in 1908. Kang Youwei escaped with foreign help. Six other reformers were captured and executed. Worse excesses were prevented by foreign intervention, but the wrath of the anti-reform faction smouldered on until, when the Boxer Rising gave a new opportunity, others who had been associated with the Hundred Days were judicially murdered in belated revenge. The six who died in the palace coup were the first martyrs of the Chinese revolution. It was said that among them, Tan Sitong, the young philosopher from Hunan, although he could have escaped chose to remain and die. 'Blood will have to be spilt for the revolution;' he is supposed to have said, 'let mine be the first.' There is no proof of this, but the fact that the story was soon believed throughout China indicates how the reformers won in having lost. China chose to believe that Tan had died the perfect model of a Confucian hero, in the cause of reforms which his murderers condemned as anti-Confucian. This belief dramatized an irreversible shift of opinion which left conservative orthodoxy stranded and doomed.

It could be said that the Hundred Days failed because Chinese public opinion was still unorganized and inarticulate. It was only after this failure, and in reaction to it, that a modern Chinese public opinion began to crystallize. Kang's efforts to mobilize opinion in order to put pressure on the conservatives had been insufficiently effective; now, ironically, that pressure began to grow with great rapidity. Out of the study societies that he had encouraged there grew in a very few years an extraordinary number and variety of political associations.

The focus of this new political movement was the protection of the young Emperor, but the burst of loyalty to his person concealed the fact that the alien dynasty which he represented was no longer a tenable object of loyalty. As the rumours of the events of the Hundred Days spread it became obvious that the desperate efforts of the young Chinese reformers to save their country from partition and extinction had enjoyed the support of not one single Manchu, except the Emperor Zai Tian himself, and had been brought to naught by Manchus. Chinese and Manchus, all but assimilated in the course of two and a half centuries, now drew apart. The next step would be nationalist revolution.

The Boxer movement

Before this growing opinion in favour of revolution could make itself felt the conservatives at court made one last effort to turn back the clock. The opportunity was provided by Boxer insurgence in northern China in 1899 and 1900. The sect was one of several which had grown out of the dispersal of the White Lotus rebels a century before, and its name was derived from the ritual exercises by which its members sought invulnerability to the arms of their enemies. Their characteristic 'boxing' exercises went much further back, and were a variant of a form of callisthenics widely practised (and still practised) in China. The sect was confined to northern China, and until 1899 was small and insignificant; stirrings of revolt against foreign influence in this area originated not with the Boxer sect but with the Big Swords society in Shandong. Nevertheless, once this revolt had begun, the Boxers' claim to invulnerability was attractive to desperate, poorly armed men who were determined to face the foreigners and drive them from China.

Anti-foreign rebellion sprang from a belief among distressed groups in Northern China that their troubles were the result of the presence of the foreigners. The causes of distress were numerous, but the numbers of the destitute were greatly swollen by three factors. First, there had been famine in the poor part of Jiangsu province north of the Yangzi, and many of its victims sought refuge in Shandong province, which was then itself struck by dearth. Second, the breakdown of the Grand Canal and the diversion of its traffic to the coast had thrown into destitution large numbers of workers whose strong mutual-aid organizations gave them considerable power to create trouble. Third, the army reorganization begun by Rong Lu involved massive demobilization of traditional forces and no provision was made for alternative means of livelihood. None of these factors had any but the most indirect connection with the foreign presence, and foreign influence was far less in the north than in south or central China. Nor did the Boxer Rising itself begin as an anti-foreign movement. In its earliest stages, the insurgents' banners bore the familiar slogan 'destroy the Qing and restore the Ming'. The change from this to 'support the Qing and drive out the foreigners' has to be explained.

The activities of the Germans in Shandong provide part of the explanation. In 1897 members of the Big Swords society, already much patronized by anti-foreign gentry and officials, murdered two German missionaries in Shandong. The Germans retaliated by seizing Jiaozhou. The Big Swords redoubled their patriotic activities. The Germans burned down their villages as a reprisal. It is at this point that the Boxers appear with their claim of invulnerability and take over the leadership of the anti-foreign movement, turning the spearhead from the Manchus to the Westerners. The change seems to have coincided with the extension of support to the insurgents by officials. One of these, Yu Xian, Governor of Shandong, was a patron of the Big Swords, and it is probable that his influence was exerted to harmonize the activities of the two societies in a common front against the foreigners.

In rural north China almost the only visible signs of foreign influence were the missionary and his converts. The characteristic Boxer operation, early in 1899, was therefore to attack the houses of Chinese converts. Occasionally they attacked churches, and more rarely missionaries. There was at this point no reason to anticipate that their sporadic local activities would grow into a full-scale attack on foreigners throughout northern China. The local authorities could have dealt easily with them had Beijing ordered suppression. Another factor was necessary, and that was the support of the Court.

The conservatives had overcome the reformers in 1898, but victory had proved almost as shameful as defeat. The foreign powers, who had hoped to see China set at last on the road of reform, were disappointed. They were sympathetic towards the young Emperor, and made it clear in the bluntest fashion that if he were 'to die at this juncture of affairs', as the British ambassador put it, the effects on China's relations with the powers would be incalculable. Yehenala was humiliated. Her brother-in-law Zai Yi, who had played a major role against the reformers and whose son would succeed to the throne should the Emperor Zai Tian be deposed or killed, was frustrated in his ambition by the attitude of the powers. He was mortified when the diplomats unanimously declined an invitation to celebrate the naming of his son as heir apparent.

The provincial and local authorities were at first uncertain as to how they should treat the insurgents. Such sects were illegal, and were usually repressed very firmly if they became openly active. Some district magistrates suppressed the Boxers in the normal way; but when they took over the anti-foreign stance of the Big Swords, many Chinese officials began to tolerate them. Many of the local gentry were bitterly anti-foreign and anti-Christian. The privileges and the power of the missionaries and their followers seemed to them to symbolize China's humiliation and their own. The fear and resentment among the gentry were shared by many officials. The educated Chinese classes, moreover, although they were the representatives of a secular and rational tradition, were not entirely without superstition. For example, astrologers flourished even in the circles of the great. The Boxers' claim of invulnerability was attractive. While at least one sceptical *xian* (county) magistrate put the claim brutally to the test in his yamen courtyard and was confirmed in his scepticism, others more than half believed. More important, however, was the ancient Chinese idea that when the people 'rise in righteousness' they are both justified and irresistible. The idea of the Boxers' invulnerability was accepted as a symbol of the invincibility of the people.

As the Boxers gathered strength with the tolerance of the gentry, officials higher up began to take note. Yü Xian openly espoused the Boxers, constituted them an official militia, and changed their name from Yi-ho Quan (the righteous and harmonious fists) to Yi-ho Tuan (the righteous and harmonious militia). France protested, Yu Xian was transferred, and his successor as Governor, Yuan Shikai, dealt firmly with the insurgent bands and restored order in Shandong, but the trouble then spread to Zhili (now Hebei) and the rest of the north.

The Court was now well aware of the movement and divided between apprehension of the power of the rebels and hope that this power might be used to defeat the foreigners. Even among the extreme conservatives who surrounded Yehenala there was opposition to the idea of giving support to the Boxers; even Rong Lu dragged his feet as the Dowager gradually shifted from hostility to tolerance and from tolerance to support. He could do no more. There was a conspiracy afoot, led by the vengeful Zai Yi, to persuade Yehenala to go to war against the powers, with the Boxers as allies. This conspiracy came to a climax when the pro-Boxer faction informed her falsely that the foreign diplomats had demanded a virtual protectorate over China. In a dramatic scene she relayed this spurious information to the assembled Court, and appealed to all to support her in a last defence of the dynasty and the country. Weeping nobles and officials knelt and pledged their lives. The sceptical could only remain silent. The Court opened the gates of Beijing to the Boxers and declared war on all the powers at once. The extermination of all foreigners was ordered.

If the secret societies throughout the whole of China had joined with the Boxers the foreigners might indeed have been driven out by the wrath of the people. In the centre and the south, however, the stirrings were feeble and were very promptly suppressed. The governors of the centre and the south had no illusions as to the outcome of a war in which Rong Lu's unblooded new recruits and the rabble of adolescent Boxers took on the soldiers of Europe and Japan. They refused to acknowledge the declaration of war, responded to demands from Beijing for troops with merely token forces, and negotiated a 'business as usual' arrangement with the foreign consuls. Of eight provincial authorities south of the Yellow River, only two favoured war and they were silenced by the rest. The imperial armies in the north failed to stop the foreign advance, and the Boxers proved only too tragically vulnerable. After a siege of two months, from 14 June to 14 August 1900, allied troops entered Beijing and relieved the foreign legations.

The conservative cause collapsed. Zai Tian's concubine (he had never loved his wife, who had been chosen for him by the Dowager) attempted to keep him in Beijing when Yehenala's supporters were preparing to flee; for if he could stay in the capital he would be restored to power, the powers being sympathetic towards him. Yehenala solved this problem in her own way: the concubine was thrown down a palace well and Zai Tian dragged off to Xi'an. Three representatives were nominated to stay behind and face the allies; two of them fled, and the third hanged himself. Li Hongzhang, now aged 78, was brought back to cope with the situation. Rong Lu's friends hurriedly patched up a forged diary (even using excerpts from the memorials of some of those who had died for their attempts to prevent support for the Boxers) to show that he, Rong Lu, had disagreed with the Court's policy. The allies accepted it.

It was the domination of the Court by purblind reactionaries rather than the protest riots of the poor of northern China that was the key to these events. Zai Yi and his brothers who shared his new power were members of the ruling Manchu house who had shown no talents and had held no posts of influence hitherto. With the reformers crushed and those officials sympathetic to reform silenced in September 1898, there had been little opposition to the assumption of power by these reactionaries. The presidents of three of the Six Boards were enthusiastic supporters of the Boxers; the presidents of the other three were hostile, but two of them were silenced by execution. The Zongli Yamen was actually in the hands of Zai Yi. Government, in fact, had been taken over by Manchu nobles and courtiers with little experience, survivals from another era who were obscurantist, superstitious, parasitic, and vengeful. For two and a half centuries the Manchu emperors had struggled to keep the bannermen of the great clans from control of affairs by ruling through the Chinese. In the civil wars of the nineteenth century the delicate balance had been upset when, the Manchus having failed to stem the Taipings, Chinese officials assumed more and more power. In 1898 the pendulum swung violently back.

The years from 1860 to 1900 were the critical years for the adjustment of China to the modern world. Those who held office within reach of foreigners were, however reluctantly, beginning to acknowledge the need for change and even to lead it. China's failure was due primarily to a virtual interregnum preserved by Yehenala from 1861 until the end of the dynasty in 1912. China faced the greatest storm in her history rudderless.

The end of the monarchy

Five years after the Boxer catastrophe the cowed Court had accepted most of the reforms for which the young reformers had died in 1898. The changes were initiated by three memorials jointly submitted by governor-generals Zhang Zhidong and Liu Kunyi. The first proposed the establishment of modern schools at all levels, and the inclusion of modern subjects in the examinations. The second proposed the end of sales of office, the reduction of the Green Standard forces, an increase in the anti-corruption allowance, the recruitment of men of outstanding talent, and a policy of frugality, including the abolition of sinecures. The third proposed the modernization of the armed forces, the promotion of agriculture, industry and technology, a programme of translation of modern books, and regulations for mining, railways and trade. In addition, the first steps were taken to codify and modernize the law, to abolish the examination system gradually by reducing the quotas of graduates, and to survey all revenues in order to make possible an annual budget. Twelve new ministries replaced the Six Boards.

The most striking feature of this new reform movement, however, was the immense voluntary, non-government effort which was touched off by the commitment of the central government to change. The Court could not stem the flood which it had released. For example, while the new official schools were established only slowly, private foundations multiplied apace and with a more modern curriculum proved far more popular than those of the Government. Control of education, the first principle of Confucian government, was thus lost. A new generation sceptical of the old values, trained in Western ideas, impatient for results, and indifferent if not hostile to the Manchu court, began to appear. In the area of projected political reform symbolized by the creation in 1901 of the Superintendency of Political Affairs (which Kang Youwei had advocated in 1898), organized pressure groups and voluntary associations multiplied; Chinese public opinion became a reality, and the press discussed issues of constitutionalism which the Manchu government was most reluctant to raise.

Foreigners were now strongly impressed by China's new willingness and ability to change, and half-gratified, half-alarmed by the strength of organized public opinion, displayed in trade boycotts and resistance to economic concessions. This was backed now by more efficiently trained military forces whose presence made the consuls hesitate before bringing up the gunboats.

After the victory of Japan over Russia in 1905 the pace of change quickened; an Asian but constitutional power had beaten a European but despotic power. Nationalism and liberalism resumed in Asia the close connection which they had displayed in nineteenth-century Europe. It was now impossible for the Manchus to evade the demand for a constitution and a parliament. In 1905 two missions were sent abroad to study foreign constitutions. The country responded with the creation of Constitution Protection clubs. Their programme was provided by Kang Youwei's disciple Liang Qichao, in exile in Japan since the destruction of the Reform Movement. He demanded responsible parliamentary government, local self-government and an independent judiciary. In August 1908 the Court issued an Outline of the Constitution. It proved to be highly autocratic. On the Japanese precedent, there was to be a tutelage period of nine years before a parliament was created. Meanwhile a cabinet was formed. It proved to consist of seven Manchus, one Mongolian and only four Chinese.

These arrangements merely inflamed the feelings of the constitutionalists. The domination of the new cabinet by Manchus and their Mongol allies seriously damaged the already weakening links between the Chinese and their foreign rulers. The Manchu nobles, sending their sons for military training in Germany and holding command of the armies of the capital and the metropolitan province, monopolizing the twelve new ministries, and now all but monopolizing the new cabinet, had broken all the rules of the balance of appointments between Chinese and Manchus. At the same time the Court sought to weaken the provincial Governors-General, the greatest of whom were Chinese. In this they were aided by the death of Li Hongzhang and of Liu Kunyi in 1901. The two most powerful political figures remaining, Zhang Zhidong and Yuan Shikai, were kicked upstairs as presidents of the Grand Council and so deprived of their provincial power. When in 1908 the Emperor Zai Tian and Yehenala died, the Regent (Prince Chun) graciously but firmly gave Yuan Shikai leave to retire to nurse an injured foot. Zhang Zhidong died in the following year.

In 1909 the Regent created elected provincial assemblies. He had no intention of promoting decentralization. On the contrary, he hoped that these merely consultative assemblies, by acting as sounding boards and transmission belts, and possibly also by acting as a check on the provincial administrations, would increase the effectiveness of central government. The result was dramatically different. Decentralization of authority had already gone too far, while the new economic interests that were developing rapidly were provincial rather than national, in their markets, their organization and their relations to government. For a gentry no longer linked to the centre by the examination system, which had finally been abolished in 1906, the effective source of the benefits which political action could gain was no longer the national but the provincial capital. It was also unwise to have created provincial assemblies while postponing the establishment of a national parliament. In the absence of an elected assembly at the national level the provincial assemblies gained all the moral authority of their position as elected bodies. Unable to operate at a national level, China's new political leaders acted with all the more vigour at the level of the province, and so far from being content with a consultative role they immediately set about the task of governing their provinces in virtual autonomy.

In addition, delegates from the assemblies came together to launch one petition after another demanding the immediate establishment of a national parliament. Their efforts won only a reduction of the period of tutelage from nine years to six; parliament was to meet in 1913 instead of 1916. This satisfied no one.

The provincial assemblies were remarkable for the speed with which they developed political competence and confidence. They were largely composed of holders of the traditional degrees, but the leaders among them were men who had some knowledge of Western ideas. Their members brought with them the experience of a commanding position in the affairs of their own localities, of practical administration of these affairs, and of the habits of consultation and compromise which such experience provided. They were untouched by social radicalism and uninfluenced by extreme nationalist opinions. If one may risk a historical analogy, they were in composition and experience much more like the English Parliament of 1688 than the French Estates-General of 1789. They were not at all republican, and would have considered the achievement of a constitutional monarchy a revolution sufficiently glorious. They were not anti-Manchu until the Manchus revealed themselves to be anti-Chinese; and then it was they, rather than the revolutionaries, who forced the ruling Aisin Gioro clan to abdicate and go home to Manchuria.

The revolutionary movement was quite separate from the constitutional movement, and its sources of support were very different. It was confined at first to the far south. The inhabitants of Guangdong and Guangxi had never been wholly reconciled to Manchu rule. North China, on the other hand, had shown little disposition to reject it. Central China, favoured under the Qing as under previous dynasties with the highest examination quotas, had not been as hostile as the south; but there was a tradition of seventeenth-century resistance to the conquest in the Yangzi valley and, in the twentieth century, a great revival of interest in the patriot-scholars who had led it. There were also folk memories, now revived, of the bloody massacres with which the conquerors had revenged themselves for the stubborn resistance of certain Yangzi cities. The Taiping Rebellion had added another dimension to these folk memories, expressed in heroic tales of the imaginary exploits of its leader Hong Xiuquan. In South-east Asia, on the west coast of America and Canada, and elsewhere there were Chinese populations who, being almost entirely southern in origin, had carried abroad with them their southern hostility to the Manchus, while their experience of life under Western rule had left them prepared for more radical solutions to China's problems, and they still identified themselves with their brethren at home and with the fate of China.

It is not surprising therefore that the revolutionary nationalist movement was founded among overseas Chinese. Sun Yatsen, its founder, had been born in Guangdong, but his peasant family had emigrated to Hawaii when he was about 9 years old. There he attended a mission school, from which he moved to Hong Kong to study modern medicine. His first political act was an attempt to persuade Li Hongzhang to support moderate reforms. It was only when he was refused a hearing that he turned to revolution. His first adherents were from among his former fellow-pupils in the mission school. His first funds came from his brother, who had made good in Hawaii as a cattle dealer. Sun travelled round the Chinese overseas communities seeking money to support risings in China.

In persuading the overseas Chinese to support him he had to contend with the influence of the constitutionalists, led by Liang Qichao. At first he made little headway. Only when the hope of peaceful change began to fade did opinion, and money, begin to swing in his direction. In 1896 while in London he was kidnapped by the Chinese Embassy, but released by the British Government. This incident brought him recognition as a patriot and a hero. His risings, however, were all failures, and as they took place on the remote southern borders of China it would have mattered little had they been successful.

Meanwhile, other groups of revolutionaries were being formed among Chinese students in Japan. Most of them were from the Yangzi provinces. They were mainly from higher social classes than Sun, they had received a formal Chinese education, and they were exposed in Japan to more radical ideas than were generally influential even among the Chinese communities abroad. On their return to China they began, often under cover of working as teachers, to organize revolution. In 1905 Sun went to Japan and established contact with them. At first the students were disposed to reject him as a man of no education—by which, in spite of their radicalism, they meant a man of no Chinese education. They found on acquaintance, however, that he was well read and by no means the secret-society bandit they had supposed. Sun persuaded their various factions to join a loose federation, the Tong Meng Hui (the Covenant Society or the United League), of which he was elected president. The advantages to the student groups were Sun's ability to raise funds outside China and his influence with foreigners. The existence of the Tong Meng Hui, however, was shadowy and Sun's role as leader was even more obscure. The various elements of the alliance pursued their own separate activities. Of these the most effective were the operations of the Hunanese returned student Huang Xing. Huang was convinced that the revolutionaries should concentrate on central China. He made Wuhan, at the strategic crossing of the Yangzi, his centre. Huang was also convinced that the revolution would succeed only if the imperial armies could be infiltrated. The recent military reforms facilitated such penetration. They included the recruitment of NCOs and commissioned officers from the literate among the rank and file. These new junior officers proved receptive to the revolutionary message.

In October 1911 an accidental explosion in Wuhan brought in the police. They discovered a revolutionary organization engaged in the manufacture of bombs. They were also able to confiscate lists of the membership of the local cells. Soldiers were implicated. A group of these, acting as much for self-preservation as for revolution, seized the Wuhan Arsenal on 10 October. Two army regiments mutinied in their support. The Manchu commander retreated in alarm. A Chinese commander, Li Yuanhong, was forced by the mutineers to proclaim himself the head of a national revolt, under threat of death. Impressed by their enthusiasm and courage, Li embraced the revolution; he was later to be a President of the Republic. When the news spread, army units mutinied elsewhere and local revolutionary groups rose, but in no sense was there a mass rebellion. There would have been little threat to a government which could have depended on the loyalty of the ruling classes.

At that moment, however, the Manchus could depend on no such loyalty. Power throughout China was in the hands of the provincial assemblies. They were disappointed by the delay of constitutional changes. They were disgusted by the manipulation of recent changes in favour of the Manchu nobles. Above all, they had been roused to anger by a recent decision of the Court to nationalize the railways. This issue turned the damp squib of a local rising into a revolution. Partly in protest at foreign railway building, and partly in hope of profit, local gentry in China had been raising capital to build lines themselves. The Beijing government, however, was concerned to create an integrated national network, and did not favour these local lines. Moreover the integration of the railway system would require further foreign loans, and to this the gentry were hostile. In Sichuan they protested, and when their protests failed they rioted. The Government brought up troops from the Wuhan area and quelled the demonstrations. But these were not the rice riots of expendable beggars; it was leading members of the gentry who faced the volleys of the imperial troops; and the imperial guns, as it proved, had fired the last salute of the Manchu dynasty. When the news of the Wuhan rising spread, one by one the provinces of China declared their independence.

In almost every case this was decided by an alliance of provincial assembly men and low-ranking soldiers. The revolutionary organizations themselves played a subordinate role and had only limited influence. When the Wuhan rising took place Sun Yatsen was in the United States, raising funds; he learned of the rising only from the American press. Hurrying home to China, he discovered the weakness of his position. The key to the situation was not Sun Yatsen but Yuan Shikai, who since 1906 had created China's new, modern Beiyang (Northern Seas) Army and for whose support Court and revolutionaries now competed. Summoned to Beijing, Yuan reminded the Manchu nobles that he had been sent home to nurse his injured foot and assured them that his foot still troubled him. Only when the Court became desperate did his foot mend. He then sought terms which would meet the demand of the moderates for a constitutional monarchy and at the same time would give him supreme military authority; but even the moderates now demanded a republic. The Court, however, accepted the constitutional principles which Yuan proposed and agreed to put him in a strong, though not yet unassailable, military position. His troops then recovered Hanyang from the revolutionaries to remind them of his power. From this point luck was with him. The Court conservatives murdered his only non-Beiyang military rival; and when they found an alternative prime minister to keep Yuan from gaining further power, the revolutionaries assassinated *him*. The young Manchu commander of the imperial bodyguard, fearing to be ordered south to face the insurgents, avowed lack of competence and resigned, to be replaced by Yuan's close follower Feng Guozhang. Yuan was now in a position to force the abdication of the Emperor at a time of his own choosing.

There was little dispute that only Yuan could be President, and when Sun Yatsen was elected by 16 out of 17 provinces as provisional President, it was only on the explicit understanding—accepted by Sun himself—that he was simply to act as caretaker until Yuan could be elected. The problem was how far Yuan's powers should be limited. There were two issues. The first was constitutional: Yuan must accept a cabinet responsible to a parliament, and in order to ensure this, the new provisional Senate and not the President would make the Constitution. The other was the question of the location of the capital: would it be in the south at Nanjing where the revolutionaries were strong? Or would it remain at Beijing controlled by Yuan's Beiyang garrison? The revolutionary assembly was disposed for reasons of sentiment to leave the capital at Beijing. They actually voted for this, and it took all Sun's eloquence to persuade them to reverse the vote.

Yuan was willing to concede the constitutional points for the moment. As for the transfer of the capital, he did not oppose it in principle, but merely expressed the view that the problem of public order in the north would for the present require a new President to remain in Beijing. Satisfied that he could become President of a republic on terms which would not limit his authority, Yuan now turned on the dynasty. One need not necessarily see in this any signal treachery: Yuan had after all offered the revolutionaries a constitutional monarchy and the idea had been overwhelmingly rejected. Virtually every organized body of opinion, even most of the former supporters of a constitutional monarchy, had rejected it. Had the northern provinces supported the Crown the dynasty might still have been saved, but with most of the north having already declared for a republic, with Shanxi hostile, and mutinous troops between Beijing and the Great Wall, the question now was one of safety—how to negotiate a secure and dignified retreat to the Manchurian homeland and private life. Even a less ambitious and devious man than Yuan might well have felt that the dynasty was beyond salvation. Yuan's Beiyang subordinates, who only weeks before had sworn undying loyalty to the child Emperor Pu Yi, now in a body advised his abdication for his own safety. Yuan, who retained the confidence of the bewildered young Dowager, Zai Tian's widow, to the end, added his own authority to the views of his subordinates. On 12 February 1912 an edict of abdication was issued on behalf of the child Emperor. The Manchus, who had first brought China's borders to a new breadth and the Empire to a new prosperity, and had then presided over the shrinking of her territory and the humiliation of her peoples, were escorted home.

The government of Yuan Shikai

Yuan, authorized by the Manchus to form a provisional government and then elected President by the revolutionary assembly in Wuhan, had now a dual legitimacy; if in dispute with a parliament, he could fall back on his imperial appointment, the last act of the dynasty. More urgent, however, was the question of his transfer to Nanjing. Yuan waited until a delegation had arrived in Beijing to escort him south, and then a sudden rash of riots and mutinies broke out in protest against his departure. The foreign powers, who had declared their neutrality in the revolutionary struggle in response to the good order which had been kept around the Treaty Ports, now moved up troops in case it proved necessary to protect their nationals. The southern delegates retreated with some loss of dignity to the safety of a foreign hotel. Yuan was then able to point out how dangerous it would be for him to leave. The capital remained in Beijing until 1928. Again there is no need to find in this event proof of deep duplicity on Yuan's part: some protest against the removal of government from the city which had been the capital for over two and a half centuries, and whose economy was almost wholly dependent upon its role, was to be expected, while the Beiyang troops were no doubt genuinely alarmed at the proposed departure of their patron. Yet it is a fact that prominent in the rash of riots and mutinies was mutiny by the highly disciplined 3rd Division, a force more likely to have acted in obedience to Yuan's wishes than in defiance of them.

A provisional constitution was now promulgated. Legislative power was in the hands of the Senate representing the provinces until such times as a parliament could be elected. The President was Commander-in-chief. He had the right to appoint all high administrative officials, but not members of the Cabinet. The Cabinet would be responsible to the President, but answerable to Parliament. This provisional constitution was a compromise, the result of negotiation between Yuan and the revolutionaries. Within a month its ambiguity caused friction which then led to civil war and thence to the tragic division of China from 1913 until 1931. China's experiment in parliamentary government lasted scarcely one troubled year.

The political forces supporting the Republic were already divided into two. The former constitutionalists created the Progressive Party. Sun Yatsen's Tong Meng Hui, up to this time a secret society, was reorganized as a legal political party, the Nationalist Party, or Guomindang. Superficially, a stable and effective two-party system was possible, especially as the Guomindang proved willing to lay aside for the present its more radical aims, such as the redistribution of land to the peasants. This, however, was not to be sustained. The two large groups rapidly split into cliques with a personal or provincial basis. None of them had an explicit programme. Membership of more than one party was common. The electorate was miniscule; Members of Parliament scarcely represented anyone except themselves. China had not developed to the stage when strong and competing social interests would give shape to politics. With so little outside Parliament to which to respond, the Members responded instead to patronage and bribes.

Chinese tradition was in most respects inimical to the parliamentary experiment. The idea of a competition for power among political factions was regarded with distaste. Majority voting was not regarded as an acceptable substitute for consensus. Strong government was identified with autocratic authority. When the Cabinet Secretary, who regarded himself as the President's representative *vis-à-vis* the ministry, chided Parliament for 'interfering in administration', most Chinese regarded this reprimand as expressing only common sense. Yuan Shikai's challenges to the constitution were not seen as matters of principle by most Members of Parliament, nor by China's journalists. The minority of the Guomindang who opposed Yuan's autocratic proceedings were decried as dangerous radicals. This minority within the revolutionary party found little support even from their colleagues. Most of these—even Sun Yatsen himself—were more inclined to see the Guomindang as a sort of national union of all men of goodwill, rather than as a political party contending for office.

The first crisis came within weeks. Yuan Shikai had appointed a cabinet in which the premier, the minister of the interior and the minister of war were his own close associates. Only the peripheral ministries were given to members of the Progressives and the Guomindang. His prime minister, Tang Shaoyi, however, although he had hitherto spent his career as a subordinate of Yuan, proved to be no one's puppet. He had studied in the United States and understood the workings of representative government. Yuan Shikai could have chosen no better premier had he wished to ensure the authority of Parliament. But this was far from his wish. Yuan was a traditional mandarin; worse, he was a traditional soldier. Hierarchy he understood, command was what he was accustomed to, and loyalty was what he expected from subordinates. In any case, to reign but not to rule was in Chinese experience a contradiction in terms. Yuan set about ruling, and found his premier, Tang, opposing him. Tang insisted on scrutinizing the President's inaugural speech. He then opposed Yuan's plan to seek a loan from the international consortium of banks recently formed to organize loans to China. Finally, when Yuan attempted to nullify the election of a Guomindang-sponsored candidate to the military governorship of Zhili by using his authority as Commander-in-Chief to post the new governor south, Tang resigned and the four Guomindang members of his Cabinet with him. Chinese public opinion responded by offering scorn rather than support.

Yuan, having learned from his experience with Tang Shaoyi, now appointed a complete nonentity as premier, but his choice was a man so ludicrously incompetent that even the Progressive Party which normally supported him rebelled and refused to confirm the Cabinet in office. Yuan therefore induced a public campaign to accuse Parliament of obstruction at a time of national danger (the British having renewed their activities in Tibet). Parliament backed down and accepted the new Cabinet so that foreign loans could be raised to strengthen defence.

Hitherto Sun Yatsen had avoided a confrontation. He had little interest in Parliament, the creation of which he regarded as premature. He had laid down what he believed to be China's most appropriate path to democracy, which lay through a period of development of democratic self-government at the grass roots. National parliamentary government, Sun believed, should come at the end of the process. Meanwhile, Yuan must as far as possible be supported, critically but loyally.

Had the Guomindang been numerous and vigorous enough to carry out this preliminary political education at the grass roots, Sun's policy might in the long run have been successful. Little, however, was done; the Party did not even have branches at village level. Moreover, the question of local government institutions could not be solved because of deep disagreement between the two major parties. The Progressives, heirs of the provincial assemblies, wanted decentralization to the provincial governments. Sun Yatsen, on the contrary, feared the power of the provinces and sought a system in which there would be no powerful intermediaries between the central government and China's two thousand counties—not least because the Progressives were strong, after 1911 as before that date, in the vast majority of provincial governments and the Guomindang in very few.

When the first regular elections to Parliament were due, Sun was persuaded by his fellow leader Song Jiaoren that the Party should fight the election competitively, and on the platform of responsible cabinet government. The Guomindang won an absolute majority.

Song Jiaoren was shot dead when about to board the train from Shanghai to Beijing. The complicity in his murder of Yuan's prime minister, Zhang Bingjun, was proved. Few doubted the complicity of the President himself. Yuan now hastened negotiations for a loan from the international consortium, and accepted it on terms which put the salt gabelle and other revenues in the hands of foreign administrators as security for the loan. He did not consult Parliament until the negotiations were complete.

Sun was at last driven to accept that Yuan could only be brought to order by force, but his position was difficult. Many Guomindang Members of Parliament were still prepared to make a last effort to control the President by parliamentary means. Even more depressing was the revelation that the military leaders in the southern provinces, to which Sun's political influence was largely confined, were reluctant to support him, mainly because the division of opinion in Parliament and the country was reflected within the forces they commanded. Yuan struck first. Having obtained parliamentary approval of the foreign loan, he attacked Jiangxi whose military governor, Li Liejun, was the only staunch military supporter of Sun's political faction. The other pro-Guomindang commanders gave only half-hearted help. Within three months they were defeated. Public opinion applauded Yuan's victory.

Yuan arrested the radical Guomindang Members of Parliament and created his own party, using funds from the Bank of Communications. With this, the support of the Progressives, and a mob calling themselves the Citizens' Corps surrounding Parliament, he secured his election to the formal presidency (10 October 1913) before the constitution under which his election should have taken place had even been drafted. As President he had power and patronage enough to secure by intimidation and bribery the promulgation of a constitution which gave him autocratic power. While forcing Parliament to draft this constitution he appealed to the provincial authorities against the Guomindang members who opposed him; they unanimously supported the President, who then claimed that he had public opinion on his side when, as his next act in clearing his way to autocratic power, he dismissed the Guomindang from Parliament. This left too few members to form a quorum. Yuan again appealed to 'public opinion', and was advised to dissolve Parliament. The steps from this to the restoration of the monarchy on 31 December 1915, with himself as the first Emperor of a new dynasty, were short and simple: the same combination of force, bribery, and manufactured opinion served.

In declaring himself Emperor, however, Yuan went too far. He could create the appearance of legitimacy and of popular acclamation, but while on the earlier occasions his machinations had probably done no more than exaggerate a public opinion which, at the worst, regarded his government as an evil less than that of the guomindang firebrands, preferring the devil they knew to the devil they knew not, this latest action had no support whatsoever. It would be difficult to find a parallel case of a reversal of popular judgement so swift and so complete.

Yet the grounds of this reversal had been prepared by the reaction of Chinese public opinion to renewed Japanese pressure, an expression of ambitions which were to culminate in 1937 in a full attempt at conquest. There was general agreement in Japan that Japanese national security required a close alliance with China and Korea in a common front against the extension of European power in the Far East. But this belief did not, in itself, dictate that Japan would attempt to assert political domination over mainland East Asia. She would have preferred an alliance of equals had her two neighbours shown themselves capable of sufficiently increasing their wealth and strength; but in the absence of successful modernization, such allies would be a liability rather than an asset. Japanese policy therefore wavered between two poles: that of an alliance of equals, and that of Japanese domination which could enforce modernization. The choice was muddled by other factors. First, the conservatives in Japan, the successors of those who had resisted the Meiji Restoration and the opening of the country to the West, were determined on conquest. Second, political pressure could yield a good deal of profit from the Chinese economy, and this prospect, which appealed particularly to the Osaka merchants involved in trade with China, weakened the resistance of the commercial classes to the expansionism of the conservatives. Third, the influence of the military on the policies of Japan's civil government grew steadily until finally by the 1930s civil government had ceased to exist in all but name, while the military groups which held the real power in Tokyo were, in turn, incapable of controlling the Japanese forces in Manchuria. Meanwhile international resistance to Japanese expansion was inhibited after 1917 by the hope that Japan could provide an effective barrier to the spread of communism from the Soviet Union, which had already transformed Mongolia into a client state.

Yet although Japanese policy towards China was ambivalent, although there was no settled determination on the part of successive Japanese governments at this time to seek political control of China, in actual fact the increase of control was always attempted whenever an opportunity offered; as far as China was concerned, Japan could resist anything except temptation. Temptation was now presented by the preoccupation of the European powers with the World War. On 18 January 1915 Japan presented China with a list of twenty-one demands. They included the strengthening of Japanese power in Manchuria and Shandong, control of the Hanyeping coal and steel complex, and an undertaking by China that she would not alienate any part of her coast to another power. In addition, it was demanded that China should appoint Japanese advisers in police, military, financial, and political matters, and would employ no foreign capital other than Japanese in any basic industries built in the province of Fujian; these were referred to as the fifth group of demands. The European powers and the United States could do nothing effective to resist the twenty-one demands. The United States protested; other nations, allied with Japan against the central powers, could not even do that much. When Japan delivered an ultimatum (withdrawing for future discussion the fifth group of demands which would have made China a virtual protectorate), Yuan had no choice but to accept. He was accused then, and has been since, of having bowed to Japan in order to obtain loans and also to gain Japanese support for his plan to assume the throne. Perhaps so, but such motives scarcely counted, for China was in no position to face Japan alone.

From the guardian of peace, stability, and international respectability, Yuan overnight became not only universally rejected but ridiculed. His closest associates, the commanders of the Beiyang forces, were as alienated as the rest. He had no option but to go through the extreme humiliation of renouncing the throne he had just assumed. He died soon after, on 6 June 1916, at the age of 56.

7

The Chinese economy

Developments between 1912 and 1938

Conventional opinions on the state of the Chinese economy and Chinese society in the first half of the twentieth century have been largely the reflection of nationalist emotion rationalized in a vulgar Marxism. These opinions are easily stated. They are that the Chinese economy was stagnant and regressing; that one major cause of this was the deteriorating conditions in which the peasant majority lived, conditions which were leading to their rapid expropriation; that the second major cause was the competition of foreign enterprise, buttressed by privileges imposed by force and served by a sycophantic class of compradors, competition which made it virtually impossible for modern enterprises in Chinese hands to thrive; and that such foreign competition also crushed the life out of the traditional handicrafts.

Modern historical research has disposed of these assertions. What we find in fact is that coastal China (the only areas of the country within easy reach of the new economic stimuli from abroad) put up a rate of industrial growth almost as high as that of the Japanese 'miracle'; that China's rural society did not change for the worse, and that for most of the period up to 1937, when the Japanese invaded, the average real income of the Chinese peasant was actually rising; that China's new industrial sector coped well in competition with its foreign rivals; and that with few exceptions Chinese traditional handicrafts, far from collapsing, thrived and grew. It is as true to say that, by the 1930s, the foreigners were serving the Chinese economy as it is that the Chinese economy was serving them—the exception being the Japanese, whose economic policies were a planned part of their effort to subjugate China. Finally it is the case that the despised compradors, far from being subservient, were the chief instruments in China's assertion of new economic strength.

Between 1912 and 1933 China's per capita gross domestic product grew from Ch$113 to Ch$123, although population was increasing at a rate of at least 0.8 per cent per annum. The rate of growth of modern industrial production (excluding Manchuria which was industrialized in Japanese hands after 1931) was, from 1912 until the Japanese War in 1937, over 6 per cent per annum. Chinese-owned steamship tonnage increased in roughly the same period by

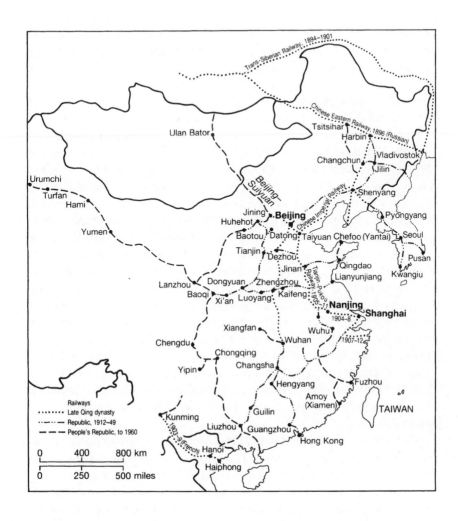

Map 6. The development of railways

about 12 per cent per annum; railway mileage by over 10 per cent; iron production by over 9 per cent; coal by over 8 per cent; and cotton-yarn spindles by
almost 12 per cent. Foreign trade grew from the 1870s onwards at about 2.5 per
cent per annum, and by 1933 China had—in addition to a still-growing hand-
loom production of cotton cloth—one of the largest mechanized textile
industries in the world, and was once again a net exporter of cotton cloth.
Agriculture, in spite of population growth which cut the average size of farm
from 1.37 hectares in 1870 to 0.92 hectares in 1930, continued to increase
production. About 1 per cent was added to the existing area of arable every

year; rice yields rose from their already historically high level of 2.3 metric tons per hectare to 2.47 in the 1930s; low-yielding food crops such as barley, sorghum (*gaoliang*) and millet were giving way to maize and yams. Cash crops increased from 14 per cent to about 17 per cent of agricultural output value. In the half century or so since 1870 the marketed surplus of agriculture had increased by about 50 per cent, in spite of the increase in the numbers which had to be fed directly by China's subsistence farming.

Most industrial development was confined to five provinces (if Japanese-controlled Manchuria is excluded): Jiangsu, Guangdong, Hebei, Hubei, and Shandong. These formed less than 10 per cent of China in area and contained less than 20 per cent of the Chinese population. Economic growth was thus geographically limited; but we should not rush to accept the notion that this division of China between developing coast and stagnant hinterland was the result of sinister foreign-controlled economic forces. The two great deltas had been for centuries more productive, populous, and commercialized as the result of climate, soil, and the availability of water transport. Partly the division was a result of the success of the Chinese Government in preventing foreigners from acquiring extensive property outside the Treaty Ports. Partly it reflected the ability of the foreign powers to hold at bay the forces of disorder which engulfed China up to the privileged walls of the foreign concessions. Finally, the new economic stimuli came from across the oceans and could easily and quickly penetrate only where the ocean-going steamer could reach. Even the strenuous efforts of the post-revolutionary government since 1949 have not entirely transformed the traditional balance of the location of industry in China.

What this concentration of industrial growth does signify, of course, is that growth and change in the affected areas were far greater than is suggested by figures which are nationwide. The population of the areas involved in industrial growth was of the same order of magnitude as that of Britain or Japan at the time. Nor should we exaggerate the concentration. In 1913, of 468 known factories in China, 229 were in areas other than those of the Treaty Ports. Of later years we know little. From 1913 to 1928 there was almost constant civil war, led by war-lords many of whom taxed and requisitioned in the areas they controlled to a degree which made investment hazardous. Even in these areas, however, the story is one of enterprise frequently frustrated rather than of stagnation, and there was probably much more development than we now know. Treaty Port industry was easily seen; but new enterprises in the interior—small, precarious, and not overwilling to bring themselves to the attention of rapacious soldiers—may in many cases have escaped the record. At the same time there was a proliferation of 'intermediate technology' workshops and putting-out networks whose numbers are certainly underestimated.

By 1933 there were about 4,000 known modern manufacturing establishments in China; about one-fifth were formally foreign-owned, although many of their sharcholders were Chinese. The total number of industrial workers was about one million. Chinese-owned steamship tonnage was reckoned in 1935 at 675,000 tons. In 1937 there were 13,000 miles of railway. Chinese corporate business (only a fraction of the total because most Chinese businesses were family firms or partnerships) represented a capital of Ch$870 million.

The new industries were mainly in the consumer goods sector, but about 25 per cent of total capitalization was in heavy industries. The range of industrial products was wide, as was the export trade, especially after the rapid decline of exports of tea and silk, the staples of the traditional trade. The image of China in the 1930s as an exporter of agricultural products and minerals and an importer of manufactures is misleading. More than one half of exports consisted of manufactured or partly-manufactured goods; almost one-quarter was of machine-made goods. Neither did imports consist entirely of frivolous luxuries for the upper classes: after the cessation towards the end of the nineteenth century of imports of opium, the main imports were raw cotton, cotton yarn and kerosene—materials directly or ultimately for mass consumption. Nor were imports of machinery negligible: the cumulative total value of machinery imported by 1938 was Ch$130 million.

Rural China

Right-wing nationalists argue that Chinese rural society was sound and needed no fundamental changes. The left wing on the other hand insist that radical revolution was necessary, on the grounds that existing rural society was bitterly exploitative and that exploitative relations inhibited growth and perpetuated poverty. Consequently, two contradictory impressions of the Chinese peasant are current: that he was a hard-working and contented yeoman farmer, and that he was an oppressed semi-serf. The latter interpretation has come to dominate Western as well as Chinese opinion.

In the immense variety of China it is possible to find evidence for almost any view the observer cares to adopt. There were farming communities whose members could consume a hearty 4,000 calories a day, and others where the average intake was 1,400. There were counties in which almost every farmer was the proprietor of all the land he farmed, and others in which almost every farmer was a tenant. There were tenants who were prosperous small-scale commercial farmers enjoying perpetual leases on insignificant ground rents, and share-croppers handing over 50 per cent of their miserable subsistence to the landlord on a precarious annual lease. There were farmers winning 169 bushels of rice per acre and others scraping 22 bushels. The inexorable increase in population had driven millions from the well-watered paddy-fields of the valley bottoms to scrape a living on forty-degree mountain slopes. Even the best harvest on a national scale was usually accompanied somewhere in

China by flood, drought, wind, hail, or locusts, which could wipe out a lifetime's labour and a lifetime's savings, forcing villagers to sell their quilts, then their tools, then their roof rafters, then their daughters, and then to wander until they died by the roadside.

In these circumstances national aggregates and national averages have only limited significance; but it is from these that analysis must begin, always bearing in mind that to find a completely adequate sample of China's one hundred million farms is not possible.

The only acceptable sample survey was made by a team from Nanjing University, led by John Lossing Buck, between 1929 and 1933. It comprised 16,786 farms in 168 localities in 22 provinces—representing virtually the whole of China proper, plus parts of Manchuria and Inner Mongolia, and of Qinghai and Xikang in western China. Buck admitted that the sample was one which yielded results 'somewhat better than average', and his results have often been dismissed by those who have felt compelled to present a more pessimistic image of the Chinese peasant; but identical methods used again by Buck in Sichuan in the early 1940s produced results as appalling as any revolutionary could have desired for his justification. There was nothing in Buck's methods which made optimistic conclusions inevitable.

Buck's sample was a sample of villages; and the whole population of each village was expected to be surveyed. Not all farmers responded, and it is on this point, not on the choice of villages, that Buck thought his sample might have been biased. It is not clear, however, why poorer rather than richer farmers should fail to respond; one would suppose prosperous farmers to be more likely than poor ones to try to conceal their assets. Buck's results are in fact broadly comparable with those of other large-scale surveys, although they often contrast sharply with surveys of particular villages or local areas; but such local reports were usually crisis reports, the area having come to notice precisely because its difficulties were dramatic. There is no reason to think that Buck's results give a grossly false picture of China and of its main regions as a whole, except in one particular, that the most distressed of the village families often moved out, and are taken account of only obliquely as a statistic of migration (4.4 per cent of the village population on average). It would be safe to assume a maximum figure of about 10 per cent to cover those who, having lost their place in rural society, escaped Buck's net in one way or another—working in urban industry, begging in the cities, serving with one of China's armies, recruited by local bandits, or on the move from seasonal job to seasonal job. As in most pre-modern agrarian communities, absolute destitution was exceptional; there were few people who did not find work of some sort, however grossly inadequate, but Buck's figure of 7 per cent (including the sick and disabled) of the rural population without work of any kind in the year of survey may be rather too low; part of the 4.4 per cent who emigrated should be added to the destitute.

The average Chinese farm was one of just over three acres. About a quarter of the farms were classified as small, varying round an average of just under one acre and a half. One in five farms was of six acres or more; and one in twelve was 'very large'—about twelve acres. Medium and medium-large farms, the two categories which straddled the average size of farm, accounted for more than half of Chinese farms. Only the large and very large farms, 17 per cent of the total, were large enough to require the employment of a permanent labourer. Hired labourers, including full-time and seasonally employed hands, accounted for only about 18 per cent of all labour expended in farming. There was almost no capitalist farming; the seasonality of farm work and the difficulty of supervising the meticulous work necessary for China's intensive agriculture made the employment of labourers on large farms unattractive to owners.

Some of China's farmers owned all the land they cultivated. Some were dependent entirely on rented land. A third group owned a part of the farm and rented the rest. Many authors did not recognize this third category and—according to their political taste and fancy—classified such farmers either as owners or as tenants. This, as well as careless methods of estimation, often accounts for the wide discrepancies in the figures given in different reports. Buck's survey found that for China as a whole 54 per cent of farmers owned all their farm land, 29 per cent were part-owners, and 17 per cent were tenants. If one includes part-tenants as tenants, the pattern changes: tenants are then 46 per cent. These national averages, however, concealed very large regional differences. In the wheat-growing north full tenancy was only 6 per cent; in the rice region 25 per cent.

Tenancy as opposed to ownership was of little importance in the north. In the rice-growing south and south-west the position was very different, with substantial minorities of tenants ranging from around 20 per cent in the undeveloped south-west to almost 50 per cent in Sichuan where there had been substantial immigration over the preceding two centuries. In Guangdong and Guangxi, if one includes part-owners as tenants, 75 per cent of farmers could be described as tenants.

It is common to equate tenancy with poverty, but such a view oversimplifies. While 29.5 per cent of the total area of farms classified as small was rented, the proportion even for very large farms was only a little less at 24.3 per cent. Land hunger was only one reason for hiring land; other reasons were the possibility of profitable commercial use, and the availability, as sons grew to manhood, of more family labour. Tenancy was most common on irrigated rice land with its capacity to grow two crops a year. Consequently tenants in the south enjoyed on average a standard of living higher than that of owners in the north.

Almost three-quarters of tenants paid a fixed rent in cash or kind; the rest were share-croppers. Rents averaged 43 per cent of the main crop, representing about one-third of total farm income; where the rent also covered the farmhouse this figure was not uncommonly high when one considers that housing in most countries represents between 20 per cent and 40 per cent of income. The landlord paid the land taxes, which absorbed about 13 per cent of his rents. The average return on capital invested in land was only about 5 per cent, or little more than half of the return available in commerce or in industry. In fact land was not bought as a means of maximizing profit; it was bought for security and for prestige. In terms of earnings, its main importance lay in the leisure and the means it provided to landlord families to acquire education, which enabled sons to enter the professions, and so increase their incomes.

There were few large landlords in China. Very few estates were as large as an average English family farm. There were in every age individuals who had acquired huge holdings, but this was so exceptional that it was always assumed that the individual concerned had acquired his wealth by nefarious means, and this was often indeed the case. A few clans also held large estates, but estates were unstable, being constantly split up by division on inheritance, and attempts to protect them by corporate clan ownership were seldom successful.

Few farmers depended entirely on agriculture for their income. Overall, 14 per cent of farm incomes came from non-agricultural sources. This proportion increased on small farms; over 20 per cent of the income of small farmers with one and a half acres or so came from other occupations. The high level of small-scale commercial activity in China, and of labour-intensive handicrafts, provided a wide range of opportunities to supplement farm incomes. These forms of employment, in descending order of the percentage of farm families engaged in any of them, were as follows: home industries 22 per cent; trade 16 per cent; labouring on other farms 14 per cent; labouring other than farm-labouring, unskilled 11 per cent, skilled 7 per cent. Nine per cent of farmers had professional occupations such as teaching, medicine, or public administration. The total incomes of the smallest farmers were thus brought up a little nearer the average by their greater participation in non-farming activities. The average of 14 per cent of farm incomes earned from non-farming sources conceals a wide range of circumstances, from full-time farming throughout the growing season to spare-time farming by families whose main income came from other trades or professions. In fact a fundamental problem in China is to define 'the peasant'. In an agrarian society everyone aspires to secure tenure of land. Land is sought not only by full-time farmers but by artisans, merchants, officials, teachers, doctors, soldiers. It is the only final security for rich and poor alike. The merchant bought land as a secure investment but stayed in his counting-house. The carpenter put his savings into a plot, cultivated it in his leisure hours, and fell back on it when times were hard for carpenters. Conversely, the full-time farming family spent the slack seasons in pursuing other occupations. The farm labourer often had his own plot. The village teacher saved hard for a bit of ground as a life insurance policy in favour of his wife and children, letting it out to a local farmer. Is the carpenter a peasant? Is the teacher's widow a landlord? The question is not merely academic. The answers chosen by those in authority can have a profound effect on land reform policy.

Generally, the picture of rural China that emerges is not one of glaring inequalities. There was no aristocracy with vast estates. The smaller farms were about half of the average size; all but a few exceptionally large farms were no more than twice the average; and over half of all farms were just above or below the average. Tenants do not seem to have been on the whole much poorer than proprietors with the same size of farms, partly because only the more fertile land was worth renting out, and partly because the tenant was, perforce, on average a more efficient farmer. All farmers except the share-croppers (about 5 per cent of all farmers), being either owners or tenants paying a fixed rent, had the incentive to increase production and earnings. The market at that time encouraged a switch to crops which were at once more profitable and more labour-intensive, thus providing opportunities for increased income on small farms where there was more labour power per acre. There is no evidence of increasing polarization of land ownership or of agricultural incomes, in spite of the contemporary belief that this was so. Land ownership did not become more concentrated, and the rate of tenancy may actually have decreased slightly.

Almost four in ten of China's peasants at any one time were in debt. Three-quarters of this debt was for purposes of consumption; to buy food in a bad year, to provide a dowry or pay for a wedding, to meet the costs of a funeral, to celebrate a festival. Such expenses did not of course occur every year. The average debt of families in debt was about equal to four or five months of family income. Over half of this debt was borrowed from friends, relatives, and neighbours. Landlords provided only 2 per cent of credit, merchants 3 per cent.

It is often argued that the merchants bought grain cheap after harvest when the peasants were forced to sell to pay their debts, and sold grain back to them in the hungry spring at inflated prices. However, Buck's analysis showed that this was not general. Certainly, more than half the grain sold by farmers was sold immediately after harvest and the need to pay off debts was a factor, as with farmers everywhere; but there are other factors to be considered. The waste and costs of grain storage on the farm, not to mention the risks, were high and account for much of the difference in seasonal prices. In fact seasonal variations of price were not great, being within 3 per cent either way of the year's average price for wheat, and about 5 per cent either way for rice. A quarter of the grain sold was not sold through middlemen but directly by the farmer to the customer, and it was the smaller farmer who sold least through the merchants. In any case a price difference of 10 per cent for a peasant selling one-third of his grain would represent a difference of only 3.3 per cent in his total annual income.

In one part of his survey Buck's investigators asked the peasants to give their opinions as to the causes of adverse conditions in agriculture. Almost one-third stated that they were aware of no adverse factors. Almost one-half of the rest named bandits or soldiers as the worst evil. More than a third (39 per cent) named natural disasters. Surprisingly, a number virtually equal to this (38 per cent) emphasized subjective factors such as lack of education, neglect of sanitation, and the prevalence of superstition. Only 10 per cent drew attention to lack of resources. Only 9 per cent blamed heavy taxes. There was no mention of land-tenure problems, or of expensive credit, or of regrating merchants. If this survey is valid, then the diagnosis of rural ills produced by the peasants themselves was very different indeed from that of their radical, self-appointed political spokesmen in the Communist and Nationalist parties. The diagnosis of the peasants does not, surely, express a revolutionary frame of mind.

Throughout most of the period up to 1931 the average standard of living of the Chinese peasant was slowly but steadily improving. From 1870 onwards there was a long, slow inflation. The prices received by the farmers increased; the prices they paid, although they increased little less, did so more slowly, so that the farmer was always ahead. Wages, the cost of land, and other farm costs rose more slowly than the prices received by the farmers. The farmers gained by the difference.

Chinese rural taxation, though relatively high, was also getting lighter. This may seem surprising in view of the continued piling up of supplementary land taxes and other extra charges, which locally could reach monstrous proportions. However, since the main land tax had been fixed in perpetuity by the Kang Xi Emperor in 1713 the prices of agricultural products had increased some 500 per cent. Without concomitant rises in taxation China's local governments would have ceased to function. In fact on average taxes rose less than prices until 1925.

China's taxation of land was made considerably lighter in reality by the fact that, there having been no survey of land ownership in China since the reign of the first Emperor of Ming, little of the vast areas of land reclaimed since then was taxed. In some areas as little as one-third of the land was assessed. Attempts at reform were prevented by the fact that the assessment books in the more prosperous parts of China had fallen into the hereditary control of tax-farming families, who found it more profitable to 'protect' their taxpayers than to encourage the Government to produce a more realistic assessment. It is often assumed that the main beneficiaries of concealed reclamation were the larger landowners, but the one survey we have (of a single village only) shows that in this case it was mainly the middle-ranking peasants who gained, at the expense (in extra taxation) of the very rich and the very poor.

At the same time a slow movement towards crops of higher value was taking place, assisted especially by the rapid growth of tube-well irrigation in the north-west. The acreage under cotton, and that under rape-seed, almost doubled between 1904 and 1909, and again between 1929 and 1933. The increase in cultivation of maize and sweet potatoes was also significant. So, too, was that of the acreage under opium—no benefit to the nation, but the most valuable of all cash crops for the farmers of western China, in spite of heavy opium taxes.

It is not therefore very surprising to find Buck's farmers, with the exception of those of the north-west region, then in the grip of devastating drought, almost unanimous in asserting that their standard of living had improved over the previous few years. Even in the stricken north-west more than half of the farmers recorded a rise in their standard of living. This near unanimity, moreover, shows that all classes of the peasantry had experienced improvement—which is to be expected, as with few exceptions all farmers in the Chinese village, regardless of the size of farm, grew the same crops in the same proportions and stood therefore to make much the same gains or losses.

So much for national averages. They undoubtedly indicate a growth in both production and prosperity, and they show clearly that China's social structure was not likely to have been a decisive, though it was certainly an important, factor in inhibiting agricultural improvement. The great question then is why a revolutionary situation developed in the Chinese countryside.

Part of the answer is that while on average, standards were slowly rising, and while this rise was enjoyed in all regions of China and by all categories of farmers, there was on a local scale much disruption and distress. Another part of the answer is that the numbers of the destitute were slowly rising, the result of increasing population. Part also is that in spite of improvement the vast majority of the farming population still lived very close to subsistence in conditions made precarious both by climate and by endemic disorder. On average 84 per cent of the farmer's income was spent on food, clothing, heat and light. Bad harvests occurred on average every third year. Two successive bad harvests brought the risk of ruin.

In the lower Yangzi region a substantial minority of farmers specialized in the growing of mulberry leaves. A drastic fall in silk exports occurred in the early thirties, as a result of the invention of rayon, the world depression, and the difficulty of inducing Chinese peasants to improve their product to meet new market needs. The distress caused was especially severe because specialist mulberry growers were reluctant to cut down mature mulberry plantations in order to revert to grain. The tea-growing areas were also hit by the virtual disappearance of their export market. The decline was not sudden, as in the case of silk, but it substantially reduced an important source of supplementary income for the peasants of Zhejiang and Fujian.

Weaving, the most important rural occupation alternative to agriculture, grew steadily but the main location of cotton textile manufacture shifted several times, moving towards the cotton-growing areas of the north and towards the new centres of population in Manchuria which came to be supplied with cotton cloth from the north of China proper. Thus within the overall increase of production and employment some areas of the south and centre suffered a decline. Although opportunities for employment in handicrafts did not diminish except on a local scale, local changes of this kind could easily wipe out the surplus available to smaller farmers whose income from agriculture itself might oscillate above and below bare subsistence.

There were two great national disasters in the years around 1930. The first was the total failure of the harvest in Shaanxi and other parts of the northwest in 1929 as a result of drought, with severe famine continuing into 1930 because most of the seed had been eaten. The second was the Yangzi floods of 1931. This was the result of the gradual accumulation of silt in the river bed, brought down from overcultivated, erosion-prone slopes up-river, and of the excessive building of dikes in the lake areas to protect newly reclaimed polders. Succeeded by a sharp downturn in agricultural prices after 1931, these disasters, besides their appalling immediate consequences, depressed the areas concerned for several years.

To natural disasters were added the disasters of war. Civil war was continuous from 1911 onwards and the destructive nature of these civil wars escalated as troop numbers swelled and weapons increased in weight and power. Direct destruction was accompanied by requisitions, forced labour, and arbitrary exactions. Normal trade patterns were disrupted, and economic life thrown into confusion by the irresponsible issue of provincial banknotes in order to sustain the military operations of the war-lords.

The disorders of wars fought by huge armies of ill-paid soldiers living off the country led to the militarization of civilian life, including the usual organization of armed protection-rackets and of armed forces in the control of clans and landlords. Banditry spread. Normal government often disappeared. An example is in the poorer part of Jiangsu province north of the Yangzi. Here, landlords organized armed gangs, built stockades and forts, and fought their neighbours for land and irrigation water, terrorized their tenants, and usurped judicial rights. An observer estimated that the landlords in some Jiangsu counties disposed of five times the armed force available to the county government. At the same time in some areas peasant protest led to organized landlord resistance and added to the escalation of militarization.

Yet by no means the whole of China was equally affected. The major warlord campaigns followed particular routes; the railways from north to south were the strategic arteries, the major railway junctions and the main river crossings the objects of attack. To this extent the principal damage was geographically limited, although there were other areas of constant fighting and intensified militarization. In the greater part of the country, however, the visitations of the soldiers were at worst occasional, and there was time for the peasant economy, with its extraordinary resilience, to recover.

From 1928 to 1931 the fighting, now between Chiang Kaishek's government and the pro-Nationalist war-lord armies whose commanders resented Chiang's power, was less destructive than earlier civil war campaigns, and the costs met by less arbitrary means, but they were paid for by increases in taxation. The increase in taxes began to exceed the rate of inflation from 1926 onwards. By 1935, however, the first steps had been taken to reduce rural taxes and the total fell somewhat.

One factor, originating quite outside China, brought a temporary reversal of the growing prosperity of Chinese farmers. The long inflation which had given so much to the peasants for two generations had been associated with the world-wide demonetization of silver, which depressed its value in China and led to rising commodity prices. In 1931, however, the Government of the United States in response to American silver producers began to buy silver heavily. The world price rose strongly. Silver poured out of China. Prices dropped sharply as trade fell off for lack of currency. Farm-gate prices were reduced by up to 50 per cent. Farm costs did not fall so fast. Thus the circumstances of the preceding period of inflation were reversed. The effect on the peasants was the frustration of optimistic expectations engendered by seventy years of increasing prosperity.

The effect on many landlords receiving their rents in kind was even more severe. To the average peasant, selling only a proportion of his crop, a drop in market prices of 50 per cent meant a fall in total income of perhaps 15 per cent. The landlord dependent on rent in kind, however, found his income from rent cut by almost the full 50 per cent. This squeeze on landlord incomes may explain in part the increased harshness towards tenants which is evident, at least on a local scale, at this time. In one in ten Chinese counties landlords began to demand deposits on entry as a condition of giving a lease. There was a slight rise in the proportion of leases of under three years and a slight reduction in that of leases of ten years or over. There was resistance by some landlords to the normal requests for reduction of rent in years of poor harvest. There were increases in rent in some places. By 1935, though, the problem had been solved. China had adopted a managed paper currency. Normal levels of trade returned, while the harvests of that year and of 1936 were the best in China's history. The slow growth of peasant prosperity was resumed.

Even when all the disruption and distress experienced locally in China is taken into account, it still cannot be argued that the cause of revolution in the countryside was the immiseration of the majority of peasants. Yet local distress, in communities whose hold on subsistence was at best precarious, inexorably added to the numbers of the destitute and the uprooted. Every poor harvest, every military campaign, every local depression of the market for handicraft products, every local abuse of taxation, claimed its permanent victims, squeezed out of the rural economy with little chance to return. Such conditions might be local and irregular in their occurrence, might only be negative exceptions to generally positive changes; but they created a destitute and alienated mass of people roughly equal to the entire population of the British Isles, and of course the beggars and the vagrants were more conspicuous than the majority of peasants who were being undramatically a little better fed, clothed, and housed every year.

More important, these setbacks were seen by China's educated classes in a framework of changed values and expectations. If the processes of industrialization had not yet transformed China, nevertheless the great message of the Industrial Revolution had been received: poverty is no longer necessary; it is no longer necessary for the vast majority of the human race to live in chronic want and frightening insecurity; poverty is therefore a scandal and a source of shame to a nation which tolerates it.

Traditional handicrafts

China's traditional handicraft sector grew slowly but steadily until the silver crisis of the early 1930s. The weaving of cotton cloth on hand-looms grew by six or seven million yards a year, stimulated by the availability of cheap, strong machine-made cotton from factories in China. The low-count, machine-made yarn that was suitable for the manufacture of cloth for the everyday use of the Chinese working population was by 1930 manufactured almost entirely by Chinese-owned mills; the higher-count yarns were manufactured mainly by the foreign-owned firms for urban markets. Chinese hand-loom weavers often used strong machine-made yarn for the warp and home-spun for the weft, a practice typical of the early stages of industrialization. The stronger warp made possible the use of cotton on the draw-loom, hitherto mainly confined to silk, and thus a whole new industry of cotton brocades and other materials of complex weave. Weaving was also much improved by the introduction from Japan of foot-treadle looms, looms with moving parts of iron in place of wood, and even Jacquard looms.

Changes in the hand-spinning industry are less certain. Some argue that it must have declined, on the grounds that the known increase of hand-loom cloth was insufficient to provide employment for all the spinners putatively left idle through the competition of machine-made yarn. Other authorities believe that there was in fact a large increase in the amount of raw cotton available to hand-spinners, and that the industry must therefore have increased in size. The latter opinion is more plausible. Cotton acreage doubled between 1913 and 1931. Of the new total output, from one-half to two-thirds was retained for use on the farm. Thus, only if we assume that the peasants had previously kept for their own use *all* the cotton they grew before the increase of acreage, would the amount then available for home-spinning be roughly equal to the amount available after the increase; and they certainly had not kept their whole product. Therefore the amount of cotton available for spinning on the farm by 1930 must have increased. On these grounds it is impossible to believe that, on the national scale, hand-spinning declined.

The most rapidly growing handicraft employment, though, was the processing of food. Over 90 per cent of this, including the processing of tobacco, was done by simple, though often improved, methods. The rate of development of oil-processing was as high as that of food-processing generally, with the strong movement which was taking place in farming towards increase in the cultivation of oil-seeds. Again, almost all the increased production was dealt with by the use of unmechanized processes.

From the first opening of the Treaty Ports, the number of junks rose very rapidly; although large sea-going junks were almost entirely replaced by steamships, the steamship traffic gave an immense stimulus to short-haul transport in traditional vessels. The consequent increase in employment was substantial.

The manufacture by simple means of soap and of new commodities such as matches and cigarettes was soon widely established and grew rapidly.

Examples of handicrafts which declined are hard to find, except for the processes of silk production and the processing of tea. Exports of tea and silk, as we have seen, had declined drastically by the 1930s. It is possible that by 1930 traditional coal-mining and traditional iron-making were declining slightly, but the figures are too imperfect to permit any firm conclusion.

China's surplus labour was a major factor in the survival of handicrafts; but the main reason was the different demands of the urban and rural markets. These were also kept apart by the costs of inland transport, as well as by the resistance of the Government to the establishment of foreign enterprise beyond the Treaty Ports. Finally, improvements in handicraft technology actually strengthened traditional handicrafts as well as encouraging the rise of small semi-mechanized workshops. That the traditional sector could respond to new challenges is well shown by the fact that some of the lines of handicraft production which grew fastest (cotton-textile manufacture, tobacco processing, sugar refining) were among those which faced most competition from imports. And China's exports of handicraft products actually grew at a slightly faster rate than her exports in general.

Public debt

Before the Sino-Japanese War of 1894 the imperial government of China was not heavily in debt. About 40 million taels had been borrowed for various emergencies. By 1894 33 million had been repaid in principal and interest, almost entirely out of the proceeds of the maritime customs.

Thereafter debts piled up. About 360 million taels were borrowed for investment in railways and telegraphs and industry, but the service of this debt was largely covered by revenue from the investments. The cost of the 1894 war with Japan (120 million taels), and the huge indemnity of 263 million taels— US$200 million payable in gold—imposed by Japan, was the main factor in reducing the Qing to near bankruptcy.

This monstrous exaction was followed five years later by the Boxer indemnities of 450 million taels. China's liability for indemnity payments was thus greater than her foreign borrowings for economic modernization. Nevertheless her indebtedness should not be exaggerated; the ill consequences were more the result of China's inelastic revenue system than of the real burden of foreign debt, which amounted only to one tael per capita. The indemnity payments actually made represented only one six-hundredth of a tael per capita per year. Internal debt was negligible before 1928.

The foreign debt was secured on various Chinese revenues, including the maritime customs and the salt gabelle which, like the customs, employed foreign senior administrators. Foreign insistence on this form of security was regarded with great hostility in China; but it is difficult to see how China could ever have raised the foreign loans necessary to meet the indemnity payments without some such guarantees. The late Qing and early republican governments represented such a bad risk that even on these terms the foreign banks of the West had to be bullied by their Governments into keeping China afloat. The nationalist image of foreign bankers falling over each other to lend to China at usurious rates is quite false.

The rates of interest charged on foreign loans were not exceptionally high. They varied with the stability of successive Chinese governments, but only in the war-lord period from 1916 to 1928, when the administration in Beijing exercised virtually no control over the country, had no command over its finances, could not pay the salaries of its servants, and had incurred secret debts of vast but uncertain magnitude to Japan, was the cost of borrowing very high. In these circumstances it was 9 per cent, and the principal might also be discounted by 5 per cent. From 1895 to 1915, however, it had been around 5 per cent and therefore little more than the international norm, and after the establishment of the Nanjing regime in 1928 the rate of interest returned to this lower figure. The difference between rates sometimes charged to China and the rates internationally current reflects not greed but a justified fear of loss.

There is no doubt, however, that the burden of debt imposed on China's creaking system of public finance inhibited government economic initiative. Of total revenue, 44 per cent, classified under 'general administration', went to the servicing of existing debts; a further 20 per cent represented loans necessary to meet normal administrative costs; 31 per cent serviced the railway loans, and only 5 per cent represented payments on industrial loans.

There is a strong contrast between the debt burden as related to revenue and the debt burden as related to national wealth. From the first point of view it was crippling; from the second, and considering that China had virtually no internal debt, it was no great burden. Thus while it hampered the Government's ability to contribute to economic growth it was not a significant burden on the economy as a whole or on potential entrepreneurs, to whom it was the irrationality and unpredictability of the tax burden, rather than its level, which discouraged investment.

Foreign enterprise and China

Investment in the form of loans to the Chinese Government was only a small fraction of total foreign investment, which by 1931 is estimated to have been well over US$3,000 million. But even this, by the standards of investment in the developing countries after the Second World War, was very low. It was rather less than 1 per cent of China's Gross National Product; it equalled only Ch$7 per capita, and it represented only about 20 per cent of total existing investment in modern economic enterprises in China. Most foreign firms were relatively small, and none enjoyed a monopolistic or semi-monopolistic position. Half of the foreign direct investment was in import and export facilities, shipping, banking, public utilities, and trade-related real estate; 16 per cent was in railways; 15 per cent was in manufacturing.

It has been fashionable (but is perhaps less so now) to assume that the operations of foreign firms in developing countries must inevitably create an intolerable degree of dependence; incorporation in the world economy on terms dictated by the economically powerful is bound to be a net disadvantage. This is not the place to discuss the general applicability of the theory of dependence, but in the particular case of China it seems scarcely to apply. Foreign economic influence was marginal, its impact largely confined to the coast. No foreign power (with the exception of Japan) depended heavily on China for any vital product. China's exports were not dominated by one product or even by two or three. Two-thirds of foreign direct investment in China was directed to creating a modern infrastructure in the Treaty Ports, and almost all of the infrastructure so created was as valuable to China's merchants and industrialists as to the foreigners. In fact a substantial part of foreign direct investment was devoted to the creation of facilities which the Chinese Government might have provided but (unlike that of Japan) failed to provide. The 15 per cent which represented foreign investment in industry was almost entirely in import-substituting industries which were of benefit to the Chinese economy as a whole.

Foreign enterprise also found markets for new Chinese export commodities which gave fresh opportunities to Chinese farmers: hog bristles, hides, egg products, soya bean products, and tung oil.

Above all, foreign enterprise introduced modern technology and modern methods of management. The shipyards, public utilities, and cotton mills of the Treaty Ports were training grounds for skilled workers, technical managers, and entrepreneurs. Many set up their own firms. Most Chinese manufacturing enterprises originated in this way. By 1931 foreign firms were in a minority, and over 70 per cent of the output value of Chinese manufacturing industry was produced by Chinese firms which, although on average smaller than the equivalent foreign establishments, and with lower capital–output ratios, were as efficient as their foreign rivals. Their profit rates were as high. They grew as fast. In the depression of the 1930s their survival rate was as high as that of foreign firms.

In many respects it was the foreign-owned firms which had to struggle against disadvantages. The language barrier prevented direct access to the sources of supply of Chinese goods and to their final customers. They therefore had to pay high salaries and commissions to their Chinese agents, the compradors. Successful compradors made vast fortunes. Foreign firms were obliged to pay higher wages, and although both wages and conditions of work in the foreign establishments were usually superior to those in Chinese firms, strikes were often directed at them and spared their Chinese competitors. They suffered frequently from highly effective nationalistic boycotts.

The Treaty Port system was universally condemned by Chinese nationalists; yet its effect, for either good or ill, was very limited. The Government of China, forced to concede to foreigners the right to trade in and from certain areas on the coast and on the navigable rivers, stubbornly defended the hinterland against foreign penetration. As a result, no foreign-owned plantation economy developed in China. Foreign control of mineral resources was generally prevented, with the one significant exception of the Han Ye Ping coal and iron complex, which as a result of its losses passed into the hands of its Japanese creditors. The whole of China's export and import trade was kept in Chinese hands, to the extent that there is a good deal of truth in a recent conclusion that the foreign firms had been 'gradually transformed into Shanghai and Hong Kong commission agents serving the established Chinese commercial networks'.

It was an odd sort of imperialism, the more so as the great developed powers of the West, having secured the minimum of acceptable conditions of trade, made no attempt to exert strong pressure on China to open up further. Concessions to build railways and to open mines were certainly sought, and not always politely; but the system by which no such important industrial undertaking could be created except by a special concession from the Chinese Government was never questioned. When after 1928 the Nanjing regime—China's first viable modern government—began to press for an end to Treaty Port Privileges and then to attack foreign interests in China, the Western governments, while they dragged their feet as best they could, did not seriously challenge China's rights. Only Japan resisted, and resisted to the point of war.

8

The war-lord era

The origins of war-lordism

From 1916 to 1931 the political history of China as a united country virtually ceases. There was a shifting system of quasi-independent states concerned to maintain or improve their positions in a struggle to control the national government, whose authority these very rivalries prevented from being more than nugatory. It was a situation which called forth explanations inspired by disillusionment and despair, explanations which stressed the selfishness of the war-lords, their lack of political principle and their indifference to the national interest. Explanation in these terms, because it could serve as propaganda for the Nationalist Party by representing the conflict between the Nationalists and war-lords as a struggle between good and evil, has become the almost unchallenged interpretation. The truth, however, is much more interesting.

In the course of the revolution of 1911–12 government throughout the provinces had been militarized. The revolution itself had been carried out mainly by mutinous soldiers, who represented thereafter the only real authority. The disappearance of traditional forms of social control and the inability of the new republic to replace them had led to an almost total breakdown of law and order. The emergence of the 'war-lords', in the sense of military governors (*dujuns*) or senior commanders with *de facto* control of whole provinces, represented not disintegration but a partial reintegration, bearing the only immediate hope of restoration of order.

The reason this hope was not realized was mainly because of the bankruptcy of the central government. Since the Taiping crisis there had developed a vicious circle in which Beijing allowed the provincial authorities to use revenues normally passed to itself; the centre, thus financially weakened, was less and less able to provide for the maintenance of the provincial armed forces; and the provinces therefore alienated further sources of revenue in order to maintain these forces. Even the most honest *dujun* was forced to maintain his troops by collecting and spending the taxes of his garrison area, and in turn was forced to accept a similar financial relationship with his own subordinates, leaving them to find their means of survival in their own bailiwicks.

Each commander had to seek to control territory which yielded revenue in order to achieve political stability in it. The result was the feudalization of government. Authority came to be based on the allocation of territory and its revenues to subordinates in return for military service. Loyalty was owed primarily to one's immediate superior, who had the power to give or take away one's fief. Most of those who wielded this authority came from the margins of Chinese society, from poor families whose members in normal times would have enjoyed little prospect of upward social mobility. A striking proportion were from families which had seen better days. Some had been involved in banditry and were thence assimilated into the army. The rapid expansion of modern armies after 1890 had provided careers open to talent without the necessity of education beyond the stage of mere literacy; and given the simplicity of warfare in China at that time, the talents demanded were simple—courage, an intuitive tactical sense and the ability to lead men. Thus many who rose to power were, as foreign observers were surprised to find, charismatic in the approved manner of the heroes of the traditional popular fiction: generous, charming, bold, and ruthless. The building of the new armies had been supported by the creation of military schools, from an elementary level to the Baoding Military Academy. The southern provincial armies, built on the model established by Zhang Zhidong, were fed by a separate but similar system. Tuition was free and subsistence provided. The most distinguished graduates of these schools were sent abroad, usually to Japan but sometimes to Germany, for further study. The new system opened entry into the officer corps to the very poorest of people. Such people now ruled China.

The split in the Beiyang army

The most senior Baoding graduate, Duan Qirui, was Prime Minister when Yuan Shikai died and remained so when Vice-President Li Yuanhong succeeded. There did not take place then, as is often implied, an immediate split among the northern (Beiyang) commanders. Duan Qirui and his colleagues appeared to have a common policy, of restoring China's unity which had been destroyed by Sun Yatsen's southern resistance to Yuan Shikai's bid for the throne. Only the wisdom of hindsight reveals the existence of a 'Zhili clique' and an 'Anhui clique'. The polarization of opinion between them, when it came, was not the result of factional intrigues for power, but of disagreements over policy.

The principal actors in the events which led to war within the Beiyang group were Duan Qirui, Feng Guozhang, Cao Kun, and Wu Peifu.

Duan Qirui was born in Anhui. His father was a brigadier in Li Hongzhang's Huai Army. He attended the first course taught at the Beiyang Military Academy, came top, and was sent to spend two years in Germany studying artillery. After his return he became the Director of the Baoding Staff College. He was the most capable of Yuan's lieutenants. Yuan appointed him Minister for War and subsequently Premier.

Feng Guozhang was born in Zhili of a peasant family which had fallen on hard times; the family sold its property in order to educate the sons, but Feng being the fourth son had to cut his education short. He was reputed to have earned his living at one stage by playing the fiddle in disreputable theatres. Enlisted, he came to the notice of a battalion commander who sent him to the Beiyang Military Academy. In 1895 he served as military attaché in Tokyo and his reports came to the attention of Yuan Shikai. He was an amenable man, and had been able to keep on good terms both with Yuan Shikai and with the Manchu nobles who had secured Yuan's retirement in 1908, but he publicly opposed Yuan's bid for the throne. In 1916 he was *dujun* of Jiangsu. When Li Yuanhong succeeded to the presidency on Yuan's death, Feng was elected Vice-President.

Cao Kun was also born in Zhili, in Tianjin. His family was poor, and Cao made a living as a peddler in his youth, but then enlisted. He had met Yuan Shikai early in life, and Yuan invited him to participate in creating the new armies. He commanded the 3rd Army, formerly the 3rd Division. In 1913, after taking part in the suppression of Sun Yatsen's southern supporters, he became *dujun* of Zhili.

Wu Peifu, the fourth principal figure in the Beiyang Army, though junior to the others, soon came to wield considerable influence because of his ability as a soldier. He was born in Penglai county, Shandong. His father, a small shop-keeper, died when Wu was 14, and the family was very poor. Wu enlisted in the army partly to earn a living and partly for patriotic reasons; in 1895 he had seen his native Penglai overrun by the Japanese. He went through the Beiyang Military Academy and was posted to the 3rd Division, then commanded by Duan Qirui but later by Cao Kun.

This generation of soldiers, trained under Yuan Shikai, were not revolutionaries except in military matters. The Beiyang Academy aimed not only to train its students in military affairs, but to inculcate traditional Confucian values. It also aimed to inspire patriotism, a patriotism directed primarily against the Japanese; so it is not surprising that resistance to Japanese demands proved to be an issue on which many Beiyang commanders held strong views. Wu Peifu in particular was fiercely nationalist. He resolved in his youth never to set foot in a foreign concession, and in the end died rather than enter the French Concession for medical treatment. As for Confucian ideology, Wu Peifu and Feng Guozhang had taken the first degree, while Duan Qirui was a capable scholar. Their political ideas were not advanced, and for all their generally humble origins they regarded the possibility of social revolution with hostility. They accepted the change to a republic with resignation rather than enthusiasm; indeed neither Cao Kun nor Wu Peifu publicly opposed Yuan Shikai's bid for the throne.

The Beiyang Army held northern China within the Wall, though not Shanxi; this was in the hands of Yan Xishan who had led the revolution there in 1911. Beiyang commanders were also the military governors of Jiangsu, Anhui, and Hubei. Beyond that their control did not extend, which meant that Beijing's authority too was limited to these provinces. Outside the Wall the north-eastern provinces (Manchuria) were in the hands of Zhang Zuolin, a five-foot-two, doll-like figure whose fragile appearance belied his formidable strength of character. He had brought his troop of brigands into the imperial service to fight against the 1911 revolution, which his power nevertheless survived. From this position, by ousting from authority virtually all those who were not native to his own Fengtian province, he rose to power. These north-eastern provinces had been settled mainly from Shandong, but they remained a frontier area where land was relatively plentiful. Of all the warlord satrapies of China it was economically the strongest. It retained a separate identity which the Japanese did everything to encourage.

The north-west had slipped from Beijing's enfeebled grasp, and its local rulers were perforce more concerned about their relations with Russia and Japan than about those with Beijing. Outer Mongolia was soon to become a satellite of the Soviet Union, while Inner Mongolia was in a turmoil of Mongol nationalist resistance encouraged by Japan. The provinces of the south and south-west, on an arc from Guangdong to Sichuan, were in the hands of military rulers who had led the opposition to Yuan Shikai's abrogation of the 1912 constitution and his subsequent attempt to found a new dynasty. In this they reflected the greater political radicalism of the south. Guangdong itself was the base of Sun Yatsen's Nationalist Party. It might have been supposed that common support for the Republic and its constitution would have given the area some unity, but in fact it was soon as murderously divided as the north.

Between north and south lay Hunan, key to the crossing of the Yangzi at the southern terminus of China's most strategically vital railway from Beijing to Hankou. Its population tended to support the southern regime; but it was inevitably the cockpit of China.

To Chinese public opinion and to the Beiyang regime alike the reunification of China was the most important issue. Preparations were made in Beijing to invade Hunan and from there to penetrate Sichuan and the southern provinces. Yet while public opinion earnestly wanted reunification, not everyone wanted it at the price of further war. Most Chinese favoured a negotiated settlement. The 'South' had repudiated its allegiance only because the 1912 constitution had been abrogated. On the death of Yuan Shikai this had been restored. If Premier Duan Qirui would respect the 1912 constitution, then a negotiated settlement would surely be possible. This, however, Duan would not do. It was on this issue that the Beiyang establishment split and China was plunged into war-lordism.

When Yuan Shikai died and Vice-President Li Yuanhong assumed power, the question was under which constitution he had done so. If under the provisional constitution of 1912, then he was President for the rest of Yuan's seven-year term of office, and the 1913 parliament was still, for lack of a new election, the legitimate assembly. If, however, he was President under the constitution which Yuan Shikai had forced through in 1914, then his term of office was limited to three days in which to arrange a new presidential election. The South insisted that the 1912 constitution was still in force. Li Yuanhong as Vice-President not unnaturally favoured this view. Duan Qirui as Premier opposed him. The navy in protest deserted to the South. Feng Guozhang persuaded Duan to yield.

When Duan Qirui finally accepted the 1912 constitution the separatist government in the South dissolved itself and China was, at least theoretically, reunited. The Guomindang members returned to Parliament, but it very soon became obvious that the Beiyang generals, with the support of most of Chinese public opinion, were unwilling to accept that the conduct of government should be hampered by Members of Parliament backed by the south-western armies. A council of provincial military governments was formed to combine against any provincial commander who threatened the unity of the country. The Progressive Party, for all its commitment to parliamentary government, soon showed that it was as willing as the southern radicals to depend on military support. When the Guomindang proposed that provincial governments should be elected, the Progressives appealed to the military, who supported them. The *dujuns* vetoed Parliament's appointment of Tang Shaoyi (the first republican premier, who had sought to curb Yuan's abuse of the constitution) as Foreign Minister. President Li Yuanhong protested at the constant flouting of his authority by Duan Qirui, and more especially by Duan's 'Cabinet Secretary' Xu Shuzheng, who was soon to play a sinister role in affairs.

Xu Shuzheng was the son of a village schoolteacher, and like Feng Guozheng and Wu Peifu a *xiucai*. He had come to the attention of Duan Qirui in 1901 when he submitted a memorandum on the military affairs of the nation; Duan sent him to study at Japan's main military academy (the Shikan Gakko). His constant interference in affairs led to a confrontation with Duan's minister of internal affairs. The Cabinet Secretary and the minister were persuaded to resign simultaneously, but Xu Shuzheng remained powerful because of his close personal relations with Duan. In any case his resignation came too late; he had done the damage which put China on the slippery slope to disintegration.

It had been decided that the Government should make new appointments to all provinces. While in China's militarized situation there was a limit to how far this could be done, there was nevertheless some room for manœuvre. Duan chose to use this to break up the south and south-west coalition by transferring some of its *dujuns* elsewhere. In the course of this he decided that the Government should oust the leading pro-Nationalist provincial commander, Li Liejun, in Hunan. In Cabinet, Xu Shuzheng argued for this intervention, although he had no right to speak. When a majority of the Cabinet opposed it he issued orders on his own initiative for an attack. The campaign began on 6 October 1917.

Duan Qirui was now evolving a plan for the unification of China by force. Close relations with Japan played a key part in his strategy. The plan was to obtain loans from Japan in return for concessions, in order to build up an armed force to use against the South, and to rationalize this military buildup by joining in the world war on the side of the Allies.

Duan and his colleagues have been universally condemned for acting as sycophants of Japan in order to serve their own power and interests. Yet this is perhaps too harsh a judgement. China was divided and the Government was bankrupt. Reunification could not be achieved (Duan believed) except by force, and force needed funds. The Government's credit was so poor that it was not possible to raise domestic loans. The Western powers were at war. There was only one possible source of finance, and that was Japan. Japan could name her price, and her 1915 list of twenty-one demands had already shown that the price would be high. Yet if China could have used Japanese loans to rebuild her unity and her strength, she might then have been able to 'astonish the world with her ingratitude', and dispose of Japan's encroachments on her sovereignty.

There were valid arguments to support China's entry into the war. She would be an ally both of Japan and of the Western powers, and this might provide some check on Japanese demands. China might also hope to gain concessions from her allies: Duan had in mind the cancellation of the Boxer indemnity payable to Germany and Austria, and a postponement (perhaps for ever) of further Boxer payments to the Allies; a raising of tariff duties on imports from 5 per cent to 12.5 per cent in exchange for the abolition of the *likin* internal trade taxes; and cancellation of the prohibition against the stationing of Chinese troops within twenty miles of Tianjin which had been stipulated in a Protocol imposed after the Boxer Rising. More generally, China's grateful allies might be prepared at the conclusion of the war to make broader concessions to China's interests; many Chinese actually had in mind the example of Cavour, who had taken Piedmont into the Crimean War in order to gain a place at the peace conference.

There was at first much opposition. The President was against participation in the war, and so was Vice-President Feng Guozhang. Chinese commercial and intellectual circles did not favour participation. Nor did most Guomindang (Nationalist) Members of Parliament. At this stage Duan Qirui and

Liang Qichao were almost alone in favouring war. However, at a special conference of provincial *dujuns* Duan was able to win a unanimous vote in favour. At the same time the balance of opinion in Parliament was changing. Had Duan shown sufficient patience he would almost certainly have secured parliamentary approval, but he rushed his fences, called out the 'Citizens' Corps', an organized mob which Yuan Shikai had employed to put pressure on Parliament, and attempted to bully the Members into voting in favour of war. Parliament responded by voting for Duan's resignation. President Li dismissed him.

The interprovincial association of *dujuns*, the chairman of which was Zhang Xun, immediately took action. Zhang Xun marched his troops to Beijing in June 1917, ostensibly to restore Duan to power. However, Zhang was a passionate monarchist. His background was much like that of his colleagues: poor, orphaned and living by his wits, he had enlisted. He fought in the Sino-French and Sino-Japanese wars, rose rapidly in rank and finally came to the notice of Yuan Shikai. An earlier experience may account for his loyalty to the Manchus: after the Boxer Rising it was he who had escorted the Dowager back to Beijing and had won her favour. His headquarters at Xuzhou in northern Jiangsu was a royalist centre, frequented by those who still favoured a constitutional monarchy, such as Kang Youwei of the 1898 Reform Movement. The idea of a restoration was always in the air. The British Government had been careful to ensure that the young ex-Emperor's tutor was British. A succession of royalist intrigues had already been exposed. And the *dujuns*, for all their acceptance of the Republic, still appeared at the ex-Emperor's court on days of ceremony and performed the kowtow.

Most provinces protested against the dismissal of Duan; notable exceptions were the three Yangzi provinces which were under the Beiyang commanders most hostile to war with the South. When Zhang Xun, *en route* to Beijing, demanded the dissolution of the old parliament, he was obeyed.

Zhang Xun, however, had not occupied Beijing with his pigtailed royalist soldiers to put Duan back in power. He announced the restoration of the young ex-Emperor and offered honours and appointments to Feng Guozhang, Li Yuanhong, and others; but he offered nothing to Duan Qirui.

The restoration was short-lived. The *dujuns* unanimously condemned Zhang's action. Beiyang forces drove him out. Their commander was a young Christian general, Feng Yuxiang, notable for his gigantic frame and his gold ear-rings. Duan was thus restored to power by the very generals—Cao Kun, Feng Guozhang, Feng Yuxiang—who are always described as the leaders of an anti-Duan 'Zhili clique', while the only man who showed any animus towards him was Zhang Xun, who according to received opinion was the chief leader of Duan's 'Anhui clique'.

President Li Yuanhong now decided to resign and Vice-President Feng Guozhang took over on 2 July 1917. Among Duan's first acts on his return to power was to prepare to send troops to Hunan as a preliminary step to reconquering the South. A few days later China declared war on Germany. Duan's policies in this and in other respects had the support of the Progressives, organized round the 'Research clique', a group of intellectual politicians led by China's most famous liberal intellectual, Liang Qichao, who had been Kang Youwei's closest and most articulate disciple, but who had since deserted the cause of constitutional monarchy and assumed the leadership of the Progressive Party.

The Progressives argued that in restoring the ex-Emperor, Zhang Xun had overthrown the first republic; there was now a second. The old parliament was therefore defunct. The argument is obviously somewhat specious; but one could hardly expect the minority to accept, apparently indefinitely, a hostile majority in a parliament whose term was long past.

The response of the South to the restoration of Duan Qirui was to form a new rival national government at Canton, and bring together a Movement for the Protection of the Constitution. At Canton 250 members of the once-more dissolved parliament assembled and elected Sun Yatsen as Grand Marshal, with two southern commanders as marshals. One of these (Lu Rongting) had, however, already been to Beijing on his own initiative and negotiated with Duan Qirui to secure the position of Inspecting Commissioner of Guangdong and Guangxi and the 'neutralization' of Hunan under a native Hunanese *dujun*.

Had this agreement been kept there might have been no war with the South, and no occasion for the split in the Beiyang ranks, but within weeks Duan appointed a Beiyang general as *dujun* of Hunan and sent an army to install him. The Southern troops immediately moved north to support the existing *dujun*, Tan Yankai, an associate of the Guomindang. He was a native of Hunan, a moderate man and well trusted. The attempt to oust him, and the breach of Hunan 'neutrality' which it involved, led to the first cracks in the unity of the Beiyang forces. The troops sent into Hunan by Duan Qirui were led by two former subordinates of President Feng Guozhang. In November these two commanders circulated telegrams asking that the war be stopped. They were supported by the *dujuns* of Zhili, Hubei, Jiangxi and Jiangsu, all men of the Beiyang Army, and all from Zhili. This was the birth of the Zhili clique.

At this point we must consider the definition of the word 'clique'. It indicates (pejoratively) a group who plan and act in concert, but who do not constitute a group authorized institutionally to take such concerted action: whose ties are personal and not official; and whose aims are inimical to wider interests which they are supposed as individuals to respect. The problem was that, there being in China no tradition of political combination on the basis of ideological values, even the most political of groupings, existing solely for the pursuit of a view of the public interest, would almost certainly be built in the first instance around personal relationships—kinship, subordination, common education, or 'blood-brother' ties of friendship. Sun's Nationalist Party had begun from his former fellow-pupils in his mission primary school in Hawaii. The constituent elements of the Communist Party of later date were largely based on kinship or shared education. There is therefore nothing surprising in the fact that when political opposition (which in the circumstances of the time was bound to take the form of military opposition) began towards Duan Qirui among the commanders whom he had charged with fighting an unpopular civil war, it should spread in the first place among the closest military associates of these commanders, who were the Zhili-born, Mandarin-speaking officers of armies recruited in the north, most of them closely associated in training and command.

Morever, the chronology of events is not compatible with the assumption of action by an existing clique. On the contrary, the narrative suggests the gradual coming together of a group of leaders in response to a political issue—whether to fight with the South or to negotiate. Throughout the story the initiative in opposing war came not from the highest Beiyang leaders but from their subordinates. The most senior Beiyang leaders came to oppose war only after much vacillation. The senior commanders took up arms against Duan Qirui only when he had made it plain that he was determined to crush them, after overriding both Parliament and President in order to build a new and formidable army. It may be added that on all the public issues which came to divide Duan Qirui from his former Beiyang colleagues Chinese public opinion was generally on the side of the Zhili clique.

When we turn to the Anhui clique of Duan Qirui, it is difficult to find anything which one could describe either as a clique or with its roots in Anhui. It is true that one major source of the Beiyang Army had been Li Hongzhang's Huai Army, raised in Anhui against the Taipings, that Duan came from Li's native county, and that his father had served under Li. But none of the few *dujuns* who supported Duan was born in Anhui. It was recognized by some contemporaries that the idea of the existence of cliques actually originated with Duan himself, whose resentment of opposition led him to suspect all who disagreed with him as being parties to a conspiracy and so to force them into a conspiracy to defend themselves.

Duan's campaign having petered out through the reluctance of his commanders to fight, he was forced to resign. President Feng Guozhang then appointed a non-partisan premier, indicating his determination to heal the breach. In the same spirit he reappointed the ousted pro-Guomindang *dujun* of Hunan. On 25 December 1917, one month after the dismissal of Duan, President Feng announced that hostilities against the South would cease.

Duan's power was nevertheless too great to ignore. The President, in appointing a commander-in-chief of the expeditionary force which was to participate in the World War, could not overlook Duan's claims, which were pressed on him not least by China's allies, including Japan. From that position Duan soon became Minister for War and again dominated the Cabinet. The South, now sure that Feng Guozhang was not in a position to make good his policy of conciliation, attacked the remaining Beiyang stronghold in Hunan. Feng was forced to allow Duan to send troops south to meet this threat. Duan then ordered Zhang Zuolin, the *de facto* ruler of Manchuria, to send troops to Beijing, ostensibly to replace the northern units. This was the first intervention by Zhang Zuolin in the politics of Beijing and perhaps it whetted his appetite. It also made it impossible for the President to resist the restoration of Duan Qirui to the premiership.

Duan's reappointment, however, could not make the commanders in Hunan any more willing to fight. It is usually said that the reason for their reluctance at this stage was that they were not adequately compensated for their victories. In fact Duan had offered Cao Kun and Wu Peifu authority over the whole of the south to induce them to carry on the war, but this inducement was rejected. Wu Peifu had been strongly influenced by Zhang Qihuang, a Hunan official. Zhang was a metropolitan graduate of 1904, but he adopted liberal views which led him to refuse to co-operate with Yuan Shikai. He preferred to return to his native province, where he served with distinction as a district magistrate. It was he who persuaded Wu Peifu at this juncture of the need for peace; it was believed then, in fact, that Zhang actually drafted the telegram in which Wu and his fellow commanders appealed for peace. Thereafter he served Wu as his political adviser until 1926, when he was shot by a sniper during Wu's final retreat.

In these circumstances the suggestion which is sometimes made that Wu Peifu in opposing further fighting was merely sulking in his tent because he had not been made *dujun* of Hunan does not do him justice. Nor was he following the instructions of his superior Cao Kun. Cao at this point was still supporting the war, in which in fact he had originally taken the initiative. Wu's actions were to show that he believed Hunan should be neutral under a native Hunanese for the sake of the stability of central China. His main object throughout his career was to preserve for his Zhili colleagues the control of the Beijing–Hankou railway, while holding only a southern bridgehead across the river in Hunan. Mobility, not territory, was his aim.

Duan Qirui's second attempt to invade the South failed, like the first, because of the response of the soldiers in the field to condemnation of the war by Chinese public opinion. Public opinion was reflected in the ranks of each and every army in China. Subordinate units could, and often did, evade the obligation to fight. Although sometimes this was from motives of self-interest, sometimes it was because they were out of sympathy with the reasons for war. It was a strong leader who could guarantee to put all the fighting strength that was his in theory into the field: 25 per cent was a good average. This 'moral' element should not be neglected in analysing the history of the times. The war-lord armies which won their battles were usually those whose commanders stood for some identifiable view of the national interest—those of Wu Peifu and Feng Yuxiang, and (later but most obviously) the Guomindang's 1st Regiment led by the cadets of the Party's military academy at Whampoa (Huangpu) on the Canton River.

In Beijing Duan redoubled his efforts to strengthen his position. He organized a political party of his own round the so-called 'Anfu Club' (the name refers to the provinces of Anhui and Fujian, said to be the main sources of Duan's support). He built up the 'European War Participation Army' under his unpopular associate Xu Shuzheng. The source of funds both for party-building and for army-building was a series of enormous secretly-negotiated loans from Japan, the Nishihara loans, the first of which was contracted on 29 September 1917. The new army thus financed was trained by Japanese officers.

Allied to the Anfu Party, which took 330 seats in the 1918 elections by blatant bribery, were 200 parliamentary representatives of the so-called 'Communications clique', a financial counterpart to the military cliques in the eyes of some contemporaries, but like these more a party or a movement than a clique. The Bank of Communications, whose operations were based mainly on Chinese railway finances, was virtually China's central bank, overshadowing the Bank of China. With it was associated a group of financiers, the senior and most notable of whom was Liang Shiyi.

Liang was born in Sanshui county, Guangdong, a place with close relations with Hong Kong. He came from a scholarly family; his father had studied under the same unorthodox teacher as Kang Youwei. Appointed a Hanlin scholar at the age of 26, Liang capped this by taking first place in the Court's special political economy examination of 1902. He became a protégé of Yuan Shikai and was soon known as China's most respected financial expert. As Yuan Shikai's Director-General of National Revenue Administration in 1914, he was the only man in that period who ever actually succeeded in improving the finances of the Beijing government. He it was who led the Communications clique, whose other senior members were experienced bank officials, monetary experts, and railway administrators. As with the other cliques, Chinese forms of personal association inevitably played a part in determining membership, which was mainly Cantonese, but there is no reason to believe that the leaders formed a self-serving cabal. Their policies are on record and they can be judged by them.

Their financial policies included the acceptance of Japanese loans, for which China had to concede favours to Japan in return; but before we repeat the accusation of treason which so many of their compatriots made against them, we might recall that Liang Qichao, whom no historian has ever seen reason to accuse of dishonesty or treachery, actually participated in the negotiation of the Nishihara loans. Most of these loans were ostensibly sought, and granted, for economic development. It was Duan Qirui who diverted the greater part of the proceeds to military purposes.

As the news leaked of the extent of China's borrowing, however, and as rumours of the price paid for them at the cost of China's integrity began to circulate, public opinion reacted strongly. The alarm was focused on the possibility, soon proved to be the case, that the main price was the acceptance of Japanese replacement of former German influence in Shandong province. This touched northerners more than southerners and therefore the generals (and their troops) from Zhili, Henan, and Shandong itself. It touched Wu Peifu most nearly as a native of Penglai county in Shandong, occupied by Japan in 1895. He was quick to make his opposition most publicly and furiously known.

Up to this point Wu's superior Cao Kun had supported the policies of Duan Qirui. What may have brought him over to support his fellow commanders from Zhili was the assassination by former Cabinet Secretary Xu Shuzheng of a retired senior veteran of the Beiyang Army, Lu Jianzhang, highly respected by all, who had busied himself to bring about an end to the war. Lu was invited into Xu's residence and there treacherously murdered on 14 June 1918.

Feng Guozhang's term as President expired on 10 October 1918. He agreed not to seek re-election provided Duan Qirui retired as Premier on the same day. Feng was succeeded as President by the veteran statesman Xu Shichang, whose election was an attempt to prepare the way for reunification. Like Liang Shiyi a Hanlin scholar and a protégé of Yuan Shikai, Xu Shichang had earlier been the architect of the Qing's changed policy of encouraging immigration and Western investment in Manchuria, and he had become Governor-General of the north-east provinces. He was one of the Chinese members of the first imperial, Manchu-dominated cabinet of May 1911 and was one of the four men whom Yuan Shikai as Emperor designated as his personal friends. He was by this time almost a professional peacemaker, having sought reconciliation between Yuan Shikai and the Court in October 1911, between Li Yuanhong and Duan Qirui in 1916, and between Duan and Feng Guozhang in 1917. His election to the presidency, backed strongly by the parliamentary representatives of the Communications clique (which had now itself reacted against the abuses of Duan's borrowing from Japan), was expected to have a healing effect on the division between North and South. Indeed it was proposed to offer the Vice-Presidency to a representative of the Southern forces.

The South rejected this suggestion, but some form of negotiation between North and South was now unavoidable. Duan Qirui had been driven from office by public opinion hostile to his policy of force. And now, with the World War over, the Western powers were putting pressure on China to find some way of recovering her unity. It was plain that no help could be expected from the West as long as there were two governments in China.

President Xu Shichang therefore called a peace conference at Shanghai at the end of 1918, but with little prospect of success. The Southern delegates were angered by the fact that their allies in Shaanxi, a Nationalist enclave in the north, had been excluded from the truce, and negotiations were delayed until Wu Peifu had persuaded Beijing to include them. The South then demanded that the military agreements with Japan be repudiated, that the National Defence Army (the renamed European War Participation Army) be disbanded, and that there should be no more loans from Japan. Beijing's reply was to announce that a further military agreement with Japan had just been signed.

In the middle of this deadlock there burst an outbreak of public protest against Duan's pro-Japanese policies. Touched off by student demonstrations in Beijing on 4 May 1919, it quickly spread to other cities and other classes. The Beijing government was forced to dismiss the three ministers who were most closely identified with the concessions offered to Japan. This May Fourth protest (as we shall see in chapter 9) was soon to transform Chinese politics.

With the failure of the Shanghai peace conference, which Wu Peifu had strongly supported, the stage was set for another attack by Duan Qirui on the South. Wu Peifu promptly made an agreement with the Southern military government by which he received funds for the expense of moving his army out of Hunan, so that the South was free to deal with Hunan's new pro-Duan *dujun*. Leaving his young lieutenant Feng Yuxiang to hold a bridgehead south of the Yangzi, he evacuated the rest of Hunan and took possession of the Beijing–Hankou railway. Wu's superior Cao Kun had meanwhile brought together an alliance with those *dujuns* who had been the backbone of opposition to Duan and who now co-operated constantly with each other. The alliance at this point included Zhang Zuolin, who came to Beijing from Mukden (Shenyang) in June in the hope of preserving peace; as a result Duan Qirui was forced to accept the dismissal of his henchman Xu Shuzheng by the President on 4 July.

Duan's response to the pressure was to rename his forces as the National Pacification Army, and force the President to dismiss Cao Kun and Wu Peifu from their commands: 'For the maintenance of order and discipline in the government,' Duan said, 'I must conduct an expedition against them.' Thus began the first of the wars fought between the Anhui, Zhili, and Manchurian forces.

The Zhili–Anhui–Fengtian wars

The first fighting lasted from 14 to 18 July 1920. Duan's apparently formidable army was crushed. Chinese public opinion regarded this as a victory over Japan. One of Duan's protégés (Jin Yunpeng), however, was then restored to power as Prime Minister by the victors, an unlikely choice if the object of the war was indeed to force on China a government drawn from the Zhili clique.

The victors insisted on certain points designed to prevent the repetition of the situation in which unconstitutional control over the Beijing government could be used to impose power on the rest of the country. They demanded that the provincial authorities should be consulted on all government appointments and policies; that they should have a right to nominate to office within their own provincial jurisdictions; that they should be able to veto appointments outside them; and that they would 'advise' provinces not accepting orders from Beijing. Such a solution was of course as unconstitutional as the activities of Duan Qirui which had created the problem, but it simply reflected in another form the low expectations by then entertained of successful government from Beijing. These had already led to the growth of a strong movement for a federal solution to the problem of disunity, a movement probably supported by the majority of thoughtful Chinese in the early 1920s.

A federal solution had much to recommend it. Power was already split among the provinces. The bulk of revenue was raised and spent in them. The new economic interests were largely provincial. As far as the development of constitutional government was concerned, there seemed more chance for it to take root if a score of provinces were free to attempt it than if it were left to Beijing, where its development had been so disgustingly perverted. Nor was there any reason to suppose that China would be weaker *vis-à-vis* the outside world if her provinces were autonomous in internal affairs; on the contrary, if a federal system was the condition of reunification then China's international position would thereby be improved. Since the Reform Movement of 1898 a federal system had been one of the forms of future government under consideration. In 1900 Liang Qichao had argued the case in an essay on Rousseau. In 1911 the declaration of autonomy by Shandong had incorporated demands for provincial rights, and these were referred to in the preamble of the constitution of the first provisional revolutionary government in 1912. The argument that federalism served the interests of the war-lords is not altogether valid: the association of *dujuns* had always in principle favoured a centralized government, and Wu Peifu was especially hostile to federalism. The war-lords who favoured it were not the Beiyang commanders but those who had come to power as natives of the provinces they ruled; and it is questionable whether they supported federalism or whether federalism as the expression of strong provincial loyalties supported them. It was mainly such militarists in the south and south-west who gave the notion of federalism their patronage.

The federalist movement died down in the chaotic conditions which were soon to prevail in China. The Guomindang came to oppose it largely because it gave countenance to the independence of the militarists of the south and south-west, control over whom the Nationalists sought. The death-blow to Guomindang support was to be their adoption in 1924 of the Soviet democratic-centralist model of party organization.

After its victory over the Anhui clique, the alliance led by Cao Kun made a division of responsibility, with Cao Kun controlling north China, another Zhili soldier, Wang Zhangyuan, controlling Hunan and Hubei, and Zhang Zuolin controlling the north-east. Zhang was also given responsibility for defending China's interests in the situation which had arisen in the north-east as a result of White resistance to the Russian Revolution of 1917 and the intervention of the Allies, and in particular the numerical domination of this intervention by the Japanese.

The new balance of forces did not last. First, Zhang Zuolin disarmed Duan's Japanese-equipped army and took the equipment back to Mukden. He then secured the appointment of his own chief of staff as commander of the Beijing 'military police', actually a force of 30,000 Manchurians. Then Wu Peifu took control of Hunan and Hubei by supporting military leaders who were natives of these provinces; he was appointed Inspecting Commissioner of Hunan and Hubei.

The position was an unstable one which the first crisis was liable to destroy. The crisis when it came was financial. By November 1921 the bankruptcy of the Beijing government, which could not pay officials, teachers, garrison troops, or police, was made manifest by a run on the banks. Attempts to raise a domestic loan foundered on disagreement between the Premier, who thought that a loan could be floated immediately, and the ministers of Finance and Communications, who believed that existing loans must first be reorganized. Zhang Zuolin stepped in to lend Beijing Ch$4 million from the Mukden treasury. The Premier dismissed the Finance Minister, and Zhang Zuolin insisted—presumably for the safety of his money—that the financier Liang Shiyi should be appointed Prime Minister. Liang, however, although he had previously come to oppose Duan Qirui's excessive financial dependence on Japan, could see no alternative in the crisis he had inherited to approaching Japan once more for a loan, and he was prepared to make the inevitable concessions.

At this time the Washington Conference (1921–2) had opened. China had high hopes that the assembled powers would agree to an alleviation of the restrictions which had been imposed on her sovereignty. The Conference had been called on the initiative of the United States, in agreement with Great Britain, in the hope of reaching arrangements which would better protect China, especially against Japan. China proposed, and the Conference accepted, five principles: respect for China's independence and territorial integrity; respect for China's neutrality in the event of war; a review of foreign rights and privileges; the removal of all limits on Chinese sovereignty; and that the powers would make no treaties among themselves, affecting China's interests, without the participation of China. Two issues were uppermost in Chinese minds. The first was the revocation of extraterritoriality and the Nanjing Treaty tariff; the second was the continued influence of Japan in Shandong.

On the first question the powers were now ready to consider the removal of these anomalies in principle, although (as it proved) they were less ready to hurry their demise. They had never regarded these arrangements as permanent. In Japan they had relinquished them as soon as it was plain that the Japanese government could guarantee to protect foreign lives and property and to provide equal justice. In war-lord China, however, there was no such guarantee; indeed China was further from the political stability which would have made such guarantees possible than she had been some years before.

If therefore the Conference had improved China's position in these respects, the improvement was not obvious to the Chinese. Nor were they much impressed when the United States and Great Britain, seeking to limit Japanese naval strength, conceded to the Japanese (who unlike the United States and Great Britain had no need to maintain warships outside Far Eastern waters) a ratio of battleships which would in practice enable Japan to dominate Chinese waters.

These disappointments came later, however. Meanwhile it was the handling of the Shandong problem by the Conference which threw Beijing into renewed crisis and China into renewed civil war. Tokyo sought increased control of the railways in Shandong. Liang Shiyi cabled the Chinese delegation ordering them to 'yield a little ground' to Japan, and the delegation promptly leaked this order. Wu Peifu denounced Liang in a public telegram. He was supported by the *dujuns* of Jiangsu, Jiangxi, Shandong, Shaanxi, Hunan, and Anhui. Public associations throughout China joined in demanding Liang's resignation. Liang then insisted to President Xu Shichang that Zhang Zuolin be ordered to send his Mukden troops to the capital to protect the Government. This made war almost inevitable. Cao Kun, who until this point had avoided giving public support to Wu Peifu, now agreed to fight, even though in the interests of unity he had just arranged a marriage alliance with the family of Zhang Zuolin.

Zhang had meanwhile made an alliance with Sun Yatsen in the south. This is usually represented as an unprincipled combination, but it is explicable in the circumstances of the time. Under pressure once more from the powers, who would not permit the international banking consortium to lend to Beijing unless China was first reunited, new moves in the direction of healing the breach with Canton had already begun. New elections had been offered under the 1912 constitution, but the South had insisted that the 1913 parliament should be restored. When Liang Shiyi became Prime Minister it was agreed that the 1913 members would be recalled and given the task of creating a new constitution, with Sun Yatsen as President and Liang Shiyi continuing as Premier. Liang Shiyi and his Cantonese associates acted as the bridge between North and South. It was therefore not unnatural that Sun should join Zhang Zuolin to defend Liang Shiyi's government.

Fighting began again on 28 April 1922. Zhang Zuolin was quickly defeated by the Zhili dissidents. This was due largely to the forces of Feng Yuxiang, whose army, though not numerous, was highly disciplined. From then on Feng Yuxiang was a power in the land. Zhang Zuolin withdrew from Beijing politics and declared Manchuria independent.

The Zhili victors took up the problem of reunification where the vanquished had left off. They accepted the 1912 constitution and recalled the 1913 parliament. Li Yuanhong was persuaded out of retirement to resume the presidency temporarily. Parliament resolved that both Northern and Southern governments should be dissolved simultaneously.

Wu Peifu exercised the chief influence in the appointment of the Cabinet. He chose men who combined distinction in Chinese public life with sympathies conducive to the restoration of unity. The new Prime Minister, Wang Chonghui, had been Minister of Justice in Liang Shiyi's cabinet. Born in Hong Kong, the son of a Protestant minister, he was a lawyer trained at Yale, had later studied in Germany and Britain, and had been called to the English Bar. Before the Revolution he had been a close associate of Sun Yatsen and had drafted Sun's first public statement of his revolutionary aims. By no stretch of imagination can he be held to have been a member of the Zhili clique or a puppet of Wu Peifu; his promotion by Wu was rather an expression of Wu's lifelong preference for those with Western rather than Japanese connections. Wang in turn chose as Minister of Finance not one of the accepted financial experts but another lawyer, Luo Wengan, then Chief Justice of the Supreme Court, perhaps with the idea that an unquestioned reputation for probity was more important than financial experience in the particular circumstances. Luo was from Canton and had been educated in Britain, reading law at Oxford; his career had been largely in the field of legal reform. As Foreign Minister the choice was China's most experienced diplomat, Gu Weijun (known in the West as Wellington Ku). Son of a property owner in the international settlement at Shanghai, Gu's education was entirely Western: he had been a distinguished student at Columbia. More recently he had served in negotiations at the Washington Conference and with the Soviet Union. Of him too there can be no suspicion that he was one of Wu Peifu's men; on the contrary, he was a close friend both of Zhang Zuolin and of Sun Yatsen. It was in his house that Sun, mortally ill, was to spend his last days in March 1925. If one judged Gu by these associations, one might expect him to be an adherent of the Mukden–Canton coalition just defeated. Finally, appointed as law officer in the new cabinet was Xu Qian, China's principal constitutional expert. Born in Anhui of indigent parents, Xu struggled to educate himself, became a *jinshi* in 1905, and joined the Hanlin Academy in 1907. As head of the late Qing Law Codification Bureau, he had played the principal part in creating the new independent judiciary. Although not a revolutionary, he had called in 1911 for the abdication of the Manchus, served in Tang Shaoyi's first brief ministry under Yuan Shikai, and then joined Sun Yatsen in the south. In 1916 he had prayed to the Christian God for the death of Yuan Shikai, vowing to become Christian if the prayer was answered; apparently it was, and he kept his vow. After Yuan's death he had returned to Beijing to become Vice-Minister of Justice, but when Duan Qirui dissolved parliament he again joined Sun in the south. He now became Minister of Justice.

Of these four principal members of the new cabinet, three had an entirely Western education and two were brought up in a Westernized environment, one in Hong Kong and one in Shanghai; none was from the north. Three of the four had close connections with Sun Yatsen and two had served a Southern government; none was in any way associated with the Zhili group. Two had already been members of the recently overthrown Liang Shiyi cabinet. None was in any way associated with Japan. It was an extraordinary government to be approved by a conservative, anti-foreign war-lord such as Wu Peifu. It can only be seen as expressing Wu's hopes of peaceful reunification of China, and his hostility to those with Japanese connections.

Their ministry was to last less than three months, however. Lo Wengan, the Finance Minister, chosen for his probity, soon found himself accused of accepting a bribe in the course of financial negotiations with a foreign bank. Although in fact he was innocent, the 'commission' having been duly handed over to the public treasury, an order for his arrest was issued by the President. Wu Peifu protested publicly at his arrest.

By this time the Zhili group were at odds with each other. Those round Cao Kun were by now almost as hostile to Wu Peifu as Zhang Zuolin was. They urged Cao Kun to take the side of Parliament, which wanted a judicial inquiry into the Luo Wengan affair, and to oppose Wu Peifu, who gave in, typically putting loyalty to his superior above his own convictions, and the next day, 21 November 1922, the Ministry was dissolved.

The new prime minister was wholly a member of the Zhili group. His appointment, secured by the bribery of Members of Parliament, was the first step to a new situation in which Cao Kun himself won the presidency by corrupt means. With the death of Feng Guozhang in 1919 and the elimination of Duan Qirui from affairs in 1920, Cao Kun was now the senior member of the Beiyang connection. As militarists go he was a man who preferred peace to war, and in every situation he had been slow to take sides and had been ready to mediate. In the constant process of negotiation which had been going on continuously he had played a key role. His immediate entourage maintained friendly connections with Zhang Zuolin in spite of the recent war. If Cao Kun saw in himself the potential to be a peace-making president this would not have been entirely without reason. His chief lieutenant Wu Peifu was at the height of his popularity in China, looked on by millions as the man who might save the nation; Cao may well have mistaken Wu's popularity for his own. Cao Kun's power, however, depended by this time on the abilities and public reputations of the two men, of whom Wu was one.

The other was Feng Yuxiang. Just before the collapse of Wang Chonghui's ministry, Feng had been ordered to Beijing, and by the end of 1922 his army controlled the capital. It was Feng's affairs which precipitated the crisis which led to the rise of Cao Kun to the presidency. Feng had been promised support for his troops in Beijing, but by early 1923 the Government was once more in a financial crisis. Government servants, police and troops were again unpaid. This time the troops were those of Feng Yuxiang, who regarded the regular payment of his soldiers as a point of honour. Feng applied for control of the octroi levied on goods entering Beijing, at that time appropriated to the upkeep of the presidential establishment. The Cabinet agreed, but the President not unnaturally refused. Cao Kun supported Feng Yuxiang.

President Li Yuanhong might have weathered the storm if there had been no other problems, but he had just laid himself open to a charge of corruption. Though the rump of the 1913 parliament was scarcely large enough to provide a quorum in debates on the draft of the new constitution, the discussions were being dragged out by the opposition of Members who wanted to proceed to the election of a new president before, rather than after, the constitution was established. Many of these Members are believed to have been in the pay of Cao Kun. Li Yuanhong responded by offering an expense allowance to Members who attended the debates, and by proposing financial penalties on those who absented themselves. The intention may have been honest, but scandal was inevitable. Cao Kun's followers were given the opportunity they sought. The 'Citizens' Corps' appeared again, as in 1914 and 1917, and Parliament succumbed. Cao then used bribery on an unprecedented scale—Ch$5,000 per vote—to ensure his election to the presidency. Chinese public opinion reacted with disgust and contempt. The cause of parliamentary government in China suffered a final blow. Soon it was the conventional wisdom, even among liberals, that China was not ready for democracy.

Until then Wu Peifu had enjoyed immense popularity for his patriotism, and Feng Yuxiang for the reforms which he had sought to carry out wherever he had enjoyed control of an area for even a few months. In an informal magazine poll in which readers at this time were asked who were the greatest living men in China, while Sun Yatsen came first, Feng Yuxiang was a close second and Wu Peifu fifth out of sixteen names. Their reputations were now dashed. Feng appeared to have seconded Cao Kun's coup; Wu, out of loyalty to his commanding officer, had refused to repeat in public his private condemnation of it.

For the first time since 1918 the Zhili group lost the support of public opinion. Zhang Zuolin quickly restored his alliance with Duan Qirui and Sun Yatsen. Zhang also appealed to the Japanese for help, claiming that the Zhili clique was backed by Great Britain and the United States, both of whom in fact had maintained the strictest neutrality. Japan was also in theory neutral, but whatever Tokyo might propose it was the Japanese army in Manchuria which now disposed, and their connection with Zhang Zuolin was being daily strengthened.

The immediate cause of the second Mukden–Zhili war arose not in the capital but on the Yangzi. There the *dujun* of Zhejiang controlled the Shanghai and nearby Songjiang areas although these were actually part of Jiangsu province. What was at stake was the Jiangnan Arsenal near Shanghai, together with revenues from 'opium fines' said to amount to Ch$2 million a year. The Jiangsu *dujun* Sun Chuanfang, a man highly regarded by the local population and a supporter of Wu Peifu, sought an opportunity to regain control. He found it when the police chief and *de facto* authority of the area was assassinated. He stepped in to appoint his own nominee, but in the ensuing struggle it was the Zhejiang nominee who won. On 1 September 1924 Jiangsu declared war on Zhejiang. Zhang Zuolin saw in this the danger of a further increase in the power of Cao Kun and Wu Peifu. In the event the Zhejiang *dujun* was defeated because of the wholesale defection of his troops, but by that time Zhang Zuolin had attacked through Shanhaiguan, where the Great Wall nears the sea.

Then, in the north, a defection more dramatic and decisive than that of the subordinates of the Zhejiang *dujun* soon took place. On 30 October Feng Yuxiang revolted against his superior Wu Peifu. Wu was soon a fugitive with a price on his head and Feng Yuxiang master of the capital.

Many explanations have been offered for Feng's 'treachery': simple ambition; alienation from Wu Peifu on personal grounds; a new radical development of Feng's ideas, leading him to favour the Guomindang; massive bribery by the Japanese. There is evidence for all of these explanations. Of his ambition there is no doubt. And there is no uncertainty about the deterioration of his relations with Wu, who blamed Feng for complicity in Cao Kun's coup and for the assassination of one of Wu's officers dispatched north to keep Feng in order. Wu was perhaps also alienated by Feng having sent him, his fondness for alcohol being well known, a present of a bottle of distilled water. It is a fact also that Japan provided Feng on the eve of his change of allegiance with a sum of money variously estimated at between Ch$1 million and Ch$2.5 million, though this is not proof of venality. Wu Peifu, with his resources stretched, had informed Feng that in the coming campaign against Zhang Zuolin his troops must live off the country, something Feng had always tried to avoid. If he was to fight a campaign on any other terms it must be paid for, and the Japanese were willing to pay. However, long before the event it was common talk in China that Feng would not this time accept Wu Peifu's orders. Feng probably took payment for what he had already decided to do.

The political dimension of Feng's action is also interesting. He had complained privately to a subordinate in Beijing at the time of Cao Kun's coup that they were both little more than 'the running dogs of the war-lords' who were dictating to the Government while the nation was in chaos and the people suffering. This subordinate, Sun Yo, who now supported Feng's move against Wu Peifu, was a member of the Guomindang. The plot was soon joined by another commander, Hu Jingyi, sent north by Wu Peifu to keep an eye on Feng; he too, secretly, was a member of Sun Yatsen's party. In 1923 Feng had been in a close relationship with Xu Qian, the Minister of Justice in Wang Chonghui's recent cabinet, who was actually Sun's representative in Beijing. At the same time Zhang Zuolin's son and heir had also begun to take an interest in Sun's party. The mould of China's conservative-dominated war-lord politics was beginning to break up.

That Feng's action had a political dimension is evinced by his policy after taking Beijing in 1924. He drove the ex-Emperor Pu Yi from his palace, to make an end, as he said, of royalist intrigues. He encouraged Guomindang activities in Beijing. He renamed his army the Guominjun (the Citizens' Army).

Feng was not in a strong position, however. The winner of the war was Zhang Zuolin, whose troops swept unimpeded to the Yangzi. In spite of Feng's control of the capital, Zhang was able to enforce his own choice of government. He chose Duan Qirui, who thus, on 24 November 1924, came back to power against all the odds. He was named 'Chief Executive', as an indication that his power was provisional, while a 'rehabilitation conference' was brought together in Beijing. The Zhili *dujuns* of the Yangzi area were in no position to resist immediately, and they were prepared to accept Duan because he now controlled no military forces of his own. This did not mean that they would accept domination from Mukden, however, and they soon began to build a new alliance against Zhang Zuolin.

Meanwhile the 'rehabilitation conference' was about to meet. Sun Yatsen was invited to attend it, for his new allies could do no less; his growing prestige made it difficult to exclude him. The left wing of the Guomindang was not enthusiastic about Sun's participation; they would have preferred no compromise with the militarists. Sun called for the eradication of the warlords, the abrogation of the 'unequal treaties', and the convening of a national assembly. There was now sufficient pressure of public opinion behind these demands to ensure that Duan Qirui promised a national assembly within three months. The foreign diplomatic corps, however, had offered recognition of Duan's government of condition that Duan gave an undertaking to respect all existing treaty obligations.

An urgent question concerned the composition of the conference. Sun, who, as will be seen in the next chapter, was now under Communist influence, wanted it to be composed of representatives of industry and commerce, educational institutions and student organizations, trade unions and peasant associations, political parties, and the army units which had opposed Cao and Wu. Predictably, however, those with power in Beijing had a different conception of it. Had Sun got his way, the Guomindang of course would have controlled the proceedings. Beijing proposed instead to invite those in authority, military and civil, and, additionally, some of 'those who have made great contributions to the nation or enjoyed special reputations or experience'. While some representation was offered to the groups proposed by Sun, they were to have no right to vote.

The conference opened on 1 February 1925, but in the end the Guomindang refused to participate; and Sun, suffering from cancer of the liver, died in Beijing on 12 March.

Sun's death at this critical juncture earned him a greater national reputation than any he had enjoyed during his life. His followers made his funeral a great public occasion, a demonstration of popular support, burying him with honours in the Western Hills outside Beijing. From now on, as we shall see, there was little doubt where the political allegiance of the Chinese people lay. The power of the militarists, which in the past had achieved a certain ambiguous legitimacy in the public's eyes, was now condemned as the unprincipled manipulation of force.

Meanwhile Zhang Zuolin's position was not strong. His lines of communications were too extended. Although he controlled the Tianjin-Pukou railway the parallel Beijing-Hankou line was largely in the hands of Feng Yuxiang, a very dubious ally.

Zhang himself was never more than half-hearted in his interventions in China proper. It was some of the younger professional soldiers in his entourage who were keenest on intervention. Under their influence the Mukden armies began to take steps to consolidate power on the south bank of the Yangzi. They rebuilt the Jiangnan Arsenal, previously dismantled by agreement among the militarists. Then on the excuse of maintaining order after the May the 30th Incident of 1925 (for which see chapter 10), Shanghai was occupied by Mukden forces. The threat to the remaining *dujuns* of the Zhili connection was obvious. They responded by announcing an alliance of five Yangzi provinces, two of which were then in Mukden hands, and attacked on 15 October 1925. Wu Peifu took the opportunity to re-enter affairs and joined them. Zhang Zuolin's Manchurian forces pulled out of the Yangzi area and retreated to Xuzhou. The attitude of Feng Yuxiang was critical. In his new and more radical phase he had accepted Soviet help and was determined to control Tianjin, through which he could receive Russian arms. Xuzhou fell to the Zhili commanders, and Zhang Zuolin was forced to concede Tianjin to Feng as the condition of an alliance; but it did not guarantee Feng's loyalty. Nor did Zhang really expect it. Indeed, Feng's increasing friendliness towards Soviet Russia had incurred the Manchurian war-lord's deep hostility, and he would have much preferred war with Feng to war with Wu Peifu. When he withdrew before the attack from the Yangzi it was to swing the weight of his armies to his flank, opposing Feng's Citizens' Army.

At this point Zhang Zuolin's most trusted commander Guo Songling rebelled against him in secret agreement with Feng Yuxiang. Guo was a Japanese-trained, highly professional officer. While he was an instructor in Mukden's military academy Zhang Zuolin's son Xueliang had been one of his students, and Xueliang had become his patron. In 1925 he was the actual field commander of 70,000 crack troops which were ostensibly under Xueliang's command, holding northern Zhili. On 22 November he launched his revolt, demanding the resignation of the father in favour of the son. How far Xueliang himself was implicated it is probably now impossible to know; his father believed he was, and would have executed him out of hand had members of his entourage not persuaded him to relent. Nor can we be sure of Guo's own motives. Xueliang had already shown favour to the Guomindang, and Feng Yuxiang's new Soviet connections made him tacitly at least an ally of the Guomindang, which was now an ally of the Soviet Union. It is possible that Guo Songling's political predilections pointed in the same direction. At any rate, on launching his rebellion he immediately summoned to his support the radical writer Liu Changyin. Liu was an adherent of British Fabian socialism and a consistent supporter of parliamentary government. He was also the most eloquent of all opponents of Japanese influence in China. It cannot be without significance that Guo Songling now sent this anti-Japanese social democrat a secret message, urging him to join the 'revolutionary cause', and engineered his escape from Beijing by a special train.

Guo Songling at first swept all before him. Mukden was soon in danger, and many of Zhang's younger subordinates defected to Guo's side. Then the Japanese army in Manchuria stepped in. They barred Guo's direct way to Mukden. Guo was forced to make a long detour in winter weather, in the course of which his flank was surprised (23 December 1925) by a force of cavalry from northern Manchuria, led and stiffened by Japanese soldiers. He was defeated and executed.

Meanwhile Feng Yuxiang, facing the forces of his former commander Wu Peifu, was engaged in one of the most stubborn and bloody engagements of these increasingly bloody wars. The battle was joined on the day before the defeat of Guo Songling. Feng's devoted army won, but his position was left desperate. Wu Peifu, re-established in Hubei and in command of a wide alliance, now combined with Zhang Zuolin against twice-treacherous Feng. Hemmed in, Feng resigned and went to Moscow. His troops still held much of the metropolitan province and the north-west, however, and his commanders were loyal. They withdrew from Beijing to the Nankou Pass and there, outnumbered five to one and short of ammunition, held out for four months, withdrawing only when the war-lord of Shanxi, Yan Xishan, fearing that they would retreat through his territory, threatened to cut the Beijing-Suiyuan railway. They then retreated north-west with their forces intact.

By this time the Guomindang forces were pressing forward in a northern expedition and had already taken Hunan. A new, formidable and committed force had entered the scene. The war-lord era was about to come to an end.

The effects of war-lordism

To argue that the chief war-lords of China were concerned with the national interest and fought their battles in pursuance of policy aims is not of course to deny that war-lordism was an appalling scourge; neither is it to say that each and every commander, great or small, was inspired by motives of patriotism. The agglomeration of forces forming war-lord armies, in conditions in which every unit was obliged to find its own territorial means of support, produced only the partial unification of an array of semi-independent forces. Some of these were derived from units of the national army. Others grew out of local militias. Others comprised co-opted local bandits. Their allegiance had to be bargained for, and freedom to commit appalling abuses was often tolerated in the process.

Some great commanders showed a determination to control their sub-ordinates, to enforce order, and even to attempt reforms. In Guangxi, pro-Nationalist commanders succeeded in virtually eliminating crime through the creation of a well-controlled and indoctrinated militia, while they expanded education, developed industry, and carried through a sustained programme of public works. Yan Xishan, who as a soldier-member of Sun's Tong Meng Hui had led the republican revolution in Shanxi and become its military governor, was famous throughout China for his comprehensive programme of primary education and his literacy campaigns. Chen Jiongming, another early member of the Tong Meng Hui, a journalist who had raised a military force to fight for the revolution in eastern Guangdong, which he thereafter controlled, took a similar interest in the development of education, and he also encouraged trade unions and peasant associations. Feng Yuxiang's forces were subjected with severity to their commander's puritan morals: no drinking, gambling, swearing, or resort to prostitutes was permitted. Opium smoking was suppressed and addicts rehabilitated. Good order was maintained in Feng's territories, and his army worked in peacetime on the building of roads, the planting of trees, and the erection of dams. Feng was a sincere reformer but military vicissitudes prevented him from maintaining power in any one place for long enough for his reforms to take root.

Other war-lords showed less interest in good government and in reform. Wu Peifu's administration was lax, but as he had no settled territorial base he had only minimal motive and opportunity to establish effective government. Some were savage brutes; and notable among them was the gigantic ex-bandit Zhang Zongchang of Shandong, whose extravagance, cruelty, and indifference to the behaviour of his troops, left the province in a state of total anarchy and impoverishment.

Yet the appalling consequences of war-lordism arose mainly not from the wickedness of individual militarists but from the incessant and increasingly destructive warfare. Supplementary taxation—for example, the collection of taxes not due until future years, increases in tax on salt and other necessities, the proliferation of tolls, the encouragement of a vast revival of opium growing (which had been all but eliminated by 1916) as a source of revenue—put unprecedented burdens on people throughout most of China. Then, if these means of raising money proved inadequate, the war-lords printed their own, with inflationary consequences.

These wars were labour-intensive, involving at their height a total of two million men, mostly living off the country. They also involved the arbitrary conscription of just as many civilians, mostly peasants; and passing armies might thus sweep an area clean of able-bodied men. Draught animals and carts too were requisitioned on a vast scale. The increasing use of artillery left ever more widespread devastation. China's simple defences against flood, needing annual repair and renewal, deteriorated rapidly from neglect and destruction. The period culminated in the famines of 1929, in which the consequences of war played a major role.

Finally it was inevitable that militarization of the countryside overturned normal social relationships and inflicted irreversible damage on the structure of traditional society.

9

The radicalization of Chinese politics

Sun Yatsen and events in the south, 1913–1923

We must now return to 1913 in order to look more closely at the parallel events in the south, and the gradual consolidation of the Nationalist regime.

From 1913 Sun struggled to maintain a foothold amid the military and political rivalries of the south and south-west. His first problem was that opposition to Yuan Shikai was by no means unanimous even among his own supporters. While the Guomindang in the south favoured war, most of the parliamentary party opposed it. Among the provincial military commanders only one, Li Liejun of Jiangxi, was determined to resist; his colleagues in Hunan, Anhui, and Jiangsu were prevented from effective action by disagreement among their officers, who were as split on the issue as public opinion generally. These circumstances account for the easy victory of Yuan Shikai's Beiyang commanders.

Even when in 1915 Yuan proclaimed himself Emperor unified action against him was difficult to achieve. The then *dujun* of Guangdong was no supporter of the Guomindang, whose members he constantly harassed. Support against Yuan Shikai therefore had to depend on the provinces of the south-west. A National Protection Army was formed. Its leaders, however, were not supporters of Sun's Nationalist Party; they were Progressives associated with Liang Qichao. This division in political allegiance remained important.

The National Protection Army, though small and hungry, held out stubbornly until support for Yuan's re-established monarchy leaked away even among those most closely associated with him. When Yuan relinquished the throne the south-western forces still stood to, demanding that he should also relinquish the presidency.

Support for Yuan Shikai by the conservative *dujun* of Guangdong threatened this continued resistance, and as a result a new factor appeared in the politics of the south, and one which was to play a major role thereafter. In order to curb the *dujun* the armies of Guangxi were invited to Canton. They soon dominated the province. In the military council which was set up as an alternative government to that of Beijing, composed of the military leaders of the National Protection Army, Lu Rongting the Guangxi commander was the most powerful member.

Yuan Shikai's death on 6 June 1916 seemed to have resolved the problem, but the solution proved to be short-lived when Duan Qirui showed the same determination to unify the country by force. The National Protection Movement was therefore renamed the Movement for the Protection of the Constitution. In this new grouping Sun enjoyed increased influence. About 250 Members of Parliament had come south and most supported the Guomindang. The Navy Minister, Cheng Biguang, had deserted the northern government and sailed his fleet to Canton. He was a staunch supporter of the Guomindang. Sun was elected Grand Marshal. The Guangxi and Yunnan commanders became his deputies.

A semblance of unity was preserved for as long as the threat of invasion from the north seemed serious; but when Duan Qirui's troops refused to fight, and the crisis was over, the Southern leaders again fell out among themselves. The main issue was whether to accept the legitimacy of the Beijing government and negotiate with it, or to repudiate it entirely. The rump parliament was divided. On the right was the Political Study Group. They favoured negotiation and had the support of most of the military. On the left were the Friends of the People who supported Sun's uncompromising line. In the centre, holding the balance of power, was the Good Friends' Association. The issues soon came to be focused on the question of the drafting of a new constitution. Sun's radicals supported this. The Political Study Group, seeing in a new constitution yet another obstacle to reunification by negotiation, resisted and attempted to filibuster the constitutional commission into failure.

Accompanying these parliamentary manœuvres was a struggle for military power. Sun Yatsen attempted to use the support of the navy to lay the basis of an armed force under his own command. The Guangxi commander, Lu Rongting, responded by murdering several members of the Grand Marshal's bodyguard. Sun brought his little navy up to Canton and bombarded Lu's yamen. Lu responded by arranging for the assassination of the commander of the navy. His power was preserved, but the native Cantonese were becoming highly discontented at the unruly and expensive presence of his 'guest soldiers' from Guangxi. This was reflected in Parliament where the centre party, the Good Friends' Association, threw its weight behind the Friends of the People, the constitutional commission, and the enemies of Lu Rongting. When the draft constitution was talked out Sun's supporters appealed to the Yunnan commander, Tang Jiyao, for military support and moved to Yunnan under his protection.

In the course of these manœuvres Sun's position of Grand Marshal was abolished, and a new council, mainly of military commanders, was set up on 20 May 1918. Although Sun was a member of the council he was without influence. He left in disgust for Shanghai and from there submitted his resignation. For the next two years he devoted himself to putting together his book, *The Fundamentals of National Reconstruction.*

When the Zhili-Anhui war of July 1920 split the Beiyang regime in two, this created from the point of view of the South the possibility of alliances aimed with more or less sincerity at reuniting the country. The first effect, however, was to throw the south and the south-west into a state of fragmentation worse than that of the North. In a general upheaval Tang Jiyao the Yunnan commander, who was the Progressives' leader, was driven from power by his own subordinates. The *dujun* of Guizhou suffered a similar fate. Sichuan broke into warring fragments. At this point Sun found a new source of military support. East Guangdong was governed by Chen Jiongming, who entertained comparatively radical ideas and was from this point of view Sun's most natural military ally. Chen arranged with Beijing a truce on his Fujian border and, thus covered, attacked Canton and drove out the unpopular Guangxi troops in October 1920.

Sun was at last able to set up a government strong enough to create a reformed and prosperous Guangdong. He and Chen Jiongming agreed on the need for reform, but unfortunately this agreement concealed a profound difference of aims. Chen had accepted the notion of federalism then fashionable, and his ideal was a strong and autonomous Guangdong within a federal system. He wanted to keep Guangdong out of the struggle and allow the province to use its resources for its own advantage, whereas Sun saw Guangdong as the base for a northern expedition. In this matter Chen, not Sun, probably had the support of most of the long-suffering Cantonese. Chen had sensible plans for economic development on which he had immediately begun to work; Sun's expensive national ambitions would frustrate them. Moreover in the search for allies in the north the two men differed completely. Sun negotiated with Duan Qirui and then with Zhang Zuolin of Manchuria. Chen Jiongming, more in tune with Chinese opinion generally, was an admirer of Wu Peifu.

Although Chen was willing to allow Sun to set up a rival national government in Canton, he would give him no encouragement to march north. But Sun had undertaken to do so while Zhang Zuolin attacked the Zhili group. When on 3 February 1922 Sun with a few military allies launched his expedition, Chen encouraged the Hunanese authorities to resist and refused to send military supplies. Then Sun's chief treasurer and fund-raiser, Deng Keng, was assassinated, at the instigation, it was generally believed, of Chen Jiongming.

Sun's forces returned and drove Chen out in August 1922. One of Sun's military staff, a young man from Zhejiang called Jiang Jieshi (later known in the West as Chiang Kaishek), advised him to press home his victory and eliminate Chen's power entirely, but Sun chose to be magnanimous. His magnanimity was soon rewarded when, having returned to his northern expedition, he found himself once more an exile when Chen's troops from eastern Guangdong again debouched into the Canton delta and took over the provincial government. Sun's forces had to turn back south in July 1922.

The May Fourth Movement

Beneath the surface during the decade (1919–28) of military struggle China was stirring. A new generation, who had still been learning their letters when the Empire disappeared, was coming of age. Their experience of the politics of their elders was uninspiring. They were ready for new loyalties and new ideas.

The centre of new thought was Beijing University. It was based on the Tong Wen Guan, (the language school for diplomats), which had been transformed into a university by the 1898 reformers; and it was the only one of their reforms to survive. In 1916 the liberal scholar Cai Yuanpei had become its president. He encouraged debate and built up a staff representing every shade of opinion. While China's own culture remained the foundation of education it was now studied critically. Typical was the work of Gu Jiegang, the young historian who applied to the classics the methods he had already used in his studies of the colloquial drama, treating the classics as accretions of tradition.

The most influential writer at Beijing was Chen Duxiu. In his journal *New Youth* he encouraged his contributors in an open-minded search for radical solutions to the nation's problems. He preached 'science and democracy' as the basis of renewed national strength. He launched a head-on attack on Confucianism, dismissing it as irrelevant to the modern world. Above all, he brusquely dismissed the central dilemma which faced China, the choice between preserving her culture and preserving her existence as a nation. 'Where are the Babylonians today?' asked Chen. 'What good is their culture to them now?'

A third young member of the Beijing staff was Hu Shi, recently returned from America. He had studied first under Liberty Bailey at Cornell, then at Columbia under the philosopher John Dewey, whose central tenet, that truth as we can know it is no more than inductively verified prescriptions for change, was an idea whose relevance to China seemed very obvious to the new generation. Dewey's pragmatism gave Chen Duxiu's appeal for openminded, radical thought a philosophical foundation.

The spark which lit this tinder came as usual from a threat to China's integrity. China's main object in joining the Allies in the First World War was that, if Germany were defeated, German privileges in Shandong province would be abolished. This had been promised, but at the same time the Allies had, in contradiction, agreed that Japan should inherit these privileges. As Japan had the power to assert her claims and China had not, the peacemakers of Versailles had only Hobson's choice as to which promise they would keep. By the spring of 1919 the situation was known in China; but the government of Duan Qirui had already 'gladly concurred'—a phrase which became notorious—in Japan's claims, and left the Chinese delegation at Versailles without instructions. On 4 May 1919, 3,000 students from Beijing University and various other institutions held a protest march. Their example touched off a national movement of demonstrations, strikes of workers and a boycott of Japanese goods. The Government responded by repression. The merchant community organized a run on the banks, and the Government gave in. China did not sign the peace treaty.

This was the May Fourth Movement. It precipitated changes which had until then been only potential. A united front of intellectuals, merchants, and workers had defeated the Government in defence of national interests. This was, its participants felt, democracy in action, successful in the streets while in Parliament the nation's representatives had been bribed into acquiescence in treachery. The youth of the nation, in colleges and schools in all the major cities, threw itself into politics, confident in the ability to lead ordinary ✗ citizens. They opened workers' night schools, wrote and published popular newspapers, and created trade unions. They joined the Guomindang in such numbers that for the first time its membership in China exceeded its membership in the overseas Chinese communities.

Yet the effects of the May Fourth Movement were greatest in the cultural sphere. For some years a few individual intellectuals had argued that the classical form of written Chinese (*wenyan*), hitherto used for all serious writing, should be replaced by the more colloquial written form (*baihua*), whose use in the past had been mainly confined to the popular literature of novels and plays. Of the literate population of China only a small minority could read the classical form with ease. If the new ideas which the radicals sought to propagate in China were expressed in colloquial form they would reach a wider, and a non-élite, audience. Until 1919 resistance to this change had been all but universal. Now, suddenly the literary revolution was accomplished almost overnight, at least as far as the new generation were concerned. From then on they wrote about politics, economics, and philosophy, they wrote poetry, and they expressed their new passions for nationalism and socialism, in *baihua*—'plain language'. The use of *baihua* became the shibboleth of radicalism. This was a change almost as significant for the democratization of culture as the replacement of Latin in Europe by the vernacular languages after the Renaissance.

Confucianism was rejected by the new generation, but, as in any revolutionary change in thought, the rejection was far from complete. In the first place the Confucian classics were still the vehicle by which children were taught to read and write; while the new generation might repudiate Confucianism as a guide to action in the modern world they were still too devoted to their cultural heritage to relinquish the classics as the basis of education. In the second place it is easier to repudiate a system of ideas intellectually than to change behaviour accordingly; even now Confucian attitudes strongly influence behaviour in China: hierarchy and patron-client relationships, face-saving, family solidarity, avoidance of conflict, are still dominant characteristics of Chinese society. However, the intellectual dominance of Confucianism ceased.

The most novel of the ideas now widely propagated was socialism. Before 1917 socialist ideas in China had little influence. Socialism as a reaction to the problems of modern industrial society did not seem relevant to China, whose problems arose from the absence of industry. Only when in 1917 a socialist revolution occurred in Russia, a country sufficiently backward to be comparable to China, was the question of the relevance of socialism to China raised. Before then, while there existed in China the vague distaste for the idea of capitalism usual in pre-modern countries, the strongest revolutionary feeling was directed not against capitalism imported from the West but against China's own authoritarian social system, which was based on familial authority. It was here that feelings ran deep.

It is not surprising therefore that, before 1919, anarchism was more popular than socialism among young radicals. China's anarchist movement had begun among Chinese students in France. There, during the First World War, a small group of anarchists published a journal called *New Society*. In Japan another group published *Natural Justice*. Two other students, Li Shizeng and Zhou Fuhai, translated Kropotkin's *Mutual Aid*, and other anarchist works were also translated. The main anarchist organization was the Society for the Promotion of Virtue, which attracted some early members of the Nationalist Party, including the left-wing leader Wang Jingwei. Its decline was as rapid as its rise, however, and by 1919 most of its influence was spent; of the young anarchists only one, Zhou Fuhai, joined the new Communist Party, and he soon left. The three other leading spirits of Chinese anarchism moved indeed to the right as they grew older, and eventually became 'elder statesmen' of the Guomindang. Yet the fact that there is no continuity of persons to be discerned between the anarchist and the communist phases of the rebellion of Chinese youth does not necessarily mean that anarchist ideas played no role in the history of Chinese communism. Anarchist ideas profoundly influenced the mass-line policies of Mao Zedong; and in so far as anarchism versus authoritarianism echoes the ancient Chinese Daoist-Legalist polarity, the contrast can never be far from the subconscious, if not the conscious, thought of Chinese social theorists.

A socialist party existed in China before 1917, but its history is obscure. It was created by Jiang Kanghu, who was born in Jiangsu province in 1883 and educated in Japan. Jiang proposed the equal distribution of land, the nationalization of production, and the abolition of war, armies, the death penalty, and prostitution. He advocated the replacement of all existing taxes by one direct tax, the elimination of inheritance, and free compulsory education. Beneath these specific demands, however, and colouring all of them, was a passionate desire to destroy the authority of the paterfamilias. To Jiang, capitalism was primarily a form of quasi-family property, family authority writ large; and although he professed sympathy with anarchism, what in fact he sought to do was to replace the family head by the State as the accumulator of capital, the organizer of production, and the dispenser of welfare. Vastly inflated figures circulated for the membership of Jiang's party, but it seems to have had so little organization as to make it impossible to determine its real membership. Jiang played his part in opening Chinese minds to new possibilities. Young Mao read his pamphlets with approval, but one cannot trace any continuity of persons between Jiang's group and the Communist Party.

If China's young radical intellectuals produced no socialist movement of any consequence before 1919, neither did China's industrial workers. There were some sporadic strikes in the first two decades of the twentieth century, and occasional temporary and local labour organizations, but nothing more.

Founders of Chinese communism

It was in the course of the May Fourth Movement that small groups of young people came together to study socialism and in particular Marxism, and the process of creating the Communist Party began. This process was in sharp contrast to that by which the communist parties of Europe came into being, which was by the splitting off of radical minorities of the existing social democratic parties with their mass working-class memberships. The Chinese Communist Party was created solely by intellectuals; to be more precise, by two university teachers.

The first Chinese to proclaim the significance of the Russian October Revolution was Li Dazhao, Professor of History and Librarian of Beijing University. Li was born in 1888 into a peasant family, orphaned at the age of 3, and brought up by his grandfather, a small landlord. Educated in the Beiyang College of Law and Political Science, he became a journalist and worked for a liberal newspaper, *Chen Bao*. He found means to study in Japan at Waseda University, where the New Village Movement profoundly influenced many Chinese students, including Li. He supported Liang Qichao and the Progressive Party and believed in the possibility of reforming China through parliamentary government. His thinking was radicalized, like that of so many other Chinese, by the violence and chaos of the war-lord period. He broke with the Progressives when they supported Duan Qirui—not long before Liang Qichao himself left politics in despair to devote himself to Buddhism. In 1918 Cai Yuanpei, the tolerant President of Beijing University, offered Li Dazhao the Chair of History.

Li, like so many of his generation, was motivated by a nationalistic reaction to China's weakness. He felt compelled to show that China might still have a future as great as her past. To do this he took the Buddhist idea of eternal flux and the Han Confucian idea of the mutual influence of *yin* and *yang*, and married them to the modern Western idea of progress. In the flux of events one country or culture may draw ahead and another fall behind, but such relations of superiority and inferiority are temporary. The country that now lies in the shadow of *yin* will burst forth again into the glory of *yang*, and beneath the phenomenal flux is the underlying dynamic unity of inevitable progress in which all countries and cultures play their part in turn. China had once led, and China would lead again. In these terms, Li looked at his own age as one in which the forces of both Western materialism and Eastern spiritualism (this naïve contrast was part of the new conventional Chinese wisdom) had exhausted themselves, and the world awaited a new synthesizing impulse. To Li the motive force of historical change was not the individual, either as hero or as free citizen, but the masses: nothing less could embody the great forces of history in which he believed. Even so, in this process the educated must provide the initial impulse; they must make the masses conscious of themselves and of their destiny. Li's interpretation of democracy is what one might expect, given his view of history and his disillusionment with China's parliamentary experiment. Democracy in Li's theory expresses the will of the people in an undifferentiated Rousseau-esque sense. Democracy does not consist of institutions; it is a question of mass consciousness.

The October Revolution in Russia burst on Li Dazhao's mind as the realization of his apocalyptic vision. Backward Russia had leapt forward to lead human progress, in a revolution in which a handful of intellectual leaders had lit the fuse of mass consciousness, to create a new synthesis in which Western materialism would be used in the service of Eastern idealism. He saw in the Russian Revolution what he wanted to see. He was not yet a Marxist. Although his philosophy clearly predisposed him to a Hegelian, dialectic view of history, and his political ideas to an acceptance of the totalitarian democracy which Marxism had inherited from the Jacobins, he still had reservations. Writing in the first *New Youth* symposium on Marxism in 1919, he rejected the materialist interpretation of history. But by the end of the year he had shifted to the position that while the moral sense is primary, the content of that moral sense is in any particular society determined by the mode of production. And then, a year later in a further article in *New Youth*, he fully accepted Marxism. He had already organized in Beijing University a group for the study of Marxism. He became a founder-member of the Chinese Communist Party.

Li Dazhao died in 1927, strangled after being captured in Zhang Zuolin's brutal raid of that year on the Soviet Embassy. His influence lived on in a young member of his Marxist study group, his library assistant Mao Zedong, and Li had been a Marxist with a difference. The difference was his stress on mass consciousness as the driving force of revolution. It was Mao Zedong who worked out and applied the implications of this for political leadership and for the conduct of social change. Mao also accepted from Li that the Chinese revolution must be a peasant revolution, and that it thus must also be a cultural revolution.

The second founder of the Chinese Communist Party was Chen Duxiu, editor of *New Youth*, a man very different in background from Li Dazhao. Born in 1879 in Anhui into a family of military mandarins, he followed the family tradition in a modernized form by studying naval science. Like Li Dazhao he attended Waseda University, but he also spent some years studying in Paris, and French influences formed his thought. In contrast to Li Dazhao with his mystical populist ideas, Chen was a rationalist and an individualist. His belief was that reason would dissolve both hierarchy and superstition and so free the energies of the individual, and the energies of the individual would transform China.

After the revolution of 1911 Chen Duxiu was appointed Education Commissioner of his home province, but when Yuan Shikai dissolved Parliament Chen retired to Japan. He returned in 1915 and founded *New Youth*, which became the most influential of all the journals created at that time. It was the influence of *New Youth* which made it possible that the student protest of May Fourth 1919 should surpass its original aims and open out into a revolution in thought. Chen was imprisoned for his part in the May Fourth agitation and was led to despair of the parliamentary experiment. While in hiding in the French Concession in Shanghai he met the Comintern representative Voitinsky; yet paradoxically it was John Dewey, the American philosopher, lecturing in China in 1920, who finally made Chen a Marxist. Chen was especially struck by two ideas which Dewey brought to China. The first was the central idea of pragmatism—that we learn to understand reality only by changing it. It is an idea which pragmatism shares with Marxism. In Chinese conditions Chen Duxiu interpreted it in the Marxist sense, that only by engaging in the process of revolutionary change can one learn the truth about society, and that therefore the only true intellectual is the revolutionary activist. The second idea reinforced the first: that (as Chen interpreted Dewey) 'facts can make laws, but laws cannot make facts'. By 1921, Chen Duxiu had founded two of China's first Communist cells.

Younger than either Li or Chen, and at this time not known nationally but destined to play a far greater role than either, was Li Dazhao's young associate, Mao Zedong. Mao's conversion to communism illustrates vividly the pressures and the presuppositions which brought together the founders of the Chinese communist movement. He was born in 1893 in Shaoshan *xian*, Hunan. His father was a self-made rich peasant, hard-working and frugal, narrowed rather than broadened in mind by his hard-won success. The son was expected to pull his weight on the farm, not to waste his time with books, and young Mao succeeded in gaining an education only by rebellion. Consequently his early education was delayed, broken, and confused. It was to a large extent a self-education with the characteristic vices and virtues; when he came to power in 1949 he was still the brilliant autodidact, mixing shrewd unorthodox insights with astonishing ignorance. After some short periods at different traditional schools, after toying with a police college and a soap-making institute, spending some weeks as a volunteer in the post-1911 revolutionary army, and a few months of independent discursive reading of translations of Western literature in Changsha provincial library, he entered Changsha's First Normal College in 1913 as a mature student to train as a schoolteacher. Here for the first time he found himself among kindred spirits. With his philosophy teacher Yang Changji, he established a close relationship. Yang, already well versed in Chinese philosophy, had studied Paulsen's development of the philosophy of Kant in Germany, and thence went to Edinburgh where he absorbed the combination of Oxford neo-Hegelianism and Scottish empiricism which was current there. On his return he created a philosophy which reconciled these Western studies with the thought of the seventeenth-century Chinese patriot-philosophers who had resisted the Manchus and had become the heroes of the modern nationalist intellectuals.

In these years Chinese youth relived the European Enlightenment, with its questioning of traditional moral sanctions and institutions, and its search for a philosophical justification of the individual conscience and for a new relationship between the individual and society. They relived it not in the detachment of academic study but in a crisis of national collapse. Kant had written that Rousseau's work was 'a prescription for the foundation of a state', and it was thus that Chinese youth read Western authors. They came to accept as axiomatic that the strong and wealthy state is built on the energies of liberated individuals. The question was how these individuals should relate to society.

In Yang Changji's philosophy the justification of individual moral judgement had been given by Kant. The mechanism of individual moral motivation had been given in Paulsen's treatment of the will, which Paulsen equates (to put it simply) with man's compulsion to try to live up to the moral image which he forms of himself. Man's relation to society had been satisfactorily given, for Yang, by T. H. Green: that society's moral progress is motivated by the contemplation of the gulf between reality and possibility, which ensures that no conscious man can feel satisfied until he knows that all men are satisfied. Yang gave these ideas a Confucian interpretation. To achieve moral consciousness requires effort: the instincts are there but they must be trained. The will must be made perfect. Action must follow knowledge or the knowledge is vain. And the knowledge must be based on the facts seen objectively in their moral significance. Yang's thought was an attractive synthesis of Chinese and Western moral philosophy. When the young Mao became a Marxist he did not repudiate the ideas of his teacher, but incorporated them in his Marxism.

At the Changsha Normal College Mao played a leading part in student affairs. As Secretary of the Student Union he founded a workers' night school programme. He created a society, the Xin-min Study Society, devoted to the practice of the ideas he had learned from Yang Changji. 'Xin-min' was a phrase from one of the classics, the *Great Learning*—'the renewal of the people'. The aim of the members of this society was 'to create for themselves a "new" personality by discussion, debate, self-analysis and action'. This formula remained built into Mao's concept of political leadership. Many of his associates in the Xin-min Study Society were young peasants like himself, attracted to the First Normal College because there were no tuition fees. Many were to follow Mao into the new Communist Party.

Mao graduated in June 1918 and was invited to Beijing to assist in organizing a movement to send students to France. Yang Changji had just been awarded a chair in Beijing University. He found Mao a post—though a very humble one—under Li Dazhao in the University library in the capital. Li had just founded his Marxist study group. Mao was interested, but most of what he read on this brief first visit to Beijing was anarchist rather than Marxist. He returned to Hunan in March 1919 to take up a post in the school attached to the Normal College.

A few weeks after he left the capital came the outbreak of the May Fourth student protest. The movement spread to Changsha. Mao and the Xin-min Study Society threw themselves into the organization of demonstrations against the *dujun*, Zhang Jingyao, who represented Duan Qirui's government in Hunan. The Hunan United Association of Students went on strike, formed lecturer corps to speak in the streets, put on plays, organized night schools and enforced an embargo against Japanese goods. Mao founded (and wrote most of) a popular journal, the *Xiang River Review*, the Hunan government suppressed it after five issues. Short-lived as it was, it brought Mao the beginnings of a national reputation. His articles showed how much his visit to Beijing had changed him. Before, his concern had been the renewal of the individual; after, it was to organize the mass of the people into 'an irresistible force'. The influence of Li Dazhao is obvious, but at this time Mao knew little of Marxism beyond the name.

Dewey's lectures in China had stirred up a great controversy within the ranks of the May Fourth Movement between pragmatists and Marxists. Hu Shi, the pragmatist leader (whom Mao at this time admired), summed the issue up in an aphorism—'-isms versus problems'—and condemned holistic theories as no substitute for patient problem-solving. Mao promptly founded in response a Society for Problems, listing 140 of them as a start to debate. This and the fact that his writings in the *Xiang River Review* almost all still expressed liberal values, shows that Mao moved no faster towards Marxism than his mentor in Beijing University library; the main enemy was still authoritarianism, the main task still the liberation of the individual, though now in a context of co-operative mass action.

In January 1920 Mao returned to Beijing. There he read his first book on socialism. It was a history of socialism by Thomas Kirkup, a late nineteenth-century Scottish minister. Mao read it 'with wild excitement'. Its theme was that there were two contrasting and contradictory ideas of socialism: the étatist, centralizing socialism of Saint-Simon, and the communal socialism of Robert Owen. Kirkup preferred the second, a preference which was generally shared by Mao's generation in China. The choice of socialist works for translation into Chinese at this time shows a strong bias in that direction; and Li Dazhao, although he had available a score of Lenin's writings, was deeply impressed only by *State and Revolution*, that impassioned description of a society of 'autonomous local communities . . . voluntarily united for the defence of the whole'.

Mao also read Kautsky, from whom he seems to have taken four ideas that were strongly to influence his own future thinking: that 'we must not think of socialist society as something rigid and uniform, but rather as an organism constantly developing, rich in possibilities of change . . .'; that 'a new social form does not come into existence through the activities of certain specially gifted men . . .'; that 'never yet in the history of mankind has it happened that a revolutionary party was able to foresee, let alone determine, the forms of the new social order which it strove to usher in . . .'; and that conflict would inevitably continue in socialist society. Ironically, these quotations from Kautsky the great revisionist could stand as the text for Mao's own attack on 'revisionism' in the Cultural Revolution.

We know the extent of Mao's reading on this second visit to Beijing, and what is striking is that he read so little of Marx and Engels. He read only the *Communist Manifesto* and *Socialism, Utopian and Scientific*; he seems to have read little more even in the course of the next twenty years.

The May Fourth Movement soon split between those who believed that a long period of education must precede the establishment of popular government, and those who believed that immediate political action was both necessary and possible. Mao saw that war-lord China gave little scope for an open educational process. The suppression of his *Xiang River Review* was the least among many experiences which showed him that this was so. Power would have to be seized before the process of education could even begin; and Russia's October Revolution showed how power could be seized. It was in this sense only that Mao had become a Marxist by 1920. Theories of class and the class struggle played no part in his thought. In an essay, *The Great Union of the People*, Mao showed himself concerned to unify, not to divide. It was not until 1926 that he made his first published attempt to analyse Chinese society in terms of class, and even then his purpose was to demonstrate the breadth of possible support for the revolution in a society which, as he was soon to write, was 'big in the middle and small at both ends'.

When Li Dazhao opened the debate on Marxism it was taken up by various groups of young radicals. Out of their discussions came the first little groups concerned specifically with Marxist socialism. They were scattered and isolated, in Canton, Wuhan, Tianjin, Jinan, and Changsha, as well as in Beijing. The tentativeness of their members' commitments is shown by the large number who either did not join the Party or having done so, soon left it. Of the five members of Chen Duxiu's Shanghai group who became prominent in Chinese life, four joined the Guomindang and one left politics for scholarship. Of four in Canton, two left the Party. Most of those who remained loyally Communist were killed in battle or executed; Li Dazhao's group was wiped out by 1930; most of Mao's fellow members of the Xin-min Study Society also perished. Of those who first joined the Communist Party, only two whose names are known—Mao Zedong and Dong Biwu—entered Beijing in 1949 to found the Chinese People's Republic.

The Chinese Communist cells formed in France and Germany showed greater capacity for survival. Many of the members of the Student Workers' Movement formed to take advantage of the scheme for the dispatch of Chinese labourers to Europe to assist the Allies on the Western Front during the First World War returned to become leaders of the Communist Party. Zhou Enlai, Deng Xiaoping, Li Fuchun, and Zhu De survived to become members of the Political Bureau and of the People's Government. The total group of Chinese cells in Europe was at first larger than all the groups in China together. The cells in France were for a while part of the French Communist Party, and thus the only section of the future Chinese Party whose members served their political apprenticeship in association with Europeans whose original background was the social democratic movement. Whether for this reason or not, these returning expatriates were to be distinguished in Chinese Party affairs and government by their relative indifference to ideology. They retained that touch of scepticism with which Chen Duxiu, also French-trained, was often to irritate his Russian advisers. Moreover it is clear from the history of the beginnings of the Chinese Communist Party that the attraction of Marxism as a social philosophy was subordinate to the far greater attraction of Lenin's assertion that the miseries of the underdeveloped world were due to the economic power exercised in their midst by foreign capital.

Soviet efforts to mould the mixed membership of the Shanghai proto-Marxist group into an orthodox communist party were not immediately successful. However, the Comintern representative Voitinsky encouraged its members to become involved in the creation of a labour movement, and here there was no hesitation. Organizing Chinese workers to oppose their often foreign employers raised no ideological doubts, while it would be a natural extension of the May Fourth agitation among the workers, agitation in which most of those who were now communists had been involved. The formal creation of the Chinese Communist Party came in 1921, after a year or so of successful experience in creating trade unions among railwaymen, miners, seamen, printers, and others.

Meanwhile the Soviet Union was seeking allies in China. The international policies of the Bolshevik government were determined by its precarious position, faced as it was with armed opposition and foreign intervention. The new revolutionary government had offered independence to the non-Russian peoples within the Soviet Union, but when movements for independence became allied with opponents of the Revolution, the Bolshevik regime found an answer. Control was reasserted by the creation within each national group of a pro-communist party which usually then came to power supported by the Red Army. While the principle of national autonomy was acknowledged by the establishment of independent republics, rule from Moscow was maintained by insistence on a single communist party organization for the whole. This was a method which by analogy could also facilitate control beyond Russia's frontiers and perhaps eventually achieve 'the complete union of the toilers of all nations'. The extension of Russian influence abroad by this means worked through the unity of the Communist International. Applied in Asiatic Russia and extended eastwards, it led rapidly to the explicit reassertion by the Bolsheviks of the Tsarist principle that the future of Russia lay in Asia. Defence of the Revolution could not in any case be easily confined within Russia's own frontiers, for overlooking these frontiers were hostile states mostly dominated by the capitalist powers. By diplomacy or subversion their influence in Turkey, Persia, Afghanistan, Manchuria, and China had to be attacked.

The greatest of the capitalist powers was Great Britain. The British position in Asia turned on India, which was therefore the prime target; but India proved impervious to Soviet penetration. China was softer. With rival governments in north and south, with local war-lord regimes whose aspirations to national power could be encouraged, and with the collapse of effective Chinese sovereignty beyond the Great Wall, China presented an opportunity made more favourable by the growth of interest in Marxism among Chinese intellectuals. The Soviet Union played every angle in this confusion: normal diplomatic relations with the recognized government in Beijing, clandestine relations with Sun's regime in Canton, negotiations with provincial warlords, the replacement of Chinese authority in the frontier regions, and the creation of a Chinese Communist Party subservient to the Communist International.

There was a second dimension of Soviet policy in China. With the failure of the expectation that revolution in Russia would be followed by revolution in Western Europe, Lenin turned his attention perforce to the possibility of allies beyond Europe. He found a parallel between the alliance of workers and peasants in Russia in 1917 and possible alliances in the countries of the undeveloped world between workers and nationalists. It was in this context that Bukharin invented the idea (since attributed both to Lin Biao of the

Chinese Communist Party and to D. N. Aidit, Secretary-General of the Indonesian Communist Party until 1965) of comparing the capitalist world to cities surrounded by a multitude of peasants.

At the Third Congress of the Communist International in May 1920, Lenin proposed that the communist parties of the colonial and semi-colonial countries should unite with 'bourgeois nationalist parties' in the struggle for independence. The Indian communist M. N. Roy disagreed. He argued that the 'bourgeois nationalist' parties of the colonial world differed in maturity, and in many cases were already too powerful to have to accept co-operation with a party aiming at socialist revolution. He was willing to accept Lenin's policy provided that leadership of the revolution was not handed over to the nationalists, and provided that the communist parties were able to 'carry on vigorous and systematic propaganda for the idea of Soviets and . . . organize peasants' and workers' soviets as soon as possible'. The debate revealed the ambiguity of Lenin's proposed alliance, which experience in China was to prove.

Maring, the Dutch communist, author later of precisely such arrangements both in China and in Indonesia—with, as it soon proved, the same tragic issue in both cases—produced a formula which enabled the Third Congress to combine the contradictory proposals of Lenin and Roy. Maring's solution was, however, merely verbal: he proposed to delete the phrase 'bourgeois nationalist' and substitute for it the phrase 'national revolutionary'. This did not in reality make bourgeois nationalist parties any less bourgeois or any more revolutionary, but it enabled the Congress to reach unanimity. The price of that unanimity, in China alone, was to be the death of tens of thousands of communists. Had the Soviet Union consistently pursued a goal of revolution in the colonial world the problem would no doubt have solved itself in the rapid breakdown of unnatural alliances between communist and nationalist parties; but when Russian national security came to replace revolution as the primary aim of foreign policy, so that a strong bourgeois ally in power was reckoned to be worth more than a weak communist party in opposition, the contradiction became intolerable.

Urgency was given to the question when anti-communist intervention in the Far East threatened the Bolshevik revolution. In the Russian Far East, Horvath in 1917 had established a counter-revolutionary government which was supported by Japan and the Western powers. Beijing was encouraged to contribute troops to the anti-Bolshevik intervention and was not reluctant, as the Chinese Eastern Railway had been taken over from Horvath by pro-Soviet forces. Chinese troops drove these forces out of Manchuria. Anti-Bolshevik resistance spread throughout the whole area from Lake Baikal eastwards. One major reason for Western intervention was fear that Japan would seize the Chinese Eastern Railway; Japan's contribution to the forces of intervention outnumbered the combined forces of all the other powers, while the Cossacks had come under Japanese command. China's interest was to prevent the establishment of Japanese power on her inner frontiers.

At the height of the crisis the Soviet Government, in an attempt to detach China from her allies, announced in the Karakhan Declaration of 25 July 1919, which was addressed both to Beijing and to Canton, that it was willing to renounce the privileges enjoyed in China by Tsarist Russia, including control of the Chinese Eastern Railway. No reply was sent by the Beijing government; neither was the message made public; nor did Canton respond to the Soviet gesture. It became known only through the efforts of the journalist and Guomindang politician Eugene Chen, who added this scoop to his earlier triumph of the exposure of the Nishihara loans. The revelation could not have been better timed. The West had just confirmed the transfer to Japan of Germany's privileges in Shandong. Many Chinese concluded that only the new revolutionary power in Moscow was prepared to relinquish imperialism.

Thanks to the Karakhan Declaration, when three Comintern agitators (Voitinsky, Maring, and Yang Mingchai) arrived in China in May 1920, they were assured of a ready welcome from Chinese radical organizations. The Soviet Government, now victorious in the East, soon forgot its avowed intention of waiving Russian privileges, and the main aim of its subsequent negotiations in Beijing was actually to negotiate Russian retention of the Chinese Eastern Railway. Meanwhile the avowal nevertheless had had its effect. Early in 1921 a small group of delegates met at Shanghai to formalize the foundation of the Chinese Communist Party, already in informal existence since the preceding year.

In August 1922 a formal diplomatic mission from Moscow, headed by Adolph Joffe, arrived in Beijing to negotiate on Russia's claims in Mongolia and Manchuria. The Chinese refused to negotiate until Russia had withdrawn from Mongolia and renounced its claims on the Chinese Eastern Railway. Joffe thereupon went south to make contact with Sun Yatsen. Sun, once more at loggerheads with his military supporters, and with his Anhui–Mukden allies having been defeated in the north by Feng Yuxiang, was desperate. Appeals to the West and to Japan had failed. Suspicious as he was of communism, the prospect of Russian help was difficult to resist. The West hammered the point home by sending a joint naval demonstration to prevent Sun's southern government from taking over the revenues of foreign trade at Canton. Sun made a last appeal, through America, for Western help. He even proposed a joint Western occupation of the provincial capitals of China in order to crush the war-lords, and a five-year protectorate to put China on the road to modernization and democracy. Such a plan, however, was too imperialist even for the imperialists themselves.

Sun's political sympathies lay with the Western powers, but his approaches to them had been rebuffed. When he turned to the Soviet Union sympathy with Marxism played no part in his motives. His opinion was that Marxist class analysis represented 'the pathology of a particular society' and not the physiology of society in general. He did not think that communism had any relevance for China where, as he claimed with some truth, there were no rich and poor but only poor and poorer. What he wanted from Moscow was material aid; he did not contemplate at that stage a bargain by which his own party and the Communist Party of China would virtually merge. However, in negotiations with Adolph Joffe (conducted largely by Liao Zhongkai, the most pro-communist of Sun's followers), Sun found that Soviet aid would be dependent upon his willingness to accept close co-operation with the Chinese Communist Party. At the end of a month of negotiation Sun and Joffe issued a joint declaration (26 January 1923) stating that communism was not applicable to China at her existing level of development. This allayed Sun's fears, or at any rate provided a disclaimer useful to him in persuading his fellow leaders to suppress their own. After further negotiation Sun Yatsen agreed that members of the Communist Party would be permitted to join the Nationalist Party as individuals, while the Communist Party would retain its identity.

In the months when negotiations with the Soviet Union via Joffe were taking place, the first efforts were being made to reorganize the Nationalist Party, in order to provide it with a formal system of decision-making, with the discipline it had hitherto lacked, and with agreed policies. In the event, all three were provided when the reorganization of the Party merged with the creation of the Communist alliance. The reorganization was dictated by Soviet advisers.

What had been mooted (even though it was never implemented) before the Soviet Union became involved is worth attention because of the profound difference between this purely Guomindang-inspired scheme, and that which followed the Soviet intervention. The manifesto issued by a meeting of provincial Party representatives in September 1922 showed little political or social radicalism. In its elaboration of Sun's political theory, the *Three People's Principles*, there was no mention of imperialism; the manifesto merely proposed equality among nations and the revision of treaties. In its section on 'people's livelihood', equalization of land rights and control of capital were included (being the two basic ideas of the corresponding section of Sun's *Principles*), but the implications drawn from them were far from communist. The first implied a gradual redistribution of land as a result of social-credit-type taxation. The second proposed the encouragement of capitalist enterprise, though under 'supervision'. These proposals represented Sun's own consistently held views. However, the documents issued from the First National Congress of the Guomindang, held at Canton in January 1924 after the formation of the Communist alliance and representing the reorganized Party, expressed views in sharp contrast to these.

The Guomindang was reorganized on the basis of democratic centralist discipline; on Taiwan it remains so today—a Leninist party with non-Leninist aims. It was 'placed above the nation in order to rebuild the nation'. China was proclaimed to be a colony of the foreign powers, and existing treaties to be unequal treaties. Unequal distribution of property was declared to be the root cause of China's internal conflicts. It was declared that capitalists could not be expected to represent the interests of the people or to be independent of foreign interests. Democracy was demanded, but 'those who betray the nation . . . will be permitted neither freedom nor rights'. Marxist terminology was eschewed; but the ideas of a vanguard party above the state and society, of imperialism, of class struggle, and of the power to deprive political opponents of their rights were all asserted. The ideology and organization of the Guomindang were transformed by these decisions, many of which proved as useful in justifying Chiang Kaishek's later dictatorship as in justifying totalitarian socialism.

The changes in Party organization did not immediately improve Sun's situation. In Canton the new alliance with the Communists earned him the hostility of the Cantonese merchants, so that his base was now threatened from within, while beyond Canton city the generals still ruled. Sun appointed the most powerful of them to the new Central Executive Committee, but the new Party discipline was lost on them; they obeyed only when they chose.

Yet there was now a fresh military factor in the situation: the Whampoa Military Academy, founded mainly with Soviet help and resources. The Whampoa units were politicized; as in the Soviet armed forces no order was valid unless countersigned by the Party representative of the unit. Its growth was slow, and made slower by Sun's immediate diversion of most of its funds to finance another northern expedition in alliance with Mukden, in an attempt to oust Cao Kun from his ill-gotten presidency assumed in October 1923. In the event, only the Hunanese and the Henanese (keen to get home), along with one section of the Yunnanese, obeyed Sun's orders. Worse, many of the 'guest soldiers' (units from other provinces) joined in a conspiracy with the Canton merchant militia and with Chen Jiongming, still powerful in his eastern Guangdong bailiwick. However, the first instalment of Soviet weapons had just arrived at Whampoa and the crisis gave the new cadets their first opportunity. They promptly proved their merit. The merchant militia was defeated and disarmed.

The next test for the Whampoa cadets came soon. In January 1925, when Sun was on his last visit to the north from which he was not to return, Chen Jiongming in alliance with the Yunnanese and the Guangxi soldiers and in support of Duan Qirui's new executive government, launched yet another attack on Canton. The Whampoa cadet regiments defeated him, then swung round on his allies and disposed of them also. Chen thus passed out of Chinese history, leaving behind him a reputation as the most persistently treacherous of Sun's military allies, though it might be more fitting to regard him as the military representative of moderate Cantonese opinion.

The Guomindang now at last controlled Guangdong province, but the independence of Guangxi remained a threat. Fortunately, in the incessant internal struggles within that mountainous province, the winners were a group of commanders who proved to be strong supporters of the Nationalist cause and who were to remain faithful—in their fashion—until the final disaster of 1949. Three soldiers who had first met as boys in the Guangxi Military Primary School had formed a remarkably lasting alliance. They were Li Zongren, Bai Chongxi, and Huang Shaohong. The last act of their rise to power came when Duan Qirui attempted to assert the power of Beijing in the south. His appointees fell to fighting each other and were crushed by the Li-Bai Huang connection. The victors then proceeded to stabilize Guangxi, put its resources at the disposal of the Nationalists, and carry through a programme of eccentric but effective reforms remarkably reminiscent of those which the Taipings from Guangxi had hoped for two generations before.

Unfortunately, however, a new form of tension now grew within the Guomindang. The power of the Communists was regarded by many with fear and suspicion. The restive right wing had been held in check only by the personal authority of Sun Yatsen.

10

The rise of Chiang Kaishek

The Guomindang and the Zhejiang connection, 1911–1926

After Sun's death in March 1925 the civilian contenders for the succession to the leadership of the Guomindang were veteran revolutionaries who had been closely associated with him since the early days of the Tong Meng Hui: Hu Hanmin, Wang Jingwei, and Liao Zhongkai. Liao, born and educated in San Francisco, a journalist by profession, was the most able of the three. His support, however, came mainly from the Communist Party and from the Comintern advisers. Of the other two, Hu Hanmin probably had the greater following; in the elections to the first Central Executive Committee he had come top of the poll. He was regarded as right-wing in the sense that he was, of the two, the less happy over the participation of the Communists. Wang Jingwei was regarded as the leader of the 'left' Guomindang—a shadowy group united only in their acceptance of the United Front with the Communist Party and led (if that is not too strong a word) by Wang, by Sun's widow Song Qingling and son Sun Fo, and by Eugene Chen. Chen was an ebullient English-speaking West Indian lawyer and writer, son of an exiled Taiping and a woman of part-Chinese and part-Negro ancestry. A British subject, he had impulsively joined Sun Yatsen as he passed through London on his return to China in the wake of the 1911 Wuhan rising.

At the far right of the Nationalist spectrum was a group determined to be done with the alliance. Although composed of men of great reputation who, like Hu Hanmin and Wang Jingwei, had joined the revolution in its earliest days and had faithfully accompanied Sun through all the vicissitudes of his frustrating career, this group had no leaders who could compete in popularity with Hu Hanmin and Wang Jingwei.

Within a few weeks of Sun's death Liao Zhongkai was murdered by an unknown hand. Hu Hanmin was under suspicion of being an accessory, along with the right-wing Party veterans who had been involved in the attempted impeachment. Hu went abroad and the others sought refuge in Shanghai.

The first challenge for the succession came, however, as one might have expected, from a soldier. Tang Jiyao, the former Progressive *dujun* of Yunnan, had been elected Sun's deputy at the First Congress of the reorganized

Guomindang and on this basis claimed to succeed him. He urged his claim by marching his army into Guangxi *en route* for Canton. All depended on the attitude of the new military masters of Guangxi, the Li-Bai-Huang connection. They chose to support the civilian leaders of the Guomindang. Tang was eliminated from the political game. Yet another, though less obvious, militarist threat was now growing. In the previous two years the Whampoa Academy had proved remarkably successful. Its small but well-disciplined force had become the backbone of the 1st Army of the revolutionary government. The commandant of Whampoa, Chiang Kaishek (Jiang Jieshi), had hitherto played no political role; his views were unknown; he had played the exemplary part of a soldier who obeyed the orders of the civil power. He was something of an outsider in the Cantonese-based Nationalist Party, having been born in Zhejiang. Yet it was his Zhejiang connections which proved to be his strength.

When the 1911 revolution spread from Wuhan to other areas, local groups of insurgents formed lasting connections. In the Shanghai area such a connection was formed round the attractive figure of Chen Qimei of Zhejiang. Chen was assassinated by agents of Yuan Shikai in early 1916, but the connection survived, with Chen replaced as patron of the group by a veteran member of the Tong Meng Hui, Zhang Renjie, who had since become a successful entrepreneur in Shanghai. The Chief bond of this group was their having participated, under Chen Qimei's leadership, in a brave attempt in October 1915 to seize a Yangzi gunboat. Zhang Renjie, the group's new leader, had been in the confidence of Sun Yatsen, whose revolutionary activities he had supported financially from an early stage, and he was anxious that his young men should play a part in events.

Some of them were already involved in revolutionary affairs elsewhere. Huang Fu, the orphaned son of a family of gentry ruined by the Taiping Rebellion, had made a name for himself as a diplomat at the Washington Conference and had then served as Minister of Education in two Beijing governments. He remained thereafter in the north, working for the Guomindang. He had close relations with Feng Yuxiang; it had been a cable from Huang Fu which gave Feng the signal to rebel against Wu Peifu, and when Feng seized Beijing he made Huang Acting President. Huang Fu and Chiang Kaishek were sworn brothers, and there was a third member of the brotherhood, Zhang Xun. Although from Sichuan, Zhang had been closely associated with Chen Qimei and his Zhejiang followers. Zhang Xun too was now in the north in the service of Feng Yuxiang. Two brothers from Zhejiang, Chen Guofu and Chen Lifu, Nephews of Chen Qimei, had also been involved in the attack on the gunboat. They were to play key roles in Chiang Kaishek's future government of China. Their family, like that of Huang Fu, had been impoverished by the Taiping Rebellion, but had rebuilt its fortunes through trade.

From 1920 to 1922 Zhang Renjie, the Chen brothers, and Chiang Kaishek were brought into an even closer association in a Stock and Commodity

Exchange business which they created in Shanghai in order to raise funds for the revolution. With them in this venture was Dai Jitao, who was also to become one of Chiang's entourage; he already had a reputation as an eloquent right-wing interpreter of Sun Yatsen's thought, having worked closely with Sun during his two years of exile in Shanghai, when Sun was writing his *Fundamentals of National Reconstruction.*

These and several other close associates of Chiang Kaishek formed a group based on the overlapping associations of Zhejiang birth, participation in the gunboat raid, and management of the Commodity Exchange. At its head was Zhang Renjie, already regarded as one of the elder statesmen of the Guomindang.

It was Zhang Renjie who recommended Chiang Kaishek for service with Sun at Canton; but Chiang's first experience there seems to have been unhappy. Although he earned the favour of Sun Yatsen he found himself isolated among the Cantonese who then dominated the movement. He was again in Canton in 1922, however, when Sun was driven by his Guangdong war-lord ally and rival Chen Jiongming to take refuge on board a gunboat. Chiang spent some days with him on board the vessel. Soon after, Sun made him chief of staff of his small bodyguard, and when the Whampoa Academy was set up he appointed him its commandant, after three months study of military organization in Moscow.

Chiang asked Chen Guofu to act as recruiting agent in the lower Yangzi provinces. Chen set to with such a will that he produced 4,000 cadets in two years, the bulk of the Whampoa classes, mainly from Zhejiang. Thus the new highly trained, highly indoctrinated Soviet-armed units, the crack troops of the revolutionary movement, came virtually to represent the Zhejiang connection. Soon two other Zhejiang natives joined Chiang at Whampoa, one (He Yingqin) as chief instructor in tactics, and the other (Shao Yuanchong) as acting director of political instruction. Even so, with few exceptions the political instructors chosen for Whampoa were not members of the Zhejiang connection. The senior appointments were largely honorary; the real work of political indoctrination was largely in the hands of the Communists, led by Zhou Enlai. At this stage Chiang showed no signs of opposition to them, and worked closely with them and with the Comintern advisers. It was in the interests of the Nationalists at that time that Whampoa should continue to be provided not only with Soviet money, arms, and military training but also with political training in so far as this could assist them to operate the system which was now being created on the Soviet model. The political power which such a system could concentrate was, for Chiang Kaishek at any rate, a very positive aspect of communism.

With access to the wider and more popular organizations of the Guomindang, which was now growing rapidly in strength with the financial backing of the Soviet Union, the Communist Party although still very small (with a membership in hundreds rather than thousands) was able to exert an influence out of all proportion to its numbers. Its main source of weakness was that Soviet funds went almost entirely to the Nationalists; what was given directly to Communist Party organizations was negligible. Such nevertheless was the vigour and single-minded devotion of the young Communists that they were able to penetrate the Guomindang most effectively. The top positions remained in Nationalist hands, but these carried more prestige than power. The offices which made day-to-day decisions, implemented policy, and supervised personnel were almost all in Communist hands. The principal check on communist activities came actually from the Comintern advisers, who in the interests of the alliance with the Nationalists discouraged any dangerously radical interpretation of policy.

The Communists set out to create mass organizations responsive to their own leadership, especially trade unions. This was their main objective and on this, tragically for them as it proved, they pinned their hopes.

The labour movement

China's industrial milieu did not encourage trade unionism. Workers in traditional handicrafts and commerce (who even in the cities outnumbered workers in the modern industrial sector six to one) were organized in guilds which included both employees and employers. Workers in modern industry had no such organization; instead they were protected, and victimized, by the secret societies. The conditions in which capitalism was established in China were not such as to encourage strong union consciousness. Workers did not yet constitute a group dependent upon and committed to industrial employment. They came from the countryside and maintained their links with it. Some returned there in the busy season of agriculture. Many were from families the rest of whose members continued to farm, so that the industrial earnings of the worker represented a cash supplement to family income rather than subsistence. When industrial workers were able to save out of their appalling wages—as surprisingly they often were—they bought land if they could.

Given this persisting relationship between farming and industrial work, the density of population, and destitution growing as a result of the political and economic disruption of the time, wages were as low as one would expect. Hours were from 12 to 18 a day, relieved by only one rest day every two weeks. Public holidays, although in China mercifully numerous, were not sufficient to compensate. Women and children worked hours unlimited by law, the children sometimes from the age of 6. As the labour force consisted largely of single migrants, there was no incentive to provide housing, except for primitive dormitory accommodation. Its recruitment depended on middle-men. The racketeering and vice-oriented secret societies of China's cities, such as Shanghai's notorious Green Gang, added recruitment of labour to their control of prostitution and the distribution of opium. Those who sought to create modern trade unions, including the Communists, had to fight against this vicious and powerful interest.

In 1920 the first Communist-led union, the Shanghai Mechanics Union, was set up; labour journals were published and workers' night schools opened; and a Committee of the Workers' Movement was brought together in Shanghai. In the following year a national trade union secretariat was set up, for which the Soviet Union provided US $1,000 a month—a pittance compared with the sums soon to be lavished on the Guomindang. The first national trade union congress was held in May 1922; there were 162 delegates, claiming to represent 270,000 members. At the second congress in 1925 the number of members claimed had doubled, and doubled again by the third congress of 1926. By the time of the second congress the Communist Party had entered the first United Front and could work through the Labour Bureau of the Guomindang. Although this was headed by Liao Zhongkai, the most left-wing of the Nationalist leaders, Liao's Communist deputy ran the labour movement as a whole.

Almost half of the modern industrial work-force was employed in firms registered as foreign-owned. But this was less of an inhibition on the growth of unions than was the traditional hostility of Chinese authorities towards unofficial social organizations deemed to offer a threat to the existing order. Whereas provincial governments usually crushed union activity savagely, the foreign employers, although by no means sympathetic to trade unions, had neither the will nor the authority to emulate such vigour, and indeed were obliged in the face of growing hostility to provide better wages and conditions than their Chinese competitors. On the two tragic occasions in 1925 when Chinese workers were fired on by foreign troops or foreign-commanded police, the foreigners were not attempting to suppress trade unions: they were defending the Concessions.

The rulers of China, national and local, had every reason to fear the workers' movement under Communist leadership, for the aim of that leadership was to use the movement as an instrument of revolution. It was hoped that railwaymen, seamen, postal and telegraph workers, and power station workers could be brought into a single organization which could, by their striking together, paralyse the country. Yet in the context of a nationalist revolution directed first against war-lord power and then against foreign power, the use of workers' unions as a political instrument was opposed neither by the Nationalist Party nor by the modern commercial and industrial classes. Indeed, the prominence of foreign ownership actually assisted unionism. The foreign firms were a target which China's native capitalists were delighted to see attacked. Chinese employers were therefore ready to encourage mobilization of the workers, and were even ready themselves to participate in so-called 'strikes' directed against foreign power.

The peaks of Communist influence in the workers' movement all occurred in the course of nationalist protests in which other classes participated and with which employers sympathized. On 3 May 1919, on the eve of the May Fourth Movement, the workers of Qingdao (Tsingtao) in Shandong struck, demanding the return of Qingdao to China. Two weeks later Beijing workers struck, demanding the return of all national territory in foreign hands. The Hong Kong seamen's strike of 1922 was directed at foreign power. The May the 30th Incident of 1925 in which Concession police under a British officer killed twelve demonstrators produced strike action in Shanghai and throughout the country on an unprecedented scale, and doubled the number of workers associated with Communist-led unions in a matter of weeks.

In strikes against large employers, as opposed to demonstrations against foreign imperialism, China's new unions seldom succeeded. A strike at the Kailan (Kaiping) mines in 1922 failed after three days. Strikes at the Hanyang ironworks and the Anyuan mines in Jiangxi also failed. The most tragic failure was the Beijing-Hankou rail strike of 1924. The railway was controlled by Wu Peifu. He was sympathetic to the creation of workers' organizations as a part of general patriotic mobilization, but when the railwaymen formed a national union he became alarmed, having come to realize that such a powerful union could close down the line and immobilize his troops. He forbade its formation. The railway workers struck, and the Beijing-Hankou line was closed. Wu responded with a massacre of union members, a tragic event which sharply checked the growth of the union movement generally.

The Communists and the peasants

The Communist Party was slower to attempt organization of the peasants than that of the workers, who presented a less difficult problem. The workers were concentrated in the major cities where a few agitators could hope to mobilize them; there was a relatively simple conflict of interest between employers and employees, at least in the modern industrial sector; and communist theory demanded that organization of the urban working class be given highest priority. None of this held in the countryside. Hopes of mobilizing the peasants of half a million villages could scarcely be entertained by a party which even in 1925 had only about four hundred full-time cadres. Rural society was so complex and China's new youthful radicals so ignorant of its conditions that there was little hope of formulating a general policy; and, as Secretary-General of the Party Chen Duxiu himself pointed out, more than half of China's peasants were proprietors and likely to resist, or at least stand aside from, any attempt at rural revolution. The Communist International proposed the mobilization of the Chinese peasantry but this was largely theoretical, for radical rural policies would have prejudiced the Russian alliance with the Canton regime, although complete failure by the Nationalists even to attempt to mobilize the peasants left a vacuum into which the Communist Party might have moved but did not.

In these circumstances the peasant movement was created by individual enthusiasts, not by the parties; and its inspiration came less from communism than from Waseda University in Japan and its New Village programme. This programme had inspired Li Dazhao, and it was to inspire Peng Pai, the founder of the first Guangdong peasant associations, having influenced Liao Zhongkai, whose important position in the Canton regime enabled him to encourage and protect the movement until his assassination in 1925.

Peng Pai, born in eastern Guangdong to a rich landlord family, was a protégé of Sun Yatsen's dubious ally Chen Jiongming, who put him in charge of a new education programme in Haifeng county. There Peng met Chen Duxiu, whom Chen Jiongming had appointed his minister of education while he controlled Canton. Peng Pai's views were already radical, and under Chen Duxiu's influence he apparently joined the Communist Party. He thereupon began, single-handed, to create China's first peasant movement. He began by approaching individual peasants, and quickly learned that he must change both his dress and his speech before they would listen to him. In the early summer of 1923 he sat daily in a crossroads rest-house where peasants stopped *en route* to and from market, and talked. After some weeks he had made three converts from the village of Red Hills. They introduced him to the village; he played his gramophone, performed conjuring tricks, put on puppet shows, and talked about justice for the peasants. When the number of his converts rose to thirty he formed in Red Hills village China's first association of peasants. Recruitment spread to nearby villages. Soon the association was strong enough to boycott local landlords who were evicting their tenants and offering the land to others at increased rents. The association ran its own arbitration courts; and – taking advantage of local custom which recognized as the owner of newly forested land whoever planted it—began to acquire common property. No radical demands were made, not even for a general reduction of rent, but such issues could not long be avoided. Inflation induced landlords to try to push up rents, as farm incomes were on average rising. Then a destructive typhoon led to a demand for a reduction in the rents of the affected farmers. Landlords were traditionally willing to offer such concessions to their own tenants, but they were less ready to make them under pressure from a peasant organization. The association was forced into actions which alarmed all the gentry: landlords feared for their rents and magistrates feared a breakdown of public order. The landlords formed their own association and got the ear of the district magistrate, whose troops, none too tenderly, closed down the peasants' headquarters. In this escalation of the conflict both sides appealed to Chen Jiongming. His view was that the peasants had as much right to form associations as workers or students, but he had not sympathy with conflicts which led to disorder. He forced the peasant association virtually to cease its activities. They were revived later, with bloody consequences, but mean while the focus of peasant activity shifted elsewhere.

After the first United Front was formed in 1924, the mobilization of the peasants became approved policy. Peng Pai was made head of a nationalist bureau of peasant affairs. However, the next initiative was, nevertheless, again a personal one. Three students from the up-river country of Guangming, who were in contact with workers from that country employed in the food-processing industry in Canton, decided to return home and organize the peasants. The Guangming workers in Canton collected money from among themselves for the initial expenses. Their efforts were rewarded by rapid local recruitment into peasant associations. Peng Pai came up-river to assist. As a result of a century of disorder, Guangming country was thoroughly militar-ized, whereas the forces of the revolution had not yet reached so far. Even so, the organizers of the peasant associations could now assume that they had the sanction of Canton for a radical policy. Peng Pai put forward demands for rent reduction which he had discouraged at Haifeng. Brutal suppression began immediately.

For the Canton government, the situation was a test of both its sincerity and its strength. Of its sincerity it left little doubt: the district magistrate hostile to the peasant associations was replaced. As for its strength, Liao Zhongkai sent a crack division to deal with the situation; when that failed Hu Hanmin, although as closely associated with the Guomindang right as Liao was with its left, despatched his own personal guard regiment to put down the landlord armies; Peng Pai was put in command of the Guomindang units; and the anti-peasant forces, besieged in two clan fortresses, were defeated. They were ordered to disband and pay compensation for the damage and loss of life they had caused. The peasants' triumph, however, proved short-lived. The precarious Canton regime could not maintain its forces in Guangming; they were withdrawn to march against Chen Jiongming and then to put down a revolt by the Guangxi troops. Canton was even forced to invite the dismissed district magistrate of Guangming to incorporate his private army in the revo-lutionary forces. Meanwhile the peasants' militia had been destroyed when they loyally opposed the Guangxi mutineers. They were not to have a second opportunity. Close on the heels of these events came the assassination of Liao Zhongkai, and then action by Chiang Kaishek in which left-wing influence was sharply reduced at Canton. The peasant affairs bureau was abolished. Landlord action in Guangming was no longer opposed.

A third effort to organize the peasants had meanwhile been made in Huaxian district, a market-garden suburb of Canton. The movement here was begun by agitators trained in the new Peasant Movement Institute, founded to train United Front agitators for work in rural China, and under the very eyes of the United Front regime. Here, if anywhere, the movement should have been successful. It was not. It ran into much the same difficulties as those in

Guangming. There was conflict and disorder; this, so close to Canton, brought Chiang Kaishek himself into the affair, his chief interest being the restoration of public order, while as the strength of the Whampoa forces increased, Nationalist interest in arming the peasants as a counter-weight to hostile local militias was fading. Chiang in any case was now preoccupied with the 1926 northern expedition. Soon he was a thousand miles away in Jiangsu, and soon after that he was embroiled with the Communist-led armed workers' pickets in Shanghai. His suppression of these was taken throughout southern China as a signal that suppression of all Communist-led organizations was in order. The Huaxian movement was destroyed.

Chiang Kaishek and the Communists, 1925–1927

The first occasion on which Chiang asserted his political influence was against the right wing of the Guomindang, not the left. Right-wing veterans who had attempted to impeach the Communists and then fled to Shanghai after the murder of Liao Zhongkai were soon joined by others of similar opinions. They protested again at Communist infiltration of the Nationalist Party. Several of their number met solemnly at Sun's tomb in the Western Hills, and from this earned the name of the Western Hills Group.

They were an impressive set of men, all Tong Meng Hui veterans. They and others associated with them renewed the oath of loyalty to Sun Yatsen, which had been exacted by Sun at a time when his party was an illegal organization, demanded the expulsion of the Communists and the removal of Mikhail Borodin, the Comintern's chief representative in China, and called for constitutional changes to prevent any renewal of left-wing dominance. They were denounced by the Guomindang leadership. They then set up a separate Party headquarters in Shanghai while seeking support from military commanders, including Feng Yuxiang, but failed to win it. Without it, they were helpless.

In Canton, Chiang Kaishek supported Wang Jingwei and the left wing in condemning the Western Hills Group. As a result he was elected for the first time to the Central Executive Committee of the Guomindang at its second national congress. Yet soon after this he chose to lead a sharp attack of his own on increasing Communist power. Claiming that there was a left-wing conspiracy to seize power, in which the gunboat *Zhongshan* was to be employed, he seized its captain, several Comintern advisers and many members of the Chinese Communist Party. Whether or not there was such a conspiracy is not known. Chiang had in fact just personally supported the appointment of a man (Deng Yanda) well known for his pro-Communist sympathies, to an influential post at Whampoa, an appointment suggesting that the *Zhongshan* incident was not the result of a premeditated move against the left.

There might well have been an end to the alliance at this point, but to end it suited neither the Comintern nor Chiang Kaishek. A compromise was reached. The left-wing prisoners were released. The two rival political societies at the Whampoa Military Academy, one devoted to communism and the other to the ideas of Sun Yatsen, were simultaneously abolished. The Communists relinquished all their senior posts in the Guomindang, although they remained in the Party and still retained considerable influence. The number of Comintern advisers was cut.

Chiang's victory was not only over the Communists but also over their left-wing Guomindang allies. Wang Jingwei, Chiang's only rival for power since the murder of Liao Zhongkai and the departure into exile of Hu Hanmin, was much weakened by rumours that he had been associated in the putative *Zhongshan* plot. Chiang was able as a result to have his old patron Zhang Renjie elected Chairman of the Guomindang, while Chen Guofu became head of the all-important organization department, which position he was to enjoy for most of the history of the Nationalist regime. The 1st Army was deprived of most of its Communist political commissars. The Zhejiang connection was now dominant in both civil and military circles.

In the course of the negotiations Chiang Kaishek forced the chief Comintern adviser, Borodin, to agree reluctantly to the launching of a new northern expedition. Borodin and the Communists feared, correctly as it proved, that war would strengthen the military wing of the Guomindang to their disadvantage. They had little influence among the Whampoa cadets, and seem to have done little to create it.

While the South was now united, the North was more deeply divided than ever. Duan Qirui, finding himself powerless in spite of his title of Chief Executive, had resigned on 20 April 1926 and retired from politics. Zhang Zuolin had been driven from the Yangzi area. Wu Peifu, having restored his military power in the confusion of Guo Songling's revolt against Zhang Zuolin, held the Hubei-Hunan river crossing. Feng Yuxiang had returned from Moscow and threatened Zhili. The Northern forces should have dealt easily with Chiang Kaishek's attack. Together they outnumbered the whole Nationalist force by six to one, but they failed to unite. Sun Chuanfang in Jiangsu, who had gained the dominant position in the Zhili group, had no desire to see Wu Peifu reassert his influence, and presumably he did not rate the threat from the Nationalists at more than the inferior numbers of their forces would suggest. It would also have been natural, in terms of war-lord manœuvres, for Zhang Zuolin, having recently narrowly escaped destruction at the hands of the rebel Guo Songling (supported by Feng Yuxiang, who had made known his sympathies with the Guomindang), to have joined in against the South, while Yan Xishan, faced with Feng's formidable army on his Shanxi borders, might well also have joined the other Northern war-lords. The explanation may simply lie in underestimation of the small Nationalist armies.

Yet there is more to the situation than this. The Beiyang command and its rival successors had, in their ambivalent way, sought to unite the country. It was the prospect of reunification that had provided them with a rationale for their manœuvres and legitimacy for the successive governments set up in Beijing. The result, however, was greater disunity than ever, and the total corruption of national government, whereas the competing May Fourth view of politics which the Guomindang–Communist alliance had grasped as its own was gaining favour with national public opinion. The war-lords were uncomfortably on the defensive.

Chiang's armies drove into Hunan in July 1926. Wu Peifu put up only weak resistance. The Guomindang was then able to swing most of its force east. In six months its armies had occupied Shanghai and Nanjing.

In the wake of the revolutionary armies a Guomindang group, elected in a joint session of the Central Executive Committee and the National Government Council, travelled to Wuhan to establish the National Government there, formally from 1 January 1927. The group went first to the field headquarters of Chiang Kaishek at Nanchang. He gave them a tremendous welcome before they went up-river to Wuhan.

There was no outward sign at this time of the rift which was to open rapidly between Nanchang and Wuhan. The group which went to Wuhan included Sun Yatsen's widow Song Qingling, his son Sun Fo, Eugene Chen, Xu Qian, and Song Ziwen (T. V. Soong). The chief Russian adviser, Borodin, was with them. Hu Hanmin was still abroad, as was Wang Jingwei, offended at Chiang's suspicion that he had been involved in the *Zhongshan* incident. There was little in the political record of the members of the Wuhan group to suggest any great radicalism although they were usually referred to as the left wing of the Guomindang. Sun Fo was actually regarded by the Communist Party as somewhat hostile. Song Qingling had played no political role during her husband's lifetime and little since; she was a figurehead. Eugene Chen was a fiery, not to say imprudent, enemy of imperialism but he had not been conspicuous as a social radical. Song Ziwen had been Sun Yatsen's chief financial expert, and was soon to serve Chiang Kaishek's Nanjing government in the same capacity; if he ever then or later entertained radical views he did not make them known. As it proved, however, the opinions of the Wuhan group were to be of little importance when the crisis of Chiang Kaishek's repudiation of the Communists occurred. It was, as before, the soldiers who mattered.

The distribution of the revolutionary armies already threatened a polarization between those who would support the Communists and those who would not. The troops most closely associated with Chiang Kaishek and the Whampoa Academy had taken the eastern route. The armies in which the left-wing commissars remained influential had taken the old Taiping route to Changsha and Wuhan. The commander of the armies in this western sector was Tang Shengzhi of Hunan, whose late adherence to the revolutionary cause after much negotiation had made the northern expedition possible. He was not a Guomindang veteran. He was disposed to favour the left, but no one doubted that his motive was simply the hope of military aid from the Soviet Union.

The eastern armies themselves were not above suspicion. In the very heart of Chiang's camp the commander of the Nanchang garrison was an old fellow student of Zhu De, future commander-in-chief of the Red Army. He appointed Zhu De as his head of public security and encouraged him to open a training unit for officers who were sent to agitate among the peasants of Jiangxi. The threat was increased when another force whose political commissar, Lin Boju, was Communist moved down-river to take Nanjing on 24 March. Chiang was thus faced with armies whose political officers were Communist extending from Changsha right down the river to Nanjing.

He was also faced with a formidable mobilization of China's urban workers. The northern expedition saw the maximum growth, the complete politicization, and finally the total collapse of the Communist-led union movement. The unions were encouraged to play their part in the campaign by delivering supplies to the revolutionary armies, disrupting the northern railway system, and closing down the Wuhan Arsenal to deprive Wu Peifu of munitions. Their contribution in this respect has been grossly exaggerated by Communist Party historians; but in the wake of the Nationalist armies left-wing agitators organized unions and mounted armed pickets, and launched virtual general strikes. In some cities the pickets attempted to impose workers' control of the factories. Business was shaken, banks failed. The employers responded by calling in Nationalist army commanders to disarm the pickets. Armed pickets were suppressed in Hangzhou, Chongqing, and Fuzhou before the right wing of the Guomindang called the conference which decided on Chiang's Shanghai purge of April 1927. The pickets remained powerful in Wuhan, tolerated by the Wuhan government; there Deng Yanda, non-Communist but a passionate believer in insurrection, executed eight non-Communist trade union leaders.

If armed attacks on business interests constituted a threat to the consolidation of Nationalist power, attacks on foreign interests were a far more dangerous threat. The British Concession at Jiujiang was attacked by a mob led by armed pickets; the British relinquished the Concession peacefully. A similar attack was made on the foreign settlements at Nanjing, although soldiers were more prominent in this incident than union members. Several foreigners were murdered, and the city was then bombarded by foreign warships. In Changsha thirty to forty Chinese businessmen associated with the foreign trade were executed. The foreign powers thus had good reason to be alarmed at the danger to their position in China; and the danger seemed greatest where their position mattered most, in Shanghai. There, as the armies of the revolution fought their way northwards towards the city, a wave of strikes broke out, and as the armies drew nearer the strikes developed into insurrection. When Bai Chongxi's Guangxi troops entered the suburbs the war-lord garrison was not disposed to resist. Liu Shaoqi and others set up a revolutionary government in the city on 29 March.

Two days earlier, a threat to attack the French Concession had been averted by the action of Nationalist troops. The insurrectionary municipal government sought to prevent a confrontation with the powers, but it was nevertheless committed to the unilateral abolition of the Foreign Concessions, and the threat remained. Chiang Kaishek on his arrival in Shanghai assured the foreigners that they were safe, while at the same time insisting that the Communists had a right to participate in the national revolution. He also insisted that the Nationalist army alone should have the responsibility of defending the Concessions. In Shanghai as elsewhere, even before Chiang's arrival there, Nationalist units often commanded by Whampoa cadets were challenging the armed workers' inspection teams and attempting to disarm them. On 7 April, in an act of defiance, the Shanghai workers' inspection team paraded, armed. This precipitated a dénouement. The Green Gang secret society rivals of the new unions were given arms. The Communist leader of the Shanghai Labour Union was invited to dinner with the Green Gang leader, Du Yuesheng, and murdered. On 12 April the Gang's forces moved out of the shelter of the Concessions, the authorities of which co-operated. The Labour Union, bewildered by uncertain orders (the final source of which was Stalin), put up only a sporadic defence. The armed labour movement was crushed with the loss of several hundred lives.

The April coup was a symptom rather than a cause of the collapse of revolutionary unionism. Hitherto the Guomindang leaders and the Chinese middle class had made common cause with the organized workers against war-lord and foreign power. Now, in south and central China at least, the battle against the war-lords had been won, while the struggle against foreign power had to be suspended until the Nationalist regime was consolidated. The armed workers had seized Shanghai from the war-lords, but they could not be permitted to attempt to seize the Concessions from the powers. The nationalist fervour of the workers had become an embarrassment, and it was clear from events in some cities that their fervour was now liable to be directed at targets nearer home.

Even so, in the following years the new Chinese capitalist class was not unwilling to accept peaceful union organization. After the Nationalist government had been established at Nanjing in 1928, a code of industrial relations was promulgated and implemented through local bureaux. The code was not illiberal and the bureaux were not ineffective. China's workers, organized in new unions, secured for a time some significant gains in wages and working conditions; they were aided by buoyant trade conditions and thriving exports, although by the mid-thirties this liberalism on the part of Chiang's regime was reversed as the Nationalist Party moved to the right. Commununist influence in these developments was negligible.

It is clear that Communist-led unionism from 1920 to 1927 flourished on nationalist, not industrial or class, issues, and faded out when these issues were no longer a matter for insurrectionary action. The attempts of the Party to rouse insurrection on class grounds in the course of Red Army attacks on cities after 1927 were a humiliating failure. The party of the working class had little or no contact with the working class until, twenty years later, it captured the cities from without.

The peasant movement, like the workers' movement, revived in the wake of the victory of the revolutionary armies. In Hunan a great explosion of peasant protest took place in late 1926, with perhaps a million and a half peasants involved. In many areas they took over local government and superseded the authority of the landlords. The peasant movement in Hunan was the nearest approach to social revolution that the radicalization of Chinese politics in the 1920s had so far produced.

The question whether or not to support such popular insurrection was the issue on which political polarization took place. In the event the commanders around Wuhan and Changsha in spite of their apparent support of the left proved to be as alarmed as Chiang Kaishek himself at the 'anarchy' in Hunan and elsewhere. When Tang Shengzhi's subordinates disarmed the Hunan peasants and Tang ordered that their arms should be restored to them, his commanders protested and he was forced to rescind the order.

Had the left-wing Wuhan government positively supported the armed mass movements Tang Shengzhi might have protected it. But Wuhan itself was wavering. Song Ziwen had already deserted to become Chiang's Minister of Finance. Xu Qian had gone on a mission to Feng Yuxiang and failed to return.

Wang Jingwei had hurried back from abroad, summoned both by his Wuhan colleagues and by Chiang Kaishek at Nanjing. Wang was soon faced by the fact that Feng Yuxiang had announced his adherence to Nanjing, and that the Guangxi generals, though no lovers of Chiang Kaishek, loved Tang Shengzhi even less, and were happy to find an excuse to oust him from Hunan and Hubei. Wang Jingwei himself, whose radicalism was very moderate, was alarmed by the indifference of many of the Communist leaders to the instructions of the Wuhan government. When the Indian Communist M. N. Roy rashly showed him a telegram from Stalin instructing the Communists to recruit their own army and to take over the Guomindang apparatus, Wang broke with them.

Immediately afterwards the Nationalist garrison commander at Nanchang proclaimed martial law, disarmed the trade unions and the peasant associations, and expelled the Communist Party activists.

In Nanjing several of the most trusted and respected veterans of the revolution took the initiative on 15 September 1927 in calling together, as a means of reconciliation, a Special Central Committee. It represented Chiang's faction, along with the Western Hills Group and the remnants of the Wuhan government, now depleted by the departure of Song Qingling and Eugene Chen for Moscow.

The Special Central Committee did not succeed in bringing all sides together. Wang Jingwei left when it became clear that its members were unwilling to regard him as the head of state. Tang Shengzhi in Hunan resisted it, and his subordinate in the south (Zhang Fakui) launched an attempted coup in opposition to it. Both were defeated; Tang was driven out by Guangxi troops, with the result that the Guangxi commanders added Hunan and Hubei to their territories.

The Western Hills Group were then eliminated from the Committee by an event in Nanjing. Right-wing-inspired public celebrations of the victory over Tang Shengzhi led to a riot in which two left-wing students were killed. The Western Hills representatives were held responsible and forced to resign. This left Chiang and his centre group in control; but he was suddenly discredited when northern forces caught Nanjing unprepared and counter-attacked across the Yangzi. Chiang resigned his posts briefly. Authority in Nanjing was put in the hands of a triumvirate of which two were Guangxi generals, and the third Chiang's chief commander He Yingqin.

While out of office Chiang on 31 December 1927 married Song Meiling, sister of Song Ziwen and of Sun Yatsen's widow, Song Qingling. A third sister, Song Ailing, was the wife of Kong Xiangxi (H. H. Kong). The Songs and the Kongs were soon to become very powerful. Both families were Christian and Westernized, and they were high in the world of Shanghai business. The father of the Songs had been taken as a child to the United States by an uncle, and baptized and educated there. He returned to China as a missionary. He was entirely Westernized; the missionary Young J. Allen criticized him as a 'denationalized Chinaman'. Faced with this prejudice he left evangelism and became one of China's most successful entrepreneurs, though remaining an active Methodist. He was an unswerving supporter of his son-in-law, Sun Yatsen. The Song children had also been educated in the West, and while they were by no means 'denationalized' like their father they were part of a cosmopolitan Treaty Port world of Western culture and Western-style business, very far indeed from the Chinese world inhabited by most of their Guomindang colleagues. Their experience was in contrast even to that of Chiang Kaishek himself: Chiang had been outside China only to study at the Japanese staff college and to visit Moscow briefly. Song Ziwen, trained at St John's College, Shanghai, and then at Harvard, had returned to China to become secretary-general of the Hanyeping coal and steel complex in 1917. Sun Yatsen, already married to Ziwen's sister, soon invited him to Canton where he became Sun's Minister of Finance and was responsible for the reform of southern finances that had made possible the successful war against the North.

Kong Xiangxi was also from a Christian business family, Shaanxi bankers who became agents for the British Asiatic Petroleum Company. Kong had attended a mission school and was converted to Christianity. He also joined a revolutionary secret society. During the Boxer Rising the family had worked to save Christians from the pro-Boxer governor Yu Xian, who had executed 137 missionaries and their children. Li Hongzhang appreciated the goodwill which their actions had created among the foreigners, and arranged for Kong to be sent to America. Kong attended Oberlin College, with which he maintained a lifelong association, and then Yale. Oberlin, in Ohio, was a university with a tradition of Christian radicalism (once famous for its stand against the extension of slavery). Kong after his return established the Oberlin-in-China programme of education in Shaanxi, and in 1914 he married Song Ailing. He was not at that time associated with Sun Yatsen; it was only after he had read and been impressed by Sun's *Fundamentals of National Reconstruction* that he joined the Guomindang and offered Sun his services. He became a member of Chiang Kaishek's Nanjing government in 1927, and became Minister of Industry and Commerce while Song Ziwen was made Minister of Finance. By then Chiang Kaishek had married Song Meiling and had accepted Christianity.

In this way was formed the notorious family connection which the left argued—and perhaps believed—was the real power in China. It was probably the world's most powerful group of Methodists, but to suggest that it ruled China is based on a misunderstanding. Song Ziwen and Kong Xiangxi were successively Minister of Finance of the National Republic. That they enjoyed the confidence both of Chiang Kaishek and of the Chinese business community is of the utmost importance, especially as the Government remained dependent, though decreasingly so, on its ability to borrow. But Chiang's power lay elsewhere: it lay in his military headquarters at Nanchang, in the organization departments of the Party, in the organs of propaganda and education, and in the control of the four lower-Yangzi provinces, through his appointment of their governors, as well as of the mayors of Shanghai and Nanjing.

Of the seventeen key positions involved in this network of control, thirteen were held by natives of Zhejiang or (in two cases) by men who although born elsewhere had been associated in their youth with Chen Qimei's Zhejiang-based revolutionary group in Shanghai. Of the four others, two were filled from Jiangsu and two from Hunan. Only one appointee, Yang Yongtai, was Cantonese but he had never been closely associated with the southerners who had dominated the Guomindang during Sun Yatsen's lifetime. None was from the ranks of Chiang's Guangxi allies. None was from the north. The 'unification' of China had resulted in its domination by a group geographically narrower than any of the pre-existing war-lord connections.

Neither can it be argued that the Zhejiang group were merely instruments of control employed by the Song–Kong connection. There was intense rivalry between them and the Nanchang headquarters, and more often than not Nanchang prevailed, especially in the perpetual struggle over public expenditure between the economizers Song and Kong and the military in Nanchang.

Behind the Zhejiang connection and the Song–Kong Westernized banking connection, linked by Chiang Kaishek himself, was the group known as the 'four elder statesmen'. Why they and they alone earned this title is not obvious: there were many Guomindang leaders who were older and who had more experience as statesmen. The name reflects their relationship not so much with the Guomindang in general as with Chiang's own regime.

Two are already familiar: Zhang Renjie, successor to Chen Qimei as patron of the Zhejiang group, and Cai Yuanpei, Chancellor of Beijing University at the time of the May Fourth Movement, both born in Zhejiang. The other two, Wu Zhihui and Li Shizeng, came together in their youth in Paris where—in their more radical days—they had been associated in founding the anarchist journal *New Century*.

There was also an ill-defined but influential group known as the Political Study clique. Opinions as to who were members of this shadowy connection were often speculative. The group, however, had a definite beginning. After the defeat of the Nationalist resistance to Yuan Shikai in 1913 a 'Society for the Study of European Affairs' had been formed by Chinese exiles in Japan. It was led by the Cantonese Yang Yongtai, who was a sworn brother of Zhang Xun of the Zhejiang connection. Yang and Zhang had brought together an association called the Political Study Society in Duan Qirui's 1916 parliament. When Duan dissolved Parliament they went south, where they formed the main right-wing opposition to Sun Yatsen. Zhang Xun introduced Yang Yongtai to Chiang Kaishek. By 1929 Yang was chief secretary at Nanchang. Shortly after this, another member of the same group, Xiong Shihui, became Nanchang chief of staff.

These appointments linked Chiang's regime, via the Political Study clique connection, with some of the most able men in Chinese intellectual and economic life. Among the entrepreneurs associated with the clique was a Zhejiang industrialist, Qian Yongming, who had taken over a moribund group of coal-mines in Shandong and transformed them into a major modern enterprise. Zhang Jidao, another member, had made his reputation while manager of the Shanghai branch of the Bank of Commerce by defying Yuan Shikai's order to the banks to suspend the issue of notes. He became manager of the Bank of China in 1929 and persuaded the Chinese banks to pool resources for a crash programme of strategic railways for defence against Japan. Another banker member, Chen Guangfa, had pioneered the mobilization of small savings, and another, Wu Dingchang, had pioneered bank support for rural credit co-operatives. Yet another member was Wang Chonghui, who had returned from Yale to become legal adviser to Chen Qimei; he had been Premier of the cabinet set up by Wu Peifu on 19 September 1922.

The clique was a loose association, strengthened by personal and geographical ties, of conservative modernizers; it overlapped with the Zhejiang connection, with Cai Yuanpei's academic followers, and with certain ex-Progressive militarists of the south-west. Its role was to guide Chiang's modernization efforts; consequently almost any figure who could be identified with his cautious reform policies came to be regarded as a member. It provided Chiang's regime with the loyalty and the advice of some of the most enterprising and successful men in China, and if his reforms mostly failed it was not for lack of will or ability on their part.

As a result of these failures, Chiang's entourage is generally viewed as relatively conservative. Yet it has to be remembered that he eliminated from positions of influence not only the Communists and their allies of the left-wing Guomindang but also the right-wing Western Hills Group.

11

The Nationalist regime

1928–1937

The legacy of Sun Yatsen

In 1927 the history of China splits again into two interlinked but separate narratives: the history of the Nationalist government, and the history of the state within a state founded in that year by the Communist Party of China. The split had another less obvious but profound significance. It had been unquestioned by both right and left that successful change in China must take place village by village—'not one revolution, but half a million revolutions' was the theme. Much of the Maoist political rhetoric which in the West is often assumed to have originated from Mao himself and to have expressed his political genius—rhetoric typified by exhortations to go back to the country-side and 'share weal and woe' with the peasants—was the current coin of political debate at that time, and in this respect the writings of right-wingers such as Hu Hanmin were scarcely distinguishable from those of the left. Yet little had been done by 1927, by either right or left, towards the political mobilization of the masses. The workers' movement and the peasant move-ment collapsed at a touch in 1927. Yet this was actually the beginning of change. The Communists, driven out of the cities, could survive only by the mobilization of rural support. Chiang Kaishek, on the other hand, alarmed at left-wing infiltration of such local branches of his top-heavy party as then existed, destroyed them in the purges which followed his April coup in Shanghai.

The future of grass-roots revolution lay with the Communists. In 1927–8, after desperate efforts to re-establish their power in the cities, they retreated to create soviets scattered throughout rural China. The most notable (or perhaps only the most noted) was that associated with Mao Zedong in Jiangxi. That regime lasted through four successive nationalist attempts to destroy it, then in 1933 it was crushed at the fifth attempt but only to be re-established in the north-west. Meanwhile the Nationalists faced a far greater threat from Japan, as well as almost continuous armed opposition from dissident groups sup-ported by surviving war-lords. In this chapter we will look at the history of the decade of Nationalist power from 1928 to the final Japanese invasion of 1937, and in the next chapter at the evolution of Communist policy during the same decade in its new and largely rural context.

The Nationalist regime was based ostensibly on the ideas of Sun Yatsen. Sun, however, was a political agitator, not a political theorist. The exposition of his political philosophy was left to his followers and proved capable of widely different interpretations. Sun learned as he ran. His mind was a palimpsest of hastily gained notions, while his situation forced him to try to be all things to all men. Consequently both the Communist Party and the Taiwan regime can and do claim to be his legitimate heir. The main source for Sun's political philosophy is his *Three People's Principles*, a text based on notes taken down by members of an audience present at a series of his lectures. Sun's political aims were democratic in the widest (and vaguest) sense: the creation of a government which would serve the people of China. The three principles are those which should inform the restoration of the nation, the operation of popular sovereignty, and the restructuring and modernization of the economy; they were named nationalism, democracy, and 'people's livelihood'.

Sun's principle of nationalism was the least ambiguous of the three. China, he believed, was a nation, not merely a culture; however, the Chinese people were scarcely aware of their nationhood. While conscious enough of the difference between 'us' and 'them', they had little commitment to the idea of mutual responsibility as fellow citizens. They had little sense of loyalty beyond the family, the clan, and the patron-client relationship. They did not look to national government as a major source of benefits, and did not regard themselves as much obliged to obey it or defend it. They showed no capacity for united national action. The clans, Sun said, must learn that 'the continuity of the blood and food of the lineage' depended on the fate of the nation.

Sun's principle of democracy was not separable from nationalism; it was primarily a means of overcoming China's lack of national consciousness. If the first step to revolution was to get rid of the emperors who regarded China as their patrimony, the second was to create a government which would be recognized by the people as their own creation, and which they would therefore honour and obey. Although Sun was not strongly motivated to proceed further in his thinking on the problems of democratic government, two ideas did emerge clearly. One was that a process of building democracy (which was at the same time a process of nation-building) must begin at the grass roots with the creation of democratic local government. In this he was expressing an idea then almost universally held. The other idea was that there is no necessary contradiction between strong government and democracy; to Sun, democracy was a source of national strength, not of weakness. This idea was less easy to accept in China.

Sun's principle of 'livelihood' was especially ambiguous. As a nationalist leader he sought to avoid proposing policies of expropriation, but as the advocate of social revolution he was obliged to stress the need to return the ownership of land to the cultivators. As a nationalist concerned with the necessity for rapid economic growth he proposed an industrial economy which would take full advantage of capitalist enterprise, but as the advocate of social revolution he was obliged to deplore the evils of capitalism and propose that it be subjected to government controls. The principle of livelihood was so vague that it might seem to imply almost anything. Yet in proposing land reform plus government-supervised, capitalist-based industrialization assisted by foreign investment, Sun anticipated the general route of development which has been taken since the Second World War in many countries. It has been most successful of all in Nationalist Taiwan, which has since come very near, avowedly on the basis of Sun's 'principle of livelihood', to resolving the contradictions between growth and equity, enterprise and planning, economic independence and foreign assistance. So perhaps Sun's economic ideas were less confused than they appeared to be.

Ostensibly, the form of government adopted in 1928 on the foundation of the Nationalist Republic was based on Sun Yatsen's proposals. Sun Yatsen undoubtedly looked forward to the creation in China of democratic government on the Western pattern, but only after a period of tutelage, during which the gradual establishment of self-government at local levels would allow the inculcation of democratic values, habits, and practices. Sun expected this period of tutelage to last for about six years.

He also proposed to modify the familiar Western tripartite division of powers (legislative, executive, and judicial) by adding two more powers, drawn from Chinese tradition: the examining power and the 'controlling' or supervising power. The Examination Yuan (court) would examine all aspirants for public office. The Control Yuan would supervise the conduct of officials and would have the power to impeach. He did not elaborate on these ideas; the relations of the five powers were not settled. The only clue he gave lay in the distinction he made between popular sovereignty and political power. This distinction could be interpreted as pointing to some sort of plebiscitory dictatorship. That this is not what Sun meant is shown by his strong insistence on the importance of the rights of referendum and recall.

The acceptance in 1924, as a result of the Comintern-directed reorganization of the Nationalist Party, of democratic centralism and the idea of the party-state, further confused Sun Yatsen's political legacy. Sun himself of course regarded it as temporary; necessary for the first phase of political development, which was the establishment by military force of a reunified China, and possibly useful as the framework of tutelage.

A further ambiguity arose from Sun's personal position. When in 1913 he had for a short time reorganized the then parliamentary Guomindang into the Chinese Revolutionary Party (Zhonghua Geming Dang) he had exacted from his followers an oath of loyalty to himself. From then on he enjoyed the power of veto over Party decisions.

The Nanjing government of 1928 incorporated Sun's Five Yuan, proclaimed the beginning of a six-year period of tutelage, and asserted the power of the Party over the State, the army, and the mass organizations. Sun's unique final authority was not formally passed on to a successor; it was deemed to have been personal to him as Father of the Revolution, and to have died with him. It was some years before it underwent a resurrection and was bestowed on Chiang Kaishek.

Many members of the Guomindang condemned as premature the establishment of the Five Yuan at this stage. When the new government was promulgated, Beijing and Manchuria were still in hostile war-lord hands and a substantial part of China proper was still beyond Nanjing's jurisdiction. It was hasty even to proclaim the end of military rule. Nanjing's authority only operated within the limits of the area directly subordinate to it. Elsewhere the fact of local, militarist autonomy was acknowledged by the creation of Branch Political Councils virtually independent of Nanjing, the civilian counterparts of regional military force.

Opposition to the Nationalist regime, 1928–1933

The creation of the new government was greeted with immense goodwill and boundless hopes, but the honeymoon was not to last. The goodwill was soon dissipated by Chiang's exclusion of all rivals from positions of authority. Within a year the civil wars recommenced. The pattern was distressingly familiar, although some of the faces were new. The South, as during the war-lord period, was hostile to the national government and more radical. A native governor ruled in Hunan, able to maintain his autonomy only for as long as both South and North tacitly agreed to respect Hunan's neutrality. In Shanxi Yan Xishan the survivor continued to survive. Feng Yuxiang, back from Moscow, had inherited the mantle of his former patron Wu Peifu and menaced the railways north from the Yangzi. The Guangxi forces had spread from their home province to Beijing. In Manchuria Zhang Xueliang had inherited the power of his father, who had been assassinated by the Japanese army. He confirmed his position by murdering a rival, Yang Yuting, while Yang was his guest, thus continuing a long tradition of war-lord hospitality.

Immediately after the triumph of the 1926 northern expedition, China's military commanders met to discuss the reduction of troops. The negotiations dragged on while the number of armed men actually grew. Chiang Kaishek insisted that all China's forces should be unified under Nanjing. His military allies saw no reason why Chiang, whose claims to legitimate power were not much better than their own, should disarm them. His civilian rivals Hu

Hanmin and Wang Jingwei were just as little enamoured of the idea that he should monopolize military power.

The Guangxi group acted first, in February 1929, in a move which was intended simply to reduce their vulnerability. Their overstretched lines extended through Hunan whose military governor therefore leant towards Nanjing. Guangxi troops under Li Zongren drove him out. Chiang responded with a typically astute move: he sent Tang Shengzhi, who had earlier been defeated and forced into exile by the Guangxi armies, north to Beijing to win back the allegiance of his former Hunan troops who were then garrisoning Hebei under Guangxi commander Bai Chongxi. Bai himself was absent. Tang's troops welcomed his return. Deprived of help from Bai in the north, Li Zongren was defeated.

Feng Yuxiang had made no move to assist Guangxi, but when defeat was imminent he concentrated his forces in Henan. Nanjing had failed in an undertaking to pay Feng's troops, and he was unwilling as always to allow them to live off the country. He marched south, but too late to gain from Li Zongren's rebellion. Nanjing secured the neutrality of Yan Xishan of Shanxi by appointing him a deputy commander of the national forces. Then Feng's most trusted and able general went over to Nanjing. Yet, although the war was thus limited, it was only after bitter and bloody fighting for four months that Feng was driven back.

Neither of these revolts, Li's or Feng's had widespread political support. In the next insurrection, however, although the actors and the action were much the same the political implications were more obvious. Feng Yuxiang secured the support of Yan Xishan and made an alliance with the Guangxi group, and this time the civilian opposition joined in. Their project was known as the Enlarged Conference Movement. The rebels formed an alternative government in Beijing in July 1930; and right and left, the Western Hills group and Wang Jingwei's faction, gave their allegiance to it.

Li Zongren and Bai Chongxi boldly threw their forces northwards from Guangxi leaving their home base weakly defended. They took Hunan; but the third of the Guangxi triumvirate, Huang Shaohong, left to defend the rear, was defeated. Li Zongren turned back to extricate him and was routed. In the north Yan Xishan was defeated, leaving Feng Yuxiang alone in the field.

The outcome was decided in a familiar way. Zhang Xueliang in Mukden had so far refused the offers of both sides, but he now intervened on the side of Nanjing. The Manchurian army, as so often before, came south through the Shanhaiguan and occupied Beijing. Feng admitted defeat.

Guangdong had played no part in these events. Its military governor, Chen Jifeng, had no ambition to become a national leader, being content to develop his province in relative independence. It was only an act of provocation from Nanjing which forced him into opposition. The Guomindang veteran Li Jishen, who was closely associated with Canton although born in Guangxi, had gone to Nanjing under assurance of safe conduct to reconcile Chiang Kaishek and the Guangxi leaders who, although loyal to the Guomindang, were far from happy to yield all power to Chiang. Chiang imprisoned him. Then, soon after the defeat of the Enlarged Conference Movement, Hu Hanmin, now President of the Legislative Yuan, opposed Chiang's proposal to establish a constitution on the grounds that this was premature in terms of Sun Yatsen's ideas. Chiang once more showed his growing arbitrariness by arresting Hu. In May 1931, with two of the South's most respected representatives in gaol, Canton rebelled and set up another alternative government. This new regime had considerable support. A rival regime in Beijing had been too reminiscent of the bad old days to attract much allegiance, but the establishment of a similar government in Canton could be accepted (if public opinion was disposed so to accept it) as a renewal of the revolution.

By this time the need for renewal was widely felt. Chiang's military regime was not what China had wished for. The extremely narrow basis of his ruling group was alarming. Of the promised reforms few had been attempted and fewer applied. The Japanese threat was growing, and soon the first murmurs of dissent were heard against Chiang's policy of appeasing the foreign aggressors while straining every resource to put down the Communists. A sudden reversal of economic improvement by natural disasters on the one hand and on the other by the abrupt deflation caused by the American purchases of silver, although neither could be ascribed to the Government, increased discontent. Chiang himself confessed that the Guomindang was now detested and that the revolution had failed.

His regime soon faced opposition from various groups outside the Guomindang. The common denominator was opposition to one-party rule. They were small groups, unarmed and therefore impotent, but their long-term effects in the erosion of loyalty to Chiang's government, and eventually in the promotion of a general acceptance of Communist rule as the lesser evil, were incalculable.

The first protest against one-party government had come even before the northern expedition came to an end. Zhang Jiasen (known in the West as Carsun Chang) was at that time Chancellor of Guanghua University in Shanghai. Established in 1923 as the National Institute of Self-Government, it had grown to university status under Zhang. Its staff were mainly former associates of Liang Qichao. When Zhang published an attack on the Nationalist Party's monopoly of politics, the University was closed down. Zhang fought back by founding an underground journal, *New Path*, but it too was closed down and Zhang was imprisoned. On his release he went to Germany, where he had studied as a youth. Then, back in China, he founded a new underground party in 1932, the National Socialist Party—an unfortunate name in the context of the times, but Zhang's party was democratic socialist. Canton gave it cautious patronage. When war with Japan came in 1937 Zhang rallied to the national government, but as was the case with many others his loyalty to it was to wear thin as the war went on. In 1941 he was to participate in the formation of the Federation of the Democratic Groups of China which brought together a united opposition to the Guomindang and was later to become the China Democratic League.

Another of the 'third force' parties of the time, the People's Front, was founded by China's chief pioneer of vocational education, Huang Yanpei. Huang had been involved in revolutionary activity before 1911, and had been forced to flee to Japan. On his return he devoted himself to education. In 1930 he took up politics again because his efforts to create popular education were frustrated by the obstructiveness and corruption of Nationalist officials. He came to believe that only constitutional democratic government could provide the necessary framework for cultural change. In 1941 his party, like that of Zhang Jiasen, was absorbed into the China Democratic League. Others forced into politics by frustration included Liang Shuming, rural reformer and philosopher, and Zhang Lan, a scholar from Sichuan, who eventually became chairman of the Democratic League. Their politics were really the politics of the unpolitical, who had learned from sad experience that in the China of their time politics could not be evaded.

To the left was the Workers' and Peasants' Party; it had different names at different times. It was founded by three men, of whom one was a former Communist and two were close associates of the Communists at the time of the Wuhan government. The chief figure was Deng Yanda. He believed passionately that the revolution required a mass uprising of the labouring classes and of the lower middle classes, but he soon became convinced also that the Chinese Communist Party was more an instrument of Russian ambitions than a truly national revolutionary movement. He said so forcibly in Moscow, and returned to China to set up a new party of the left. Nanjing was implacably hostile. He was arrested and executed in 1931. Leadership of his party passed to Zhang Bojun, who was from a scholarly Anhui family and had studied philosophy at Berlin. There he had become associated with Deng, and with the future Red Army marshal Zhu De. Zhang had been one of the propaganda chiefs of the left-wing Wuhan government, and was one of the few non-Communists to participate in the Communist-led Nanchang Mutiny of 1927 (see chapter 12). The Workers' and Peasants' Party advocated popular risings to establish a socialist state, a planned economy, and the nationalization of land.

Zhang Jiasen's National Socialist Party was based on Liang Qichao's 'Research clique'; Zhang Bojun's Workers' and Peasants' Party was derived from the left-wing of the Guomindang which had been created by Liao Zhongkai in Canton but defeated and scattered with the fall of Wuhan. Other existing 'third force' parties had no basis in pre-1927 politics and therefore commanded less support.

Two other organizations played an important role in the formation of opinion, although they were not political parties but single-issue pressure groups. The first was the Chinese League for the Protection of Civil Rights, which embraced a wide political spectrum. Many of its members were not otherwise involved in politics; its chief martyr, indeed, was one of China's foremost scientists and Secretary-General of the Chinese Academy of Science. He was assassinated for agitating for the release of the Communist woman writer Ding Ling, who had been kidnapped by one of the Guomindang's strong-arm units (she was to suffer worse persecution under the Communist regime). The League was unable to prevent the increasing persecution of dissent, but it kept the conscience of the nation alive, with consequences from which Chiang Kaishek was to suffer in the end.

The second pressure group was the National Salvation Association, which was formed to demand resistance to Japan. The Japanese occupation of Manchuria in 1931 and gradual absorption of north China thereafter, while Chiang's government appeased Tokyo and fought the Chinese Communists, produced a growing and ever more clamorous reaction. Chiang, however, had little choice but to attempt to suppress the Communists.

The only rebellion against Nanjing to be inspired by 'third force' ideas took place in 1933. On the surface it was another 'militarist' revolt, and it was identified with one force, the 19th Route Army. This was descended from the 4th Regiment, founded in 1921 and therefore pre-dating the Whampoa Academy. The soldiers of the 19th Route Army had become heroes when in January 1932 they held the Japanese off for three weeks at Shanghai until outflanked by a Japanese naval landing. The most politically prominent and articulate of its commanders was Chen Mingshu. He had been chairman of the Guangdong provincial government, but had refused to support the 1931 Canton separatist government. He was then appointed commander-in-chief of the anti-Communist forces in Jiangxi, and this had brought him back into contact with his associates in the former 4th Regiment. In January 1932, just before the Japanese attack, he had held a meeting with these associates, along with Trotskyists and followers of Eugene Chen, with the support of Sun Fo, the son of Sun Yatsen. After the fighting at Shanghai, Chen Mingshu and the 19th Route Army had accused Nanjing of failing to support them. Chiang offered Chen the position of chief of staff, which Chen refused. He had then gone to Paris, and came back to launch the rebellion. Its main political support was the Workers' and Peasants' Party, but the ex-Communist Tan Pingshan, Guomindang veteran Xu Qian, and Eugene Chen were also involved. From the beginning it was hampered by tension between Zhang's group and Tan Pingshan, who wanted alliance with the Communist Party, and there was constant disagreement over the question of revolutionary versus peaceful means.

The 19th Route Army had made west Fujian a 'third force' stronghold. They had cleared out local war-lords and forced Chiang Kaishek to accept their nominee as governor. They had pursued a vigorous reform programme which included abolition of excessive local taxes and experimental land reform. But the corvée and forced levies they imposed had created opposition. Moreover they were Cantonese 'guest soldiers'. Their popularity was already fading when they launched the rebellion.

The rebellion came as no surprise. Chen Mingshu had made his intentions public, but he allowed six months to pass before Fujian actually declared independence while he attempted to win over the two military leaders on whom success would depend: the commander-in-chief of the 19th Route Army and the governor of Guangdong. The former agreed reluctantly, the latter remained aloof. The revolt was joined by quite disparate elements united only by their opposition to Chiang's regime: for example, even the Youth Party, China's most right-wing group, chose to be associated mainly out of admiration for the 19th Route Army's resistance to Japan. Chen Mingshu believed he would also have military support from Yan Xishan and Feng Yuxiang; it was even rumoured that Song Ziwen, Chiang Kaishek's brother-in-law who had recently resigned in protest at Chiang's increasing military expenditures, was in support; and help was also expected from the Communists of the Ruijin Soviet in Jiangxi with whose leaders a preliminary pact had been signed, although because of disagreements among themselves the Communists had not offered military assistance.

Little of the hoped-for support was forthcoming. Perhaps one reason was the rebels' repudiation of the Guomindang and of Sun Yatsen and his 'Three Principles'. Sun's portrait was even removed from public offices. This drastic rejection of the usual legitimation of rebellion alienated potential allies and offended Chinese opinion.

Furthermore, the divisions within the movement widened. The Workers' and Peasants' Party, although formally disbanded in favour of a new and wider group, the People's Revolutionary Alliance, still sought to dominate. The Alliance in turn fell under the dominance of the soldiers who formed yet another group, the Producers' Party. Then the movement's Communist adherents sought by subversion to take it over, but they succeeded only in dragging it into coercive paths which ruined its reputation. As a result the rebellion received remarkably little public support, in spite of a demonstrated ability to carry through reforms.

Chen Mingshu had misjudged the public mood. Fear of Japan had rallied opinion to Nanjing in spite of growing doubts concerning Chiang's willingness to resist, so that what Chen saw as a protest against Nanjing's reluctance to oppose the Japanese was now regarded by public opinion as a sort of treason in the face of the Japanese threat. Thus the most principled, the most practical and the most hopeful non-Communist alternative to Chiang's regime faded away.

The record of the Nationalist regime

The Nationalists had a decade at most, from 1928 to 1937, in which to transform China. The subjugation of reluctant war-lord allies took until 1930, and was followed by the Canton secession in May 1931. War with the Communist soviet areas continued until 1936. In 1933 came the 'third force' rebellions in Fujian. In 1936 Canton was to break away once more. Meanwhile the Japanese took over Manchuria in 1931, and in 1933 established their power, through Mongol and Chinese puppets, in Jehol, Chahar, and Suiyuan. They spread their influence into the metropolitan province by the terms of the Danggu (Tangku) Truce of 1 May 1933.

In these circumstances it might be argued that Chiang had no alternative to a policy of reuniting the country by force. To criticize him for attempting to do so can only be on the grounds that his government, lacking legitimacy, had no right to impose its writ on the whole country. But the fact is that the politically conscious section of the public accepted Guomindang rule, which could only mean the rule of Chiang, for better or worse. No other Guomindang leader combined the support of the Party's military establishment, the Party bureaucracy, the bankers, and (with whatever reservations) most politically conscious people. Perhaps most important of all, China's bond-holders had a very strong vested interest in the survival of Nanjing. There was no reasonable alternative.

Yet in 1930 Chiang's government directly controlled only 8 per cent of the area of China and 25 per cent of its population; and, although his defeat of the Communists and his pursuit of them during their Long March to the northwest enabled him to extend control over larger areas of south and west China, by 1936 the Nationalists still ruled mainly through allied military governors whose obedience had to be constantly renegotiated. Chiang had no authority even to make appointments in those provinces which he did not control militarily. There was no means by which he could enforce his new policies outside the lower Yangzi area, and even there local power had long before passed into the hands of local gentry who, with their local knowledge and connections with the class of 'brokers' which had grown up in the disorders of the nineteenth century, formed a barrier at the grass roots very difficult to penetrate. Only in the 'bandit suppression zones', where the campaigns against the Communist Party allowed Chiang to assert greater political pressure, was it possible to replace this local élite with representatives of the central government. Nevertheless, throughout China there was at this time a wholesale replacement of local officials, although, on account of a lack of trained and committed people, they were for the most part merely political appointees with sinecurist views of their posts, and were so grossly underpaid that corruption was inevitable.

Nanjing inherited the problems created by the slow decline of effective government over the previous 150 years. China's defences against flood and drought had decayed physically and the countryside was left vulnerable to appalling catastrophes, the worst of which struck before the new government had yet got into its stride. Nanjing also inherited vast debts. While most of the Boxer indemnity was returned to China to be used for education, much of it still had to be paid in the first place. No such mercy was shown by the Japanese in the case of the 1895 war indemnity. Although the First Congress of the Guomindang, under Comintern influence, had resolved to repudiate the old debts, Nanjing decided to honour them in order to restore China's credit. Tacitly, some distinctions were made: the Government did not acknowledge the Nishihara loans, which had been negotiated secretly and unconstitutionally; but even without them the burden was heavy because the obligations had to be met out of the very limited revenues available to Nanjing. Not all the debt burden came from foreign loans (of the total of which in any case at least one-third was now owned by Chinese citizens). Much of it was the result of profligate internal borrowing during the years following 1912. In total, about 35 per cent of the 1930–1 budget represented the servicing of foreign loans, leaving the Government in a position of having to borrow more in order to meet existing obligations. Had such obligations not existed Nanjing could have balanced its books in spite of its high military expenditure.

The most severe limitation on the Government's revenue was the loss of the land tax to provincial governments. This process had begun in the stress of the Taiping Rebellion and spread as a result of the independence of the war-lords. It had been confirmed perforce, in the constitution established by Cao Kun when he became President in 1924 and was accepted, perforce, by Nanjing. For the most part, Nanjing lived off the maritime customs revenue and other indirect taxes, and was compelled to make the most of them, even at the expense of economic efficiency and of the social consequences of the regressive taxation of necessities. Unlike the developing countries after 1945, China during the Nationalist decade received relatively little foreign investment and no foreign loans, with the exceptions of a Famine Relief Loan of US$9 million in 1931, a Wheat and Cotton Loan in 1933–5, and some credits arranged by the railway administration. The Government had to provide for economic development, as well as for educational and welfare services, out of severely limited resources.

The most cruel and undeserved disadvantage that Nanjing suffered was the devastating deflation from 1931 to 1935—the four most peaceful years in the regime's history. At first, with the onset of the world depression in 1929, the value of silver fell. This stimulated the monetarization of the Chinese economy, and also made China's exports cheaper. As a result, China boomed while the rest of the world slumped. Then came the drastic reversal. The consequences that China would suffer from an American policy of purchasing silver were obvious, but China's appeals were in vain. Silver poured out of

China. The new national silver dollars were melted down; the country was drained of its currency. Prices tumbled, imports poured in, banks lost their silver reserves and collapsed, and industrial firms went bankrupt for lack of cash. As much damage was done to the Chinese economy and the fabric of Chinese society by this American policy (which Roosevelt himself deplored) as had been caused by the preceding twenty years of civil war.

Japan added all she could to the troubles of these bitter years. In 1931 she detached Manchuria, China's most rapidly growing internal market. In January 1932 she forced the Chinese Government to a partial repudiation of its internal debts by her invasion of the Shanghai area. She used her increasing power in north China and her position in Taiwan to sabotage the Government's revenues from the maritime customs by encouraging smuggling, and in particular maintained loopholes for the illegal export of silver. The Japanese in fact pursued a deliberate policy of economic destabilization of the Nanjing government. It is a miracle that Nanjing achieved anything. Yet its achievements were by no means negligible; since 1945 many countries of the world, in circumstances much more hopeful and with massive international assistance, have done worse.

There were subjective as well as objective constraints. For all the ambivalence of Chinese attitudes to democracy, and for all the excesses into which Nanjing was goaded by Communist insurgency and infiltration, the Guomindang was committed to the evolutionary development of a free society and a mixed economy. Revolution, in the sense of the expropriation of landlords and capitalists without compensation, was not the aim.

There is one last simple point to make. The gestation period of modern basic industries is at least five years. The Guomindang regime was in power for only ten before the Sino-Japanese War began. The first years were spent in attempting to create the fiscal and financial infrastructure of growth, and with some success. They were succeeded almost immediately by the deflation caused by the silver crisis, which lasted until 1935. That China emerged from the whole decade economically stronger than she entered it is remarkable.

On the other hand it would be too much to give credit to Nanjing for everything positive that developed. The foundation for much that occurred after 1927 had been laid—surprisingly—in the preceding decade of warlordism. A large proportion of the successful economic ventures took place in and around the Treaty Ports, beyond the reach of the more rapacious representatives of the regime; indeed the hated Foreign Concessions were an indispensable haven for Chinese capitalists and Communists alike, and one can scarcely conceive what the history of modern China would have been had there been no Concessions in which freedom, both political and commercial, was comparatively well protected. Moreover there was in China in this period a remarkable number of men, outstanding both for their talents and for their public spirit, who successfully pioneered modernization and reform within their own fields of endeavour, sometimes with the help of the regime, sometimes in spite of official obstruction. And to these must be added a number of foreign advisers, missionaries, and seconded overseas academics whose devotion to China's interests was as single-minded as that of the most patriotic of China's own citizens.

Largely as a result of such individual enterprise, one can also say that by the end of the 1928–37 decade China had proved that means existed to solve the country's manifold problems of economic development and social reform. The evidence is derived from local successes of limited scope, and the reader must judge for himself if such locally-produced solutions were capable of national application. Much of this work is little known: John Lossing Buck complained that no Western journalist bothered to visit the area in Sichuan where a successful pilot scheme for the redistribution of land had been carried out; foreign journalists preferred the more dramatic scenes of Communist Yan'an. And generally it is true that the social experiments of the Nationalist period which have since borne fruit in Taiwan are scarcely known inside China or out.

China's pioneering traders and industrialists had shown that China was thoroughly capable of rapid economic modernization. By 1937 most major branches of basic modern industrial production were represented in China: for example, after the successful building of a railway through the Nankou Pass by the engineer Zhang Tianyu in 1907–9, China had the capacity to design, construct and operate her own railways and increasingly did so. There were similar successes in the agricultural field. As a result of research and agricultural extension work begun by Buck at Nanjing University, continued by T. H. Shen, and supported by many other distinguished agricultural scientists both Chinese and foreign, China's imports of rice, wheat, and cotton were reduced to an insignificant amount by 1937, due to increased domestic production and improved quality.

The mobilization of China's savings for use in economic development was vigorously carried out by individual pioneers, who were often motivated to relinquish secure positions for the risks of novel enterprises by a conviction of their importance to national development. Modern banking methods were introduced; limitations on the strength and scope of the traditional Chinese banks based on personal credit were overcome; the monopoly of foreign exchange dealings by foreign banks was broken; nationwide operations were developed; small savings were encouraged. Banks backed the introduction of American strains of cotton through agricultural credit and marketing co-operatives established for the purpose. Through such means they also provided the initial finance for agricultural co-operatives and capitalized silk, tea, and tung oil production. A consortium of banks provided most of the funds for an extensive railway building programme; insurance services were created; industrial development was financed. The new banking system proved that it could survive flood, drought, foreign invasion, partial financial default by the Government, and the economic devastation caused by the American Silver Purchase Act. By the end of the decade the foreign banks had been reduced to a modest role.

In the realm of education China's progress was even greater, although for the most part it was confined to the region of direct Guomindang rule, where higher education was already concentrated. This geographical concentration was perhaps inevitable at this stage. The region was the richest and the most populous part of China; it was the most open to new intellectual influence, and had been the main centre of scholarship for many centuries. There was not much the Nanjing government could do about educational deprivation in Gansu or Guizhou, and its record should be judged rather by what took place where its power was sufficient. Foreign, usually missionary, institutes initially set the standards: Nanjing, Nankai (Tianjin), and Yanjing (Beijing) universities, the Peking Medical Union created on Rockefeller money, and many others. It is a debt which it should be possible to acknowledge without embarrassment because of the speed with which the Chinese of the day learned from their foreign mentors, grasped the concepts of modern science and scholarship, and then reassumed the leading role in the nation's intellectual life.

Primary education was less well served; it depended on local effort which the central government could scarcely influence, and it did not bring to provincial rulers the prestige they could earn by opening a university. Yet individual pioneering showed what could be done. 'Jimmy' Yen (Yan Yangchu) in Ding Xian county showed how effective a mass education system could be when closely related to the peasants' life. Tao Xingzhi took Dewey's theories of 'life education' to pilot areas in the countryside of twenty-one provinces; it was Tao's (and Dewey's) ideas, rather than anything derived from Marxism, that provided the precedents for Mao's later attempts to revolutionize education in China.

In this decade the intellectual level of public debate was high. Nanjing's fitful and inconsistent censorship and its erratic attacks on journalists did not prevent the growth of an intelligent, responsible, courageous, and critical press. Indeed in spite of all the restrictions imposed (or half imposed) by Nanjing, China possibly enjoyed more intellectual freedom then than ever before or since.

In the field of public health the way forward had been shown, foreign philanthropy having primed the pump through the Rockefeller Foundation which provided the largest grant in its history to create the Peking Medical Union and its teaching hospital. The Foundation has been criticized for having created an élite institution, but although the Foundation specifically and quite reasonably set out to provide China with one medical institution whose work would be carried out at the highest of international standards, there was nothing else that was élitist about it. From the beginning it stressed public health rather than private practice. Professor of Public Health John B. Grant, who had been born in China as the son of a Canadian medical missionary in Fuzhou, was the pioneer of grass-roots medicine in China. It was his students, not Mao Zedong, who invented the 'bare-foot doctor', providing simple treatment which peasants could afford, through the use of locally recruited paramedics. The first factory medical services were also Grant's creation; so too was the first municipal health service, in a ward of Beijing where it cut the death-rate by half in ten years. Grant was a man of considerable political acumen and was able to ensure, through his political contacts, that when the Nanjing government was set up its ministry of health was staffed by Peking Medical Union doctors and not by political carpet-baggers. Of the Union's graduates only one is known to have left China after 1949, and he soon returned; and the vast majority chose low-paid public health work rather than lucrative private practice.

In general it is surprising how many of the policies and institutions associated since the late 1950s with the left wing of the Chinese Communist Party and with Mao Zedong were first introduced to China by missionaries and other foreigners since condemned as 'cultural imperialists'. For example, the idea of sending educated youth to the countryside to participate in manual labour originated not with the Communist Party but with the missionary-founded University of Nanjing which, when setting up China's first department of agriculture, refused to admit any student unwilling to do manual work in famine relief areas. And for another example, the idea of co-operative village industry, which plays so great a part in Chinese Communist economic strategy and which perhaps represents China's greatest contribution to development in poor peasant countries, began with an American missionary (who was as much a disciple of Kropotkin as of Christ) who encouraged his congregation in the countryside near Shanghai to create their own co-operative economy; this merged with the 'apprenticeship' project of the New Zealand engineer and poet Rewi Alley—and from this the chain of descent to the wartime industrial co-operative movement, thence to Mao Zedong's south Yan'an co-operative, thence to the Great Leap Forward and the communes of 1958, and thence to China's present policies for rural industry, is clear in all its links.

To sum up our judgement of the Guomindang regime, there is no doubt that by 1937 in every respect China under the Nanjing government was solving her problems, at least on an experimental scale. How then can one reconcile this with the sweeping condemnations so often made? How can one reconcile it with Chiang Kaishek's own often repeated despair of the revolution, his belief that his party was hated and feared rather than loved by the Chinese people? Part of the reason why more progress was not made is that the handful of zealous reformers who took over responsibility for national affairs in 1927 was too small to rule China effectively. They were immediately overwhelmed by place-seekers, carpet-baggers, and the nominees of war-lord allies, who brought into the new administration all the faults of the old regime and almost none of its virtues. The administration was also hijacked by its military wing, whose members reinforced the authoritarian mandarinism, imposed on Government and Party alike by the wave of traditionally-minded opportunists which all but drowned them.

Many including Chiang himself soon began bitterly to complain that the revolution was already in decay. Hostile commentators seized on this to paint a picture of continuing retrogression to which the regime's final collapse in the late 1940s in an orgy of corruption induced by hyperinflation, lends colour. Yet in fact there was in almost every aspect of Chinese life a slow but certain improvement until war broke out in 1937. The vices of the Nanjing government in its early years were the traditional vices, inextricably involved with the traditional values. They were not imposed on China by the Nationalist Government, but inherited by it. There is some evidence that gradually they were being overcome. Bureaucratic inertia, arbitrary imposition of taxes, indifference to poverty, nepotism, disruptive unpredictable corruption (as opposed to predictable, institutionalized squeeze made inevitable by the low scale of salaries), all these evils were beginning to give way. Many branches of the public service were by 1937 capable of providing competent, honest, and just administration. The whole vast, unwieldy bureaucratic mass was beginning to move. It was China's growing strength, not growing weakness, which caused the Japanese in 1937 to decide that time was no longer on their side.

Chinese Fascism, 1928–1937

The Nationalist Government nevertheless presented an ugly face to the world. Its situation was one which has since become familiar in other countries. It was drained and demoralized by its protracted struggle against Communist insurgency and infiltration. Paranoia set in: every sort of radicalism was seen as tainted with communism, until all opinions which differed from its own were equated with those of the mortal enemy, the Communist Party. In Europe similar political circumstances had created Fascism, and among its own more right-wing elements Fascist proclivities soon appeared. Within the Guomindang a group called the Blue Shirts was formed. Its original creators were socialists; its ideals of social responsibility, public honesty, and personal austerity were admirable; its blue shirts were the plain, indigo-dyed cotton clothing of the peasants. It was one of those movements which opposed social revolution (though not social change) by stressing the prior importance of individual moral regeneration. Such ideas represent a half-truth, and perhaps a significant one, but they have always proved very easy to draw into the service of reactionary violence. Such was the case in China, and the blue shirt, adopted to symbolize democratic and socialist aims, soon became identified in the public mind with kidnappings, beatings, shootings, and all the thuggery of Fascism.

At the same time Chiang Kaishek launched his 'New Life Movement', which was also a demand for moral regeneration, but one which appealed explicitly to traditional Confucian values. Chiang believed, or made himself believe, that all China's problems came from foreign influence; foreign vices had been imported along with foreign commodities. To read Chiang, one would sup-pose that until the foreigners came to China there had been no corruption, no theft, no prostitution, and no indiscipline. Sun Yatsen, although avowing his devotion to Confucian morality, had been willing to acknowledge that in practice, if not in theory, Westerners often exhibited more charity, more for-bearance, and more loyalty than was common in China. Chiang made no such admission. He reverted, in fact, to the comfortable nineteenth-century illusion that China could combine 'Chinese values and Western methods'. *Mutatis mutandis*, that is still a recurring theme in China.

Chiang's 'New Life Movement', like the Blue Shirt movement, was soon drawn into the new Chinese Fascism, providing it with the necessary historical myth of national purity threatened by alien wickedness. It was a myth of imperialism, but unlike left-wing interpretations it left no place for the possi-bility that China's own internal deficiencies played a part in her problems. On the contrary, by throwing the entire responsibility for material and moral failure on the foreigners, Chiang helped to divert the attention of China from the internal and divisive evils. Thus the theory of imperialism, left-wing in origin, often ends by serving reaction.

As the decade wore on, the widening scope for 'bandit suppression' gave increased opportunities to the Fascist elements in the Guomindang. The 'rehabilitation' of areas retaken from the Communists was in their hands. They were, it may be said, very successful in their endeavours at restoring central governance. They carried through a revolution in local control, oust-ing the local gentry and their yamen parasites, and replacing them with administrators loyal to Nanjing. But the price paid was heavy in terms of loss of public confidence in the democratic professions of the regime.

To the discredit thus suffered by the Nanjing government and the Guomin-dang domestically was added discredit arising from the external threat. The most popular political movements in the country were all directed against Chiang Kaishek's reluctance to put up an immediate defence against Japanese encroachment. Chiang may have been correct in believing that time was on China's side; but his policies became increasingly unpopular. The Communist Party took full advantage of this to influence patriotic organizations, espe-cially among students. The Guomindang responded with heavy-handed and indiscriminate repression. The result was that the Communists, long before they had become involved in the guerrilla war against Japan, which was to lay the basis of their power and their prestige, were coming to be regarded as the true patriots and the true democrats.

12

The Chinese Communist Party

1927–1934

The policy of insurrection

The Fifth Congress of the CCP was held in Wuhan two weeks after Chiang's Shanghai coup in April 1927, with anti-Communist purges sweeping through China. Yet all did not seem lost. The Wuhan government was still hostile to Chiang Kaishek. Feng Yuxiang in Henan was assumed to be favourable to the left-wing Guomindang, and Tang Shengzhi had made plain his support for the left. The allegiance of the rest of the Nationalist forces was unknown, but it was a reasonable assumption then that only about one-third of the total owed any great loyalty to Chiang Kaishek. Perhaps the United Front could still survive.

Party histories written after 1945 when Mao dictated official history assert that a minority at the Congress argued for withdrawal from the United Front; specifically those who later supported Mao, or died before they opposed him—Liu Shaoqi, Ren Bishi, and Qu Qiubai—as well as Mao himself. Sources closer to the event do not confirm this. Mao had retired from the Congress, claiming to be ill, but perhaps incensed by the fall in position and influence he suffered in the elections as a result of hostility to his radical report on the peasant movement in Hunan. Most of the members of the Congress seem to have supported Borodin's reluctant acquiescence in Communist International demands for the maintenance of the United Front. It seems that only one man, Ren Bishi, demanded immediate withdrawal. The fact is that no one knew what to do. At one stage the idea was mooted of retreating to north-west China and direct Soviet protection; at another of marching east against Chiang Kaishek; and at another of retreating to the Guomindang base at Canton and starting the revolution over again. Later Party history accuses Secretary-General Chen Duxiu of having advocated surrender to the Nationalists, overlooking the fact that Chen as Chairman had to mediate between the Chinese party and the Comintern. The internal arguments were beside the point. Moscow wanted the United Front to continue. M. N. Roy, the representative of the Communist International, made this plain.

Had the International's orders laid down what specific policies were to be followed in maintaining the United Front, the Chinese Communist Party could perhaps have taken some positive action. As it was, the Party was simply now faced, in a more acute form, with the fundamental dilemma which Soviet policy had all along imposed upon it. Its own future strength, and perhaps its immediate survival, depended upon increasing the power of the mass organizations which it had made, by choice, its political base. On the other hand, the continuation of a united front with the left-wing Guomindang at Wuhan made it impossible to pursue the radical policies on which to appeal to the masses. This was no academic question, with the Hunan peasant rising at its height.

The Fifth Congress discussed the possibility of more radical policies, but Wuhan's alarm and distaste were becoming more obvious daily, and the armies around Changsha and Wuhan proved in the event even less disposed to tolerate rural insurrection. On 18 May one of the subordinate commanders of Tang Shengzhi, the chief military supporter of the Left, attacked Wuhan 'to save China from Communism', and was beaten off only after a week's resistance.

Land redistribution was debated, with Mao Zedong, Peng Pai, and the Hunan peasant leaders arguing for unconditional redistribution. It was in relation to the Hunan peasant rising that Mao made his first original contribution to China's political debates. He was present in his home province of Hunan when peasants in five counties rose in the wake of the revolutionary armies. The movement was almost entirely spontaneous, although a handful of Communist agitators, including Mao, were active. The Communist Party was more alarmed than inspired. Mao, however, wrote a glowing account of the peasant insurrection. In this *Report on the Peasant Movement in Hunan* he argued that peasant disaffection was the main potential force for revolution in China; if the new government in Wuhan supported the peasant movement the revolution could be victorious. It has often been argued since that Mao's *Report* was heretical from the point of view of the Marxist theory of revolution, in that it stressed the role of the peasants and minimized the role of the urban working-class, who should be the leaders of revolution. Yet to argue that peasants were the 'main force' was not to imply the repudiation of working-class leadership. The *Report* was in any case addressed to the Wuhan government and not to the Communist Party and was not therefore expressed in Marxist terms. Although his fellow leaders were not prepared to accept Mao's argument in the political circumstances of the time, his *Report* was not regarded as heretical, and was in fact later published with approval in *Inprecor*, the journal of the Communist International. The idea that the peasants were the main force of the Chinese revolution was eventually accepted, perforce, when the Communist Party were driven out of the cities. There was, however, a second important implication in the *Report*, important in the context of the

May Fourth debate on education versus revolution. Mao drew from his experience in Hunan the conclusion that the peasants formulated their aspirations clearly only *after* they seized power. The seizure of power was the first step in political education, not the last. This conviction was fundamental to Mao's political strategy from then until the Cultural Revolution of 1966.

In 1927 the Communist Party adopted the least radical of the land reform policies proposed: everything was to be done to 'curb the excesses' of the peasant movement, on orders direct from Stalin: 'by curbing it we will enlarge our influence over it'. When the Hunan committee tried to organize a mass march of peasants on Changsha, Tan Pingshan refused to sign the order, and Borodin cut off the funds. Many thousands of peasants nevertheless marched. They were turned back with an appalling loss of life. Stalin responded with a telegram of instructions. He demanded the trial, by a tribunal of prominent members of the Guomindang, of the 'untrustworthy generals'. These generals were now laying about them on the middle Yangzi, with Guomindang approval, making short work of the Communists' mass support. He demanded the introduction of more peasants and workers into the Central Executive Committee of the Guomindang. And he ordered the creation of an army of 20,000 Communists and 50,000 peasants and workers. Borodin himself described these orders as 'ludicrous'.

M. N. Roy, with more honesty than tact, showed the telegram to Wang Jingwei, to whom it was clear that the intention was to take over his government by military force. The impossibility of subjecting Communist activities to his orders was already plain. A few days later Feng Yuxiang withdrew his support from Wuhan, in all probability persuaded by Wuhan's own envoy, Xu Qian. Tang Shengzhi remained the last lifeline, but his own generals opposed his pro-Communist policies. By 15 July the Wuhan Guomindang had expelled the Communist Party members, and the United Front was over. Only the Communist International still clung to the illusion that it could be revived.

The disastrous end to the United Front was almost the end of the Chinese Communist Party. When it began to revive later, from 1930 onwards, it was beyond the reach of the Communist International, so that it is tempting to ascribe the Party's failure in 1927 entirely to the imposition upon it of policies dictated by Russian national interest. This would be too simple. In order to consolidate their political influence the Communists would have had to overcome obstacles which would have been formidable even if they had been free of Communist International pressure and of the inhibiting effects of their consequent attachment to the Guomindang.

China's society, as Mao himself had formerly accepted, was not sufficiently polarized to offer much encouragement to revolution. Most workers still worked for small firms, and the style of life of their employers often differed little from their own. Most peasants still owned land. Many 'landlords', perhaps most, were small men largely dependent on employment as officials, army officers, teachers, traders, even in many cases as workers. While poor tenants, agricultural labourers, and rural vagrants were numerous, they were still a small minority in comparison with those who owned land or had secure access to it, as Chen Duxiu had reminded the Communist Party.

On the other hand, since about 1912 China's new industrial and commercial middle classes had been growing in numbers, wealth, influence, and confidence; and the Nationalist party, if it can be said to have represented any particular class, represented this new social stratum. About half of the Nationalist leaders were derived from it, and the switch in power within the Guomindang from the Guangdong group to the Zhejiang group increased their influence.

Nationalist feeling was a far more powerful motive force in China than social radicalism. Until 1927 the Communist Party had been successful only in so far as it propagated the nationalism of the Guomindang; but until the party of Sun Yatsen itself seemed to deny that heritage by failing to oppose Japan, it was inevitably the Guomindang who reaped the benefit in popular support. The Communists were scarcely aware themselves of the extent to which their influence in 1926 was the result of patriotism rather than radicalism among workers. They must themselves bear some responsibility for the exaggerated hopes entertained in Moscow by making such claims as, for example, that in 1930 there were 30 million Chinese in organizations affiliated to the Party. Such claims could not easily be gainsaid by Russian representatives on the spot; they dared report only what Moscow wanted to hear. After the breach with Chiang Kaishek the Communists met little except indifference or hostility among peasants and workers. Everywhere, as they themselves freely admitted, they had an uphill fight to gain the confidence of the masses.

In these circumstances, one may question if the policies imposed by the International were really the decisive cause of the 1927 defeat. The argument is that Moscow's influence prevented the Communists from pursuing policies sufficiently radical. However, in the social situation we have described, the International was probably correct in believing (in its more sober moments at least) that the best route to power lay through co-operation with the Guomindang in creating a modern nation-state in which organized workers and peasants would have a place, leaving social revolution to the future. But Moscow could not be consistent in this. The world's communist parties were after all an outcome of, rather than the cause of, the October Revolution. They arose and flourished on the delusion that what had happened so unexpectedly in Russia would surely happen soon in the rest of the world. Their political activity was dominated by this belief, so that in a situation in which their own Marxist analysis, coolly applied, would have shown them that the dynamics of socialist revolution did not yet operate, they were under a compulsion to force the pace. Consequently in China they contradicted their conviction that it was necessary to support the Guomindang with constant conspiratorial action designed to undermine it. Inevitably this led to suspicion, then alarm, and then bloody suppression. There is nothing in Chiang Kaishek's record to suggest that his April coup was a long-premeditated act of treachery; he was goaded into it, as the left-wing Wang Jingwei three months later was goaded into repudiation of his Communist allies.

In the nation-wide suppression of Communists and their supporters which was touched off by Chiang's April coup, Party membership fell from 58,000 to 10,000, and even this figure was more nominal than real. For the remaining Chinese Communists only quick victory could purge them of the guilt of having survived, and justify the martyrs. For Moscow, only quick success could prove that Trotsky's withering condemnation of Stalin's policies in China was wrong. The effect therefore was not, as one might have expected, that the Communists moderated their activities and accepted the need for a long haul. On the contrary, they plunged into a policy of insurrection which demanded for success a combination of military strength and popular support, although it was plain that they did not command the one nor enjoy the other. In three successive hopeless adventures before the end of 1927 they succeeded only in forcing their local leaders to expose themselves, and so to suffer another wave of arrests and summary executions.

First of all, however, the prestige of the Communist International had to be restored; or to put it another way, Stalin's face had to be saved. Borodin in Moscow told Qu Qiubai frankly that the blame would have to be borne by Chen Duxiu. An emergency conference was called on 7 August 1927 by Besso Lominadze, Borodin's successor. Only twelve full members of the Political Bureau of twenty-nine were present; many senior members were absent, involved in the Nanchang Mutiny, the first of the insurrections to be attempted. Some of those involved later declared that the conference had deliberately been called together while these leaders were absent, in order to ensure the removal of Chen Duxiu. He himself was not present.

The Chen leadership of the Political Bureaux was replaced by a group of Communists who were in the confidence of Lominadze. The main figure was Qu Qiubai, whose education had been in Russian language and literature. The Communist International now forced on this new provisional Chinese Political Bureau the slogan 'transfer of power in the villages to the hands of the peasants', backed by the confiscation of the land of large and medium landlords. A Communist army was to be created. Trotsky's idea of 'permanent revolution' could not be accepted without a surrender on Stalin's part; so instead it was asserted that while China was engaged still in a bourgeois, not a socialist, revolution, this would now have to be led by a 'workers' and peasants' democratic dictatorship' on the grounds that the Chinese bourgeoisie had deserted the bourgeois revolution. This allowed Stalin to assert that all that had occurred had been foreseen and policy was correct and continuous. The claim was further assisted by the ludicrous fiction that the 'true' Guomindang (wherever that was now to be found) was identical with this democratic dictatorship.

Meanwhile the Chinese Communist Party had launched a rising at Nanchang, the provincial capital of Jiangxi, and the headquarters of Chiang Kaishek. The International, in spite of its radical rhetoric, hedged its bets. It allowed no Russians to take part; it advised against acting 'if there was no chance of victory'; and it finally sent Zhang Guotao to Nanchang to persuade the conspirators to postpone the rising. They refused; it was too late to reverse the course of events.

Prospects did not seem entirely hopeless. Twenty or thirty thousand men under the future Red Army marshals He Long and Ye Ting could be depended upon, greatly outnumbering Chiang Kaishek's forces in and around Nanchang, and Zhang Fakui, whose troops were near by, was still believed to be radical. The city was easily mastered. A revolutionary government was set up in the name of the Guomindang and claiming the support of Sun Yatsen's widow Song Qingling, Liao Zhongkai's widow, Deng Yanda, and Zhang Fakui. None of them was present. The population proved completely apathetic. In these circumstances the city could only be held until the Nanjing forces had gathered sufficient strength. When they arrived they were actually led by Zhang Fakui. The Communists evacuated the city and began a long and debilitating retreat south.

Nanchang had shown that the Party no longer enjoyed influence among the urban workers. The next adventure, the Autumn Harvest Uprising, was to show similarly that the prevarications of Stalin had also lost for the CCP the confidence of the Hunan peasants. In pursuance of the more radical agrarian line of the 7 August conference Mao Zedong—only recently disgraced for his advocacy of just such a line—was put in command of a force to invade Hunan and Hubei and rekindle peasant insurrection. His force consisted of one mutinous Guomindang guards battalion, a body of coalminers from Hunan and Jiangxi, some peasant militiamen, and another small force of mutinied soldiers. This last group changed allegiance again and attacked the others. The rest of the force broke up. Meanwhile in Hunan only two small peasant risings had occurred. In Hubei, although the local Party there claimed that peasant enthusiasm was running so high that it was 'impossible not to propose insurrection', nothing happened; the Communists robbed a train, then dispersed when attacked. Throughout there was constant friction between the Party centre and Mao Zedong. Mao was accused of treating the operation as a purely military one. Given peasant indifference, however, he had no choice. Finally, the remnant of his little army retreated south, halting finally on the barren mountainous ridge of Jinggang Shan, on the borders of Hunan and Jiangxi.

Even this second failure did not end the policy of insurrection. A special enlarged plenum decided that the Autumn Harvest failure had been due to lack of attention to the mass line, an insufficiently radical programme of land reform, and failure to use terror to destroy village authority. Meanwhile the Communist forces retreating from Nanchang were undergoing experiences which gave the lie to such analysis. They were having to fight off a hostile peasantry.

The next plenum ejected Tan Pingshan, who as Wuhan's minister of agriculture had borne the responsibility for curbing the peasant movement (he later joined one of the third-party organizations which were soon to appear). Mao was suspended from his position as an alternate member of the Political Bureau for having taken a purely military viewpoint. Zhang Guotao was also suspended on the grounds that when sent to Nanchang he had distorted the International's instructions by attempting to secure postponement of the rising.

Another plenum of the Central Committee in November moved even further to the left, removing the distinction between 'bourgeois democratic' and socialist phases of the revolution and calling for unconditional land redistribution. The Communist Party thus embraced, in effect, Trotsky's views; but Trotsky had argued for these when the Party had (or supposed it had) a large mass following, and Trotsky himself was now calling for a retreat.

The International nevertheless plunged on to a third adventure, the December insurrection in Canton. The Party there wanted a rising, desperate because Communist influence in the city's trade unions was rapidly melting away. When the remnant Communist forces retreating from Nanchang were defeated in east Guangdong, the Party centre explicitly forbade action in the city. But Moscow demanded action. Trotsky asserted that the insurrection was forced on the Chinese Party in order to give Stalin a victory which he could use at the Fifteenth Congress of the CPSU. Li Aung, who claimed to have been the Chinese Political Bureau's corresponding secretary at this time, states that daily telegrams from the International left the Party with no choice. The insurrection, when it came, was virtually run by the Communist International representative, Heinz Neumann. Circumstances seemed to offer some prospect of success. Zhang Fakui, whose troops had returned to the south, was at loggerheads with the Guomindang military governor of Guangdong, Li Jishen. Near by, peasant insurgents led by Peng Pai held the two *xian* towns of Haifeng and Lufeng, so that rural and urban insurrection might be combined. It was assumed that the Canton workers would give support.

On 11 December 1927 the Communist forces seized the city. They proclaimed a revolutionary government with an uncompromisingly socialist programme, including the nationalization of land, banks, factories, and bourgeois property.

They held the city for only two days. Zhang Fakui joined his rival the military governor against the insurgents. Virtually no assistance came from the peasants of the Hailufeng rural soviet. The city's workers proved apathetic, even hostile; some unions actually joined in attacking the Communists. Some 1,400 pro-Communist cadets of a training regiment and 4,000 Party members put up a heroic but hopeless defence against 50,000 troops. Foreign gunboats shelled the city. Defeat was followed by savage reprisals.

In the wake of these three successive tragedies—Nanchang, Hunan, and Canton—Stalin had no victory to lay before the Fifteenth Congress of the CPSU. Instead, he had to find excuses for defeat. His supporters still argued that there was a 'new upsurge' and that the policy of insurrection should be continued. Trotsky, on this occasion supported by Bukharin, argued now that China was still feudal and still needed a bourgeois revolution; this in spite of his own former insistence that capitalism already dominated Chinese rural society. Stalin compromised. He characterized the Chinese situation as an ebbing tide which would soon turn to the flow; meanwhile, he asserted, the CCP should work for 'a United Front from below'. Yet while this might seem to suggest a retreat from insurrection to preparatory organization of the masses, and while it was emphasized that 'to play with insurrection . . . is a sure way to lose the revolution', it still left room for urban insurrections in support of the new rural soviets. And this was the interpretation adopted in China.

The rise of the rural Soviets

The Sixth National Congress of the Chinese Communist Party was held in Moscow. Organization in China had been so shattered that the Congress could not be held there in safety. In fact a far greater number of delegates met in Moscow than it had ever been possible to assemble in China. A new and smaller Political Bureau of only seven members was chosen. It was said that Bukharin nominated three and Stalin three. The seventh member was Zhou Enlai, acceptable to everyone as always. Qu Qiubai lost the secretaryship of the Party to Xiang Zhongfa, but Xiang, a working-class labour leader, was a nonentity, and the real power was held by Li Lisan, a school-master's son from Hunan. Although Mao Zedong was elected to the Central Committee, the Congress treated his rural soviet as a side-show. The new leadership retained a strong urban bias. The possibilities created by the establishment of rural soviets defended by a Red Army were recognized, but at the same time the creation of political and military power by the recruitment almost exclusively of peasants was regarded as a poor—and indeed positively perverse— substitute for urban insurrection. At the time this was a not unreasonable view. Mao Zedong was still beleaguered in Jinggang Shan. His mountain base was about 35 miles in diameter. It was barren, and its grain production insufficient for the maintenance of an armed force of any size.

Mao had arrived in October 1927 with a few hundred men. He joined with 120 resident bandits who were then subjected—though with less than perfect success—to the 'proletarian education' which Mao substituted for proletarian origins among his troops. Zhu De arrived in April 1928 from the south with perhaps a further 1,000 men. Peng Dehuai, defeated after an insurrection at Pingxiang ordered by the Party centre, also brought his small force in the autumn. From these beginnings the Red Army grew, and from these beginnings the future Maoist leadership of the Chinese Communist Party was established. Estimates of its strength in late 1928 vary from 10,000 to 50,000, but estimates of the number of rifles vary less: there were about 4,000. Eventually this force partly controlled six counties at its greatest extent, but the area fluctuated. Meanwhile a number of other small Communist-controlled areas sprang up elsewhere.

In a small-scale preview of the later 'bandit suppression' campaigns, three successive Nationalist attacks were launched against Mao's little base. The first was completely mismanaged. The second ended in a quarrel, followed by a battle, among the Nationalist commanders. The third was successful; and in another small-scale preview, this time of the Long March, Mao's forces moved out with no certain destination, until they settled eventually at Ruijin on the Jiangxi–Fujian border.

Throughout the brief history of Mao's first base in Jinggang Shan there was tension between the Party centre and the guerrilla leaders. The concern of Mao and Zhu De to conserve their small force was predictably condemned as militarism. Their concern to avoid alienating the more prosperous peasants and smaller owners by excessively radical policies in order to maintain a political foothold in the area, and for this purpose to evade the 'kill and burn' terrorism demanded by Li Lisan from the security of the Shanghai Concessions, was also condemned. The Front Committee in Jiangxi (with Zhu De as commander-in-chief and Mao as Party representative) was actually abolished by the centre for its 'military opportunism'. In the narrow confines of Jinggang Shan these differences were theoretical. Their practical implications were to appear only when the base moved to the richer and socially more diverse area of Ruijin.

Mao's year in Jinggang Shan laid the first foundations of his future political methods. Hitherto he had been only on the fringes of decision-making. Now he had a territory of his own. True, his army was miniscule, half-armed and hungry, and his territory only a mountainside. But he was its king, and he used his authority from the beginning to set his stamp firmly on the fragment of the Communist movement which he controlled. The process had begun when his forces paused at Saiwan on the retreat south to consider their future. It is ironical that Mao was accused of taking a purely military viewpoint at the very time when he, and he alone, was striving to turn into practical policies the centre's vague pieties about the necessity of a close relationship between military and mass organizations. The principles on which Mao had begun to work were that the army must be deeply involved in the political tasks of creating mass organizations, popular local government, and the political conditions for social change; that conversely, the mass organizations should be involved in military tasks such as supply, intelligence, medical services, guarding the rear, and harassing enemy units; and that the relations of the army with the civilian population must be based on strictly enforced rules of honesty, courtesy, and helpfulness. The corollary was that policy must be modified to ensure that the people would accept it and come to regard the Red Army as the military expression of their own aspirations. This was the formula which, long practised, greatly elaborated, and given a philosophical foundation, was eventually to carry Mao and the Chinese Communist Party to power.

To gain the confidence of the local population was not easy. A report in 1929 said: 'The masses completely failed to understand what the Red Army was. In many places it was even attacked like a bandit gang ... There was great difficulty in finding encampments, carrying on military operations and securing information.' Mao himself confirmed the aloofness of the masses. Even when confidence had been established there were still serious problems, Mao reported. It was difficult for the Party not to be drawn into the clan feuds and communal struggles of south China and to become identified with one side or the other. The new elected local governments did not function as such because Chinese hierarchical expectations ensured that the elected assembly left everything to its standing committee, and the committee to the secretary.

The combination of consent and terror by which Mao's guerrillas—like any other guerrillas—ruled was an unstable mixture. To secure the necessary degree of consent involved the rejection of extreme and egalitarian policies which, while they might win the support of a nominal majority, would at the same time create intense hostility among a minority large enough to destabilize the regime. The conventional Marxist analysis divided the Chinese peasants into poor, middle, and rich. In reality there were no such clearly discernible groups. In the typical case, the amount of land owned by each family was a continuum across the whole village population. Also, the income a given amount of land would yield depended heavily on the life cycle; a peasant rich in terms of land but with several small children might be struggling for subsistence, while a peasant poor in land but with few or no dependents and perhaps a grown son to help him could be better off. There was only an imperfect correlation between poverty and tenancy, which was common among middle peasants and not at all uncommon among rich peasants. At the same time, the middle peasants, as defined for purposes of policy, owned more land per capita than the village average, so that while as a group they would gain from a land reform which simply abolished tenancy. they would lose from a reform which redistributed all land in equal shares. On the other hand, the middle peasants as a group were net debtors, and so would gain from the cancellation of debts.

Clan and family relationships were so ramified that a policy might be as injurious to one branch of a family as it was advantageous to another. The clan system itself posed problems. A tenant on a clan estate, although he paid the usual rent, was in effect paying it into a common fund and did not usually regard his rent as exploitation. Even a poor clansman renting land privately from a richer member of his clan was likely to look on his landlord as a patron rather than as a parasite; and indeed as the man-land ratio worsened with the growth of population, the farmer who found a secure tenancy on good land, even on the land of a stranger, was often more inclined to be grateful to the landlord than to resent his demands. And after all the tenant, unlike the small owner, was at least shielded from the rapacity of the tax farmer; he had turned an unpredictable taxation risk into a predictable rent cost. In these circumstances class-consciousness, however justified, was not always easy to arouse. Mao admitted that in its early years half of the Red Army were recruited not from peasants but from rural vagrants, the lumpenproletariat of the countryside.

The creation of a disciplined and committed army largely out of such material provided another set of problems. Mao solved them by putting the army firmly under Party control. Branches and cells were created in every unit from the platoon upwards. He sought to ensure that one soldier in three was a Party member; a ratio of one in four was achieved very quickly. Proletarian education of the troops, while it was rationalized for the benefit of the Party centre as a means of infusing peasant recruits with working-class virtues, had the simpler purpose of instilling self-respect, self-discipline, and an *esprit de corps* into a force which was recruited to a substantial extent from deserters, vagabonds, and bandits who were thereafter to be engaged, though from the highest of political motives, in activities not entirely dissimilar to those to which their own proclivities might have led them. Proletarian education also helped to solve the two major problems of all insurgent guerrilla forces, desertion and sectarian strife.

The onset of the world depression radicalized Moscow's international policies by reviving flagging hopes that world revolution was imminent. Capitalism appeared to have reached its terminal crisis. What the International failed to see, however, was that the paradoxical effect of the depression on China in the first stages, as a result of the initial reduction in the value of silver, was not a slump but a boom, especially in exports. With buoyant trade and rapid economic growth the new non-Communist trade unions made considerable gains and the attempts of the Communist Party to induce workers to participate in political strikes completely failed. Peasant incomes also continued on average to rise, and this may partly explain the disappearance of most of the rural bases created in 1927 and 1928.

The Li Lisan Line

In these conditions the tasks facing Li Lisan were formidable. He was charged to complete the agrarian revolution, revive Communist power in the cities, and prepare for insurrections. He was instructed to achieve these ends by radical demands. It is not surprising that he soon met strong opposition from those in the Party who bore the actual responsibility for mobilizing peasants and organizing workers. Nor can it be a matter for surprise that as a last resort he fell back on the use of military force to capture the cities from outside.

Li did not launch into 'ultra-left' policies as soon as he found himself in power. He did not, for example, take a radical line on land reform. It was Moscow which forced him to the left, for reasons of Russian state security. The Japanese threat from Manchuria was one problem. Another was the fact that Nanjing had seized the Chinese Eastern Railway. The Soviet Union was alarmed. The Chinese Communist Party was forced to justify Russia's recapture of the Railway, and in its resolution of 11 June 1930, which marked the real beginning of the Li Lisan Line, it was asserted that 'the chief danger at the moment is a war of aggression against the Soviet Union'. It was Chen Duxiu's protest against this subordination of Chinese to Russian interests which caused his final expulsion from the Party.

The 11 June resolution was entitled the 'New Revolutionary Rising Tide, and Preliminary Successes in one or more Provinces'. It was a response to Communist International accusations that the Chinese Communist Party was 'still lagging behind the growth of mass discontent and revolutionary power . . . the Party must encourage and accentuate class conflict in every way'. The instrument for achieving these preliminary successes was to be the Red Army. Hitherto, Li Lisan had regarded it as useful only in supporting rural insurrection, and in February 1929 he had actually ordered Mao Zedong and Zhu De to disperse their forces in order to mobilize the peasant masses over the widest possible area. Mao refused; his policy was to consolidate the base area politically, and then to expand on its frontiers. The move to Ruijin in January 1929 had transformed the prospects of his soviet. It was now sufficiently large to provide a flow of supplies, revenues, and recruits. From late 1929 to 1930 the Red Army's numbers rose from the 2,000 who had reached Ruijin to 60,000 or 70,000. It was now a force to be reckoned with, and Li Lisan saw in it the means of resolving his dilemma. In a letter to the Jiangxi Front Committee he laid down the principle that the essential task of the Red Army was to capture the cities of central China.

Mao Zedong and Zhu De did not disagree with this as a principle. Mao himself had written that 'only after wiping out comparatively large enemy units and occupying the cities can we arouse the masses on a large scale and build up a unified political power in adjoining counties'. Thus there was no difference between Li and Mao in principle. Mao's objections to Li's demand for immediate attacks on the cities was precisely the same as his objection to Li's earlier demand for the dispersal of the Red Army in guerrilla operations. The Red Army was strong in its base, where it could achieve the popular support on which its strategy depended; outside that base it was as yet no match for Guomindang numbers and equipment.

It may be that Li Lisan was now evolving a visionary plan, in which Mao's vision of the preservation and development of the Red Army for a long revolutionary haul played no part. Li seems to have believed that world revolution was now imminent; that China was the weakest link in the imperialist chain; that large-scale insurgency in China, aimed at the commercial and industrial centres, would bring in the imperialist powers; and that the Soviet Union would then perforce intervene. He did not express such hopes explicitly. Yet his own hints and the rumours of the time fit with his actions and his policies to suggest that if he was not actually looking to launch Armageddon he was at least prepared to court the possibility.

Li was perhaps also influenced by a sense of the precariousness of his own power, which could only be consolidated by some dramatic success. The 'real work' faction under He Mengxiang led the Jiangsu Bureau, which was responsible for Shanghai and its workers, and was adamantly hostile to Li Lisan's demands for impossible political strikes. The 'real power' faction so-called— the leaders of the rural soviets and their armed forces—had shown themselves prepared to ignore Li's instructions. The North China Bureau protested at Li's hostility to intra-Party democracy. Chen Duxiu, with his prestige by no means altogether dimmed by his ejection from the Party, eloquently seconded Trotsky's condemnation of the International's forward policy. However, the most influential of Russia's China experts, Pavel Mif, Director of the Sun Yatsen University, supported Li Lisan and had the ear of Stalin; and Stalin, busy with the destruction of Bukharin and the kulaks, was himself in a radical frame of mind. On 23 July a Communist International letter arrived; 'The Red Army must be organized and strengthened in order that it may be able to take one or more key cities in the future.'

By then Li's plans were already laid. Central China had been denuded of Nanjing troops by the combined revolt of Feng Yuxiang, Yan Xishan, and the Guangxi generals. There might never be a better moment. Mao and Zhu were to march on Nanchang, Peng Dehuai on Changsha, Fang Zhimin on Jiujiang. All would then join to attack Wuhan.

Peng Dehuai took Changsha on 27 July but the population proved hostile. The Nationalists recaptured the city ten days later. Mao's wife, the daughter of his old teacher Yang Changji, was among those executed. Mao and Zhu De attacked Nanchang, but failed to take it. The attack was perhaps less than whole-hearted. Their forces then moved to join up with those of Peng Dehuai. Li Lisan ordered a second attack on Changsha although it was now strongly defended, as Chiang Kaishek's forces, having defeated the Beijing revolt, poured back. The attack was defeated. The Red Army, against orders, retreated south.

A plenum (the third) was called to judge this latest failure. Zhou Enlai attempted to exonerate the Party leadership without putting the blame on the International. He admitted on behalf of the Political Bureau only to mistakes of tactics. By this time Pavel Mif had been sent to China along with twenty-eight very young graduates of Sun Yatsen University who had distinguished themselves by support of Stalin's line; they were known as the Young Bolsheviks. Mif rejected Zhou Enlai's prevarications; Li Lisan (like Chen Duxiu three years before) had to be sacrificed to save Stalin's prestige. A fourth plenum was called.

Between the two meetings He Mengxiang and the 'real work' faction made a bid for a change in leadership and a reversal of policy. He Mengxiang demanded moderate policies in both the cities and the soviets. From outside the Party, Chen Duxiu was arguing on the same lines, with the support of another, in this case anti-Stalinist, group of graduates also from Mif's Sun Yatsen University. Chen's manifesto of 29 December argued for the relinquishment of insurrection in favour of concentration on economic improvement of the conditions of workers and on the extension of democratic rights under bourgeois rule. Most of the Party below the level of the central leadership were probably in favour of these ideas, but they had been unable to influence policy. Hence the demand of the North China Bureau for real elections and full discussions within the Party. Li Lisan had responded by sending supporters to take over the North China and Jiangsu bureaux and the soviet areas. They were not accepted, and now therefore when his crisis came, he had few friends.

At the third plenum Zhou Enlai in his report had sought to protect the Li Lisan leadership by concentrating criticism on He Mengxiang's faction. They replied by demanding an emergency conference which others as well as Central Committee members could attend. In return they were dismissed from the Party. He Mengxiang then formed his own rival party in Jiangsu on 17 January. The following day he and twenty-two of his supporters were arrested in the International Concession by the British and handed over to the Guomindang. They were executed. That this was coincidence is hard to swallow. It stretches credulity to suppose that the British in Shanghai, who were only just learning to make a distinction between the Communists and the Nationalists, were in a position to pick out with accuracy the particular Communists who were followers of He Mengxiang. They were certainly betrayed by some of their colleagues. Suspicion at this time pointed to the leader of Pavel Mif's group of young Stalinists, Chen Shaoyu, as the instigator and to the head of the Party's secret police, Gu Shunzheng, as the perpetrator.

Thus the 'real work' faction was eliminated. Mao's 'real power' faction were absent in Jiangxi. The fourth plenum therefore consisted of the Li Lisan leadership in the position of the accused and Pavel Mif's triumphant twenty-eight Young Bolsheviks as the accusers. The Communist International provided the script: Li Lisan had ignored the uneven development of world revolution and failed to see that China could be revolutionized independently; this was 'opportunist passivism'. His stress on the importance of China in the world situation was 'petty bourgeois chauvinism'. Taken together, these two charges are evidence that in Moscow's eyes at least, Li had assumed, and perhaps sought to court, the possibility of Soviet military intervention in China.

Li's *putsch*ist line, wrote the International, did not represent only 'individual or accidental errors'; it expressed 'a repetition of the theories of Trotsky' which denied the bourgeois revolution. Yet it was of course the International which had insisted that the world was experiencing a revolutionary upsurge, in which China had a crucial place. And it was Moscow which had insisted, though only with the help of metaphors, that the bourgeois revolution in China could 'grow into' the socialist revolution. Finally, it was the International which had created all the premises of the attempt to secure 'a preliminary success in one or several provinces'. And it was urgent Russian interests of state which had led the International to do so.

The conclusion of the fourth plenum was that Moscow's line had been correct but that the Chinese Party had distorted it into *putsch*ism. An observer might have continued to assume that there were some vestiges of sincerity in the conclusion had the International not proceeded, on the basis of this conclusion itself, to change Moscow's line.

Mao Zedong and the Jiangxi Soviet, 1931–1934

The new line was spelled out in a Communist International letter of 16 November. It called for the organization of a consolidated Red Army of workers and peasants, the immediate establishment of a solid soviet regime, and the organization of the masses in the soviet area under the banner of Bolshevism. Thus Moscow at last accepted that the rural soviets were the centre of gravity of the Communist movement in China.

Moscow also at last accepted that persistent defeats in the cities dictated realistic and moderate policies there and no more military attacks on them from without. By then, however, the damage had been done. The follies of the past had exposed so many active Communists in the cities that Guomindang penetration of the network was easy; there were enough prisoners taken to ensure that through disillusionment, by bribery, by the taking of family hostages and if necessary by torture, the necessary information could be obtained. Communism in Chinese industry was finished. A leading participant reckoned that almost 40,000 trade unionists died in violence and war from April 1927 onwards, 25,000 in fighting, and 15,000 by execution.

The elimination of He Mengxiang was followed by the execution of General

Secretary Xiang Zhongfa and by the capture of Gu Shunzheng, the chief of the Party's secret police. Gu was arrested in Hankou disguised as the leader of a troupe of jugglers. He collaborated with his captors, and the information he gave enabled the Guomindang virtually to destroy Communist organization in central and east China. By 1932 the Political Bureau could no longer operate from Shanghai, and moved to the Jiangxi Soviet. Its members then sought to direct the policies of the Soviet, and there was constant tension.

In 1930, in the aftermath of the defeats at Changsha and Nanchang, an obscure purge, known as the Futian Incident, occurred in the Jiangxi Soviet. As Mao retreated south, he arrested all but two of the action committee that Li Lisan had created, and at the same time imprisoned over 4,000 men of one of the Red Army units, the 20th Corps. In return the prisoners were rescued, and a rival soviet set up. Mao struck back ruthlessly; it was generally believed that there were several thousand executions. Mao asserted that most of those who were arrested were members of the 'Anti-Bolshevik League'. It need hardly be said that this was highly unlikely; so much so that one is forced to speculate as to what this opposition did or believed which could give even the most spurious colour to the accusation. We do know, however, that a year later there was further trouble in the Jinggang Shan area, when it was said that most of the Red Army officers and most of the leaders of the Youth League were 'social democrats'. One of the groups thus accused again set up a rival soviet, and again the accusation was that 'soviet power in West Jiangxi was completely in anti-Bolshevik control'. In the same year in the Oyuwan Soviet (on the Hubei-Henan-Anhui borders) there was a similar purge, involving a Communist leader, Xu Dishan, who had for a short time joined the Third Party of Deng Yanda. One report states that 170 members of the Oyuwan army's political department were executed; another report says that 700 Party members and 4,000 rich peasants were executed. These developments suggest that Chen Duxiu's demand for moderate action within the context of the 'bourgeois state' enjoyed a significant degree of support within the Communist Party.

With the rise of the importance of the rural soviets and the decline of Communist influence in the cities, the influence of the Communist International on the Chinese Party declined sharply. Partly this was due simply to lack of communication. (So poor was contact that *Inprecor* actually published an obituary of Mao Zedong.) Yet the remoteness of the Jiangxi Soviet is not a sufficient explanation for the sharp reduction of Moscow's influence. There was a withdrawal of Russian interest in China. Little is heard thereafter of any activity by Soviet political agents, although Braun continued to serve as military adviser to the Jiangxi Soviet. Russian foreign policy was gradually moving from the encouragement of class conflict to a united front against Fascism. The years 1931 and 1932 were years of transition, and of some uncertainty, in Moscow's China policy, so that the Chinese soviets were free to develop without haranguing from Moscow and systematic intrigue by Comintern agents within the Party. A new leading group gradually emerged, composed mainly of those who were identified with the Jiangxi Soviet and especially with Mao's policies there. A score of names emerged of men who were to dominate Chinese politics from the late thirties until the seventies.

Meanwhile the old conflicts continued in the new Jiangxi context. The centre persisted in demanding the rapid expansion of the soviets and Red Army attacks on cities. Mao was forced into a series of offensives down the Gan River in February 1932. Zhou Enlai was the main spokesman for this policy. The attacks failed. Yet in spite of defeats, Zhou and the 'international-ists' as they were now called still demanded attacks on cities. Their aim was to join up the various bases in Jiangxi and Fujian, extend power to the towns, and from there once more attack Nanchang, to achieve a position from which they could attempt to seize the Yangzi cities.

Several leaders who were actually in future to be closely associated with Mao Zedong concurred in criticizing his prudent strategy; Liu Bocheng was sarcastic at the expense of those who thought that the traditional novel *The Romance of the Three Kingdoms* and the writings of Sun Zi (China's ancient military theorist) and of Zeng Guofan were an adequate basis for revolution-ary war: Mao was in the habit of quoting such authorities. The international-ists also demanded that the soviet territory should be defended at its borders. With Nationalist attacks growing in strength this became the major issue. Mao's defensive method was based on 'luring the enemy in deep'. The Red Army was hugely outnumbered and had little artillery and no air cover. It could not ring the frontiers of the soviet area and wait for the enemy to attack. It had no choice but evasive, semi-guerrilla tactics. Mao's (or perhaps Zhu De's) unique contribution to military science was to raise these tactics to the strategic level. The Communist forces retreated, encouraging the enemy to move into unfamiliar and hostile territory. The Red Army would then move with great rapidity to concentrate against one enemy division. The remarkable result was that during the first four of Chiang Kaishek's five encirclement campaigns the Red Army, though so heavily outnumbered overall, actually enjoyed superiority of numbers in every battle. The key to such extraordinary success was military intelligence: 'the communists moved in broad daylight,' wrote the Nationalist commander Chen Cheng, 'while we blundered about in the dark'. And the key to intelligence was the support of the population. Mao's strategy had a political foundation.

One must, however, define popular support. At one pole, no guerrilla force can survive amid a hostile population ready to betray its every movement. On the other hand, popular support does not imply that the population or a majority of it applauds all the policies of the insurgents. It is enough that an 'us-versus-them' situation is created in which the guerrillas are part of 'us'. To betray them then becomes shameful. One must not therefore assume that there was among the population of the soviets an extraordinary high level of identification with Communist policies. Moreover, popular support is stiffened by terror. If it is shameful to betray the guerrillas, it is by the same token praiseworthy to betray their opponents among the population, and so lay them open to terror. Then when support has made terror possible, terror prevents the withdrawal of support.

Although the achievement of a sufficient degree of popular support did not depend on agreement between the Party and the population on detailed policies, it did depend on the general thrust of policy and on its effects on the interests of various segments of the population. The basis of the appeal of the Communist Party in the rural areas was the promise of land reform. This can be defined as the reform of the conditions on which land was held and worked, and included questions of ownership, tenure, rents, taxes and debts. Some of the complexities of Chinese rural society in these respects have already been indicated. The Party at different times proposed widely differing policies, but they can be summed up in terms of two contrasted assumptions. On the one hand, there was the assumption that the more radical the policy of land reform the more solid would be the peasant support created. On the other hand, there was the assumption that the most solid support would be attained by compromise policies which would ensure firm majority commitment to the revolution, while doing no more injury to the interests of the more prosperous than was necessary to attain that end. Clearly, if the object was the creation and gradual extension of the soviet—a Communist state within the state—then the second assumption was more realistic. The priority was then to preserve the Communist state. Its preservation depended both on political stability and on economic viability. Political stability demanded that the creation of inveterate enemies be minimized. Economic viability demanded that production and distribution, and above all the marketed surplus of agriculture, be maintained. This required the preservation of the larger farms which could provide most of the surplus. It dictated that land reform should be so designed as to increase rather than decrease production.

Clearly these needs were such as to preclude a doctrinaire and egalitarian redistribution of land which would shatter the existing pattern of cultivation, depress the modal size of farm below the level at which substantial surpluses could be produced, dissipate taxable accumulations of income, destroy the existing sources of farm credit, and at the same time drive the totally dispossessed landlords and rich peasants into a resistance made desperate by the completeness of their destitution. Yet the internationalists demanded such radical doctrinaire measures, in relation to their demands for an aggressive policy of military expansion. On the other hand Mao Zedong, although in the beginning he had shared this extremism, was rapidly sobered by the responsibilities of government and argued consistently for moderation.

The main issues were: should the land of middle peasants be included in the redistribution? Should rich peasants be wholly expropriated or should they be given a share of the redistributed land, and if so should this be land of average quality or poor land? Alternatively, should they be deprived only of land which they rented out or cultivated with wage labour and left with full rights to the rest? Should the owners of small estates worked by tenants (a category which included land which was the support of widows and orphans, and land owned by local handicraftsmen and others) be expropriated, or subjected only to the reduction of rent? After redistribution, should the owners be free to buy, sell, and mortgage land? Should private traders be expropriated and replaced by state or co-operative trading organs? What was the definition of a rich peasant: that over 15 per cent of his income came from exploitation, or over 25 per cent? How many members of a family had to work on their land before it was classified as a labouring family: all able-bodied males, or only one? These are some of the questions which were raised by the conflict between doctrinaire egalitarianism and pragmatic state-building.

Mao Zedong won the argument. By 1933 the more moderate view had been implemented—as far as land reform ever was actually implemented, that is to say only on about 25 per cent of the Communist territory. This programme of relatively limited reform was retained as the basis of the later and final nation-wide redistribution of land between 1948 and 1953. In the main, tenancy was simply abolished and the existing cultivators left in ownership, subject to modifications which allowed for allocation of land to landless labourers and village craftsmen; thus the 'middle peasants' were left with their land intact, and those among them who had been tenants or part tenants actually gained from the reform. Rich peasants were left with as much land as they could cultivate with family labour. Expropriated landlords were given an allocation of land which they could cultivate for a living like the rest of the village. There was the least possible disruption of production. The marketed surplus was not seriously depressed. Debts were cancelled, and this was actually more of an advantage to the middle peasants, who were often heavily in debt, than to the poor peasants who were often debt-free for the melancholy reason that having no credit they could not borrow.

This pragmatic compromise was not reached without bitter struggles. These culminated in the campaign of 1933 against the 'Luo Ming line'. Luo Ming, acting secretary of the Fujian committee, was accused of luring the enemy in deep and evacuating the inhabitants rather than 'hitting the enemy beyond the gates'. The charge shows that he was being used as a stalking-horse for Mao. When dismissals followed, not only Luo Ming but various other close associates of Mao were among the victims—his brother Mao Zetan, his secretary Gu Bai, and Deng Xiaoping. A Land Investigation Movement was launched at the same time as Mao was once more criticized for the moderation of his land policies. But these policies survived and were reasserted in two documents on land reform written in October 1933.

In that month Chiang Kaishek launched the fifth of his encirclement campaigns. Some 800,000 men surrounded and attacked the soviet area, with ample artillery and air cover. Their advance was slow and methodical and backed up by political consolidation. The *baojia* (hundred and tithing) was reimposed in the wake of the Nationalist armies, and turned into an all-purpose means of control. The Blue Shirts directed these efforts, while a new special semi-secret surveillance force was created to enforce discipline and unity on those army units not directly under Chiang's own control.

The question of whether to use Mao's 'people's war' defence or a conventional defence of the borders of the soviet area now became academic. Later recriminations against those who were said to have favoured the latter were to play an important part in Mao's final rise to predominance during the Long March, but the brutal fact is that the Red Army was given no choice. Chiang's forces refused to be 'lured in deep'. They advanced yard by yard, imposing a strict blockade with barbed wire and blockhouses. The Communists had no opportunity to use their superior mobility.

The Fujian revolt of the 19th Route Army in 1933 (for which see Chapter 11) gave them what was perhaps their last opportunity to stem Chiang's advance. Argument still goes on as to why the opportunity was missed. Mao later claimed that he had been in favour of a military alliance with the third-party regime in Fujian, but the evidence belies his claim.

From late 1932 the Communist International, now committed to a united front with other left-wing parties, pressed the Chinese party to pursue a 'united front from below' and to create an anti-imperialist alliance. 'From below' meant an attempt to organize against the Guomindang government in favour of resistance to Japan, rather than to offer it co-operation. In February 1932 the Chinese Soviet Republic formally declared war on Japan. In January 1933 the Central Soviet Government publicly declared its willingness to co-operate with any military group which would cease to take part in the (fourth) encirclement campaign, guarantee democratic rights and arm the people against the Japanese. Such a declaration would suggest that the Fujian regime was the most obvious potential ally.

Zhou Enlai and the internationalists favoured the immediate despatch of forces to assist the rebels. Mao did not support them. He signed a condemnation of the rebels, and said after their defeat that the movement had been without revolutionary significance. We do not know why Mao, supported by Zhu De, chose to decline this opportunity of alliance with the most famous fighting force in China and so to allow the Red Army's eastern flank to be uncovered, and to miss the chance to launch a united front from below by a dramatic reconciliation with old enemies. Mao himself later agreed that the decision had been a grave error of judgement, but he did not acknowledge his share of responsibility for it.

From 10 to 12 April 1934 the decisive battle of the fifth encirclement campaign took place at Guanchang north of Ruijin. The Red Army was defeated.

Thereafter the choice was between evacuation and annihilation. The Young Bolsheviks who controlled the centre even more firmly after the fifth plenum of the Sixth Central Committee still shouted for 'victory or death'; but preparations for evacuation went on nevertheless, and on 19 October 1934 the Red Army broke through the Nationalist cordon and began to stream westwards.

13

The Chinese Communist Party

1935–1949

The Long March, 1934–1935

Of the 90,000 men who broke out of Jiangxi, only one in ten reached the new base in the north. The Long March is often described as an epic victory. An epic it was, but to call it a victory is only wisdom after the event. In itself it was a disastrous retreat following a devastating defeat. The three main soviets had been rooted out; now nine out of ten of the Red Army were killed or scattered.

The First Front Army from the Jiangxi Soviet was already reduced, almost entirely by desertion, to half its number by the time it had broken free of Chiang's net. The remainder marched north-west in the hope of joining up with He Long's forces in western Hunan, but the Nationalists barred the way. The First Front Army was forced to turn westwards, in the hope of joining the forces of Zhang Guotao who, driven out of the Oyuwan Soviet in the fourth of Chiang Kaishek's campaigns, had established a base in western Sichuan. By the time they crossed the Xiang River in Hunan the First Front Army was down to one-third of its original number. They were driven further west into Guizhou. There, at the town of Zunyi, They halted to consider the future.

Formally Mao's position had been much weakened. His power was derived from his presidency of the Soviet Republic, now destroyed. On the other hand, his moral position had been much strengthened by the defeat which had discredited the Young Bolsheviks. He took full advantage of this, but wisely confined his criticisms to the military policies of his opponents; on the other issues, which were less clear-cut, he could not depend on the same degree of support. Later, Mao accused the Young Bolshevik leadership of leftism, but at Zunyi he made no such charge. On the contrary, he charged them with right opportunism in military affairs. In the end a compromise was reached. The Standing Committee of the Political Bureau was not changed, but Mao Zedong now became its Secretary and replaced Zhou Enlai as Director of the Military Affairs Commission. Thenceforward he was the dominant figure in the Party.

The army moved on, but the direct route to Sichuan was blocked. They marched and counter-marched across Guizhou until forced out of China proper into Xikang. Pushing north, they crossed the Gold Sand River and the Dadu River in two heroic battles. They struggled through the swamps and climbed snow-filled mountain passes. On 16 June 1935 the 10,000 battle-weary survivors made contact with Zhang Guotao in Sichuan. His Fourth Front Army numbered 40,000–50,000 rested men. In these circumstances Zhang Guotao, whose reputation was no less than that of Mao and whose Sichuan base of twenty *xian* and nine million people had flourished and grown while Mao's Jiangxi base was being destroyed, was unlikely to accept a junior role. He condemned the Zunyi conference as illegal on the grounds that only half of the Political Bureau had been present. He also asserted that the Long March had been a failure. This charge, however, won him the hostility of all those who had led it. In the event Zhang accepted the Zunyi decisions, on condition that eight of his Fourth Front Army leaders were co-opted to the Central Committee and he himself appointed political commissar of the Red Army. Conflict nevertheless continued. The issue was the destination of the reunited Red Army, soon to be joined by He Long's troops, which had performed their own long march in which 3,000 had survived out of 20,000.

Zhang was reluctant to move too far from western Sichuan, arguing that a strong base there could threaten the rich Chengdu Plain, while its rear would be covered by Xinjiang, whose war-lord ruler, Sheng Shicai, was then in alliance with the Soviet Union. Mao preferred a location in Shaanxi, a position which would give greater credence to the anti-Japanese stance which the Party had already asserted. Here, Soviet help might still be expected. At a conference at Maoergai on 5 August 1935, it was agreed that both armies should move north-east to Shaanxi and join Gao Gang's still surviving soviet there. This plan, however, did not work out. The pressure of the Guomindang's forces in the north-west was heavy and ubiquitous. The move north became something of a *sauve qui peut*, in which Zhang Guotao was forced west while the First Front Army split into one force accompanied by most of the political leadership and another led by one of Zhang's commanders. Recriminations flew, and unity was as far away as ever. Zhang Guotao formed a rival central committee; Mao's closest supporter Zhu De joined it. In the event the problem was solved when combined Nationalist and Muslim forces wiped out all but 2,000 of Zhang's men. The remnant joined Mao.

More Red troops straggled in from other bases, and when the Party's headquarters made the final move to Yan'an in December 1936 the total force was about 20,000, including the local forces of Gao Gang and some new Shaanxi recruits. Weapons were very much fewer. The Nationalists held Suiyuan to the north, and Zhang Xueliang, having been driven out of Manchuria by the Japanese, held Xi'an to the south. The hostile Muslims who had destroyed Zhang Guotao's forces lay to the west. Yan Xishan held Shanxi to the east. The Communists should not have survived.

It was the Japanese who saved them. If the Long March, although a military defeat, was a great propaganda victory it was so only in the context of relentless Japanese pressure on China and the reluctance of Chiang Kaishek to offer resistance until he had united the country. Ironically, he had already decided that resistance was now possible. The Communists were on the point of elimination. The pursuit of the Long March had established Nanjing's power in central and western China. In 1936 the last revolt of the south had collapsed. Chiang's speeches on the question of Japan had assumed a new note of truculence. As far as resistance to Japan is concerned, his opponents were now beating at an already open door. That, however, was not the issue. The issue was whether Chinese should continue to fight Chinese. The Long March had dramatized the question.

The Second United Front, 1937–1945

Throughout the period of its odyssey in the remotest parts of China the influence of the Communist Party in the cities had been reviving, not through revolutionary appeals to workers, which continued to fall on deaf ears, but through nationalist appeals to the intelligentsia. Following the Mukden Incident of 1 July 1931, when the Chinese executed four Japanese spies, the Japanese seized Manchuria. This was succeeded by war at Shanghai in 1932. Jehol was occupied by the Japanese in February 1933, and in May the Danggu Truce forced Nanjing to evacuate eastern Hebei. In 1935 a Japanese-supported regime was set up in Inner Mongolia. In July 1935 China was forced to sign the He-Umetzu Agreement closing all Guomindang offices in Hebei and Chahar. In 1936 the new Hirota government in Tokyo adopted a policy of unrestrained expansion in China, and signed the Anti-Comintern Pact.

The Soviet Union responded by substituting for advocacy of a 'united front from below' (that is, a combination of anti-Chiang forces) the demand for a united front 'from above' (that is, a common front with Nanjing). A more urgent problem was the recent Japanese invasion of Suiyuan; a local united front of all those threatened was necessary for common security. Negotiations began with Yan Xishan in Shanxi and Zhang Xueliang at Xi'an. The Red Army could now concentrate its forces to defeat the Nationalist expedition sent against it. This was the background of Chiang Kaishek's two visits to Xi'an in October and December, during the second of which he was kidnapped by Zhang Xueliang.

Chiang's object on his second visit was to secure the co-ordination of all the north-western forces to complete the destruction of the Communists. When Zhang Xueliang refused to participate he was dismissed from his command. Encouraged by massive anti-Japanese demonstrations in the streets of Xi'an, Zhang Xueliang seized his guest. He then proclaimed a united front with the Communists and released all political prisoners. He demanded the convening of a national salvation conference and the end of war against the Red Army.

The first response of the Communist leadership was that Chiang should be publicly tried and executed. This satisfying prospect was, however, soon disposed of by the Moscow newspapers, which condemned the kidnapping as an attempt to frustrate Chiang's efforts to unite the country, and accused Zhang Xueliang of being a Japanese agent. Furthermore, the strong and unexpected public feeling in Chiang's favour, the degree of consternation expressed throughout China at his imprisonment, made it clear that to execute him would be politically disastrous. Finally, reflection made it plain that if Chiang was removed from the scene he was likely to be replaced by members of the right-wing Guomindang even less likely to oppose Japan than he. Zhou Enlai said later, 'We didn't sleep for a week trying to decide.' In spite of resistance from Mao Zedong the internationalists secured a decision to echo Moscow's condemnation of the kidnapping. In fact, however, this played no part in Chiang's release, which had already been ordered by Zhang Xueliang on his own initiative. Chiang Kaishek returned to Nanjing convinced of the neccessity and the possibility of a united front and ready at last to resist any further Japanese encroachments. Zhang Xueliang in return loyally surrendered himself to Chiang Kaishek and was sentenced to ten years' imprisonment.

Thus we have the extraordinary fact that the Second United Front, which started the Chinese Communist party on the road to national power, was created while the Party fretted and fumbled and failed to take a decision. And the man who was so brilliantly to exploit the opportunities of that United Front, Mao Zedong, was the man who most persistently argued against it. The proposal for the United Front was probably discussed in terms of the precedent of the 1923–7 alliance which had ended so disastrously; the assumption may have been that a new united front would entail similar subordination to the Guomindang. It soon proved that some of the internationalists in the Party expected this and were prepared to accept it, while Stalin's future actions towards the Nanjing and Yan'an governments, in which he co-operated with the Nationalists and virtually ignored the existence of the Communists, suggests that his view was similar. If this was what the United Front meant to Moscow, then Mao remained consistently hostile to it, while he evolved a different relationship with the Nationalists which allowed the Communist Party to reap to the full the advantages the situation offered—the expansion of Communist territory, the creation of a powerful Red Army and the end of the Guomindang's monopoly of political power and legitimacy.

The arrangement of the new United Front took nine months of negotiation, and might have taken longer had not the Japanese Guandong army concentrated Chinese minds by launching its final invasion of China on 7 July 1937. By the following month Nanjing and the Soviet Union had signed a non-aggression pact. By September the United Front was confirmed. In retrospect it seems inevitable. Chiang Kaishek, already prepared to resist Japan, could not depend on the Western powers for the military equipment he so desperately needed, and could only turn to the Soviet Union; and this being so the Communist Party had virtually no choice but to accept Nanjing as the legitimate government of China and to co-operate with it.

On 15 August 1937 the Chinese Communist Party issued a statement of Ten Great Policies as the basis for co-operation with the Nationalists. Only two of these were concerned primarily with resistance to Japan: an anti-Japanese foreign policy, and the destruction of Japanese imperialism. The other eight points concerned domestic policies. They were:

1. Grant freedom of speech, publicity, assembly, and association, and of armed resistance in the anti-Japanese fight for national salvation, to everyone except traitors.

2. Abolish laws preventing patriotic popular movements.

3. Release all 'patriotic and revolutionary' political prisoners.

4. Mobilize and arm the Chinese people.

5. Mobilize the national minorities on the basis of self-determination and self-government.

6. Convene a national assembly.

7. Create a government of national defence, including all parties and interests except the pro-Japanese factions.

8. Ensure local autonomy.

In return, the Party undertook in September 1937 that their base areas would become part of the Nationalist Republic and their armies part of the Nationalist army. Their radical policies, such as land distribution and sovietization, would be suspended.

It has been argued that the suspension of these policies deprived the Communist Party of the opportunity of continuing their radical appeal to rural society and that therefore the support which they won from the rural population must have been a response not to the offer of revolution but to the patriotic role of the Party in leading the peasants against Japan. There is truth in this, but not the whole truth. First, the policy of rent reduction, accompanied by low and equitable taxation and by participation in a system of elected government, was radical enough, considering the failure of the Nationalist Party to deliver as much. Second, although the Communists certainly appealed primarily for loyalty to the nation, it was to the nation as it could be rather than to the nation as it had been. To look at nationalism and revolution as two mutually exclusive kinds of appeal is false, not only for China but for much of the Third World.

These arrangements could be represented to Chinese public opinion as a sacrifice of Communist independence to the cause of resistance, and as support for democratic rights and representative government. In reality, they put the initiative firmly in the hands of the Communists. If Chiang Kaishek objected to the expansion of Communist territory, he was obstructing their reconquest of China from the invaders. If he forbade an increase in the Communist armies he was weakening China's defensive capacity. The same applied if he opposed the arming of peasants and workers. If he checked Communist political activity in the Guomindang areas—activity explicitly aimed at the eventual overthrow of his government—he was denying democratic rights to the Chinese people, although in their own areas the Communists claimed the same one-party control as Chiang sought to assert in his, and did so with an effectiveness which concealed their failings, while the failings of the Nationalist government were public knowledge.

The course of the war also put Chiang at a disadvantage before public opinion. The Japanese sought to take over the coastal cities and the main communication routes, especially the railways. To do this they had to defeat mainly Nationalist, not Communist, forces. The Nationalist government suffered a series of humiliating defeats and enormous losses of territory. On the other hand, the Japanese had neither the means nor the desire to establish power throughout the rural areas where the Communists were established; these areas were subjected only to occasional attacks. The 8th Route Army participated, with honour, in opposing the first Japanese attacks in the north. Thereafter the Japanese largely ignored them, and left rural China mainly to Chinese puppet troops. Only once—in 1940—did the Red Army launch a major attack on the Japanese, and it brought down such retribution on their heads that they did not repeat it. Yet by their guerrilla activities they appeared to be winning back Chinese territory. Thus although the Nationalist armies bore almost the whole brunt of Japanese attacks, it was the Communist armies which impressed the Chinese public.

The fact is that neither party in China covered itself with much military glory.

To judge thus is not to impugn the courage of China's soldiers, Nationalist or Communist. The Nationalist army's stubborn defence of Changsha is one of the epics of modern war. The success of the Nationalist contingents in the Burma campaign showed what Chinese troops could do when well led and adequately armed. And while the Communist guerrilla campaigns could not win the war, they left no doubt of the tenacity, skill and daring of the peasant volunteers of the Red Army. However, the Japanese had by the end of 1938 taken as much of China as they wanted. They then sat back waiting for China to surrender. Major Japanese operations revived only in 1944 when the United States forces were threatening Japan's maritime lines of communication and establishing air bases in China; but by that time it was clear that Japan would be defeated by the West, and the two Chinese parties were not much distracted by the Japanese presence from their primary concern with fighting each other.

For China there was no prospect of successful independent resistance. The defeat of Japan depended on others. The only hope was that Japan would finally be involved in war with the United States and the West. Japanese forces were well equipped, with massive naval support and air cover. Behind these forces were the resources of a modernized and industrial nation. China had little heavy industry, and lost all of it in the first stages of the war. Her arsenals were crippled by lack of supplies, especially of explosives and non-ferrous metals. She did not have the capacity to build planes or even trucks.

The Soviet Union offered prompt assistance in munitions, training, planes, and pilots. A credit from the Soviet Union of US$250 million was matched by credits from the USA, Great Britain, and France of US$263 million. International assistance was hampered, however, by the rapidity of the Japanese advance in China: by the end of 1938 all China's ports and the entire railway system of eastern China were in Japanese hands. China had to be supplied overland.

The outbreak of war between Japan and the Western Allies was partly caused by the determination of Japan to cut the Burma Road by which the Chinese armies were supplied from Western sources, although of course Japanese ambitions in South-east Asia extended far beyond that aim. Indo-China and Burma were overrun and the Burma Road was cut. To replace it, an air route over 'the Hump' (from Assam across the southern Himalayas) was established and by 1943 was capable of carrying as great a tonnage as the Burma Road had carried, and its Assam base was successfully defended by British and Indian troops. The Hump airlift kept China in the war, but it was incapable of providing the Chinese armies with more than a small fraction of their needs.

The international situation was not such as to make China's allies either able or willing to equip and train her armies to play, as China hoped, a major role in the defeat of Japan. The defeat of Germany was given strategic priority by the Western powers. The Soviet Union, locked in its desperate and destructive battle with the Germans, could give no further assistance. Finally, the realization that Japan could best be defeated by using her Pacific island bases as stepping-stones to bring the Allies into a position from which they could attack Japan itself, added to the prospect of eventual Soviet participation in the Pacific war and therefore the containment or destruction of the Japanese armies in Manchuria, led to a situation in which the Allies were concerned only to maintain the Chinese armies in the field in order to pin down Japanese forces and to make use of Chinese territory for the establishment of air bases from which to bomb Japanese positions. When the island-hopping campaign had brought American planes within striking distance of Japan itself even this latter motive was lost. Meanwhile, the United States was becoming utterly disillusioned by the appalling state of the Chinese Nationalist armies. To the problems of extreme scarcities of supplies and equipment was added the effects of hyperinflation which so corrupted the military, as well as the civilian, establishment as to destroy all confidence between officers and men and between soldiers and civilians. Add that the best of the Nationalist forces were used not against the Japanese but to contain the forces of the Communist Party, while a large proportion of the rest was still under the command of warlords resistant to Nationalist orders, and one can see why the Allies pinned their hopes on the slow and costly process of approaching Japan via the Pacific islands rather than on the Nationalist Chinese armies, in which manacled conscripts were dying of starvation and maltreatment before they ever reached the front. The fact is that under the pressures of hyperinflation Nationalist China, military as well as civil, was sinking into chaos. The contrast with the sober good order and honest efficiency of the Communist areas became ever more apparent. As Chinese protest grew, Nationalist repression grew in response. As repression grew, China's liberal elements turned to the Communists as the only hope of reform. The repression was redoubled; government became as arbitrary as it was corrupt. By the time of the surrender of Japan, Nationalist China as an ally was not an asset but a liability.

There is little point in making any judgement of the decay of the Nationalist wartime regime in personal terms. It is doubtful if any leader could have succeeded in the circumstances, and it is also doubtful if any leader other than Chiang Kaishek could have won even as much unity and obedience from China as he succeeded in maintaining almost to the end. He had to fight a major war without arsenals and almost without revenues, with military satraps of doubtful loyalty and with colleagues many of whom would have preferred alliance with Japan against communism to alliance with the Soviet Union and the Chinese Communist Party against Japan. He could have imitated the Communists, armed the people, and resorted to a guerrilla defence, but to do so would have guaranteed immediate Communist domination or alternatively, when such domination threatened, the desertion of most of his fellow leaders to Japan. Chiang's only option was to attempt to keep a Chinese army in the field until the industrial strength of the West had borne Japan to the ground. China paid an appalling price, but she emerged from the war as an acknowledged great power; and this transformation of her international status, ill-based as it might be, was victory enough for the former 'colony of all the powers'. It was not enough, however, to save Chiang's regime from the now powerful and prestigious Communist Party and the Red Army.

The Nationalist government had at first allowed Communist political centres to be established in its territory, permitted the publication of the Communist *New China Daily*, and created a People's Political Council representing all parties including the Communist Party. The Red Army received a share of military supplies, pay for three divisions, and a financial subsidy. On the Nationalist side co-operation was punctilious, if wary. On the Communist side, however, the original undertakings were already being ignored in spirit if not in letter. Alarm at the expansion of their territorial bases came to a crisis in Shanxi where three new bases were created in the territory of Yan Xishan. Yan fought back. The result of this and of similar developments elsewhere led the Nationalists to stiffen their attitude. The Wuhan Communist headquarters was closed down and Communist-influenced youth organizations put under surveillance. Communist expansion nevertheless went on; the Red Army had grown far beyond the 45,000 men originally agreed with Chiang Kaishek, and the Communist New Fourth Army operating in east central China had become powerful south of the Yangzi although Chiang had expected it to operate only north of it. It was this penetration of the south which led to the final crisis of the United Front. Chiang became alarmed at the rapidity with which the New Fourth Army had expanded in an area which he was determined not to yield. He offered to recognize north China, except for Yan Xishan's Shanxi, as the Communist sphere of influence if the New Fourth Army would move north of the Yangzi. This was agreed. The Communist troops were already moving out when their rearguard was attacked by Guomindang troops and defeated with heavy casualties.

The two sides of the United Front were now at open enmity. The Nationalist subsidy was cut off. Some 200,000 Nationalist troops blockaded the main Communist base round Yan'an. Communist activities in the Nationalist areas were repressed, and with them the liberals who protested at the repression.

The withdrawal of government subsidies and the imposition of a blockade had drastic economic effects on the Communist areas. Worse, however, were the consequences of the Hundred Regiments offensive of August 1940, which although successful brought swift retaliation from the Japanese. By a campaign of military counter-attacks backed up by indiscriminate terror against villages which had sheltered guerrillas, the Japanese reduced Communist territory from areas containing 45 million people to areas containing 25 million. In the long run, the brutality of the 'kill-all, burn-all, loot-all' policy was counter-productive; it drove the population into the arms of the Communist Party and was the main factor in creating a Red Army of a million men by the end of the war. In the short run, however, it was highly effective. Hitherto, in spite of the appalling poverty of the areas, their economies under Communist administration had been viable. Communist administration had fed its people. It had maintained the army and the apparatus of government with only minimal taxation. After the Japanese counter-attack this was no longer possible. There had to be profound changes of policy to meet the crisis; and it was out of these that 'Maoism' was born.

'Maoism' in the 1940s

The conditions of the Border Regions (as the Communist areas were known under the arrangements for the United Front) showed three characteristics. There was little or no capital available for development; labour had to be used instead—the technique which Lord Ritchie Calder later called the technique of 'a million men with teaspoons'. The Border Regions were under siege; they had to improvise their industrial technologies. Finally, they were scattered and could not be centrally planned; their development depended on local initiative, mainly at village level. The experience of economic development gained in this situation was unique. It coloured the views of those leaders involved, especially the views of Mao Zedong, and it was natural that later, in the mid-1950s, when Mao was searching for an alternative to Stalin's centralized command economy, he should cast back to the Border Region experience. What was attempted here in the early 1940s sowed the seeds of the 1958 Great Leap Forward and the communes, and has had a permanent influence on Chinese economic theory and organization.

Mao's main proposals for economic development were based firmly on two principles: that in these poverty-stricken regions, increases of revenue were only possible out of increased production; and that the continued commitment of the population could be expected only if their gains in income were greater than their losses in taxation. Mao argued that this was the only possible basis of protracted war—a handsome tribute to material incentives by a man so often since accused of demanding their elimination.

The first measure was to cut down the now top-heavy central bureaucracy, and distribute its surplus members to the villages to assist in economic development. The regular army was also cut down in size, and the spare-time guerrilla forces relatively increased.

In the event, the attempt to cut down on the number of administrators failed and their number actually grew. Nevertheless, many former central bureaucrats were sent down to the villages 'released downwards', *xiafang*—losing status in the process. For further economies, all members of the administration and all army units were required to participate in production and to attempt to make their units self-sufficient in food and cotton. Self-sufficiency was never achieved, but by 1945 about 40 per cent of their basic needs were supplied in this way.

At village level, effort was concentrated on co-operative land reclamation, mutual aid in farming, the creation of supply and marketing co-operatives, and the establishment of small co-operative workshops. Mao bitterly attacked the existing Communist co-operatives which he said were run by and for the Government and 'only added to the burdens of the people'. He insisted on voluntary co-operatives directed at increasing the incomes of their share-holder members.

This policy of village-level development based on labour-intensive construction, simple semi-industrial technologies, and co-operative organization had strong implications for the nature of political leadership. Orders from above would be ineffective. Dreams entertained by some Party leaders of large-scale steelworks and munition factories and large-scale collective agriculture were irrelevant and dangerous. To make a success of the new policies required leaders who could show flexibility, practicality, willingness to study local conditions, and the ability to communicate with ordinary people, who could take the initiative independently of their distant superiors, and who were willing to become involved in production and to get their hands dirty in the process. There was no place in this scheme of things for the heavy-handed Party boss, the dogmatist, the bureaucrat, or the status-conscious.

The whole project depended on the ability to motivate peasants and other small producers, including members of small co-operatives, to invest their surplus labour and their savings in the improvement of their own lives.

The problem was complicated by the fact that the Party's cadres were recruited from two very different sources: from peasant resistance volunteers, and from young urban intellectuals who had trekked across China to join the resistance. The new economic policy brought the potential conflicts to a head. Most of those sent down from Yan'an to the villages were educated young people from the cities. They were now forced to work directly with the peasant leaders, to whom their habits, manners, and language were alien and often offensive. While they had been educated and so could take the long view, the broad view, and the theoretical view, they knew nothing of local peasant life. The local peasant leader might know little beyond his own ravine in the loess hills but he knew how to scrape a living out of it. The incomers had to learn—and even unlearn—before they could teach. Humility was the first necessary virtue, a difficult lesson for Chinese intellectuals to accept.

This was the background against which, in the course of the Rectification Movement of 1941–4, Mao first systematically elaborated his philosophy of political leadership. His 'mass line' was not merely a political style, but a strategy of social change. Thus the Rectification Movement was a great deal more than a tactic to overcome his remaining political rivals, although it certainly involved such a power struggle. It had begun in 1939 from an apparently straightforward decision to provide systematic education for Party cadres. The Party had grown so rapidly, its sources of recruitment and the political motivation of the recruits were so diverse, the Communist areas so scattered and so different in social conditions, and the contradictions, temptations, and pitfalls of the United Front so dangerous, that the creation of a common framework of ideological reference was an urgent need.

Yet this educational programme could not possibly be carried through without bringing to the surface the latent conflicts within the Party. It was divided on lines not dissimilar to those of earlier times. Observers had distinguished in the Chinese Communist Party three main groups: the 'inter-nationalists', the 'real power' faction, and the 'real work' faction—in other words, the central leadership group imposed by the Comintern, the leaders associated with the soviets and the Red Army, and those directly concerned with practical work in the Nationalist-controlled cities. The first two groups still existed, while He Mengxiang's 'real work' faction had, in a sense, been reincarnated as that section of the Party concerned with underground work in the Nationalist areas. This was led by Liu Shaoqi and included Bo Yibo, An Ziwen, Peng Zhen, and Lu Dingyi (all to be purged along with Liu himself twenty years later in the Cultural Revolution). Mao's 'real power' connection had been strengthened by the adherence of the leaders of the Shaanxi soviet, the terminus of the Long March. Their Shaanxi base had suffered from the same division between radical theorists and pragmatic administrators. On his arrival Mao took the side of the pragmatists. Liu Shaoqi's group had been strengthened when Chiang Kaishek closed down the Party's Central China office headed by internationalist Chen Shaoyu and so destroyed internationalist influence in the Guomindang areas.

The internationalists, trained in Marxist theory in Moscow, still remained powerful in the Party's education and propaganda apparatus, precisely the area of activity which was to be sensitized by the new education campaign. One, Zhang Wentian, was director of the Marxist-Leninist Institute. Another, Qin Bangxian, ran the Central Committee press bureau. Yet many other institutions concerned with education and propaganda were not under their control, being administered by the government of the Shaanganning Border Region in Shaanxi–Gansu–Ningxia and therefore under Gao Gang. The most notable of these institutions was the University of the Anti-Japanese Resistance ('Kang Da') whose dean was Lin Biao.

Kang Da and the Marxist-Leninist Institute were already at loggerheads. Gao Gang and Kang Sheng, the latter the ex-internationalist but pro-Mao director of the Party's 'social affairs department'—a euphemism for the secret police—stepped in to emphasize empirical investigation as opposed to theory. As the corpus of set texts to be used in the campaign was decided and extended there proved to be no writings by the internationalists on the list, while writings by Mao Zedong increased in relative importance, with writings by Liu Shaoqi in second place. It soon became obvious also, in Mao's contri-bution to the campaign, that the internationalists were cast in the role of the representatives of arid theory and foreign dogma. It was a one-sided debate. The opposition was searcely heard. All we can say is that the attitudes ascribed to them at that time are consonant with the attitudes they had earlier displayed.

At the level of policy the only specific charge made against any of the internationalists was that Chen Shaoyu had promoted the slogan, 'everything through the United Front', that is, the sacrifice of the Party's independence to the war effort. Chen Shaoyu, returning from Moscow in 1938, might be expected to represent Stalin's emphasis on support for the Nationalist government, and Mao's condemnation of 'imperial emissaries' certainly suggests that one element in the conflict was resistance to Moscow's attempts to continue to dictate policy. As Stalin was then supporting the Nationalists in distant Chongqing (the new seat of the Nationalist government) while ignoring the Communists who were virtually on the Soviet border, some indifference to Moscow's orders could be expected; as the Chinese proverb says, 'Don't expect the chickens to come if you have no corn in your hand'.

Mao set out to give his own interpretation of Marxist philosophy in order to defeat the Moscow-trained theoreticians on their own ground. This attempt had begun in 1937 with the publication of *On Practice* and *On Contradiction*, and was now elaborated.

The core of his philosophy appears in two paragraphs which although from different essays on ostensibly different subjects are parallel and complementary. One is on the Marxist theory of knowledge:

Discover the truth through practice, and again through practice verify the truth. Start from perceptual knowledge and actively develop it into rational knowledge; then start from rational knowledge and actively guide revolutionary practice to change both the subjective and the objective world. Practice, knowledge, again practice, and again knowledge. This form repeats itself in endless cycles, and with each cycle the content of practice and knowledge rises to a higher level. Such is the whole of the dialectical-materialist theory of knowledge, and such is the dialectical-materialist theory of the unity of knowing and doing.

The other, parallel, passage is on the mass line:

In the practical work of our Party, all correct leadership is necessarily 'from the masses, to the masses'. This means: take the ideas of the masses (scattered and unsystematic ideas) and concentrate them (through study turn them into concentrated and systematic ideas), then go to the masses and propagate and explain these ideas until the masses embrace them as their own, hold fast to them, and translate them into action. Then once again concentrate ideas from the masses and once again go to the masses so that the ideas are persevered in and carried through. And so on, over and over again in an endless spiral, with the ideas becoming more correct, more vital, and richer each time. *Such is the Marxist theory of knowledge.*

Thus the exposition of the mass line ends by identifying it with the Marxist theory of knowledge. The dialogue between leaders and led is inseparable from the dialectic between theory and practice. Mao went further by seeking to assimilate other contradictions, or rather unities of opposites: intellectuals and the masses; centralism and democracy; the centre and the localities. Even the relationship between industry and agriculture partakes of these others. They are similar in that the action of the superior, the more general, the more intellectual, the more central, or the more sophisticated term of the contradiction is a *response*; and that the test of truth or efficacy lies with those who represent the other, inferior, term of the contradiction. It is also to be noted that the dialectical process is not simply from thesis and antithesis to *final* synthesis; it is an eternal, open-ended spiral of development.

In this way, Mao resolved in his own mind the great intellectual conflict of his youth between Marxism and pragmatism.

Mao's statement of his mass-line philosophy and its practical application to the critical situation of the Border Regions was only the prelude to rectification. The Party had to be brought to accept his ideas and those who were irreconcilable ousted. For the purpose, Mao produced two aphorisms to guide the process of intra-Party conflict. The first was 'unity–criticism–unity'. In the West this has been interpreted as a demand for uniformity of thought, but this is wrong. Mao's argument was that if all discussion begins from acknowledged unity of purpose, then it can be carried on without rancour, after which unity can be reaffirmed at a higher level of rationality and mutual understanding. There is nothing extraordinary about the idea; it is a prescription for successful committee work which any experienced chairman would recognize. The extraordinary thing is only that the Chinese, because of their negative attitude to conflict, had to be taught it as a novel principle.

The second aphorism was 'cure the sickness to save the patient'; in other words, a man who is in error is not necessarily in sin, and is a case for help, not punishment. The actual means of political therapy, however, were often less benign than the aphorism would imply; intense small-group discussions, criticism and self-criticism, the demand for repeatedly rewritten confessions of error, and at the extreme the use of brainwashing—the destruction of the personality of the 'patient' by a combination of psychological pressure and physical deprivation—all these techniques first came into general use in the Rectification Movement. One can see why they arose: the Chinese have protected themselves for many centuries from the pressures of authoritarian hierarchy by developing a capacity for convincing displays of conformity, to the extent that they can even fool themselves. How can one be sure that a man is sincere if he cannot even be sure himself? But the fact that the excesses which culminated in brainwashing are culturally explicable does not make them less heinous, nor less appallingly at variance with Mao's gentle metaphor.

It is also characteristic of Chinese Communist history that a movement which began as a programme of spare-time reading for Party cadres should end as a purge. When the process of rectification was spread throughout the rank and file of the Party it followed that each cadre's record would be scrutinized. In the United Front situation the extent of legitimate co-operation with non-Party elements could never be satisfactorily defined, and new tensions and suspicions naturally arose following the break with Chongqing. Scrutiny of cadres' records was followed by a campaign, still under the banner of Rectification, to ferret out traitors and to eliminate counter-revolutionaries.

Confessions under torture and executions followed; this became so serious that the Central Committee took over all but special cases from Kang Sheng's secret police. The Party leadership later admitted that 'some good comrades' had suffered in error. Similar admissions have had to be made after every major political campaign in China since.

In theory the mass line was a democratic process. In practice it was seldom so. Its precedents lay in the Jiangxi Soviet's combination of consent and terror. Its use implied a degree of popular support, but it also implied the use of that support to destroy the opposition.

The victory of the Chinese Communist Party

The growing threat to Japan's sea lanes by the inexorable progress of the island-hopping strategy of the United States, and the building of American air bases on the Chinese mainland, had forced the Japanese into motion again in 1944 in an attempt to join up a land route through China to Burma and South-east Asia. In June 1944 General 'Vinegar Joc' Stillwell, the American commander of the China–Burma–India theatre of war, was accepted by Chiang Kaishek as Chief of General Staff to the Chinese armed forces, but his nickname proved to be a good indication of his powers of diplomacy. Within four months Chiang was insisting on his recall. He was replaced by General Albert Wedemeyer in October. At the time that Stillwell had been appointed, Vice-President Henry Wallace had visited Chongqing and emphasized American interest in a peaceful settlement between the two major Chinese parties. Soon after, Major-General Patrick J. Hurley was sent as American Ambassador to China. He was quite without experience in international affairs. *En route* to China he visited Moscow, where he allowed Molotov to convince him that the Soviet Union did not regard the Chinese Communist Party as a true Communist party, and had no interest in supporting it. He reached China convinced, therefore, that there was no reason to look on the Yan'an regime with hostility. He proposed that three Communist regiments should be armed and advised by the United States to operate against the Japanese in Nationalist territory. Chiang refused.

Hurley then visited Yan'an and brought back, after discussions with Mao, the Communist Party's proposals for a settlement. These proposals in effect demanded a coalition government. Hurley had signed them, but only (he insisted) as an observer, so that they were not binding on his government.

At this time the Yan'an regime had come to look on the United States with much less hostility. Plans for co-operation were mooted, and it even seemed possible that Mao Zedong or Zhou Enlai might go to Washington. Hurley's incautiously given signature brought these possibilities to an abrupt end. The Guomindang refused to consider the Communist proposals unless and until the Red Army had accepted integration with Government forces, and the

United States had no means of forcing Chiang to relent. Yan'an pointed to Hurley's signature and accused the United States of bad faith. It is unlikely that Mao, well briefed by Zhou Enlai from Chongqing, had really supposed that Hurley could bind his government in this way. It is more likely that Yan'an simply now accepted that the United States could not get for them what they sought from the Guomindang. The Communists began to publish anti-American propaganda. Hurley for his part had by then embraced hostility towards the Communists with the same volatility as he had previously come to favour them.

On 14 August 1945 Japan surrendered. The question of the future of China now became critical for the United States and its allies. At the insistence of a new US Ambassador, John Leighton Stuart, Mao was invited to Chongqing. He arrived on 28 August. Shortly before, from April to June, the Seventh Party Congress had been held. Its aim was to display the Communist Party as a necessary participant in any future Chinese government, and to project Mao Zedong as a national leader. Every speech extolled him. A Political Bureau was elected which included no one who had not been associated with him since the Ruijin days. A 'Resolution Concerning Some Questions on the History of Our Party' condemned the internationalist leaders by name. At the Congress Mao gave a report, 'On Coalition Government', in which he made public, and virtually non-negotiable, the Party's terms for a unified Chinese government. It was backed with figures to show the strength of the Communist position: a population of 95,500,000; a regular army of 910,000 and a militia of 2,200,000; and 1,121,000 Party members.

By the end of the war the prestige of the Communist Party in China was high. They had won the propaganda war, if not the Pacific war. They were regarded in liberal circles as courageous and incorruptible, capable social reformers, and democrats. Their strength was regarded as the reward of their virtue.

The Chongqing government could project no such image. This was partly because all its actions were open to public scrutiny, in spite of attempted censorship, while Yan'an's actions were seen only by visiting journalists on guided tours. It was, however, mainly because it had now little positive to project. Even its achievements in having finally secured the end of the 'unequal treaties' and the acceptance of China as one of the five great powers, which in other circumstances would have been hailed as the triumph of triumphs, did it no good; its war record was so bad that these triumphs were seen for what they were—gifts of the Allies.

Repression had grown throughout the war. It was first intensified when Wang Jingwei and his followers, in despair of victory, defected to Japan in 1938. It was vastly increased in response to successful Communist infiltration of all branches of Chinese public life and successful Communist appeals to liberals and to students. Chongqing came to be wholly identified with the

olitical freedom. The assassination of the gentle poet Wen Yido on
5, after he had protested at the appalling treatment of Nationalist
, was the watershed of liberal opinion.

was hyperinflation. China's financial resources had long been
exhau d, and the war had been maintained by the Government's printing
presses, until in 1948 prices were 5.5 million times those of 1937. The consequence was universal corruption. Those living on public salaries, now made
worthless, had no choice but to sell their services.

Chiang Kaishek was well aware of the situation. Personally honest and well-
meaning, he was hemmed in by the untrustworthiness of provincial leaders,
the Byzantine intrigues of his Chongqing court, and the ubiquity of
Communist influence. He leant more and more on a few sycophantic con-
fidants. He no longer expected even then to get his will carried out, and had
no more hopes of the Guomindang as a reforming party than had the Chinese
population at large.

China, in fact, was in a classical eve-of-revolution situation. The ruling élite
had lost its confidence and its will to rule. In these circumstances the final
victory of the Communists, although it was gained by war, was actually a
political victory. In 1947 the Communist armies faced Nationalist superiority
in men and materials of two-and-a-half to one. After less than a year of
fighting, they had reversed the proportion, as a result of the corruption,
demoralization, and frequent defection of the Nationalist armies. In a further
year they had driven the last of the Nationalists off the mainland to the shelter
of Taiwan. The actual military events of the Communist conquest of China
are of little interest. The Nationalist armies, as Lenin had said of the soldiers of
the Tsar in 1917, voted with their feet. The war-lord allies of the Guomindang
retreated into their own bailiwicks and from them made their peace with
Mao Zedong. Only the old Whampoa regiments stood firm until they were
overwhelmed by numbers.

14

The Chinese People's Republic

1949–1957

The early years of Communist rule, 1949–1953

The new Chinese People's Republic was proclaimed in Tian An Men Square, Beijing, on 1 October 1949. Mao Zedong from the rostrum announced, 'China has stood up.' It was the nationalist message which most Chinese wanted to hear; to most of his vast audience, socialism in 1949, as in 1919, was first and foremost a means to national revival. The institutions which were created by the conquerors were ostensibly in this spirit. They expressed Mao's view, held since the days of the May Fourth Movement, that the vast majority of the Chinese people could unite behind revolution, and that its only opponents would be the landlords and the handful of businessmen whose fortunes, he believed, depended upon the exercise of foreign economic privilege.

An assembly representing all areas, political organizations, and interest groups except those in direct enmity to the revolution, was called under the title of the Chinese People's Political Consultative Conference. The Conference passed an Organic Law as a temporary constitutional basis for the new regime, and a Common Programme defining its fundamental policies. These two documents were meant to display the acceptance by the nation of Mao's proposals in his two speeches, 'On New Democracy' and 'On Coalition Government'. The essence of what they expressed was that capitalist commerce and industry would be encouraged under socialist controls, while the land would be restored to the peasants to be worked individually for their own profit. These policies were to last 'for some time'. They were at once the fulfilment of Sun Yatsen's democratic revolution and of the Communists' minimum programme.

Mao Zedong was elected Chairman of the Chinese People's Republic, holding this post along with his chairmanship of the Party. A State Administrative Council was elected. While all vital posts were put in the hands of members of the Communist Party, lesser positions were given to members of the various 'third force' parties which had decided to support the Communist Party against the Guomindang.

Potential resistance to the regime was much reduced by the fact that both Taiwan and Hong Kong offered escape routes for the disaffected. Many took with them skills or capital or both, to create (at China's loss) two of the world's most vigorous and efficient new industrial economies. Many moved on to South-east Asia, the United States, Australia, Europe, or elsewhere. Yet by no means all of China's intellectuals and enterpreneurs became *émigrés*. The number of those who stayed is more striking than the number of those who left. The vast majority of China's scientists chose to stay. China's writers and artists, who had suffered much under the Nationalists, mostly remained. Most social scientists had long despaired of the Nationalists and took their chance with the new Beijing regime. The industrialists who stayed at their posts also probably outnumbered those who fled.

Beijing's confidence in nation-wide support was shown in the relaxed policies of the time, which were generous towards capitalists, rich peasants, and even the landlords who, though deprived of their estates, were permitted to retain their commercial and industrial interests. This honeymoon period was brought to an end by the outbreak of war in Korea.

At the end of the Second World War the Korean people had looked forward to independence, after almost half a century of Japanese rule. At Yalta, however, the Allies had agreed that for an interim period Korea would be governed by a four-power commission. Meanwhile, the Soviet military authorities would accept the surrender of the Japanese north of the 38th parallel, and the American forces south of it. It was agreed that Korea should be united, but this broke down on the refusal of the Soviet-installed provisional regime in the north to accept free elections. By 1947 two separate governments, each claiming to be the legitimate government of the whole country, had been set up north and south of the 38th parallel.

On 25 June 1950 the forces of the North, numerous and well-equipped by the Soviet Union, invaded the South whose forces were few and carried little more than small arms. The communists swiftly occupied virtually the whole of the peninsula. The United States responded within twenty-four hours of the invasion. The United Nations Security Council condemned the North Korean Government as the aggressor and approved UN intervention. (The Soviet representative, absent in protest at the refusal of the Council to offer a place to the Chinese People's Republic, could not veto the resolution.) Under the UN flag, American troops and token forces from fifteen other nations arrived in time to preserve only a toe-hold at Pusan.

Yet North Korea's sweep south had been all too successful: General MacArthur, commander of the UN forces, had no difficulty in making a landing near Seoul, cutting the communications of the North Korean army, and eliminating it. The UN forces in turn swept north to the northern capital of Pyongyang, with a UN mandate to unite the country.

China could scarcely be expected to maintain neutrality in these circumstances. She had no wish for war, the outbreak of which had surprised and alarmed Beijing as much as Washington. Yet Korea was a pistol pointed at the heart of China—her industrial heart, just north of the Yalu River. When the UN forces landed at Inchon and set about destroying the North Korean army China immediately sent a force of 'volunteers', intitially 1,200,000 in number, under Marshal Peng Dehuai, to rescue the Korean regime. This massive force, although poorly armed, overwhelmed the UN forces by sheer weight of numbers. But Chinese casualties were appalling; they numbered almost one million; there can scarcely be another major campaign in modern history in which the victors suffered such losses. And the victory was short-lived. American hardware told in the end. The Chinese and the North Koreans were forced back to the 38th parallel. General MacArthur was ready to invade the North again, but President Truman decided that it was enough to have restored the status quo. MacArthur was dismissed in dramatic circumstances.

Negotiations began in July 1951, but they quickly came to a deadlock over the refusal of the Western forces to restore those prisoners-of-war, about 20 per cent of the total, who did not wish to return to communist China or North Korea. Negotiations dragged on. Stalin died in March 1953. Eisenhower was determined to break the deadlock, if necessary by renewed war. The communist side therefore yielded on the issue of the prisoners. An armistice was signed, but no peace.

One measure taken by the United States in response to the despatch to Korea of a Chinese army was to adopt the Taiwan regime as a client. The United States also began to patrol the Taiwan Straits, and secured a United Nations embargo on trade with China in strategic goods. These developments strengthened Beijing's apprehension that the capitalist world had launched its war of intervention via Korea. When disaffected elements at home began to spread a rumour that 'Chiang Kaishek would be back in time to eat his moon cakes' (at the Autumn Festival), the Communist Party swung from generosity to severity.

Land reform and economic recovery, 1949–1953

The new severity affected the course of the land reform. Policy here, however, had never been entirely stablized. There were differences of opinion within the Party; there were changes of policy as the political situation changed throughout the final civil war; and as the People's Liberation Army moved south, differences in the local societies through which it passed produced further modifications in policy. The first land reform draft law was issued from Yan'an in 1946, before the final civil war began. Its provisions were part of an appeal for unity against the Nationalist regime and it was published, significantly, on the anniversary of May Fourth. Only large estates were to be taken over for redistribution, and compensation would be paid except to estate owners who had collaborated with the Japanese. This proposal was never implemented because civil war ensued. The next draft was produced when the Communists were facing Chiang's armies in Manchuria, and the radical nature of its provision reflected the need to maximize the recruitment of peasants to the PLA. It swung back to the uncompromising egalitarianism of the first days of the Jiangxi Soviet: all land was to be taken over and distributed equally to the whole rural population. One of its authors was Liu Shaoqi. Mao Zedong immediately made his objections plain, damning the draft law with faint praise, both on grounds of its egalitarianism and of its use of 'poor peasant leagues' as the instrument of redistribution. Mao insisted that the reform should be carried through by elected village assemblies in which all except landlords should participate. He then revived the 1933 Jiangxi Soviet land law, which left the holdings of middle peasants undisturbed as well as that part of the land of rich peasants which they cultivated with their own labour. This policy by no means eliminated inequality in the village; the ratio of the largest to the smallest farms after redistribution remained about two to one— the cost, in terms of surviving inequality, of avoiding the disruption of the existing pattern of cultivation.

The new moderate policy reckoned without the ambitions of the poorest peasants and the zeal of local Party cadres. As the PLA pressed south, excesses of all kinds occurred. In Henan in 1949 the villagers seized all rich peasant land, and interpreted the category of rich peasant in such a way as to include large numbers of middle peasants whose support the Communist Party regarded as vital. They also disobeyed the instruction to leave movable property untouched and to protect landed property devoted to industrial purposes. They carried off and divided everything that could be moved. In spite of instructions, beatings and killings were widespread and not all the victims were landlords. In mitigation it may be said that many prosperous peasants whose holding were not large enough to bring them within the scope of the reform had acted as bailiffs or bullies for landlords, or had been involved in the detested *baojia* system, and in this way had incurred the hatred of some fellow villagers. Land reform in Henan was halted abruptly while a new method was worked out.

The method was to lead the newly occupied village through the events which had taken place in the old liberated areas. There, the process had taken a decade. In the new areas it would take a few months only, at most a year; but it might make possible the same orderly process of change. The creation of peasant institutions and the attack on the landlords went on together, with one operation supporting the other. First, a peasant militia was created to guard the village against raids from Guomindang remnant forces. This militia was then employed in a 'bandit suppression campaign' directed not only at these armed remnants but also at those landlords who collaborated with them. When the peasants had thus tested their strength and won, a peasant association was formed. The association then took the pressure on the land-lords a step further by enforcing the reduction of rents and the cancellation of old debts. When this had been successfully carried out an elected village government was formed and it was this representative village body which ruled on land ownership and enforced the distribution of land. It was an ingenious policy, making possible a revolution which, though taking place from the bottom up, might still be carried through in a non-violent and quasilegal way. It also involved most of the village in committing themselves to the revolution. Finally in the course of it the natural radical leaders of the village would emerge to make possible the establishment of a Communist Party branch whose members would enjoy the confidence of the community. This policy had the further advantage of requiring a minimum of administrative control on the part of a regime then so short of experienced personnel that it could not have found even one cadre per village.

When the lower Yangzi provinces were occupied new problems appeared. While on the one hand a far higher proportion of the farmers there were tenants, on the other hand agriculture was commercialized to a significant extent. Disruption of production in this area would have serious economic consequences: a Chinese proverb says that when Tai Cang, Kun Shan, and Chang Shu (three contiguous areas on the south bank of the Yangzi estuary) have a bad harvest China tightens her belt. A controversy began in the Communist Party on the question of whether Yangzi agriculture should be considered 'feudal' (in which case the land would be redistributed) or 'capitalist' (in which case it would not). Farming in that area was, of course, neither feudal nor capitalist in any recognizable sense. What was at stake was the fate of the commercially orientated rich peasant. In the event, although it was ruled that Yangzi society was feudal and land tenure must therefore be reformed, national policy was changed in order to respect the interests of these Chinese 'kulaks' and so to protect the marketed agricultural surplus. Under the final national Agrarian Reform Law of 1950 rich peasants retained not only the land which they worked with family labour but also that which they worked with hired hands and that which they rented out, provided that no more than half of their total land was in these categories.

The land reform process also changed. It was now carried out by administrative means. The result was perhaps not entirely advantageous to the new regime, at least in the long run, for although it was possible to carry the redistribution through with less risk of locally inspired excesses, the poor peasant received the land as a gift and not through his own committed political action. Mao Zedong later commented on the effects of this difference on the peasants of south China.

China's land reform was the greatest act of expropriation in human history. While the official figures, suggesting that half of China's 240 million acres of arable land had changed hands, were probably based on the usual left-wing exaggeration of the degree of concentration of land ownership, one can safely assume that at least 200 million acres were distributed to about 75 million peasant families. In theory it was to be carried out without violence; but this is more than could be expected. The method of mobilizing the peasants by the use of 'speak bitterness' meetings, during which they were encouraged to recount their grievances and to accuse the landlords paraded before them, involved the risk that emotions would get out of hand. There was an inevitable ambiguity between the desire to conduct land reform justly and peacefully and the desire to terrify the rural upper classes in order to neutralize them politically. The Korean War tipped the balance. A new 'Campaign Against Counter-Revolutionaries' put every landlord or former landlord in danger of denunciation. This increased the tendency towards illegal excesses. As for the landlord class, they offered little opposition. Both main political parties had been committed to land reform for a generation. The local gentry had slowly but surely lost their prestige as society's values and institutions changed. They had little will to resist. Consequently there was no need for a general policy of severe repression, and in spite of peasant excesses, the Korean War and the Campaign Against Counter-Revolutionaries, the vast majority of China's two million landlords, while they lost their estates, survived the land reform. However, to those who were accused by the peasants of criminal acts in the past—beatings, murder, arson, rape—no mercy was shown.

At the same time as the redistribution of land was taking place the Government began the task of restoring the economy, battered by over thirty years of war. The hyperinflation inherited from the preceding government was dealt with by a guarantee that the value of savings would be tied to the price of a basket of necessities. This was accompanied by price controls made effective by the fact that the Government disposed of a substantial part of the stocks of commodities. The method worked remarkably well. The stability of the currency was restored within months.

China now had, for the first time in her modern history, a government whose writ ran everywhere. Normal trade relations were restored. This was the most important factor in the rapid economic recovery which now took place. By the end of 1952 the indices of production of most important commodities had surpassed the record levels of 1936. Policy towards private business was at first generous. Its owners were assured that they would be protected for a 'fairly long time' and could therefore invest in safety. The demands of workers were moderated. Fine words, however, did not solve the unfamiliar problems of relations between free enterprise and a communist administration exercising supervision over the economy. Mao had warned his rural cadres that when they reached the cities they would face 'sugar-coated bullets'; and when one reflects upon the fact that a regime can be corrupted by nothing more than, for example, the consequences of exchange control, the extent of the danger in

China where economic controls were comprehensive in their scope can be easily guessed.

The Korean War, in the same way as it led to a greater severity towards the landlords, also brought about a change in the Party's attitude towards the relations between cadres and capitalists. It was in Manchuria, the area of China directly threatened by the operations in Korea, that the first action was taken. A campaign against three evils was launched (the so-called 'Three Antis' campaign), to investigate and punish cadres whose relations with the private sector had led to their corruption. The evils were graft, waste, and bureaucracy. A high percentage of cadres in the cities were found guilty. Inevitably the campaign spread to involve the business community. The 'Three Antis' became the 'Five Antis'. The evils now were bribery, tax evasion, theft of state property, cheating on government contracts, and theft of state economic information. Every private business in urban China came under investigation, with its employees put under pressure to reveal the misdemeanours of their masters. Whatever its origins were, and however justified the investigation of commercial corruption may have been, the campaign was used as an opportunity to pulverize China's capitalists politically. The numbers actually convicted were small far smaller than the number of cadres punished under the preceding 'Three Antis' campaign but an atmosphere of terror was created, and the way was paved for the eventual takeover of the private sector. Foreign business, missionary and charitable institutions were meanwhile frozen out or taken over.

The imposition of intellectual control

Intellectual life was brought quickly under control. In 'On New Democracy' Mao Zedong had appealed to the Chinese people against the oppressiveness of Guomindang censorship, suppression of intellectuals, brutality towards students, murders of political opponents, and increasingly Fascist methods. 'On New Democracy' offered freedom, and promised tolerance towards all but the immediate associates of the defeated and discredited regime. This freedom scarcely lasted eighteen months before a campaign was launched to exert full command of China's intellectual life. It was heralded by an attack on Liang Shuming, one of the most admired writers of China. Liang was a philosopher who had sought to combine with the democratic socialism of the modern West what he saw as the virtues of Eastern civilization, with its stress on social harmony. He had become a leading member of the Democratic League, now ostensibly a part of the new ruling coalition. Essentially, however, his philosophy was anti-Marxist; there was no place in it for class struggle. Moreover, the values which Liang's writings expressed were widely shared in China; indeed the dilemma of the choice presented—Confucian social harmony, the radical individualism of the West, or Marxist class conflict—was the central issue of twentieth-century Chinese history. This unresolved contradiction had paralysed the educated classes and rendered them politically impotent. Perhaps it was Mao's consciousness that he himself had been vulnerable to the Confucian-liberal blandishments of Liang Shuming that gave his treatment of Liang an unusually vicious edge. Mao set out, personally, to discredit, humiliate and disgrace Liang, and to drive him from Chinese intellectual life. Liang Shuming defended his beliefs with vigour, but in the end was overwhelmed by the flood of insult and calumny to which he was subjected.

A second campaign was begun in May 1957 against a film based on the life of Wu Xun, an orphaned child of poor peasants who in the late nineteenth century had devoted his life to rural education, raising money for the purpose from officials and gentry. He was honoured at his death by the young Guang Xu Emperor. The film, its makers, the Party critics who had praised it, and the Party leaders (including Liu Shaoqi) who had been naïve enough to accept it, were criticized. Mao again took the lead by writing (anonymously) the article on 10 January 1957 in the *People's Daily* which lauched the attack. Wu Xun, it was argued, had in his slavish dependence on the feudal upper classes helped to perpetuate the old system and had actually helped to propagate its ideology among his fellow peasants. He was not a hero but a traitor—so much for the many admired figures among China's intellectuals, some of them now associated with the new Communist government, who had patronized, participated in, or led one or other of the various rural education movements of the 1930s.

These two warning shots having been fired across the bows of Chinese academia, the boarding parties soon followed. The universities and research institutes were taken over. Their members were subjected to a process of 'thought reform' in courses of treatment lasting normally for about six months. The course began with small group sessions, using methods reminiscent of group therapy. The members were encouraged to talk freely about their beliefs and doubts in an atmosphere of sympathy, relaxation, and encouragement. They were then each taken individually and their confessions used against them; isolated, physically deprived, and constantly under frightening pressure, their feelings of class guilt, their intellectual contradictions, and their yearning to be good patriots were used to break down and change their personalities by a process akin to religious conversion. It was effective only because of the moral confusion which China's twentieth-century situation had produced among the educated. It has been observed that the classes of men who most successfully resist such practices are religious fanatics, Communists, and aristocrats. They have no doubts. But the twentieth-century Chinese intellectual was full of doubts. Yet the evidence shows that in most cases the effects were temporary. The 'transference', as psychoanalysts would express it, to their Communist mentors seldom had a permanent effect. In the end all the Communists earned was fear. Liberal humanism lived on; most of the young men who created Democracy Wall in 1978 were not even born in 1951.

The symbol of the intellectual liberalism under attack was Hu Shi, the pragmatist follower of John Dewey. Hu had been a principal leader of the May Fourth Movement, and the inspirer of the 1919 literary revolution in which the vernacular had replaced the old literary written language. In 1949 he had chosen exile in Taiwan, but his influence persisted in China through his many students. As in the case of Liang Shuming, the fact that Hu Shi's philosophy had so strongly influenced Mao in his youth perhaps gave him a special interest in laying the ghost of Hu's pragmatism.

In July 1954, however, opposition to the tight control of intellectual life appeared within the Communist Party itself. The Party writer Hu Feng wrote to the Central Committee in protest. In the thirties Hu Feng had been a close associate of Lu Xun, the most distinguished Chinese imaginative writer of the twentieth century, a radical socialist and Mao's favourite among modern authors. Hu Feng was an important figure in the Party's literary establishment, and a member of the national People's Congress. In his letter he accused the Party administrators of pointing 'five daggers' at the heart of Chinese literature. These were the demands that the lives of workers and peasants should be the sole source of literary inspiration, that writers must submit to thought reform, that the Party should dictate the forms of literature, that the Party should determine the subjects of literature, and that all writers must accept Communist ideology.

Again Mao led the attack with an anonymous article in the *People's Daily*. This induced Hu Feng's colleagues to turn on him, and the result was the unedifying spectacle of China's greatest authors joining in the vicious personal denigration of the only man who displayed the courage of the convictions which all of them shared. Hu Feng was imprisoned.

Within three or four years the educated classes of China, on whom the regime was very dependent, and even more dependent when with the First Five Year Plan the drive began for planned economic growth, were demoralized. Cowed into obedience, they carried out their work perfunctorily and avoided the risks of offering advice or pursuing innovation. In January 1956 Zhou Enlai admitted that the pressure had been counter-productive, and proclaimed a new and more liberal policy.

China's First Five Year Plan, 1953–1957

By 1953 the economy had recovered, land reform was complete, the private sector had been reduced to subservience, and the Korean War had ended in a protracted truce. China had been assured that 'New Democracy' would last for some time, but by 1953 there was no obvious obstacle to the initiation of the 'transition to socialism'. The decision to begin China's First Five Year Plan was not, in itself, a decision to press on beyond New Democracy; but it was unlikely that in the effort to mobilize resources for the creation of a planned economy the control of agriculture, trade, and industry would be left in private hands.

The Plan was based on Soviet experience. Resources were centrally allocated, including intermediate goods. The task of managers was simply to deliver to sellers or to other producers the goods specified in the Plan. Production was controlled by setting targets not only for output but for all major inputs. The individual manager was responsible to the Ministry for the performance of his enterprise, under the general supervision of the Party branch.

In line with Soviet precedent, priority in investment was given to heavy industry, followed by light industries, with agriculture last. Within heavy industry the leading factor was steel production; the steel target was fixed first, and all other parts of the Plan set in relation to it—even the targets set for agriculture. In industry the aim, again in line with Soviet precedent, was to create urban, high-technology, capital-intensive, large-scale enterprises. No provision was made for local, small-scale labour-intensive forms of employment. On the contrary, such pre-modern enterprises were regarded with contempt and neglected when not actually suppressed, so that so far from the possibilities of non-farm employment in the rural areas being increased in the planned economy they were severely reduced.

Trade in grain was taken over by the State in 1953, and the farmers were obliged to deliver a specified quantity of grain or of an equivalent crop to State purchasing agencies at a fixed price, in order to ensure supplies at low prices to the growing urban industrial work-force.

The Plan would have been virtually impossible to achieve without large-scale Soviet assistance. Its backbone consisted of almost two hundred large turnkey factories provided on credit by the Soviet Union.

The Chinese, however, took a cautious view of their own Plan. Although begun in 1953, it was not until 1955 that its general contents were made public. And by 1956 some elements in the Chinese Communist Party, including Mao Zedong himself, were becoming critical of it. The First Plan proved, in fact, to be China's only exercise in totally central planning. Yet it was highly successful in its own terms. The main targets were met. The rate of industrial growth was very rapid, and the rate of growth of heavy industry remarkable.

Planned economic growth was accompanied by the socialization of agriculture and of private commerce and industry. The collectivization of agriculture, however, was no longer quite the shibboleth of Marxist socialism that it had been. Its performance in Russia had been disastrous and its achievements in East Europe little better. Its original architect, Stalin, died in 1953. Its supporters everywhere were on the defensive. In China it was accepted—publicly at least—as a desirable end, and from as early as 1951 experiments in co-operative forms of agricultural production were being encouraged in the wake of land reform. But most Party leaders set collectivization in a long perspective, and expected that China's agricultural production would remain individual for a long time. A careful long-term strategy had been worked out. The Chinese peasant would be led to collectivization in stages, and led to it by the demonstration effect of the increased production, incomes, and security which co-operation could bring.

The first stage was the mutual-aid team, in which groups of farmers co-operated in the busy seasons of agriculture. The teams were dissolved at the end of each season. The second stage was the primary co-operative. In this the farmers pooled their land and shared the proceeds; but each farmer retained title to his land, and in addition to remuneration for the labour he contributed was paid a dividend on the value of his land share. The third and final stage was the full collective, in which dividends on land were abolished.

The most interesting aspect of China's method, however, was the gradual development *within* each stage. The seasonal mutual-aid teams were encouraged to take up simple infrastructural developments between the busy seasons, and so to become continuously operating organizations. They were encouraged to acquire common property—equipment, a field reclaimed from wasteland, an orchard planted on a hillside—and so to move one stage nearer to collectivism. At the primary co-operative stage similar methods were used. At first the dividend on land might be the major part of the distribution of the proceeds; sometimes as much as 70 per cent to land and only 30 per cent to labour. As inputs of other resources grew, and especially as labour inputs were intensified, it would become acceptable to reduce the dividend on land. Eventually it would become irrelevant and the co-operative would thus become a full collective.

If this policy had been maintained over several years collectivization might have been achieved with no loss in absolute income to any peasant. This could have been achieved well within the average increase in production which actually took place. The process had scarcely begun, however, when it was overtaken by full collectivization abruptly imposed from above. This was the first occasion, but tragically not the last, on which the Chinese Communist Party, having created development policies of an intelligent, realistic, and liberal kind, have then thrown away the benefits by a reversion to crude and dictatorial means of implementation. The traditional political genius of the Chinese finds itself at loggerheads with the dogmatic demands of Marxism. In fact these sensible policies were created by Mao Zedong, the man who himself was to ride roughshod over them.

In the early 1950s there had seemed to be general agreement in China that unless and until industry was capable of providing agriculture with the means necessary for large-scale farming, there was little point in pushing the pace of collectivization. Larger farms are an advantage only in so far as they make possible economies of scale, and these can only be realized by mechanization. Most of China's leaders made this point publicly. Mao Zedong kept silent.

In 1955 a decision was taken to speed up the process of collectivization. The experience of the preceding year had suggested that greater control of the marketable surplus of agriculture was necessary. The resale of grain to villages which claimed to be deficient in food supplies hampered the flow of grain to the cities. False reporting of grain deficiencies was difficult to prevent among a hundred million peasant families who consumed most of their produce and kept their own stocks. A second problem was that an attempt in 1954 to increase the quotas for grain procurement had failed; its only result was to discourage the sowing of grain. Pressure therefore began to be put on the peasants to enter primary co-operatives. By the middle of the year, however, the opinion had gained ground that this pressurized collectivization was destroying peasant incentives and endangering food supplies; 35,000 newly formed agricultural co-operatives were therefore abolished.

At this point Mao Zedong took a hand. Since the beginning of the era of planned development he had intervened little and was apparently happy to accept the advice of the Soviet experts on economic matters, of which he was modest enough to confess his ignorance. Now, however, he stepped into the controversy with dramatic effect. He made a speech accusing those who favoured a slower pace of collectivization of acting like 'old women with bound feet', dragging behind the masses, the majority of whom he asserted favoured collective agriculture. This was in July 1955. He followed it up by convening a huge conference of co-operative activists from the grass roots, who delivered a succession of favourable reports on the movement. The opposition on the Central Committee was silenced.

At the end of the year the reports from this conference were published with an introduction and notes by Mao himself, under the title *The High Tide of Socialism in the Chinese Countryside*. Each report presented a community or an area which had solved at least one of the problems of co-operative organization. The reports provide a comprehensive view of the actual practical problems of the collectivization movement, although they give an optimistic view of the possiblity of solving them. The aim was not simply to justify Mao in having overreached and defeated the opposition. The reports also provided detailed instruction on how to succeed in collectivization. And they were intended, through Mao's own contributions to the volume, to provide a new perspective on the development of rural China. His opponents saw no point in collectivizing until China could provide agriculture with modern inputs. Mao's argument, however, was that China's peasants might never reach the stage at which they could afford modern inputs unless they first pooled their resources to increase production by the means to hand.

Mao's economics were not irrational. A glance across the water in 1955 would have shown that Taiwan's agricultural production was growing well on the basis of a similar package of simple improvements grouped around the more intensive use of labour, requiring little capital, without mechanization and with only marginal use of chemical fertilizers in the early stages.

Implied in the *High Tide* materials was a new strategy for Chinese rural development. The key article was a description of one co-operative—the Wang Guofan Co-operative—which provided an *a fortiori* argument for the rest. Wang was the leader of a mutual-aid team which included both poor peasants and 'middle peasants'. When he proposed that it should form itself into a primary co-operative, the middle peasants withdrew. The poor peasants could see no way in which, without the resources of their more prosperous neighbours, they could possibly succeed in collective production. Wang, however, persuaded them that it was possible. He proposed that they should spend the winter cutting brushwood on a hillside some miles away for sale as fuel, and that they should then save the proceeds for investment. The amount to be earned was trifling, the labour enormous; but Wang argued that if he and his fellow peasants did not earn from that, they would earn nothing. To put it in the language of economics, the labour spent cutting faggots had no opportunity cost. It was agreed and it was done. The earnings enabled them to make a start. The next winter they cut more brushwood, and again invested the proceeds, and by the second year their farming was doing well. By the third, we are told, the middle peasants were asking to join, as the incomes of the members of the 'paupers' co-operative' rose to exceed their own.

This story of Samuel Smiles self-help in the collective context was blazed throughout the nation. Its achievements may have been exaggerated but, true or false, as a myth it carried conviction. In fact, whatever the eventual success or failure of Mao's strategy in the nation as a whole, China thereafter could always show village communities whose self-reliant achievements, though less dramatic than those of Wang Guofan, were real and inspiring.

Analysis of the *High Tide* volumes shows the course of development which Mao hoped would follow. It is a spiral of growth and diversification. In its first year the co-operative, during the winter season, would carry out a plan of labour-intensive construction, most often to improve irrigation. This would involve almost no capital and would pay off in increased production in the following harvest. Savings out of the increased production could be invested in simple equipment, so that in the following winter a bigger job of construction could be undertaken. At the same time, almost any form of land development undertaken would result in the following year in an increase in the routine demand for farm labour. Very quickly, at least in the busy seasons (and especially where new irrigation construction made possible two crops a year in place of one), the first strain on labour resources would be felt, while the extra income gained from the improvements would provide the means to meet this strain by investment in the first labour-saving equipment. A spiral of growth would begin, which would eventually create both the demand and the means for the diversification of the local economy into simple industries serving agriculture, or producing consumer goods to satisfy the peasants' increasing purchasing power. Part of the profits of these industries could be fed into agriculture for its further improvement. As production became more varied and sophisticated, a demand would be created for better education and better cultural facilities. As co-operative enterprise paid off, willingness to accept higher forms of co-operation, a larger scale of operation, and more long-term investments would grow. As needs grew, the new demands of half a million rural communities would stimulate and guide the State sector of the economy, and create new economic relationships between State and local community. Mao saw no reason for this process to stop before, in its self-generation of capital, it had modernized agriculture, industrialized the rural areas, eliminated the 'three great differences', and created an effective socialist consciousness among the peasants.

The *High Tide* concept of rural development had another potential advantage, and one which undermined the argument of those who believed that rapid agricultural mechanization would create a problem of rural under-employment. The mechanization of agriculture would be undertaken gradually, as the increasing strain of labour scarcity came to be felt, with the profits of each stage of mechanization paying for the next.

In 1956, however, with the abrupt speeding up of collectivization, both the economic and the organizational strategies were cast aside. The *High Tide* material did not justify hasty collectivization, and most certainly it did not justify the immediate establishment of full collectives. In fact it showed clearly the very special circumstances in which a few full collectives had been successfully established before 1956. Some were in areas where horticulture based on the intensive use of skilled labour reduced the perceived value of the land as opposed to the value of labour, to the point where the abolition of the dividend on land was acceptable to the peasants. Others were in communities exceptional for equality of land ownership, making the payment of a dividend to land unnecessary.

Hasty collectivization immediately brought trouble, but the previous gradualist policies had in most places been implemented for long enough to take some of the sting out of the change. The post-socialization troubles of the Chinese countryside were insignificant compared with those experienced by the Soviet Union. Perhaps what grieved China's more prosperous peasants more than collectivization itself was the attempt which followed hard on its heels to 'equalize the resources' of the brigades into which the collective farm was divided. Land, beasts, and tools were to be redistributed to ensure that each brigade had the same endowment. This was the first, but not the last, occasion on which attempts were made to redress the historic economic differences between adjacent villages, and then as later it produced stubborn resistance from the more prosperous peasants, stubbornly supported by the local Party branch. 'Worse than land reform was for the landlords,' the peasants declared. The policy was abandoned, to be revived, however, in a different form in 1958 in the communes.

Ten Great Relationships and a Hundred Flowers, 1956

At this point a new factor entered China's situation. On 20 February 1956, Khrushchev condemned Stalin at the Twentieth Congress of the Soviet Communist Party. The morale of the world's communist parties was shattered. China was least affected, except perhaps for Yugoslavia. Both these countries had made their own revolutions. Their leaders were former nationalist partisans, with sources of political strength outside the Party apparatus. Tito in Yugoslavia had already created his own national road to socialism. Mao Zedong was now free to do the same.

The admiration of Mao and his fellow leaders for Stalin was—to say the least—qualified. Nevertheless, he had been presented to the Chinese people as the great symbol of communist endeavour, and China had not been informed beforehand that Khrushchev's ideological mushroom cloud was about to fill the skies of the communist world. From the beginning therefore the Chinese publicly stated their disagreement, insisting that Stalin's virtues outweighed his faults, and that he was still a great socialist hero though a flawed one. Mao could hardly have guessed that thirty years later his colleagues would use the same formula to save their faces again by applying it to Mao himself.

The more important problem, however, was what to put in place of Stalinism. The Political Bureau met for three months. The problem was considered in the light of the successes and failures of China's Stalinist Five Year Plan, now approaching its end. Mao summed up his sense of the discussions in a draft entitled *On the Ten Great Relationships*. It was only officially released after his death, but the ideas it expressed were soon incorporated in articles in the newspapers. He was later to say that it was his first attempt to formulate the difference of approach to socialist development between the Soviet Union and China.

In the *Ten Great Relationships* Mao summed up the Political Bureau's discussions under ten headings, each stating a fundamental relationship in need of adjustment:

1. Heavy industry on the one hand and light industry and agriculture on the other.
2. Industry in the coastal regions and industry in the interior.
3. Economic construction and defence construction.
4. The State, the units of production and the producers.
5. Central and local authorities.

6. The Han nationality and the minority nationalities.

7. Party and non-Party.

8. Revolution and counter-revolution.

9. Right and wrong.

10. China and other countries.

'In the Soviet Union,' Mao began, 'certain defects and errors that occurred in the course of their building socialism have lately come to light. Do you want to follow the detours they have made?' He went on to criticize the Soviet Union for neglecting agriculture in favour of heavy industry, pointing to its 'prolonged failure ... to reach the highest pre-October Revolution level in grain output' as the consequence. He accused the Soviet Union of having failed to reconcile the interests of the State with those of economic enterprises and collectives and with those of the individual, and of emphasizing only the demands of the State. He condemned Soviet overcentralization, which deprived enterprises and lower administrative levels of all initiative. He asserted that the system of squeezing the peasants to accumulate capital for industrial development was counter-productive—it was 'draining the pond to catch the fish'. 'What kind of logic is that?' he asked. He asserted that the relation between Russia and her non-Russian minority peoples was 'very abnormal'. And he accused the Russians of showing towards China all the 'arrogance and conceit' of an imperialist power.

In economic policy, Mao rejected the zero-sum-game assumptions of Russian planning. His proposals are a series of paradoxes. If you sincerely want to develop heavy industry, invest in agriculture and light industry. If you sincerely want strong defence industries, invest in the economy generally. If you sincerely want to develop industries in the rural interior of China, continue to develop the existing coastal industries as the seed-bed of high technology and advanced management skills. If you sincerely want central direction to be effective, decentralize to the enterprises and the localities. The speech is an assertion of the possibility of dynamic relationships, the substitution of multiplication sums for subtraction sums.

The most fundamental change from Soviet economic orthodoxy lay in the implication that the accumulation of capital depends in the last analysis, in Chinese conditions at least, on the development of agriculture. It is the increasing purchasing power of the peasant majority, and the response to that increased purchasing power by the consumer goods industries, which create the conditions for the rapid development of heavy industry. The historical basis of Marxist theory is the assertion that the original industrial revolution in Britain was made possible by 'primitive capital accumulation' and that capitalist industry then grew by further accumulation of capital at the expense of the consumption of the people. The Russian Marxists, coming to power in an undeveloped country, asserted—explicitly on the basis of this historical analysis—that the socialist regime would have to conduct the same process of forced saving. Hence Preobrazhensky's 'objective feudalism' and Stalin's ruthless exploitation of the peasants. But Marx's theory had no basis in historical fact. Nor had it a basis in economic logic: capital cannot be accumulated continuously unless real purchasing power continuously increases as innovation cuts the cost of production. And in this process the producers' goods industries are not primary; they are a secondary response to rising demand for consumer goods. Mao Zedong was neither an economist nor a historian; but he had the genius to rise above the distorted conventional wisdom of orthodox communism and restore the common-sense view that the best way to make people better off is to make them better off, not to make them worse off.

As far as the wider political issues were concerned, Mao proposed the decentralization of decision-making: 'Centralisation must be enforced where it is possible and necessary; otherwise it should not be imposed at all.' While insisting that the regime must retain the right to execute saboteurs and spies, he nevertheless condemned execution as a normal means of dealing with counter-revolution: 'If one such criminal is executed, a second and third will be compared to him in their crimes, and then many heads will begin to roll . . . If you cut a head off by mistake, there is no way to rectify the mistake . . . killing counter-revolutionaries . . . will only earn you the reputation of killing captives, and killing captives has always given one a bad name.' Ninety out of one hundred counter-revolutionaries should simply be sent down to the agricultural co-operatives to work under public supervision. In general, the policy should be one of 'few arrests and no executions'.

Mao emphasized again his view that people who made mistakes should not be debarred from further part in the revolution, but criticized, encouraged to reform, and allowed to continue to contribute. While he insisted that 'a clear distinction must be drawn between right and wrong, for inner-Party controversies over principle are a reflection inside the Party of the class struggle in society, and no equivocation is to be tolerated', at the same time he poured scorn on those who found an issue of principle in everything.

The *Ten Great Relationships* expressed Mao's conclusions from the Party's first considered reaction to Khrushchev's speech. These conclusions proved to be only the first step in a journey which was to take him far away from the soviet model, and to embroil him in bitter conflict with his fellow leaders.

The first division appeared very soon, and concerned the question of intellectual and political liberalization. Zhou Enlai had promised that policy towards intellectuals would be eased. In May 1956, following the *Ten Great Relationships*, Lu Dingyi, head of the propaganda department of the Central Committee, expressed this more liberal view by quoting the Chinese classical aphorism, 'Let the hundred flowers bloom and the hundred schools contend', stressing that variety (within limits) is creative. At the National People's

Congress a month later, Mao pressed for the widest possible interpretation of this offered freedom, but the reluctance of his fellow leaders to accept it was evident, while few intellectuals dared to take up the offer.

In September, however, the communist world received a further shock, from the Hungarian uprising. Mao condemned the Nagy regime for its attempt to leave the communist bloc, but at the same time emphasized that the opposition to Rakosi had been justifed by his excessive authoritarianism.

China was then suffering from similar problems—strikes, withdrawals from the new agricultural collectives, and other forms of protest—though on a scale insignificant as compared to similar events in eastern Europe. Mao, following out his own diagnosis of the Hungarian situation, began to press for freedom of criticism in China. The Hundred Flowers policy had been announced but not really implemented. At the same time a new rectification movement was being prepared within the Party. Mao sought to combine the two, to create a movement in which the Party would be rectified by criticism from the non-Party public.

In February 1957 he launched his movement with a speech 'On the Correct Handling of Contradictions among the People'. It was made not to a Party meeting but to a meeting of the Supreme State Conference. It was an attempt to appeal to society against the Party. Mao admitted that 90 per cent of the Party opposed the idea of being forced to submit to public criticism, Gradually the opposition was worn down, however. In April Liu Shaoqi accepted the hundred flowers rectification, but stated that public criticism should be like 'a gentle breeze and fine rain'.

'On the Correct Handling of Contradictions among the People' was not published then, and we do not have the original version. It was published only when freedom of criticism had been brought to an end, and then only in an edited version; but even this doctored version is significant. Mao argued that conflicts (contradictions) must inevitably continue under socialism, even when class conflict itself has ceased. He condemned the Soviet insistence that socialist society is conflict-free as a view which merely provided an excuse for outlawing anyone who offered opposition. He distinguished between class conflicts which are 'antagonistic contradictions' and can only be resolved by force, and contradictions 'among the people' which could, and should only, be solved by discussion and education. 'The people' included all who accepted the revolution. He also argued that it is precisely these contradictions within socialist society which propel it forward. Conflict is the motor of progress. Among these contradictions, he argued, are conflicts between the people and the socialist State. In particular there is conflict between the State and the collectives, and between the collectives and their individual members.

The speech was followed by a short-lived period of free criticism. Some have seen in this an indication of Mao's liberality. Others have seen in it only a sinister excuse to coax the opposition out into the open in order to destroy it.

The truth is rather different. In the speeches in which Mao urged his policy on his fellow leaders he several times used the metaphor of immunization against disease. This is the clue to his motives. He believed that in Hungary and elsewhere in the communist world the discontent which flared up in 1956 was justified by the repressive policies of the preceding years. At the same time, he believed that elements hostile to socialism had taken advantage of the situation. He decided that a campaign in which the Chinese public were encouraged to criticize the Party would enable the regime to respond to popular discontent and restore relations with 'the masses'. At the same time, if complete freedom was allowed, hostile elements would soon be isolated. The main point was not to secure the suppression of those who were hostile, but to secure a renewed and strengthened consensus. In this way, to return to his metaphor, China would be innoculated with a benign form of the Hungarian distemper, and so saved from the real disease.

The fever of criticism which soon raged was perhaps some degrees higher than Mao Zedong had anticipated. His fellow leaders reacted by demanding that the movement be brought immediately to an end. Mao insisted that freedom of discussion can do good, and that even violent protest may have good consequences. He expressed regret that relatively few workers in Shanghai had protested; if there had been ten times as many, 'that would have been the end of bureaucracy'. We find him defending the large numbers of students from all over China who had assembled in Beijing to express their grievances (a foretaste of the Cultural Revolution). We find him justifying the Muslims in north-west China who had protested at the interference of Communist cadres in the slaughter of meat: 'they beat up a few cadres, and that solved the problem.' He exhorted his fellow Communists to 'toughen their scalps' and endure public criticism whether it was just or unjust.

He lost the argument. Not only was the movement abruptly brought to an end but the critics were dismissed from their posts and sent into rural exile or worse. That Mao had intended them to be criticized severely in their turn is certain; that he intended their punishment is improbable, for at this point he insisted on the distinction between the man and his political beliefs, emphasized his continued personal friendship for some of those under attack, and had himself photographed in Shanghai dining with a group of 'rightists'.

Yet within two years it was his fellow leaders who pressed for the rehabilitation of the intellectuals they had condemned and Mao Zedong who resisted. In between came the Great Leap Forward, which profoundly changed the whole pattern of political relationships in China.

15

The Great Leap Forward

Economic problems, 1956–1958

Free criticism during the Hundred Flowers period had culminated in demands for the fulfilment of the democratic rights offered in the 1954 constitution, but no Chinese leader was willing to interpret these rights as offering anything analogous to Western Democracy. Mao went further in this direction in 1957 in permitting criticism, approving protest, emphasizing the distinction between Party and State, and defending the right to strike even though the constitution did not legalize strikes. Yet even Mao made a distinction between democratic rights within a system of one-party control and 'bourgeois democracy'. The published version of 'On the Correct Handling of Contradictions among the People' laid down six criteria as the limits of legitimate opposition. They meant that no challenge to the supreme authority of the Party could be permitted.

Nevertheless, criticisms had shown how widespread was opposition to the authoritarian State–Party bureaucracy built up since 1949. Mao and some other members of the Chinese Communist Party were as sympathetic to this hostility towards authoritarian bureaucracy as they were opposed to a Western democratic cure for it. The Stalinist type of bureaucracy—based on ministerial chains of command with highly specialized functions, was quite at variance with Chinese tradition. Chinese bureaucracy had been based on general moral control of a largely self-governing population. It was also at variance with the experience of the Chinese Communist Party in guerrilla conditions in which mass mobilization had been more appropriate than administrative fiat. As a consequence, when the Party came to consider the other, economic, aspect of past experience of centralized control, it was against this political background of the manifest unpopularity of centralized bureaucracy.

There was agreement that the rate of central accumulation and investment had been too high; that heavy industry had been given too great a priority; and that planning had been over-centralized. There was another perplexing problem: the population census of 1953, the first modern census which any Chinese government had undertaken, had shown that the population of mainland China, so far from numbering 450 million as widely accepted estimates had suggested, was actually 582 million; it was therefore obvious that some simple means, requiring a minimum of capital, must urgently be found to provide new forms of employment, especially in the countryside. Here Mao's spiral of rural growth and diversification could prove relevant. It was agreed at the same time that greater funds for central investment could not be raised by increasing the amount of grain compulsorily purchased from the peasants, as the failure of the attempt in 1955 had clearly shown.

There were also disagreements. Recent changes of policy in the Soviet Union, initiated by Khrushchev, had given sanction to a degree of decentralization of economic management. In China decentralization was generally accepted; but the word proved to mean different things to different people. To the more orthodox planners it meant that more power should be given to the enterprise managers. To the Maoists it meant that increased power should go to the communities; local governments, agricultural collectives, and the work-force (not the managers) of industrial enterprises.

These disagreements were revealed in contradictory policy statements at the end of 1957. On 14 September the Central Committee issued a cautious directive expressing the conclusions of a national conference on rural work. It confirmed the policy of cutting down the size of collective farms and promised that there would be no further changes for ten years. It made no reference to Mao's own more radical Twelve Year Plan for Agriculture, already accepted by the Party 'in principle'.

Within a few days, at the third plenum of the Eighth Central Committee the conservative view was reversed. Mao also secured agreement on this occasion for the assertion (against a previous decision of the Eighth Session of the Communist Party Congress) that the principal contradiction in Chinese society was that between 'the people and the bourgeoisie'. This assertion would justify further changes towards the consolidation of the socialist system, and Mao's Twelve Year Plan for agriculture was readopted at the same time.

One section of the Party was content simply to reduce the rate of accumulation, give more autonomy to industrial managers, relax the intensity of collectivism in agriculture, and modify the proportions of sectoral investment. The left wing, however, was reluctant to accept what they regarded as merely negative policies. Mao was searching for an alternative strategy which would incorporate his new sense of dynamic relationships. With his eloquent amanuensis Chen Boda at his elbow, he cast back to China's wartime experience for a solution.

Mao and Chen Boda actually looked back to the industrial co-operatives of the Border Regions decade, although this was never openly acknowledged. These rural co-operatives used intermediate technologies and little capital. They were led by young patriotic technologists who had escaped from the Japanese-controlled industrial cities, who accepted the way of life of the peasants among whom they worked, and who took no extra wages. The management of the co-operatives was democratic, sometimes extravagantly so; in some, no decision could be taken without unanimity; in others, workers acted in rotation as officers of the day and there was no formal manager. Each factory was independent and responsible for its own profits and losses, under the general supervision of Indusco, the national organization.

Their economic characteristics were relevant to development in a poor peasant country. A well-run co-operative could turn its small capital over in two or three years, pay back its loans, and begin to modernize by ploughing back profits. Gestation periods were nearly nil. In the undeveloped conditions of rural China, the co-operative usually had to diversify its production, having to create for itself many of the complementarities which would have existed in a more developed economy, and this tendency to diversify was further stimulated by the great variety of urgent uses to which its new, semi-mechanized productive capacity could be put. Beginning with the production of army uniforms, simple medical supplies, and simple contributions to weaponry, they moved forward into consumer goods and back into the production of raw materials.

From these aspects of the Indusco firms Mao drew two conclusions: that in the short term small firms using appropriate technologies could accumulate capital more rapidly than large, and contribute immediately to increasing wealth, employment, and incomes; and that freedom to widen into complementary operations was necessary to the success of rural development; 'simultaneous development' was the key.

It was virtually impossible for these Indusco firms to operate simply as production enterprises. In the appalling health conditions of the Chinese hinterland the factory clinic was a necessity. The education of the mainly peasant membership of the co-operative was also necessary. And the clinic and the school could not be closed to the rest of the community. In this way the Indusco factories rapidly became communities rather than enterprises; and sometimes, at their most successful, they absorbed the entire population and resources of a whole village or even of several adjoining villages.

In this example Mao found the seeds of co-operative economic communities, democratically organized, providing their own education and welfare services, capable of rapid growth, diversification, and modernization, self-governing but assisted by educated volunteers from the cities who humbly took their place among the other co-operative members. Nor was it irrelevant in 1958 that the Indusco co-operatives had been able to produce weapons to arm the local guerrilla forces.

The American missionary whose efforts to create self-help communities had contributed to the establishment of Indusco had quoted Kropotkin on mutual aid as one of the sources of his ideas. Mao, like the rest of his generation, had also read the works of that gentle anarchist. He had also read Kirkup's description of Robert Owen's planned socialist communities.

Indusco seemed to have proved for Mao the practicality of Kropotkin and Owen, while in the revolutionary implications of these democratic co-operatives and in their close association with the 'People's War' against Japan, there was more than a hint of analogy with the Paris Commune. More immediately, the Indusco model might serve to create employment in the countryside; to help to maintain a high rate of accumulation and investment not through central monopolization of resources but locally and through the enthusiasm of local communities, and for nil-gestation projects which could immediately add both to consumption and to savings. Part of these savings could be fed back into the gradual transformation of agriculture, and rising agricultural production and incomes would in turn feed community industry. Mao's spiral of rural development had found its incarnation. This was the origin of the Great Leap Forward and of the communes.

The new movement, launched in late 1957, was preceded by a campaign designed to ensure that it was democratically conducted. Democratic persuasion and organization formed the major premise; only free commitment could ensure success in this process of grass-roots development. Every kind of institution in China was made to go on record with solemn promises to lead democratically, to listen to criticism, to be patient with opposition, and to create policy out of the aspirations of the people themselves. The new economic strategy was to be the supreme mass-line exercise.

Ironically, all the problems which in the event occurred and which were to bring the Great Leap to disaster, were anticipated. Once more was to be seen the conflict between intelligent humanistic Chinese planning and crude, hasty, ruthless implementation.

The Great Leap Forward consisted of three related movements. The first was a vast campaign of labour-intensive farmland construction for defence against flood and drought. The second was a campaign to develop local industry in the ownership of the collectives. The third was to develop the modern sector at the provincial level to ensure that each province would have, at the disposal of local development, a backbone of basic industries, with whose assistance and guidance the counties would be able in turn to create their own industrial minicomplexes to support industries lower down.

In economic terms the Great Leap was not irrational. It represented in a Chinese form the widespread contemporary reaction against planning principles which had been current throughout the world in the late forties and fifties, a reaction which by 1958 was becoming the conventional wisdom of development specialists throughout the world. The rejection of the idea of giving false priority to heavy industry; the acceptance of the necessity of creating labour-intensive industries in the rural areas; the high hopes entertained of rural community development; the belief that popular participation in the process of development was both socially and economically necessary; the appreciation of the fact that surplus rural labour was actually a resource which could be used to create new rural infrastructure; and finally the growing awareness that increased agricultural production and increased peasant incomes were the true key to rapid growth; all these ideas were by 1958 widely current.

Built into Great Leap policy was another idea which was then becoming familiar throughout the world: the concept of deliberately unbalanced growth. The central planners normally aimed at a balance in which the demand for and supply of all inputs would be carefully equalized. Mao rejected this as too static. In an economic parallel to his assertion that political conflict was the stimulus of progress, he now affirmed that it was economic imbalances which drove the economy forward. For this reason in 1958 planning was in abeyance; every unit sought to maximize production; the resultant imbalances, it was asserted, would stimulate lagging sectors which in turn would take the lead and so create new fruitful imbalances.

With such excellent theory behind it, and with the successful precedent of the wartime Indusco co-operatives to provide a tried form of practice, it might seem surprising that the Great Leap failed so dramatically. The answer is to be found not in its economics but in its politics.

The Chinese communes

The fundamental idea of the Leap was that the local communities should take the initiative in self-development. The role of the Party was to induce the process by democratic methods. The duty of the State was to respond by providing the means: credit, equipment, expertise. The question was, at what level of local society would the co-ordination take place. The average village was too small a unit for planning and resource mobilization. For overall local planning the obvious level was the *xian* (county) administration which still remained, as it had been in imperial China, the point at which state and local society met. The *xian* Party committee became the headquarters for mass mobilization. The populations of China's two thousand *xian*, however, now averaged between three and four hundred thousand people, and this was far too large for the actual management of most of the new enterprises, while on the other hand the existing collective farms were too small for the effective mobilization of resources. In the course of great water conservancy campaigns in the winter of 1957–8, and then more urgently in certain areas threatened with floods in the summer, some of the collectives began to combine to form larger units. On one such *ad hoc* federation of collectives in Henan it was decided that the constituent farms should be combined together in a single unit of account and distribution. This announced itself as China's first commune. It was named the Sputnik Commune. The word 'commune' was chosen with care. The Chinese word is a twentieth-century neologism, created specifically to refer to the Paris Commune: the 'Bali Gongshe'. The implications of the choice of this word to describe China's new social institutions are obvious. It had always been a part of Marxist belief that the proletariat on achieving power would not take over the bourgeois state but replace it with popular institutions, the adumbration of which Marx and Engels had perceived in Paris in 1870. The Chinese choice of the word commune shows that the institution was Mao's proposed solution to the problem of State bureaucratism in China, revealed so forcefully in the Hundred Flowers movement a year before.

An immense emphasis on the popular militia as an essential part of the commune (for some months the commune militia units were actually left independent of the command of the PLA) suggests that what Mao had in mind was indeed the dissolution of the bourgeois state. The name 'Sputnik' was perhaps significant in this respect. The Soviet Union, by launching the first satellite, had just demonstrated its military superiority: 'The East wind prevails over the West wind,' said Mao. Under the protection of Soviet superiority in ballistic missiles, the State under socialism could now perhaps begin to wither a little.

The first task of each new commune was to carry through the programme of the Great Leap. It was to be a collective, owned by its members and making its own economic decisions. It was, however, more than an economic enterprise; when the process of communization was complete, the *xiang* (parish) and the commune became one, so that the commune inherited the political functions of the *xiang*, to become an autonomous social and political unit.

This was the theory, but in practice the assumption of political responsibilities by the commune compromised its position as an autonomous economic enterprise; it inevitably became simply a new, lower level of the State–Party hierarchy, carrying out orders from above. Its leaders were paid by the State and were responsible to the State, not to the commune members. The commune did not function as an autonomous community. It became a means to thrust the power of the State directly into the village for the first time in Chinese history.

A controversy soon began, in fact, as to whether the communes should be considered to be collective or State organs. Many on the far left believed it possible to move on immediately from collective ownership to full national ownership, under which China's peasants would be State wage-earners. This was dismissed by Mao as impractical; it would oblige the State to pay all China's peasants a national wage, regardless of the size of the harvest. So the communes would have to be responsible for their own incomes, yet at the same time their operations were dictated by the higher levels of State and Party. It is a familiar enough situation in communist countries, but was thrown into relief in China in 1958 because it so sharply contradicted the whole theory of development through community initiative on which the Leap was theoretically based.

The new system was also compromised by the attempt to use the resources of more prosperous villages to improve the lot of the poorer, by including both in the same unit of ownership and distribution. In this, the commune system sought to do what had been tried within the original collectives through the attempt to equalize the assets of the constituent brigades. It had failed then in the face of peasant resistance, and *a fortiori* it could be expected to fail again with communes which took in not just a dozen brigades but a dozen collectives. At the beginning, this scale was not intended. There were to be three levels of commune organization: the production team of thirty or forty families which would remain the unit of ownership and distribution in farming; the brigade which would assume the ownership and operation of small-scale industrial production and of agricultural machinery; and the commune which would assume the ownership of all-the-year-round industries and the management of tasks requiring a large scale, such as water conservancy construction. It was expected that as farming was mechanized and as the local economy was diversified the level of ownership of all assets would be raised to brigade, and eventually to commune level; but this was to be a gradual process. Predictably, this gradualism was soon overtaken by the pace of coercive mobilization; within weeks the original concept had been forgotten and the commune had become a single huge farm. The familiar gigantism of Stalinist socialism had thus, paradoxically, reasserted itself.

In the Great Leap process of economic development, as in the commune organization, gradualism soon disappeared. Mao's rural spiral had been conceived as operating from harvest to harvest; to attempt to push its speed beyond that was to break the organic connection between agriculture and local industry. It was conceived as a process which generated its own resources in a circular flow that included increasing purchasing power; it came to depend instead on the massive withdrawal of resources from consumption for huge local investments in grandiose, often duplicated, projects of uncertain value, forced on the peasant communities by local authorities which were themselves under irresistible political pressure from higher levels. It was supposed to operate by gradually and rationally increasing labour productivity in order to free labour for continued diversification; instead, it worked by increasing the hours and the intensity of work to intolerable levels.

China's Communist cadres did in fact the only thing they knew how to do: they took the system of authoritarian allocation of resources, created in the First Five Year Plan, and thrust it down into the grass roots. The results were politically intolerable and economically disastrous.

The failure of the Leap, 1958–1960

Yet in the summer of 1958 one would not have said so. At that point the results were astonishing and the enthusiasm overwhelming. Indeed, part of the explanation of the failure of the Leap lies precisely in its early success, which created a state of euphoria in which everything seemed possible. Production targets, at first moderate, were increased and increased again as dramatic reports of local successes were made the basis of universal demands. Local cadres were forced into promises they could only hope to fulfil by coercion. they responded to pressure from above with false claims of success, which misled even the Political Bureau, and committed the cadres and their community to impossible tasks. All this was foreseen, but none of it was prevented.

Euphoria also created problems on another dimension. Many radicals convinced themselves that the Leap was not only an economic leap, but a bound from socialism to communism, from 'to each according to his work' to 'to each according to his needs'. The policy of the free supply system, by which the greater part of the earnings of the commune member was in the form of a free ration of food and other necessities, given without reference to his performance at work, suggested this possibility. The creation of communal mess halls, through which much of this ration was provided, increased these hopes, as well as hopes that the 'bourgeois family' was about to disappear. The result was to increase the influence of those who favoured extreme egalitarianism. Private plots were abolished and the very fruit trees in the cottage courtyard taken into communal ownership.

Even in March 1958, however, when the euphoria was at its height, the first notes of alarm were being sounded. At the Chengdu Conference (March 1958) it was agreed that the Leap must be conducted with more circumspection; Liu Shaoqi drew apart a little from Mao in his stronger insistence on caution. Pregnant with future trouble was the cool reception given at Chengdu to the proposal by Mao that China's State-owned tractors should be handed over to the communes; this was to become one of the ignition points of the Cultural Revolution. The modest reassertion of right-wing influence, however, did not prevent the promotion of three left-wing figures to positions of greater power, when Marshal Lin Biao was made vice-chairman of the Party, and Tan Zhenlin, Minister of Agriculture, and Ke Qingshi, First Secretary of Shanghai, joined the Political Bureau.

More cautious policies might have been reasserted had it not been for the alarming deterioration in China's security which took place at this point. The United States decided to provide Taiwan with modern missiles. This revived the fear of war with the Nationalist regime. At the same time, Khrushchev had begun to make it plain that he would take advantage of Russia's new ballistic superiority not to redouble pressure on the West, but to reduce it. China, faced with the possibility of American-supported invasion from Taiwan, was not interested in *détente* but in an assurance of support from her Russian ally. The assurance offered proved to be rather more generous than China was willing to accept; it would have meant in effect Soviet control of China's airspace and of her coastal waters. China evaded this bear-hug, but remained unsure of

Soviet intentions. To test them, she began to shell the Nationalist positions on Quemoy and Matsu islands, close to the Fujian coast. The United States responded by reasserting support of the Taiwan government; but there was no matching response from Russia. Only when the crisis was safely over did Khrushchev affirm that an attack on China would be regarded as an attack on the Soviet Union.

At this point the commune militia was again expanded, with the aim of creating an 'armed people'. Within this new institutional context, with its obvious emphasis on a guerrilla defence, the Great Leap production drive again accelerated. The pace remained frantic until the end of the year.

A further plenum of the Central Committee met in Wuhan on 28 November. Mao admitted that the movement had shown serious shortcomings, and accepted important changes, including a partial restoration of hierarchical control, the abolition of the free supply system, and the partial revival of free markets. He then announced his retirement as chairman of the Republic.

Mao emphatically accepted responsibility for some of the worst mistakes of Great Leap policy, and particularly for the attempt to spread the manufacture of iron and steel to the villages by the use of small-scale blast furnaces. This policy was condemned then, and has been ever since, as completely irrational. Ironically, in the early 1980s when the rapid increase in peasant purchasing power caused great scarcities of goods in the countryside, the 'back-yard blast furnace' was revived in the hands of individual peasant enterpreneurs, in spite of strenuous discouragement by the Government, and proved highly profitable. It was not so, however, in the collective context of 1958.

To do Mao Zedong justice, he was apparently among the first to recognize where and how the Great Leap had gone wrong. He condemned the arbitrary requisition of peasant resources, reminding his fellow leaders that even the property of China's capitalists had not been confiscated without compensation, asserted that the requisitions were 'sheer banditry', and supported the resistance of the peasants as 'right and proper'. Having acknowledged his personal responsibility Mao asked that his self-criticism should be circulated throughout the Party, but this was never done.

Although no longer Chairman of the Republic Mao remained Chairman of the Party. He fought back in an effort to prevent the Leap being altogether brought to an end. He won no ground. His cause was saved, however, by Khrushchev. The Soviet leader had made his distaste for the Leap and the communes very plain, and done so with offensive crudity. Within China, opposition to Mao's policies was gathering round Marshal Peng Dehuai. Peng, as China's Minister of Defence, went abroad to meet Khrushchev to discuss military co-operation. He returned in time to attend the enlarged meeting of the Political Bureau at Lushan on 21 July 1959. On 14 July he condemned the Great Leap and the communes as 'petit-bourgeois fanaticism'. On 18 July Khrushchev delivered a speech in which he echoed Peng's condemnation. It was difficult to resist the conclusion that Khrushchev and Peng were acting in collusion. Peng's position was undermined by this suspicion; a majority of the Political Bureau were as disillusioned with the Leap as Peng himself, and the failure of the majority to support him can only have been due to resentment at his apparent willingness to be the instrument of Soviet pressure. The conflict was made sharper by the fact that Peng Dehuai was identified with belief in the virtues of a conventional, as opposed to a guerrilla, defence. Conventional defence would inevitably depend on Soviet assistance; Khrushchev's speech had implied that the price of such assistance would be a humiliating retreat from the communes; and Peng was by implication, ready to pay that price. He was dismissed. Lin Biao replaced him as Minister of Defence and Luo Ruiqing became Chief of Staff.

The Leap was then revived, but not for long. The 1958 harvests had been splendid, but the summer harvest of 1959 was poor, and the harvests of 1960 were disastrous. One-third of China's arable was stricken with drought and another sixth was flooded. Grain production, which had been about 185 million tonnes in 1957 and perhaps 200 million in the Leap harvests of 1958, sank to 170 million in 1959 and to 160 million in 1960. There has been a deep division of opinion, in China as well as in the West, as to how much of this disaster was due to bad weather and how much to the dislocations caused by the Great Leap and the communes. Liu Shaoqi affirmed that it was due 70 per cent to 'man-made disaster'. The left denied this. It is difficult to know. The two policies which had the most severe effects on the production incentives of the peasants—the free supply system, and the combination of prosperous and poor villages in the single commune unit of distribution—had already been rectified. But the indiscriminate creation of non-farm enterprises continued to stretch the rural labour force to such an extent that it could not easily be redeployed to deal with natural disasters. There is also evidence that decentralization to the new communes had made it more difficult to secure the movement of grain from surplus to deficit areas.

It was the acute scarcity of food which brought the Leap to an end. The growing of industrial crops was relinquished in favour of food production, and light industry was suffered to run down. Private plots were restored: more than this, a blind eye was turned on private land reclamation and on local revivals of independent family farming. Collective agriculture was in danger of collapse.

At this juncture, in August 1960, Khrushchev withdrew all Russian aid, technicians, and blueprints from China, in revenge for Chinese hostility to his policy of *détente*. This brought to an abrupt halt virtually the whole development of new industries and the introduction of new technology. It was a crippling blow, delivered at the worst possible time.

The harvests of 1961 were little better. Only in 1962 was there a full recovery. It has been suggested in China that twenty million people died as a result of the agricultural disasters of these three bad years. If that is so, it was one of the greatest recorded famines in history. The figure is the result of indirect inferences drawn from the movement of China's population figure, and cannot be taken literally. But there is no doubt that the number of deaths from famine and from the results of malnutrition were at least of the order associated with the great famines of the past.

None the less, the Great Leap was not from the long-term point of view a complete failure. The simple methods of labour-intensive construction of flood control and irrigation works developed out of the winter campaigns of 1957–8 and subsequent years, although they proved inadequate then, have since contributed to the elimination of serious famine in China.

The Leap also established as part of Chinese socialism the ideas of community development, of local appropriate-technology enterprise, and of labour-intensive agricultural construction assisted by the profits of local, collectively owned enterprise. It broke the dominance of the Russian, urbanized, heavy-industry model, and made room for a concept of economic growth based on the increasing purchasing power of peasant communities able to improve their own productivity by diversified development. However, although these positive aspects of Maoist strategy were separable from the negative aspects more immediately obvious—the excessive egalitarianism, the extreme collectivism, the pressurized mobilization of people and resources—it would be too much to expect the Chinese people, in a situation in which these new policies had collapsed in hunger and unemployment, to make such distinctions. The majority, from the Political Bureau to the grass roots, condemned the whole experience of 1958–60 in one judgement: 'Never again!' Yet in the end the positive aspects were to be reasserted, and by Mao's opponents.

As a result of the disasters the configuration of politics in China had suffered a great change. The anti-rightist campaign had profoundly shocked China's intellectuals, as well as millions more who had agreed with the criticisms made of the Party in the 1957 rectification. Mao's role in defending the critics was not known; he was indeed regarded as personally responsible for their persecution. After the Great Leap, many intellectuals, already alienated from Mao, joined the right-wing majority of the Party in condemning him as responsible for the disasters of the Leap. From Mao's point of view the intellectuals had thus made common cause with the bureaucrats he had sought to put under control. The right wing now attempted to rehabilitate those condemned in the anti-rightist campaign, while Mao, their former defender, opposed this.

Mao, however, now had little power. His colleagues preferred to assume that his retirement was total. Many intellectuals, including many who were members of the Party, began to create a literature of criticism focused on the Leap and on Mao himself. The criticism was oblique, expressed in parables and poems. China's senior poet and journalist Deng To produced a 'notes and queries' column in the Beijing *Evening News,* each brief article ostensibly on some antiquarian triviality, but each hiding a political barb. Deng To had many imitators. Historical dramas also become a fashion, each one again with a political point; usually the hero of the play was one of the figures of the past who had stood up to the Emperor and given him unwelcome counsel. With Wu Han's play *The Dismissal of Hai Rui,* it became obvious that the political aim of these authors was to defend the dismissed Peng Dehuai.

The right were virtually in complete control. They had won the benevolent neutrality, if not the support, of Liu Shaoqi, Mao's successor as Chairman of the Republic. Under his aegis new economic policies were attempted, whose precedents were to be found in the reforms in Eastern Europe, especially in Hungary.

These policies were successful. The economy made a remarkable recovery in 1962. How far this was due to the new policies and how far simply to the return of normal weather is difficult to determine. The left in China were not impressed. They saw grave danger in the relaxation of control, especially over collective farming. These fears were not entirely the result of an attachment to ideological aims and of an indifference to economic growth. Communist China's greatest achievement, after all, had been to create a system which ensured the satisfaction of the basic needs of virtually the whole population. This the left now felt to be at risk. Moreover, as our analysis of the Leap has shown, the left were by no means indifferent to economic growth; their theory was that in the conditions of rural China a system which maximized local *collective* incentives would ensure the highest possible rate of growth, while offering a guarantee of equitable distribution of the product. They believed that their strategy not only reconciled rapid growth with equitable distribution but made these two apparently contradictory social aims mutually supporting. These ideas were not in principle entirely irrational.

The unimpaired operation of the new right-wing policies did not last long enough to permit us to judge them. In September 1962 the Eighth Central Committee met in its tenth plenary session. It resolved that 'class struggle continues after the foundation of the socialist state'. This formulation showed that the left had regained its influence. Deng To in the Beijing *Evening News* wrote the last of his series of satirical 'third leaders', 'Evening Chats on Swallow Hill'. In one of them, he urged his readers to plant the pine cabbage which stands unharmed through the icy Beijing winter, ready for use when the spring thaw arrives. In the last of all he discussed the 'thirty-six stratagems' and concluded that the best was to 'fight and run away, and live to fight another day'. The satires and parables ceased.

China's foreign policy, 1949–1963

China's repudiation in the Great Leap Forward of orthodox Soviet means of economic growth and social change was accompanied by and closely related to the repudiation of the Soviet alliance.

The Second World War had left Western Europe and the Soviet Union exhausted, Japan prostrated, and the United States dominant. By October 1949, when the Chinese People's Republic was founded, this situation had begun to change. With the help of the Marshall Plan, Western Europe was recovering strength. Although in most places European colonial power had been reasserted, a process made possible only by the indirect help of the United States which, by supporting the defence of Europe, allowed the European imperial powers to maintain their empires, nevertheless the process of decolonization was under way, and partly as a result of American pressure. The Soviet Union, with access to the raw materials and skills of the countries of central and eastern Europe in which communist regimes had been installed by force or by subversion, was also on the way to recovery. Then in September 1949 Russia successfully tested an atomic bomb.

The distribution of power had thus shifted somewhat to the advantage of the Socialist bloc, but although the Soviet Union now had a nuclear capacity she was still without the means of delivering a nuclear attack on the United States, which on the other hand could attack Russia from a ring of bases close to Soviet territory. Although the economies of Comecon were growing at a faster rate than those of the capitalist world they still could not at all match the West. The West remained dominant and the Soviet Union without significant influence beyond its own immediate sphere of influence. The exception was the accession of a Communist regime in China, although this had come about in the face of Soviet discouragement, so apprehensive was Moscow of a possible conflict with the United States.

By 1949, when the Chinese People's Republic was founded, wartime hopes of the creation of an effective system of control of international conflict had faded. Stalin's failure to honour his undertaking to permit the countries of Eastern Europe to hold free elections and to choose their own social systems had wholly alienated the West, which responded by incorporating West Germany into the anti-Soviet alliance—an act which has wholly alienated the Soviet Union.

American strength, increased rather than diminished by participation in the Second World War, was combined with that of a recovered Western Europe whose economic driving force was the German Federal Republic, and with a resurgent Japan. From the point of view of the Soviet Union and China, former allies and former enemies now seemed to be combined in a formidable coalition against them.

Then in 1957 came a dramatic change in the pattern of world power. The

Soviet Union astonished the world by the successful launching of the first satellite. The United States was no longer out of range of Soviet atomic weapons. The Soviet Union could now negotiate from strength. Ironically it was this new-found strength of the Socialist bloc which led to its division.

When Mao proclaimed on 1 October 1949 that China had 'stood up', he was anticipating the future rather than describing the present. For the moment China's security as a nation was little better protected than it had been in the previous century. Although the People's Liberation Army was large, battle-hardened and well led, it lacked modern equipment. It was unmechanized, it had no air cover, and its armoured units were negligible. The coast was defenceless for lack of a navy, and the inner frontier was equally open for lack of means of defence against armoured attack. No doubt China's advantages of size, terrain, population, and sheer underdevelopment made her in the last resort invulnerable to conquest; but her industries, virtually all located on or near the coast, were at the mercy of attack from the sea, while Beijing stands on the eastern edge of the world's greatest sweep of good tank country, and could be taken at negligible cost by a Soviet attack. The Chinese Communist leaders might publicly express complete faith in the possibility of a 'people's war' defence, but such tactics could not, in 1949 any more than in 1939, have prevented powerful enemies from occupying virtually every part of China that was of much value to an invader.

In 1949, as before, China could only react to events. If events should produce a situation in which China were threatened on two fronts—from the sea and from the steppe—China's new People's army would no doubt resist with more honour than its predecessors, but probably with no more success. And if the very dangers of the world-wide conflict of the superpowers should force them into local collusion in the Far East—a possibility of which the Chinese were acutely aware—then there would be little that China could do.

In more settled times it might have been possible for China to pursue a policy of non-involvement—an attitude which tradition encouraged. However, with the Russians exerting strong influence in Manchuria, the Western powers in occupation of Japan, and the Nationalists actively preparing a return from Taiwan, splendid isolation offered no great security. A choice had to be made.

It was inevitable that the Chinese, obliged to 'lean to one side', would choose the Soviet side; they could in good communist conscience do no other. Yet how far they would choose to depart from the perpendicular was by no means pre-ordained. Past relations with Stalin, and the fate of Eastern Europe, did not encourage hopes for an alliance of equals.

In this situation American policy towards China was decisive. The United States adopted the assumption that China was a satellite of the Soviet Union, and a wholehearted participant in a conspiracy of communist expansion. Chinese approaches to America were repulsed. Beijing was obliged to take account of the possibility that an invasion from Taiwan would receive American support. This might be accompanied by an attack on China through Korea.

China therefore sought from the Soviet Union more than fraternal goodwill. She sought security and economic assistance. Mao Zedong went to Moscow, and on St Valentine's Day 1950 China accepted a marriage of convenience with Russia. A Treaty of Alliance and Mutual Assistance was signed.

This treaty guaranteed Soviet military assistance against an attack by Japan 'or any state allied with her'. It provided Soviet credits of US$300 million over a period of five years. In return the Soviet Union reasserted control of the Chinese Eastern Railways and of Port Arthur and Dairen (Dalian). Sino-Russian joint-stock companies were set up in Manchuria and in Xinjiang to exploit minerals and construct railways. Citizens of third countries were excluded from these regions. China conceded recognition of the 'independence' of Outer Mongolia. Almost every clause in the treaty had a precedent in the unequal treaties of the nineteenth century. China paid a heavy price for Russian protection.

The test of the treaty's value to China's security came soon, when the Korean War broke out in June 1950. While the situation was not, literally, one in which the treaty would automatically come into operation, because China herself was not the object of attack, yet it was certainly one which in Chinese eyes called for prompt and generous help from her Soviet ally. Assistance was given in the form of shipments of arms, but China later complained of their inadequacy, and that she had been made to meet the whole cost of the war; this offset substantially the Soviet development credits offered under the terms of the treaty.

The Korean War confirmed American hostility to the Chinese People's Republic and support for the regime on Taiwan. The American interpretation of events in Korea, a reasonable deduction from their false premise that China was a Soviet pawn, was that the war had been a Russian initiative to which China was a party. On the initiative of the United States, a severe embargo on trade with China was accepted by the Western democracies. The result was to throw China into almost total economic dependence on the Socialist bloc. Trade with the communist world as a proportion of China's total trade leapt between 1949 and 1952 from 8 per cent to 87 per cent. In the same way the communist world became China's only source of credit and of aid. With Soviet imports and Soviet loans came, inevitably, Soviet advisers, institutions, and methods. The factories supplied by Russia formed a complex of industries planned and operated in the Soviet manner. The economy, education, military organization, almost every aspect of Chinese public life was reorganized on Soviet lines. The American prophecy of a satellite China had proved self-fulfilling.

That the Chinese Communist leadership would be content with this situation, however, is more than one could expect of a nation of such passionate and irritable nationalism. Slowly China began to exert a certain independence. The Chinese Communist Party claimed as early as 1949 to have charted a new path to revolution, suitable for the conditions of underdeveloped countries, and so challenged the Soviet monopoly of ideological leadership. In international economic relations China diversified her trade to the utmost degree which the Western embargo allowed, reducing to some extent her dependence on the Socialist bloc. The Soviet loans were paid off rapidly, leaving China debt-free.

In the diplomatic field, however, the Chinese took no independent action, for two reasons: the solidarity of the Socialist bloc was China's security, while inexperience combined with ideological expectations led the Chinese leadership to exaggerate both the will and the capacity of the capitalist West to inflict damage. China therefore remained content to accept Stalin's crude division of the world into two camps, socialist and capitalist. This division allowed no exceptions: it neglected all differences of interest and experience among the Western powers and between the Western powers and the newly independent states which emerged as colonialism retreated.

After Stalin died in 1953 the Chinese, although they remained of necessity firmly wedded to the Socialist bloc, no longer felt obliged to project an image of unquestioning identity of views. Khrushchev, for his part, was ready to slacken somewhat the Soviet grip on the other socialist powers, and to release China from its dependent position. He accepted the termination of Russian privileges in Xinjiang and Manchuria, and showed himself apparently prepared to treat China as an equal ally.

The Geneva Conference of 1954, which virtually ended French colonial authority in Indo-China, formed a second landmark in China's move towards an independent foreign policy. At Geneva China played a major role. She also discovered there that the West was not monolithic, and that differences among the Western powers offered some room for manœuvre.

At the same time, one assumption behing the 'two camps' theory—that the independence of the former colonies was sham—was wearing thin. It was clear that, on the contrary, the ex-colonies jealously and for the most part successfully guarded their independence. In 1955, at the Bandung Conference of Asian and African states, China recognized that their independence was a fact, and one which could be put to use to improve China's international position. The Conference was a Chinese initiative. It did not win China any specific allies, but it provided an opportunity for the Chinese to allay fears in the Third World, and especially in South and South-east Asia, that China was prepared to exploit communist-led insurgency or to take political advantage of the large Chinese communities abroad. At Bandung China took the first step to the development of foreign policies based on two related Maoist concepts: the importance of the intermediate classes (for foreign-policy purposes the intermediate zone), and the united front. In 1955 this new Chinese view did not seem to be specially significant; the Soviet Union had already relaxed Stalin's 'two camps' view of the world to the extent of courting good state-to-state relations with Third World countries without reference to their ideology.

It was later, when China had broken her links with the Soviet Union, that these Maoist concepts offered the basis for an independent Chinese policy, and one so pragmatic that it could eventually embrace a *rapprochement* with the United States.

The Sino-Soviet split

'The East wind prevails over the West wind', Mao's comment on Russia's successful launch of the Sputnik, was not the expression of a naïve assumption that the socialist camp was now in a permanent position of ballistic superiority. Mao had too much respect for American technological capabilities to suppose that the advantage—which in 1957 was in any case merely potential—would be allowed to last. What he instantly recognized was that the new ability of the Soviet Union to strike at the heart of America would produce a balance of terror, which would inhibit the superpowers from risking the escalation of local conflicts. And in these conflicts the forces of revolution, Mao believed, would inevitably win. This analysis also reveals the significance of another of Mao's aphorisms which alarmed the West by its appearance of naïvety: that the atom bomb was a 'paper tiger'. By this Mao did not mean that nuclear war is tolerable but that it is highly unlikely: the bomb is a weapon which no one dares to use. To Mao, the implication for the policy of the Soviet bloc was that local 'liberation' movements should henceforth be unambiguously supported. To Khrushchev, however, the policy implications were precisely the opposite. The socialist camp could now exert its influence through direct negotiation with its opponents rather than by the devious and uncertain processes of subversion by proxy. In this view local liberation movements were of less importance.

In subsequent polemics the Chinese argued that Khrushchev's motives differed profoundly from their own. They themselves, they claimed, were continuing Lenin's pursuit of world revolution, while Khrushchev was prepared to betray the revolution in the interests of the Russian state, now secure behind its enhanced deterrent. In fact the pursuit of world revolution was no more a concern of Beijing than of Moscow. For both, national security was the aim. The means was co-existence, which in practical terms meant acceptance by the capitalist world. The encouragement of revolutionary movements was primarily a form of pressure exerted to induce the capitalist world to yield that acceptance.

Khrushchev could now claim such acceptance, and assumed that China would share the benefits of the increased security which negotiation from strength would bring. The Chinese, however, did not agree. They suspected that when bargains were made between Russia and the United States Chinese interests would not be likely to loom very large. By virtue of the Sputnik, the United States would have to share its world dominion with the Soviet Union. Global conflict might come to be mitigated by regional collusion—at whose expense? American forces remained in South Korea. American support maintained Taiwan as an armed camp. The Nationalists still maintained island bases in two of China's very harbours, at Quemoy and Matsu. The principle of an unarmed Japan had been modified, if not relinquished. The United States, though with reluctance, was supporting the attempts of France to restore her power in southern Vietnam.

In this uncomfortable position two things were clear to the Chinese Government. On the one hand the United States would be unlikely to accept with the Soviet Union any negotiated agreement which would relieve the pressure on China. On the other hand no one had any doubt that if Russia could reach with the West an agreement which would give her security in Europe, she would not hesitate to sacrifice Chinese interests.

In 1958 the Chinese put Soviet intentions to the test by bombarding Quemoy and Matsu. The purpose was clear; it was to show the superpowers that there could be no settlement of the world's problems without Chinese cooperation, and to force Khrushehev to show his hand. The results were not reassuring. Khrushchev made it clear that Russia would run no risks to support China. There was another point which Mao Zedong sought to demonstrate by this action: that for all the strength of the United States it would not be difficult to induce the Americans to overstretch their forces. Mao described in amusing terms to the Central Committee the hurried movements of American warships as they tried to cope at once with a crisis in the Mediterranean and another in the Pacific. The conclusion Mao drew from this was that there was more to be gained by stirring up trouble for the United States than by negotiating with her, in a situation in which fear of precipitating nuclear war inhibited American action.

In 1959 there was a revolt in Tibet against the Chinese, who had in 1950 restored their historic suzerainty there. The revolt was supported by both Taiwan and the United States and had Indian approval. Khrushchev refused to allow this to prejudice his attempts to improve relations with India, to which he offered large credits at the same time as he withdrew Soviet assistance to China's nuclear programme.

In 1956, when anti-Soviet movements had occurred in Poland and Hungary, China had shown how much importance she then still attached to the unity of the Soviet bloc. While expressing sympathy with the Polish protesters she had condemned the Hungarian reformers because Nagy proposed to take Hungary out of the Warsaw Pact. Her hostility to Tito's non-aligned Yugoslavia had been unremitting. By 1960, however, the Chinese had begun to believe that too great a dependence on Russia would simply inhibit China's own attempts to improve her position.

Two further events confirmed China's worst fears. The first was the Cuban crisis in 1962 when Khrushchev, after attempting to install rocket bases in Cuba, backed down in the face of American threats, saving his face by procuring from Washington a promise that America would not invade Cuba, an action which, in view of the farcical failure of the recent Bay of Pigs venture, the United States was very unlikely to attempt again. The Chinese took much the same view of the Cuban crisis as the rest of the world. They condemned Khrushehev for his dangerously provocative act, which could bring no advantage commensurate with its risks, and they held him in contempt for his subsequent pusillanimous withdrawal. Their conclusion was that the Soviet Union under Khrushchev could not even consistently pursue its own policy of co-existence.

The second was the Test Ban Treaty, concluded in 1963 by the Soviet Union and the United States. In effect it sought to bestow a monopoly of nuclear arms on those powers which already possessed them. The Chinese regarded the Treaty as aimed mainly at China. Further, they regarded it as decisive proof that the two superpowers were being drawn, however reluctantly, into the creation of a world-wide dyarchy. It was at this point that the Chinese broke openly with the Soviet Union. They did not do so lightly, but only after seven years of protest, negotiation, attempted compromise, and politely veiled polemic. In these years they had suffered Khrushehev's sarcastic condemnation of the Great Leap Forward and the communes, the cancellation of Russian nuclear assistance and the abrupt withdrawal of Soviet advisers.

During the Cuban crisis a further irritant was added to Sino-Soviet relations. While Khrushchev was embroiled with the United States, China's relations with India had been deteriorating to the point of crisis. Hitherto, potential disputes over the uncertain boundary between Tibet and India had remained no more than potential, but Indian support for the Tibetan rebels had disturbed the amicable relations between the two great Asian powers in a manner which was bound to be most acutely manifested on this frontier. Charges and countercharges flowed, and in these exchanges India proved the less amenable party. On 20 October 1962, two days before President Kennedy ordered the naval blockade of Cuba, Chinese troops invaded the disputed territory on the Tibetan border with India. Indian resistance collapsed by the 24th. The Chinese, having thus dramatically demonstrated their ability to occupy the territory they claimed, withdrew unilaterally. Khrushchev meanwhile pursued his policy of befriending India and supplying her with arms, unmoved by this dispute.

The disagreements between the two major communist powers were, publicly, couched in terms of ideological argument. China's only means of putting pressure on Russia was to appeal to the world's communist parties against the apparent betrayal of the cause of world revolution by the Soviet Union in the interests of the Russian state. The conflict was therefore carried on mainly by apostolic blows and knocks. In fact ideology had little to do with it. The situation was simple and familiar: the stronger of two allies seeks peace with the common enemy; the weaker ally fears that its interests will be sacrificed, and finally concludes that the alliance offers no security. When China was at last forced to launch an independent foreign policy, ideology played very little part in it, and China was as prepared as Russia to sacrifice revolutionary principle to the security of the State.

16

The Great Proletarian Cultural Revolution, I

The Socialist Education Movement, 1963–1965

Between 1962 and 1965 Chinese politics appeared to be stable. The Great Leap had been ended and the damage repaired. The rate of economic growth had increased satisfactorily. Progress in agriculture under the new policies was especially gratifying, so that even though these new policies had begun simply as an improvised response to the threat of hunger, their success disposed some of China's leaders to accept them for the future. The oblique reassertion of left-wing views at the tenth plenum of the Eighth Central Committee in September 1962 passed virtually unremarked in the West. Yet, behind the façade of national unity that China presented to a hostile world the issues of the Great Leap period were still alive. A new process of polarization had begun as the right wing sought to protect its policies and its position against renewed left-wing manœuvres.

Most of the details of this muted struggle came to light only in the revelations of the Cultural Revolution. The revelations were heavily biased against those in power, but when they are compared with the public record of the years concerned it becomes clear that the substance of the accusations was true, even if the implications which the left drew from the facts are a matter of opinion. The struggle was not, as the Red Guards and their mentors insisted, one between good and evil, socialism and capitalism, but between two equally sincere and tenable views of how to give communism a human face. These two views, implicit in the whole history of socialism, were now to work themselves out in China.

The first stage was a Socialist Education campaign in the countryside. Its aim was simple: to restore collectivization, damaged by the disasters following the Leap. However, the first experimental work done in the villages soon revealed that the *malaise* was far deeper than had been known. Corruption among grass-roots rural cadres was rampant. The focus of the movement was therefore switched from the restoration of collectivized agriculture to the rectification of the village leadership. In February 1963 a draft resolution of the Central Committee on 'Some Problems in Current Rural Work', written by Mao himself, was circulated, indicating that the Socialist Education Movement would concentrate on the administration of collective accounts, communal granaries, public property, and work points (the 'four clean-ups').

This resolution, the 'Early Ten Points', changed not only the aim of the Movement but its methods. Hitherto, Party work teams had controlled it. This would have been an appropriate method had the problem been simply, as was first supposed, to ensure that collectivized agriculture was restored; but when the problem was seen to be one of widespread peculation in which cadres worked in collusion with each other and with the former village élite, and used their authority to stifle protests, work teams were unlikely to achieve much. They were outsiders, and they were composed of Party cadres who might only protect their village subordinates.

The 'Early Ten Points' made it clear that Mao was not content that the Party should be left to reform the Party by such administrative means. His solution was political: the task of the work teams was to mobilize the non-Party masses, resurrecting the old 'poor peasant leagues', to reassert their authority, and to identify the errant cadres while the work team held the ring. As in the 1957 Rectification Movement, the Party was to submit itself to non-Party criticism.

In the autumn of 1963 Deng Xiaoping was given the task of updating this resolution in the light of experience. The directive he produced, the 'Later Ten Points', differed sharply from Mao's original. 'Class struggle' was not mentioned; instead the problems of the rural areas were said to be 'non-antagonistic contradictions' (using Mao's own 1957 phrase) to be resolved by educational means. The poor peasant leagues were to be under the control of the work teams. There was to be no interference with the 'prosperous middle peasants' and no disruption of existing organizations. Deng Xiaoping seems to have been concerned mainly that the more flexible system of farming which had established itself in the preceding two or three years should not be put at risk.

In June 1964 Mao once more asserted his ideas. He insisted that the Socialist Education Movement should be judged by its success in mobilizing the poor peasants, and that erring cadres should not be hauled off for judgement by higher authority, but simply 'struggled against' by the masses. Mao's solution would have two advantages: that the judgements would be made by the villagers who alone could know who had transgressed, but that at the same time the cadre force would not be decimated by arrests and punishments. Mao made these points at a central work conference, but the resolution subsequently published ignored them.

In September of that year Liu Shaoqi was given the task of producing yet another document. This was to be known as the 'Revised Later Ten Points'. At first sight it seemed that Mao had won; the 'Revised Points' took a much more radical view. Yet it was this document which was used in the Cultural Revolution as evidence of Liu's right-wing proclivities. It was said to have been 'left in form but right in essence'.

Liu's wife Wang Guangmei had taken a vigorous personal part in the campaign. She had gone down to a sample of villages, incognito, to lead the reform. The members of her work team lived with the peasants, won the confidence of individuals, and collected information on the behaviour of the cadres. She was soon horrified by the evidence of corruption, brutality, and demoralization which she uncovered. She communicated her alarm to Liu Shaoqi, and his 'Revised Later Ten Points' expressed it. In particular, his directive emphasized the problem of collusion between village cadres and their friends and patrons at higher levels of the Party: 'Cadres in basic level organizations who have made mistakes are usually connected with certain cadres of higher level organizations ... and are instigated, supported and protected by them ...'. The content of the 'four clean-ups' was widened to 'politics, economics, ideology and organization'. The poor peasant leagues were given a commune-level organization so that they could exert influence at commune headquarters to prevent retaliation by threatened village cadres. The militia were called in to strengthen the leagues.

Mao did not approve. Liu's attack was directed against cadres only, and not against the 'capitalist' elements among the peasantry whose ambitions provided the scope for corruption. Liu also regarded all cadres as under suspicion, and all found guilty were to be severely dealt with. While Liu's directive appeared to give the poor peasant leagues an important role, in practice they were swamped by huge 'human wave' work teams. Finally, although Liu himself attached importance to the problem of collusion between higher and lower levels of the Party, in effect (so it was stated) the campaign was still directed against relatively low levels, leaving Liu vulnerable to the accusation that he had 'hit at the many to protect the few'. Dependence on work teams from the higher levels of the Party made this inevitable.

Mao returned in January 1965 with a new set of instructions, later known as the 'Twenty-three Articles'. He demanded a 'triple alliance' of peasants, cadres, and work teams, expressing again in this his technique of building the widest possible alliance in order to isolate the offending minority. He sought (although neither the right nor, as it proved, the left chose to obey him) the regular re-election of grass-roots cadres. Dealing with various points for decision in the village—both with points of discipline such as whom to punish and how, and also with policy points such as the question of private land reclamation—he insisted repeatedly throughout the Articles that these decisions must be taken by the peasants themselves. He advocated leniency towards those found guilty of misdemeanours; they were to make restitution, but only the most serious cases were to be dealt with by law, leaving the rest to village opinion.

At the same time Mao asserted that the evils under attack existed at all levels, even up to the Central Committee itself, some of whose members were 'taking the capitalist road'. The implication was that the targets of the campaign should include those in high places who encouraged the attitudes which led to corruption. At this point the movement as an attack on corruption merged with the attack on individualistic agriculture in the countryside. The recent relaxation of collective control had created an ambiguous situation, with the definition of what was permissible left largely to the discretion of local cadres who, by colluding with peasants who sought greater scope for individual enterprise, could find opportunities for corrupt gains. In so far as such collusion tended to involve members of the former rural élite because of their greater skills and experience, the left wing saw danger of a rural counter-revolution.

Mao's assertion that even the Central Committee was tainted was ominous. It implied that the urban centres of Party power might have to be purged before the villages could be reformed. In this way the 'Twenty-three Articles' prefigured the Cultural Revolution nine months later. At the same time the implied criticism of Liu Shaoqi anticipated the attacks which were later to be made on him during the Cultural Revolution in reaction to his heavy-handed use of work teams against the students in the summer of 1966, similar to his use of the work teams in the Socialist Education Movement. Mao later told Edgar Snow, an American journalist who had enjoyed Mao's confidence since the Yan'an days, that it was in January 1965 (the month when Mao produced the Twenty-three Articles) that he decided that Liu Shaoqi was not a suitable successor.

The documents of the Socialist Education Movement revealed, however, not two but three different points of view. Mao stood for a political, massline solution, anticipating that this policy would solve both the problem of corruption and the problem of the spread of individualistic agriculture, believing that the reassertion of the political power of the poor majority would dispose of both at once. Liu Shaoqi, perhaps as a matter of personality rather than of ideology, chose to attempt a legalistic solution, which might well have solved the problems only at the cost of shattering the existing Communist leadership in the villages. Deng Xiaoping seemed less interested in political methods than in agricultural policies, seeking to preserve the economic gains which had been won through the relaxation of collective farming. It is interesting that Mao's greater wrath was kept for Liu Shaoqi's faults of political method, and not for Deng Xiaoping's opposition to the tightening up of collectivization.

Although in the Twenty-three Articles Mao had made the definitive pronouncement on the future course of the Socialist Education Movement, in the event his policy was not applied. In the month following, the United States began to bomb North Vietnam, and with this threat of war the Chinese Communist Party turned its attention to more urgent concerns.

The polarization of Chinese politics, 1963–1965

In these years there were other potentially divisive issues which were to provide further fuel for the explosion to come. Every aspect of life was involved: philosophy, literature and the arts, education, medical services, planning, and industrial management. The striking feature of the controversies in all these fields was the inability of Mao Zedong to get his will carried out. He retained sufficient influence to secure favourable decisions, but he no longer had the authority always to ensure that the decisions were implemented. He was defeated by passive resistance. Yet he clearly believed with increasing force that China was threatened with the fate of the Soviet Union, through the creation of a post-revolutionary ruling class whose relationship with the people (Mao believed) was not significantly different from that between capitalists and workers. Six years before, in his marginal comments on the Russian *Textbook of Political Economy*, Mao had written that the change to public ownership of the means of production, although it is the necessary beginning of revolution, merely provides the *opportunity* to create socialist relationships but does not in itself create them. 'There must be a process,' Mao wrote, 'there is still work to be done'. The privileges of this new ruling class, he thought, were institutionalized in the sharing of power among bureaucrats, technocrats and Party leaders, were expressed covertly in an apologetic literature, and were perpetuated through élitist education.

To represent Mao, on account of what followed, as a latter-day Stalin attempting to prevent the liberalization of the Communist system is to ignore the fact that he acted out of hostility towards some of the features of Stalinism to which the Western liberal tradition itself is most hostile. Although his alternative was much less than fully democratic, and indeed in the Cultural Revolution proved to be a cure worse than the disease, we will not understand Mao's proceedings unless we recognize that his condemnation of the 'new class' in the Soviet Union, and his fear that China was developing in the same direction, were the springs of his actions.

There is ample evidence that his fears were justified. In spite of his efforts in 1958 to create an egalitarian education related to production and to problem-solving—an ideal which owed more to John Dewey, whose ideas Mao's generation had so admired, than to Soviet Marxism—Chinese education remained élitist and bookish. Medical services were concentrated on the privileged in the cities. 'The health service,' said Mao in 1964, 'should be called the city health service, or rather the city gentlemen's health service'. Privilege in education and health was matched by privilege in housing, transport, entertainment, and all the amenities of life. Salary differentials were small but the perquisites of office gave the official a life-style which made a most unsocialist contrast with the life-style of the majority. The whole of Chinese society was dominated, as it always had been, by patron–client relationships which determined success or failure in finding employment, in promotion, in access to social services, even in obtaining permission to move from country to city. It was consequently (and still is) a system in many respects more feudal than feudalism. It still ran (and runs) on the authoritarianism of the privileged who can exploit the traditional deference of the many. Mao set out to break this deference with his assertion that 'to rebel is justified'. That, he said, is the whole message of Marxism. From 1963 onwards he began to press for changes.

He was able to prevent the general implementation of the proposals of the economist Sun Yefang, who argued that profit was the best index of efficiency, that profits should be used to provide incentives, and that China's main economic problem was not how to maximize production but how to minimize costs. Such ideas were already familiar in some European communist countries, but the Chinese left wing regarded them as 'revisionist'. Mao's explanation of this judgement was characteristic: Stalin had prevented popular participation and replaced it with bureaucratic command. His successors substituted material incentives for Stalinist coercion; they replaced the stick with the carrot, but they changed nothing else; there was still no participation. Meanwhile the provision of new material incentives in the form of profits only strengthened the position of the bureaucrats by adding money to power. In spite of the considerable influence which Sun Yefang's ideas exerted on many members of the leadership, Mao was able to prevent these ideas from being fully applied. Some incentive bonuses were paid, but in industry the main target remained output, not profit. Managerial autonomy remained negligible, and Sun Yefang's proposal that enterprises should be charged for the capital they used (which would actually have had an equalizing effect between factories using old and new equipment) was not accepted.

Mao was also able to elevate the Daqing oilfield in Manchuria to the position of a model for industrial organization. Daqing was an industrial base without a consumer city. The workers were settled in villages where their families grew the food and provided the services. Little attempt, however, was made to apply its lessons elsewhere. Mao's Anshan Constitution (named after the Anshan iron and steel complex in Manchuria) which provided for full workers' management, was not even published, far less adopted, while the right wing maintained instead an ineffective system of workers' congresses controlled by the official trade unions.

In agriculture, while Mao was able to publicize the Da Zhai Production Brigade as the model, he was unable to ensure that its methods were generally adopted. Da Zhai was a poor brigade in Shanxi, deep in eroded gullies. Its people, by their own efforts (so the story said) and without State subventions, terraced the cliffs and carted soil to the terraces to create fertile land where there had been none before. Three times their work was swept away by flood, but they persisted and won. In their commitment to this communal struggle against the elements they abolished the work-point system prevalent elsewhere, and settled for a more egalitarian method of remuneration.

Not only was Mao unable to secure general imitation of Da Zhai, but the brigade came under pointed attack from the right wing during the Socialist Education Movement. This choice of Mao's own model as a target for criticism could only have been a challenge. It was found, according to those who investigated it, that its production figures had been grossly exaggerated and that so far from being self-reliant it had received exceptional State help. Mao responded by giving the Da Zhai party secretary a personal interview and ensuring his election as a member of the National People's Congress. Nevertheless the 'Learn from Da Zhai' movement was stalled.

On the cultural front Mao had no more success. The philosophy, the fiction, and the dramatic arts of the time had four characteristics which Mao found distasteful. The first was a preoccupation with the failure of the Leap. The second was oblique support for Khrushchev's theory of a 'Party and State of the whole people' as opposed to a State representing the working class. The third, shown especially in opera (China's commonest form of drama), was the neglect of modern social themes in favour of traditional themes. The fourth characteristic, scarcely noticed in the West, was the writing of historical novels to promote the reputation of individual Party patrons who had an eye on the succession.

The reassertion of class struggle at the tenth plenum in September 1962 proved to be a sufficient warning for most of the literary opponents of the Leap; but they had suffered a check, not a rout, and had only retired to plant, metaphorically, the pine cabbages which Deng To had recommended. On the theme of a 'Party and State of the whole people' the opposition to Mao was more stubborn. Many leaders believed that since the socialization of agriculture and industry in 1956 there had been no more need for class struggle in China. This sentiment was powerfully reinforced by the fact that the motivation of so many founding members of the Party had been primarily nationalistic, so that while they might accept the need for class conflict to remove from power those who appeared to stand in the way of the recovery of the nation, when this was accomplished their instinct was towards unity rather than strife. Mao himself in 1957, in his speech 'On the Correct Handling of Contradictions among the People', had asserted that the great and turbulent class struggles of the past were over, although he was too canny a politician not to qualify this and leave himself room for manœuvre. Many were prepared to accept Khrushchev's advocacy of a Party and State of the whole people and to build on the constitution of 1954, whose civil rights provisions had never been honoured. Foremost among these was Peng Zhen who as the Party Secretary of the capital had tolerated, perhaps even encouraged, the anti-Maoist literature of 1960 to 1962.

In August 1964 a challenge was issued to the left in an article by the Director of the Higher Party School, Yang Xianjian. Yang argued that the essential course of dialectical change was towards combining 'two into one' and that 'one into two' was no more than an analytical device: this was an appeal for unity, against the continuation of class struggle, an attempt to give Khrushchev's formulation a philosophical rationale. It also implied that China had reached a satisfactory resolution of her social contradictions and need not go on to further basic changes. Other writers were more explicit in their arguments: for example, that collectivized agriculture was fully socialist and so need not give way in time to nationalized agriculture. Such views were unacceptable to Mao, who had so strongly criticized the Soviet Union for accepting as permanent many institutions which had been meant to be merely transitional; and Mao linked this complacency to the power of the 'new class' which had nothing to gain from further changes.

The right refused to recognize the manifest political intent of Yang's article, and defended him by insisting that the question of 'two into one' was merely academic. The left, however, won. Yang was denounced and disgraced.

Mao persisted in his criticisms of current literature, determined that China's writers should provide a climate of opinion which would permit the advocacy of further social change. In May 1963 a national conference of artists and writers was held, on the theme of resistance to revisionism. Mao appealed to those present to 'accept conflict'—one of his lifelong themes—and also to identify with workers and peasants. The conference accepted his proposals, but nothing changed. A year later he warned China's writers that if they did not change soon they would become a 'Petöfi Club'. In the following month the Party agreed that there should be a rectification of literature and art. Again, however, there were no changes, nor were changes likely when Peng Zhen, patron of the satirists, was put in the charge of the rectification.

At another conference one year later, in September 1965, the frustrated Chairman threw down the gauntlet by demanding the criticism of a specific literary work, a play which had been written by the historian Wu Han, Peng Zhen's deputy as Mayor of Beijing (and Deng Xiaoping's bridge partner). The hero of Wu Han's play, *The Dismissal of Hai Rui*, was a Ming dynasty official, legendary for his courage in opposing tyranny and corruption. Having been appointed Governor-General of 'Jiangnan' (China south of the Yangzi), he arrives incognito, and finds that the local officials are corrupt and vicious. They are taking the land from the people and persecuting those who resist. He finds himself, however, in a moral dilemma: the chief villain of the Jiangnan scene is an old associate, who once saved Hai Rui from the consequences of a palace intrigue. Where does his duty lie? Will he honour his personal debt? Or will he honour his public responsibilities? Hai Rui decides that his public responsibilities come first, reveals himself, and condemns the culprit and his henchmen. Meanwhile, his enemies have been at work and the order for his dismissal comes post-haste from the capital. Hai Rui, however, stubbornly holds on to the seal of office until he has disposed of the wrongdoers. He then accepts the responsibility for this illegal act.

The parable is plain. For the requisition of the peasants' land and the punishment of those who sought to resist it, read the Great Leap and the communes. For Hai Rui's moral dilemma, read gratitude to the Communist Party for its earlier achievements, and condemnation of its acts in 1958. For Hai Rui, read Peng Dehuai, dismissed for his bold condemnation of the Great Leap. For the retention of the seal of office, read Peng's determination to persist in his condemnation in spite of all warnings. For the Emperor, misled by bad counsellors, read Mao Zedong.

By this time (1965) Mao clearly felt that he was in a strong position to attempt to restore his full authority. He enjoyed one great political advantage, in the support of the Minister of Defence Lin Biao, who had been appointed to replace Peng Dehuai. China's armed forces consisted of four million recruits hand-picked for their 'political consciousness'. Of demographic necessity the vast majority were peasants. Brought together in the armed forces and given a political education, they were a formidable political force even without their weapons. Lin Biao chose to line them up with the left. From 1964, under the slogan 'Learn from the PLA', army personnel moved into civilian life to become in effect the political commissars of civil institutions. The army led the rural militia to act as the backbone of the revived poor peasant leagues. It launched in its ranks a rectification of its own literary and artistic establishment. Thus in several critical areas of controversy the army under Lin Biao presented a challenge to the anti-Maoist establishment.

In the summer of 1965 there seems to have been one further veiled conflict, this time over the question of methods of defence, following the escalation of the war in Vietnam. On the anniversary of VE Day, Luo Ruiqing, the Chief of Staff, made a commemorative speech. Lin Biao followed suit on the anniversary of VJ Day with a speech entitled 'Long live the victory of people's war!' These two speeches seemed to have represented irreconcilable views of the defence of China. The evidence depends upon the interpretation of apparently unremarkable differences in wording, and not all readers have found this evidence convincing. Yet the fact is that in the following year Luo Ruiqing was among the first victims of the Cultural Revolution, harassed to the point of attempted suicide, while Lin Biao's speech was held up as one of the most revered texts of the left. The differences in nuance were enough, it seems, to destroy one leader and elevate another to the highest eminence below Mao himself. Subsequent accusations made against Luo Ruiqing strengthen the case. Apparently Luo in his comments on the Second World War obliquely proposed active intervention against America in Vietnam, backed by renewed alliance with the Soviet Union. Lin Biao on the other hand argued for nonintervention and for a self-reliant defence of China based on guerrilla strategy.

It would have been surprising if no such disputes had occurred in China, faced in Vietnam with the most alarming threat to her frontiers since the end of the Korean War. What could not have been predicted was that the left would treat Lin's speech as a public avowal of support for their whole programme. We will perhaps never know of what manœuvres and negotiations Lin Biao's speech was the consummation. At any rate the speech seems to have given the signal. It was made on 3 September. It was in that month, at the Party's next central work conference, that Mao demanded an investigation of Wu Han's play. When the response was lukewarm he turned to a newspaper in Shanghai to get his criticism published. When the Party press in Beijing refused to reprint the critical article, Lin Biao's *Liberation Army Daily* published it and forced the Party's hand. The Great Proletarian Cultural Revolution was about to begin.

The aims of the Cultural Revolution

The Cultural Revolution produced such confusion that it is almost impossible to know what its aims actually were. The number of groups pursuing their interests and aspirations in the name of Mao's exhortation to rebel were so diverse that it is almost impossible to point to a dominant line of policy which had the support both of the Cultural Revolution Group and of a majority of their professed supporters. Mao's own 'directives' were general and vague. At the outset he may only have sought certain changes in cultural policy. On the other hand he may have intended from the beginning to launch a revolution. There is a third possibility: that he courted a struggle to see what came of it, determined to manipulate that struggle to gain certain ends which he had in view.

On the evidence, the best hypothesis seems to be that Mao began with limited aims; that the resistance of the Party machine then produced a succession of reactions from the left which drove the movement far beyond its original scope; and that Mao, along with other left-wing elements—some of them far to the left of Mao himself—then saw opportunities to secure more radical changes during the ensuing breakdown of Party authority.

We can with some confidence infer the wider aims which Mao, given the opportunity, would be expected to pursue. His fundamental fear was that a new ruling class was being created. He believed that the source of this new élite lay in the centralized and authoritarian nature of the economic system which provided little scope for popular participation in the process of development. (It is a premiss which has, since Mao's death, been inherited by the present democratic opposition, in spite of their condemnation of the Cultural Revolution.) He had come to believe that the Party's hostility to criticism from outside its own ranks protected this new class, and that China's writers and educators had provided a further perimeter of defence around it, making it almost impossible for critics to gain a hearing. His positive alternative had already been shown in the decentralized, community development policies of the Great Leap, accompanied by the participation of workers in industrial management and a part-work, part-study system of education.

Mao saw the conflict between these alternatives as a form of class struggle, and explicitly referred to those who opposed his policies as 'those taking the capitalist road'. The use of the word capitalist in this context need not be taken literally; Mao in reply to Edgar Snow agreed that its use was meta-phorical, but justified it by the fact that the relationships between leaders and led in the centralized socialist economic system he deplored were in his eyes little different from those between employers and employees under capitalism.

Mao was not accusing his fellow leaders of nefarious conduct. His point was much more interesting. It was that in working conscientiously to build up a system of paternalistic socialism they were unwittingly creating something which, if they foresaw its end, they would abhor as much as Mao himself. In the end, Mao believed, they might create in China a sort of Fascism.

Some years later Zhang Chunqiao, one of the radical leaders of the Cultural Revolution, in describing the central character of a proposed revolutionary drama, made clear how the Maoists viewed their opponents. This character, wrote Zhang, was as an individual a hero: 'not a landlord nor a capitalist in his family for four generations . . . joined the Party before the Long March . . . fought courageously in the Resistance War and the War of Liberation . . . became a cadre . . . a man of infinite conscientiousness and absolute integrity . . .'. Yet he was not to be the hero of the play but rather its villain: a tyrant. But it was the system which forced him to play the tyrant, not his own nature.

In 1965 Mao asserted that 'the officials of China are a class, and one whose interests are antagonistic to those of the workers and peasants'. And on this assumption he was ready to encourage vigorous protest: 'Let those who will make fierce attacks, demonstrate in the streets and take up arms to provoke change. I definitely approve.'

Such words might suggest that Mao deliberately embraced the strife and bloodshed to which his cultural revolution led, but the precedents which he probably had in mind were less alarming. One was the May Fourth Movement of 1919, when a few thousand students, Mao among them, had so successfully dramatized the issue of Duan Qirui's pro-Japanese policy and stirred up millions of their elders to respond. The other was the Rectification Movement of 1957 when the non-Party public had been persuaded to criticize the Party. Mao's idea at the end of 1965—or at any rate by the spring of 1966—was probably to use student protest to touch off a movement in which the public would participate, critically, in a debate on the policies that had dominated China since 1961.

The course of the Cultural Revolution

The publication of the attack on *The Dismissal of Hai Rui* was a deliberate challenge by the left to the Group of Five which had already been set up to reform the cultural establishment. The article criticizing *The Dismissal of Hai Rui* had taken seven months to prepare and had been frequently revised by Mao's wife Jiang Qing, the journalist Zhang Chunqiao, and the literary critic Yao Wenyuan. Mao does not seem to have been directly involved in its preparation, for after it was published he was critical, asserting that it had not made the essential political point, that the dismissal of Hai Rui was a parable for the dismissal of Peng Dehuai. The *Hai Rui* play itself had been prepared by a similar process of repeated consultation and rewriting, in the course of which its political message was carefully shaped.

When Yao's article was published, Peng Zhen asked the Party's Director of Propaganda, Lu Dingyi, to telephone Shanghai and demand to know who had authorized publication. Zhang Chunqiao, it was reported, replied that it was Mao himself. Thus the seriousness of the challenge was left in no doubt. Nor was there any doubt that it was a challenge to the authority of the Party as an institution. Mao had circumvented it by going outside Beijing and evading the official Party organs to secure the publication of his attack.

On 29 November 1965 the *Liberation Army Daily* reprinted Yao's article. It was then broadcast nation-wide; it was thus impossible for the rest of the Party press to remain silent. Peng Zhen attempted to represent the problem as merely an academic one, a question of the accuracy or otherwise of Wu Han's interpretation of the role of the real Hai Rui. The *People's Daily*, forced at last to print Yao's attack, did so in its academic pages, in its column entitled 'Let a Hundred Flowers Bloom'. It was accompanied by a note from the pen of Peng Zhen himself calling for academic discussion. An extraordinarily elaborate diversionary exercise was launched, in which China's university departments of history, law, and social sciences switched their resources to research on the life and times of Hai Rui. In December, Deng To, author of the former 'Evening Chats', wrote for the *People's Daily* an article on Hai Rui which studiously avoided the political implications, and the editors commented in such a way as to suggest that the subject was now exhausted and the matter closed. Wu Han wrote a perfunctory self-criticism in which he denied that his play was a political parable. Mao's supporters condemned this as inadequate. Peng Zhen meanwhile ruled that no articles were to be published in major organs without the permission of the Group of Five, and turned down an article submitted (as a further challenge) by the Beijing radical Qi Benyu. At the same time he was assuring his colleagues that 'Chairman Mao agrees with my point of view that Wu Han is not a political question', and that 'the question should not be related to the Lushan Conference' (where Peng Dehuai had been purged): 'Wu Han is not opposed to the Party and to socialism—that is what the Chairman said'.

By this means he secured the assent of a majority of the Group of Five for a decision known as the February Outline. Deng Xiaoping later claimed, 'I ratified it because I was told that Chairman Mao had agreed with it.'

How far Mao was from agreeing he soon showed. He called a meeting of the Standing Committee of the Political Bureau (17–20 March). He demanded that young people should be free to express their ideas 'without having to fear that they will "break the king's law" '. He issued a scarcely veiled threat: 'For a long time I have begged the local authorities to rebel against the Central Committee if those in power have not done their job.' Having won over—or at least silenced—the members of the Standing Committee, he then summoned a Central Committee work conference, where he repeated his strictures with greater emphasis. The Propaganda Department, he said, was 'the Devil's own headquarters'. He condemned Peng Zhen by name. And he made good his threat: 'I call upon the local provinces for a rebellion and an attack on the Centre.'

Peng Zhen appeared no more in public. The Group of Five was dissolved and replaced by a new Central Cultural Revolution Group which included the chief members of Mao's own entourage and their radical supporters in cultural circles. Among those now gathered round Mao in support of his cultural revolution were his wife Jiang Qing, Yao Wenyuan the author of the attack on Wu Han's play, Chen Boda who had been Mao's secretary and had risen to be the chief interpreter of his thought and senior Party member in the Chinese Academy of Sciences, Zhang Chunqiao the noted Shanghai journalist, and several associates of Chen Boda in the Academy. Deng Xiaoping, Liu Shaoqi, and Zhou Enlai concurred in condemning Peng Zhen. His dismissal made it possible to launch a full campaign against the anti-Maoist writers in Beijing. Led by the *Liberation Army Daily*, the Press published several thousand articles on *Hai Rui* within a few weeks. Half a million copies of Yao's critical article were printed, the text being distributed by telegraph to provincial printers. Yao produced another article, this time condemning Deng To, the author of the satirical 'third leaders' in the Beijing *Evening News* referred to in chapter 15, the 'Evening Chats on Swallow Hill'. These attacks soon widened into a general assault on the Beijing press.

Soon after, a most serious charge was made in unofficial sources against Peng Zhen and his closest associates. They were accused of having conspired in December 1961 to remove Mao Zedong from office. The conspirators were said to have met secretly in a pavilion, the Chang Guan Lou, in Beijing Zoo. Their purpose was to assemble evidence that Mao, during the Great Leap period, had habitually issued orders without the sanction of the Party. The reports given of their discussions show their belief that 'mistakes are never corrected by those who make them'; in other words, that Mao must go. Peng Zhen assured the rest that Liu Shaoqi would support them.

While the Chang Guan Lou meeting certainly took place, we have no corroborating evidence that there ever was such a conspiracy; but the accusation may be true. Given the strength of the revulsion against the Great Leap at that time, and given that the revulsion was all but universal, that Liu Shaoqi clearly shared this feeling, and that Mao was held personally responsible for the disasters of the Leap, some move against Mao was all but inevitable. Given that Mao had indeed circumvented the Party apparatus, and that of all the members of the CCP leadership Liu Shaoqi and Peng Zhen were the most likely to regard such circumvention as incorrect, it is plausible that Peng Zhen should appear as the initiator and should expect Liu's sympathy. The detailed nature of the account of the conspiracy now published and the consistency of the reported dialogue with the style and characteristics of such participants as Peng Zhen and Deng To also lent the accusation a certain conviction.

So, too, do the circumstances in which this revelation was made. The dependable Yugoslavian news service Tanjug was then reporting from Beijing that special commando units in the capital had been deployed and the municipal Party's headquarters occupied by soldiers. Tanjug also reported that Mao could not risk returning to Beijing and that Lin Biao had brought up more troops.

That Mao and his supporters feared an armed coup is also suggested by Lin Biao's speech on 18 May 1966 when he stated that 'Chairman Mao in recent months has paid particular attention to the prevention of a counter-revolutionary *coup d'état*'. Against this background, the revelation of the so-called 'Chang Guan Lou conspiracy' was perhaps intended to warn that what Peng Zhen had sought to do once he might try again.

Looming over the events of this stage of the Cultural Revolution was the question of the succession to the ageing Mao. His appointed successor was Liu Shaoqi. Hitherto secure in his expectations, Liu's position was now badly shaken by Mao's disillusionment with his part in the Socialist Education Movement, while Lin Biao's rising power was obvious. A coup against Mao could have been justified as supporting Liu's 'legitimate' claims against those of Lin Biao; and it was soon to be seen that Mao, by accepting dependence on Lin Biao in launching the Cultural Revolution, was indeed in danger of losing his independence of action. In this way a coup might well have been justified to 'save' the Chairman from Lin Biao. If it were to be planned, who more likely to lead it than Peng Zhen, stickler for forms, Liu Shaoqi's old associate and client, strong in his control of the capital, now the most consulted member of the Political Bureau, perhaps the only CCP leader who was not in awe of the Party Chairman, and himself the focus, and potentially a victim, of the Cultural Revolution counter-attack.

After twelve days of debate the Central Committee produced the 'May the

16th Circular'. This condemned the February Outline because it had failed to make it clear that the point of *The Dismissal of Hai Rui* was precisely the dismissal of Peng Dehuai. The Circular also condemned the attitude, presented by the February Outline, that the Cultural Revolution must proceed under Party control: the Revolution was aimed at the unrestrained mobilization of the masses. Finally, the Circular put the 'class struggle' point of view in emphatic terms: 'The representatives of the bourgeoisie who have sneaked into the Party, the Government, the army and various cultural circles are a bunch of counter-revolutionary revisionists . . . Some are still trusted by us and are being trained as our successors; people like Khrushchev, for example, who are still nestling beside us.'

This threatening statement has been interpreted as the opening of the attack on Liu Shaoqi. It was certainly to provide the rhetoric of that attack, but Mao was still insisting privately that his differences with his fellow leaders were 'contradictions within the people', to be resolved by persuasion.

At this time, too, we cannot always be sure who was writing the script: Mao or Lin Biao. Lin was soon to make statements crude in content and minatory in tone. Parts of the 'May the 16th Circular' sound much like Lin's style.

At any rate, on 18 May Lin made a speech in which he said that 'reactionaries who had infiltrated the Party should be suppressed,' and added, 'Some should be sentenced to death.' Such ferocity was completely at odds with Mao's attitude to differences of political opinion among Party members who shared a common purpose and common values.

Finally, Lin Biao took the same occasion to launch his campaign for the adulation of Mao, describing him as a genius and insisting that 'one single sentence of his surpasses ten thousand of ours'. Mao's response to this was given in a letter to his wife Jiang Qing in which he expressed his alarm at the prospect of being hoisted on to such a dangerous pinnacle of worship, but admitted that he was in no position to condemn Lin's alarming proceedings in public: 'Our friend and his colleagues have presented me with a *fait accompli* . . . This is the first time in my life that I have had to agree with other people about an essential problem against my will.' And there is other evidence of Mao's alarm at Lin's creation of a Mao cult.

The role of Lin Biao in the Cultural Revolution is obscure. By this time (May 1966) the cliques and connections which determined the chaotic history of the next five or six years were crystallizing out. It was a nominee of Lin Biao who succeeded Luo Ruiqing as Chief of Staff. An old 4th Army colleague, Tao Zhu, was soon to be brought north from Canton to replace Lu Dingyi as head of propaganda. It was a niece of Marshal Nie Rongzhen, another old comrade of Lin Biao, whose dramatic defiance of the Beijing educational establishment in early June was to provide the next step in escalation of conflict; she had close connections with certain philosophers of the Chinese Academy of Sciences who, through Mao's close supporter Chen Boda, became linked with

Lin Biao. And it was this group which launched the campaign against Liu Shaoqi. Lin worked in the background, said little, and appeared seldom; but there always seems to be a link between Lin and extremism.

By early May what Mao sought to do was becoming clear. His immediate aim was to make possible a debate in which the Party would be subjected to popular that is, non-Party—criticism. Through this debate he hoped to change the climate of opinion, so that his non-bureaucratic, non-élitist policies would again gain a hearing.

The first necessity was to ensure that young people had freedom of access to the media. Throughout the manœuvering from November 1965 to May 1966, Mao's most constant theme was a demand for freedom of criticism for the young.

At the same time the 'May the 16th Circular' condemned 'abstract bourgeois' ideas of freedom, and Mao's supporters were to assert repeatedly throughout the Cultural Revolution that freedom was not an inalienable human right but an instrument of class struggle. Yet freedom for the citizens of communist countries to criticize, and even to change, their rulers, even without the right to challenge the communist system, is better than no freedom at all. As for the Liu Shaoqi regime, while it appeared to offer greater freedom to Chinese intellectuals than they had perhaps enjoyed at any time since 1949—except for the few ambiguous weeks of the Hundred Flowers movement in 1957—those intellectuals who chose to challenge the paternalistic system of the 1960s rather than lend it their support had found themselves silenced. Leftwing writers could not get their work published, protesting students were exiled to the villages, and the very real discontents of millions of Chinese—soon to be most vehemently expressed—were not heard.

Up to this point in the evolution of the Cultural Revolution the object of criticism was culture: the arts and literature, the media and education. However, as the *Hai Rui* case showed (and was chosen to show), the culture in question had political implications. And these implications did not represent merely some tenuous and oblique ideological relationship between culture and politics: current literature and thought were dominated by hostility to the Maoist policy alternative. The favoured, influential Chinese writers of the early sixties emphatically shared with the leaders in power an outlook on policy and organization which precluded that alternative.

The publication of the May the 16th Circular, which included news of the condemnation of Peng Zhen, changed the face of events in the colleges. The immediate result was the posting up in Beijing University of a wall newspaper which made an uncompromising attack on the Party administration of the University. Its author, Nie Yuanzi, was a junior member of the academic staff. She had been for years at loggerheads with the University's Party boss, Lu Ping, over the need for more political education, and had already won a signal victory by defeating the official candidate in the election for the position of her own department's Party secretary. The Party brought out the Youth League to stop the distribution of the text of Nie's poster. In response, Mao ordered that it should be published in the newspapers and broadcast nationally. On 2 June it was printed in the *People's Daily*, accompanied by an editorial entitled 'Sweep Away all the Freaks and Monsters'. On 3 June Lu Ping, the Party leader of the University, a protégé of Peng Zhen, was dismissed from his University office. The background of these events was that many students had since 1964 been active in criticizing the University establishment but had been suppressed. Six thousand of them had been exiled to the countryside; they now returned in triumph.

In the first days of June Party work teams were sent into the universities. Work teams were a normal means of organizing campaigns against errant cadres. In the Socialist Education Movement, however, Liu Shaoqi had given the work teams a dominant and controlling role. Now he angered Mao once more in the same way. His teams, sent into the schools and colleges in the early days of June, imposed eight rules laid down for the purpose by Liu and accepted (in Mao's absence) by the Central Committee. It was not unreasonable that these rules should forbid insulting behaviour, sabotage and the besieging of residences; but to forbid the writing of wall newspapers, and rallies and demonstrations in the streets, and to demand a clear distinction between 'inside and outside'—that is, between Party and non-Party matters— was in flat contradiction to what Mao sought. Liu also insisted there should be no liaison among students in different institutions, and his teams came down hard on 'outside agitators'. He opposed the new Red Guards and condemned them as an illegal organization. According to his daughter, he told her that 'he regarded all students opposed to the work teams as bourgeois elements and gave them no freedom or democracy'. He made a distinction between students of 'good' (that is, of working class or peasant) background and others. The former could take part in the Cultural Revolution and the latter could not. It was thus Liu Shaoqi himself who created the distinction which was to prove the main source of factionalism and violence in the events which followed.

The arrival of the work teams was greeted at first with joy, but their repressiveness soon led to a change. Those hostile to the teams then formed their own 'revolutionary' organizations. Those who supported the teams followed suit. The latter organizations tended to be led by the children of high cadres; the former were often led by the children of bourgeois families which had suffered discrimination at the hands of the regime. In this way, the Red Guard movement was split from the beginning.

The split expressed hostilities already powerful in China's schools and colleges. There the children of cadres, organized in the Youth League, and less circumspect than their parents, paraded their belief that they were a hereditary élite. They were especially hostile to bourgeois pupils who sought by hard scholastic work to overcome the political disadvantages from which they suffered, and which had been increased since the tenth plenum of September 1962 had reasserted the necessity for class struggle. In education one form of the expression of class struggle was the imposition of a quota system for admission to higher education in favour of the children of workers and peasants; this actually meant, in practice, in favour of the children of cadres. Chinese schools in fact presented in microcosm the national situation in which the revolutionary leadership was on their way to becoming a new élite. Anita Chan, in *Children of Mao*, presents in the words of a former Red Guard an image which vividly expresses the source of these tensions. In his school the members of the Youth League (which was monopolized by pupils of 'good background') built the classroom desks into a pyramid: the son of the highest cadre whose family was represented in the school sat at the apex, the rest in hierarchical order of their fathers' positions. From there they laid down the law to their fellow pupils. Through the Red Guards these tensions now exploded in the streets.

In the West the two opposing groups of Red Guards were referred to as the 'radicals' and the 'moderates', but while those who protested against work-team control might reasonably be called radical, their opponents scarcely deserved or earned the epithet of moderate. The distinction between them was not a difference of degree, but a fundamental difference of aim—the one determined to criticize the regime, and the other concerned to defend it and to defend their fathers who ran it.

The climax—a feeble one in comparison with much that was to come, but shocking at the time—was a pitched battle on 19 June between the radical students and the work teams. Liu Shaoqi's wife promptly condemned the students' attack (or resistance) as a 'counter-revolutionary incident'. Mao (absent in the south) informed the students, through Jiang Qing, that on the contrary their resistance was a 'revolutionary act'.

On 16 July the ageing Mao swam in the Yangzi. Aided by the river's rapid current, he swam several miles downstream in an impressive display of physical vigour. In this dramatic way he convinced China that it was too soon to dismiss him and think only of the succession. Two days later he returned to Beijing, called a series of meetings, demanded the withdrawal of the work teams, and put the responsibility for their actions firmly on Liu Shaoqi. He did not win easily. On 24 July Liu Shaoqi decided that he would nevertheless not withdraw the work teams, but Mao convened another meeting the following day, and forced the withdrawal through. Further, the students were advised to reject candidates who had been nominated by the work teams for the elections soon to be held to replace those cadres dismissed in the course of the campaign.

Then, on 1 August, Mao wrote his own wall newspaper: 'Bombard the Headquarters'. He published it while the eleventh plenum of the Eighth

Central Committee was actually in session. It was an explicit invitation to the radical students to direct their criticism at the highest leaders of the Party and the State. It was clear that Liu Shaoqi, as the man responsible for the 'fifty days' of work-team control, was the main target.

Liu had by no means opposed Mao at all points. He had accepted the dismissal of Peng Zhen, though concerned that Peng should not be judged with unnecessary harshness. He had accepted the purging of the Beijing committee and the dissolution of the Youth League. He pursued with vigour the educational reforms proposed by Mao, which included the abolition of the academic admissions system and the promise of an alternative system of admission by recommendation, along with a plan for new teaching materials. On the Party authorities in the universities his hand fell heavily. Eleven high officials in thirteen universities were ejected from office. In Qinghua University, Beijing, where the work team was led by Liu's wife Wang Guangmei, all Party cadres were made to present self-criticisms. Only 30 per cent passed the test; the remaining 70 per cent are said to have been sent to the labour camps.

This was a purge as drastic as anything Mao could have wished. His quarrel was not with any lack of vigour on Liu's part. His objection was that the purge was an irrelevant exercise in paternalism, in which the high leaders of the Party pre-empted the right of the non-Party public to criticize and condemn. The fact that the resulting purge was severe was no compensation; indeed rather the reverse, for the virtual destruction of the Qinghua University Party machine by the work-teams' drumhead justice, while Party leaders at higher levels were spared from any criticism, was neither just nor expedient. In Mao's eyes Liu Shaoqi had repeated precisely the errors which he had committed in the Socialist Education Movement.

The withdrawal of the work teams was a triumph for the radical students. But perhaps what gave them the greatest satisfaction was the disbandment of the Youth League, which had not only shown its hostility to the Cultural Revolution but had also become an embarrassing manifestation of the Party's failure to appeal to young people. Recruitment was falling, and the average age increased as numbers declined. Few of its members were under 20, and very few were girls. In the countryside it was almost non-existent. In common with other attempts to involve students more closely in public affairs, such as militia training in the universities and student participation in the Socialist Education Movement, the League had done little to overcome the apathy of the majority or the disaffection of the minority.

Party resistance was, however, scotched rather than defeated. 'Moderate' Red Guard organizations continued to work closely with the Party to oppose the radical students, who at first formed only a small minority. Indeed at one stage the young radical Kuai Dafu of Qinghua University, son of a peasant, stood almost alone there. He demanded that no liaison committee of Red

Guards should be formed without consultation with all students or without elections, in order that the students could produce their own leaders. He was imprisoned and went on hunger strike.

The dominant right wing of the Red Guards formed the United Action Committee which openly supported the establishment and attacked Lin Biao. In order to divert criticism from Party members, these right-wing Red Guards concentrated their attacks on 'bourgeois intellectuals'. They organized privileged skilled workers in the capital and prosperous peasants in its suburbs to oppose and attack the radical students. They arrested and imprisoned their opponents.

Mao took a hand to redress the balance. He wrote a letter to the radical Red Guards of Qinghua University on 1 August, assuring them: 'I will give enthusiastic support to all who take an attitude like yours to the Cultural Revolution.' He observed that 'organizations of workers and peasants have been formed, and are opposed to the students ... the Centre must issue a declaration forbidding this sort of thing anywhere'. On 10 August, ignoring normal security procedures, he went down among the crowds to talk to the students.

A new Sixteen Points directive issued on 11 August by the eleventh plenum for the conduct of the Cultural Revolution asserted that the socialist revolution had entered a new phase, and that the direction of the Cultural Revolution was correct. It emphasized that the method of the Cultural Revolution was to 'mobilize the masses without restraint' and added: 'Do not try to act on behalf of the masses; they will educate themselves in the course of the movement.' It insisted that the difference between 'antagonistic and non-antagonistic contradictions' should be respected, and differences resolved through discussion. It asserted that the vast majority of cadres were good or were capable of improvement; only a small minority were incorrigible. It encouraged the formation of Cultural Revolution congresses, groups, and committees. It warned that no cadre should be criticized by name in the press without the permission of the Party committee at the same level; that the movement must not hinder production; and that in the armed forces it should be carried out only under the instructions of the Military Commission of the Central Committee and of the General Political Department of the PLA. It called for a radical reform of the education system, and for the integration of the Cultural Revolution in the countryside with the Socialist Education Movement. Finally, it laid down that the guide to action should be the thought of Mao Zedong.

The key to the process of 'cultural revolution' as it was anticipated in the Sixteen Points lies in the instruction that 'the masses' were to be given the opportunity 'to educate themselves in the course of the movement'. Some months later Zhou Enlai, in congratulating the members of a scientific research organization on having successfully exposed and ejected its former leaders, remarked: 'We could have got rid of these people simply by administrative action; but from that you would have learned nothing.' In this comment is revealed the whole difference between the two concepts of reform already expressed in the Socialist Education Movement, Liu's reform from above and Mao's reform from below.

The tone of the Sixteen Points was moderate. In this respect it contrasted strongly with the attitude maintained by Lin Biao. A few days after the issue of the Sixteen Points directive in a speech at the first great Red Guard rally, he said: 'We must launch fierce attacks on bourgeois ideology, old customs and the force of old habits. We must thoroughly topple, smash and discredit the counter-revolutionary revisionists, bourgeois rightists and reactionary bourgeois authorities.' It was Lin Biao who had defined the task of the Red Guards as 'the destruction of the four old things', and so given justification—or at least encouragement—for the excesses committed by some Red Guard groups and for releasing a *jacquerie* against everything from traditional dress and Western hairstyles to the works of art in the museums of the capital. Mao obliquely showed his opposition to this cultural iconoclasm by giving a published interview to his niece, in which he not only defended China's cultural heritage but proposed that his niece, a student of English, should make a new translation of the English Bible into Chinese.

The Sixteen Points directive did not prevent the conservative Red Guards from continuing their opposition to the radicals. Liu Shaoqi's instruction that only students of 'good' family background could participate in the Cultural Revolution was now taken up. Paradoxically, it was the so-called 'moderates' who insisted that no one from a non-labouring background could be a good socialist, and the radicals who argued that one could. The reason was simple: the fathers of the leaders of the conservatives, being high cadres, were working class by courtesy—although few of them were actually so in family origin. The radicals, on the contrary, were frequently of middle-class origin, and were forced to argue that political attitude and not class origin was the hallmark of a socialist. It was such bourgeois students and their families who had suffered most at the hands of Party authorities from suspicion, and from discrimination in university entrance, jobs, and selection for service in the countryside. Beneath the idealistic slogans of the student movement lay this bitter conflict between the children of the new privileged class and the now underprivileged children of the former dominant classes.

Policy questions in the Cultural Revolution

Meanwhile, the scope of protest and criticism had now spread beyond the area of culture to include policy. Mao's 'Bombard the Headquarters' wall newspaper had justified criticism of members of the central leadership, and (whether deliberately or not) had especially implicated Liu Shaoqi who had organized the work teams. Policy questions, as we have seen, were implicit in the attack. One policy question at least had perhaps already played a part in events. While Peng Zhen was still engaged in resisting the attack on the Beijing satirists, another and different challenge had been presented to him. The Hubei Party Committe (Hubei was the native province of Lin Biao) submitted to the Central Committee a group of proposals for agricultural mechanization. These were in fact the proposals which Mao had made in Chengdu in 1958 in the course of the Great Leap, advocating that the ownership, operation and, as far as possible, the manufacture of agricultural machines should be decentralized to the communes themselves, and not controlled by the state as in the Soviet Union. The Chengdu proposal had not been implemented seriously, and died the death with the rest of Mao's 1958 policies. To bring these proposals up again in April 1966 was to spring another mine under the Liu Shaoqi regime. The Central Committee actually passed the Hubei document to Peng Zhen, of all people, for his comments. By this time Mao had made his own notes in the margin. They included criticism of Soviet agriculture. They also included a request for the proposals to be circulated throughout the Party. Peng Zhen apparently struck out some of Mao's comments, including those critical of the Soviet Union, and then advised the Central Committee that it should not be distributed. At the same time a document written by Liu Shaoqi during 1958 was revived and circulated; it was a paper which, by emphasizing the importance of modern technology, implicitly denied the value of grass-roots, appropriate-technology mechanization.

There was no issue between right and left which more strongly manifested the essential differences between their respective strategies for economic growth and social change than the question of agricultural mechanization. During the First Five Year Plan, Kang Sheng (by 1966 a member of the Cultural Revolution Group) had been sent to the Soviet Union to examine mechanized agriculture. His conclusion was: 'Soviet farms have many machines, and yet the productivity of Soviet agriculture is not high. We should not imitate the Soviet machine tractor stations. If we do, agricultural mechanization will be divorced from the peasants . . .'. He concluded that the machine tractor stations of the Soviet Union simply 'held the peasants to ransom'. The alternative, which Mao embraced in 1958, was to encourage the collectives (by then communes) to buy their own machines. This possibility had been raised in the Soviet Union (by Sanina and Venzher) but dismissed by Stalin on the grounds that to give State-owned tractors to collectively owned farms would be a retrograde act. Mao opposed Stalin's argument and denied that (in Chinese conditions at least) collective as opposed to State ownership of agricultural machines would be a retreat from socialism.

The left did not see the tractor only as a means of pulling the plough, but as a versatile source of power which could considerably increase yields—by pumping water, by use in post-harvest operations, by use in soil improvement, and in other ways: but this would be effective only if the tractor was on the farm and in the farm's control. As for the inability of the collectives to buy standard tractors, the left's reply was that mechanization could start with small machines accompanied by improved traditional equipment; the profits from their use would provide funds for eventual full mechanization.

The left saw many other advantages in commune ownership and operation of agricultural machines. Ownership would motivate the peasants to use the machinery fully and in every profitable way. Responsibility for and use of the machines would have in the villages an educational effect which no other policy could so well provide. The maintenance and repair of the machines, and the manufacture of ancillary equipment, could be, along with local processing of crops, the natural starting-point of industrialization of the village. In fact, the small tractor with a power take-off was the key tool for Mao's spiral of village development. The seasonal arrival from the machine tractor station of a tractor which ploughed and then vanished was no substitute.

Perhaps the greatest objection of the left to State operation of agricultural machines was that these machines would almost inevitably be used in areas where they would bring the biggest financial returns; as a result the more prosperous farming regions would be modernized while the poorer areas remained backward. The gap in average income between the developed and the underdeveloped areas of China would grow, and so assist in creating the 'internal colonialism' which China's inherited pattern of location of industry and markets already threatened.

Liu Shaoqi was accused of having taken the lead in advocating State control, central manufacture, and maximization of profit in operation. Of the innumerable charges made against him, this was perhaps the most nearly true. In the early sixties he had indeed personally advocated precisely such a policy. He had proposed that a trust should be formed to control the manufacture and operation of farm machines; that its policy should be to choose one hundred out of China's two thousand counties and mechanize their agriculture. Out of the profits made by the trust, a further one hundred counties would then be mechanized. The trust would operate through tractor stations whose distribution would be so planned as to avoid any control of their operations by local authorities. This project was offensive to the left at every point.

The Cultural Revolution campaign of criticism of existing policies did not end with the question of farm mechanization. It continued with a Press campaign against one of China's most influential economists, Sun Yefang. Sun was highly critical of the wastefulness of China's planned industrial production. He insisted that economic progress should be measured by increased returns to factors of production, above all to labour. He argued that the only satisfactory measure of efficiency is profit, which provides the most unambiguous index of the efficient use of labour and capital. Sun went further and advocated the use of profit not merely as a measure of efficiency but as an incentive to effort. He proposed therefore to make profit the most important target in the plans imposed on industrial enterprises. And it followed from this that enterprise managers should be given the autonomy necessary to arrange production in the most profitable way. His proposals were not original; such an alternative was already being tried out in various East European communist states, and Sun freely admitted his debt to the Soviet economist Liberman, who had given his name to similar ideas.

Sun's ideas were anathema to the Chinese left, who saw in them only a widening of the possibilities of the creation of a highly paid technocracy, an exacerbation of what they saw as China's deepest political problem the repolarization of society into the managers and the managed. Far from entertaining the possibility of using profit as the index and motivation of industrial success, the left opposed even the existing system of piece-work. Mao's own opposition to this, however, was expressed in practical terms familiar enough to any Western industrialist: that piece-work leads to neglect of quality, resistance to innovation, and disputes among workers. He was never opposed to the use of material incentives in general to stimulate production. His objections were particular: excessive differentials between managerial salaries and industrial wages, urban and rural incomes, and rich and poor regions. He was also critical of the failure of Soviet theorists to distinguish between individual material incentives and collective material incentives, believing that the latter could be effective. Stripped of jargon, his ideas on material incentives were neither novel nor extreme; but many of his followers made an absolute of equality.

The question of collective versus individual incentives was at its sharpest in agriculture. Agricultural policy since 1962 had accepted the relaxation of collective control. This was expressed in documents drawn up without consultation with Mao. He had complained of this at the conference of Seven Thousand Cadres in January 1962: 'Sixty regulations on our work in the countryside; seventy regulations on industrial enterprise; sixty on higher education; forty on scientific research . . . all already implemented!' The regulations on agriculture sanctioned increased private plots, more private trade in rural fairs, and wider scope in general for private peasant enterprise. In comparison with similar changes in some other communist countries at that time the sixty regulations were cautious; but from a left-wing point of view they threatened to undermine the rural strategy of which collective agriculture seemed an essential part, by diverting scarce resources away from the communal effort.

The right wing saw these left-wing protests (and most Western commentators agreed) as indicating a predilection for Utopian values to the neglect of the needs of economic growth, but we should acknowledge that what Mao and his supporters believed was more interesting: it was that the fastest means to economic growth was identical with the proper means of transition to socialism—maximum popular participation in the process of development. If this view was anti-revisionist it was also anti-Stalinist.

Equally offensive to the left was the destruction of commune and brigade industries. Of these Mao had said in 1958: 'Here lies our great and glorious hope for the future.' His successors since 1976 have now accepted and vigorously developed the village enterprises, and continue to quote Mao's words; but in the wake of the Leap, during which the first attempts to industrialize the villages had been a wasteful failure, the right wing condemned the enterprises outright and abolished most of them. Worse, they expropriated those which had been successful, turning them into State enterprises. Liu Shaoqi was especially severe on them, condemning them as 'the black bag of cadre corruption'; but to abolish the commune and brigade industries was to deny Mao's whole perspective of rural development.

17

The Great Proletarian Cultural Revolution, II

The 'Paris Communes', January 1967

Once questions of policy were brought into the struggle, virtually the entire membership of Liu Shaoqi's government became vulnerable. Even Zhou Enlai, although perhaps the most widely respected figure in the whole leadership, was not immune. However, his sincere support for the Cultural Revolution and his close identification with its leaders saved him from more than sporadic attacks, and enabled him eventually to save most of his ministers—perhaps even to save the regime—by keeping government intact and functioning.

Meanwhile the hard-pressed radical students had sought allies among certain groups of workers. While skilled workers in the State-sector establishment, with high wages, pensions, and security for life, opposed the radicals vigorously, by no means all of China's industrial workers did so. Between 30 and 40 per cent of them were virtually casual labourers; they were on short contracts, paid at lower rates, with no security or pensions, and no right to housing, medical attention, or the education of their children. They were the biggest and most natural constituency of the radicals. Besides these 'contract workers' were several million who worked in pre-modern or semi-modern handicraft co-operatives or in service occupations who were also denied the benefits enjoyed by those on the official State-sector payroll. They too supported the radicals. As the Cultural Revolution went on, many other groups were to express their grievances and to support the Red Guards' initiative. They published their own tabloid news-sheets. The proliferation of such publications was extraordinary, and was matched by the millions of handwritten wall newspapers (*dazibao*) which turned every bare wall in urban China to account. The wall newspapers were strongly encouraged by Mao. They were, he claimed, 'classless' because their production was virtually cost free; anyone with a grievance could find the simple means to express it in this way. They were almost impossible to censor and their authors were anonymous, so that retaliation against them was not possible. There was a good Marxist precedent for praise of wall newspapers as a political weapon;

Engels had expressed his admiration for them and stressed their importance when they were used by the German working class during the revolution of 1848.

The alliance between radical students and disaffected workers took the Cultural Revolution into the factories. An intense struggle began. Its centre was Shanghai, but similar events took place in most cities. The left-wing workers formed organizations called Red Rebels, while the conservative workers formed rival groups calling themselves Scarlet Guards. Shanghai's Party organization and the official trade unions sided with the conservatives. This concerted resistance produced a new and even more explosive head of radical steam. Moreover the left wing, from the student–worker rank and file to Mao's supporters on the Cultural Revolution Group in Beijing, had by this time taken their criticisms and condemnation of the Party's leaders so far that they felt they must oust the Party establishment from power and replace them, or suffer retribution sooner or later. At the same time this situation offered to those who sought it the possibility of the replacement of the Party's rule by some more participatory and democratic form of government. The seizure of power and the creation of alternative institutions became at once a possibility and a necessity.

In August 1966, Red Guards from Beijing, frustrated in their attempts to interview Shanghai's governors, seized the city hall. The authorities organized the establishment workers, via the trade unions, to oppose them. After several days of fighting the Red Guards were ejected. They then summoned from Beijing the two principal radical Red Guard leaders, Nie Yuanzi and Kuai Dafu, to assist in creating an alliance with young workers and casual labourers. When these working-class allies tried to send a delegation to the capital, hostile railway workers shunted their train into a siding and left them stranded. This incident roused radical tempers, and clashes brought chaos to the whole city.

The struggle was primarily directed against the offical trade unions. They were abolished on 27 December, but they were immediately reincarnated as the Scarlet Guards. The rebel workers meanwhile spontaneously created their own new unions under the name of 'friendly societies'. Their demands were mainly economic: higher wages, better bonuses, shorter hours; above all they wanted contract workers to enjoy equal pay and to be officially registered as city residents. The right-wing leaders in Shanghai responded by granting to those groups of the industrial workers who supported them large increases in wages and bonuses. The left condemned this as a cynical trick, but it may well have been unavoidable; discontent with the Party's policy of keeping down money wages was not confined to casual labourers, and the pay rises may have been the necessary price of support for the Shanghai Party establishment. Especially embarrassing to the left wing were the demands from the contract workers. On the one hand, Beijing could not add enormously to the State payroll by giving them equal status; on the other, they could not abolish the system because of the pressure of rural underemployment.

In November Zhang Chunqiao arrived from Beijing, and with Mao's authority forced the city authorities to give way to the rebels. The Scarlet Guards, however, refused to acknowledge the agreement and launched strikes which paralysed the city. It was largely in an attempt to bring the strikes to an end that the radicals then began to organize seizures of power, factory by factory and unit by unit. Finally on 14 January they seized the government of the city. However, by this time there were no less than seven hundred rebel organizations competing for a share of power, and they were unable to form an effective administration. It was in the hope of finding a rubric under which all the radicals could unite that it was proposed to form a 'Paris Commune' government of the city, with direct elections, the right of recall, and officials paid no more than the wages of workers. A Preparatory Committee for the Shanghai Paris Commune was formed on 5 February. It was announced as 'a new form of local organization of the dictatorship of the proletariat'.

The committee had been formed from organizations in the factories and the units, each of which had elected a new management by secret ballot and with the right of recall. The bureaucracy had been ousted, and the industrial managers and Party authorities with it. For a brief space there was a sort of democracy: complete freedom to criticize, elected workers' management, an elected city government and free trade unions. 'We are the masters of the country and of our own concerns,' some workers said.

There was tremendous enthusiasm among radicals everywhere for the new Paris Commune form of government. In about half of the provinces and cities of China moves were made to imitate Shanghai. Nevertheless the rebels were actually in a minority in Shanghai, in whose relatively advanced industries skilled workers predominated. The Japanese newspaper *Asahi Shimbun* reported that while the Red Rebels numbered 400,000, the Scarlet Guards numbered 800,000. Moreover the attitude of the central Cultural Revolution leadership was ambivalent. It is true that the idea of a Paris Commune type of organization had been sanctioned by the Cultural Revolution leaders in Beijing, that *Red Flag* had proposed it, and that the Sixteen Points directive, accepted by the Central Committee, had recommended it. Lin Biao had said: 'The people's democratic rights are being instituted in accordance with the principles of the Paris Commune.' However, it was one thing to recommend this as a form of organization for the Cultural Revolution groups themselves, and another to accept it as an alternative form of government which would deprive the Party of its *raison d'être*. Zhang Chunqiao himself, in accepting the Shanghai Paris Commune, had already quoted Mao's reservations on the point: 'With the Commune inaugurated do we still need the Party? I think we need it because we must have a hard core . . .'. And then he added ambivalence to ambivalence by continuing, 'whether it is called a communist party or a social democratic party . . .'.

Mao soon forbade the Shanghai Paris Commune outright. It was already clear that the Cultural Revolution Group in Beijing was not ready to support the most radical demands being made in Shanghai. The economic demands of the rebel workers were mostly refused. The new 'friendly society' trade unions were condemned. The contract-labour system was reasserted, although city registration was given to those contract workers already in Shanghai. Zhou Enlai had deplored seizures of political power and tried to confine such to Cultural Revolution organs and economic institutions. The rebels in Shanghai had been warned off interfering with the secretariat of the East China Bureau on the grounds that it was an organ of the Central Committee. Mao's condemnation of the Shanghai Paris Commune did not come entirely as a surprise.

By the end of 1966 the armed forces were becoming deeply involved in the movement. At the beginning, the PLA had simply provided the logistics for the huge assemblies and vast movements of young people which took place with the growth and spread of the Red Guards. In September, on Mao's orders, the soldiers began to play a more active role in trying to maintain public order; but this was on the basis of preserving neutrality in the struggles of the different factions, and the essential aim was to minimize violence and the disruption of services, and so to make possible the sort of free and peaceful process of debate and demonstration that had been envisaged by the Central Committee when the Sixteen Articles were agreed. A second army intervention of December, again in response to orders from Mao, was of a different kind. Its orders were now to support the left against those Party organizations which were resisting the Cultural Revolution. When Mao recommended that the Paris Commune organization should be replaced by 'revolutionary committees', the army was given representation on them, along with radical delegates and those existing cadres who had not incurred severe criticism.

The 'revolutionary committees', 1967–1968

Mao Zedong told a foreign delegation in 1967 what his perspective was: a year of agitation, a year to establish new power structures, and a year of consolidation. This was probably to be followed by a Party Congress. The revolutionary committees represented the new power structure Mao had in mind. It is not likely that he was happy to see the army playing the dominant role within them, but military dominance could scarcely be avoided and it was almost bound to have conservative implications. While the PLA was certainly much more disposed to favour Mao's policies than the civilians of the Party and the State, nevertheless its commanders, like soldiers everywhere, disliked indiscipline and disorder, and they were bound to regard the radicals as a threat to the discipline of the army itself. This threat was dramatized by radical control of the military academies, whose students had illegally arrested and maltreated Luo Ruiqing and Peng Zhen, and dragged Peng Dehuai out of retirement to be tried before a kanagaroo court.

Lin Biao, by changes of personnel which began with the purge of Luo Ruiqing, had established firm control of the forces directly commanded by the Ministry of Defence, but half of the army was under decentralized regional and provincial commands. These regional commands still represented the pattern of the conquest of China in the Third Civil War; the field armies which had occupied different areas in 1949 were still the garrisons of these areas. Among them Lin Biao's 4th Army occupied the largest territory, but it did not dominate the country. The provincial armies had sufficient independence to be in a position to define 'the left' which they had been ordered to support according to their predilections. Lin Biao's appointees in the Beijing military establishment, Xiao Huan and Yang Chengwu, attempted to reduce the powers of the provincial commanders in a series of ordinances, but failed.

The first revolutionary committee, which provided the model, was set up virtually by the army, and throughout China the process of the formation of the new committees was dominated by the soldiers. At the same time, these events cannot be seen simply as a military seizure of power. If that had been so the committees could have been formed very quickly, but in fact the process took eighteen months of discussion, factional struggles, and painstaking negotiations before the last provincial revolutionary committee was formed. The PLA should perhaps be praised for its patience rather than condemned for its intervention.

Forbearance on the part of the soldiers, however, was not sufficient to win them friends among the extreme left, and in Guangdong, Hubei, and elsewhere the blatant bias of many army commanders in favour of the Party establishment and of the pseudo-revolutionary organizations which had been created to protect it goaded the left wing to new extremes. By the middle of 1967 a distinct though by no means unified 'ultra-left' movement became obvious. Its leaders included new editors of the two principal national newspapers, the *People's Daily* and the *Guangming Ribao*, and the editor of the Party's chief theoretical organ, *Red Flag*. This group had strong links with the Institute of Philosophy, which had three representatives, Guan Feng, Wang Li, and Qi Benyu, on the central Cultural Revolution Group itself. Among the Red Guard organizations, it could work through Kuai Dafu's student group in Qinghua University with its highly effective national network.

The so-called ultra-left gained the confidence to operate openly as a result of an alarming incident in Wuhan. There, from April to July 1967, an armed confrontation between radical students and workers on the one hand and conservative workers on the other rapidly increased in intensity. The radical workers were drawn largely from the steel industry. They were opposed by a federation of conservative groups called the Million Workers. The commander of the provincial forces, Qian Zaidao, took the conservative side. The Cultural Revolution authorities in Beijing sent a delegation to make a judgement as to which groups were truly revolutionary. The composition of this delegation showed the increasing strength of the left wing of the Cultural Revolution movement. Most of the group were men soon to be identified as members of the ultra-left: Wang Li, a close associate of Chen Boda (the leftwing exegesist of Maoism and Mao's former secretary). Air Force Commissar Yu Lijin, and extremist Red Guards from the Aeronautical Institute in which Lin Biao's son was influential. To send such a group was a direct provocation to the conservative faction in Wuhan. The conservative Million Workers, led by one of Qian Zaidao's regiments, seized the city and the new Yangzi Bridge. They besieged the hotel where the members of the deputation were staying and beat up Wang Li. The authorities in Beijing were forced to launch a military campaign in which troops under central command, supported by warships, occupied Wuhan.

Wang Li returned to Beijing as a hero, to put himself at the head of the ultra-left and help to push the Cultural Revolution to an extreme which proved to be its final peak. The ultra-left made three demands. The first was to 'drag out the handful of capitalist-roaders in the Army'. The second was that the further formation of revolutionary committees, which were dominated by army units and old cadres, should be suspended until both the army and the cadres had been further purged. Their third policy was an escalation of the attack on Liu Shaoqi.

When in March 1967 the Central Committee ruled that while Liu's policies and writings should be criticized he himself should not be subject to personal attack, the ultra-left had promptly responded with personal accusations against Liu of a kind which in the circumstances of the time could not be glossed over or suppressed. The attack began with an article entitled 'Patriotism or National Betrayal?' Its author was Qi Benyu. In form, Qi stuck to the rules; ostensibly he criticized Liu Shaoqi only for having praised a film, *The Secret History of the Qing Court*, in which the young Guang Xu Emperor of the 1898 reforms was made the hero while the Boxer rebels were shown in a derogatory light. The immediate implication was that Liu Shaoqi, in approving this view of the Boxers, had shown that he was hostile to the mass line. There was, however, a further implication. The article was a parable, worthy of Wu Han himself: for the Boxers read the Communist Party; for the Guang Xu Emperor read Chiang Kaishek and his futile half-measure reforms. Thus the scene was set for the direct accusation, which was soon to follow, that in the 1930s Liu Shaoqi had secretly favoured Chiang Kaishek and had betrayed the Communist movement by advising a group of Communist Party members held prisoner by the Nationalists to save their lives by denying their faith. It was also asserted that these apostates now ruled China as Liu Shaoqi's clients. At the time in question Liu Shaoqi had been the leader of underground work in the Nationalist-held areas of China, and possibly some such incident actually occurred; perhaps Liu Shaoqi judged it better to save valuable lives by persuading the prisoners to deceive their captors than to encourage futile martyrdom. It is certainly true that several of these prisoners remained closely associated with Liu after their release and that by the 1960s they were playing a major role in the government of China. This new move thrust the burden of proof of their integrity on half of the members of the Party centre, on a charge which perhaps could never be in a literal sense refuted.

The question of how to handle the State–Party cadres who represented the establishment was shown at this point to be a major issue between the left and the ultra-left. Mao had agreed with Zhou Enlai that perhaps only 5 per cent of existing State and Party place holders need be dismissed. The rest could be 're-educated' by working under the authority of the mass organizations. The ultra-left would not accept this; they wanted a clean sweep of the administration at all levels. They saw the role of the revolutionary committees as popular executive governments which would replace the State–Party hierarchy. In fact although they had been forced to drop the form they would not relinquish the substance of the Paris Commune. Revolutionary committees in which the old cadres combined with an unreformed PLA to dominate the mass organizations, accompanied by a process of rebuilding the Party apparatus from which the representatives of the mass organizations were excluded, seemed to the ultra-left to be a complete betrayal of the whole movement, and of themselves. One recalls the dilemma of England's victorious seventeenth-century rebels: 'Though the King be defeated, yet is he still King, and all our posterity will be made slaves.' The Cultural Revolution rebels could no more trust the Communist Party not to retaliate against them than the parliamentarians could trust Charles I; now the Party was being restored, and its revival was directed by Mao himself, who advised that 'the masses should not be in too great a hurry to supersede the organs and associations of the Party'.

His influence was not sufficient to bring the movement to a halt at this point. The struggle over the revolutionary committees and the campaign to 'drag out' the conservatives in the armed forces continued. So, too, did the mounting attacks on Liu Shaoqi, again in spite of Mao's disapproval and his attempts to redirect the rebels' fire to Liu's writings rather than his reputation.

It was undoubtedly the intention of the Cultural Revolution Group that the representatives of the mass organizations should play the dominant role in the new revolutionary committees. State and Party cadres were to work, in effect, under mass supervision. The army was at once to support the left and to protect the cadres against excessive pressure. If the committees had been created from below, as the Shanghai Paris Commune had been created, then the mass organizations might indeed have been dominant. They were not. In

Heilongjiang, where the idea of the revolutionary committee first appeared, it was formed when the provincial Party secretary criticized himself, joined the rebels, and proposed that the provincial commander should be a member. In Guizhou a senior PLA political commissar joined the Cultural Revolution forces and took the lead in forming a revolutionary committee with himself as chairman and the provincial PLA commander as his deputy. In Shanxi the deadlock between mass organizations and the State–Party apparatus was resolved when the deputy political commissar of the provincial army formed a revolutionary committee on which the majority were cadres and soldiers. In Beijing, after prolonged strife, the revolutionary committee was formed by the Minister of Public Security, Xie Fuzhi, with a composition which gave a majority to an alliance of cadres, soldiers, suburban peasants, and State payroll workers.

The ultra-left protested at a process which seemed to them to be no different from the sham power seizures in the Beijing ministries in late 1966, but the breakdown of public order made it inevitable that the army would exercise the authority to choose among competing factions. In vain the centre protested that 'ideas and actions which imply that the Party committee of a military zone has authority over the local revolutionary committees must be criticized severely and corrected'. The protest could scarcely be sustained when Zhou Enlai himself was forced to admit that 'a quick survey of the situation today shows that most departments need military control'.

The influence of the extreme left was short lived. Even their apparent triumph in the Wuhan incident was a hollow one, for the offending provincial commander, Qian Zaidao, suffered no penalty. Their own extreme actions destroyed them. Allied with the recently returned Chinese chargé d'affaires in Jakarta who accused the Liu Shaoqi regime of having failed to protect the Chinese community in Indonesia, they attacked the Ministry of Foreign Affairs. They sacked its archives. They then organized or encouraged a Cultural Revolution outbreak in Hong Kong, delivered an ultimatum to its British administration, and burned down the British legation in Beijing. Soviet diplomats, Japanese communists, and other foreign nationals were molested or assaulted. Chinese diplomats abroad (the most senior having been ordered home) were constrained to demonstrate their 'Maoist' convictions in foreign capitals. China's relations with many other countries were thus threatened by actions which were more often ludicrous than dangerous, and as futile as they were distasteful.

Mao and his associates promptly reacted to destroy the influence of the extreme left; but although the reaction was abrupt it was only the culmination of a process of increasing control which had begun months before. It was confirmed by Mao's condemnation of the Shanghai Paris Commune, and his expression of a preference for the Heilongjiang revolutionary committee. His decision changed the course and nature of the Cultural Revolution. From an attempt to subject the Party to the authority of new popular institutions, it became a struggle for control within the Party between left and right, a struggle in which the advantage lay with the undamaged Party apparatus within the army, allied with the beleaguered but far from defeated members of the civilian State–Party hierarchy.

The efforts at control began as early as January 1967 in the wake of the chaos in Shanghai. The right of free travel enjoyed by the Red Guards and other rebel groups was withdrawn. The schools and colleges were declared reopened. The Cultural Revolution leaders themselves now actually revived Liu Shaoqi's ruling that rebel groups should be confined to their own institutions and not form federations. These first efforts failed; although mass Red Guard peregrinations ceased, some important groups had already established nation-wide means of communication. The schools could not be reopened because the teachers were afraid to teach, the textbooks had been destroyed, and no one dared to impose a syllabus which might become a target for renewed attack. Nor was it possible to prevent liaison among rebel groups in different institutions; in fact the attempt to do so was counter-productive in that it encouraged a mulitiplicity of small groups impossible to control. Nevertheless the attempt persisted and this persistence shows clearly the limits which the majority of the Cultural Revolution leadership were prepared to impose on the 'participatory democracy' which they themselves preached: they wished to keep not only their opponents but their allies fragmented.

The Little Red Book

The ineffectiveness of the first attempts to bring the rebel groups under control was partly due to differences of opinion as to the best means of creating effective unity among them, and these differences were related very closely to the original split between Mao and Liu. Those of a more authoritarian cast of mind—on both the right and the left of the Cultural Revolution—wished to suppress organizations which held opinions different from their own. The Maoists, on the other hand, sought to identify and strengthen within each and every organization a nucleus of support. In the critical and bloody summer of 1967, when factional strife was being carried on with the aid of looted weapons, home-made tanks and anti-tank devices, Molotov cocktails, and even crude chemical weapons, the Maoists sought to bring all factions into a common discussion, based on the famous 'Little Red Book'. This had been designed in the first place (by Lin Biao in the course of political education in the PLA) to redefine the revolutionary consensus. Divisive in its rejection of routinized bureaucratic authoritarianism, the 'Little Red Book' was meant in every other respect to create unity round the concept of the mass line.

This is plain from its form and content. Its title, literally *Sayings of Chairman Mao*, employed the word (saying: *yulu*) which had been used for centuries as a title for collections of informal aphorisms; the implication is that its contents were not *ex cathedra*. At the same time the word *yulu*, in this use, had strong Buddhist and therefore religious associations. Which of these contradictory implications would be uppermost depended on the manner in which the 'Little Red Book' was presented. Lin Biao settled this by using it as an instrument in his campaign of quasi-religious adulation of Mao.

The book contains few statements about specific policies. It is rather moralistic and general. It is, taken as a whole, a re-statement of Mao's mass line to which everyone paid at least lip service in China. Its publication was an invitation to Party and people to reaffirm their acceptance of the mass line. It was also an invitation to debate its implications for policy; the item which heads all the rest is a comment by Mao on the supreme importance of policy. This is where the challenge lay. The quotations in effect asked for a renewed revolutionary consensus, but one whose centre of gravity would be left of centre at least in the sense that it assumed continued social change. How far left of centre would, again, depend on how the contents were presented, and it was the insurgent radical left which laid down the parameters of debate. There is, in fact, the most shocking contrast between the book itself, with its rather sober and simple message, and the violence in which the Cultural Revolution became involved.

However, the new consensus was not to include the ultra-left, which was willing to carry divisiveness to an extreme by destroying the whole existing State–Party machine, invading the army and carrying the challenge into friendly foreign countries. Already the new Minister of Public Security had arrested three extremist students to check further attacks on Zhou Enlai's ministries; this inevitably encouraged the right to resist once more, and again this resistance merely fed the fury of the extremists. Mao toured China, encouraging unity. In response, the printing workers of the New China News Agency went to Qinghua University to appeal to the students to lay down their arms. They were fired on and several of them were killed. Mao summoned Kuai Dafu and Nie Yuanzi before him. They complained to him that some 'black hand' had organized this group of workers against them. Mao replied, 'I was the black hand.' He condemned both them and their followers for their behaviour. 'You have let me down,' he said, 'and what is more you have let down the workers and the peasants.' The Red Guards were forced by Mao's authority to admit groups of workers to the schools and colleges, and it was these workers who formed the first 'Mao-Zedong-Thought-Teams', bringing all sides together to discuss the issues in the light of Mao's principles. Meanwhile the ultra-left editors were dismissed from their posts. Qi Benyu disappeared from politics—though leaving the venom of his attack on Liu Shaoqi to work. The ultra-left in Beijing was broken up.

Its destruction in the provinces took much longer. The ultra-left 'Victory Alliance', the Sheng Wu Lian, in Hunan province issued its programme in

January 1968, over the name of a girl pupil in a Hunan high school: Mao, this document averred, had put forward a vision of a new society in his May the 7th letter to Lin Biao. The opportunity to create this new society had been provided by the January 1967 seizures of power, when authority had passed into the hands of the people in the new Paris Commune government. But the three-in-one combinations on which the revolutionary committees were based was simply a reinstatement of the bureaucrats. The 'January storm' did not even touch the most vital problem of all revolutions, the army. The supporters of Sheng Wu Lian asserted that Mao had been in favour of the Shanghai Paris Commune but knew that it could not succeed until the PLA had been purged. They now demanded an end to the formation of revolutionary committees, a purge of hostile army commanders, the mass dismissal of cadres, the creation of a new Communist Party dedicated to Mao's mass-line vision, and the arming of the people. By this time, however, the fight had already been lost.

The fall of the Beijing ultra-left did not leave the highest leaders of the Cultural Revolution unscathed. Jiang Qing herself took a voluntary holiday, after revoking her earlier instructions to the left to defend themselves by force if necessary. Chen Boda, the link between the leading group and the radical philosophers of the Academy, who had been Mao's closest adviser, retreated under a cloud which presaged his later fall; the purge of the Beijing radicals had deprived him of his three chief supporters in the leading group.

The involvement of both Jiang Qing and Chen Boda in the disgrace of the ultra-left obliges one to ask just how far beyond the spectrum of acceptable Cultural Revolution politics the so-called ultras really were. They professed to act according to the thought of Mao: perhaps at this point, then, we should pull together and summarize what Mao's thought implied.

Mao's emphasis on 'mass-line' political leadership had been constantly expressed over the years. What institutions and practices does such a concept require? It demands leaders who process popular demands, rationalizing them, reconciling them, and making operational sense of them—that is, translating popular aspirations into policy, with the results always subject to popular criticism. It assumes a high degree of decentralization of decision-making so that those who have to carry out decisions can as far as possible be party to them. It implies the acceptance of the right of citizens to criticize their rulers, if necessary protected from retaliation by the anonymity of the wall newspaper which puts the burden of proof on the cadres under criticism and not on the critic. Finally, although the leading group has total authority in the last analysis, it is only for as long as it enjoys popular support. The ultimate authority of communism is derived from the laws of history but it does not necessarily reside in any particular communist party. A communist regime can become alienated from the people. It can become corrupted by power and privilege. If as a consequence it loses popular support it may and should lose its power. The influence of the traditional idea of 'the mandate of heaven' is plain in this. At the same time, if persuasion and 'education' are the main means by which the Party exerts its authority among non-Party citizens, by the same token offending cadres are due equal patience and consideration, and having been criticized must be given the chance to reform. The dismissal of offending cadres should be a last and reluctant resort.

If we look at the demands of the ultra-left from the Maoist point of view we have thus presented, it is clear that they far exceeded Mao's intentions. They were not content to be associated in decision-making but wanted to take it over entirely. They were prepared to eliminate the Party as the leading factor and virtually replace it with popular assemblies of elected delegates subject to recall. They were prepared to use against the members of the State–Party establishment and any other opponents the authoritarian methods of which Mao's mass-line theory was a condemnation.

Yet it was Mao himself who had insisted on the 'Mandate of heaven' view of Party authority, and this was what the Sheng Wu Lian were assuming. Mao also recommended that the rebuilding of the Party should take place 'with an open door'—that is, that the non-Party public as represented by the mass organizations should participate in the choice or election of Party members and functionaries; but he then largely negated this, first by his prescriptive assertion that 95 per cent of existing cadres were good or capable of becoming good, and then by the 'three-in-one combination' which gave the representatives of the cadre force and of the army each a position equal to that of the mass organizations.

Mao's insistence on the 'open door' was in fact seldom honoured. It was bitterly resisted by the Party, and when the last of the left eventually fell from power after Mao's death in September 1976, the most persistently repeated charge against them was that they had sought to enforce it.

The question is, did Mao betray his own cultural revolution? The answer must be yes; but dependence on the army to prevent a total breakdown of public order and public authority gave him little choice. The creation of the revolutionary committees was partly at least a device to disguise the necessity of military control.

On the other hand the left wing did not entirely fail to leave its mark on the system. By the end of the period of left-wing rule at the end of 1976, more than half of the cadre force at middle and lower levels had been appointed during the Cultural Revolution, and subsequent events showed that many of them were ready to defend left-wing policies with a stubbornness which even by the late eighties had not been entirely overcome.

The restoration of Party power, 1968–1969

Gradually Mao's campaign for unity had its effect. Disorder died down. By mid-1968 the new system of revolutionary committees had been in the main completed. This new unity was won at the expense of Liu Shaoqi. The Party establishment seems to have accepted his disgrace as the price of the preservation of its power. Mao Zedong and Zhou Enlai ceased to attempt to defend him. Attacks on most other figures stopped. Liu became almost the sole target. In September 1968 he was removed from all his posts and expelled from the Communist Party. The accusations against him referred (obliquely) only to his so-called treachery in the 1930s. Of all the charges which had been made concerning his actions since 1949 not a word appeared in the final indictment.

With the fall of Liu the dominant influence of the left, though in a coalition with more moderate elements, was assured. The system of revolutionary committees also assured that the policies enunciated by Mao's supporters at the centre might now be implemented. No longer would the Party *apparat* pay only lip service to his appeals for a more egalitarian education system and more equitably distributed medical services. No longer would those hostile to the Great Leap strategy take decisions unchallenged.

Yet if the fall of Liu Shaoqi was a victory for the left, and ought to have been succeeded by the full implementation of their policies, this did not prove immediately to be the case. The fall of Liu entailed the confirmation of Lin Biao's position as heir apparent. Although he had hitherto been identified with the radical left (partly perhaps by their will rather than his own) his immediate interest on the attainment of power was to widen his support. In the circumstances of the time this had to involve reconciliation with still powerful groups who were hostile to the more extreme manifestations of the Cultural Revolution. Chief among these were the members of the State bureaucracy, still protected by Zhou Enlai, and the commanders of that substantial part of China's armed forces beyond Lin Biao's direct control or personal influence. At the same time, the most ready means of ensuring his own predominant influence over a reorganized Party was to maximize the military element, already pre-eminent in the revolutionary committees. The aim therefore was to increase control of the revolutionary committees through a form of restoration of the Party hierarchy directed by Lin Biao's military supporters, but at the same time to offer policies which would reduce polarization.

As a result, the Cultural Revolution proved to be something of a non-event, in comparison with the chiliastic aspirations with which it had begun. The replacement of authoritarianism by a Paris Commune type of democracy— the destruction of the 'bourgeois state apparatus'—did not take place. The mobilization of this 'democracy' in the form of powerful collective organizations which could exercise a countervailing power *vis-à-vis* the bureaucracy, was now checked, ostensibly in the interests of efficiency. The insistence on continued transition to socialism, the assertion that if socialism did not go forward it would go backward, was now surrounded by so many caveats that it was drained of most of its meaning. The assumption that the new collective democracy would spontaneously launch a new great leap in investment and production was never tested; the old 'great leap' phrase and its new euphemism the 'flying leap' were disowned from Beijing every time they were used at a lower level.

The Ninth Congress of the CCP met on 1 April 1969. If the associations of that date had been the same in China as they are in Europe, the left might have seen a wry significance in the choice. Jiang Qing, Zhang Chunqiao, and Yao Wenyuan were given no opportunity to address Congress. The new Central Committee consisted 40 per cent of soldiers, and—even more striking—of the Politburo of sixteen, no less than ten were military men. No Red Guard leader became a full member of the Central Committee, and several purged former ministers reappeared. The message of the Congress was not one of continuing the revolution, but of unity, stability and reconciliation.

After the Congress the reassertion of Party control was intensified, although the length of time which passed before the complete hierarchy was once more in place was considerable. How far this delay was due to resistance, and how far to the insistence of the left that the non-Party Public should participate in rebuilding the Party, is impossible to determine; both factors operated. The Cultural Revolution had led to the autonomy of many mass organizations, non-Party political bodies, and pressure groups. Many were reluctant, as a matter of principle, to accept the reassertion of Party control. Many were still at loggerheads with each other. The question of whether former cadres condemned in the Cultural Revolution should be re-employed, or which, or how many, and under what sort of control, was still bitterly controversial. There were accounts from certain areas (published because they illustrated a problem sufficiently widespread to be serious) of armed resistance to the restoration of Party power. In many factories the work-force refused to accept managerial authority, perhaps (as the Party press asserted) because they anarchistically rejected all authority, or perhaps because the new managerial authority was too reminiscent of the old—or indeed was the same.

Control was patiently recovered. The Party committees were declared to be the leading body in the revolutionary committees, and although the distinction between the two continued to be drawn it was at the same time prescribed that Party branches and revolutionary committees would share the same office and the same administrative apparatus. Party building was accompanied by the rehabilitation of former cadres. Discredited ministers reappeared. The State Planning Commission began to function again with many of its old personnel. The Red Guards were persuaded that their duty lay in the villages, and were sent to the countryside by the million; this was consistent with one aspect of Cultural Revolution theory, but it eliminated them as a political force. Executions of those guilty of crimes of violence during the political upheavals of 1966 to 1968 were reported. All attempts at further rural revolution in the form of raising the level of ownership from team to brigade or commune were deplored. The rights of the production team were reasserted, and private plots, limited handicrafts and limited private trading were protected. The use of wall newspapers for political agitation and the expression of grievances, although guaranteed in the new constitution, was curtailed.

One should not, however, interpret this swing to the right entirely as the result of Lin Biao's attempt to consolidate his power. It was partly a response to the alarming threat from the Soviet Union, coming at a time when China's southern frontier had been rendered vulnerable by the American operations in Vietnam. While Warsaw Pact troops moved into Czechoslovakia, the Soviet Union in 1968 sharply increased her forces on the Chinese border, began to foment disaffection in Xinjiang, and to accept if not provoke border disputes with China on the Aigun River. The new call for unity and stability accompanied measures to improve China's defence, of which the most dramatic was the campaign to dig a huge honeycomb of air raid shelters beneath the cities. It was a situation in which Lin Biao, as military leader, enjoyed every advantage.

Yet even in this new political climate the gains made on behalf of Cultural Revolution aspirations were not negligible. The 'four great freedoms' (great blooming, great contending, large-character wall newspapers, and great debate) were written into a new State constitution. Insistence on the necessity of Party leadership was accompanied by equal insistence that the Party must operate through the mass line, while Party decisions at all levels must be taken by the whole Committee in consultation with members, and not by the Party Secretary alone; that this was seriously intended was shown by the numerous detailed examples of good practice which were promoted as models.

There was as much emphasis, and as much display of concrete examples of proper practice, on the question of cadre participation in physical labour. The practice became general at this time, and was more than merely symbolic. The May the 7th cadre schools, in which cadres, especially from industrial concerns, were retrained partly by study of the new ideology and partly by physical labour, were continued. In some places members of a factory revolutionary committee, including Party cadres, spent one-third of their time in the office, one-third at a May the 7th cadre school, and one-third working on the factory floor.

Strenuous efforts were made to ensure that the reopening of schools and colleges and the admission of new students were not accompanied by a complete reassertion of the old practices which the left had condemned as élitist. To some extent there was a reaction; examinations were restored, and the authority of teachers, who had been humiliated and abused since 1966, was protected. On the other hand, admission policy, on Mao's orders, gave a high priority to workers, peasants, and soldiers who had been recommended by their committees or their units, to which it was expected they would return on graduation. Political education was stressed. Students were expected to spend two months of the year in productive labour, usually of a kind related to their subjects. There was at the same time a considerable development of informal, part-time, and locally financed education of all kinds, closely related to production, as in 1958.

By far the most significant gain for the forces of the Cultural Revolution was the restoration of the development of small industries owned and operated at commune and brigade level. Such development had been at the centre of the Great Leap strategy. It was given an added point in 1969 by the threat from the Soviet Union which, if it should lead to war, could be met only by guerrilla defence; and decentralized defence required decentralized industry. The localities were urged to create in every country, as far as means allowed, a minicomplex of basic industries. The main purpose was to service the modernization of agriculture, but many of these industries could in the event of invasion be switched to defence.

The revival of local industrial development proved to be the most stable of the achievements of the Cultural Revolution. The other victories of the left were to prove less permanent, but for the moment one aim had been achieved: to create a climate of opinion in which the threat of a new élitism would be recognized, and in which it would be accepted that the aim of Chinese politics was a continuing transition to socialism, however gradual. The other and related aim, the institutionalization of public criticism and public supervision of the Communist Party, was only partly achieved if at all.

The fall of Lin Biao

In September 1971 the Mongolian press revealed that on the 13th a Chinese-owned Trident had crashed in Mongolian territory, and that its nine occupants had been killed. It was soon reported that the victims were Lin Biao and several of his senior military associates. Rumours pieced together seemed to show that Lin Biao had plotted the assassination of Mao Zedong, and had fled when the plot was discovered. This explanation was later confirmed by Mao himself to Edgar Snow, and by Zhou Enlai at the Tenth Party Congress. Direct evidence is wholly lacking but no more acceptable account of the disappearance of Lin Biao has appeared.

Its political significance is not clear. Lin Biao spoke little and wrote less. After his death the charges against him (in which he and his supporters were referred to by the epithet 'swindlers like Liu Shaoqi') were so indiscriminate and contradictory as to carry no conviction. However, if we bring together his known previous attitudes, the controversies which preceded his fall, and the changes in policy which succeeded it, it becomes at least possible to separate the accusations made against him into the credible and the incredible.

On the eve of his fall an apparently esoteric discussion took place in the Chinese press on the question of whether industrial investment should give priority to electronics or to steel. After Lin Biao's fall no more was heard of the debate, except that Liu was accused of having favoured the electronics alternative. To concentrate on electronics would have meant a heavy dependence on imported technology. The Western embargo on trade with China made it unlikely that new technology would be supplied from the West. The source would have to be the Soviet Union. Such dependence was not an acceptable prospect, only ten years after the Soviet Union had crippled Chinese development by withdrawing its technologists and advisers, and the dependence would have been military as well as economic. One of the main charges against 'swindlers like Liu Shaoqi' (that is, Lin Biao and his supporters) was their underhand dealings with foreign countries; the allusion was to the Soviet Union, and it was *en route* to the Soviet Union that Lin Biao and the other fugitives apparently crashed. Finally, it was soon revealed that these 'swindlers' had also been less than enthusiastic about further recruitment to the militia and had thus cast doubt on the doctrine of people's war. The author of 'Long Live the Victory of People's War' had perhaps revised his opinions and sought—like his predecessors Peng Dehuai and Luo Ruiqing—to modernize the PLA at the cost of renewed dependence on Russia.

The other major issue of the time was the prospect of a diplomatic revolution in which Mao sought a *rapprochement* with the United States. According to Mao, Lin Biao opposed this, and it could certainly not have been easily reconciled with willingness to seek Russian military assistance.

Mao also informed Edgar Snow that Lin Biao had opposed the rebuilding of the Communist Party. Whatever this meant, it probably referred to his interest in maintaining the independent power which the army had won. Some colour is given to this by the constant demands in the Chinese press in the year preceding Lin's disappearance that the Party must be supreme over all other institutions and that the army must not pre-empt the decisions of the revolutionary committees; and Lin's death was immediately succeeded by the most sweeping changes in the command structure of the Chinese army ever to have taken place in the history of the CCP, and by the restoration of the supremacy of the Party over the military.

On questions of policy and organization, evidence of Lin Biao's opinions is even more difficult to find. There is no doubt that he had been associated during the Cultural Revolution with some of the most radical groups. On this evidence one would have expected him, on assuming power, to pursue the more radical policies which had been mooted between 1966 and 1968. In fact the period during which he was at the height of his influence was, as we have noted, one of 'unity and stability', of reconciliation and of caution. There are, however, degrees in such matters, and immediately after Lin's death there was a further sharp move in the direction of moderation, and a sustained campaign against those 'swindlers like Liu Shaoqi' who had encouraged exaggerations of Party policy, forced teams to merge into brigades, suppressed private plots and side-occupation handicrafts, and treated simple service trades with contempt. It seems then that Lin Biao's elimination made possible a more rapid dissolution of the extremes of the Cultural Revolution. It seems to have made possible the adoption of policies more consistent with Mao's own combination of boldness in strategy and caution in tactics, with the Cultural Revolution as an exercise in restoring socialist perspectives rather than in immediate social change, and more consistent also with the substance of Mao's own many recommendations, the moderate tone of which throughout the Cultural Revolution had stood in such contrast to the wild actions of his self-professed followers.

The period after late 1971 was one in which the language of policy sometimes bears a striking resemblance to that of the post-Mao era, with constant insistence on the rights of the production teams and the limits of their obligations to the State, on the necessity of material incentives, and the importance of costs, etc. The context, however, remained firmly collectivist, and the economic ethos was non-market—'develop production to increase supply' was the bottom line. Yet it is not surprising that at this point Deng Xiaoping should reappear, and soon rejoin the Political Bureau. Although he was ranked only nineteenth in the leadership, as Zhou Enlai's health failed Deng began to exert considerable influence.

Deng was only one of many former leaders who reappeared at this point. However, none appear to have been members of the Liu Shaoqi connection which had been formed in the late thirties in the Guomindang areas of China. And there was as yet no rehabilitation for the many thousands of appallingly persecuted 'bourgeois intellectuals', still languishing in prison or forced to humiliating drudgery in distant exile. They were people of no political account. It was not worth the risk for anyone to propose that they should be freed. The intellectual left—Jiang Qing and her Shanghai supporters—having little direct influence on policy outside the intellectual and cultural spheres made the most of their control of these spheres; Yao Wenyuan was reported to have complained in his cups (referring to Zhou Enlai) that 'he has the Party, the State and the army, and what do I have? Nothing but the worker–peasant–soldier Mao-Zedong-Thought-Teams. And this is by the will of Chairman Mao!' As their influence was thus confined to matters cultural, they used this power to its utmost. If they no longer had the power to suppress the 'bourgeois state', at least they could bully poets and ballet-dancers.

They were far from reconciled to leaving Zhou Enlai in control of all the institutional levers of power, to hand them on perhaps to Deng Xiaoping, the former 'number two capitalist roader'. That such a restoration was possible was indicated, as so often in China, by a new literary parable, a play, called *Climbing Peach Mountain Three Times*. During the years of the Socialist Education Movement, when left and right had been promoting the rival merits of Mao's Da Zhai Production Brigade and Liu's Peach Garden Village, there had been a play called *Going Down to Peach Garden Three Times*. To Jiang Qing's group, this new or revived play was a provocation comparable to that of the *Dismissal of Hai Rui*. The Hai Rui play had been launched to rehabilitate Peng Dehuai; the Peach Mountain play may have been launched in an attempt to rehabilitate Liu Shaoqi. The left attacked it on lines reminiscent of the attack on the *Dismissal of Hai Rui*, but this time the attack petered out.

Then there began another of China's esoteric academic debates, heavily loaded with political implications; but in this case the possible implications proved ambiguous: they could serve both the Jiang Qing group in its attempts to maintain its power, and its opponents who favoured the continuation of populist democracy. The debate provided contrasting rationales for both dictatorship and dissent.

It was begun by a professor of philosophy, Yang Rongguo. Its starting-point was the appeal which Lin Biao in power was said to have made for 'restoration of the rites', a phrase quoted from Confucius. Presumably it was an appeal for a return to some degree of normality. Yang used it, however, as a text to contrast rule by ritual, which he associated with arbitrary power over a slave society (it being Marxist dogma that Chinese society in the age of Confucius was based on slavery), with the rule of law introduced by the Qin (Ch'in) dynasty (associated with a change from slave society to feudalism). This positive view of the First Emperor of Qin was startling. To praise the emperor who burned the Confucian books and buried Confucian scholars alive was the equivalent in China of praising King Herod who massacred the innocents. At this point in the Cultural Revolution, however, the paradox made a certain amount of sense. In the chaotic unpredictability of a situation in which men found themselves at the mercy of anyone who could enforce a claim to be acting in the spirit of Mao Zedong Thought (which had been only too obviously ritualized), against whom the law was no defence, the idea of the Qin dynasty's system of precise laws had some attraction: progress should be sought through changes in the law, not through ideological slogans. Lin Biao had appealed for the 'restoration of the rites'; Yang countered by appealing for the restoration of law. Lin Biao, of course, was gone. The object of Yang's attack was the Cultural Revolution leadership which survived him.

They in turn took up the debate but with different implications. They agreed that the Qin tyranny had been 'progressive', but on the grounds of its destruction of slave society, and they urged that the historical necessity of this destruction justified Qin Shi Huang Di's brutal elimination of his intellectual opponents, the Confucian apologists of slavery. The argument was a defence of their own persecution of China's intellectuals.

This was the message of a new campaign by the left 'to root out Lin Biao and Confucius'. The campaign, however, had a more precise target. Confucius' hero was the Duke of Zhou. The campaign dwelt constantly on that name. It was clearly aimed at Zhou Enlai. In such matters in China there is no such thing as coincidence; consciousness of the political use of historical parallels is too keen to permit any accidental or careless use of analogy. In imperial China an author could lose his life for making an unfortunate pun which seemed to reflect on the Emperor. No one in China makes such verbal parallels by accident.

At the same time the alternative interpretation of the progressive role of Qin Shi Huang Di was taken up in a document which was to become the basic text of democratic dissent. It first appeared as a wall newspaper in Canton in 1974, signed with the fictitious name Li-Yi-Zhe, which combined elements from the real names of its three authors.

The Li-Yi-Zhe statement was posted up on the eve of the fourth National People's Congress, and as an appeal to it. The object of attack was 'the Lin Biao system' which, it was argued, had survived Lin Biao, especially among some of his 'literary associates'—a clear pointer to the left-wing intellectual followers of Jiang Qing.

The argument of this document began from Yang Rongguo's contrast between Confucian ritual and legalist law, but met the left wing's defence of Qin Shi Huang Di's tyranny by pointing out that his dynasty collapsed soon after his death in the face of popular revolt. The implication is clear: law must be based on consent; socialist legality is inseparable from civil rights.

The poster was not, however, an attack on the Cultural Revolution, which its authors judged to have been positive, and indeed to have been a democratic movement of great significance—the first successful exercise of rights theoretically offered in the 1954 constitution:

The fact that the mass of the people were actually able to exercise their constitutional rights to freedom of speech, publication, assembly and association as well as the right, which is not in the Constitution, to travel around exchanging experience, and were able to do so with the support of the Central Committee headed by Chairman Mao, is the great achievement of the Great Proletarian Cultural Revolution. But the Revolution has not yet fulfilled its tasks.

Lin Biao used the popular movement to establish his power, and then, from the summer of 1968:

socialist legality suddenly lost its force, and the theory that 'State power is the power to suppress' came into vogue ... Everywhere there were arrests, repression and miscarriages of justice ...

The four great freedoms were out of date ...

The authors then argued that the basis of the repressive dictatorship of the 'Lin Biao system' is precisely the sort of privilege which the Cultural Revolution had in the first place set out to crush:

The fundamental theoretical question in judging the Great Proletarian Cultural Revolution is whether or not there is emerging in China the type of privileged stratum which has already emerged in the Soviet Union . . .

How has it come about that 'getting in through the back door' has become common in our society? . . . How has it come about that so many senior cadres have been able to turn the prosperity and the privileges, which they have undoubtedly earned, into forms which their children can inherit? On what do these new bourgeois forms of ownership and the political means to defend them depend? Literature and art, education, admission to May 7th Cadre Schools, service in the countryside and in remote areas, admission to the universities, the training of revolutionary successors, almost any aspect of what are now called 'new-born things' can become a stage on which privilege vaunts itself . . .

Can we ignore the aristocracy and the new bourgeoisie which are now being created before our eyes?

Thus to these young democrats the problem was still that from which the Great Proletarian Cultural Revolution had begun, the crystallization of a post-revolutionary élite protecting its privileges by the abuse of political and economic power.

Zhang Chunqiao's *On Exercising all-round Dictatorship over the Bourgeoisie*, published in early 1975 as a theoretical justification of the policies of the left, began from the same problem of privilege. It was in the explanation of the causes of its emergence that Zhang Chunqiao and Li-Yi-Zhe differed. Zhang took the conventional view of Lenin that 'small production engenders capitalism and the bourgeoisie continuously, daily, hourly, spontaneously and on a mass scale'. Privilege was the consequence of the capacity of capitalism to regenerate itself even within socialist society. To prevent this process, collectivism must be extended and income differentials minimized. This theory was hardly likely to convince the majority of Chinese, who could see very well that the new privileges were associated with macro-economic socialist control and with large-scale bureaucratic enterprises, and not with peasant peddlers and handicraftsmen.

The Li-Yi-Zhe authors did not even allude to Lenin's famous or infamous dictum. Instead, they found the source of privilege in China's inherited Confucian political culture:

Socialism in China was born from the womb of semi-feudalism and semi-colonialism. Traditions formed during thousands of years of feudalism and aristocracy cling stubbornly on in thought and in culture, in law, and in all other parts of the superstructure.

The cure cannot lie in the enforcement of higher levels of collectivism, which will simply increase the opportunities for power and privilege. It lies in the enforcement of the rule of law through democratic institutions.

The authors then outline their appeal to the forthcoming National People's Congress. The principle is simple:

The people are not simpletons. They know where the shoe pinches. What they attack is the Lin Biao system, not the revolutionary policies and line of Chairman Mao . . . The people they hate are Lin Biao . . . and those who have developed a vested interest in his system. What they are demanding is democracy, a socialist legal system, the revolutionary rights and the human rights which are the defence of the mass of the people . . .

For any Marxist willing to face up to new questions, the experience of class struggle, reflected in factional strife among the people, has thrust to the fore the problem of factional democracy. The class struggle has been reflected on both sides and both sides must have democratic rights; one side destroying the other won't work.

On this basis they put the following proposals to the National People's Congress. First, that democratic rights should be laid down in black and white: 'The masses of the people (must) exercise the right of revolutionary supervision over Party leadership at all levels.' Second, restrict privilege. Third, 'specific provisions should be made for the people to replace at any time those cadres (especially senior cadres in the organs of the Centre) who lose the confidence of the broad masses of the people'. Fourth, strengthen sanctions against those who 'trump up false accusations, use the machinery of state to settle personal scores, set cases in motion for their own private ends, run private gaols, inflict corporal punishment, and treat the lives of the people as dirt'. Fifth, put into operation policies long agreed: 'Congress should reaffirm that those of the Party's policies . . . which have been proved correct in actual practice must be applied for a long time to come, and it should express this in appropriate legal forms.' Sixth, the principle of 'from each according to his ability, to each according to his work' should be put into practice, to bring to an end the stagnation of industrial wages and the economic pressures on the peasants, and to prevent 'nepotism in appointments, punitive transfers . . . and general reshuffling of jobs'. In fact, the authors argued, the principle of 'to each according to his work', so far from generating privilege, is the most effective way of restricting it.

The aftermath, 1975–1976, and a summing-up

The Fourth National People's Congress met on 13 January 1975, ten years after the preceding Congress. It was convened soon after the second plenum of the Tenth Central Committee, which produced significant changes in leadership. Deng Xiaoping became a member of the secretariat of the Political Bureau. The State appointments subsequently made by the NPC (voting by secret ballot) reflected the new balance of forces, with many familiar figures from the days before the Cultural Revolution back in office, and only one of the left-wing leadership, Zhang Chunqiao, in a leading position in the State. At the same time an absolute majority of the delegates were workers, peasants, and soldiers.

A new constitution reflected this balance of forces. It was introduced by Zhang Chunqiao. The left wing were able to secure the inclusion in the constitution of Mao's thought as the theoretical basis of the nation's thinking, of a statement that China was a class state practising the dictatorship of the proletariat, and that workers, peasants, and soldiers would form the main body of people's congresses at all levels. The communes, explicitly stated to 'integrate government administration and economic management', were made a part of the constituted State system.

The purpose of the dictatorship of the proletariat was defined as being to ensure that State organizations and State personnel maintained close ties with the masses, and to exercise similar control in the fields of education, health, scientific research, and cultural matters. Study of 'Marxism-Leninism-Mao Zedong-Thought' was prescribed for all State officials, and participation in physical labour was made obligatory.

The four great freedoms were guaranteed, as was the right to strike. At the same time the Constitution sought to ensure some control over the application of policies by guaranteeing to commune members the right to cultivate a private plot, and to engage in limited individual spare-time occupations, while production teams were protected from arbitrary requisition of their resources by communes and brigades.

In the major speeches at the Congress the left-wing line was further asserted. The key phrase, 'continue the revolution under the dictatorship of the proletariat', was prominent. 'Bourgeois rights' were to be restricted. Further, the principle that 'the principal contradiction in a socialist society is the contradiction between the proletariat and the bourgeoisie' was reasserted. Thus, while the new constitution seemed to go some way towards meeting the demands expressed in the Li-Yi-Zhe poster, this was more than offset by the reaffirmation of class struggle and of the restriction of bourgeois rights, the two main sources of the authoritarianism which the left exercised in spite of its theoretical insistence on the mass line.

The Congress fully accepted the premisses of Mao's alternative economic strategy. It was emphasized that the order of priorities in economic development would be agriculture, then light industry, and then heavy industry. The Da Zhai Production Brigade, Mao's model of the egalitarian, and self-reliant collective village, remained the model of rural development; and the Daqing oilfield, his industrial centre without a consumer city, was retained as the model for industry.

Mao was not present at the Congress, but its decisions reflected his views: the danger of a new élite, the need for continued revolution, and the need for direct mass supervision of the superstructure; the key importance of agriculture in development; the need to restrict but not eliminate income differentials and to limit but not deny the use of individual material incentives.

The second dismissal of Deng Xiaoping

One might at this point have predicted that China was now likely to enjoy a period of stability. The left had won much ground, but at the price of shedding its millennial hopes and its more extreme interpretations of Mao's policies. Industrial discipline had been restored and the left-wing economic strategy appeared to be working well; economic growth had been restored and in 1975 reached an astonishing rate of 11.9 per cent. An appearance of unity was given by the presence of both Deng Xiaoping and left-wing leaders at a great national conference held in the famous Maoist Da Zhai Production Brigade.

In early 1974, in his last speech before entering hospital, where he died of cancer on 8 January 1975, Zhou Enlai had put forward proposals for a new economic strategy, under the title The Four Modernizations. He had actually put these proposals forward in 1964, with Mao's full approval, but they were stillborn because the Great Proletarian Cultural Revolution began in the following year. This time they were enthusiastically supported by Deng Xiaoping. They covered agriculture, industry, science and technology, and defence. There appeared to be general agreement on the proposals; at any rate, neither Mao nor the Gang of Four objected.

With Zhou Enlai's death while Mao was in the last paralysing stages of Parkinson's disease, the question of the succession came to the fore. Mao was by now thoroughly disillusioned with his own close supporters, and much inclined at this point to favour Deng Xiaoping, for his combination of administrative ability and political acumen. However, three controversial documents were now sponsored by Deng, as an interpretation of the Four Modernizations. The first, 'Several Questions Concerning the Acceleration of Industrial Development', seems to have been written by Deng himself. The second, 'Promote Scientific Research and Application', was drafted by Deng's supporter Hu Yaobang. The third, 'General Working Programme of the Party and Country', curiously, was written by two conservative ideologues, Hu Qiaomu and Deng Liqun, who were to give Deng great trouble in the 1980s by opposing some of his economic reforms. Their participation suggests that Deng's interpretation of the Four Modernizations had fairly wide support. However, the three documents produced a strong reaction from the left wing. Some of the comments in the documents were harshly pragmatic and scarcely even Marxist, scornful of egalitarianism, scornful of national self-reliance ('self-conceit'), and insistent on the primary importance of the leading role of scientists and technologists. The left wing damned the documents as 'the three big poisonous weeds'. This initiated a new attack on Deng Xiaoping, once more reviled in wall posters as the 'number two capitalist roader' in the Party.

However, another issue arose on which Deng was at this point more vulnerable. Academic authorities had begun a campaign to reverse Mao's policies on education which, so far from promoting specialized training in science, were aimed at preventing the development of an elite of technologists. Mao's anti-intellectualism had a cause. Since 1949, higher education had remained as bookish as ever; for example, China's soil science students never saw a farm, but sat in their studies reading Soviet textbooks about Russian soils. However, Mao never succeeded in creating a viable alternative which would still ensure specialist training. Deng supported the campaign; he had argued that the development of science should be given the highest priority among the Four Modernizations. Mao was obdurate, Deng just as stubborn.

Then on 4 April 1976, several hundred thousand people, mostly young, assembled in Tiananmen Square to lay flowers in memory of Zhou Enlai. Similar demonstrations took place on the same day throughout China's major cities. These co-ordinated demonstrations were in effect an oblique call for Deng Xiaoping to succeed Zhou Enlai as prime minister; to many Chinese Deng was the rightful heir to 'our revered and beloved Premier Zhou'. To Mao, Deng's vast popularity thus acclaimed must have seemed to narrow even further his options for the appointment of his successor. The demonstrations were roughly put down, and on 7 April Deng Xiaoping was dismissed from all his posts. On the same day Hua Guofeng, the former Maoist Party leader in Hunan, already Minister for Public Security, was made First Vice-Chairman of the CCP. The dismissal of Deng and the promotion of Hua was the last political act of Mao Zedong. Five months later, on 9 September 1976, he died.

Mao Zedong in retrospect

Mao's two great attempts to transform socialism, the Great Leap Forward and the Great Proletarian Cultural Revolution, both ended in apparent total failure. The chaos into which the Great Leap sank caused famine on a vast scale: Mao's opponents calculated that 5 per cent of the population died of hunger. His Cultural Revolution deteriorated into civil war.

Until the failure of the Great Leap, Mao Zedong had enjoyed the reputation of being the most pragmatic of communists. Then overnight he was condemned as the most Utopian and unrealistic.

Four charges were made against him. First, he was accused of being more Stalinist than Stalin himself. Second, he was deemed to have put his Utopian dreams before China's need for economic growth. Third, he was condemned as a 'voluntarist' who believed that the human will could overcome all material obstacles. Fourth, he was regarded as an ideologist whose policies were no more than the application of dogmatic a priori Marxist theory.

One is often warned in these days of computers that you get out of the computer only what you put in. The principle applies to all analysis. In this case, if the analyst reads only Mao's ideological statements, then his assumption determines his conclusion, and Mao is 'proved' to be an ideologist. The late and great Alex Nove once wrote that in studying what communist leaders do, one should never accept an ideological explanation, even when they themselves assert it, unless and until all possibilities of explanation in terms of practical responses to practical problems have been exhausted.

Exegesis is not enough. To understand Mao's actions requires the study of China's history, of the problems of modernization in poor peasant countries, and of the history of socialism. Space cannot be given here to a full analysis of Mao's thinking on these problems, but it is possible to suggest the lines on which such an enquiry might be conducted.

The fundamental aim of the Chinese revolution since it was launched by Sun Yatsen had been to strengthen China to the point at which she was secure from attacks on her sovereignty and on her independence. This demanded rapid industrialization. Meanwhile, given the absence of industrial strength, it was not irrational to believe that China's only possible means of defence was by the sort of guerrilla warfare which was perceived to have succeeded against Japan. British staff officers accepted that this was China's best resort, and Chinese staff officers accepted 'people's war' not as a virtue but as a temporary necessity.

Industrialization was the prime necessity. The Soviet Union had industrialized rapidly, until she was strong enough to destroy the invading German forces in the Second World War. She had done so by exacting from her peasants the capital needed to build industry. This Stalinist paradigm of development became generally accepted when, from the late 1940s, the attempt began to modernize the underdeveloped countries of the world, although it was seldom outside the Soviet Union applied with the ruthlessness of Stalin.

However, this strategy had not gone unchallenged even in the Soviet Union, where in the 1920s Shanin and Bazarov had argued for an alternative route of development. Shanin pointed out that relatively small investments in agriculture could make possible very large increases in production and therefore in peasant incomes. Increased peasant purchasing power would then fuel the growth of industry as it responded to increased demand. Bazarov argued that most economic development was essentially local, that electricity made possible the diffusion of development throughout the country, that what Russian agriculture needed in order to rise above subsistence level was 'dirt roads and spur lines', and that the most effective organization of development was that in which 'the labourers were also the beneficiaries'. Bukharin came to support them. Preobrezhensky, who had actually been the author of the Stalinist paradigm, was won round. The Shanin–Bazarov paradigm was probably what most Soviet socialists hoped for, but Stalin won the argument by executing Bukharin.

Mao was never wholly convinced by the Stalin paradigm. It is now known that before coming to power in 1949 he had publicly stated, in the first version of 'On New Democracy', that China would have to build a mature capitalist system before attempting to impose socialism. During the period of the Border Regions he had asserted that 'an increase in peasant incomes year by year is the only possible basis of protracted war'. Nevertheless in 1953, faced with American threats following the Korean War, he felt compelled to accept massive Soviet aid, and with it the Soviet economic system. Stalinist organization was rapidly imposed during the First Five Year Plan from 1953, But Mao soon became highly critical of the Stalinist command economy. He condemned Stalin's ruthless procurement policy as 'draining the pond to catch the fish'. In emphasizing the difference between the collectivization of agriculture in China and in the Soviet Union he wrote: 'in thirty years the Soviets have failed to create a truly collective system; all they have done is to perpetuate the counter-productive exploitation of the landlords.'

In the collectivization campaign of 1955–6, as *The High Tide of Socialism in the Chinese Countryside* shows, Mao's aim was to achieve collectivization village by village by encouraging each village community to unite in the pursuit of specific plans to increase production and incomes by co-operative means, and he saw in this the possibility of a spiral of increased production, incomes, and investment through which the villages could modernize themselves.

Thus, in the *High Tide* we find the beginnings of an alternative development paradigm. It was close to that of Shanin and Bazarov. And as the 1950s wore on, Western development specialists began to think along the same lines. Nurkse argued that surplus rural labour could substitute for capital if it was employed in improving the infrastructure of agriculture, diversifying crops, and establishing small labour-intensive industries, carried out through integrated village plans.

Such a concept applied with particular force in China, which has the worst man–land ratio of any major country, and as a result the largest rural labour surplus. The consequence is that the burden of maintaining this unproductive mass of rural labour continued to press Chinese agriculture back to subsistence levels, so that it would become even less able to supply the capital for industrialization. The Nurkse concept also has political implications: if the peasant population pay in the market for industrial goods out of purchasing power increased by village development, then they are paying for industrialization voluntarily, in their own interests, and not being forced to pay for it by the imposition of high taxes and low farm-gate prices. The failure of the attempt by Beijing to increase procurement norms after the good harvests of 1954 and 1955, in the face of passive peasant resistance, was to Mao the turning point.

Finally, the Hundred Flowers criticisms showed how violently the imposition of the Stalinist system of comprehensive centralized bureaucratic command was resented. The revolutionary consensus was threatened. Mao himself detested bureaucracy and was sceptical about centralization. He said: 'Centralize only what must be centralized and leave the rest alone.' He believed (and here he had Soviet experience in mind) that over-centralization is counter-productive; it forces the lower levels to protect their interests by evading orders, distorting policy, and resorting to the use of misinformation.

For centralization to be efficient, he argued, the local levels must be allowed room for autonomous initiative. His response to attacks on centralized bureaucracy during the Hundred Flowers was therefore to enlarge the possibilities of local autonomy. Indeed, already before the Hundred Flowers he had, in *The Ten Great Relationships*, adumbrated the possibility of a more mutually profitable relationship between the three sections of the economy—heavy industry, light industry, and agriculture—essentially a relationship between the centre and the rest.

Thus the problems of preparation for a dispersed guerrilla defence, of surplus rural labour which made the Soviet model inappropriate, and of popular hostility to bureaucracy, all pointed to the need for drastic decentralization and to the maximization of autonomous local development.

In this way what Mao attempted in the Great Leap Forward can be justified without resort to ideology; and Mao himself justified all of it in documents and speeches written in plain, practical, non-Marxist language. These common-sense documents, however, have received scant attention in the West where most scholars have preferred to study Mao's Marxist rhetoric.

Gradually, from the *High Tide* in 1955 to his critique of Stalin in 1959, Mao built up his alternative to Stalinism. One would have expected that Mao's critique—far more devastating than that of Khrushchev in 1956—would have been recognized in the West as one of the key documents in the history of socialism. Yet it has been all but neglected. It is therefore perhaps worth summarizing here.

In a series of speeches and documents he condemned Stalinism on five grounds. (1) It was counter-productive to impoverish the peasants in order to build industry. (2) The high priority given to the development of heavy industry was also counter-productive: 'If you are really serious about developing heavy industry, you will give attention to agriculture and light industry.' (3) Stalin's command economy offered no place for popular participation and popular initiative: accumulation and investment sprang not from the communities' consciousness of new possibilities but from state coercion, and accumulation was therefore severely limited. (4) Stalin argued that in socialist society there were no contradictions: Mao argued that contradictions continued, including contradictions between the people and the government, and he also argued that to deny and suppress such conflict was to 'abolish politics', and so to abolish progress, for conflict is the motive force of progress. (5) His fifth point arose from the fourth: that a socialist society cannot stop merely at the nationalization of the means of production and treat the first institutions thus created as if they were permanent. The first institutions created by the revolution can become an obstacle to further progess if they are reified. These first institutions are only the beginning, and they are not in themselves socialist: 'there is still a process to be gone through . . . there is work to do', to create new and truly socialist relations of production.

The way to overcome all these faults is to decentralize decision-making as far as possible to the local communities: the job of socialist planners will then be to respond to community initiatives, not to dictate from above.

The documents in which these criticisms were made were also in plain straightforward language. It is obvious that any Western democrat can acknowledge that the points made are rational. The critique stands or falls without resort to Marxist discourse. There is no hidebound ideology here.

Even in his use of Marxist analysis, Mao bent the whole theory towards pragmatism. First, in 1937 he subsumed the Marxist theory of knowledge under his own idea of mass-line leadership, to propose a system of trial-and-error experiment in which all whose interests are involved participate; this owes more, as a theory of knowledge, to John Dewey than to Engels. Second, he ignored the esoteric categories of the Hegelian-Marxist dialectic, and employed only one Hegelian principle—the unity of opposites—and this he virtually reduced to a heuristic device for the analysis of conflicts of interest.

Thus it can clearly be shown that Mao was not Stalinist; that, far from being indifferent to economic growth it was his primary concern; and that his policies, far from being merely an application of ideology, can be, and were, justified on practical grounds already familiar among democratic development specialists.

The charge of 'voluntarism' is equally false. The accusation was first made in the Soviet Union, and it refers to the long-running controversy within Marxism over the respective roles in the process of revolution of economic determinism and revolutionary will. The satiated second-generation leaders of the Soviet Union were all for leaving the future of communism to economic determinism: the advance of technology alone would bring communism. In other words, there is no need to rock the boat, to the possible disadvantage of the entrenched elite. To Mao, however, the establishment of an entrenched elite was a threat to continued social progress, and so he was on the side of revolutionary will; but his faith in it was not excessive. True, Mao referred to the legendary Chinese hero 'the old man who moved the mountain'; but the old man did not succeed by a miracle; it was determination and perseverance that did it.

We must see Mao's so-called 'voluntarism' in two contexts. First, in the context of China's needs: her peasants had to be persuaded to relinquish their age-old worst-case planning, and open their minds to new possibilities of technique and organization. Second, in the context of Mao's early intellectual experience: the Western idea of 'will power' was not involved. Via his teacher Yang Changji, Mao learned from T. H. Green that consciousness motivates; and he learned from Paulsen that consciousness, in motivating, creates aspirations to which the individual feels obliged to devote himself consistently and with resolution. The lesson from this is: do not expect people to act in an enlightened way if they have not yet reached the necessary pitch of consciousness and resolution, which will be achieved only in the light of new experience. Paradoxically, Mao's view is thus a warning to fellow leaders not to push policies further than popular consciousness permits. However, it is at the same time a demand that leaders must act positively—even coercively—to create opportunities which can provide the new experience which can then create new consciousness.

His practice did not always follow his theory; but the hurried extremes of policy implementation—the 1953 resort to Stalinist organization, and the repudiation of this in the even more hurried Great Leap—came at times of crisis in that ever-present area of preoccupation, the threat to China's independence. Stalinism in China was a response to American threats after the Korean War. The Great Leap was hastened (and distorted) by the fear of military dependence on Khrushchev's Soviet Union. The Cultural Revolution began from a public controversy between those (led by Lin Biao) who argued for self-reliant 'people's war' and those (led by Luo Ruiqing) who argued for a conventional defence which would entail renewed dependence on the Soviet Union.

That Mao was an authoritarian ruler, prepared to be ruthless towards those he believed to be conspiring against the revolution, is not in question. What is in question here is the idea that he was some sort of closed-minded orthodox fundamentalist. Why then did his two great campaigns fail?

The Great Leap did not fail because it was a Utopian exercise. Beneath the many factors which contributed to the disaster lay one fundamental flaw: the authoritarian, totally unaccountable Party hierarchy which Mao himself had created was a useless instrument for the inculcation of new consciousness. In preparation for the Leap, there was a vast campaign in the Chinese press in which all the institutions concerned pledged themselves to honour democratic procedures. This was elaborated by warnings of the problems which would otherwise occur. These warnings proved to be a remarkably prescient account of precisely the problems which did occur. Yet their occurrence was not prevented. Mao was aware of this; no one among his fellow leaders condemned these appalling distortions more trenchantly than he himself. He defended the growing resistance of the peasants to the increased tyranny to which the Leap had led. Yet he could do little. Encouraged by the media,

China's local authorities turned every report of exceptional successes into universal demands. The village cadres were forced to promise more than they could deliver. Having then claimed, for example, to have achieved vast increases in grain production, they faced vastly increased procurement demands, and they met these by emptying the barns. This was essentially a bet on the continuation of good weather. But the weather that succeeded was appalling. Hence the famine.

The Great Proletarian Cultural Revolution failed for different reasons. First, the discontents of the younger generation whom Mao mobilized proved to be far more furious than he had supposed, and the young were soon joined by other alienated groups, of which the most important were the millions of casual (as opposed to established) workers in State industry. Second, the threatened Party leaders fought back by force and fraud, most obviously through the creation of sham Red Guard organizations. The resulting chaos ensured that the Party's authority was eventually restored by the PLA, with the support of Mao himself.

Yet neither of these campaigns proved to have been entirely futile. It is seldom recognized that the ideological condemnations of senior Party leaders published by the Red Guards were almost always accompanied and illustrated by condemnation of the policies of those they opposed. These indictments in policy terms, put together, show that one of the objects of the Cultural Revolution was to re-establish the Great Leap strategy, shorn of the excesses which had prejudiced it. And in 1970, Mao's commune and brigade enterprises, the heart and soul of the strategy, were re-established. This time they succeeded. By the time Deng Xiaoping came to power in 1978 they had become indispensable and were soon to become the fastest growing sector of the economy, expanding at rates of up to 33 per cent per annum.

The importance of Mao's economic legacy is now being recognized both in China and abroad. In *China Quarterly*, 144 (Dec. 1995), Andrew G. Walker writes: 'China's Maoist legacies are . . . increasingly seen as a foundation for post-Mao success . . . Some see the decentralisation of the Chinese economy as a structural factor that allowed China's reform strategy to work.' Steven M. Goldstein adds:

Mao's reforms . . . created an institutional pattern that would decisively shape the course of the reforms initiated after his death . . . Those who look for the roots of the entrepreneurial and profit-seeking behaviour that has been the major force for growth of the 'non-state sector' must look to the legacy of the man to whom such activities were anathema.

It should be pointed out, however, that the accumulation of capital in the hands of collective firms, or in the hands of the community's economic commission which draws on that accumulation to develop the local economy, was not at all regarded as anathema by Mao. And one should recall that Wang

Guofan, the hero of the collectivization movement, organized his fellow villagers to raise the funds to make a start by cutting firewood on the hillsides and selling it in the towns: collective entrepreneurship.

The Great Proletarian Cultural Revolution was launched when Mao said: 'To rebel is justified.' That instruction was not forgotten, but many of those active in the Red Guard movement realized that the objects of cultural revolution could only be realized if rebellion led to the establishment of the rule of law and of democratic procedures. The first result was the Li-Yi-Zhe poster. The second was the 1978–9 Democracy Wall protest. From then on, through the Tiananmen demonstrations of 1989 to the present day, former Red Guards have led the only part of the democratic movement in China seriously concerned to mobilize all classes to achieve democracy from below. Moreover, Mao's conviction that the system of comprehensive central economic command was the main source of privilege and the abuse of power became the shibboleth of the democratic movement.

In this sense, Mao built better than he knew. He himself, both in the Great Leap and in the Cultural Revolution, drew back from the brink; committed in the last resort to the idea of the necessity of a Leninist 'vanguard party', he was reluctant to discipline the offending cadres in the Leap, and in the Cultural Revolution he drew back from supporting Paris-Commune-type government. However, the forces he released—former Red Guards committed to real democratization, and an economic system which created millions of new centres of economic decision-making outside the system of central planning—strengthened the preconditions for future democratization.

His final contribution to China's future was the rapprochement with the USA which he pursued and achieved. This made possible the relaxation of the policies of self-reliance which had so hampered and distorted development. These policies now proved to have had everything to do with defence and nothing to do with ideology.

18

China since the death of Mao

The re-emergence of Deng Xiaoping, 1976–1981

On the death of Mao in September 1976, Hua Guofeng succeeded. His position as Party Chairman was publicly confirmed one month later. He claimed, and the Party leadership accepted, that Mao had nominated him as successor. Mao had always emphasized his belief that experience of government in the provinces was the best preparation for power at the centre. Hua had served virtually his entire career in Mao's own home province of Hunan, where he had conscientiously carried out Maoist policies. He had been brought to Beijing by Mao and appointed Minister of Public Security on 17 January 1975.

It seemed as if the left wing had peacefully inherited power. Two days later, however, it became known that the Cultural Revolution leaders Jiang Qing, Zhang Chunqiao, Yao Wenyuan, and Wang Hongwen, along with a score of others, had been arrested by the PLA unit which had served as Mao's bodyguard. The arrest was carried out by its commander, Wang Dongxing, but was credited to Hua Guofeng. We know little or nothing about the political background of this sudden event. The Jiang Qing faction, later referred to derisively as 'the Gang of Four', were accused of having prepared to seize power by a *coup d'état*, which was nipped in the bud by Hua Guofeng.

That the Gang of Four actually prepared to seize power by force is not proved, although the circumstantial evidence is impressive and there is ample information to show their desperate attempts to strengthen their political position as the death of Mao Zedong approached. Renewed ideological attack, with the issue of the historical role of Qin Shi Huang Di, the first emperor of a united China, as a means of esoteric communication with their followers; attacks on the reviving establishment in education, industrial management, and other walks of life; the creation of new and the revival of old mass organizations as potential rivals of the Party; strikes and other disruptive activities in factories, docks, and railways; the renewed mobilization of the militia—all this shows their concern that with Mao's death their power and their liberty, and perhaps their lives, would be at risk.

However, the question of whether, after the death of Mao, they actually sought to mobilize the militia in order to seize power by force is not of great importance. A division between the Gang and Hua Guofeng was quite clear. Hua did not share the Gang's hopes of continuing to exclude from the top councils of the Party the many veterans whose prestige was far greater than that of Hua himself. That the veterans would now compromise with the Jiang Qing group, on any terms, was not possible. Hua's choice was therefore between alliance with the Gang of Four or alliance with the Party veterans and there can be little doubt where his interests lay, although, as it proved, his alliance with the right wing did not last long. He did not succeed in establishing his authority. His attempts to create even a modest personality cult failed.

In fact, the reason for Hua's dismissal from power was much more specific. It was generally accepted that after the chaos of the Cultural Revolution there must be a return to a greater degree of central control, regular administration, and predictability. As a professed Maoist, Hua might have been expected to minimize such changes. Instead he produced, as a response to the Four Modernizations, a Ten Year Plan which actually sought to destroy Maoist decentralization entirely. His new Plan was as Stalinist as the First Five Year Plan. The provincial State-owned enterprises were deprived of their discretion in the use of their depreciation allowances. The central planning system was made comprehensive. County and village economic autonomy was swamped by the revival of forced labour for agricultural construction, on such a scale that in Hua's first winter a quarter of the rural population were thus engaged. At the same time, investment in heavy industry was given a higher priority than ever before. In the course of the year, the extravagantly ambitious targets first set were raised several times.

On the other hand, Hua took advantage of the Four Modernizations to seek foreign loans. His borrowings were enormous, threatening China with massive indebtedness. Hua proposed to cover the debt by a huge increase in the export of oil. One of the economic successes of the period of the Cultural Revolution had been a large increase in oil production. Hua assumed on the basis of further surveys that this rapid increase could continue. This assumption proved to have been extravagantly optimistic. It seemed that China, for the first time since the communist revolution, was incurring debts which she might never be able to repay. The avoidance of such debts had hitherto been an agreed principle, and the early debts to the Soviet Union had been paid off as rapidly as possible.

The moderate reformers called in Deng Xiaoping who reappeared in 1977 as one of five vice-chairmen of the Party. By December 1978, at the third plenum of the Eleventh Central Committee, he was in a position of dominance, although he enjoyed no top post. From then on the Cultural Revolution was gradually dissolved. The demonstration of 4 April 1976 in memory of Zhou Enlai, as a result of which Deng had been put out of office for the second time, was declared a 'justified revolutionary act'. Liu Shaoqi was posthumously rehabilitated; so were over 2 million other and lesser victims of the Cultural

Revolution, and with them most of the victims of the anti-rightist movement of 1957; but as Deng Xiaoping himself had actually been in charge of the anti-rightist movement, to save his face a number of the 1957 rightists remained condemned.

Wang Dongxing, who had arrested the Gang of Four but who was firmly on the left, resigned; so did the left-wing Mayor of Beijing, Wu De, who had suppressed the 5 April 1976 demonstration. Finally, at the sixth plenum in June 1981 the Party laid down its judgement of Mao himself: a great leader, but one who made serious errors in later life, including his mistaken class analysis, which had led to the Cultural Revolution. The Great Leap was also condemned as the result of error.

By 1980 Deng Xiaoping, although refusing supreme office, had secured the appointment of Hu Yaobang as head of the CCP, and Zhao Ziyang as premier. Both were close associates of Deng and firm supporters of his policies. A rectification campaign was launched to bring to order the middle ranks of the Party, more than half of whom had won their positions during the Cultural Revolutions.

The third plenum of the Eleventh Central Committee (18–22 December 1978) made no significant statements on economic policy, but decisions thereafter soon disposed of Hua's revived Stalinism. His high targets were cut down

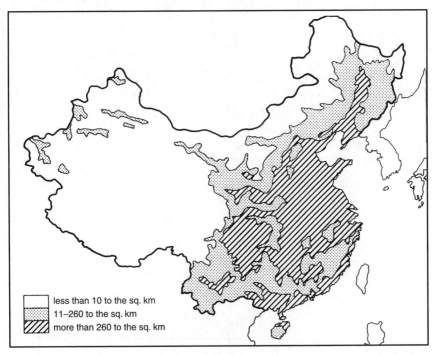

less than 10 to the sq. km
11–260 to the sq. km
more than 260 to the sq. km

Map 7. Population density

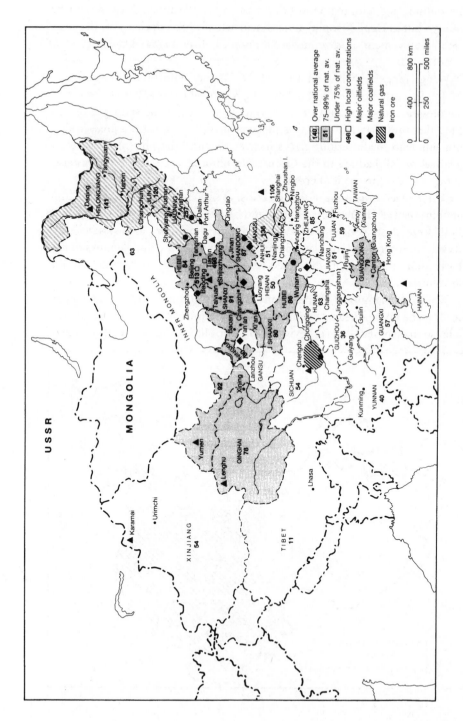

Map 8. Industrial production (per capita, by province), 1979

and a period of retrenchment was announced. Agricultural procurement prices were increased by 20 to 30 per cent. Commune and brigade enterprise was accepted, and then encouraged. No further massive foreign loans were sought. The provincial State-owned industries were again freed to use their depreciation allowances. The first tentative steps were taken towards reform in the State sector of industry and commerce.

The most significant decision was the acceptance of the reversal of sectoral priorities, already proposed before the death of Mao, who had always argued for greater emphasis on the other sectors of the economy. Thus Deng Xiaoping's reforms began with a total reversal of sectoral priorities unparalleled in the rest of the communist world. Within three years, 1979–81, while heavy industry's output fell marginally, the production of light industry rose by over 30 per cent.

In this way, economic reform in the actual event was by no means a total reaction against the economic strategy of Mao and the Cultural Revolution, but against Hua Guofeng's attempt to repudiate it.

Deng may have won the authority to carry through his reforms, but he was not in the position of an autocrat. There was a collective leadership in China, with Deng no more than *primus inter pares.* Deng, Hu Yaobang, and Zhao Ziyang were balanced by more conservative figures such as Chen Yun, one of the architects of the First Five Year Plan. Chen Yun was the most sophisticated economist among China's Party leaders. Since the 1950s he had played a moderating role in which he had continually stressed the need for a market dimension. However, Deng's reforms were soon to surpass what Chen Yun was willing to accept and Chen was soon to reassert his consistently held view that the market should be 'like a bird in a cage', strictly subordinate to the planned economy. In this he had the support of many retired veterans like himself, and many more who were to prove hostile as Deng's changes gathered force. Deng, as a result, had to argue his case, to move one step at a time, and sometimes to retreat from positions which opposition had made untenable.

On 25 January 1981, after a lengthy trial, followed by two months of silence between the end of the trial and the delivery of the verdicts, the Gang of Four along with five senior members of the defence establishment associated with them were sentenced. Jiang Qing and Zhang Chunqiao were sentenced to death, with two years' reprieve; Yao Wenyuan received a sentence of twenty years; Wang Hongwen was given life; Chen Boda was given eighteen years. The rest received sentences of seventeen or eighteen years. Jiang Qing subsequently committed suicide on 14 May 1991 while still in prison.

The first steps to economic reform

Movement away from Stalinist centralized control of the economy and material-balance planning was taking place in varying degrees, though in an uncertain and halting way, in all communist countries; even the Soviet Union, which as the supreme guardian of Marxist-Leninist morality was the most reluctant to move, was prepared to consider some degree of change. The reforms in China were therefore already familiar in their general direction and in much of their detail.

Some such change was made almost inevitable by the very course of socialist economic development; it was as much the consequence of success as of failure. Extensive development—the accumulation of machines—once successful, has to give way to intensive development in which attention to costs becomes vital, and continued growth comes to depend increasingly on innovation. When the worst problems of poverty have been solved and the people begin to acquire greater purchasing power, they demand a greater choice of goods, and central planning cannot cope, overwhelmed by the task of planning the production and distribution of commodities which, counting all shapes, sizes, models, and specifications, run into millions even in economies where scarcity is still the rule. In particular, the rise in incomes leads to demands for a more varied diet; this requires the diversification of agricultural production, formerly devoted largely to a grain monoculture. Here the central planners are even less likely to be able to cope, as mixed farming depends so much on local conditions and local knowledge, and is extremely sensitive to the market—even where for ideological reasons no market is deemed to exist.

It is wrong to write off the communist experiment which began in Russia in 1917 as something which did not work and never could have worked. The Soviet system brought the Russian Empire from immemorial poverty to the position of the world's second greatest economy in a generation. It enabled Russia to defeat the German invasion. It produced universal education and universal free health services, and maintained full employment. China's socialist development was also impressive. From 1952 to 1975 China's gross domestic product grew at an average rate of 6.7 per cent per annum. Industry grew from 20.9 per cent of gross national product to 45.7 per cent. Absolute poverty came to be largely confined to certain western provinces, although because of the high rate of national investment, running at about one-third of gross national product, there was little general increase in the standard of living. Health standards had been raised enormously. The growth of agricultural production at 3 per cent per annum compared very favourably with that of most underdeveloped countries, and the rate of agricultural growth may actually have been substantially higher because by 1975 the village populations had at their disposal almost 50 per cent more arable land than appeared on Beijing's land registers, as a result of surreptitious land reclamation, which Mao had been willing to tolerate.

However, as in the Soviet Union, the capital–output ratio deteriorated. In China it changed from an investment of 2.51 yuan of gross capital formation to produce an output of 1 yuan per annum to an investment of 15.49 yuan. Because of the rapid increase of population, the available food supply per capita actually fell slightly, although good distribution eliminated malnutrition across most of the country.

Growth suffered a check during the Cultural Revolution. Production in the state-owned enterprises was seriously disrupted. Higher education was virtually suspended and as a result the number of qualified technicians and scientists fell by half. However, at the same time, as grass-roots industrialization proceeded apace, local cadres were gaining valuable entrepreneurial and management experience. At Mao's insistence a process of agricultural diversification had begun, in response to his slogan 'on the basis of grain production, diversify agriculture', and was successful in spite of the sort of egregious local errors which one would expect.

Yet the success of the communist systems during their first generation concealed the essential problems of the Russian-style command economy. The system of central planning is deficient in two fundamental respects; the planners lack information, and the managers lack incentives. Socialist governments were therefore forced to accept the necessity, for some purposes, of the market, which can signal its needs to the enterprises and reward those enterprises which satisfy them.

The attempt at change began as soon as Stalin died in 1953, and speeded up after Khrushchev's speech of February 1956 in which he condemned Stalin's crimes. Yet the response of the Soviet regime was feeble. The reaction in China, however, was the revolutionary Great Leap Forward. When the Leap failed, the Liu Shaoqi regime began to consider a very different alternative by then being urged in the rest of the communist world. In the course of the reform debate which Khrushchev encouraged in Russia, the economist Liberman had put forward in 1962 a plan for the transformation of the bureaucratic State enterprises into market-oriented entrepreneurial organizations.

The central change advocated by Liberman was the granting of a measure of autonomy to the enterprises. Having fulfilled certain contractual responsibilities to the State, they would be free to use their remaining resources to operate in the market. Their continued obligation to the State would take the form of a contract to supply certain goods, or simply to pass on a stipulated sum out of profits or to pay a tax. The remuneration of the managers would be in proportion to profits. The firm would find its own raw materials and intermediate goods by trade with other enterprises, and would pay a charge on funds received from the State. It would be responsible for its own profit and loss. Prices would be as far as possible freed, or at least made more flexible.

Liberman's idea was taken up in China after the Great Leap Forward by the economist Sun Yefang. Mao was utterly opposed. He condemned the proposals as 'the capitalist road' and contrasted this with 'the socialist road' represented by his own decentralized collective economy, with its commune enterprises and its workers' management of the State enterprises. In fact Mao's 'two roads' were on the one hand the road to reform proposed by Liberman and partly adopted in the European communist states, and on the other hand the road opened by his own strategy in China, based on dispersed autonomous collective enterprises.

The 'two roads' had hitherto been considered, not only by Mao but by Liu Shaoqi and his allies, as mutually incompatible; and there is no doubt that Mao's collective village enterprises, the main plank in his platform, were not generally regarded with great favour even in 1979. The conservatives condemned them as a threat to proper socialist control; the reformers saw them as of marginal importance and largely a waste of resources. But they were there. They had grown since their restoration in 1970 at a remarkable pace. They numbered millions of firms. Attempts to curb them failed. The first measure taken against them was to close down vast numbers of the local collective steelworks and coal mines; but new ones were opened at a faster rate than the rate of closure; two years on, there were four times as many as before the closures.

Deng Xiaoping therefore accepted the existence and headlong growth of local collective industry as a *fait accompli*. Having done so, he then made changes which widened their opportunities and strengthened their incentives. Hitherto they had been restricted to their own local markets; he opened the whole country to all collective enterprises. Hitherto their workers had not been paid wages, but continued to be paid in work-points, that is, by a share of the total production of the collective, including its agricultural production, but Deng now instituted a wage system. The system of taxing local authorities was changed so that the amount of local tax remitted to the centre was fixed, and the additional revenues created by the expanding operations of the enterprises were retained for reinvestment, thus turning China's local bureaucrats into enthusiastic entrepreneurs. Deng was not inspired here by ideology; he was simply determined to extend all opportunities for initiative; but in favouring these Great Leap village enterprises his pragmatism led to the acceptance of a system which, when Mao created it, had been condemned by the world as an example of crazy ideology.

It soon proved that the 'two roads' were less incompatible than had been supposed. Deng Xiaoping perhaps foresaw how the buoyancy and vigour of this new rural industrial economy would prove critical for the Libermanist reform of the State-owned enterprises, as the monopolies enjoyed by State industry were broken by the competition of local industry, and as the two sectors were brought into fruitful relationships through mutual trade and through the spread of subcontracting. Nor on the other hand did Mao ever conceive that a major factor in creating such fruitful intersectoral relationships, the search for which was fundamental to his economic strategy, would be Libermanist reforms in the State sector, which allowed and encouraged its managers to enter into the profitable market system made possible by the growth of local collective industry. Thus the 'two roads' were to a significant extent reconciled.

Meanwhile in the Soviet Union reform was stalled. The attempt in 1957 to decentralize state enterprise was soon reversed. Agriculture was left virtually unchanged, except for Khrushchev's ploughing up of a large part of the steppe to grow maize, a policy which proved environmentally disastrous. Liberman's proposals were attempted experimentally, but soon dropped. There was no great urgency; economic growth continued and the standard of living was rising.

Slowly, however the strains were beginning to show. While labour productivity remained stagnant, the stress of the high-tech arms race grew rapidly, culminating in the threat presented by Reagan's star-wars programme; the cost of this military competition grossly restricted the possibility of increased investment where it was most needed, in agriculture and consumer goods industries. For China however the strains of Cold War competition diminished just as those for the Soviet Union increased.

By a series of decisions, Deng Xiaoping with characteristic perseverance led his party through small changes to great. There was no blueprint for economic reform, and this was probably an advantage. Abrupt and comprehensive change of the kind which later occurred in the Soviet Union would in all probability have had the same kind of disastrous results. The Chinese did not so much adopt a policy of gradual change as accept that they had no option but trial and error. There were no convincing precedents in 1979 for economic change in other communist countries. There was a good deal of hostility towards any serious reform among China's Party veterans. In the debates on reform which Deng now encouraged, many different and often contradictory views were expressed, even though the debate among the reformers was remarkably free from ideology and was thoroughly pragmatic and increasingly sophisticated.

The decentralization of a certain amount of authority to the provincial governments and to provincial branches of State-owned enterprise both set limits to what the centre could do, and at the same time left room for a variety of provincial initiatives towards reform. Many important changes were in fact first attempted by one province and then subsequently approved for national application.

Changes in rural China

The most dramatic provincial initiative was in relation to collective agriculture. In the province of Anhui, China's poorest coastal province where the Great Leap famine had claimed a quarter of the national total of victims, a movement began at country level during 1980 to set up small groups within the collective teams to carry out contracted tasks in return for incentive payments. This was already a commonplace idea in the communist world in theory, but had only been fitfully and unsuccessfully attempted. In Anhui the provincial Party secretary Wan Li approved it. Zhao Ziyang, then in Sichuan, followed suit. It spread. Then some of these small groups were given responsibility for the whole year's process of cultivation; soon this was followed by the offer of similar contracts to individual families. Thereafter, these annual contracts were gradually extended from the initial single year; they are now generally for thirty years or more. The centre dragged its feet, and tried to confine this *de facto* restoration of family farming to places with exceptional conditions, but the idea was so popular that only ruthless action could have reversed its general acceptance. No doubt many party leaders recalled the success in Anhui of the *sauve-qui-peut* return to individual farming in the face of the Great Leap famine, and were disposed to think that the restoration of the incentives of individual cultivation might be as successful again. The *fait accompli* was accepted.

The change touched off a period of quite remarkable growth of farm production, although we cannot be sure exactly how important the return to family cultivation alone may have been; the change was accompanied by total increases of 50 per cent in procurement prices. A substantial amount of the revenue derived from rural collective industries, since their restoration in the 1970s, had been invested in the infrastructure of agriculture, especially in improved irrigation, as well as in the creation of sources of steel and cement within the local community's control. What is certainly true, however, is that this acceleration in the growth of agricultural production increased peasant incomes to such an extent as to transform their standard of living.

About half of the increased income came from farming. The rest came from employment in the 'town and village enterprises' (the new name for commune and brigade enterprise). The rural enterprise sector was now growing at 20–33 per cent per annum and continued to grow far more rapidly than the other sectors of the economy. This apparent economic miracle can be explained. First, Deng's fiscal changes gave it a tremendous stimulus. Second, the CCP as a whole had, to a great extent, shared the orthodox Soviet contempt for small-scale industries, so that in spite of Mao's efforts a far smaller proportion of China's total industrial output still, in comparison with that of other countries at the same level of development, came from small firms. Third, with cheap rural labour and using simple methods requiring little capital, it was not difficult to compete with the sclerotic State-owned enterprises. Fourth, China was starved of simple consumer goods, the more so as the purchasing power of the peasants who were still almost 80 per cent of the population, was now rising so rapidly. Finally, some credit must be given to the well-known entrepreneurial abilities of the Chinese peasant. Traditionally, clans and extended families had provided the capital needed for diversified economic activities, and in this sense the township and village enterprise complexes are old-style family enterprise writ large.

The importance of township and village enterprises went far beyond the mere fact of their contribution to total industrial production. They gave employment to many millions among China's surplus rural labourers; to a significant extent they turned this problem of surplus population into an advantage, as Mao (and Nurkse) had predicted. In doing this they reduced the flow of rural migrants to the cities, a flow which had revived when the new regime relaxed the existing tight residence restrictions. The rapid rise in peasant incomes led to a vast increase in peasant savings. They matched the increase in peasant purchasing power with a flow of consumer goods. They competed powerfully with State industries, helping to force the State sector to become entrepreneurial. Although relatively undeveloped in the poorer areas as one would expect, they substantially raised incomes even in such places, thus further reducing regional poverty. Overall, they helped to raise the average per capita income of the Chinese peasant from a level characteristic of those countries internationally classified as poor to a level typical of middle-income countries, and to do so within five years—something, it has to be said, of a great leap forward.

The revenues which accrued to the local governments out of the profits of township and village enterprise were reinvested in the enterprises, used for the improvement of the infrastructure of agriculture, the strengthening of social security, the development of schools and local clinics, and the general improvement of rural amenities. In particular their investments in the local production of modern agricultural inputs and in the infrastructure of farming actually tended to decrease inequalities, at least in the short term, among the rural population because those who had most to gain from such improvements were those on the poorest land.

Of course they had their downside, as the conservatives were not slow to point out. About 13 per cent of them failed. This is a very small proportion compared with the failure rate normal among new small businesses in capitalist countries, but it was perceived as a sign of weakness and a form of waste. Their primitive technologies were very hard indeed on the environment, and this mattered politically because China had begun to take environmental problems seriously during the Cultural Revolution. They borrowed heavily from the banks, and this was deemed by their enemies to increase inflation; but the critics chose to forget the enormous stream of peasant savings the rural industries helped to create and the consumer goods they produced to match the higher incomes; it is possible that their total economic influence reduced rather than increased inflation, though no full calculation has as yet been made.

Above all rural industry created a new and vigorous alternative economy which vastly offset the difficulties experienced in the reform of the State sector. By the early 1990s the sector was producing 50 per cent of the gross value of industrial output, and 45 per cent of China's manufactured exports.

Opinion abroad was just as hostile to township and village enterprise as in

China. The attitude of Western economists who worked on China was that, being beneath the level of the economies of scale, these little primitive factories were beneath the level of serious consideration. Entire books on the Chinese economy were written without reference to them or with only contemptuous dismissals. Such underestimation was not only bad economics, it was bad history. In underdeveloped China there were still pockets of easily won resources almost everywhere, and pre-modern techniques for their exploitation were not wholly lost. In these respects, China was more like sixteenth- than twentieth-century Europe. In fact the 'backyard blast-furnaces' of the Great Leap, so jeered at in the West, sprang up again in the hands of individual peasants after the abolition of collective cultivation, and were profitable.

The result of this historical myopia was that township and village enterprises were written off. The number of Western experts who believed that they had a future could be counted until the 1990s on the fingers of one hand. It took thirty years for even the World Bank to recognize their value.

If we look at this new socialist economy in broader terms, it can be seen first as the partial triumph of the communalist strain of socialist aspiration over the étatist strain, Robert Owen over Saint-Simon. At the same time it can be seen as the triumph of the idea of economic development based upon the increase of peasant purchasing power, as opposed to that based upon the pillaging of the peasant majority for the means to develop heavy industry in the Stalinist manner, which was so widely influential in the less developed world in the 1950s and which is still powerful today. Chinese authors now accept that the revolutionary increase in peasant purchasing power, the object of Mao's Great Leap Forward, has been the main driving force of reform.

If we look at it in terms of future democratization, we could hazard the hypothesis that the creation of millions of dispersed centres of economic decision-making, side by side with the increase in individual autonomy created by the restoration of family farming, must, other things being equal, contribute to the creation of a potentially democratic society in which consultation, discussion, and negotiation largely replace command as the prevailing mode of politics.

The contrast between the success of China's gradual economic reform and the disastrous consequences of the abrupt abolition of the communist system in the Soviet Union demands explanation; but no explanation which assumes that reform in China began only in 1979 under Deng Xiaoping, and in the Soviet Union only in 1985 with Gorbachev, is satisfactory. In both countries the final reforms had a long prehistory, which largely determined what followed. The contrast begins here.

In the Soviet Union, Stalinism had lasted for thirty years, and such was the power of the entrenched vested interests it had created that it took a further thirty years and more to change it. In China, however, the Soviet system was adopted only in the year of Stalin's death, and then its moral authority was destroyed by Khrushchev's 1956 speech before China's first plan had even been completed. The Soviet Union was a principal protagonist in the Cold War which China had deserted. The Soviet Union was a polyglot empire, of which almost half the population was non-Russian, so that any attempt to relax rigid central control was perceived to incur the danger of the disintegration of the country; but China is exceptional among large states in that 93 per cent of the population are of common race and culture; thus a high degree of economic decentralization, although it may increase provincial differences of interest, does not threaten national unity. In the Soviet Union, the Stalinist system had originated in the assertion, by terror, of Bolshevik power and bore the stamp of its origins; it was ruthlessly centralized and had no significant element outside the circle of material allocation by the planners. China, however, had not had the time, or perhaps even the possibility, to subject the whole economy to centralized material allocation; and then by 1957 the inevitability of a degree of decentralization had been formally accepted, to be vastly extended in the Great Leap Forward and after the Cultural Revolution. Thus on the eve of Deng's reforms, vast resources were already being deployed outside the control of the planners in Beijing, through horizontal, quasi-market local relationships among the state enterprises and the new local collective firms.

Liberman's proposals—at least as they were interpreted by communist regimes—were focused on the State-owned industrial enterprises. They were not seen as relevant to agriculture. But the relationship between industry and agriculture was of vital importance. In the Soviet Union no serious efforts were made to increase rural production and incomes. One significant result of this was that two-thirds of the foreign exchange earned by the Soviet Union's oil exports had to be spent on imports of fodder; this is typical of the constraints imposed on the Soviet economy by its failure to improve agriculture.

In China, in contrast, while the necessity of feeding the growing industrial labour force at tolerable retail prices continued to dictate that farm-gate prices should be controlled, there was always a strong sense that this was not enough, and that some means must be found of increasing peasant incomes, although this opinion was not shared by Liu Shaoqi. In fact the most striking contrast between the Soviet Union and China was the absence in the Soviet Union, and the presence in China, of a realistic perception of intersectoral relationships which, properly handled, could provide a new context for the reform of State-owned industrial enterprises. This perception was first expressed in Mao's *Ten Great Relationships*.

While one problem of Libermanism was its focus on State-owned industries, another was the fact that the difficulties of the transition from directed enterprises to autonomous enterprises were not systematically examined nor was any programms for the transition proposed.

Deng Xiaoping was widely regarded as a pragmatist, but the word in his case needs definition. He continued to profess socialism: his three successive slogans were 'socialism with Chinese characteristics ... the first stage of socialism ... socialist market system'. The question is whether these slogans were sincere, or were simply meant to placate the ideological opposition. His pragmatic determination to exclude no individual or institution that might contribute to the increase of China's wealth and strength is not incompatible with a continued determination to dictate the terms on which such contributions were to be made, and to do so for what could be widely accepted as socialist reasons. There is nothing in his actions to suggest that his covert aim was to change China into a society dominated by free enterprise; indeed it is part of his pragmatism that he is unlikely to have entertained so dogmatic an aim. It must be recalled that until the very eve of China's adoption of Stalinism in 1953, the general view in the CCP was that China would have to develop capitalism to the full before the transition to socialism, in order to create the abundance that would make socialism possible. Mao then shared this belief. However, it was also firmly held that in Chinese conditions successful development of capitalism could occur only under communist leadership, and under the direction of the State. Communist beliefs in this respect, before the 1953 acceptance of Stalinism, were little different from what one might call the May Fourth consensus expressed by Sun Yatsen, since applied with great success in Taiwan.

Expressed in Marxist terms, Deng defended his reforms by insisting that the main force behind the creation of socialism was the development of 'the forces of production' as opposed to 'the relations of production'. Further changes in the relations of production which could bring about the transition to full socialism would thus occur simply as the result of improving technology. This was an emphatic break with Maoism. However, before congratulating Deng on his common sense, it must be remembered that in embracing the idea of the primacy of the forces of production he was returning to Stalin, and that this proposition had provided in the Soviet Union a convenient rationalization of the continuing power of the new elite. Deng's acceptance of this Stalinist view was a denial of Mao's insistence that China's officials had become a class hostile to the majority, an appropriate target of class struggle and of continued revolution in the relations of production. Yet in fact his proposed economic reforms involved massive changes in existing production relations, although these changes were perhaps, from a Marxist-Leninist point of view, regressive.

Deng Xiaoping was not dealing with a *tabula rasa*. On the one hand, the vested interests of the State industrial sector remained a barrier to reform. On the other hand, local collective industry outside the Plan had grown, in a decade, to the point where it, too, represented vested interests, massive in total.

The communes were abolished in 1982. The change, however, was largely nominal; the local authorities remained just as capable as the communes had been of organizing and co-ordinating local economic development. In addition, as 75 per cent of the evaluation points a local official could earn were awarded for his success in developing the local economy, China's local bureaucrats had a powerful incentive to become entrepreneurs.

The official line was still that township and village enterprise had been wholly invented by Deng Xiaoping. Mao was given no credit. Alternatively, it was admitted that they had existed before 1979, but that the Gang of Four had destroyed them. Pushed from this position, the argument then became that they had existed but were uneconomically focused on heavy industry and were merely a source of loss. The author, working on local industries in 1982, living in villages in three provinces, was always given one or other of these stories when first meeting the local leaders; but when the individual factories were visited, to the question 'when was your factory founded?' the answer was usually 1970, 1971, 1972. In other words, they were the creation of the Cultural Revolution. Some even went back to 1958, having evaded Liu Shaoqi's abolition of the original commune and brigade enterprise of the Great Leap.

The new system of individual contracts in agriculture has generally been interpreted as the end of collectivized agriculture in China, but this is a misunderstanding. The land is still publicly owned. The farmer still has to produce his contracted amount of grain or cotton; his freedom is confined to the use of his remaining resources, if any. His market is still, for the most part, the local State trading organizations. He is dependent for supplies of farm inputs on the local authorities who can, and do, withhold them from peasants who do not do as they are told. If his family members change in number, relative to those of his neighbours, the land is redistributed under new contracts. A sharp rise in contractual obligations could, *de facto*, wipe out his precarious autonomy. His prosperity is still cruelly dependent on the relative movement of agricultural against industrial prices, and in recent years the terms of trade have moved against him. He is frequently paid for his produce only in IOUs, and responds by joining his fellows in riotous protest. Local government is still authoritarian, and this authority is constantly abused.

In more positive respects, however, the village is as collective as ever, largely via the disbursement of the profits of local collective industry. Indeed, the Rural Responsibility System (that is, the system of individual contracts) was quickly accepted by the reformers as evidence that individual incentives need not after all undermine collectivism, and was therefore used as a model for the reform of State-owned enterprise through the use of analogous contracts.

As a result of vast and increasing new rural prosperity, the entire Chinese economy surged forward at an extraordinary rate, so that in contrast to the rest of the communist world, where reform generally took place in conditions of economic stagnation or regression, in China it took place in an economy whose rate of growth was exceptionally high. This was the encouraging milieu in which China's reform of the State sector was able to proceed.

The eventual aim of economic reform was never clearly stated, and perhaps could not be as long as there was ideological opposition; by the same token, reforms were always justified publicly in ideological terms. The necessity for a gradual experimental approach was accepted, and expressed in the slogan 'crossing the river by groping for the stones'.

During the 1980s however a strong body of opinion was growing in the communist world that because the institutions of the command economy were so interlinked, nothing would work except the simultaneous abolition of all of them. This opinion naively assumed that free markets would immediately and spontaneously take over. It ignored the fact that the creation of a market economy requires new laws, institutions, networks, skills, and expectations. Fortunately for China, this 'big bang' strategy had not yet appeared when Deng's reforms began.

Reforming the State sector

There were several stumbling blocks to reform. First was the fear of inflation: any step towards more entrepreneurial behaviour by the State firms was likely to involve a massive creation of credit, while the very pace of economic growth itself pushed prices up. Second was the reluctance of the regime to face the vast unemployment which any serious attempt to increase the efficiency of the grossly overstaffed State-owned enterprises would incur. Most inhibiting of all, however, was the fact that among the State firms there was no level playing field; their assets and their location had been determined too often by social or by strategic considerations rather than by economic rationality. As a result, any attempt to impose uniform rules immediately raised the need to make so many exceptions that the old bargaining relationship between firm and ministry was simply revived.

In any case, autonomy for the State-owned enterprises had to be defined. Autonomy from what or whom? The ministry? The local authority of the area in which the firm was located? The factory's all-powerful Party committee? And even if decisions were arrived at in this respect, there was the further problem that autonomy, in the absence of many other important changes, was almost meaningless. Its effect would critically depend on what proportion of profits the firms would be allowed to retain. It required that firms should be able to sell their surplus over State targets freely on the market; many already did so and under Mao always had done so; but without a reduction in their obligatory deliveries to the State their market operations could not be more than marginal. Autonomy could not operate in reality as long as most essential materials were allocated by the ministries. If firms were to be responsible for their own profit and loss, they would have to enjoy the right to hire and fire, and they would have to be relieved of their welfare responsibilities, the burden of which could turn a profitable firm into a losing one; and as the original industrial workforce recruited in the early 1950s aged, the costs of these responsibilities (especially for pensions) were growing rapidly.

Prices would sooner or later have to be freed from State control so that they would reflect relative efficiency. The remittance of their profits to the State (the major item in the revenues of the central government) would have to be replaced by a uniform tax. Loss-making firms would have to be declared bankrupt. The reformers soon realized that if they were in for a penny they were in for a pound: to make autonomy good, they would sooner or later have to accept comprehensive change, even if the changes were introduced as slowly as was feasible.

After a successful experiment by Zhao Ziyang in Sichuan, the State-owned enterprises throughout China were offered, and most accepted, autonomy. The firms were permitted to sell their surpluses on the market, as indeed many were already doing. They were allowed to keep a proportion of any profits made on the sale of surpluses. An attempt was made to oblige them to pay a charge for the capital received from the State. It was officially decreed that the economy would thenceforth have two sections: the planned and the market. The State's planning targets were reduced annually for three successive years. An attempt was also made to substitute taxes for the remittance of profits to the State. The firms were encouraged to shed surplus labour, in the first instance by encouraging early retirement on pension. These measures, however, had only very limited effects.

It is important also to appreciate the paradox pointed out by Barry Naughton that the spread of markets was pushed forward as much by recession (usually caused by resort to deflationary policies when inflation threatened) as by boom. In times of high demand, non-State market-oriented industry grew; in times of recession, planned production was less necessary, while at the same time the highly priced goods of the State-owned enterprises could not compete in a slack market. The machine-tool industry offers a dramatic example. When demand was high it could not be met by State industry; when demand was low, State firms could not sell at government-fixed prices. In a short time it became pointless to allocate materials for the production of machine tools.

In spite of all the difficulties, by 1984 a fairly clear and agreed reform project had been created by Zhao Ziyang. Zhao sent a letter to the standing Committee of the Politburo on 9 September. While first paying lip service to the importance of the planned economy, he proposed that planning should be indicative, not prescriptive, and urged that all goods should come to be exchanged voluntarily. Following the approval of this letter, the Central Committee issued a new document (October 1984). It was now stated that enterprises should become responsible for their own profit and loss, should determine their own labour force, design their own form of organization, set their own prices, and adopt their own wage and bonus policies, 'within the scope of the State plan'. Implementation, however, would take a long time: the Central Committee document was merely a statement of aims.

Following this, the vital decision was taken to freeze planned State investment, and eventually to limit it to certain priorities. From then on, all further growth would be outside the system of planned allocation. This meant that China would increasingly become a market economy, although one in which the major actors would perhaps continue to be State and collective institutions. The decision left as many problems as it solved, but at least the direction of reform was now made clear. In particular, the reforms could not work at all if the problem of freeing prices was not solved. The difficulty was, again, the disparity in resources and opportunities, over and above differences of efficiency, among the State-owned enterprises. The idea was that prices should be set at costs plus a margin, but whose costs? A debate began: should price reform precede enterprise reform, or vice versa? The fact is that the two were mutually dependent. Gradually, a system of dual prices was set up, with in-plan prices on the one hand and market prices on the other. This was not really sustainable, however, and it was an open door to corruption.

Meanwhile, a change in personnel was encouraged. Political figures gave way to technocrats. Fifty per cent of city mayors (who had considerable economic power) and almost 50 per cent of industrial managers were now engineers by training. How far this actually increased efficiency, however, must be doubtful; the Soviet Union was ruled largely by engineers throughout an entire generation of unsuccessful attempts at reform. More recently in China engineers have begun to be supplemented by economists and lawyers—rightly, for the new market economy controlled not by bureaucratic orders but by the use of macroeconomic levers, in which planning is concerned primarily with the prediction of growth paths, requires economists and, being based on free contracts, requires lawyers.

Gradually the idea of contract, pioneered in farming, was introduced to industry; first, new workers were given contracts instead of lifelong employment. Then managers were given long-term contracts. Finally, even the ministries were put on contract.

Autonomy was now properly defined in terms of legal rights. However, severe difficulties of implementation remained. In spite of the new right to hire and fire, relatively few redundant workers were sacked in the mid-1980s. Managers were most reluctant; lifetime employment was a shibboleth of Chinese socialism as well as a reflection of traditional hostility to 'breaking rice-bowls'. There was constant interference by Party cadres and bureaucrats in industrial management. The expanded banking system, on which Chinese industry now largely depended for external funding, was lacking in discipline: decisions were often made as a result of Party seniority (if, for example, the enterprise manager requesting the loan was senior in the Party to the bank manager). The autonomy of the enterprise was not consistently respected, nor indeed were the rights of the peasants under the Rural Responsibility System. Yet gradually the economic culture was changing, and marketization was spreading through its own inertia of motion.

Meanwhile, however, a new problem emerged. After 1985 the rapid increase of agricultural production slowed drastically, for two different reasons. First, the terms of trade between agriculture and industry had been reversed to the disadvantage of the cultivators, as inflation drove up the prices of farm inputs. Second, with the diversification of agriculture into crops whose prices were not so rigidly controlled, and with the continued growth of employment in local collective industry, grain-growing had become the least profitable activity. In some coastal areas where there were many nearby city markets, and where township and village enterprise was most developed, local authorities even in the early 1980s were actually forced to subsidize grain-growing in order to meet their State obligations. In a famous case in central China, the peasants of one village had totally relinquished farming to concentrate on the manufacture of a successful design of kitchen knife which had proved popular throughout China. By the 1990s, peasants were resisting grain-growing: 'we will not grow more grain next year no matter what you do to us.' The problem remains unsolved. Agricultural production has continued to grow as a whole, but much more slowly. In 1985 most of China had been permitted to abolish the grain procurement system but it soon had to be reimposed.

Problems of political reform, 1978–1989

The new regime attached importance to political as well as economic reform. Political reform expressed a reaction to the turmoil of the Cultural Revolution, a reaction shared as much by the Party leaders restored to power, who had themselves been victims of Cultural Revolution lawlessness, as by persecuted intellectuals, disillusioned Red Guards, and the ordinary people of China who had suffered a decade of unpredictability and political and economic constraint. The restored leaders had every reason to be sincere in their new-found respect for the rule of law and for constitutional process. At the same time the prestige of the CCP had been so badly damaged that it was forced, in order to reassert its authority, to offer a new deal to the Chinese people, and to seek a new legitimization. Part of this legitimization was a less rigid and oppressive form of goverment.

A few of the restored leaders would have been content simply to put the clock back to 1964; most, however, perceived that this would not be sufficient, and that some attempt must be made to deal with the discontents which had made the Cultural Revolution possible. Of the latter, the chief spokesman was Deng Xiaoping. He was not content simply to condemn the Cultural

Revolution and to rehabilitate its victims. He was prepared to accept a wider area of freedom of discussion and criticism than had hitherto been permitted in the history of the CCP. Further, he was prepared to acknowledge and within limits even to tolerate the fact that the influence of Marxism itself had been thoroughly undermined, especially among the young. He appreciated that the sort of widespread economic initiative needed, if his hopes were to be fulfilled, demanded a considerable relaxation of political control and supervision. More immediately, Deng Xiaoping was quite happy to encourage the free expression of discontent as long as that sentiment was likely to be directed against his political opponents on the left rather than against his own faction.

Deng had an able assistant in Hu Yaobang, who had been associated with him since the days of the Sichuan Soviet in the late 1920s. Hu was a Hakka, with the stubborn courage and the intellectual bent of his race. Since 1952 he had headed the Young Communist League, and from there, after the end of the Cultural Revolution, had become deputy head of the Central Party School and then head of the Organization Department. In 1980 he became the leader of the CCP, Secretary-General of the Central Committee. His first act was to rehabilitate the victims of the Cultural Revolution and of the 1957 anti-rightist campaign. At the same time, class labels were abolished. Hu Yaobang soon became the foremost advocate of democratization within the Party.

By the end of 1978, the lines of battle for the democratization of China had been drawn up. In this respect, there was no clear distinction of opinion between members of the CCP and those outside the Party, as indeed had already been proved to be the case with ruling communist parties elsewhere by public opinion surveys. In fact the democratization movement began from the Central Party School.

Before the third plenum of the eleventh Central Committee met in December 1978. Hua Guofeng asserted that 'whatever policy decisions were made by Chairman Mao must be resolutely upheld by us. Whatever instructions were given by Chairman Mao must be firmly and unswervingly followed by us.' The Central Party School, under the influence of Hu Yaobang, put forward in opposition to this slogan the assertion that 'actual practice is the only criterion for the examination of truth'. Hu had the article in which this idea was elaborated published in the major Party newspapers. It was a stronger form of the slogan put forward by Deng Xiaoping on his reappearance in 1977: 'seek truth from facts'; ironically, this was a quotation from Mao. In June Deng made a speech confirming his support for pragmatism thus defined.

The democracy movement

This speech seemed to invite wide-ranging debate, which was begun in *China Youth*, the organ of the China Youth League. An article asked why China's millions had not been able to deal with the Gang of Four. The answer was the absence of a 'disciplined judiciary' and 'the right of the people to elect, supervise and dismiss the personnel of the state's executive and administrative organs', a free press to expose abuses, and the secret ballot. The article went on to state that the Four Modernizations were impossible without democratization. Deng did not demur.

It was in these circumstances that the democratic movement of 1978–80 began, effectively in the autumn of 1978 when it was known that at the third plenum Deng Xiaoping would seek to launch his programme of reforms, against the opposition of Hua Guofeng. In October 1978 a large group of young people assembled before a blank wall in one of Beijing's main streets and began to cover its surface with wall newspapers, in the manner of the CR. The posters were soon supplemented by mimeographed journals which could spread the message further. The vast majority of these posters and journals, obstensibly at least, supported Deng Xiaoping; their purpose was to strengthen his hand at the forthcoming plenum. Their authors professed to recognize in Deng a champion of the democratization of socialism. There was also an implication that support for him was conditional on his meeting democratic aspirations. Some of the journals (such as the *April 5th Forum* and *Beijing Spring*) clearly had the support of certain Party leaders; they had access to inside political information. The authors rejected the epithet 'dissidents' and insisted that they were loyal supporters of the communist regime. And indeed much of the rhetoric of the movement had already been made familiar in the official press. Deng Xiaoping and Hu Yaobang visited the demonstration, praised it, and encouraged more posters.

Inevitably, however, the Party-linked moderates were soon drowned out by more radical voices. These condemned Party rule as 'feudal monarchy', dismissed Marxism-Leninism-Mao-Zedong-Thought as a 'deceitful hoax', called on people to 'circulate petitions . . . hold demonstrations . . . organize citizens' petition groups for human rights', and demanded the abolition of the communist one-party system.

The most radical of the democratic writers was a young electrician, Wei Jingsheng, editor of the journal *Explorations*. On 5 December 1978 his poster 'The Fifth Modernization' was posted on Democracy Wall. His fifth modernization was the establishment of democracy. In fact, Hu Yaobang's supporters had already made the point in public that without democratization, modernization was impossible. But Wei went far beyond this. He made no distinction between Deng Xiaoping and the rest of the Party; all stood condemned before Wei's uncompromising insistence on full democratic rights: 'When people ask for democracy they are only asking for what is theirs by right . . . Are they not justified in seizing power from the overlords?'

Equally radical, and at that time perhaps more influential, was a publication called *Crossroads Socialism* by a 27-year-old democrat, Chen Erjin. Little is known about him except that he was of peasant stock, worked as a peasant for some years, then as a labourer, before being given an opportunity (as a result of the Cultural Revolution) to train as a schoolteacher.

The Li-Yi-Zhe poster of 1974 had ended with a question: 'Can we ignore the aristocracy and the new bourgeoisie who are being created before our eyes?'. The poster was of course directed at the Cultural Revolution leadership (although naming only Lin Biao, who was already disgraced and dead) who had perverted the democracy of the Cultural Revolution into a privileged dictatorship more severe than its predecessor. But its main significance in the debate was its denial of the CCP's assertion that the faults of the communist system were the result of survivals from the old society, with the threat that on this basis capitalism might reassert itself. This was Lenin's theory which Mao, in spite of his condemnation of China's officials as a hostile class, had not explicitly repudiated. If Lenin was wrong and it was socialism itself which had spawned a new class, then the faults of the system were not incidental and contingent, but systemic. The Li-Yi-Zhe poster did not explicitly assert this; but Chen Erjin did so. He sent the manuscript of his book to Mao, three months before Mao's death. It is unlikely that Mao, in the last stages of mortal sickness, could have read it. The manuscript was published only during the Democracy Wall movement, as a samizdat entitled *Crossroads Socialism.*

Chen argued that post-revolutionary socialist society was in reality a specific, new social formation, even more exploitative than its predecessors. Given that authoritarian government was necessary in order to crush the old exploiting classes, the appearance of this new post-revolutionary exploiting class was an inevitable stage of history. And its appearance made a second revolution necessary in order to put power into the hands of the people, in reality as well as in theory. Chen put this forward as a contribution to Marxism.

The Cultural Revolution had been an attempt at this second revolution. It failed because of inexperience. This inexperience was partly the result of the lack of a guiding theory, which Chen claimed he was now providing.

He called the authoritarian society created by the original revolution the system of 'unicorporate public social production'—a clumsy phrase in translation, but one which indicated a society in which the ruling group controls all economic resources and shares out, in the form of privileges, the surplus value which the economy creates. This system is even more oppressive than the capitalist system because the workers are deprived even of the freedom they had under capitalism to sell their labour to the highest bidder.

The second revolution, which would create true socialism by democratization, might have to involve the use of force like the first, but it would certainly be established from the bottom, by mass action, and not from above.

Chen then turns to the question of the nature of the democratic system required. And here he is even more daring. His democratic model is the United States. He justifies this by making a distinction between the content and the form of democracy. The content in the United States is bourgeois, but the form is of universal validity. He demands the protection of civil rights, the separation of powers, and valid elections. He calls for political competition; but at this point he departs from the Western model. There will only be two parties, and they will both be communist parties. Chen in fact assumes that just as American democracy takes place within a bourgeois consensus, so Chinese democracy will operate within a socialist consensus. This being so, two parties competing within that consensus will be enough, as they are in the United States.

There is one other difference between Chen's projected democracy and that of the West. Chen asserts that democracy must also apply to economic institutions—factories and communes. He accepts Mao's Anshan Constitution which proposed workers' management, and saw producers' communities as the basic blocs of socialist society. Chen agrees in fact with Mao that the nationalization of the means of production is only the first step to socialism, which merely provides the opportunity for the socialist transformation of management and control.

His book touched off a vigorous debate within the democratic movement. Its importance was its assertion that the existing system must be overthrown, and that its overthrow would only be achieved by grass-roots mass action. To this message many former Red Guards were responsive, and Chen's book certainly played a part in creating the radical, ex-Red-Guard wing of the democratic movement whose strength was to become apparent in the Tiananmen movement of 1989, even although Chen Erjin himself disappeared from view after the suppression of the Democracy Wall movement. His fate is unknown, but as his ideas represented perhaps the most mortal threat which the movement offered to the power of the Party, it is unlikely that he was left at liberty.

Chen's debt to Mao is obvious. His theory is a rationalization and an elaboration of Mao's condemnation of China's officialdom as an exploiting class, and of his justification of grass-roots revolt. Even if one were to concede that Mao's motive in this attack on the Party establishment was simply to re-establish his own power, yet the terms in which this attack was rationalized had transformed the political possibilities and created a radical democratic movement which still persists in China in spite of over twenty years of persecution.

The authorities became alarmed. The movement had spread throughout China's cities. Dissident journals multiplied. Petitioners for rehabilitation, unemployed youths in the cities, rusticated young people back from the countryside, distressed peasants in tens of thousands, and protesting victims of vicious behaviour on the part of communist cadres, were more than ready to accept the politicization of their grievances. For example, the case of one young woman, trying to get justice for having (as she alleged) been raped by the party secretary of her unit, was turned into a massive demonstration demanding 'freedom, democracy, and food'. Much of China was still in disorder in the aftermath of the Cultural Revolution; the fuel existed for another conflagration. The posters and tabloids of the democracy movement were too reminiscent of those through whose influence China had so recently been torn apart. The call of Wei Jingsheng to the people to rise and seize power not only alarmed the government but was deplored as premature by most of the democrats. Until this point Deng Xiaoping had publicly defended Democracy Wall, but now abruptly he changed his mind. The wall was stripped of its posters by the security police. The Beijing city government offered a new site to the poster writers in a park remote from the city centre where posters were allowed only if registered with the authorities.

Wei Jingsheng was arrested on 29 March 1979 and sentenced to fifteen years in prison on two charges, of counter-revolution and of passing military secrets to foreigners. The other leaders of the democracy movement protested at the severity of the sentence and the perfunctoriness of the trial, but few openly supported Wei's political demands. In the following three months the democratic journals were suppressed and some fifty of their editors imprisoned.

The suppression of Democracy Wall did not halt the democracy movement. Although Deng Xiaoping had suppressed Democracy Wall, he was not opposed to continued debate on democratization within limits. The debate became increasingly sophisticated. There was a return to the early writings of Marx, with their passionate emphasis on individual liberty. There was a strong interest in the new developments of Marxism in the West and in the socialist bloc. There was a revival of Confucianism, with the democrats stressing its teachings on government by consent and on the value of individual judgement; Huang Zongxi of the seventeenth century was again quoted on the need to institutionalize checks on despotism. Attention swung back to the ideas of the European Enlightenment. In the field of literature, twentieth-century developments including such writers as Kafka and Sartre were used as models. There was something like a revival of the intellectual ferment of the May Fourth Movement.

The first group involved was the network which Hu Yaobang had built up within the Party. When the Maoists were cleared out after the third plenum of the eleventh Central Committee, Hu secured the advancement of his followers to positions of influence from which they virtually controlled China's intellectual institutions and the major organs of the media. Hu supported their radical demands. His own opinions can be summed up in his public assertion that democracy was not a means but an end—a shocking heresy against Marxism-Leninism. The group which he brought together in January 1979 at a Theory Conference provided most of the prominent writers of the democratic movement thereafter, and most of the *bêtes noires* of the conservative veterans.

At the same time, Zhao Ziyang as Prime Minister was also creating a network, based on the new think-tanks which he patronized. Their primary concern was economic reform; their interest in a degree of democratization was that it was necessary for economic efficiency, in an economy designed to be more pluralist. Their position was closer to that of Deng Xiaoping himself. However, as the pluralist economy developed, even they came to recognize that economic reform would have to embrace a far higher degree of democracy than Deng was willing to concede.

Among these supporters of Zhao Ziyang there grew up an eloquent and able group who, paradoxically, believed that democratization would first require a period of continued authoritarian government. They believed that immediate democratization might paralyse further reform by polarizing conflicting interests, old and new, and they advocated the postponement of full democratization until economic restructuring had been completed. There was less distinction between these neo-authoritarians and the democrats than the sharpness of the debate between them would suggest. Almost no one in China was in favour of immediate democratization even had it been possible against the opposition of the regime. The real question at issue was the pace at which gradual democratization should proceed.

The neo-authoritarian view chimed in with the view, taken in the 1980s by most Chinese intellectuals, that democratization could only come from the top: the regime must be persuaded because it could not be successfully confronted.

In contrast to these, however, were groups, usually led by former Red Guards, who sought to build a coalition of the discontented and the disadvantaged and attempt to create democracy from below. They devoted themselves to grass-roots political organization. The position and significance of former Red Guards has been underestimated in the analysis of the democratic movement. They had been taught, by Mao himself, to believe in revolution from below. We have seen the development of their ideas through the Li-Yi-Zhe poster and Chen Erjin's *Crossroads Socialism*.

Wei Jingsheng and his fellow radicals in the Democracy Wall movement were former Red Guards. So were those who at that time attempted to organize peasant protests, and so were those who, during the Tiananmen demonstrations of 1989, were to take the initiative in forming autonomous organizations of students, workers, intellectuals, and citizens. Their attitude contrasts with that of the rest of the democratic groups, who were essentially appealing to the Communist Party to take the initiative in democratization. However, given the profound differences of opinion on democratization inside the Party, this was not altogether unrealistic. The fact is that if and when democracy comes to China it will of necessity arrive through joint action inside and outside the Party.

Opposed to democratization were the group of orthodox communists, mostly but not wholly consisting of veteran Party leaders who had been retired in 1978 and nominated to the new Central Advisory Commission which, to the dismay of the more open-minded members of the Party leadership, they turned into a centre of power. Many of them were as opposed to radical economic reform as to political reform.

Associated with the orthodox veterans was a group who proclaimed themselves to be Maoist, but in fact consisted mainly of unreconstructed Stalinist control freaks bitter at their loss of power, and terrified that attacks on Mao's reputation would reflect on their own past. Their ideas had little to do with Mao.

Deng Xiaoping held the balance, sometimes supporting the democrats, sometimes opposing them. His successive statements were often contradictory, but it cannot be assumed that these swings in his opinions were wholly tactical. He swung from insistence on the absolute and final authority of the Communist Party to acknowledgement of the virtues of bourgeois democracy and back again. However, on some things he was firm. The first was that economic reform must give opportunities to all who could make a contribution—to the state sector, the collective sector in countryside and cities, and private enterprise, and to scientists and technologists and social scientists who could contribute to policy-making. This at least meant a substantial relaxation of Party control The second, as the first principle implied, was that in the sort of pluralist economy which Deng's economic strategy would entail, China's institutions should be left to run themselves by delegated power, in matters which did not involve questions of principle. The third was that, subject to the Party's ultimate authority, affairs should be carried on according to specific laws enforced by satisfactory legal procedures.

The fourth point, on the other hand, was his belief that only a system which was in the final analysis authoritarian could prevent instabilities, which might threaten economic reform. He rejected the argument, constantly made by the democratic groups, that democracy was the best guarantee of stability. His belief may have been wrong, but it was not without substance: one cannot predict whether, as the inevitable losses and frustrations of economic reform built up, democracy would have served to reconcile these conflicts or to polarize them dangerously.

On these points he was in the main consistent; and they determined in successive crises on which side he would put his weight.

The democratic debate went on against changing conditions abroad. The first Solidarity strikes in Gdańsk and elsewhere took place in the summer of 1980. Gorbachev came to power in 1986. In Czechoslovakia the democrats had set out consciously and systematically to re-create civil society, as a parallel and rival to the communist system. Meanwhile in Taiwan, Chiang Kaishek's son and successor had brought martial law to an end and instituted a process of democratization, since completed. South Korea and the Philippines were democratized by 'people's revolutions' while the Chinese debate over democracy was going on.

The orthodox veterans were frustrated. Because of the grip which Hu Yaobang had on the press, their opportunities to participate in the debate were sorely limited, just as for the Maoists in the early 1960s. Ironically, at one stage they became advocates of a free press, because of the frustrations they faced.

However, they were able on several occasions to apply pressure and to limit the freedom of debate, but only briefly and only as far as Deng Xiaoping would permit. The first occasion was at a second meeting of the Theory Conference. Although the meeting was proposed by the conservative veterans, as an attempt to restore ideological consensus, in fact it was Hu Yaobang who chose the delegates. It met and then was adjourned for the Spring Festival, and met again. In the first session radical proposals for democratization were pressed by Hu's supporters. During the adjournment therefore the conservative veterans intervened. The number of delegates was doubled, the new arrivals being representatives of the conservative faction. Deng Xiaoping made a speech attempting to limit the debate by asserting 'four cardinal principles': the socialist road, the dictatorship of the proletariat, the leadership of the Communist Party, and the thought of Mao Zedong.

This formulation was in the circumstances of the time too vague to work. All four principles were now ambiguous. The socialist road was in the process of experimental redefinition; the dictatorship of the proletariat, proposed by Marx as the means by which capitalism would be expropriated after the socialist seizure of power, was of somewhat doubtful meaning in a phase in which capitalism was being reinvented by a socialist government; the proper nature of the leadership of the Communist Party was now in debate; and Mao Zedong Thought was whatever anyone in power chose to make of it. All four principles could be interpreted to rationalize a return to totalitarianism, or to promote a large measure of democratization. At any rate Deng's intervention did not inhibit the continued advocacy of democracy. Perhaps it was not seriously meant to; perhaps its purpose was simply to find a formula which would for the moment satisfy both sides. The democratic debate went on unchecked throughout 1980. On 18 August Deng made a speech in which he praised bourgeois democracy.

Then in the summer came the Solidarity strikes in Gdańsk. It was perhaps this and subsequent events in Poland which now changed his mind, because at the end of the year he made a further speech in which he condemned bourgeois liberalism and asserted the need for continuing class struggle. Encouraged by this change of heart, the conservative veterans once more intervened. Since 1977 there had been a stream of literary works vividly describing and condemning the Anti-Rightist Campaign, the Great Leap Forward, and the Cultural Revolution. The latest was a film script published by a PLA writer Bai

Hua, called *Unrequited Love*—love for China and socialism, unrequited by the Communist Party. It was attacked in the *Liberation Army Daily*, and the conservative veterans joined in, expanding the attack to everything they regarded as bourgeois liberalism. The attack was embarrassing to Hu Yaobang, but Deng Xiaoping supported Hu's efforts to bring it to an end. Deng was hostile to *Unrequited Love*, but was not prepared to face the uncertainties of a political campaign. He repeated his rule against such activities, a rule which few were ready to dispute. The campaign was smothered. Bai Hua even received a poetry prize.

Since 1977 one of Hu Yaobang's associates, Wang Ruoshui, deputy editor of *Guangming Ribao*, had been writing and publishing on two related ideas; one was 'Marxist humanism'. The other was Marx's idea of the alienation of the working class in capitalist society, which Wang now applied to socialist society. Both ideas began to be widely debated in the early 1980s, to the alarm of the conservatives. In 1983 they made an attempt to forbid the discussion of these two dangerous topics. The first threatened the validity of class-based morality, and did so from the pages of Marx's 1844 *Economic and Philosophical Manuscripts*. The second threatened the legitimacy of communist government by asserting that the people were alienated from the system, just as the working class was alienated by capitalism. Once again, Deng Xiaoping supported Hu Yaobang's attempts at damage limitation. Wang Ruoshui lost his job, but kept his salary and his official car, and was soon rehabilitated, although his book on humanism was not published for several years.

Such interference with writers as went on was relatively mild. Few writers were attacked and, in contrast to the days before 1978, such attacks did not involve the destruction of the victim's career or the disgrace of his family and his colleagues. Little pressure was put on his peers to join in the attack. As far as the public was concerned, such attacks merely enhanced the reputations of those persecuted. And in spite of them, intellectual organizations, old and new, worked with increasing autonomy, while increasingly such organizations were formed independently, sustaining themselves out of their own revenues. Electronic communication was spreading. Foreign contacts had multiplied manyfold.

Meanwhile tentative experiments went on to establish a few slightly more democratic rules. A new electoral law provided for direct elections at the district (xian) level, and in urban constituencies at the same level of administration, including Beijing. Polling was largely by work units rather than by wards. This gave an opportunity for students to be adopted in their colleges as candidates. Some of the democratic leaders took advantage of this. The same was also possible in factories. The political demands of the democrats were thus made an issue in the new elections. Again after conscientious and not illiberal attempts at tolerance the authorities finally reacted when some candidates asserted that they were not Marxists. It had been accepted that a man in his private views need not be Marxist, but for him to stand for public office on a non-Marxist platform was more than the regime could stomach. Subsequent local elections were held under great restrictions, although there was a choice of (communist) candidates and a secret ballot. The rules for elections were again to become an issue in the democratic protests at Kei Da University in Anhui in late 1986.

The Deng Xiaoping administration nevertheless persisted in reforms which liberalized the Chinese legal system to a significant extent. The criminal law and criminal procedure were codified. Some Party elections and elections in some social organizations such as the Writers' Federation were, like local elections, by secret ballot and offered a choice of candidates. In the economic enterprises, some shop-floor and section managers were elected, and the election even of enterprise managers spread. The People's Congresses, up to and including the National People's Congress, were allowed to exercise a little more power, at least to the extent that debate became more real, and resolutions were no longer passed unanimously. It was reasserted that the 'double hundred policy' (let a hundred flowers bloom and a hundred schools contend) was intended to provide for the widest discussion of different points of view and was not merely an instrument of struggle between Marxists and their opponents. It was also laid down that there would be no 'forbidden zones' in academic research. Attempts were made to define the relative duties of Party, State, and expert management, although without much practical success; a newspaper cartoon showed three doors, one marked 'Party', one marked 'State', and one marked 'Enterprise'—but all of them opened into the office of the Party Secretary.

In October 1984 the Fourth Congress of the All-China Federation of Literature and Art Circles took place. The conservative veterans tried to pack the meeting with their own supporters, in an attempt to raise the issue of 'spiritual pollution', but Deng Xiaoping and Hu Yaobang prevented this. The Congress became a writers' revolt. Passionate speeches were made, and wildly applauded, condemning the Party's history of repression, and demanding freedom. Deng and Hu ensured that the closing speeches conceded freedom to write, although still subject to rules preventing 'decadent capitalist thinking and feudalism', and insisting that China's writers must support economic reform. The delegates gave themselves a new constitution. The proceedings of the Congress were published, and as a result virtually all China's professional associations demanded the same autonomy.

A brief thaw took place, during which another issue was raised by the democratic writer Liu Binyan in an article 'A Second Kind of Loyalty', which distinguished between loyalty to China and loyalty to the regime, and condemned the demand for blind obedience to the Party. However, the thaw ended in April 1985 when Hu Yaobang, presumably under pressure, made a speech against the freedom of the press and acknowledged the existence of 'spiritual pollution'. The autonomy which the professional associations had demanded was denied, and the conservatives felt encouraged to attempt to launch yet another campaign against spiritual pollution and bourgeois liberalism, but with the focus this time on the idea of the two kinds of loyalty. Liu Binyan, who had first raised the issue, was forced to write a self-criticism, but he used it to defend himself and to put the democrats' case once more.

By this time Hu Yaobang seems to have been in control again. The conservative ideologue Deng Liqun was removed from the directorship of propaganda and replaced by one of Hu's supporters. Hu was also able to ensure that new directors of the Institutes of Political Science, Literature, and Marxism-Leninism were elected by their peers. Finally, he revoked his attack on freedom of the press. Another period of increased freedom began. Even *Red Flag*, usually controlled by the conservatives, demanded that academic freedom should be protected by law.

Then a new crisis arose. A young economist, born in 1957, Ma Ding, published an attack on Marxist economics and called for the use of Western economic analysis. At first applauded, it was soon condemned. At this point, however, there occurred student demonstrations in protest against the Japanese Prime Minister Nakasone, who had made a speech honouring the Japanese soldiers who had fought in China. The demonstration, encouraged by the Chinese authorities, quickly widened into demands for democracy and spread throughout the country. The authorities managed to placate the students but the conservatives were alarmed. Chen Yun attacked Hu Yaobang for neglecting the problem of spiritual pollution and Li Peng, the protégé of the veterans, was made a member of the Secretariat of the Politburo. An attack was launched on Ma Qing and on the Institute for Economic Structural Reform whose members shared his beliefs. This attack, the real target of which was economic reform, was, as one would expect, too much for Deng Xiaoping, who remained determined to prevent any interference with his plans. The Chinese press was therefore allowed scope to elaborate Ma's ideas.

In April 1986 Deng Xiaoping in a speech blamed the evils of bureaucratism and corruption not on abuses of the system but on the system itself. The solution he suggested, however, was only the separation of Party from government, a change which had already been attempted for several years without success. Nevertheless his speech touched off a new wave of democratic demands and at the same time strengthened the hand of Hu Yaobang. Scientists and social scientists were now called upon not merely to give advice when requested, but to launch their own programmes of policy-oriented research. In response, calls were made for legal protection of those involved.

In 1985 Hu Yaobang had organized a series of seminars on the rule of law. In June 1986, speaking abroad, he quoted Montesquieu: 'Liberty means doing anything permitted by law.' Seminars and forums began to be held on a scale which made Party control difficult. The focus of democratic agitation then swung back to freedom of the press and a call for independent newspapers. Marx was quoted: 'Without freedom of publication, all other freedoms would just be an illusion.'

By this period, the demand of the democrats, though still stated in principle rather than in detail, was for virtually full (though not necessarily immediate) democratization. Yan Jiaqi, Director of the Chinese Academy of Social Sciences created as a measure of liberalization in 1980, took the lead. He asserted that democracy needs 'a web of rules, regulations, institutions, laws, morals, public opinion and conventions'. Demands were made for a civil code, an independent judiciary, power to sue the government, the principle that the accused is innocent until proved guilty, and the right for minorities to continue to argue their case even after majority decisions had been taken.

For the first time the right of the peasants to participate in democratized politics was asserted by democratic intellectuals, as opposed to the former Red Guard agitators who had never doubted it. Also for the first time it was asserted publicly that intellectuals should join other groups in political action. The idea that some sort of democracy could be created within the system of one-party rule had been all but relinquished. It was now asserted that the National People's Congress should be sovereign.

Up to this point the only major feature of full democracy which had seldom been demanded was the creation of a multi-party system. At the same time, however, China's existing minor parties, which had been squeezed out of the position, weak as it had been, which they had enjoyed in China's political decision-making processes before 1956, began to assert themselves. Since 1979 their membership had almost quadrupled to 290,000. They were the obvious points from which a multi-party system might grow. They had some support from the economic reformers, who recognized the value of their connections with the private entrepreneurs and with the Chinese communities abroad, members of which were contributing substantially to investment in China. These minor parties now demanded legal protection of their independence. At the same time, it was proposed that the Chinese People's Political Consultative Conference, whose existence was even more nugatory than that of the minor parties, should become a second chamber.

The conservative veterans then launched another attack. *Red Flag* published an article which asserted that political freedom could not 'be separated from the existing relations of production', i.e. from class struggle, and this was followed by a spate of similar articles. This renewed conservative intervention came to its climax at the sixth plenum of the twelfth Central Committe at which there was an argument as to whether 'bourgeois liberalism' should be referred to in the Resolution. Deng Xiaoping asserted that it should be retained, but Hu Yaobang withheld transmission of Deng's speech from the lower levels of the Party.

Hu Yaobang was becoming more assertive, because Deng Xiaoping was considering retirement from his remaining offices. Emboldened, Hu, in a speech in the United States, said that socialism had been discredited not only by its poor economic performance but by its failure to protect democracy and human rights. This offened Deng Xiaoping. Hu Yaobang was replaced by Zhao Ziyang as the head of the Central Research and Discussion Group on Political Structural Reform, on which two veteran conservatives were now given places.

Nevertheless, the democratic agitation continued unabated. Liu Binyan at the end of the year, after visits to the Soviet Union and the United States, called for a multi-party system. China's distinguished astrophysicist Fang Lizhi, too well known internationally to be easily stifled by the authorities, began a series of uncompromising speeches. He had joined the movement for political reform because his research was prejudiced by Marxist-Leninist ideology. Engels had stated that the universe was infinite; Einstein stated that it was not. Modern cosmological research in the communist world was forced to follow Engels. Fang Lizhi pursued the subject on Einstein's premises none the less. His hostility to political interference in research led him in the end to total condemnation of socialism and of Marxism, and he demanded equal and inalienable human rights.

By this time the democratization of South Korea and of the Philippines by 'people's revolutions' had taken place. Partly as result, the assumption, which had up till now dominated the democratic movement, that democratization in China could not be achieved by confronting the system, was weakened. New student demonstrations began in late 1986, starting at the University of Science and Technology (Ke Da for short) at Hefei in Anhui of which Fang Lizhi was Vice-Chancellor, and rapidly spreading to other cities. The demands of the students were the same everywhere and foreshadowed the demands of the 1989 protest in Tiananmen. However, these demonstrations proved to be counter-productive; Hu Yaobang, whose position they were intended to strengthen, was instead destroyed. Deng Xiaoping ordered Hu to stop the demonstrations and he refused. On 2 January 1987, at a meeting of the Polit-buro which had been unconstitutionally enlarged, Hu was dismissed from his post as Secretary-General of the Party. At the meeting Zhao Ziyang supported Hu's dismissal.

The veteran conservatives made a triumphant return to power, determined to reverse political reform. A general persecution of the democratic leaders took place. A new censorship office was set up and used to attempt to destroy the independent press. However, the conservatives overreached themselves. Their victims became heroes; in particular Hu Yaobang, hitherto regarded as a rather uncouth figure, like Khrushchev, became the symbol of the fight for democracy. To make matters worse the veterans, in order to illustrate the evil ideas of spiritual pollution and bourgeois liberalism, published long excerpts from the works of the guilty, and so spread their message throughout the country.

In the same campaign economic reform began to be condemned once more as the return of capitalism. The veterans held their own conference at Zhuozhou. Tapes of the proceedings reached Deng Xiaoping, who was enraged by attacks on the market economy, and brought the campaign to an abrupt end. Deng nevertheless was becoming alarmed by the democratic movement and at this point made little attempt to protect the democratic writers.

Yet when the Thirteenth Party Congress met in December 1988 the final Report was remarkably encouraging for the democrats. A draft of the Congress report was drawn up months before it met and sent to a sample group of 5,000 cadres, to the leaders of mass organizations and of the small parties, and to representatives of minority nationalities and religious groups. A Politburo meeting then discussed the response. The Report deferred to Deng Xiaoping by treating political reform merely as a question of the reform of administration. Yet important concessions were made to the democratic movement. It was accepted that Chinese society was now pluralistic. Party cells were to be eliminated from government and academic institutions, except for the top institutions of government. The Trade Union Federation, the Communist Youth League, and the Women's Federation were to be given independence. It was acknowledged that different people have different views, and need channels for the exchange of ideas. Government should be more open. The media were exhorted to support the masses in their criticisms. The People's Congresses, including the NPC, were to have fixed rules and procedures, an improved nomination system, and competitive elections, and the CPPCC should become a forum for policy debate. Members of small parties should be given appointments up to vice-ministerial level. There should be an independent judiciary and a system of appeals over breaches of constitutional rights. China should be open to 'ideological trends of different sorts'.

Deng Xiaoping retired from the Politburo and the Central Committee, but he remained Chairman of the Military Affairs Commission, and as the Central Advisory Commission was not reformed he retained his influential contacts with the veterans. In fact, as was later revealed, an agreement was made at the plenum by which in the event of disagreement within the Politburo Secretariat, Deng would be consulted. There was a considerable change in the composition of the Central Committee; many younger men were elected and fewer representatives of the armed forces. For the first time there were 5 per cent more candidates than places; as a result, those who had led the attack on Hu Yaobang were voted out of office.

Hu Yaobang was still formally a member of the Politburo but remained inactive. The new Secretariat of the Politburo was evenly balanced. Zhao Ziyang succeeded Hu Yaobang as Secretary-General, but shortly after, the veterans' protégé Li Peng became Prime Minister. Zhao Ziyang's associates assumed positions of power and the associates of Hu Yaobang were still vocal and influential, so there was no slackening of democratic agitation.

Two independent institutions had begun to play major roles. The first was the most powerful (and favoured) of China's new private enterprises. This was the Stone Corporation, the leading firm in the development of information technology. It had begun as a township and village enterprise in the back premises of a village shop. Its founder Wu Rannan was a former Red Guard.

The second of these independent institutions was created by two former Red Guards, Wang Juntao and Chen Ziming. Both had taken part in the demonstration in memory of Zhou Enlai in 1975; both had been involved in Democracy Wall as close associates of Wei Jingsheng. Chen opened a number of politically oriented enterprises, including highly profitable correspondence schools. In 1986 he founded the Social and Economic Research Institute, the first independent think-tank in Beijing, followed by the first centre for public opinion polls. Chen was also involved in a number of publishing houses translating Western books. In 1986 he bought an important journal, the *Economic Weekly*. Wang, engaged in similar activities, joined Chen in that year. A whole network of such institutions was set up. There were now many such independent networks, but the one surrounding the *Economic Weekly* was by far the largest. The organization was mainly staffed by former Red Guards. Wang and Chen and their associates were not, however, sectarian. They had good relations with the other democratic groups. They published a wide variety of opinions in the *Economic Weekly*. Their importance lay in their willingness to go beyond political debate to political organization.

The tug-of-war between democrats and conservatives continued, with freedom of publication erratically acknowledged. There were several further crises. The conservatives successfully stifled the 1988 Congress of the Writers' Federation. They attempted with less success to prevent the publication of the proceedings of a meeting held to celebrate the tenth anniversary of the Theory Conference; the democrats decamped and held their own meeting, and went on to publish most of the proceedings of the original Conference of 1978, as well as papers defending Hu Yaobang.

The most serious crisis, however, was over the showing on national television of a series called *River Elegy*. This film, made by former Red Guards, used the image of a dried-up Yellow River to assert that China had been made arid by feudalism, which the communist regime had actually perpetuated. Some of the veterans reacted in horror, but some, including Yang Shangkun (president of the state), refused even to read the script, on the grounds that comrade Xiaoping had advised them not to interfere in literary affairs. Zhao Ziyang actually permitted the series to be shown again.

By this time, democratic demands had become comprehensive. Yet few of the democratic leaders advocated immediate democratization; even Fang Lizhi believed that democracy should be introduced gradually, and so did Cao Siyuan, the spokesman of the Stone Corporation. In Chen Zimin's *Economic Weekly* it was argued that China's political problem was not a weak political system but a weak society, for lack of popular participation; the implication was that even if authoritarian government would have to be tolerated for a time, agitation for increased popular participation in politics should still continue.

The democratic movement had begun with attempts to humanize Marxism, but Marxism had now been almost entirely repudiated by the democrats. The other transformation in the movement was that the hope of democratization from the top had suffered a severe blow with the dismissal of Hu Yaobang. More effort now had to be invested in strengthening the possibilities of democratization from below. Yet still the intellectuals who led the movement made no organized effort to build a democratic coalition, although with inflation running at 19 per cent from 1988, followed by severe deflationary policies, with the cessation of the rapid increase in peasant incomes of the early 1980s, and with the increasing unemployment caused by the shaking out of surplus labour from the State-owned enterprises, there was massive discontent in many parts of the country, and an opportunity to create such a coalition.

Meanwhile, the Communist Party was finding it more and more difficult to control the democratic movement as seminars, forums, salons, and independent think-tanks and journals grew in number. Moreover, because of the divisions within the Party, leaks constantly frustrated attempts to stifle the debate. The National People's Congress and the CPPCC began to flex their muscles. The NPC at its March 1989 meeting voted for new procedures which would have considerably strengthened its powers and also passed an Administrative Litigation Law permitting citizens to sue Party and government officials and protecting defence lawyers. These proposals, however, were overtaken by the Tiananmen demonstrations which began the following month. Meanwhile the CPPCC demanded the return of Hu Yaobang to power, and then in a forum of its members organized by Cao Siyuan called for a new constitution.

The process of economic reform had inevitably increased individual autonomy. It had also led to the growth of associations which the Party had to negotiate with rather than command. The need for predictability in an increasingly marketized economy had led to a considerable, though far from complete, assertion of the rule of law. In these proto-democratic developments, the appetite grew with what it fed on. The increased tolerance of debate, in the same way, led to the expectation of even greater freedom. The Chinese people stood, frustrated, on the brink of the attainment of real citizenship. Their hope of improvement now seemed to lie with Zhao Ziyang.

The road to Tiananmen

On 8 April Hu Yaobang, attending a Politburo meeting, suffered a heart attack. He died on the 15th. Beijing students were already planning a demonstration on the anniversary of the May Fourth Movement. State Security had already reported in June 1988 that many students were disaffected. In a survey at that time, fewer than half the students wanted to join the Communist Party, and fewer than half thought that economic reform should be socialist. To mourn for Hu's death was to mourn for the loss of the prospect of democratization for which, the students believed, he had stood. Memorial gatherings were held on university campuses, but on 17 April they moved to Tiananmen Square. They were led by students from The Chinese University of Political Science and Law. They were accompanied, to the alarm of the authorities, by embassy-registered limousines, from which foreign diplomats descended to mix with the crowd. The Political Science students announced radical demands for democratization. These went far beyond the limited but significant proposals for democratization accepted by the Thirteenth Party Congress in the previous December.

The Party leaders were fairly relaxed at this point, but already the more conservative members were warning that inflation, corruption, and growing inequalities offered political dangers which the students might exploit. The same conservative veterans were also already disposed to see conspiracy rather than spontaneity in the demonstration; they sought refuge in the idea that behind the demonstrations there was some 'black hand'. They stuck to this conspiracy theory thereafter, and thus strongly prejudiced the possibility of any dialogue with the students. The more liberal members of the leadership nevertheless, although they did not deny the possibility of a conspiracy, insisted that the vast majority of those involved were well meaning and patri-otic, and that their specific immediate grievances were largely those which the Party had already acknowledged in public and had indeed attempted to address in policy.

Then even the more liberal Party leaders grew alarmed as the students launched further initiatives. The lead in these was taken by the students of Beijing University, where Fang Lizhi's wife Li Xuxian was a professor of physics and where she had been encouraging the democratic forums. Within a few days, plans were announced to form an Autonomous Federation of Students in Beida; other colleges followed suit, and soon there was a plan for a national autonomous federation. Demonstrations spread to other Chinese cities. Students began to mobilize high school pupils. They also planned to form a national network among the leaders of demonstrations throughout the country. Representatives of a new Autonomous Federation of Workers joined the students in the Square. Demands for democratization usually began with condemnations of corruption in high places, an issue which could attract widespread sympathy and support from all classes, and even from the armed forces. The apparent involvement of foreigners was perceived to be dangerous.

It was not difficult to find evidence that the students were being advised by people whose reputation for radicalism was already known. First, Fang Lizhi and his wife; second, the former Red Guards of the *Economic Weekly*, Wang Juntao and Chen Ziming; and, more generally, some of the intellectuals who had been associated with Hu Yaobang.

Two events quickly hardened the attitude of the students. The first occurred when a crowd gathered at the Xinhua Gate of Zhongnanhai where the top leaders of the Party lived and worked. Driven off, they returned and appeared to be attempting to break in. Some shouted for Prime Minister Li Peng to come out—the first expression of hostility towards him. On this second occasion the police used force to remove the demonstrators. Soon after, a student in the street was badly beaten by the police, who used their belts, although President Yang Shangkun's orders were that the police should leave both their belts and their batons at home.

Hu's funeral and memorial service took place on 22 April. Orders had been issued that the public were not to enter the Square, but 100,000 people assembled. The demonstrators were enraged to learn that Hu's eulogy did not refer to him as a 'great Marxist'. After the ceremony, three students attempted to present a petition from the steps of the Great Hall of the People. They knelt in the traditional way. They remained kneeling for forty minutes, but no one came to receive the petition.

There is some evidence that on the eve of the demonstrations, a conservative coup was being planned within the Party leadership. On 1 February the journal *Qiushi* (*Truth Seeker*), founded by the reformers, published a coded warning that the power of Li Peng was increasing, and that if it was not reduced there would be bloodshed. In April the pro-reform news agency *Zhonqquo Tongxun* (*China Bulletin*) issued a 'denial' that there existed a 'regents' party' of veterans who were acting for the 'heir apparent', meaning Prime Minister Li Peng. The victim of this possible coup would of course have been Zhao Ziyang. Thus to the tension between the leadership and the student demonstrators was added the tension of an intrigue within the central leadership, of which the demonstrators were well aware.

At this point it will be helpful to describe the decision-making process at the level of the Standing Committee of the Politburo. The Committee had five members, of whom the Secretary-General of the Party was one. He chaired the meetings. However, the Central Advisory Committee of veterans was represented by two of their number, Bo Yibo and Yang Shangkun; they had no vote, but joined in discussions. Deng Xiaoping had no place on the Committee, but by the secret decision of the Thirteenth Congress it had been agreed that in the event of disagreement he would be consulted. This could be seen to be unconstitutional, but it was not strictly so; the Committee could presumably seek advice where it chose. In practice, this agreement enabled Deng to hold the balance between those who were reluctant to accept serious reform and those who sought to push reform too quickly. Standing committee meetings might also be attended by other members of the

Politburo who had particular responsibilities, and others who attended to make reports.

In January 2001 a collection of documents was published in the West, under the title *Tiananmen Papers*. These were transcripts of the discussions which took place among the handful of people who ruled China—half a dozen men at most—and of the intelligence reports on which their information was based. Their authenticity is accepted. The broad outlines of what happened and why were already known from other and more oblique evidence, but the *Papers* allow us to be certain of what until now was only inference.

On 23 April Zhao Xiyang left on an already planned visit to North Korea. The Standing Committee met the following day without him, and then the day after met at Deng Xiaoping's house. By the 23rd it was reported that 60,000 students were boycotting classes, which meant on average 1,000 from each of Beijing's 60 colleges. There had been further demonstrations in several provincial capitals, in some of which dangerous slogans were being used. Banners in Wuhan said 'Down with corrupt government . . . Catch the murderers . . . The Four Principles are the source of the nation's misfortunes, freedom and democracy are the root of the nation's revival.' Thereafter, demonstrations in the provincial capitals closely followed the agitation in Beijing. At the peak of the crisis, in response to the final declaration of martial law and the students' hunger strike, over 130 cities were involved, and about 4 million students and citizens.

When these and other new developments were reported to the leaders it was obvious that even the more liberal members of the Committee were becoming anxious. Even Hu Qili said that 'we must not underestimate the power of the tiny minority'. Qiao Shi said, 'We certainly do not want to see any harm done to the growing democratic atmosphere, but . . . we need contingency plans for emergencies.' Yang Shangkun said, 'Above all, we must not let this question of the student movement harm our hard-won stability and unity'—an oblique reference to the Cultural Revolution. One must bear in mind that among the victims of the Cultural Revolution was Yang himself; he had spent eleven years in jail.

At the meeting in Deng Xiaoping's residence on the following day, 25 April, Li Pang said to Deng, 'The spearhead is now directed at you.' Deng replied, 'Saying I'm the master mind behind the scenes, are they?' Li Peng, describing the situation, ended by saying 'illegal student organizations have already sprung up'. 'What?' exclaimed Deng. The head of the State Education Commission, present to give a report, said that the students were networking the high schools. He added, 'We have to remember the lessons of the Cultural Revolution.'

Deng then asserted, 'This is a well-planned plot whose real aim is to reject the CCP and the socialist system.' With this even Hu Qili now agreed. Li Peng suggested that an editorial should be published in *People's Daily* expressing Deng Xiaoping's views.

This was decided. The editorial condemned the demonstrations as 'turmoil'; this translates the Chinese word *daluan* which has a very loaded meaning; it indicates chaos following the breakdown of government. The turmoil was blamed on the 'tiny handful'. Zhao Ziyang sent a telegram from North Korea agreeing with the editorial.

At this point it was being reported that the students were flagging, and the demonstrations might well have come to an end. But the editorial brought a hurricane of nationwide protest. Many Party institutions condemned it as too harsh. The army accepted the editorial, but from many units there were warnings to the effect that there were real problems, with corruption at the top of the list; and one provincial command stated that 'only methods of education and guidance should be used'. The editors of China's national Party newspapers came to Hu Qili to protest, in effect, that they would take no responsibility for the editorial, nor for its consequences. At this meeting the Secretary of the Central Secretariat was also present (Rui Yingwen), and he told the journalists, 'The big forces of social change in society are forcing reforms on the newspapers. Reporters have to tell the truth.' Li Peng was forced to order another editorial which was meant to be conciliatory; but as it simply defended the accusation of turmoil instead of withdrawing it, it only added fuel to the flames.

Qiao Shi said that there must be dialogue to enable the students to appreciate the real meaning of the editorial and Yang Shangkun agreed. This was at a meeting on 27 April.

Yang Shangkun then drew attention to another source of apprehension: that the eyes of the people of Hong Kong were on them, 'connecting our treatment of the movement with the return of Hong Kong', negotiations for which were then already in train.

It was agreed that dialogue should be opened with the students. The representative sent to meet the students (Yuan Mu) took a truculent line that only further inflamed the situation: he asserted that there was no serious corruption in the Party, and he denied that there was any censorship of the press. These claims were received with derision. The tapes of the dialogue were then made available by the leadership, in the hope of carrying on the dialogue, but this only made matters worse.

Zhao Ziyang returned from North Korea on 30 April, and summoned a Standing Committee meeting for the following day. There was some inconclusive discussion on whether the demonstrations were likely to continue, but the main event was a head-on clash between Zhao and Li Peng. Li was in favour of restoring order immediately, and then tackling the necessary reforms. Zhao argued for the announcement of reforms first. This difference in priorities became fundamental. There was, however, otherwise a fairly calm atmosphere in which the problem of democratization within a one-party framework was discussed. Zhao stated that in view of the spread of democracy in the world, 'if the Party does not hold up the banner of democracy in our country, someone else will'. He then reasserted the promises made at the thirteenth Congress. Yang Shangkun said: 'One-party rule has to solve the question of democracy as well as the problem of supervisory mechanisms to guard against negative and unhealthy phenomena within state and Party organs.'

Li Peng repeated his argument that the restoration of stability must be given priority. Hu Qili replied: 'True stability will only come when socialist democracy is fully in place.' Bo Yibo agreed. But Li Peng said that the illegal student organizations were aiming to repudiate the Four Principles: 'If they get their way, then everything—reform and opening, democracy and law, building socialist modernization, you name it—will vanish into thin air.'

The *World Economic Herald* in Shanghai had just published articles asserting that reform had brought about 'extensive social transformation from below', but this had been obstructed from above. It called for intellectuals to co-operate with workers, peasants, and people of all strata. When the *World Economic Herald* attempted to cover the intellectuals' special separate memorial service for Hu Yaobang, a work team was sent in by the Shanghai Party, but it was defied. The journal then produced another issue with the title 'We need an environment in which we can speak freely'. This was suppressed and the staff arrested, but 60,000 copies of the new issue had already been surreptitiously sent to Beijing. The journal was then shut down. The staff brought a civil suit against Jiang Zemin, under the new administrative litigation law. (The *World Economic Herald* was independent.) Hundreds of journalists protested. Journalists were then the first professional group to join the students in the Square.

In mid-May several thousand students in the Square launched a hunger strike. The following day a group of twelve democratic intellectuals went to meet the student leaders; they were led by Dai Quing, one of the neo-authoritarians. She asked the hunger strikers to desist, as they were putting at risk all that had been gained. She said both sides should make concessions, but that the Party leaders must make concessions first. The students insisted on three conditions: leaders must announce in person that the student movement was patriotic and democratic; that the autonomous student organizations were legal; and that there would be no recrimination. The government's reply was that there could be further dialogue only if the students stopped trying to bargain. However the students had gone past the point of no return and many feared that they would be in danger of reprisals if they retreated before winning victory. And their morale was restored when 30,000 intellectuals marched to the Square and urged them to stand firm.

The Standing Committee met on 16 May to consider the hunger strike. On that day in Shanghai student demonstrators carried banners reading 'workers arise! . . . peasants arise!' In Beijing student leader Wuerkaishi from Xinjiang defied the government: 'a bunch of corrupt rotten eggs. They can think what they like.' He said that if the police cracked down on them, the students would fight to the death. Zhao Ziyang warned his colleagues that the hunger strikers had put themselves in a position where they would lose face if they made concessions; the problem was how to get them to decouple the hunger strike from their demands.

At this meeting Li Peng made an open attack on Zhao Ziyang. Zhao on 4 May had made a speech to a meeting in Beijing of the Asian Development Bank. The speech played the movement down by insisting that China was not facing serious turmoil nor were the demonstrators attacking China's under-lying system. He played down the 'tiny handful'. He admitted that there was serious corruption in China and that only greater democracy could solve it. Li Peng accused him of having made the speech without having cleared it with his colleagues. Then the conservative Yao Yilin joined in to condemn the fact that Zhao, in conversation with Gorbachev, had revealed the existence of the secret agreement making Deng Xiaoping the final arbitrator.

The attacks were unwarranted. The speech to the Bank conference attempted to minimize the conflicts in China so that foreign investment would not be discouraged, and Zhao pointed out that Li Peng had praised it. And speeches to foreign visitors were not normally cleared beforehand by the Standing Committee. Chen Xitong, the Mayor of Beijing, had already told a group of Beijing workers about the secret agreement. It is difficult not to see in Li Peng's criticisms an unscrupulous attack on Zhao's authority.

Deng Xiaoping now joined in the criticism of Zhao: 'Comrade Ziyang, that talk of yours on 4 May to the Asian Development Bank was a turning point. Since then the student movement has become steadily worse.' Deng then went on to explain his hostility to immediate democratization:

Of course we want to build socialist democracy, but we can't possibly do it in a hurry, and still less do we want that Western-style stuff. If our one billion people jumped into multi-party elections, we'd get chaos like the all-out civil war we saw during the Cultural Revolution . . . Democracy is our goal, but we'll never get there without national stability.

By this point even the more liberal members of the leadership had come to agree that the student demonstrations must somehow be brought to an end. Qiao Shi said, 'Their goals are quite clear: to overthrow the leadership of the CP and change the socialist order.' Yang Shangkun said, 'Our backs are to the wall.' Hu Qili said, 'We can retreat no further.'

Deng Xiaoping then said, 'After thinking long and hard about this, I have concluded that we should bring in the PLA and declare martial law in Beijing.'

Zhao Ziyang replied, 'Comrade Xiaoping, it will be hard for me to carry out this plan.'

Deng Xiaoping: 'The minority yields to the majority!'

Zhao Ziyang: 'I will submit to Party discipline.'

However, a further meeting showed that Zhao could not reconcile himself to the decision. He persisted in arguing that the forcible suppression of the students might prove to be a mistake of such magnitude as to destroy the legitimacy of the regime. Hu Qili agreed. A formal vote was taken for the imposition of martial law. Li Peng and Yao Yilin voted in favour; Zhao Ziyang and Hu Qili voted against. Qiao Shi abstained. With the Secretariat thus evenly split, Deng Xiaoping made the decision that martial law should be imposed. Zhao Ziyang offered his resignation, but was dissuaded on the grounds that this would make the split in the leadership public.

The decision to impose martial law was not in itself a decision to suppress the demonstrations by force. Subsequent discussions show that President Yang Shangkun, who as vice-chairman of the Central Military Commission would be in charge, believed that a show of massive military force would be enough to disperse the students, and from then until the critical moment on 4 June he repeatedly insisted that there should be no violence. At the same time, the Party authorities pulled out all the stops to persuade the students to withdraw. Dialogue was several times offered. Unfortunately, it was offered on terms which the student movement would not accept. The students insisted that dialogue must be with their own new autonomous organization, and not with the official student federation. This, however, was precisely the point on which the Party leadership were adamant. Independent associations they perceived to be a long, and perhaps irreversible, step towards the creation of a multi-party system.

The decision on martial law was not meant to be made public at that stage, but Zhao Ziyang's secretary Bao Tong leaked the news promptly. The public reaction was massive. At this point, for the public and for a substantial number of Party members at every level of the hierarchy, the urgent issue was the fate of the hunger strikers. Seven hundred of them were already in hospital. Demonstrations in the provinces, hitherto sporadic, now spread to virtually all of China's cities, and all urban classes of China joined in. There were appeals against martial law from the official student federation, the Communist Youth League, and the national Youth Federation. The Tiananmen demonstration was then joined by Beijing workers, organized in work units and carrying food and blankets. A few carried Solidarity banners. They brought with them cash contributions to support the hunger strikers and the students. Similar contributions poured in from other quarters, including Y200,000 from Wan Runnan's Stone Corporation. China's national association for the disabled, the president of which was Deng Xiaoping's own son Pufang, gave Y100,000. Large donations also came from abroad. Wang Juntao and Chen Ziming encouraged the formation of independent associations of intellectuals and Beijing citizens as well as workers. This was the beginning of an attempt, which was soon made fully public, to organize a democratic coalition of all classes. This attempt, with its echoes of the Cultural Revolution and with former Red Guards as leaders, was a new and alarming development which confirmed the worst fears of the conservatives.

A one-sentence note was addressed to the Central Military Commission and to Deng Xiaoping from eight generals: 'We request that troops should not enter the city and that martial law should not be carried out in Beijing.' The students made an approach to China's two surviving veteran marshals Nie Rongzhen and Xu Xiangqian, and both of them after some prevarication issued statements. Nie: 'Under no circumstances should there be shedding of blood.' Xu: 'Let us hope it [martial law] is never directed at the students.' One of the commanders of the 38th Army refused to participate. The PLA issued a statement saying, 'The PLA extends resolute support to the broad masses, who demand that we punish official profiteering, oppose corruption, and promote the construction of socialist democracy and the rule of law.'

Although all the provinces indicated their support for martial law, in several cases there were oblique statements of misgivings.

Some of the slogans of the demonstrators attacked Li Peng by name, and sometimes Deng Xiaoping; one banner addressed to Deng said, 'Thank you and Goodbye!' Many of the intellectuals joined in student demands for the dismissal of Li Peng and others. Public Security reported that Wang Juntao and Chen Ziming had held a secret meeting at Beijing Normal College with groups from the autonomous student federation, the Chinese Academy of Social Sciences, and other associations. At this meeting they agreed to change their headquarters daily and to use a secret code. The 'conspiracy' which the conservative Party leaders believed existed had now come into being as a result of their own intransigence.

On 21 May the Elders and the rump of the Politburo Standing Committee met at Deng Xiaoping's house. Deng admitted that the threat of martial law had not worked. For this he blamed Zhao Ziyang.

Throughout the world Chinese communities made their protests. Six hundred thousand people assembled in Hong Kong. To the exasperation of the Party leaders in Beijing, Wan Li had made speeches in Canada and America which echoed the statements of Zhao Ziyang. The leaders were reluctant to order him home immediately in case this should betray a sense of crisis. They did so subsequently, but ordered him to Shanghai instead of Beijing; he was kept there under virtual house arrest until he publicly stated his support for martial law.

Meanwhile the Hong Kong press, as well as the press in Taiwan and Japan, were predicting in apocalyptic terms the dawn of democracy in China. Some of them also predicted that China would soon accept capitalism, adding that this depended on Zhao Ziyang. They detected a conspiracy within the CCP to set Deng Xiaoping aside and give Zhao unfettered power. They fulminated about 'senile tyrants'. The Hong Kong journals were familiar in democratic circles in China, and further encouraged their radicalization. Thus student demonstrations reflected once more the fact of a struggle for power, a polarization, within the top leadership. The use of force against the demonstrators should be seen in the light of this crisis in the CCP, which was catalysed by the students gathered at the gates of Zhongnanhai.

The demonstrators were now calling for an emergency meeting of the Standing Committee of the NPC, and an emergency Party Congress. Ironically, this echoed Qiao Shi who had said, 'I wish the NPC and the CPPCC could do something.' Three petitions were sent to the NPC Standing Committee by the democratic intellectuals requesting that the Committee should meet. A sufficient proportion of the NPC Standing Committee agreed, but in fact only the Politburo could call a meeting, and none of its other members agreed with Qiao Shi.

On the early morning of 18 May six leaders including Zhao Ziyang and Li Peng visited the hunger strikers who were in hospital. Zhao said, 'The aims of the Party and the government are the same as your aims', and pleaded with them to give up their strike, but they were adamant. Zhao immediately returned to his office and tried again to resign, and was once more prevented. The following day Zhao and Li again visited the Square. Zhao again begged the hunger strikers to give up and again they refused. Zhao said, 'We have come too late!' and wept. When Deng Xiaoping heard of this later in the day, he was appalled: 'Tears streaming down his face' he exclaimed to Yang Shangkun. He took this occasion to state his position again:

Our economy has improved a lot in recent years. The people have food to eat and clothes to wear, as anybody can see. The economy is still the base; if we didn't have that economic base, the farmers would have risen in rebellion after only ten days of student protests, never mind a whole month. But as it is, the villages are stable all over the country, and the workers are basically stable too. This is the fruit of reform and opening. When economic reform reaches a certain point, you have to have political reform to accompany it. You know I have never opposed political reform. But you have to consider the realities, *you have to think about how many of the old comrades in the Party can accept it right now.*

Deng took the occasion to sound a personal note: 'I have to give the nod on every important decision. I carry too much weight, and that's not good for the Party or the State. I should think of retiring. But how can I right now?'

On 21 May Deng Xiaoping and the Party Elders agreed that Zhao Ziyang and Hu Qili should be replaced. The question of a successor was considered. Given the position on martial law taken by the Elders, one might have supposed that Li Peng would have been appointed to succeed Zhao as Secretary-General of the Party, and indeed the precedents suggested that as Zhao's second-in-command he should have been chosen to succeed. Clearly, however, Li Peng was too unpopular. A number of possible successors were considered including, surprisingly, relatively liberal figures such as Wan Li and Qiao Shi, both of whom had expressed strong reservations about martial law. In the end there was a consensus on the appointment of Jiang Zemin, partly on account of his calm handling of the demonstrations in Shanghai. Li Ruihuan from Tianjin, another moderate figure, was appointed to the new Secretariat. He was joined by two men associated with economic planning proposed by Chen Yun and Bo Yibo.

In the Square the situation was changing. The original student leaders were exhausted and divided over whether or not to withdraw, but this decision was complicated by a massive influx of students from other cities who were reluctant to disperse until they had had a chance to make their protest. The chief leader of the autonomous student federation, Wang Dan, was now closely allied with Chen Ziming and his supporters among former Red Guards who proposed on 26 May that the demonstration should be continued until 20 June, when the next regular meeting of the Standing Committee of the NPC was due. Wang Dan put up a poster calling for a nationwide hunger strike. Then two more threats appeared. The first was the formation of a group called the United Conference of Patriotic Organizations in Support of the Constitution, which issued a statement which said that anyone who opposed the democratic movement would lose legitimacy and then power. The second was a secret decision by Wang Juntao and others to shift the focus of effort directly to the mobilization of workers, peasants, and soldiers.

The attitude of the Elders was also influenced by reports from Security of the considerable part being played in the event by foreigners including diplomats, and teachers and experts sent to China by Western foundations. Li Peng conveyed this intelligence to the leadership. It was then exploited in an attempt to influence the demonstrators by a campaign against the influence of the United States. This became a major theme of the government-organized counter-demonstrations, but the preaching got no further than the converted.

There was no clear idea in the new Standing Committee of the Politburo (not yet formally elected) as to what should be done next. Bo Yibo said to them, 'Now that we have got the problem inside the Party solved, we should turn to ending the turmoil. But it's not easy to say just what we should do.' Yang Shangkun, who was responsible for the implementation of martial law, could only say, 'We must be equally firm about stopping the turmoil and about avoiding bloodshed in doing so.'

At this point the eighteenth meeting of the seventh CPPCC took place, chaired by Li Xiannian, who managed to persuade the members that while democracy and the rule of law were needed, the demonstrations, railroaded by conspirators, were counter-productive. He was supported by a speech from a member who had studied and taught in the USA in Caltec and MIT who warned against 'superficial democracy' which might wreck economic reform.

In spite of their divided counsels the students were able to offer fresh provocations. On 29 May there appeared in the Square the Goddess of Democracy, a plaster figure inspired by the Statue of Liberty. Its ideological implications were obvious, and fed the xenophobia of the Elders. Then the student leader Wang Dan expressed the hope that a Walesa figure would appear in China. The Centre responded by arresting the leader of the Autonomous Workers' Federation and several of his associates. At the same time, however, Wang Dan and Chai Ling were superseded as the leaders of the students by figures who tacitly dissociated themselves from extreme demands and actions; but even they accepted that the demonstration should continue until the NPC meeting on 20 June.

There were also provocations on the other side. The Security report on the activities of foreigners was one. The other was a report by Chen Xitong which called the demonstrators 'terrorists' and described the demonstration as a 'counter-revolutionary riot', a phrase which normally indicated an armed rising. The report had been ordered by Li Peng. It did not succeed in revealing any nefarious activities, except for the appearance of one isolated poster calling for the creation of a citizens' army. However by marshalling together all the information on the escalation of the demonstrations it clearly aimed to support the demand for a prompt and final clearing of the Square. It does not seem to have had any effect on the decision-makers, who had already deprived themselves of any option but to clear the Square by force.

On 2 June at midnight the troops deployed in the suburbs were ordered to move into the city, but this decision was taken with the same doubts and apprehensions and warnings against loss of life as had been displayed throughout. This time Deng Xiaoping himself repeated the warning.

What followed gave the lie to the 'tiny handful' theory. The people of Beijing rose against the advancing troops; it is estimated that a million took part in the resistance, barricading every route into the Square, every intersection of the streets, and the bridge which gave access from the west. Among the number it is estimated that several hundred thousand were CCP members and of these 50,000 were cadres. Their weapons were mainly stones, lumps of concrete, and occasional Molotov cocktails. Their success, it has to be said, was possible only because of the forbearance of the troops; but that forbearance dwindled as the soldiers suffered casualties, and in the end they began to fire into the crowds. They entered the Square in the early hours of 4 June. They broadcast repeated calls for the students to leave the Square. Eventually it was arranged that they should leave, which they did, singing the International, with their monitors linking hands to keep order. Troops then fanned out into the surrounding streets to restore order. There they met obstruction and abuse, and again they used their weapons.

This is not what the world saw on television. We saw the Goddess of Democracy crumble and fall. We saw a casualty being rushed away spread over a bicycle. And we saw one brave young man defy a column of tanks. That is all we saw. It is not much help in the matter of estimating casualties. Foreign observers variously reckoned from 1,000 to 3,000 dead. The figures given in Chinese military and security reports were far lower. Reports of casualties treated in hospitals, because they were made while opposition to and hatred of the troops were still high, are probably the best guide; the horrified medical staff could have had no motive to minimize them. Informed guesswork is all we can manage, and that suggests that total casualties were probably in the hundreds. However, there is some suspicion that the representatives of the Autonomous Federation of Workers were surreptitiously targeted, with the consequence of further deaths, if any, unreported. Certainly the animus of the authorities against the members of this potential Solidarity movement was soon shown in the mass arrests of workers and the long sentences imposed upon them, in contrast to the far easier treatment suffered by the students. When the army entered the Square in the middle of the night, the lights were cut off for a time. What may have been done in the dark we will probably never know.

Those brief moments on television suggested the actions of a brutal, paranoiac leadership, ruthlessly defending their authoritarian regime against a democratic protest. I watched it with horror, as millions did. I thought that I had seen one tiny corner of an indiscriminate massacre of students and intellectuals, a bloodbath. However a cool head and much study eventually convinced me that the story was much less crude. It has long been obvious, and is now confirmed by the *Tiananmen Papers*, that no massacre was intended. It was the old story of troops involved in restoring public order goaded into a loss of discipline. Stoned and fire-bombed in the streets and trapped between high buildings, they reacted in fear and anger.

It is clear that the leaders of the CCP had no intention of perpetrating a massacre. Most of them had accepted the idea of proclaiming martial law reluctantly. They hoped its proclamation would be enough. When that failed, they hoped that a show of overwhelming force would prove to be sufficient. When they ordered the troops to move in, there is no evidence that they expected the massive popular resistance which then occurred; they were too obsessed with their 'tiny, tiny handful' theory. Throughout all the discussions they emphasized that there should be no bloodshed, and this warning was uncompromisingly restated in orders meant for the military authorities alone and unknown to the public.

Led by Deng Xiaoping, the CCP was attempting an orderly march from command communism to market socialism. They sincerely believed that immediate democratization in the midst of fundamental economic restructuring might be fatal to their plans for gradual, measured economic change. Change thus far had been in the main successful; it had substantially raised the standards of life of the vast majority of the Chinese people. For a decade it had maintained a remarkable pace of economic growth not, as in the earlier days of communism, directed to an irrational extent towards heavy industry, but geared to increased consumption. However, there had inevitably been losers, and the inflation which in 1988 followed the attempt to reform prices had increased the number. There were severe social strains. China's leaders believed that immediate democratization, instead of serving to reconcile the conflicts of interest created by economic change, might instead exacerbate them. The chaotic history of the Soviet Union in the next few years, when glasnost and perestroika were offered simultaneously, suggests that China's leaders may have had some reason on their side.

In fact, no influential figure in the Chinese democratic movement was at that time arguing for full democratization. The arguments were about the speed of progress. The tragedy of Tiananmen is that bungling on both sides obscured the considerable measure of agreement which existed. Up to that point, Deng Xiaoping had been extraordinarily successful in balancing the more radical against the more conservative members of the Party—largely, as he saw it, a conflict of generations. In this way he had kept the wheels of economic change going, had granted China more freedom than she had enjoyed at any time since 1949, and had cautiously advanced towards creating the rule of law. As of the 1980s most of China's democratizers prided themselves that China was further along the road to democracy than the Soviet Union.

At what then did he baulk? On this he was quite explicit: a multi-party system would be a step too far. And the 'autonomous associations' created at Tiananmen, he reasonably believed, could only lead to such a system. Control of measured advance might then be threatened. There should meanwhile only be that measure of democratization which would serve to liberate and to protect initiative.

As for the Elders, when it came to the point at which they believed that socialism was in danger, they remembered the past. The guilt of the survivors can be a powerful emotion. What is owed to the martyrs can be an inescapable obligation.

The course of the demonstration was described and its suppression by armed force justified in a report by the Mayor of Beijing, Chen Xitong, presented to the National People's Congress and then broadcast by the official New China News Agency. (A full translation is available in volume 120 of *China Quarterly*.) Although the object of his report was to defend the suppression of the demonstration, nevertheless it gives a valuable account of events. In the usual manner of Chinese polemics, Chen used only facts which the opposition could not deny: the bias is not in what he records, but in what he omits, and in how he interprets the accepted facts.

Chen, in writing his report, trapped himself in a contradiction. He sought to establish two things: on the one hand, that the 'turmoil' was due entirely to a conspiracy on the part of a 'tiny, tiny handful' of reactionary conspirators who sought to overturn communism; on the other hand, that the mob attacks on the troops revealed a situation so dangerous that it justified the decision to bring in the army. Also, in his thoroughness in exposing the 'tiny, tiny handful' he confirms that almost the entire Chinese intellectual establishment, headed largely by Party members, supported the students. In his anxiety to stress the severity of the crisis, he confirms with detailed evidence the furious rising of the people of Beijing. Ironically, therefore, Chen ends by proving that the movement had the support both of China's intellectuals and of the people of Beijing.

Chen shows that virtually all of China's centres of political and economic research supported the students: the Chinese Academy of Social Sciences and even the Institute for the Study of Marxism-Leninism-Mao Zedong-Thought participated. So, too, did the reform think-tanks. The main leader in the encouragement of the students was again the astrophysicist Fang Lizhi. He argued publicly, at home and abroad, that socialism had 'lost its attraction'. He urged China's new entrepreneurial class to ally with the students and demand democracy. He urged the new free association of students to mount a 'turbulent' movement for liberty and democracy. Worst of all, in a speech in Australia, he asserted that the communist leaders held secret accounts in Swiss banks.

Since then, apart from Deng Xiaoping, who could in no way conceal his responsibility, no one involved has stepped forward to share it unequivocally. Indeed, after the short period of conservative triumph which followed the suppression of the students, scarcely any leader implicated in that suppression has been allowed to hold high office. In 1992 Yang Shangkun and Yang Baibing were quietly dropped from the Politburo; both died in the following year. Their dismissal was followed by massive changes in PLA commands, which until then had been controlled by Yang Baibing. Only Li Peng has survived politically, but he is the adopted son of Zhou Enlai, and Zhou's widow was still alive and honoured; and even then, Li Peng had to undergo a Pauline conversion in order to stay in power. Jiang Zemin, who succeeded Zhao Ziyang as the head of the CCP, when faced in America with a question on the Tiananmen massacre, could only mumble that 'mistakes are sometimes made'.

19

Reaction and renewed reform

Jiang Zemin was from Shanghai which, recently opened to foreign trade on much the same terms as Shenzhen, had a strong interest in continued economic reform. Nevertheless, the conservative veterans, with Li Peng as their protégé, had for the moment regained power. A period of attempted reaction followed. They issued orders for continued retrenchment and recentralization. Price controls were reimposed. Wages were frozen. Credit for fixed investment was cut, and each province received a quota. Planning was restored in steel, chemicals, and agriculture. The Rural Responsibility System was threatened by renewed emphasis on its remaining collective aspects, and proposals were made to encourage peasants to join 'voluntarily' in a revival of collective agriculture. Remittances from State-owned enterprises to the government were increased. Township and village enterprises and private enterprises suffered discrimination. In late 1989, 3 million township and village enterprises were closed, ostensibly for producing shoddy goods, wasting energy, and polluting the environment. In the State-owned enterprises, Party committees again took over management.

This reaction, however, could not be sustained. At a national Party work conference, the provincial authorities, led by Guangdong and Shanghai, protested. Li Peng deserted to the reformers. The head of the State Planning Commission (Zou Jiahua) announced in February 1991 that State mandatory plans for industry would be reduced (Zhao Ziyang had only frozen them at the existing level), in order 'to push the enterprises towards the market'. China's local authorities were given back their former autonomy. Part of the reason for the failure of reaction was that State-owned enterprise managers were refusing to renew their contracts.

In October 1992 Deng Xiaoping visited Shenzhen, and in that wellspring of bourgeois liberalism, that reincarnation of imperialism (in the conservative view), he made a speech in which he demanded the speeding up of reform. However, one year in power had already been enough to show the new regime that continued reform was inevitable. The following year was one of rapid change. The number of commodities subject to State allocation fell to only eighteen. Grain and oil prices were freed, in spite of an annual inflation rate of 22 per cent.

In the same year, most of the State-owned enterprises were transformed into joint-stock companies, enjoying limited liability. This followed the creation of a Stock Exchange in 1992; but only 7 per cent of the shares issued were bought by individuals; 7 per cent were bought by foreign companies, and 24 per cent by institutions. The rest were bought by the government.

In 1993 the Central Committee offered as a guiding slogan, 'a socialist market economy'. This was not an unreasonable description. The bulk of production and distribution was now via the market, but the actors in the market were mainly State firms and collective firms; although private enterprise was growing apace, the State and collective sectors continued to grow even more rapidly.

From 1991, in spite of the international sanctions imposed on China in response to the Tiananmen incident, foreign investment began to pour into the country, especially into Guangdong and Shanghai, and by 1993 this had come to account for one-fifth of China's total fixed investment. Meanwhile, the rate of economic growth continued to be very rapid.

Parallel with the reaction against economic reform following Tiananmen, there was an attempt to rein in the freedoms which China had enjoyed under Zhao Ziyang. Many journals were closed down. The number of registered journalists was reduced by about 60 per cent. The study of Marxism was intensified. The majority of the most prominent figures in Chinese intellectual life who had supported the students were in jail or had escaped abroad. Fang Lizhi and his wife had sought the protection of the American Embassy.

Yet this reaction, like the reaction against economic reform, was short-lived. In his speech Deng Xiaoping also asserted that at this point the 'left'—by which he meant the conservatives—were a greater danger than the 'right'—by which he meant the democrats. The new administration under Jiang Zemin, although forced at first to acknowledge the revived power of the conservatives, was not of that complexion. Jiang interpreted the conservatives' reassertion of intellectual control in a fairly liberal way. His main supporters, such as Zhu Renzhong, took a similar attitude. An autonomous popular culture began to develop and the CCP tolerated it.

The last political act of the conservatives was to write a letter of protest in response to Deng Xiaoping's 1992 'southern speech'. It was signed by all the prominent conservative veterans. It had no effect. The new leadership accepted Deng's recommendations without reserve. The Central Advisory Commission of retired veterans was abolished.

The economy since 1993

The economy continued to grow very rapidly, but the same problems remained. Renewed inflation was met by retrenchment which slowed growth and caused distress in the State-owned enterprises and prejudiced their continued reform. This reform was still inhibited by fear of the unemployment which it would cause, although as a system of unemployment insurance was gradually put in place the rationalization of the labour force became easier. By 1995, 95 million State-owned enterprises' workers were covered by unemployment insurance. From 1997 pensions were paid by the State and no longer by the enterprises. However, this insurance applied only to former employees of the State-owned enterprises; 70 per cent of the urban population were outside this protected circle and had to create their own arrangements for welfare. Those unprotected included 'contract' workers, workers in the co-operative sector and the private sector, the self-employed, and peasants who had migrated to the cities. For these, welfare was provided through families, street committees, organizations of migrants, and commercial insurance.

In the rural areas, welfare depended largely on the local authorities using township and village enterprise profits, while extended families, lineages, and clans resumed their traditional responsibilities. The provision of social welfare was politically vital; there was a universal expectation that the socialist regime should provide security from the cradle to the grave. Moreover, as far as security was becoming dependent on the old intergenerational responsibilities, the problem led to resistance to population control. Nevertheless, the mutual responsibility of the generations was now reasserted and written into the marriage contract, an admission that the family must again be the first line of protection against disadvantage. The government also encouraged the provision of insurance by charitable associations, many of these based in Hong Kong. Eventually a scheme of welfare for the cities was created, based on obligatory contributions by employers and employees plus voluntary insurance payments. These arrangements, however, did not include the migrant peasants.

Thus the average citizen, while now enjoying much more individual autonomy, also faced greater hazards. There was a widespread sense of insecurity, reflected in a remarkably high level of savings even among the relatively poor.

It is sometimes asserted that China's attempt to preserve and reform the State-owned industrial sector has been a failure. It is true that a large part of the sector continued to record losses or falling profits, but there are problems of interpretation here. Some Chinese analysts argue that much of this loss is the result of the method of accounting used and is more apparent than real. Much of the recorded loss was at that time also the result of the heavy welfare responsibilities which the firms carried. This burden could turn profit into loss; but if the firm's welfare payments had been regarded as a positive economic contribution, a part of the wealth they generated, and not as an operating cost, many more State firms would have shown a profit. It should also be recognized that falling profits when combined with rapidly rising productivity may be a healthy sign which indicates some success in coping with the new competitive economy. The reformers however were impatient, and the

State-owned enterprises were under constant criticism from the central government.

Pessimism was reflected in pressures for privatization. The strength of opposition is indicated in the firmness and frequency with which Jiang Zemin and his supporters had to insist that public ownership would continue to be the backbone of the socialist market economy. However, the definition of the responsibilities of the State sector was gradually changed. Li Peng, as Prime Minister, stated that it would continue to dominate only natural monopolies, transport, public utilities, and industries of vital national importance. Meanwhile, the number of commodities subject to State allocation had dropped from 800 before 1979 to a varying figure around 20. The new Stock Exchange was not intended to be used as an instrument of privatization. It was mainly part of a move to strengthen the autonomy of the State-owned enterprises by making possible a more rational distribution of capital among them, through cross-shareholding and mergers. This, rather than bankruptcies, was the means used in dealing with failing firms.

At the same time, State enterprise prices and market prices were now rapidly converging, while measures were taken to bring Chinese prices into line with world prices.

It is remarkable that in China's economic success, privatization has played only a marginal part. No major enterprise has been sold off. Privatization has been confined largely to small losing firms, mainly in the commercial sector. Many of these have passed into the hands not of individuals or private shareholders but of co-operatives. The responsibilities transferred to a new private owner are usually so great that the transfer is more like a conditional lease than a change of ownership. Outside the State sector many township and village enterprises have been 'privatized', but such firms are usually in a position little different from that of firms which continue to be owned by the local authorities; they are obliged to conform to the local economic strategy and to contribute to the pool of community capital. Private enterprise in China is in fact private in only a restricted sense. Firms operate under licence. They are often dependent on State sources of inputs. They are obliged to conform to a co-operative ethic. Even the provision of amenities by local authorities to encourage private enterprise serves to keep these enterprises under control. The number of registered private enterprises is impressive; by 1998 it was reported that there were 960,000, with a total workforce of 13.5 million. The overwhelming majority, however, are extremely small, often little more than a peasant family, and all private enterprises, in spite of their number, still contribute only 15 per cent to the value of industrial output. Theoretically their status has been improved by an amendment to the Constitution of the PRC: they are no longer simply 'complementary' to the publicly owned economy but are now an 'important part' of the socialist market economy; however, legal protection is far from dependable. It is important to bear in mind that very little of the private sector in China is the result of privatization; most of it represents new growth outside the State and collective sectors.

The state of agriculture has continued to make difficulties, but like so many other problems in China they are problems only in relation to the rapid development of the economy generally. The growth rate in agriculture of about 4 per cent per annum would be regarded with very great satisfaction in most of the world's poorer countries, but this 4 per cent or so has to support industrial growth which has been increasing at up to three times that percentage. In spite of all the rhetoric in giving priority to agriculture in the allocation of state investment, the proportion allocated to agriculture has fallen steadily. It has been clear that the peasants cannot easily protect their interests against those of other sectors and other claimants. In 1993 the net outflow of funds from the rural economy was 52 billion yuan. Nevertheless, in spite of the problems, there were three record grain harvests in ten years.

Perhaps the worst rural problem, however, was the continued abuse of power by local cadres. In the late 1990s, legislation was introduced in an attempt to provide effective local elections and in other ways to make rural cadres accountable. The local population now have at least a choice of candidates but the nomination process is still controlled by the Party. However, accompanying measures might make possible some control of arbitrary exactions and uncontrolled spending. This will take time. Meanwhile, abuse continues and peasant riots are commonplace. Indeed, Wan Li has publicly warned of the possibility of a peasant revolt.

The township and village enterprise sector continued to grow and flourish until the late 1990s; but its headlong growth could not be expected to go on forever. The scarcities on which it has flourished have been much alleviated by its own performance, and fierce competition has set in. Yet its role remains indispensable, and this is now recognized. After Deng's 'southern speech', township and village enterprise was at last fully accepted and its vital role recognized. In 1997, it was said that it was 'likely to be the primary and strategic focus of national growth'. Between 1984 and 1996 the enterprises grew at 33.9 per cent per annum. New laws were passed in 1997 to protect their rights although this was achieved only over strong resistance in the NPC. Even Li Peng is now an enthusiast, and the Chinese Academy of Social Sciences has argued that labour-intensive development remains fundamental to China's economic future, and this means the further growth of township and village enterprise. In particular, there is an enormous disparity between the high level of development of the enterprises in the coastal provinces and the much lower level of development in the poorer provinces of the west. It is therefore regarded as important that everything should be done to further their development in these deprived areas as part of a policy package to eliminate the last areas of absolute poverty; this again implies further development of township and village enterprise.

These regional disparities are politically critical. The poor regions provide a constituency for those who are worried about the pace of economic reform which tends to leave them trailing, just as, on the contrary, highly developed Guangdong and Shanghai are the main centres of support for rapid reform. However, the problem can be exaggerated. It has been shown that even if the rich coastal provinces are excluded from the figures for national economic growth, the remainder of China has nevertheless experienced very satisfactory growth and a very great reduction in poverty. The government hopes that the mineral riches of the interior will eventually be fully exploited, to the advantage of some of the poorest areas. It has had some success in encouraging foreign investment in the inner provinces. It is pressing the bigger State-owned enterprises to enter into direct relations with firms in the north-west and often poor areas, by vertical integration; some State-owned enterprises in the richer coastal provinces are now investing in local coal mines and steelworks in the poor areas.

Reform is not proceeding even now without political controversy. Those who regard the reforms as concessions to capitalism are still vocal. They have their own organizations and they publish freely. They deplore the creation of large numbers of unemployed and of the vast communities of migrant peasants who threaten to form an underclass in the cities. They continue Mao's opposition to revisionism and argue that the fate of communism elsewhere has proved that Mao was right. However, they are of marginal importance. They have no access to power. The old veterans are disappearing. Yang Shangkun died in 1993, and Chen Yun in 1995. Deng himself died in 1997.

Perhaps the most important change has been the change of generations and this change was driven home by political action. The Cultural Revolution had already removed many of the cadres who came to power in the 1940s and early 1950s; they were mostly replaced by younger people. The reaction against the Cultural Revolution under Deng Xiaoping removed many of these new cadres, and economic reform has been punctuated by campaigns to dismiss local cadres who opposed it. The Party has grown enormously in numbers and the new recruits are relatively young. Life tenure for cadres has been abolished. Public posts are now filled by examination, and this increases recruitment from among the young. Among the ruling elite, there has been a 50 per cent turnover.

There has also been a considerable change in the background of those in power. The level of education is much higher. The sources of Party recruitment are now much more diverse and even include some of China's successful capitalists. Party cadres are becoming more differentiated functionally, into administrators, economic managers, and leaders of non-profit-making institutions; this has led to a revival of the worry expressed so often in China for the preceding century and a half that expertise is taking over from moral commitment. Although the Party's system of control remains unimpaired, functional specialization within it is tending to institutionalize conflicting interests and viewpoints.

Corruption remains the 'slipping clutch' of China's progress. In spite of strenuous efforts, it is still perhaps China's most serious problem. The most highly placed victim of the campaign against corruption was Chen Xitong, a member of the Politburo, the former Mayor of Beijing, and the apologist for the suppression of the Tiananmen demonstration. He was sentenced to sixteen years and dismissed from the Party. Convictions for corruption are numbered year by year in six figures, but the convicted have been mostly of much lesser political stature. The democrat Bao Dong, formerly secretary to Zhao Ziyang, in a letter to Jiang Zemin from prison which was revealed in the Hong Kong press, argued that only democracy can eliminate corruption. Perhaps the recent legislation on village government means that Beijing is at last beginning to learn this fundamental lesson.

Political reform since 1992

After Deng Xiaoping's 'southern speech' asserted that the conservatives were now the problem, the democrats felt free to renew their pressure. The atmosphere became fairly liberal once more. However, the configuration of opinion had changed from that of the eve of Tiananmen. Hopes of rapid democratization had been damaged. Meanwhile, the collapse of communism elsewhere had produced, especially in the Soviet Union, a chaotic situation such as no one in China was ready to risk. Until the rise of Gorbachev the Soviet Union, for all its defects, had long enjoyed internal stability even if this was only the result of appalling tyranny. Communist China, however, had undergone two drastic breakdowns, the Great Leap Forward and the Cultural Revolution. In 1989 chaos had threatened again. To most Chinese stability is worth more than liberty. The Soviet experience after 1990 confirmed this. In spite of the strength which the democratic movement had displayed in the nationwide agitation during the Tiananmen movement, to the majority of Chinese, dissidents are still suspect, and the burden of proof lies with the dissenters rather than with the authorities; comparative research has revealed that these suspicions are exceptionally high in China. The resulting pattern of opinion includes a reinforcement of opposition to rapid economic reform, indeed to rapid change of any kind; some of the younger generation have joined in the conservative reaction, and in its call for the reversal of decentralization and the reimposition of Party–State controls to prevent instability. In this increasingly conservative atmosphere there has been a revival of nationalism among the new generation, and with it a restored interest in Confucianism; but this time it is the Confucianism of hierarchy, not of government by consent. Jiang Zemin's regime exploits this while at the same time curbing any extravagant expression of anti-American or anti-Japanese feeling.

The death of Deng Xiaoping in 1997 caused little change in the policies of the Jiang Zemin regime. Economic reform continued systematically, and the denial of democratization on the grounds of the need for stability still determined the degree of freedom of expression permitted. As under Deng, this freedom was by no means negligible, but it was incomplete, erratic, and precarious. Jiang, like Deng, swung back and forth between hostility to democracy and a desire to meet at least some of its criteria. He allowed President Clinton on his visit to China in 1998 to discuss on television the necessary relationship between economic and political freedom. He permitted Li Shenzhi of the Chinese Academy of Social Sciences to argue that no one could act as a citizen who did not have political and civil rights and that China having now provided livelihood for all could now permit rights for all, and to argue also (like Chen Erjin) that democratic institutions and procedures are of universal validity. Jiang tolerated for some time the circulation of proposals for a system of checks and balances and direct elections on Western lines, but then changed his mind and imprisoned their author, Fang Jue; this reversal was the result of fear that the Asian economic crisis which arose in 1997 would lead to instability in China, which indeed it did, with protests from workers, most notably in the north-eastern provinces whose trade relations with the rest of the Far East were especially strong. In 1998 he reasserted Deng Xiaoping's Four Cardinal Principles. Having encouraged to some extent an increased degree of political pluralism, when former Red Guards attempted to establish an independent political party, the China Democratic Party, he imprisoned its three founders, Wang Youcai, Xu Wenli, and Qin Yongmin. When members of the Falungong, a religious society, held a meeting in the capital on 25 April 1999 the sect was suppressed, and is still being persecuted.

At the same time, nevertheless, Jiang Zemin pushed forward steadily with legal reforms which were more and more based on Western precedents and practice. By the end of the 1990s, these were on paper impressive and almost comprehensive, but in practice their effect was limited. In the first place, there was little consciousness or experience of either the principles or the practice of democratic jurisprudence; in the second place, as usual the centre lacked the power, even had its members had the real will, to enforce the new rules at lower levels of government; and in the third place the new laws and procedures remained subject to the Party's self-proclaimed right to intervene and overrule the law in the last resort. The trial of the three leaders of the China Democracy Party simply set aside the principles for which the new laws stood.

The National People's Congress now exerts much more influence on decision-making than formerly. Although legislation still usually originates from the State Council and is always overseen by the Politburo, the Congress is now permitted to propose amendments, it is empowered to oversee the application of laws passed, and it has specialist committees. Votes are no longer unanimous, and on occasion the vote against a proposed law can be significantly large, as in the case of the legislation on the Three Gorges Dam, which was only narrowly passed. In the case of a proposed law to replace highway tolls with a fuel tax, the Congress voted against the measure and sent it back to the State Council, on the grounds that a fuel tax would be against the interest of farmers.

There have thus been some gains. Progress has been such as to raise the question of how far the preconditions for sustainable democracy in China are being laid down. We do not have as yet any general theory of democratization which has much predictive value, but many of the conditions which help or hinder progress have been empirically identified. On most of these conditions China scores well.

She is less encumbered by intractable divisions than most large countries; almost all of her population are of the same Han race and culture. Religious divisions have played little part in her history. The great historic class division, that between landlords and peasants, was destroyed by the revolution.

There is now a consensus on fundamentals, certainly a necessary condition of sustainable democracy, with 89 per cent of the population, according to a recent sample survey, favouring economic restructuring in principle, though less than 70 per cent are content with the results so far.

As we have seen, Confucian culture can, with a plausible change of emphasis, provide a Chinese rationale for democracy. There are also strong elements in Chinese social behaviour which could lend support to democracy: the idea that the best solution to a conflict is one from which both sides gain, and the avoidance of damage to an opponent's dignity.

Another basic condition of sustainable democracy is that the machinery of government should be effectively honest and competent. While Chinese administration has very serious flaws, it has nevertheless proved its adequacy in the course of the economic reforms, in obvious contrast to the failure of government in the former Soviet Union.

It is essential for successful democracy that the government's writ runs everywhere. Given China's vastness and variety this is a difficulty which has resulted throughout China's history in tension between centralization and decentralization. This is the great hen-and-egg problem of democratization. It can succeed only if China's local authorities are made accountable, but only democracy can enforce accountability.

There are also factors in China which militate against democracy. One is traditional indifference to precise law. Another is the difficulty of accepting that strong government and democratic government are not antithetical and that in fact democracy can be the strongest form of government.

Another problem is the instinctive elitism of Chinese intellectuals. Very few of China's democrats, with the exception of some former Red Guards, appear to have any effective relations with discontented groups among the population, although this is partly because the communist government is very vigilant indeed in preventing the development of such relationships. The Communist Party remembers how in the May Fourth Movement, and indeed in the foundation of the CCP itself, alliance between intellectuals and workers or peasants overturned governments.

Economic reform is undoubtedly contributing to the strengthening of the preconditions of democracy. An economy based on contracts requires a dependable legal framework, and a society based on free contracts must to that extent be a free society. It is significant that Guangdong, the province in which private enterprise and joint ventures with foreign investors are most developed, has taken the lead in legal reform.

It is usually argued that if economic development creates a strong middle class, this class will lead democratization; but so far this has not proved true in China. We have noted that with individual exceptions China's new free entrepreneurs refrained from supporting the Tiananmen students, in spite of appeals from Fang Lizhi and others. They are still clients of the State. It may take many more years before they can risk confrontation with the communist regime.

Nevertheless as a result of economic reform the economy has become to a substantial extent pluralist. The single central locus of economic decision-making has given way to many millions of autonomous economic actors, both collective and private. The breakdown of the *danwei* system which ensured that the individual's identity was determined by membership of the factory or the collective has given way to personal autonomy and personal choice. Moreover, the operation of this pluralist economy and of the consequent increase of personal choice has led to the rapid proliferation of societies and voluntary associations which now number about 1 million. It is difficult to deny that China's civil society is in the process of being recreated. It is true that the Party does its best to control these organizations, and indeed the associations themselves more often than not actually seek Party patronage, but in time the Party representatives may well begin to see themselves as mediators rather than bosses.

The degree of freedom of opinion, the press, and associations has varied from time to time. The severe restrictions applied after Tiananmen did not last, but in the 1990s freedom in these respects remained ambivalent, though generally fairly wide. The main change has been that literature and the arts are no longer compelled to be instruments of propaganda. A new popular non-political culture has grown up. Side by side with this is a new kind of fiction which is cynical, brutal, obscene, and often surrealist. This too is apparently non-political, but strict Marxists would say that a non-political culture is actually as political as any other, and while this is a dangerous idea, it can in some circumstances be true. It is difficult not to see in this new fiction a rejection of the system more profound than the politically explicit fiction tolerated in the 1980s by Hu Yaobang and Zhao Ziyang, and it is astonishing that a communist regime should, for the most part, refrain from interfering with it.

The one fixed principle which limits freedom is the Party's determination to tolerate nothing which might lead to the establishment of any political or potentially political association which might set out to rival the Party's authority. Even here, however, it was actually a move by the government to allow more freedom of association which encouraged the formation of the China Democratic Party. Yet the founders of the new party were promptly imprisoned.

From the point of view of future democratization the most important development is simply that, given a decentralized and pluralist system, the government is no longer in a position merely to command. It has to consult, negotiate, bargain, and compromise, and these habits are inevitably growing. In this way the polity is gradually democratizing itself. One cannot of course predict that this tendency will not be halted or even reversed: anything can happen in a dictatorship. However, it does not seem likely. The economic and the political tosts would be high.

Conclusion: the modernization of China

When great civilizations go into decay a satisfactory explanation is never easy; but in China's case we can at least eliminate some of the explanations now current.

There were no signs in the late eighteenth and early nineteenth centuries that Chinese society was undergoing structural changes for the worse. While with the rapid increase of population the man–land ratio was deteriorating, there is no evidence of a decline in the standard of living of the average Chinese family. Agricultural production continued to rise; moreover, the rate of marketed surplus of agriculture also grew substantially, showing that the subsistence needs of the increased population were being met by land reclamation and by more intensive use of labour. The pressure of the increase of population certainly caused increasing destitution at the margin of society, but such a tendency is compatible with the maintenance or even the improvement of the standard of living of the majority.

In spite of the tensions produced by the continued increase in population, there is no convincing evidence of increased concentration of land ownership or of any general decline in peasant proprietorship. The steady increase in rice prices until about 1825 and again after 1850 does not suggest that the majority of the farming community were likely to have been suffering a decline in incomes, although the same circumstances might have caused increasing distress to the landless minority.

The idea that foreign influence in China was the major cause of decline is no better supported by the evidence. The symptoms of decay in Chinese government were obvious before this influence was brought to bear. They first became manifest towards the end of the reign of the Qian Long Emperor: the gross corruption; the rapid spread of disorder; the inability of successive emperors to reform the inelastic, corrupt, and regressive taxation system; the effects of the debilitating pressure of Manchu censorship on Chinese intellectual awareness, increased by the consequences of the isolation imposed on China by her rulers for several centuries; and the gradual hardening of the arteries of a system thus shielded from competition and external stimuli—all these factors were already at work.

It is indeed possible that the chief cause of political decline was the phenomenon most familiar of all to Chinese historians: the flagging energies of a dynasty already two centuries old, whose very success encouraged a relaxation of vigilance. In the absence of vigorous action by the sovereign himself the Chinese system of government was liable to cease to function. It required an emperor willing to be at his desk from dawn to record his personal decisions in his own vermilion ink in the margins of the state papers daily heaped before him. The system required a ruler not only of great industry but of intelligence, decisiveness, and political acumen. The legitimizing myth was that the emperor was the supreme sage; and there was this much truth in the myth that if he was not remarkably sagacious then government faltered and failed. The successors of Qian Long were inadequate to the task.

Yet even had China's normal efficiency, impressive by any pre-modern standards, been maintained, the new problem of Western pressure would have been difficult to solve. With the exception of Japan no pre-modern country faced with this pressure was able to rise rapidly to a position from which it could deal with the Western powers from equal strength. Japan was able to cope because Confucian government there was grafted on the vigorous rootstock of Japan's military tradition; where Confucianism was inadequate, *bushido* (the way of the warrior) more than compensated. Paradoxically, Japan's military feudalism, less 'progressive' than China's individualistic property relations, proved to be a force for change. It made possible the enforcement in Japan of a degree of discipline quite impossible in China. When the great feudal lords ordered their peasants to get the disease out of their export silk they had no choice but to obey, but the Chinese peasant was his own master. When they committed Japan to industrialization their samurai vassals threw themselves into industrial enterprise with an almost kamikaze indifference to losses, but China's cautious bureaucrats could not act so.

Nor did they want to. The Chinese were the mentors of the Confucian world, and pride kept them committed to the ideology. Confucian behaviour, both public and private, was so ritualized that even the most minor changes could be deeply offensive; the rituals had become the reality, while on the preservation of this pattern of behaviour depended the prestige of the ruling class. Yet there was more to mandarin resistance to modernization than class interest and the reification of ritual. Conscience was involved. Men such as Li Hongzhang and his associates responsible for the Tong Zhi restoration which followed the Taiping Rebellion were well aware of the possibilities offered by Western technology and organization, and their ambivalent attitude to them expressed the fear that the increased mobility which industrialization would bring would undermine the social foundations of that harmony which it was their first duty to preserve.

When in the late nineteenth century the attempt was made to square the circle by a policy of limited industrialization under the control of the official class, the officials, for all their virtues as administrators, proved utterly inept in business. For example, Zuo Zongtang, so shrewd a statesman when on familiar ground, built his new woollen mills where there was actually no soft water within a thousand miles; he did not even know enough to realize that he should have sought advice.

Only after defeat at the hands of Japan in 1895 showed the failure of limited official industrialization, and then only after another decade of disasters, did the Manchu government accept a policy of encouraging private enterprise and accept the necessity of a legal system to protect it and a modern education system to support it, changes which seriously compromised the traditional ideology. By then, however, the revolution of 1912 was at hand. And when the Empire came to an end the values, the expectations, the symbols, and the sanctions of Confucian government were thrown into confusion. Sun Yatsen, who had led the attack on the monarchy, was shocked to find that, after the revolution, many of the Chinese clans had scratched the character for 'loyalty' out of their ancestral tablets. To whom was loyalty now owed? The personal bond of allegiance to the Son of Heaven was broken before China was ready for the possibility of loyalty to an abstraction such as the State or the nation. Modern national feeling, defined as a strong sense of the mutual obligations of fellow citizens, had scarcely appeared in China at this time. National feeling in this sense is modern not only because it is recent but because it depends so largely upon other modern phenomena such as economic integration, the break-up of more local loyalties by the processes of economic evolution, the replacement of the family and the local magnate by the State as the main protector and the main dispenser of benefits, a unified system of mass education, and other consequences of economic development. None of this had yet happened across China's vast area. China was still, as Sun Yatsen said, 'a rope of sand'.

Although the warlord struggles of 1916–27 were less unprincipled than has often been asserted, they nevertheless reflected the fact that the republican governments in Beijing inspired little loyalty or respect. Had Yuan Shikai or Duan Qirui been willing and able to resist Japanese encroachments they might have gained the allegiance of China, for at this time a threat to further invasion of China's sovereignty was the one issue on which Chinese public opinion was already firm and articulate. Both these rulers, however, chose to defer to Japan in order to borrow the means to suppress the southern Nationalist regime whose claims to legitimacy were more and more perceived in Chinese opinion to be no worse than their own. In a similar way, after 1928 Chiang Kaishek's new Nationalist government temporized with Japan while bending every effort to destroy the Chinese communists. Only when he was forced to fight Japan did Chiang Kaishek win the allegiance of the nation, to lose it again in the disasters of the war. Ironically, it was left to the CCP, in spite of its divisive theory of class struggle, to unite the nation and to create in the course of the guerrilla war against Japan the mass nationalism which Sun Yatsen had sought in vain.

By 1949 when the CP won national power, almost a century had passed since China had taken her first tentative and fumbling steps towards modernization. Thirty years had passed since the May Fourth Movement had expressed aspirations for the future of China which thereafter were generally accepted. Yet little had been achieved. While in the early twentieth century the pace of economic modernization had been gratifyingly rapid in and around the Treaty Ports, the country as a whole had changed little. It is wrong, however, to believe that the competition of modern foreign industry destroyed China's handicrafts. On the contrary, many of them flourished under the new stimulus. Foreign money spent on tea and silk was largely spent in the interior, on China's own manufactures. We have seen that the traditional Chinese economy was very capable indeed of development; the resources, the organizing ability, and the entrepreneurship were by no means lacking. This does not, however, mean that China was about to undergo *sui generis* the technical and structural changes of an agricultural and industrial revolution. There was no great economic incentive for such changes. The existing technologies, given China's plentiful labour supply, were capable of meeting any likely demand; and this demand was in turn limited by the limitations of China's pre-modern levels of labour productivity. In these circumstances only a foreign demonstration of how labour productivity could be transformed by modern industrialization could provide the incentive for structural change. However, something more is always needed—a government, whether national or colonial, which will ensure the creation of the infrastructure of a modern economy and the protection of enterprise. Chinese governments failed to do either. China's failure was not a failure of economic entrepreneurship nor, to the extent which would have inhibited a vigorous government, a failure of social structure. It was a failure of political will.

The aspirations of politically conscious Chinese having been formed in the May Fourth Movement, there was little dispute over ends as opposed to means, and there has been little change since: the wealth and strength of the nation should be increased by the modernization of the economy; its independence should be secured and its sovereignty unimpaired; there should be equality in Chinese society, at least to the extent that absolute poverty should be eliminated, that there should be no unbridgeable gulf between the lifestyle of one class and another, and that there should be equality of opportunity and equality before the law; there should be greater individual freedom from the authority of both the family and the State, and the State should be responsive to the demands of citizens.

Wealth and strength

How much of this has been achieved? Progress towards the modernization of the economy has been rapid and impressive. The position of China in the world as a producer of industrial resources by 1986 was second in the case of coal, fourth in that of steel, fifth in oil, and fifth in the generation of electric power.

Table 1 Production of key commodities in the Chinese People's Republic to 1986

	Pre-1949 peak	1986
Foodgrains (metric tons)	138,700,000	391,100,000
Steel (tons)	923,000	52,050,000
Coal (tons)	61,875,000	870,000,000
Electricity (kilowatt-hours)	5,955,000	445,500,000
Crude oil (tons)	nil	131,000,000
Sulphuric acid (tons)	227,000	7,510,000

Figures derived from Carl Riskin, *China's Political Economy* (OUP, 1987).

The mileage of China's railways increased from the 15,500 miles which existed in 1949 to about 35,000 miles in 1987. Of almost equal importance has been the double-tracking and partial electrification which have taken place since. Even then the total is not very great, and the Chinese government admits that there has been too little investment in railways; lack of the means of long-distance haulage of bulk commodities is a severe constraint on further industrial development. On the other hand, China's roads have been rapidly developed. From the point of view of agricultural marketing and supply, flexible small-scale transport by truck or tractor is much more efficient than transport by rail. Starting in 1949 at only 50,000 miles, the total mileage of roads by the end of the Great Leap Forward (during which there was a massive expansion of rural highways built by the communes) reached 325,000 miles, of which 156,000 miles were metalled or paved. By 1987 the total road mileage had risen to almost half a million miles and virtually all villages were linked to the national transport system. Water transport has always been highly important, and the extent of navigable waterways (mostly in eastern China) was more than doubled after 1949, from 46,000 miles to over 100,000 miles, while an immense effort of dredging and wharf building has made it possible to bring steamships far further up the major rivers and so to link much more of the interior with the outside world than was the case before.

Since 1986, further growth has been rapid, in spite of a reduction in growth rates after the Tiananmen Incident, and during the Far Eastern economic crisis of 1997. Gross National Product has grown at an average of over 10 per cent per annum. The gross output of farming including arable cultivation, animal husbandry, forestry, and fishery grew by 4.8 per cent to 1990 and over 7 per cent in the subsequent decade. Grain production, however, has grown only very slowly since 1986, and this will remain an intractable problem as long as Beijing thinks it is necessary to control farm-gate prices.

Steel production has grown by about 7 per cent per annum, and the production of crude oil has grown to 160,000,000 tons. Industrial output value has grown by 17.8 per cent.

Population growth has been reduced, the rate having fallen from 1.6 per cent in 1986–90 to 1.2 per cent in 1991–99.

Urban per capita incomes grew from 739 yuan in 1985 to 5,854 yuan in 1999. Rural incomes lagged, but still grew at about 4 per cent per annum to reach 2,210 yuan in 1999.

Inflation has inevitably remained a problem in conditions of very rapid growth, prices having risen throughout the period, except for two brief dips in the aftermath of Tiananmen and in the Far Eastern economic crisis. Price rises, however, have never got out of hand, although discontent caused by the relatively high inflation of 1988 played a part in stimulating the Tiananmen protest in 1989.

The development of China's foreign trade, limited for many years after 1949 by autarchic policies, speeded up rapidly in the decade 1974–84. In 1950 the value per capita of foreign trade in merchandise was only 2.06 yuan; by 1984 it had reached 50.05 yuan. Total foreign trade then quadrupled between 1985 and 1999, bringing per capita foreign trade to over 200 yuan. This great development, however, still leaves China's foreign trade marginal to the economy as a whole.

During the First Five Year Plan, trade and aid relations with the Soviet Union were indispensable and shaped China's Stalinist phase. Then came the Sino-Soviet dispute and the withdrawal of Soviet technicians and advisers. China's response was to resolve to be self-sufficient. Foreign trade sank to a very low level.

Then came the 1972 rapprochement with the USA, and Mao and Zhou Enlai took the decision to restore economic relations with the outside world. China's foreign trade had already begun to grow before Mao's death. The rapid growth of Chinese exports thereafter was largely due, as in Taiwan, to the availability of cheap labour for low-tech production. At the same time, special zones, like those in Taiwan, were established as enclaves within which foreign firms and firms jointly owned by foreigners and Chinese could be set up, in privileged conditions. These privileges were rapidly extended to other areas until they became virtually nationwide. At first the results were disappointing. Most of the foreign firms concerned did not, as expected, concentrate on producing goods for export; they preferred instead to produce for China's own rapidly growing domestic markets. Gradually, however, the programme began to produce what was wanted.

Foreign investment in China began to grow rapidly from 1985 onwards. Utilized foreign investment in fact rose 30 per cent per annum, until by the end of the 1990s it accounted for one fifth of China's total capital formation.

In the initial stages most overseas investors were from Hong Kong and

Taiwan, but 200 of the world's 500 largest multinationals now operate in China. This has given China greater access to high technology. Township and village enterprise has played a considerable part in the growth of China's exports, partly through joint ventures with foreign companies; the sector now produces almost half of China's manufactured exports. China's foreign trade is now the seventh largest in the world. Rather little of this is with the former communist bloc; it is overwhelmingly with the world's market economies.

At the same time, China entered into relations with the international economic institutions, including the World Bank, and from these institutions she has enjoyed vast support. Her national housekeeping has been good. She enjoys a strongly favourable balance of trade. Although her foreign debts are large, they are not large enough to give cause for concern. The international institutions have thus had no reason to impose the sort of conditions on the provision of aid sometimes deemed necessary elsewhere. As a consequence. China has been the world's largest recipient of World Bank assistance. The contrast with the reluctance of these institutions to underwrite the reform effort of the Soviet Union is very obvious.

Industrial output value having doubled from 1978 to 1986 then continued to grow at an average of 17.8 per cent per annum until 1999. From 1978 the gross value of rural output, including both agriculture and rural industry, grew at about 10 per cent per annum, but from 1986 the growth rate diminished to 6.4 per cent. Average per capita peasant incomes rose from about 150 yuan in 1979 to 424 yuan in 1986; even allowing for the inflation which accompanied the speedier growth of 1976–86 peasant incomes doubled in that time, but incomes grew more slowly thereafter. In 1985 the average peasant family had savings equivalent to almost six months' income in the bank; their rate of savings then grew until the end of the century at an annual average of almost 30 per cent. The application of chemical fertilizers rose from about 5 kg. per acre in 1952 to 175 kg., approaching application rates in the developed world. In the same period the quantity of electric power available in the villages rose from 0.4 billion kWh (mostly in the suburbs of the cities) to 28.27 billion kWh, and thanks to China's enormous hydroelectric potential this capacity began to extend even into remote mountain areas. Growth of total national electric power continued at 4.2 per cent per annum for ten years and then dwindled almost to nothing.

Thus by 1986 China could be considered a major economic power, and this new capacity was at last being reflected in rapidly increasing consumption; and both production and consumption have grown since then at even faster rates. By the 1990s the major risks of economic restructuring had been successfully faced. These risks were much the same in all countries attempting the transition from the command economy: inflation, unemployment, shrinking national revenues, the appearance of gross inequalities of income, and general economic disruption. China weathered these, although not without considerable difficulty, by a strategy of gradual change, by avoiding massive privatization and reforming rather than destroying the State sector, and by the encouragement of both collective and individual initiatives. Township and village enterprise played, as even the more conservative elements in the CCP now recognize, a vital part in economic reform, providing a rapidly growing alternative economy during the attempts to reform the State sector. The creation of a modern economy is still far from complete, but it is within sight.

After prolonged negotiation, China joined the World Trade Organization in November 2001. In the light of China's previous, and long-held, perceptions of the dangers of exposure to international capitalism, the decision to join the WTO is of great significance. Hitherto, economic reform has been based upon a firm resolve to ensure that China would keep the initiative firmly in her own hands, and to allow no penetration from abroad which would limit her power to protect Chinese interests. The Chinese government in particular feared two threats. One was that extended foreign operations in China might lead to increased unemployment, which is already of critical proportions. The other was that the increase in peasant incomes, which has since the mid-1980s been very slow, might be further reduced or even reversed. The 1997 crisis in the Far East had shown that China was already vulnerable to the effect of economic changes abroad, and there is great fear that, if China becomes more deeply involved in the globalized economy, her power to deal with the consequences of recession elsewhere could be destroyed.

A furious public debate took place. It represented not only a clash of opinions but of interests. It is very probable that the State-owned enterprises would be the first sector to suffer from new international competition, especially in heavy industry. And this suffering would be to a great extent regional: the north-east would suffer worst. Hence much of the opposition represents particularly the interests of the threatened provinces of that region as well as State-owned enterprises throughout the country. On the other side of the argument, the southern coastal provinces are more inclined to favour an increase in free trade because the managers of their labour-intensive light industries are confident that they would win more than they would lose. The Shanghai region agrees for the same reason. The interest of the peasants has been less obviously articulated in the debate, but peasant discontent is already alarmingly obvious.

Of course, the debate involves principles as well as interests. Given China's perception of imperialism, formed since 1837, many Chinese have reacted to the prospect of membership of the WTO by repudiating it on patriotic grounds.

Yet in the face of this opposition the deed has nevertheless been done. What the economic consequences will be in the future cannot be readily predicted, but it seems probable that the overall long-term effects will be positive. The Chinese are good entrepreneurs, and will miss no opportunities. The Beijing government is able and, one can be sure, willing to act to limit severe damage in spite of its WTO treaties. Globalization can devastate the economy of a small country with an ineffective government. It has much less power to dictate to a great nation with a government which is determined, competent, and honest enough (and Beijing is not entirely corrupt) to control the situation.

The long delayed decision to join the WTO might perhaps not have been reached had the relatively conservative Li Peng not been replaced as Prime Minister by Zhu Rongji, the most robust economic reformer who has been in power since Tiananmen. Zhu is confident of the long-term advantages and prepared to deal with the short-term problems. The negotiations have been long, and, like most negotiations with the WTO, they have involved many compromises, some of them enshrined in related bilateral treaties. The details have not yet been fully analysed at the time of writing, but one could hazard the guess that whether membership of the WTO turns out to be a significant triumph or a significant disaster, it is likely in either case to hasten the dissolution of much that still remains of Chinese communism into something which will resemble the guided capitalism of China's former Confucian protégés in the Far East rather than freewheeling American capitalism.

Part of the debate has been over the possible consequences of increased foreign influence for the process of democratization. Both sides agree that this influence is likely to speed it up, but while one side in the debate welcomes this, the other side associates growing corruption, insecurity of life, and increasing inequality with the reduction of social and political control which the process of economic reform is perceived to have already entailed, and so regards the probable political consequences of further trade liberalization with horror. Speculation on this has formed an important part of the debate. China's democrats have tended to support membership of the WTO because they are confident that the result will be to strengthen the process of democratization. In some ways it must do so. The expected further proliferation of foreign and joint-owned enterprises in China must be met by precise laws properly administered. Questions of ownership will have to be defined. Arbitrary command must further give way to negotiation and to the reconciliation of conflicts by legal means. Closer cultural ties may reduce hostility to Western institutions. On the other hand, if the results of free trade prove disastrous, this will strengthen those who see in economic and political reform nothing but increased unemployment, increased insecurity, increased inequality, and increased corruption. In these circumstances there could be a dangerously powerful backlash.

The standard of living

The aspiration to greater equality has been partly realized. China's rapid growth has not been accompanied, as in some other developing countries, by sharply increasing inequalities in the distribution of wealth. While the proportion of total national income going to the poorest 40 per cent of the population is not especially high and not significantly greater than the proportion in India and Bangladesh, China scores better at the other end of the distribution curve; the proportion of total national income going to the wealthiest 10 per cent is very low in China, while at the other end of the scale there is little destitution. This low degree of inequality is now believed by some analysts to be threatened by the course of economic change, but the calculation is difficult and the results ambiguous. Much depends on the terms of trade between industry and agriculture. These moved rapidly in favour of agriculture until 1985, having since 1949 been marginally unfavourable as compared with the terms of trade in 1930–6, but since then they have moved against the farmers as input prices soared. However, as recent research has shown, comparison of urban and rural incomes has neglected the rental value of rural housing and this biases the comparison in favour of the towns. This problem goes right back to the rural surveys of the 1930s.

The expectation of life in China's cities has risen to Western levels, and in the countryside it is not far behind; this is the result of improved diet, changing habits of hygiene, and public health policies which have virtually eliminated China's old killing diseases, including plague, cholera, poliomyelitis, tuberculosis, and schistosomiasis. In particular, the diversification of agriculture since 1978 (grain now for the first time represents less than 50 per cent of agricultural output value) has made available a more varied diet in all but the least developed parts of the country. Improvements in the quality of life are assisted by a successful if draconian policy of limiting family size, bringing population growth rates down.

Education has not developed as rapidly in China as in other communist countries, and in 1978 Deng Xiaoping, in his criticisms of the existing system of economic priorities, pointed out that China was actually spending less on education than India. In general all children attend primary school, although not all finish because many are taken from school to work on the farm, a habit which the new agricultural responsibility system actually encourages, so that the government has been forced belatedly to make school attendance legally compulsory. Illiteracy is said to have been reduced to 20 per cent of the total population, but the measure of literacy used is not very realistic: a knowledge of 500 ideographs is taken to represent literacy, and it is not possible to read even simple Chinese with a knowledge of less than 2,000—the standard demanded by State enterprises from workers seeking employment. Yet it is clear that illiteracy is now mainly a dying problem of old folk and remote areas.

Higher education, however, has been horribly neglected, in contrast to the policy of other communist countries and in as sharp contrast to the policies of other Confucian countries of the Far East, where education has played a dynamic role in economic development. This may well be due to the hostility of Mao Zedong to mere book-learning. This was not unreasonable in a country whose still powerful intellectual traditions were essentially pre-scientific and divorced from both systematic observation and practical application. However, Mao's extreme attitude discouraged higher education. Thus even in 1985 and after a considerable effort by the new regime, only one primary school graduate in twenty reached middle school, and only one in thirty-two middle school graduates went on to a college or a university. Thus a Chinese child had about one chance in 600 of getting a higher education. By 1999 this had improved to one in 300. To develop education in China to the point at which imported high technology can be rapidly absorbed and diffused will still take a long time and immense resources. Until that point is reached, Chinese industry, although impressive in the growth of gross output, will remain backward, ill managed, and extremely wasteful of capital, labour, energy, and materials. And until China's resources are efficiently used, her achievements in gross output will not be fully reflected in increasing standards of living. The Chinese have wiped out mass poverty, but they still have to create mass prosperity. In that respect they look with some chagrin at the four capitalist 'tiger cubs' of the Far East—South Korea, Taiwan, Singapore, and Hong Kong—which in one generation have brought the standard of living of the mass of their people up to Western levels by a system (except in free-trading Hong Kong) of controlled capitalism responsive to inductive planning, a system that has now attracted the attention and the interest of the reform group of the Chinese Communist Party.

Foreign policy

The 1972 rapprochement with the United States removed the perceived threat from America, but the threat from the Soviet Union continued until Gorbachev came to power. By 1979 a tacit alliance with the United States against 'social imperialism' (that is, the communist bloc) had come into being. From 1978, the USA shared intelligence with China, consulted regularly on regional and worldwide issues, sold her arms, and relaxed export restrictions. The USA agreed in 1982 to limit arms sales to Taiwan. Then came Tiananmen and the right-wing reaction which followed; but this did not last, and China made gestures to placate the USA. Permitting Fang Lizhi to leave for America helped the passage of Most Favoured Nation legislation through the US Senate. China did not use her veto in the Security Council to oppose the Gulf War, and this brought an end to post-Tiananmen punitive international sanctions. By then, communism had collapsed in Europe, and Russia, thrown into chaos and weakness, was no longer a threat.

The focus of foreign policy changed from concern with national security to concern with the opportunities of international trade and investment to assist the Four Modernizations which remained the basis of Deng's economic reforms. This required good relations with the outside world generally. In order to lessen the possibility of economic dependence on any one power, China cast the net of friendship wide. The first step was to make a formal peace treaty with Japan in 1978, under Hua Guofeng. Then throughout the 1980s and 1990s the settlement of differences first with India, Burma, and Mongolia, and then with the Soviet Union, Vietnam, Indonesia, and South Korea, was reached.

Gorbachev relaxed the tension on the Chinese border. He freed Eastern Europe, burying the Brezhnev doctrine. He withdrew the Soviet forces from Afghanistan. In 1990 a definitive settlement of the border problem was reached. Cordial relations were restored.

By the mid-1980s China's involvement with the world economy had become so productive as to be virtually irreversible, as the effects of the brief imposition of sanctions after Tiananmen showed. Hong Kong was the biggest source of foreign investment in China, but this reflected the island's importance as a trade entrepôt as much as its importance as a separate source of new technology. Excluding Hong Kong, the main source of imported technology in the 1980s was Japan, but by the 1990s the United States predominated. The United States was also China's greatest export market; China's trade surplus with the USA rose from $US66 million in 1989 to $US18.3 billion in 1992, in spite of the post-Tiananmen dip.

This profound economic involvement with the USA did not, however, lead to an alliance. Free of threats, China constantly stressed in word and deed her determination to have no such entangling alliances. Her relations with America remained edgy and uneasy. There were continuing tensions over US patronage of Taiwan and over China's record on human rights. There were crises over the bombing of the Chinese Embassy in Belgrade during the Kosovo campaign, and in 2001 over the destruction of an American surveillance plane patrolling the Chinese coast. The participation in various ways of foreigners in the Tiananmen demonstrations roused the hackles of the regime, and produced among the veterans (including Deng Xiaoping) an almost paranoiac reaction; fear of 'enemies within' created by contact with foreigners, proved to be as lively as ever. And to most ordinary Chinese America is still the potential enemy, determined to thrust her power and her ideology on the whole world. Continuing fear of the United States has been an important factor in China's determination to extend mutual friendship with foreign countries as widely as possible, to the Third World, the European Community, and the countries of the former communist bloc.

From 1984 China began to participate in international institutions, and to subscribe to international agreements. Her participation, however, has been grudging and often ambivalent. She has signed several agreements on human rights, but broken most of her commitments. In spite of her agreement to desist from exporting nuclear know-how and missile technology, she persistently sold both, to Pakistan and to many countries of the Middle East. She refused to accede to the international treaties which seek to limit the dissemination of nuclear weapons and to halt nuclear tests, until confident that she had created an adequate deterrent. She regarded the Nuclear Non-proliferation Treaty as being directed particularly at her, as a relative latecomer to nuclear weapons. However, on 11 March 1992 she finally signed a non-proliferation treaty and then on 24 September 1996 signed the Nuclear Test Ban Treaty. Her negotiations towards joining the WTO were stubborn and protracted, and although she eventually accepted membership in November 2001, it remains to be seen what her interpretation of the responsibilities she has thus assumed will be. Globalized free trade is not an idea which China will find comfortable.

The return of Hong Hong

In the early 1980s China made it clear that in 1997, when the 99-year lease of the New Territories was due to end, she would expect to resume power in Hong Kong. For Britain to retain Hong Kong (ceded by China in perpetuity) would not be practical when the New Territories returned to Chinese administration. So there was no question of opposing China's demands. The question was simply how to ensure that Hong Kong's separate and highly successful economic life could be preserved; but this, in British eyes, would involve the preservation of the rule of law (based on English common law) and the establishment of democratic political representation. China's interest, however, was simply in recovering sovereignty. Her solution was expressed in Deng Xiaoping's proposal for 'one country, two systems', which would permit Hong Kong to continue to operate her capitalist economy.

In 1984 the two countries agreed to a Joint Declaration as the basis of discussions. It was drawn up by China. At this stage China rejected formal representation of the people of Hong Kong in the negotiations, but clandestine contacts were made, although almost entirely with Hong Kong Chinese businessmen.

The Joint Declaration was a treaty between China and Great Britain. The Basic Law which was negotiated thereafter was, on the contrary, to be incorporated in Chinese law and was duly passed by the NPC. In theory, Britain was not involved with the Basic Law, except in so far as she had a treaty right to ensure that the Law corresponded with the Declaration. However, neither document contained any statement of means by which such concurrence could be enforced.

Meanwhile, between the signing of these two instruments the Tiananmen incident had occurred. In the reaction which followed it in China, the negotiations over the Basic Law were used by China to minimize the concessions already made. On the other hand, Tiananmen alarmed and horrified the vast majority of people in Hong Kong, and led to a rapid growth of democratic sentiment, while the consequent protests on the island in response to Tiananmen made the new regime in Beijing even less disposed to make concessions to the British-inspired democratic political culture of Hong Kong.

It became obvious to the population of Hong Kong, and to the British government, that an effort must be made to provide guaranteed democratic institutions. This the last Governor of Hong Kong, Chris Patten, did his utmost to secure, with the support of the island's democratic parties.

However, Beijing had allies in Hong Kong of decisive strength. It had been obvious from the beginning of the negotiations that most of Hong Kong's Chinese businessmen had already made their peace with China as the best way to protect their interests, which for many of them now included large investments in Guangdong and elsewhere in China. The business group was in any case hostile to democracy; their ideal was Lee Kwanyu's authoritarian government of Singapore. Their attitude was comparable to that of China's own new entrepreneurs who had refused to support the Tiananmen demonstrators; by virtue of their Guangdong investments, many Hong Kong Chinese businessmen had joined their mainland brothers as clients of the Beijing regime.

In these circumstances Chris Patten could secure only marginal concessions on democratization. China would not accept universal suffrage. The question of whether the Basic Law was Hong Kong's constitution, to be amended by Hong Kong, or was part of Chinese law, to be amended by Beijing, was never resolved. The whole settlement was full of ambiguities, leaving Hong Kong's continued autonomy in serious doubt.

The ex-colony's main protection lies in China's hopes of recovering Taiwan under a similar 'one country, two systems' arrangement. Thus the settlement in Hong Kong must be shown to give real autonomy, and now that since the late 1990s Taiwan has been democratized, Beijing has a strong incentive to interpret the political arrangements under the Basic Law in the most liberal way. So far China has interfered very little with judgements made by the Hong Kong courts.

Modernization versus Westernization

While China is being rapidly modernized, the word 'modernization' itself is ambiguous, as a result of its partial identification with 'Westernization'. The original Western nineteenth-century route to modernization was associated with laissez-faire capitalism, individualism, and democracy. Yet even at this time the association was much less than perfect, and since then new models of modernization have arisen. One is represented by the Soviet centralized, authoritarian economy. Another is represented by the Japanese economy which, within a system of free enterprise and constitutional democracy, operates largely through a hierarchy of patron–client relationships with the national government at its apex. Thus modernization in Russia appears to have been conditioned by Byzantine Caesaropapism, and in Japan by Japanese feudalism. Perhaps modernization in the West was, in a similar way, conditioned by the traditions of individualism and constitutionalism which pre-dated the process of industrialization and had their roots in English common law and in Reformation theology.

Modernization nevertheless involves a degree of convergence. It entails certain consequences which are inescapable. Pre-modern social systems mitigated want and insecurity by family or clan solidarity and sometimes by dependence on local patrons. By vastly increasing social and geographical mobility the creation of a modern industrialized economy weakens such relationships. Industrialization thus on the one hand encourages individualism while on the other it encourages the growth of new interest groups. The process, therefore, tends to create demands for increased democracy. At the same time the increasing complexity of economic and social life forces the government into increased dependence on feedback from citizens, and so democratization (at least within limits) has come to be seen, even by the rulers of countries which have modernized by an authoritarian route, as a necessary condition of continued economic modernization.

One might therefore argue that the achievement of democracy has become one of the criteria of modernization. If this is so then the Western liberal model may prove after all to have been more than a local variant. Democracy, however, is another ambiguous word. How it is interpreted by different peoples depends on the complex of assumptions and expectactions which different nations bring to it. It depends on their relative weighting of the value of order, justice, liberty, and equality in different conditions. It involves different degrees of democratic consciousness, confidence, and competence.

In the economic field there is also a degree of convergence. The contrast between the socialist planned economy and the free-enterprise economy, which Marxists see as the most fundamental of all, is actually much less historically significant (as Marx well knew) than the difference between the natural economy and the mass-production economy. In the first, goods are produced mainly for the use of the producer or are bespoke directly; in the second they are produced for a future market which has to be anticipated. In this respect, both the social planner and the private capitalist are engaged in the same operation: forecasting demand. While on the one hand governments in capitalist countries have to attend to needs with which the operations of the market cannot adequately deal, on the other hand governments in socialist countries are forced to recognize that without the signals which only the market can provide, the efficient forecasting of demand is not possible; but this acceptance of the market does not mean that all economies will of necessity converge on the Western system of freewheeling capitalism.

The other China: Taiwan

China's modernization includes elements both of convergence and of divergence; it will not necessarily involve complete Westernization. The communist revolution of 1949 represented the repudiation of the Western liberal model; the Great Leap Forward represented a repudiation of the Soviet model. Perhaps a new and specifically Chinese model is now emerging; but perhaps at present, in order to see what a Chinese model of modernization might be, and to what extent it would correspond to Western expectations, it is better to look across the Straits to Taiwan, where remarkably succesful modernization has taken place. There is enough analogy between Taiwanese policy and the reforms being pursued in China to suggest that there exists a certain common ground of assumptions and expectations, in spite of the profound difference in ideology.

The extraordinary success of Taiwan's economic growth offers both a challenge and a model to China. When the Japanese occupation of Taiwan ended with the defeat of Japan in the Second World War, the average per capita income on the island was $US110 per annum. It is now $US13,000 and still growing. Taiwan, with a population of only 20 million, is now the fourteenth largest industrial power in the world, although the island has almost no minerals or sources of energy. This was all the greater miracle because its Guomindang rulers had had such an indifferent record on the mainland.

Taiwan certainly enjoyed important advantages. The Japanese had treated it in many ways as a part of Japan; most importantly, they extended to it their system of mass education, so that Taiwan's peasants were well educated. The island's government enjoyed massive aid from the United States for several years, although much of this was spent on maintaining a disproportionately large military establishment. Taiwan enjoyed favoured access to the American market. She also had the advantage of the advice of the Japanese *shogoshosha*, companies which make their profits solely from commissions earned through the identification for their clients of new markets, products, and processes— perhaps the world's most successful economic futurologists. The American Commission for Rural Reconstruction moved from the mainland to the island when Beijing fell to the communists; they persuaded the Taiwan government to carry through land reform with compensation, and gave indispensable advice on the development of agriculture. Finally, when China was taken over by the communists many of her most succesful entrepreneurs fled to Taiwan with the Guomindang armies.

The Guomindang landed on the island as corrupt and incompetent as ever. In 1947 they consolidated their power over the existing Chinese population by a massacre. So intolerable was their rule that in a public opinion poll a substantial proportion of Taiwanese respondents voted for the option of the return of the Japanese.

The turning point was the decision of the United States to include Taiwan among its allies against China. American pressure and advice led to a rapid improvement in government. A determined policy of economic development was launched. The strategy applied the ideas of Sun Yatsen, which expressed the May Fourth consensus: land reform, intensive rural development, the encouragement of private enterprise but under control and with the commanding heights of the economy in public ownership, and the maintenance of one-party rule until the economy and society had been modernized.

Rural co-operatives were set up, and although they were parastatal organizations controlled by the Guomindang, they were remarkably successful in introducing new crops, new methods, fertilizers, and insecticides. Although it was accepted that the capital for industrialization would have to come from the peasants through high taxes and low fixed prices, the rapid rise in farming incomes through increased production and through access to alternative employment helped to make this tolerable. Geography largely did for Taiwan what policy did for China; it dictated that industry as it developed would have to spread up the narrow coastal plain. The result was that within a few years industrial employment was within the reach of most peasant families, and 70 per cent of peasant household incomes came from industry.

The strategy was to begin by using Taiwan's cheap labour in simple low-tech industries and then ploughing back the profits in order to climb the technological ladder, all but the highest rungs of which Taiwan has now reached. At first the emphasis was on import substitution, but when the domestic market showed signs of saturation in spite of enormously increased purchasing power, a bold switch was made to an emphasis on exports, with very great success. The first step in this move was to create special zones which offered privileges to foreign investors. China, of course, some years later imitated these.

Some authors refer to Taiwan as evidence of the efficiency of a free-enterprise economy, but in fact it operates under a system of inductive planning through which the government by a variety of incentives and disincentives is able to exert considerable pressure on firms. Development has conformed to a systematic strategy imposed by the one-party regime. Other authors point to Taiwan as an example of the superior success of development under authoritarian regimes which can hold down popular demands for redistribution of income. This opinion, however, is equally misleading. The authoritarianism of the Guomindang was not imposed to outlaw trade unions. In so far as its object was not simply to protect the privileges of the new elite of carpetbaggers from the mainland, it was there to crush any demands either for incorporation with the mainland or for independence which would have denied the Guomindang claim to be the national government of the whole of China. It is by no means proven that this authoritarianism had a positive economic function, if only beause the economic strategy chosen was one which produced few losers; in fact, in contrast to most other developing countries, growth in Taiwan was accompanied by a remarkable reduction in income differentials, which are now as narrow as those of Sweden. This being so, one must suppose that authoritarian control of the economy was not necessary to hold down social demands.

Until 1967 Taiwan remained ostensibly under martial law. Then Jiang Jingguo succeeded his father Chiang Kaishek as President, brought martial law to an end, and began a process of democratization spread over almost twenty years but now complete. This provides China's neo-authoritarians with exemplification of their argument that full democratization should wait for economic maturity.

Chinese intellectual tradition and Western influence

At the intellectual level, change in China in the course of the last 150 years has expressed an ambivalent response to Western ideas, both liberal and Marxist. They have been mediated through traditional Chinese concepts and adapted to the realities of China. China's own language was not replaced for the purpose of serious writing by the language of a colonizing power, and thus Western ideas are still expressed in words encrusted with 2,000 years of Chinese associations, and often carry implicit meanings different from the terms they are used to translate; for example, the Chinese word for 'politics' carries associations not of political debate and competition but of paternalistic administration; the Chinese word for 'economics' is not associated with the analysis of economic laws but with executive action to maintain equity in economic life; the word for a political party means a clique, and the word for 'liberalism' implies irresponsibility. Thus many Western concepts have to struggle in China with the very language itself. Another result of the continuity of language is continuity of culture; there remains a Chinese realm of common discourse so rich that the Chinese scarcely have to go outside it to point the moral and adorn the political tale; in reaction to a modern situation, the first historical analogies that spring to Chinese minds are likely to be from Chinese history. There is often good reason for this: some of China's present problems are as old as her history, and ancient controversies may still be relevant. Some of these can scarcely be discussed without recalling, consciously and subliminally, the ancient debate between Legalists and Daoists; for example, the problem of centralization versus decentralization in which the choice was, and perhaps still is, between an uncontrollable central elite in the capital and an equally uncontrollable local elite in the regions.

While the Western ideas introduced in the nineteenth century collided head on with an orthodoxy fostered in their own interests by the Manchu conquerors, yet in fact beneath the surface Confucian thought in the early nineteenth century was more varied than for centuries before; it might indeed be argued that Chinese intellectual life at that time was already on the brink of change. We have mentioned the Jingshi (statesmanship) school whose members returned to the public-service emphasis of Confucianism after the severe political censorship imposed by the Qian Long Emperor. At the same time this censorship itself had a paradoxical effect: the apparently apolitical textual criticism to which it forced scholars back actually produced results which shook faith in the classical texts, and so invited new, and sometimes politically loaded, reinterpretations of China's past. The scholarship of the times was becoming increasingly eclectic, and consequently when Western liberal philosophy came to China certain ideas from the Confucian tradition which had formerly been regarded as marginal and perhaps heretical had already been revived, and some of these provided a bridge to the new foreign ideas. One was the assertion by Wang Yangming, already alluded to, that contrary to the orthodox Confucian belief the moral order does not exist in the objective world but is imposed upon it by the innate moral sense of human beings, and that such moral judgements are individual. There was enough of an analogy here to ease China's reception of the Western emphasis on the value of the individual conscience.

A second important influence was that of the patriot-scholars who had resisted the Manchu conquest and who had sought an explanation for the disastrous fall of the Chinese Ming dynasty: Gu Yanwu's argument that China's strength lay in her local communities and that over-centralized government was a source of weakness; Wang Fuzhi's naturalistic twist to the idea of the Mandate of Heaven; Huang Zongxi's assertion that the true custodians of Confucian tradition were not the emperors but the scholars, organized in their autonomous local academies, and his demand that the emperor's councillors should be drawn from them. All of these theories, implicitly at least, made a new distinction between the State and civil society and gave the latter primacy, and this prepared the ground for the reception of Western constitutionalism (by one of the uncanny coincidences of history, this Chinese Whiggery was created in the generation of the English Civil War). At the same time Wang Fuzhi's new view of the Mandate of Heaven, in which the moral laws of history worked themselves out through a process apparently amoral, eventually eased the reception of Marxism.

Gu Yanwu, stressing that China existed in her local communities rather than in the emperor and his bureaucrats, adumbrated modern mass nationalism: 'When the Empire falls,' he wrote, 'every man is responsible.' When in the early twentieth century the Chinese turned from the defence of their elitist culture to the defence of their national existence, Gu's assertion became the text of the new patriotism. And the racial emphasis of the new nationalism implied a sort of democracy; the word *guo*, a fief or commandery and by extension the Empire as the feudal patrimony of the imperial clan, came to mean the Nation. A new word was coined: *Zhong-guo-ren*, China-man.

Thus much of the force of modern Chinese democratic thinking was mediated through alternatives within the Confucian tradition, but these alternatives did not in any way invalidate the general norms of Confucian behaviour; behaviour as usual changed less than belief. Intellectual acceptance of individualism does not necessarily guarantee that the individual is in a position to neglect or repudiate the obligations to family and to patrons which are traditionally expected. For good or ill, few Chinese even today feel free to act against these norms. It is in the persistence of traditional patterns of behaviour, rather than in questions of intellectual conviction, that China resists Westernization. This pattern may be summed up as an expression of the survival of the prevalence of hierarchical assumptions and of patron–client relationships, and the obligations thereby entailed. For this reason, in China patronage is still power, however deplored this may be in theory. Those below look for patrons, those above for clients. One result is to weaken resistance to privilege and the abuse of power; the Chinese instinct is not to expose and condemn privilege, but to seek to share its advantages by becoming the client of a privileged individual. Moreover, the acceptance of hierarchy militates against the success of peer groups, and thus against the creation of organizations devoted to universalistic aims; peer groups in China tend to shake down quickly into a hierarchical form based on personal loyalties.

Yet the implications of China's traditional behaviour are not all necessarily negative from the Western point of view. They imply, among other things, an awareness of others' interests, a willingness to compromise, a readiness to seek reconciliation, and an acute consciousness of the dignity of others. They offer the possibility of building social structures which, albeit highly personalized, can often embrace people from different classes high and low. Such behaviour has proved to be compatible with dramatically successful modernization in other parts of the Confucian world—not only in Taiwan, but in Japan and in South Korea. It is not conducive to Western democracy; it is a sort of substitute for it, through its ability to solve (or at least to fudge) problems which, in the societies of the West, would probably become the subject of political action.

Most Chinese continue to feel (rather than to think) that conflict is deplorable; that any sectional interest is likely to be inimical to the public welfare; that democratic government cannot but be weak government; that personal obligations between superior and inferior, rather than impersonal and impartial relationships, provide the better ethical basis for the conduct of public affairs; and that public office bestows a moral authority over and above the specific powers derived from the remit which defines the function of the particular administrator.

Human rights in China

Meanwhile, the undoubtedly sincere efforts of Deng Xiaoping and his successors to extend the bounds of freedom a little may succeed in protecting some authors of reputation, the persecution of whom would cause an international scandal, but they have not succeeded completely in protecting the less famous and the less articulate. Contracts are still often broken at will by rural Party cadres and the protesting peasants beaten up. Torture is still used to exact confession from those too humble to defend themselves. The patronage of the Party secretary of the factory still extends not only to jobs and promotion but to housing, health care, education, and opportunities for recreation. His factory is his fief. The village Party secretary dispenses contracts, determines who gets the new economic opportunities, who gets loans, who gets fertilizers, and who has access to welfare services. His village is his fief. When Chinese dissenters claim that Chinese socialism is a form of feudalism they know whereof they speak.

Political relaxation and the theoretical improvements in law and judicial procedure have done little to protect human rights in China. The most recent Amnesty International investigation has revealed a degree of barbarism which sits ill with China's professions of political reform. Arbitrary arrest, police beatings, torture to extract confession, the persecution of defence lawyers, and the intimidation of witnesses are widespread. Part of the problem comes from legislation which created political offences, but this is only a part. The rest, and the worst, comes from failure to control vicious practices by the police and by those in local authority.

China signed the Vienna Declaration and Programme of Action at the UN World Conference on Human Rights, 1993, but she has resisted participation in subsequent international treaties. She had already in 1991 stated her position in a White Paper, 'Human Rights in China', and in two subsequent White Papers the following year. In these she declared that in China's undeveloped conditions 'social turmoil' could threaten the most important right of all, the 'right to subsistence'. But the Vienna Declaration which she subsequently signed denied that lack of development could be invoked to justify breaches of human rights. She also defended her record in Tibet. In fact, China is now a party to no less than seven UN treaties on human rights, yet the abuses go on. She has also refused to ratify two further instruments, the International Covenant on Civil and Political Rights and the International Convenant on Economic, Social, and Cultural Rights. She has made scrutiny of her own record as difficult as possible. For example, when the Fourth World Conference on Women was held in Beijing in 1995 it was made the occasion of restricting, harassing, and detaining dissidents and the relatives of prisoners of conscience to prevent contacts with foreigners.

The death penalty is imposed for a wide range of crimes, some of them petty, and increases in the use of the death penalty occur at every moment of political tension. The horrors of widespread execution are made worse by the constant breach of China's own laws with respect to judicial procedures.

Thus a permanent member of the Security Council continues to flout the decisions of the UN on matters of human rights and plays the part of a spoiler rather than a supporter of every attempt to apply effective international curbs on human rights abuses.

Recommendations for further reading

In the past twenty years about six thousand books have been published on modern China in English alone. The best introduction to this large literature can be found in the book review pages of *China Quarterly*. This present list has the simple aim of suggesting such further reading as will allow the reader to form his own conclusions on the many controversial issues which have been commented upon, often all too briefly in this volume.

The best guide to chronology is Colin McKerras, *Modern China: A Chronology from 1842 to the Present Day* (1982). *The Times Atlas of China* (1974) is indispensable for maps. The most comprehensive history, for the purpose of reference, is provided by vols. 10–13 (vol. 14 forthcoming) of the scholarly *Cambridge History of China*. There are several survey histories; each has its own character. Immanuel C. Y. Hsu, *The Rise of Modern China* (3rd edn., 1983) is in the tradition of Chinese nationalist history, an eloquent and scholarly exposition of China's struggle to regain strength and dignity. Li Chien-nung. *The Political History of China, 1840–1928* (trans. and abr. by Teng Ssu-yu and Jeremy Ingalls, 1956), written by a notable Chinese historian who lived through much of the times he describes, is enlivened by the author's irony and scepticism. O. Edmund Clubb, *Twentieth Century China* (1964), written by a former servant of the US Government in China, provides the most systematic narrative, backed by both experience and scholarship. The authors of three related volumes, Frederic Wakeman, *The Fall of Imperial China* (1975), James E. Sheridan, *China in Disintegration* (1975), and Maurice Meisner, *Mao's China* (1977), use a looser form which allows them to lay emphasis on what each regards as most significant. John K. Fairbank, E. O. Reischauer, and A. M. Craig, *East Asia: Tradition and Transformation* (1973) similarly develops, in its China sections, the ideas which John K. Fairbank, doyen of American studies of modern China, has developed in a long lifetime of concern with Chinese affairs. Jonathan Spence, *The Gate of Heavenly Peace: The Chinese and their Revolution, 1895–1980* (1981) expounds the history of the revolution through the experience of its intellectual participants in a book distinguished for both style and imagination, a book to be enjoyed for its own sake—one of the few history books one could read in bed. Lucien Bianco, *The Origins of the Chinese Revolution, 1915–1949* (1971) is full of interesting ideas.

In addition to these survey histories, there are several symposium volumes which contain much material indispensable to an understanding of modern China: W. E. Willmott (ed.), *Economic Organization in Chinese Society* (1972), Jack Gray (ed.), *Modern China's Search for a Political Form* (1969), Albert Feuerwerker, Rhoads Murphey, and Mary C. Wright (eds.), *Approaches to Modern Chinese History* (1967), and James B. Crowley (ed.), *Modern East Asia: Essays in Interpretation* (1970).

On Chinese traditional society the following books, whose titles are self-explanatory, can be recommended: Chang Chung-li, *The Chinese Gentry* (1955), Hsiao Kung-chuan, *Rural China: Imperial Control in the Nineteenth Century* (1960), Martin C. Yang, *Chinese Social Structure: A Historical Study* (1969), and Ho Pingti, *The Ladder of Success in Imperial China: Aspects of Social Mobility, 1368–1911* (1962). In addition, Mark Elvin, *The Pattern of the Chinese Past* (1973) provides an idiosyncratic but impressive interpretation, not to be missed even if to be argued with.

The First Anglo-Chinese War with its background of smuggled narcotics has produced many books more conspicuous for their emphasis on the picturesque than for their scholarship, but the following are good. Michael Greenberg, in *British Trade and the Opening of China, 1800–1842* (1951), was the first to analyse the British trading pattern in South and East Asia and its growing dependence on opium as the lubricant of exchange. W. C. Costin, *Great Britain and China, 1833–1860* (1937) provided, many years ago, a careful study of the British public records which disposed of many of the myths surrounding the war and British policy. Chang Hsin-pao, *Commissioner Liu and the Opium War* (1964) and Peter Ward Fay, *The Opium War, 1840–1842* (1975) give balanced, well-documented accounts of the events, John K. Fairbank in *The Chinese Traditional World Order* (1968) describes the preconceptions concerning international relations on the basis of which the Chinese sought to meet the crisis, and in *Trade and Diplomacy on the China Coast: The Opening of the Treaty Ports, 1842–1854* (1953) he provides a thorough and thoughtful account of the formation of the new Treaty Port system in the years after the Treaty of Nanjing.

Four books are important for the study of the disorders in China which provided the tumultuous background of the Taiping and other major rebellions in the early nineteenth century: Philip A. Kuhn, *Rebellion and its Enemies in Late Imperial China: Militarization and Social Structure. 1794–1864* (1970). Frederic Wakeman, *Strangers at the Gate: Social Disorder in South China, 1839–1861* (1966), and Jean Chesnaux, *Peasant Revolts in China, 1840–1949* (trans., 1973) and *Popular Movements and Secret Societies in China, 1846–1950* (1972). Jen Yuwen's *The Taiping Rebellion* (1973) is the classic of Taiping studies, the fruit of a lifetime of devoted scholarship. Vincent Y. C. Shin, *The Taiping Ideology* (1967) provides a study of the sources and development of Taiping ideas and beliefs. Franz Michael, *The Taiping Rebellion: History and Documents*, vol. 1 (1965) represents the beginning of a projected comprehensive history of the rebellion. These are flanked by good studies of the other two great contemporary rebellions: Chu Wen-djang, *The Moslem Rebellion in North-West China, 1862–1878* (1960) and Chiang Siang-tseh, *The Nien Rebellion* (1954).

On the rehabilitation of the Empire in the wake of the defeat of the Taipings, and the tentative and limited moves towards modernization at that time, Mary C. Wright, *The Last Stand of Chinese Conservatism: The T'ung Chih Restoration, 1862–1874* (1957) gives a full account of the 'restoration' in a thoughtful book which will not be superseded for a long time. Stanley Spector, *Li Hung-chang and the Huai Army: A Study in Nineteenth-Century Chinese Regionalism* (1964) explores the threat of regional autonomy which rose out of localized defence against the rebels. Albert Feuerwerker, *China's Early Industrialisation* (1958) gives a very able and trenchant but rather unsympathetic account of 'government-supervised, merchant-managed' enterprise.

There is not yet a survey history of Chinese international relations in the modern period which might both continue and amplify Hosea Ballou Morse's *International Relations of the Chinese Empire* (3 vols., 1910–18), written before most of the archive materials for the subject were accessible. The tendency has been to direct research to particular critical issues and developments. Some distinguished studies of this kind are Lloyd Eastman, *Throne and Mandarins: China's Search for a Policy during the Sino-French Controversy, 1880–1885* (1967), Banno Masataka, *China and the West, 1858–1861: The Origins of the Tsungli Yamen* (1964), and Immanuel C. Y. Hsu, *The Ili Crisis: a Study of Sino-Russian Diplomacy, 1871–1881* (1965). *Studies of the policies of the various powers towards China include* William L. Langer, *The Diplomacy of Imperialism* (1935), O. Edmund Clubb, *China and Russia: The 'Great Game'* (1971), John E. Shrecker, *Imperialism and Chinese Nationalism: Germany in Shantung* (1971), Alistair Lamb, *Britain and Central Asia: The Road to Lhasa, 1767–1905* (1960), Marius B. Jansen, *Japan and China from War to Peace, 1894–1972* (1975), and John F. Cady, *The Roots of French Imperialism in the Far East* (1967). The relation between imperialism and the building of China's first railways is explored in Lee Enhan, *China's Quest for Railway*

Autonomy, 1904–1911 (1977). Owen Lattimore's classic study of Chinese central Asia, *Pivot of Asia: Sinkiang and the Inner Asian Frontiers of China and Russia* (1950), is still not superseded. Jansen (op. cit.) explores the ambivalent relations between Japan and China in the twentieth century.

Meribeth Cameron, *The Reform Movement in China* (1931) has now been supplemented by William Ayers, *Chang Chih-tung and Educational Reform in China* (1971) and Charlton M. Lewis, *Prologue to the Chinese Revolution: The Transformation of Ideas and Institutions in Human Province, 1891–1907* (1976), which deal with the background in Hunan and elsewhere of the changes attempted in Beijing by the young reformers of 1898. The political philosopher Hsiao Kungchuan, in *A Modern China and a New World: K'ang Youwei, Reformer and Utopian, 1855–1927* (1975), has added a comprehensive account of the ideas of K'ang Youwei. Victor Purcell, *The Boxer Uprising* (1963) examines the origins of the Boxer insurgency, and Chester C. Tan, *The Boxer Catastrophe* (1955) gives a full analysis and account of the rising.

By far the most perceptive account of the revolutionary movement which led to the end of the monarchy in 1912 is Mary C. Wright (ed.), *China in Revolution: the First Phase, 1900–1913* (1968). Good biographies of the leaders are Hsueh Chun-tu, *Revolutionary Leaders of Modern China* (1971), Harold Z. Schiffrin, *Sun Yatsen and the Origins of the Chinese Revolution* (1968), and Hsueh Chun-tu, *Huang Hsing and the Chinese Revolution* (1961). For Sun Yatsen's political ideas, see Frank W. Price, *San Min Chu I: The Three Principles of the People* (1927) and Paul M. A. Lineberger, *The Political Doctrines of Sun Yatsen* (1937). Michael Garsten, *Chinese Intellectuals and the Revolution of 1911* (1969) deals with the role of young intellectuals in the revolution. There are two good studies of Yuan Shikai and his rule: Jerome Ch'en, *Yuan Shih-k'ai, 1859–1916* (2nd edn., 1972) and Ernest P. Young, *The Presidency of Yuan Shih-k'ai: Liberalism and Dictatorship in Early Republican China* (1977). George T. Yu, *Party Politics in Republican China: the Kuomintang, 1912–1924* (1966) and K. S. Liew, *Struggle for Democracy: Sung Chiao-jen and the 1911 Revolution* (1971) cover the history of the Nationalist Party during the Yuan Shikai period. There are two important studies of particular aspects of Sun Yatsen's ideas and policies: Marius B. Jansen, *The Japanese and Sun Yatsen* (1954) and Shao Chuan Leng and N. D. Palmer, *Sun Yatsen and Communism* (1960). The role of the young Chiang Kaishek is described in Pichon P. Y. Loh, *The Early Chiang Kaishek: A Study of His Personality and Politics, 1887–1924* (1971).

Ch'i Hsi-sheng, *Warlord Politics in China, 1916–1928* (1976) gives a general account of the period of war-lordism, while F. F. Liu, *A Military History of Modern China, 1924–1949* (1956), examines the military aspects of regional power. There are three good studies of individual war-lords: James E. Sheridan, *Chinese Warlord: The Career of Feng Yu-xiang* (1966), Gavin McCormack, *Chang Tso-lin in North East China, 1911–1928* (1977), and Donald Gillin, *Warlord: Yen Hsi-shan in Shansi Province, 1911–1949* (1967). Diana Lary, *Region and Nation: The Kwangsi Clique in Chinese Politics, 1925–1937* (1974) pursues the continuing story of regional military power up to the Japanese invasion of 1937.

In the revision of earlier impressionistic views of the twentieth-century Chinese economy, the following are important: Albert Feuerwerker, *The Chinese Economy, 1912–1949* (1968), Dwight H. Perkins (ed.), *China's Modern Economy in Historical Perspective* (1975), John K. Chang, *Industrial Development in Pre-Communist China* (1969), Ramon H. Myers, *The Chinese Peasant Economy: Agricultural Development in Hopei and Shantung* (1970), Evelyn S. Rawski, *Agricultural Change and the Peasant Economy of South China* (1972), and Dwight H. Perkins, *Agricultural Development in China, 1368–1968* (1969). John Lossing Buck, *Land Utilisation in China* (1937) is still absolutely indispensable; his data have not even yet been fully analysed. So is Fei Hsiao-t'ung's classical study, *Peasant Life in China*

(1943). For the effects on the Chinese economy of foreign economic operations, see Frank H. H. King, *A Concise Economic History of China, 1840–1961* (1969), Hou Chi-ming, *Foreign Investment and Economic Development in China, 1840–1937* (1965), Cheng Yu-kwei, *Foreign Trade and the Industrial Development of China* (1956), and Rhoads Murphey, *Shanghai, Key to Modern China* (1953).

China's intellectual revolution, that massive and painful shift from twenty centuries of domination by Confucianism to the acceptance of Western values, ideas and expectations, has fascinated scholars and there is a long bibliography on the subject. General studies include Y. C. Wang, *Chinese Intellectuals and the West, 1872–1949* (1966), the subtle and witty book by Joseph R. Levenson, *Confucian China and its Modern Fate: The Problems of Continuity* (1958), and the first volume of Ho P'ing-ti and Tang Tsou (eds.), *China in Crisis: China's Heritage and the Communist Political System* (1968). The influence of missionaries is examined in K. S. Latourette, *A History of Christian Missions in China* (1929), Paul A. Cohen, *China and Christianity: The Missionary Movement and the Growth of Chinese Anti-Foreignism, 1860–1870* (1963), and John K. Fairbank (ed.), *The Missionary Enterprise in China and America* (1974). Jerome Ch'en, *China and the West* (1979) describes in more general terms the nature and effect of the foreign presence. James C. Thompson, *While China faced West: American Reformers in Nationalist China, 1928–1937* (1969) is indispensable. One key figure in the transmission of ideas derived from missionary sources is dealt with in Paul A. Cohen, *Between Tradition and Modernity: Wang Tao and Reform in Late Ch'ing China* (1974). Liang Ch'i-ch'ao, the dominating intellectual figure of the first decade of the twentieth century, has had three good biographers writing in English: J. R. Levenson, *Liang Ch'i-ch'ao and the Mind of Modern China* (1953), Hao Chang, *Liang Ch'i-ch'ao and Intellectual Transition in China* (1971), and Philip C. Huang, *Liang Ch'i-ch'ao and Modern Chinese Liberalism* (1972). Liang's own influential *Intellectual Trends in the Ch'ing Period* has been translated by C. Y. Hsu (1959). Chou Tse-tsung's path-breaking study, *The May Fourth Movement* (1960), has now been supplemented by Benjamin Schwarz (ed.), *Reflections on the May Fourth Movement: A Symposium* (1972). Studies of individuals associated with intellectual change in the May Fourth period are given in Jerome Grieder, *Hu Shih and the Chinese Renaissance* (1970) and Lawrence A. Schneider, *Ku Chieh-kang and China's New History: Nationalism and the Quest for Alternative Tradition* (1971). Guy S. Alitto, *The Last Confucian: Liang Shuming and the Chinese Dilemma of Modernity* (1978) deals with the social philosopher who did so much to set the parameters of debate in the clash between Western and Chinese values. Thomas H. Metzger, *Escape from Predicament: Neo-Confucianism and China's Evolving Political Culture* (1977) examines the continuities of thought which underlay all the dramatic changes. R. H. Solomon, *Mao's Revolution and the Chinese Political Culture* (1971), with its questionnaire analysis of Chinese political opinions in the late 1960s, confirms the tenacity of tradition. For the emergence of Marxism as an intellectual force in China, see Benjamin Schwarz, *Chinese Communism and the Rise of Mao* (1951) and Maurice Meisner, *Li Ta-chao and the Origins of Chinese Marxism* (1970). A. Scalapino and George T. Yu, *The Chinese Anarchist Movement* (1961) examines the rise and fall of anarchist influence.

There are two general histories of the Chinese Communist Party: James P. Harrison, *The Long March to Power: A History of the Chinese Communist Party, 1921–1972* (1972) and Jacques Guillermaz. *A History of the Chinese Communist Party, 1921–1949* (1972). Chang Kuo-t'ao, a founding member of the Party, labour leader and subsequently the ruler of the Sichuan Soviet area, a rival of Mao who left the Party soon after the Long March, has left his own account of the Party's early history, *The Rise of the Chinese Communist Party*, 2 vols., *1921–1927* and *1928–1938* (1971–2). To these should be added Lyman P. van Slyke, *The Chinese*

Communist Movement: A Report of the United States War Department, July 1945 (1968) and *Enemies and Friends: The United Front in Chinese Communist History* (1967). Agnes Smedley, *The Great Road: The Life and Times of Chu The* (1956), looks at the history of the Chinese Communist Party through the experience of one of the architects of its military strategy. Early communist activity is well analysed in Jean Chesnaux, *The Chinese Labour Movement, 1919–1927* (1962) and Roy Hofheinz, *The Broken Wave: The Chinese Communist Peasant Movement, 1922–1928* (1977); our account of the early peasant movement has leant heavily on this most valuable analysis. For the subsequent development of agrarian policy, see Hsiao Tso-liang, *Chinese Communism in 1927: City v. Countryside* (1970). Harold Isaacs was a participant in the events he describes in *The Tragedy of the Chinese Revolution* (2nd edn., 1961), and Robert C. North and Xenia J. Eudin, *M. N. Roy's Mission to China: The Communist-Kuomintang Split of 1927* (1963) complement this with a documentary study. Dan Jacobs, *Borodin: Stalin's Man in China* (1981) examines the role of the best-known and most influential representative in China of the Communist International. The best account of the Long March is Dick Wilson, *The Long March, 1935* (1971). Chalmers H. Johnson, in *Peasant Nationalism and Communist Power: The Emergence of Revolutionary China* (1962), first put forward the controversial hypothesis that the rise of the Chinese Communist Party to power was due to an appeal to the national, rather than the revolutionary, feelings of the peasantry.

The Nationalist Republic has had a bad press; the following list of books, however, should provide the means to make a more balanced judgement: Carsun Chang, *The Third Force in China* (1952), Ch'ien Tuansheng, *The Government and Politics of China* (1950), Parks Coble, jun., *The Shanghai Capitalists and the Nationalist Government, 1927–1937* (1980), Lloyd Eastman, *The Abortive Revolution: China Under Nationalist Rule, 1927–1937* (1974), Charlotte Furth (ed.), *The Limits of Change: Essays on Conservative Alternatives in Republican China* (1976), Pichon P. Y. Loh (ed.), *The Kuomintang Debacle of 1949: Collapse or Conquest?* (1965), Paul K. T. Sih (ed.), *The Strenuous Decade: China's Nation-Building Efforts, 1927–1937* (1970), Barbara W. Tuchman, *Stillwell and the American Experience in China, 1911–1945* (1970), Arthur Young, *China and the Helping Hand, 1937–1945* (1963) and Arthur N. Young, *China's Nation-Building Effort, 1927–1937: The Financial and Economic Record* (1971).

The career, philosophy, and policies of Mao Zedong have been sufficiently dramatic to ensure that Mao has been the subject of many books. By far the best studies of him are by Stuart R. Schram, *Mao Tse-tung* (1967) and *The Political Thought of Mao Tse-tung* (rev. edn., 1969); they are concerned more, however, with Mao as thinker than with Mao as policy-maker. Frederic Wakeman, *History and Will: Philosophical Perspectives of Mao Tse-tung's Thought* (1973) is even more sharply focused on Mao's thought, but it complements Schram's work by putting Mao's ideas in a wider context of intellectual history. Jerome Ch'en, *Mao and the Chinese Revolution* (1965) supplies, as a further complement, an account of Mao's development in the context of the conditions of twentieth-century China. Critical junctures in his rise to power are analysed in John E. Rue, *Mao Tse-tung in Opposition, 1927–1935* (1966) and Boyd Compton (ed.), *Mao's China: Party Reform Documents, 1942–1946* (1966). The origins of Mao's policies of economic development and social change are described in Mark Selden, *The Yenan Way in Revolutionary China* (1971); Mao's own account of the Border Region economy is translated, and well introduced, in Andrew Watson (ed.), *Mao Zedong and the Political Economy of the Border Region* (1980).

Bill Brugger, *Contemporary China* (1977) gives a clear and well-documented introduction to the history of the Chinese People's Republic up to and including the Great Proletarian Cultural Revolution of 1965. Jacques Guillermaz, op. cit., vol. 2, *The Chinese Communist Party in Power* (1976), along with the latter part of James P. Harrison (op. cit.), provides the later history of the Chinese Communist Party. Study of the economic history of the regime has often produced more heat than light. The most informed volumes, and the most judicious in the opinion of the present author, are Audrey Donnithorne, *China's Economic System* (1967) and Carl Riskin, *China's Political Economy: The Quest for Development since 1949* (1987). John Gurley, *China's Economy and the Maoist Strategy* (1976) stresses the positive aspects of Maoist economics; so (within limits) do the present author's essays on the subject, to be found in Alec Nove and D. M. Nuti (eds.), *Socialist Economics* (1972), pp. 491–510, and H. Bernstein (ed.), *Under-development and Development* (1973), pp. 254–510. The process of land reform was described at first hand in William Hinton's best-selling *Fanshen* (1966), and analysed by John Wong (himself a participant in the land reform campaign) in *Land Reform in the People's Republic of China: Institutional Transformation of Agriculture* (1973). Rural social change generally was analysed with authority and perception in C. K. Yang, *Chinese Communist Society: The Family and the Village* (1965). The general development of urban policy is fully described in Ezra Vogel, *Canton under Communism* (1969), the best study of the establishment of Communist rule in one of China's cities. Theodore H. E. Ch'en, *Thought Reform of the Chinese Intellectuals* (1960) describes the process by which China's intellectuals were brought to heel.

The explosion of the Great Proletarian Cultural Revolution led to a matching explosion of publications attempting to explain the event; only a few of the most serious efforts are referred to here. General accounts of value are Jean Daubier, *A History of the Chinese Cultural Revolution* (1974), Jean Esmein, *The Chinese Cultural Revolution* (1973), and Thomas W. Robinson (ed.), *The Cultural Revolution in China* (1971). William Hinton was providentially present as he had been during land reform, and described his experiences vividly in *The Hundred Days' War: The Cultural Revolution in Tsinghua University* (1972). Victor Nee, *The Cultural Revolution at Peking University* (1969) provides a parallel account. By far the most perceptive analysis of the Red Guard movement, however, is in Lee Hong-yung, *The Politics of the Chinese Cultural Revolution* (1978). Richard Baum, *Prelude to Revolution* (1975) deals with the Socialist Education Movement of 1963–5. Lowell Dittmer, *Liu Shao-ch'i and the Chinese Cultural Revolution* (1974) is a dispassionate account of the tragic end of the career of Liu Shaoqi. Jack Gray and Patrick Cavendish, *Chinese Communism in Crisis: Maoism and the Cultural Revolution* (1968), a book written at the height of the struggle, attempted to head off the more ridiculous explanations of the Cultural Revolution then current in the West; it has perhaps not yet been entirely superseded. Stuart R. Schram (ed.), *Authority, Participation and Cultural Change in China* (1973) is indispensable. Anita Chan, *Children of Mao: Personality Development and Political Activism in the Red Guard Generation* (1985) casts a brilliant light on the sources of the Revolution in her study of the tensions within Chinese schools in the early 1960s. Two books deal with the influence on politics of the changing pattern of interest groups in Chinese society: David S. G. Goodman (ed.), *Groups and Politics in the People's Republic of China* (1984) and Gordon White, *The Politics of Class and Class Origin: The Case of the Cultural Revolution* (1976).

The best general analysis of foreign relations since 1949 is Michael B. Yahuda, *China's Role in World Affairs* (1978). On the split with the Soviet Union, see Donald S. Zagoria, *The Sino-Soviet Conflict, 1956–1961* (1962), Klaus Mehnert, *Peking and Moscow* (1963), William E. Griffith, *The Sino-Soviet Rift* (1964), and John Gittings, *Survey of the Sino-Soviet Dispute* (1968).

The immense changes which have been attempted in China since 1978 and the return to power of Deng Xiaoping have generated much writing in the West. The following books have been chosen as those providing the best introduction to the complex subject of the reforms. Jack Gray and Gordon White (eds.), *China's New Development Strategy* (1984) provides a series of views (and varied viewpoints) on the reforms at an early stage. Elizabeth J. Perry and Christine Wong (eds.), *The Political Economy of Reform in Post-Mao China* (1958) carries the story forward through another three years of rapid change. Keith Griffin (ed.), *Institutional Reform and Economic Development in the Chinese Countryside* (1984) deals with the nature and implications of the return to individual farming. Pat Howard, *Breaking the Iron Rice Bowl* (1988) reports on two years of field-work on the new agricultural policies in north-west China. Vivienne Shu, *The Reach of the State: Sketches of the Chinese Body Politic* (1988) is most perceptive. Carl Riskin (op. cit.) gives the best summary of the reforms and their implications.

Democratic dissent in China is documented in two excellent volumes: Anita Chan, Stanley Rosen, and Jonathan Ungar (eds.), *On Socialist Democracy and the Chinese Legal System: the Li Yizhe Debates* (1958) and Chen Erjun, *China: Crossroads Socialism*, trans. and intro. by Robin Munro (1984). Andrew J. Nathan, *Chinese Democracy* (1985) puts the 1978–80 democratic movement in China in a wider perspective.

Several more surveys of events in China since 1976 have recently been published. The following books introduce a variety of approaches. B. L. McCormick and J. Unger, *China after Socialism: In the Footsteps of Eastern Europe or East Asia?* (1996); Dick Wilson, *China: The Big Tiger: A Nation Awakes* (1997); W. J. F. Jenner and Delia Davin (eds.), *Chinese Lives: An Oral History of Contemporary China* (1987) puts flesh on the bones of more abstract analyses. B. Yang, *Deng: A Political Biography* (1998). The author left Beijing University in 1981 for Harvard, and subsequently returned to China to become professor of international politics at the People's University. He combines academic research with his considerable inside knowledge of China's top-level politics. C. McKerras, D. H. MacMillen, and A. Watson, *Dictionary of the Politics of the People's Republic of China* (1998). This substantial handbook, put together by a large team of distinguished contributors, is well worth keeping at one's elbow. F. Christiansen and S. M. Rai, *Chinese Politics and Society: An Introduction* (1996). An excellent survey with many insights. The preface states the refreshing approach of the authors: that 'ideology represents a rationalisation of political behaviour and is not an independent motive force in history'. *China Quarterly*, 159 (1999) is a symposium volume covering every aspect of China and has the high quality one expects from this distinguished journal.

The literature on China's economic reforms has become enormous. The selection of books which follows is intended to introduce the different points of view expressed in this literature. The best introduction to economic change in China is the cross-section given in *China Quarterly*, 144 (Dec. 1955), Special Number: *China's Transitional Economy*. The papers are full of insights. Chris Bramall, *The Sources of China's Economic Growth, 1978– 1996* (1999) is an original and indispensable study. Peter Nolan, *China's Rise, Russia's Fall* (1995) contrasts the disastrous consequences of the abrupt abolition of the command economy in the Soviet Union with the success of China's gradual reforms. The contrast is strongly argued. Barry Naughton, *Growing out of the Plan* (1995). This indispensable study analyses the reform process in an excellent reasoned narrative. Susan Young, *Private Business and Economic Reform in China* (1995) describes the ambiguities in the position of private enterprise in what is still essentially a socialist state. Paul Cook and Fred Nixon (eds.), *The Move to the Market* (1995) widen the perspective by showing that other East Asian communist regimes have taken much the same path as China in the transition from full communism, while the communist states of Europe followed (or anticipated) the Soviet strategy of reform. Harry G. Broadman, *Meeting the Challenge of Chinese Enterprise Reform* (1995) gives a view from the international economic institutions. D. Brown and R. Porter,

Management Issues in China, i: *Domestic Enterprises* (1996). (Volume ii is about to be published.) Improved management is obviously vital but, as this book shows, cultural factors can inhibit change: there are often hidden agendas.

Two books outline and analyse the debates which took place over the extent and direction of reform: Wei-Wei Zhang, *ideology and Economic Reform under Deng Xiaoping 1978–1993* (1996) and Feng Chen, *Economic Transition and Political Legitimacy in Post-Mao China* (1995). Zhang emphasizes the ideological aspects of the conflict, while Feng deals primarily with the controversies among the committed reformers.

The following books cover the consequences of economic reform for income distribution and welfare as well as the political implications of structural economic change. They examine by different modes of analysis the controversial question of whether reform has increased or decreased social inequalities. T. McKinley, *The Distribution of Wealth in Rural China* (1996); E. B. Vermeer, F. N. Piecke, and Wei Lian Chong, *Co-operatives and Collectives in China's Rural Development* (1998); F. Christiansen and Shang Jenzuo, *Village Incorporated: Chinese Rural Society in the 1990s* (1998); Xiao Bolu and J. Perry, *Danwei: The Changing Chinese Workplace* (1997); L. Wong, *Marginalisation and Social Welfare in China* (1998); G. White: *Riding the Tiger: The Politics of Economic Reform in Post-Mao China* (1993); and Jude Howell, *China Opens its Doors: The Politics of Economic Transition* (1993).

China is vast and her economic institutions now widely decentralized. The regional dimension of Chinese life has become of great importance. Two excellent books cover the issues: V. C. Falkenheim, *China's Regional Development: Trends and Implications* (1994) is a good introduction to the problems involved; Y. M. Yeung and K. Y. Chu, *Guangdong: Survey of a Province Undergoing Rapid Change* (1994) applies the analysis to a province whose interests have come to differ substantially from those of the rest of China.

China's democracy movement expresses a wide variety of opinions and of sectional interests. Merle Goldman, *Sowing the Seeds of Democracy in China* (1994) is the classical account of China's democracy movement. Note also her article in *China Quarterly*, 159, which brings her story up to the end of the century. Shi Tianjian, *Political Participation in Beijing* (1997) shows that there is a higher level of genuine participation than has hitherto been supposed. C. Li Wing-hung, *China's Legal Awakening* (1995). A careful account of China's ambiguous, but not entirely insignificant moves, towards the rule of law. G. Benton, *Wild Lilies Poisonous Weeds* (1982) is an indispensable anthology of the writings of the radical democrats of Democracy Wall. Roger Garside, *Coming Alive after Mao* (1982) gives a vivid eyewitness account of Democracy Wall, and reports a dramatic interview with Wei Jingsheng. An excellent study of Chinese students in politics is S. M. Rai, *Resistance and Reaction: University Politics in Post-Mao China* (1991). A. J. Nathan, P. Link, and O. Schell, *The Tiananmen Papers* (2001). A translation of tapes and reports on the Tiananmen incident, materials to which only China's five top leaders normally have access, smuggled out of China. Chen Erjin, *Crossroads Socialism*, translated and introduced by Robin Munro (1984). This is one of the publications of the Democracy Wall movement. It argues that Marxist theory must now accept that violent socialist revolution always creates a new revolutionary ruling class which itself becomes an obstacle to socialist democracy. Geremie Barme, *Shades of Mao: The Posthumous Cult of the Great Leader* (1996).

The question of whether a new civil society is successfully developing in China is highly controversial. The following books deal with the issue from differing points of view: T. Brook and B. M. Frolic, *Civil Society in China* (1997); Gordon White, Jude Howell, and Shang Shaoyuan, *In Search of Civil Society: Market Reform and Social Change in Contemporary China* (1996); Baoguang He, *The Democratic Implications of Civil Society in China* (1991);

D. S. Davies (ed.), *Urban Spaces in Contemporary China: The Potential for Autonomy and Community in Post-Mao China* (1995).

Several distinguished scholars have been attracted to the study of changes in rural China: Mark Blecher and V. Shue, *Tethered Deer: Government and Economy in a Chinese County* (1996); Jean C. Oi, *State and Peasant: The Political Economy of Village Government* (1989); Jean C. Oi, *Rural China Takes Off: The Institutional Foundations of Economic Reform* (1998); A. Walder (ed.), *Zouping in Transition: The Process of Reform in Rural North China* (1998); Xu Guohua and L. J. Peck, *The Agriculture of China* (1991).

Township and village enterprise (formerly commune and brigade enterprise), begun unsuccessfully in the Great Leap Forward and then successfully revived in the Cultural Revolution to become the most vigorous sector of the Chinese economy, was all but ignored until the 1990s. The following books illustrate its significance; but there is still little acknowledgement of its Maoist origins before 1978. W. A. Byrd and Lin Qingsong, *China's Rural Industry* (1990) is the report of a large study of rural industry by the World Bank. Samuel P. S. Ho, *Rural China in Transition: Non-agricultural Enterprise in Rural Jiangsu, 1978– 1990* (1994). John Wong, Rong Ma, and Mu Yang (eds.), *China's Rural Entrepreneurs* (1995). C. Findley, A. Watson, and Harry X. Wu, *Rural Enterprises in China* (1994).

The best introduction to China's recent foreign relations is T. Robinson and D. Shambaugh (eds.), *Chinese Foreign Policy* (1994). A symposium volume, it is comprehensive and is also valuable for its theoretical contributions. It ends with a very valuable bibliographical essay by David Shambaugh.

China's new and often savagely satirical or cynical literature is well introduced in the following: Lu Tongliu, *Running Wild: New Chinese Writers* (1994); Jianying Zha, *China Pop: How the Soap Operas, Tabloids, and Bestsellers are Transforming a Culture* (1995). See also Bonnie Macdougall in *China Quarterly*, 159.

Although China has signed several international treaties on human rights, her record has been far from satisfactory. The following books cover all the main issues involved. M. Svensson, *The Chinese Conception of Human Rights* (1996). D. Seymour and R. Anderson, *New Ghosts, Old Ghosts: Prisons and Labour Reform in China* (1985). Amnesty International, *China: No One is Safe: Political Repression and the Abuse of Power in the 1990s* (1996).

Human rights in China's traditional culture are dealt with in W. T. de Bary and Weiming Tu, *Confucianism and Human Rights* (1997); and W. T. de Bary, *Waiting for the Dawn: A Plan for the Prince* (1993) is a translation of the major work of one of the seventeenth-century patriot scholars so influential in the twentieth century.

Several new books on the Cultural Revolution appeared in the 1990s. Yan Jiaqi and Gao Gao, *Turbulent Decade: A History of the Cultural Revolution* (1996). Yan Jiaqi was a major figure in the democratization movement. E. J. Perry and Li Xun, *Proletarian Power: Shanghai and the Cultural Revolution* (1997). Shao Reng Huang, *To Rebel is Justified: A Rhetorical Study of China's Cultural Revolution* (1996).

Index